THE SCOTT AND LAURIE OKI SERIES
IN ASIAN AMERICAN STUDIES

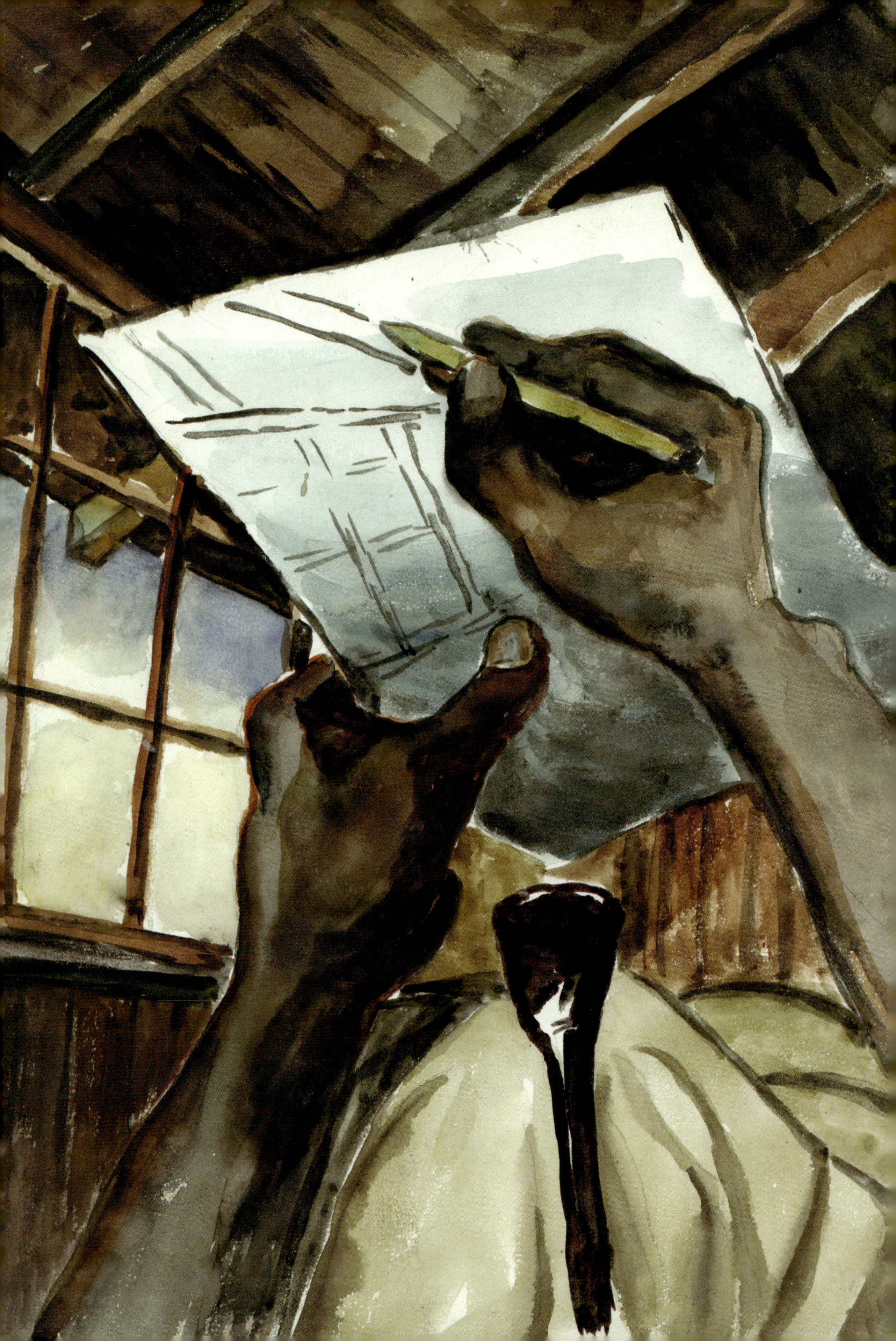

The Hope of Another Spring

TAKUICHI FUJII, ARTIST AND WARTIME WITNESS

Barbara Johns

FOREWORD BY Roger Daniels

INTRODUCTION TO THE DIARY BY Sandy Kita

UNIVERSITY OF WASHINGTON PRESS
Seattle and London

The Hope of Another Spring is published with the assistance of a grant from the Scott and Laurie Oki Endowed Fund for publications in Asian American Studies.

Additional support has been provided by the Hugh and Jane Ferguson Foundation, Alida and Christopher Latham, George and Kim Suyama, the Family of John and Virginia Bigelow, and Dr. Joseph T. and Jean Davies Okimoto.

Printed and bound in China
Design by Thomas Eykemans
Composed in Minion, typeface designed by Robert Slimbach
21 20 19 18 17 5 4 3 2 1

UNIVERSITY OF WASHINGTON PRESS
www.washington.edu/uwpress

Unless labeled otherwise, works of art are by Takuichi Fujii and in the Sandy and Terry Kita Collection.

Frontispiece: Drawing by flashlight (detail). Watercolor on paper, 14 3/4 x 10 1/2 in.

Poetry by Hakushu, Keiho Soga, and Kamekichi Tokita used by permission.

LIBRARY OF CONGRESS CATALOGING-IN-PUBLICATION DATA

Names: Johns, Barbara, 1942– | Daniels, Roger, writer of foreword. | Kita, Sandy, 1950– | Fujii, Takuichi, 1891–1964. Works. Selections.
Title: The hope of another spring : Takuichi Fujii, artist and wartime witness / Barbara Johns ; foreword by Roger Daniels ; introduction to the diary by Sandy Kita.
Description: Seattle : University of Washington Press, 2017. | Series: The Scott and Laurie Oki Series in Asian American Studies | Includes bibliographical references and index.
Identifiers: LCCN 2016036743 | ISBN 9780295999999 (hardcover : alk. paper)
Subjects: LCSH: Fujii, Takuichi, 1891–1964. | Fujii, Takuichi, 1891-1964—Criticism and interpretation. | Japanese American painters—Biography. | Japanese American painters—Diaries. | World War, 1939-1945—Personal narratives, Japanese American.
Classification: LCC ND237.F785 H67 2017 | DDC 759.13 [B]—dc23
LC record available at https://lccn.loc.gov/2016036743

The paper used in this publication is acid-free and meets the minimum requirements of American National Standard for Information Sciences—Permanence of Paper for Printed Library Materials, ANSI Z39.48–1984. ∞

CONTENTS

FOREWORD

Roger Daniels

Barbara Johns, the author of this fine monograph, is a Seattle-based art historian and curator who has been engaged for some years in creating pathbreaking studies[1] of immigrant Japanese American painters who flourished in Seattle during the decades before World War II. The book in hand, the capstone of her project, is a biography of Takuichi Fujii (1891–1964), a once well-known Issei artist who had been all but forgotten.

The cumulative effect of her studies demonstrates that neither the historians of Asian American art nor those of Seattle's Japanese American community have given these Issei artists their due.[2] It is remarkable that in 1936, when local cultural leaders selected ten artists to display works representing the state of Washington at the *First National Exhibition of American Art* in New York City, three of them were Issei painters: Fujii, Kenjiro Nomura, and Kamekichi Tokita. That result, which is surprising given the severe discrimination that Japanese Americans endured, has been ignored by historians. (No Japanese person was so honored by any other western state.) The three Issei painters were already well known in local art circles as members of Seattle's Group of Twelve, prominent artists whose interracial membership was rare, if not unique, in 1930s America. The three of them, businessmen, had mundane day jobs. Nomura and Tokita ran a sign-painting business in Seattle's Nihonmachi, where Nikkei artists and would-be artists used to hang out.

Fujii is a particularly difficult subject for a biographer, since much of his life and career can only be sketchily documented, largely from official records, newspapers, and the letters of his fellow artists. Born in Hiroshima in 1891, he had ten years of schooling in Japan, including study in a private art school, significantly more than most immigrants of that era. He emigrated to Seattle in late 1906, as a postwar slump gripped Japan, joining his father and an elder brother. Although the latter, like so many of the immigrants of the era, were sojourners, laboring abroad while maintaining families at home and eventually returning to

Japan, Takuichi, the second son, whatever his original intent, became a lifelong American. After a long decade in Seattle, first as an employee of an ethnic seafood company and then as a proprietor of a stall in the city's public market, he went back to Japan for six months, met and married Fusano Marumachi, and brought her back to Seattle in early 1917. Barbara Johns has pieced together some of the details of the life that the family, which soon included two daughters, created in the United States. Apart from a few of his early paintings, we have nothing created by his own hand until his fifty-first year.

Sometime in May 1942, Fujii began a diary that would become the most remarkable document created by a Japanese American prisoner during the wartime incarceration. Fujii, his wife, and their two American-citizen daughters were taken by armed soldiers to the temporary concentration camp that the United States Army threw together on the state fairgrounds in nearby Puyallup.[3] He wrote about and illustrated the family's imprisonment there and on the train that took them in late August to the more permanent Minidoka Relocation Center in desolate southern Idaho. His daughters soon left the camp, the elder to work on a Utah farm, the younger to work in a Minneapolis war plant and then to enlist in the Women's Army Corps. The elder Fujiis remained imprisoned until October 2, 1945, leaving as the camp was closing. His entry for that date ends the diary.

Covering three years and nearly five months, the diary is a combination of words and works of art. Its six thousand words are all of Fujii's writing that remains. The diary contains 249 inked drawings; the family collection also includes nearly two hundred paintings, drawings, and carved pieces, the majority of which relate to the diary.[4] Some of the final touches on watercolors related to the diary may have been done in Utah, where the elder Fujiis went after leaving camp, but he made no additions to the diary. However, he continued to paint for the rest of his life, which he spent in and around Chicago. After his death, in 1964, Fusano gathered and preserved the diary and his postwar works in the family home, where they remained, unseen, for more than a generation.

As Johns relates, only after the Fujiis' grandson Sandy Kita (b. 1950), who had earned a doctorate in art history and become a university professor, examined the documents his grandmother had so carefully saved was anyone aware of the hidden treasures. Kita eventually translated the diary text, whose Japanese was already archaic when written. It is the most detailed and informative work produced by an Issei prisoner in a War Relocation Authority camp. Johns's book is thus doubly significant: it not only illuminates the work of an important Issei artist but also gives us a telling alternative view of the wartime ordeal of the West Coast Japanese Americans.[5] The vast majority of what we have is from a Nisei perspective. This Issei view provides an important corrective.

ACKNOWLEDGMENTS

In 2011 Terry Kita was once again searching online for information about Takuichi Fujii, the grandfather-in-law she never knew, when she found a surprise. The federal Institute of Museum and Library Services had awarded a grant to the Wing Luke Museum in Seattle to conserve a painting by Fujii in its collection. When Sandy Kita, the artist's grandson, wrote the museum to inquire, he was told of the conservation under way and directed further to me. As we began communicating I learned about the Kitas' astonishing collection of the artist's work, heretofore unseen by the public, dating from World War II to the end of his life. I am profoundly grateful to Sandy and Terry for their trust in me and their unfailing generosity, helpfulness, and commitment to this project. Sandy's scholarship adds immeasurably to the substance of this book. Literally, the book would not be possible without them.

My work in recent years has focused on immigrant-generation Japanese American artists, and I am exceptionally fortunate to have been guided by scholars in fields outside mine of art history. Foremost among these is the distinguished historian Roger Daniels. I am honored to call Roger my teacher, mentor, and friend; he has saved me from wrong turns, led me farther down other roads, and shown me a superb model of exacting, deeply thoughtful scholarship. Literary scholar Stephen Sumida has expanded my viewpoint by his nuanced readings of texts (and images) from a transpacific perspective and many times has clarified my way forward. This book has benefited greatly from two unnamed readers, both well-versed in the history of the Japanese American wartime incarceration, whose advice led me to deeper inquiry; I am indebted to each of them.

Others closely connected to Japanese American studies have provided ongoing support and encouragement. I thank especially Tom Ikeda, founding director of the respected online resource Denshō; Roger Shimomura, whose artistic career is inspired by his grandmother's wartime diaries; and historian Tetsuden Kashima, whose guidance as I began work in the field continues to be meaningful. Tom and Denshō collection manager Caitlin Oiye Coon provided digitized images of the diary for this book. My warm thanks to Shokichi Tokita for spurring my study when he proposed to the University of Washington Press that I write about his father, Kamekichi.

In researching Fujii's life and artistic career, I have been helped by dedicated archivists and educators, in particular Karen Kanemoto, former head of the Legacy Center at the Japanese American Service Committee in Chicago; Carol Ash, chief interpreter at the Minidoka National Historic Site, National Parks Service; Traci Timmons, Seattle Art Museum librarian; Nicolette Bromberg and her colleagues at the University of Washington Libraries' Special Collections; and archivists at the Chicago History Museum. Gerard Tsutakawa generously allowed me to read the papers of his father, George Tsutakawa, and Kimi Kodani Hill shared insights about the artwork of her grandfather Chiuro Obata. Margaret Bullock and Ellen Ito gave me access to the Tacoma Art Museum's collection of Kenjiro Nomura's wartime paintings and drawings.

The preparation of this book, together with an exhibition that began touring shortly before publication, entailed sometimes elaborate and atypical arrangements. The Kitas and I live a continent apart, they on the East Coast, I on the West. A uniquely important contribution to this book was that of the Wing Luke Museum, which stored and insured the Kitas' collection so that it could be conserved and photographed; we are grateful to Beth Takekawa, executive director, and Bob Fisher, collections manager, for this invaluable service. David F. Martin, owner of Martin-Zambito Fine Art, offered his expertise in appraising the collection for insurance. Conservators Lisa Duncan (paper), Eric Eshenbach (oil paintings), and Carolina Veenstra (books) cleaned, stabilized, and repaired individual objects for their safekeeping and presentation. Assisting Lisa with the large number of works on paper to be conserved were interns Jennifer Myers, Kayla Boland, and Alexia Symeonidou. Each of the owners of Fujii's extant 1930s paintings readily agreed to their reproduction: the Wing Luke Museum, David F. Martin and Dominic Zambito, and a private collector. Richard Nicol provided new photography for many of the artworks pictured here.

The University of Washington Press has enthusiastically supported this book since I first proposed it. Given the press's outstanding record of Asian American publications, I am honored to be among its authors. My thanks especially to director Nicole Mitchell for her steadfast support, to Ranjit Arab for his guidance during the preparations of the manuscript, editors Jacqueline Volin, Nancy Cortelyou, and Margaret Sullivan for managing production, and copyeditor Bonita Hurd for help in honing the text. Tom Eykemans, who brought his design sensitivity to my previous book, has created a beautifully conceived visual presentation of Fujii and his work.

The Hope of Another Spring is part of the distinguished series supported by the Scott and Laurie Oki Endowed Fund for publications in Asian American Studies. I deeply appreciate the Okis' commitment to its inclusion. Art books are expensive to produce, and I am grateful to the individuals who saw the value in illustrating Fujii's work as fully as possible. Ellen Ferguson, trustee of the Hugh and Jane Ferguson Foundation, made a critical lead gift. Alida and Christopher Latham, George and Kim Suyama, the family of John and Virginia Bigelow, and Joe and Jeanie Okimoto joined her in generous support. Each brings a personal connection to this history and the social justice issues it represents that makes their contributions all the more meaningful.

The recovery of Fujii's work has led not only to this book but also to a nationally traveling exhibition. Although the two projects are independent of one another, the early commitment of Sandy Harthorn, former curator of the Boise Art Museum, ensured that the import of Fujii's achievement would be appreciated beyond Seattle, where he first made his home in the United States. My thanks to Graham Howe, CEO of Curatorial Assistance, for his keen interest in managing the tour.

Finally and foremost I am grateful to my husband, Richard Hesik, and our beloved family for their unwavering encouragement. Richard is my firsthand support, my first reader, and my cheerleader. All of them inspire me to keep going.

THE HOPE
OF ANOTHER
SPRING

Introduction

> In the snow remaining in the advent of spring, I can see various kinds of birds singing and playing. The beautiful stripes of yellow sunlight peek through from among the dry willow trees. Although it is still very cold, the hope of seeing another spring gives me a warm feeling.
>
> —Takuichi Fujii, Minidoka Relocation Center, circa December 31, 1942

THE HOPE OF ANOTHER SPRING is the story of an individual whose artwork opens a window to historical events and issues far greater than one person. Takuichi Fujii (1891–1964) bore witness to his life in the United States and especially to his experience during World War II. He left a remarkably comprehensive visual record, indeed a unique one for someone of his generation. The verb *witness* is defined as "to see, hear, or know by personal presence and perception" and to "give or afford evidence of."[1] Among the varying definitions in print and online, this one links perception to presence, thus emphasizing the active apprehension and interpretation of experience. Such is the artist's skill that we can see and gain some intimation of events most of us did not live through but whose lessons remain salient to our lives today.

Fujii was an Issei, or first-generation Japanese in America, and a well-recognized artist in Seattle before World War II.[2] He left Japan in 1906 and made his home in Seattle, where he established a business, a family, and an artistic practice. When war broke out between the United States and Japan, he was forced from his home and incarcerated in one of ten remote "camps" along with 120,000 other first-, second-, and third-generation Japanese Americans on the West Coast.[3] After the war he settled in Chicago, and memory of him soon faded; a decade later he was reported as having returned to Japan.[4] Until public records became accessible online, the few published references to him gave only a question mark for his death date.[5] He left almost no personal papers other than artwork and a wartime diary, and little evidence exists to trace his family history or offer insight into his motivations and intentions. Moreover, his own actions contributed to the missing record when, for unknown reasons, he moved to Chicago for a two-year period in the 1930s. In doing so he relinquished the invitation for a solo exhibition at the Seattle Art Museum, together with the likelihood that the museum would have acquired one or more of his paintings and thereby established a material institutional record. It is all the more surprising, then, that through a completely unexpected connection as I began another project, I was introduced online to Fujii's grandson, Sandy Kita.[6] Several months after our introduction, I visited Sandy and his wife, Terry, who showed me their comprehensive collection of Fujii's artworks: a wartime diary, oil and watercolor paintings, drawings, sculpture, and craft objects dating from 1942 until the end of the artist's life—a collection that Sandy had learned about only years after his grandfather's death. By far the majority of the work focuses on World War II incarceration.

In the early 1990s, as the fiftieth anniversary of the forced removal of Japanese Americans approached, the late art historian Karin Higa led an intensive effort to recover previously unknown work in preparation for an exhibition of art produced during the years of confinement.[7] Expecting to find mostly amateur production, she and her colleagues were surprised by the number of professional artists—some previously well known, others not—as well as by the quantity of art that had been preserved.[8] Like memories of incarceration for many Japanese Americans, the works of art had been stored away and kept separated from the rest of their lives. To Higa, such work seemed to have functioned like an icon. It was physical evidence of events now distant from daily life. "Literally, a history could be isolated, wrapped up, and stored . . . but be very present none the less."[9] The war left many who had been segregated and confined with internalized guilt and lingering shame; most wanted to bury such memories in the effort to rebuild their lives. Families may not have talked about their experience but retained objects whose physicality invoked the reality of the past. So it appears to have been with Fujii's collection until his grandson's discovery. Having shown me what they held, and wanting to correct the record about Fujii's life and legacy, Sandy and Terry readily agreed when I proposed a book and an exhibition, and they entrusted me with the undertaking.

Many other artists produced substantial bodies of work during incarceration that approach or exceed Fujii's production in number and scope. Fujii's work, however, is distinctive for its viewpoint and detail. Several of the professional artists featured in Higa's project, *The View from Within*, have since become the subjects of monographs. The most prominent is Chiura Obata (1885–1975), an Issei and an art professor at the University of California, Berkeley, when the war began. In Japan, Obata had studied *nihonga*, a painting style that combines sumi, or ink, brushwork with Western naturalism, and after immigrating to San Francisco he became an active, nationally recognized member of its art community. Facing incarceration, he began documenting his experience in sumi sketches that became the basis for larger paintings. In a different mode, he depicted the Topaz incarceration camp in hauntingly luminescent landscape paintings of the Utah desert. Convinced of art's affirmative value, he was instrumental in establishing schools at the temporary detention site at Tanforan and at Topaz. Although art classes were held at other camps, Obata's schools were unique in their level of organization, the experience of their teachers, and the number of students who participated. The instructors included incarcerated Bay Area colleagues and many of his former students. Among them was the schools' cofounder, Issei artist George Matsusaburo Hibi (1886–1947), who had been associated with the California School of Fine Arts and exhibited throughout the Bay Area, and who became director of the school at Topaz upon Obata's release. Hisako Shimizu Hibi (1907–1991), also Issei, had studied painting at the California School of Fine Arts, where she met her husband, and at Tanforan and Topaz painted scenes of the camp environment and most distinctively of mothers and children.[10] Among younger Nisei, or American-born, teachers, Miné Okubo (1912–2001) had earned a master's degree in art from UC Berkeley and won several Federal Arts Program mural commissions, one of which was still in progress in the spring of 1942. Her drawings of incarceration at Tanforan and Topaz would come to national attention with their publication in 1944 and 1946. Her book *Citizen 13660* was the first published and remains the best-known first-person document of imprisonment.[11]

Elsewhere, experienced artists produced significant visual records. Issei Henry Sugimoto (1900–1990) had studied in San Francisco and Paris and been deeply impressed by Diego Rivera's socially engaged painting during a trip to Mexico.[12] Sent to the Jerome, Arkansas, camp, he painted bold, modernist compositions that protest the injustice of incarceration. Gene Sogioka (1914–1988), who was born in California and educated as a youth in Japan, and who returned to study at Chouinard Art Institute in Los Angeles, was working for Walt Disney Studios in 1942.[13] At the Poston camp in Arizona he was employed as an artist after his work attracted the attention of a naval psychiatrist who was studying the impact of confinement.[14] Another artist in the government's employ was Estelle Peck Ishigo (1899–1990), the Euroamerican wife of Nisei Arthur Ishigo

(1902–1957), whom she met at the Otis Art Institute in Los Angeles. Choosing to accompany her husband to camp at Heart Mountain, Wyoming, she was hired by the War Relocation Authority to document daily life there; years later she published a book of her drawings and narrative descriptions.[15] Kenjiro Nomura (1896–1956), the most widely exhibited Issei artist in Seattle before the war, produced figurative scenes and landscapes of the Puyallup temporary detention site and the Minidoka camp in more than seventy oil paintings, watercolors, and pencil sketches.[16] Another, Atsushi Kikuchi (1918–2016), a Nisei and former student at the California School of Arts and Crafts, drew what he described as "I don't know how many sketches . . . drawings of camp life, social conditions, political ideas, and so on" at the Santa Anita and Amache camps, but destroyed them all when he was inducted into the army.[17] Kikuchi would resettle in Chicago after military service, where he and Fujii displayed paintings in the same exhibitions for Chicago artists.[18]

The creative work of these and many more, both professional artists and amateurs, has come to light during the past thirty years. Within days of the attack on Pearl Harbor, cameras were declared contraband for West Coast Japanese Americans; the ban was enforced in the camps before being gradually relaxed in long-term detention. Artistic expression provided an important means of recording experience and expressing emotion. All of the camps offered popular art and craft classes to fill the tedium of confinement and, as Obata intended, to provide uplift amid grim conditions. The extent and quality of all kinds of artistic production was recognized by folk art champion Allen H. Eaton, who began to document and collect it before the camps closed and, in 1952, published a book on the subject, the first of its kind.[19] The extent of wartime work has become increasingly evident since the 1980s in an expanding field of scholarship. An early retrieval was the discovery of documents at Cornell University in 1982, which included a cache of Sogioka's watercolors of Poston left by Alexander Leighton, the former naval officer (and later Cornell professor) who had employed him there. The resulting book, *Beyond Words* by Deborah Gesensway and Mindy Roseman, preserves valuable first-person accounts by artists who have since died.[20] Exhibitions such as the Smithsonian's *A More Perfect Union: Japanese Americans and the U.S. Constitution*, which opened in 1987, presented art and craft objects as supporting evidence in a historical narrative.[21] More recently *The Art of Gaman*, an exhibition of wartime art and craft, has toured nationally for a decade at the time of this writing, bringing the breadth of artistic production to renewed public awareness.[22]

An art-historical account has developed more slowly alongside these larger historical narratives. In addressing Asian American art history as a whole, historian Gordon Chang notes that as Asian American studies was established as an academic discipline in the 1970s, it focused on political and social relations rather than intellectual and artistic pursuits, with the result that there is "virtually no" mention of art or individual artists in Asian American studies before the 1990s. He attributes the absence to the perception of artistic endeavor as elite and not relevant to social struggle.[23] Higa's 1992 exhibition and catalogue represent a landmark, having been among the first to present paintings and drawings of the Japanese American incarceration in an art-historical context, rather than as evidence in a standard history, and the first to tour nationally.[24] In the Northwest, Mayumi Tsutakawa's accounts of Seattle's Asian American artists began the recovery of a local art history outside California.[25] More recently, *Asian American Art*, in which the essay by Chang appears, provides a major compendium of essays, chronology, and artists' biographies that locates artistic production during incarceration within an ethnically specific framework. Published the same year, critical studies of Okubo's wartime work demonstrate the complicating readings of agency, resistance, generation, and gender to be found in such work.[26]

What, then, makes Fujii's story special? Fujii produced what I believe is a visual record of wartime incarceration that is unique among his generation. It is, moreover, primarily a private record, unlike others' work that was intended for a viewing public. It presents the perspective of an Issei man unmediated by the need to buffer, explain, or elaborate to a censoring authority or a mainstream audience. The central feature of his wartime production is an illustrated diary, nearly four hundred pages of image and text that spans the period from his forced departure from his Seattle home to the closing of the Minidoka Relocation Center, where he spent more than three years. In chronological scope alone it may be the most extended visual document of incarceration. Image and text complement one another to intensify meaning in a way that neither does alone; the reader seeks in the active space between the two the deeper insight the diary offers.

Step by step in the opening pages, Fujii describes in spare terms his move from freedom to incarceration. The diary is replete with images of the barbed wire fence, armed soldiers, and watchtowers as he surveys the temporary detention site at Puyallup and then the long-term Minidoka camp. He pictures the daily routine, kinds of work, and leisure activities, but the fact of confinement is always his preoccupation. Dozens of watercolors augment the diary's narrative. In more formally considered compositions, the watercolors emphasize the built environment rather than activities, and his selection of subjects underscores his constant awareness of his confined and controlled environment. Alongside artists' work of similar scope, Fujii's remains distinctive for his generational viewpoint, the restrained but revealing voice of text in relationship to image, and, in both the diary and watercolors, an insider's methodical survey of the site of imprisonment.

In creating such a record, Fujii demonstrates his resistance to the conditions of control and conformity in which he was forced to live. His work signifies an insistence upon self-representation and his determination to relate circumstances as he experienced them. In some, he depicts scenes to which no administrator, sentry, or outsider would be privy. In others he emphasizes his personal presence and perspective. He states simply, "Me," in picturing himself sketching from a rooftop in the Puyallup camp (diary 44); elsewhere he specifies his position and viewpoint, as, for example: "In the north: looking in the direction of the front gate from the back" (diary 16).[27] The diary as a whole and related wartime work demonstrate his extraordinary resilience and perseverance in continuing his project until leaving Minidoka, nearly two months after the end of hostilities and a month after the war formally ended with Japan's signed surrender.

The epigraph that begins this introduction reveals Fujii's aesthetic sensibility as well as his cultural understanding of human experience as part of the all-encompassing flow of nature. The diary entry can be dated to or about December 31, 1942, only ten days after the solstice, or "advent of spring" (on the following page he reports frostbite in the extreme cold weather).[28] The months since his arrival at Minidoka had been made all the more difficult by the deprivations he experienced in addition to those of freedom and privacy. Barracks and many other buildings were still under construction; for more than two months there were no plumbed toilets; and despite the bitter cold, there was little coal until late December.[29] Yet Fujii finds in the first winter of desert confinement "beautiful stripes of yellow sunlight" as birds sing in the bushes. His response is visual, aural, and in its evocative distillation, poetic.

None of Fujii's work other than the paintings from the 1930s has been seen outside the family. *The Hope of Another Spring* introduces the artist and brings the fullness of his accomplishment to public attention for the first time. In keeping with his extant production, the book focuses on his work of wartime. It consists of two parts: the first, a biographical and art-historical narrative that places Fujii's life and artistic production in the context of the time; and the second, a selection of entries from his diary that represents more than half of the original document. The diary and all works of art illustrated here are in the collection of Sandy and Terry Kita unless otherwise noted.

In his introduction to the diary, Sandy Kita, Fujii's grandson, a scholar of Japanese art, and the diary's primary translator, provides a personal view of his grandfather, one informed by his own understanding of Japanese art and culture. He describes the challenge of the translation and credits the assistance of scholar and native speaker Honda Shōjō. Fujii wrote in an idiosyncratic vernacular rather than a literary form of Japanese, in which many of the kanji can be read in various ways. The published text represents their collaboration in carefully rendering the diary's meaning and nuance. While my approach to the diary in English translation places it in its American context, the translators treat the diary as a Japanese text, as Sandy explains in his introduction. In order to maintain the integrity of their work, the events and circumstances to which Fujii refers are not annotated in the diary but instead incorporated into the main narrative.[30]

Unlike such notable artists of Fujii's generation as Yasuo Kuniyoshi and Chiura Obata, or his more locally known Seattle colleagues, Fujii left almost no published writings or personal papers other than the diary. Moreover, nearly all of his artwork is undated. Many of the personal details of the biography that follows are based upon Kita's memories of his grandfather and of family lore, which he has shared in personal conversations, phone calls, and e-mails over the course of more than four years. These are augmented by primary sources such as War Relocation Authority records, immigration and residency documents, museum records, periodicals, and others' personal papers. Framing Fujii's story is the larger narrative of the Japanese diaspora in the United States, one that is shaped by generation, gender, place, immigration history, and political and social relations in the United States and Japan and between the two nations. My account is indebted to many scholars who have contributed fundamentally to the field.

I come to this project as an art historian whose primary field is modern American art, rather than as a historian of Japanese America and wartime incarceration. In the past decade I have written about several Issei artists, and each project has taken me more deeply into Japanese American studies in an ongoing learning process. Additionally, the extended period of researching and writing this book has enabled me to see increasingly more layers of meaning in the diary as it continues to come alive with insights; every page yields a story worthy of retelling. Finally, I must add that as a longtime Americanist, I neither read nor speak Japanese and depend upon others for necessary translations. While my previous subjects' personal papers provided a sampling if not a complete record of newspaper or other references to them in Japanese, no such guide exists for Fujii, and consequently the book makes no account of anything that might have been published about him in his native language.[31]

Art historians as well as historians must address the terminology of what is commonly called "internment." Once the U.S. government determined to confine the West Coast ethnic Japanese, it adopted euphemisms to disguise the fact that most of them were American citizens who were being imprisoned without due process of law. All were described as "Japanese"; citizens were often called "non-aliens"; the process was called "evacuation," a term normally applied to rescue operations; and once they were locked in camps, the War Relocation Authority called them "colonists." Fujii and his family, like the others confined by the WRA, were charged with no crime and were imprisoned solely because of their ancestry. While contemporary scholarly usage of terms varies, I follow many historians in referring to *incarceration*, and to those confined as *inmates*, to describe the conditions under which most were held.[32]

The recovery of Fujii's personal history and artistic achievement adds to the growing body of art about the wartime incarceration and, in doing so, expands, complicates, and enriches American art history. Stephen Sumida argues for the recognition of Issei poetry in American literature, despite its having been written in Japanese, emphasizing that its content derives from the specific experiences of place, local conditions, and vernacular knowledge. "For the immigrant in Asian American literature," he writes, "definition of the self and identification of his or her actual culture in America depend critically" on such localized expression, enabling us to "see and hear people thought to be invisible [or] silent."[33] He reimagines ethnic-specific production in a cultural pluralism composed of "centers without margins" that contribute to, energize, and elucidate the whole.[34] Sandy Kita emphasizes that his grandfather, an Issei, remained essentially Japanese in not only language but also thought process and worldview. Without contradicting this firsthand understanding of the person, one can distinguish between the individual and his production: Fujii's work, produced in the context of and in response to his life in America, partakes of and contributes to the greater whole of American art. I have elsewhere examined his paintings of the 1930s in this context, and in this book I place his late work within contemporary American art of its time. It is equally important to claim a place in American art history for his artistic production during World War II. Fujii's work shares in the lineage of American realism and, more particularly, the vernacular realism of the 1930s. While it is restrained rather than strident, it shares also in the protest art of that era by giving legibly expressive visual form to gross social injustice. While it is documentary, it is more than documentation: each image, selected from the flux of experience, is a conceptualization and formal realization of the experience of forced removal and confinement. With an immediacy that words cannot provide, we see and feel a Japanese immigrant's perception of a historical episode we did not witness, but which is a critical part of this nation's history.

Whether in realism or new forms of abstraction, artists across the country sought to give expression to a world war of unprecedented scope. In the 1940s the leading artists in Seattle cited Asian and Western precedents as they searched for a means to express the essential unity of humankind in the face of wartime devastation. They made no mention of the Issei artists like Fujii, whose work they had praised, whom they had considered peers, and who by then had been removed from sight to isolated, segregated camps.[35] The incarceration of ethnic Japanese on the West Coast was a historic violation of the Constitution. Mass removal and confinement, without charge, of an entire population based solely upon ancestry was a wholesale denial of legal process and civil rights. As I complete this manuscript we are hearing calls again for the rounding up and confinement of an ethnic minority in the United States, something that seemed hardly believable even as I began the writing process. Fujii's work, like that of others in wartime, gives lasting visual expression to the reality of the experience. It represents a critical contribution to an inclusive picture of America built by many visions and voices.

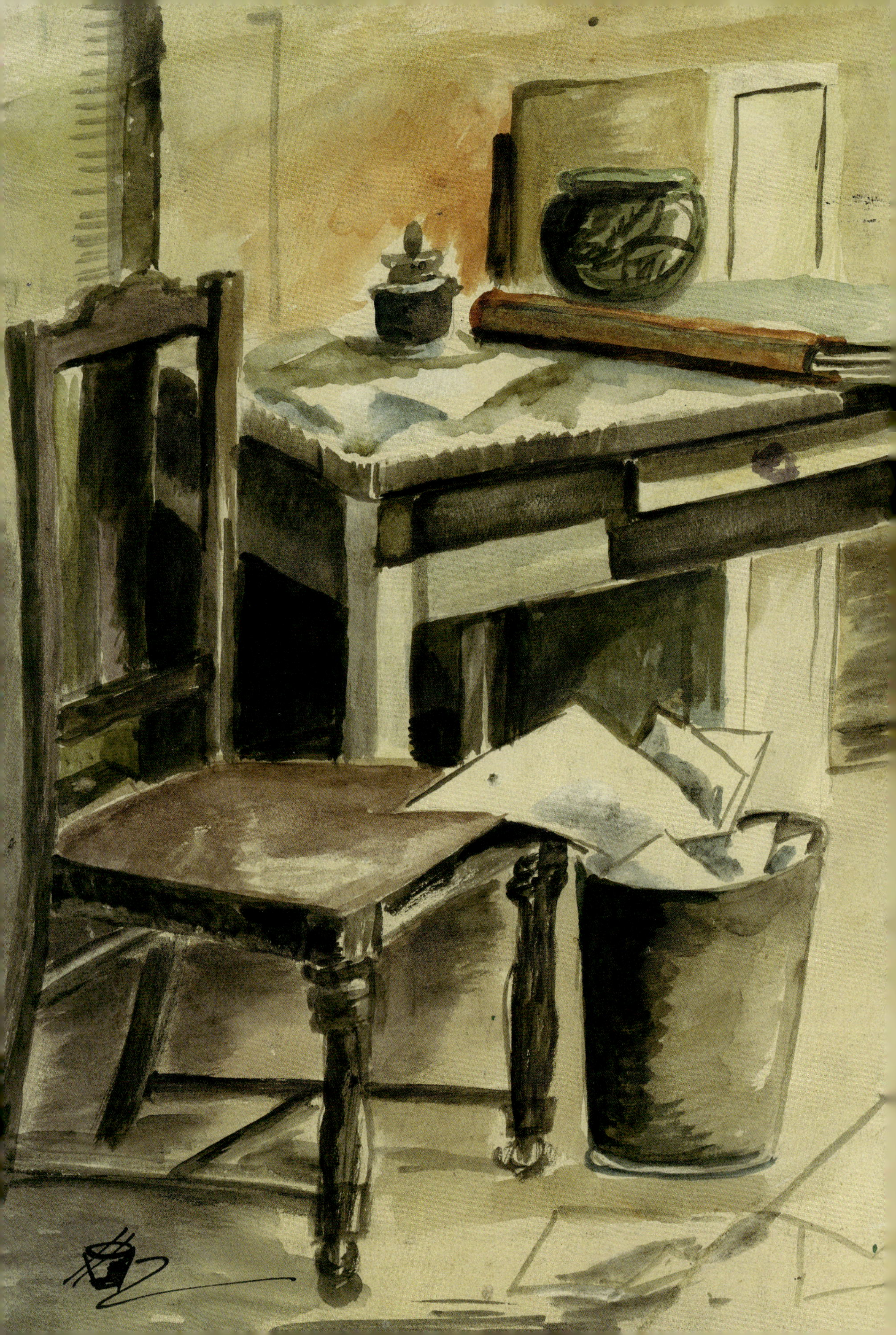

1 Another Spring

BIOGRAPHY

Fujii's painting of his desk can be seen as a self-portrait. Composed in watercolor on paper, it is undated but related to work he produced during World War II. It depicts a table and chair and a wastebasket overflowing with rejected attempts. On the table are more papers, an inkpot, and a large portfolio made to hold the finished watercolors of his wartime experience. There's also a ginger jar, the same jar that is featured in a still life oil painting from the 1930s, a sign of continuity in a disrupted life. The earlier painting bears the signature "Takuichi Fujii" in clearly written script and, on the back, a label from the Seattle Art Museum's 1935 *Annual Exhibition of Northwest Artists*. By contrast, the signature on the watercolor is a rice bowl with chopsticks, a motif that Fujii featured in a 1944 painting following news of a Japanese military defeat. The view of his workplace flickers with life even though no figure is present: the desk drawer stands open and the chair faces forward as if the subject had just left. In Fujii's portrayal of his desk, we can imagine the artist amid the meditation, conception, and trials and errors of studio work.

The signature suggests, however, the more complicated view of an immigrant artist negotiating his identity in the United States. Like most immigrants, Fujii remained grounded in his native culture while he adapted to the economic and social conditions of the American society in which he lived. His artistic method was Western, based on principles that had been introduced and practiced in Japan before he was born; his subjects were local and contemporary. Unlike European immigrants, however, he was ineligible under U.S. law, as an immigrant from Japan, for naturalized citizenship, and he remained a subject of Japan. Thus, when war erupted between Japan and the United States, he became an enemy alien. The American government's subsequent decision to incarcerate all

1.1 Desk and chair (detail), undated. Watercolor on paper, 11¾ × 9 in.

persons of Japanese descent on the West Coast, with no charge of wrongdoing, defined him solely on the basis of race and gave no recognition of his years of commitment to his American home.[1] In these circumstances, Fujii signed the painting of his desk, a deeply personal work space, with the image of a rice bowl. He left no record other than art to offer insight into his relationships to the nation of his birth and his adopted home, but his extensive body of work provides a richly nuanced visual record from a first-generation perspective.

YOUTH IN JAPAN

Fujii was born in 1891 in Hiroshima Prefecture and immigrated to Seattle in 1906.[2] He grew up in a rapidly modernizing Japan, which in little more than twenty years had transformed itself from a medieval society to a rising world power, even as it remained economically and socially divided by the inconsistency of its development. When he sailed to Seattle as a teenager, he became part of a transpacific diaspora in which the Japanese traveled abroad for education and work, many, at first, returning to Japan, and eventually many, like Fujii, making new homes for themselves in North and South America. In the new country he became an Issei, or first-generation Japanese American, a status that would shape his experience.

The transformation of Japan that defined Fujii's youth was the result of a determined, government-led effort. As the country had become increasingly threatened by the imperial interests of Europe and the United States, a revolutionary group led the overthrow of the Tokugawa shogunate, which for 250 years had tightly ruled Japan and closed it to nearly all contact with the West. The revolutionary leaders restored the position of emperor, giving name to the Meiji period (1868–1912), and formed a new government with the goals of building a modern social framework, a strong military, and an industrial base in order to compete on an equal footing with Western nations. Western knowledge was considered essential to modernization; American and European teachers and advisors were invited to Japan and Japanese students sent abroad. In the mid-1880s, driven by pressure from international labor markets and by economic and social dislocation at home, Japan opened emigration to contract laborers.

Labor emigration, which the Japanese government intended as only a short-term solution, was a response to an economic crisis in the wake of unsustainable inflation and budgetary deficits resulting from rapid modernization. The government's deflationary policy to stabilize the economy produced crippling losses among the nation's small entrepreneurs and farmers, and it hit rural areas, which benefited little from modernization, particularly hard.[3] To ease the pressure, the government lifted its ban on contract labor emigration to Hawai'i and mainland United States in 1885. The decision opened a major period of Japanese immigration that lasted for two decades, until political events in America slowed the pace in 1907 and brought immigration to an end in 1924.[4]

The years of Fujii's youth coincided with a period of competing forces as the rapidity of change brought a conservative political reaction, while a generation who had come of age during the Meiji period continued to push for modernization. The result was an assimilation of indigenous and foreign practices that produced a new, distinctively Japanese modern culture. During these years Japan also proved its new military strength. Its 1895 victory in the Sino-Japanese War and its surprise 1905 defeat of Russia in the Russo-Japanese War gave the country access to badly needed raw materials on the Asian mainland. The latter victory of a small nation over a large one, the first by an Asian over a European nation, gave credibility to Japan's ambitions to become a world power. Culturally as well as economically, however, modernization was inconsistent and the impact throughout Japan uneven. Beneath the official and intellectual surface, the country retained many of its old ways.[5]

Fujii's place of birth was shaped by these events. With the abolishment of samurai domains, Japan had been divided into prefectures and Hiroshima declared the capital of Hiroshima Prefecture. The capital grew rapidly as the economy began to shift from rural to urban, and in 1889 it was one of thirty-nine population centers designated "cities" as the Meiji regime continued to institutionalize a highly centralized government. It was home to one of seven English-language schools in Japan built by the national government in the early Meiji years. The city was located on the Seto Inland Sea and became a major port when the government constructed a harbor a decade later. The railroad was extended to Hiroshima in 1894, then to the harbor during the Sino-Japanese War. Industrialization spread as transportation capacity increased and was further spurred by the Russo-Japanese War. The region, however, was far from the seat of power in Tokyo and shared rural Japan's economic dislocation.[6]

Little is known about Fujii's family and youth. His father was Matsuzo Fujii, his mother, Kane Fujii. He had at least one brother, Nobuichi, twelve years his senior.[7] Takuichi Fujii attended eight years of grammar school in Hiroshima (six years were required under the national system), followed by two years at the private Shudo school.[8] The curriculum included moral education that instilled the core value of loyalty to emperor, country, and family; Western learning was introduced progressively and dominated the upper grades. Fujii's family was well enough situated to provide him the opportunity of private study in brushwork (*sumi-e*, or ink painting) and watercolor, although there is nothing to indicate whether that study was independent or part of the Shudo curriculum.[9] In September 1906, a few days after his fifteenth birthday, Fujii boarded the *Shinano Maru* in Kobe bound for Seattle, where his father and brother were already working.

MAKING A HOME IN SEATTLE

When three weeks later the *Shinano Maru* sailed into Seattle's Smith Cove, Fujii found himself in a raw young city only fifty years from its frontier beginnings, a striking contrast to the centuries-old home he had left behind. Sited on the eastern shore of Puget Sound, Seattle is a city of steep hills reaching down to the water, an isthmus squeezed between the Sound on the west and Lake Washington on the east. It is the American mainland port closest to Asia and historically a port of entry. City fathers had determinedly rebuilt after a fire destroyed downtown in 1889, but it was the discovery of gold in the Yukon Territory that brought the greatest new wealth and opportunity to the city. From Smith Cove southward past downtown, hundreds of ships docked at side-by-side piers.

The city's growth and modernization paralleled the major period of Japanese immigration to the United States, which spanned from about 1890 to 1924. Seattle claimed the first direct shipping service between Japan and the mainland United States, a deal negotiated by railroad magnate James J. Hill, the "Empire Builder," whose trains stretched across the West to the Seattle port. On the initial direct-transport voyage to Seattle in 1896, the *Miike Maru* carried freight and two hundred and fifty-three Japanese passengers and was wildly greeted by hundreds of boats, fireworks, and cheering bystanders upon its arrival.[10] In 1903 the *Seattle Times* reported that twenty thousand Japanese were arriving in the United States annually, with the greater number of them coming through the ports of Puget Sound.[11] It was an inaccurate boast—more sailed to California ports, and many who were headed to Seattle landed first in Vancouver—but its swagger nonetheless suggests the new visual presence of ethnic Japanese. In fact, they represented less than 3 percent of Seattle's population, which overall nearly tripled during the first decade of the century.

Despite the *Miike Maru*'s enthusiastic reception, Seattle had a mixed reaction to the newcomers. A number of civic and business leaders eagerly sought to capitalize upon the opportunities for trade with Asia, particularly with the modern nation of Japan, and enthusiastically promoted the city as the "Gateway to the Orient." Highlighting these aspirations was the Alaska-Yukon-Pacific Exposition in 1909, just three years after Fujii's arrival, in which Japan was prominently featured and celebrated (fig. 1.2). As part of their claim of a

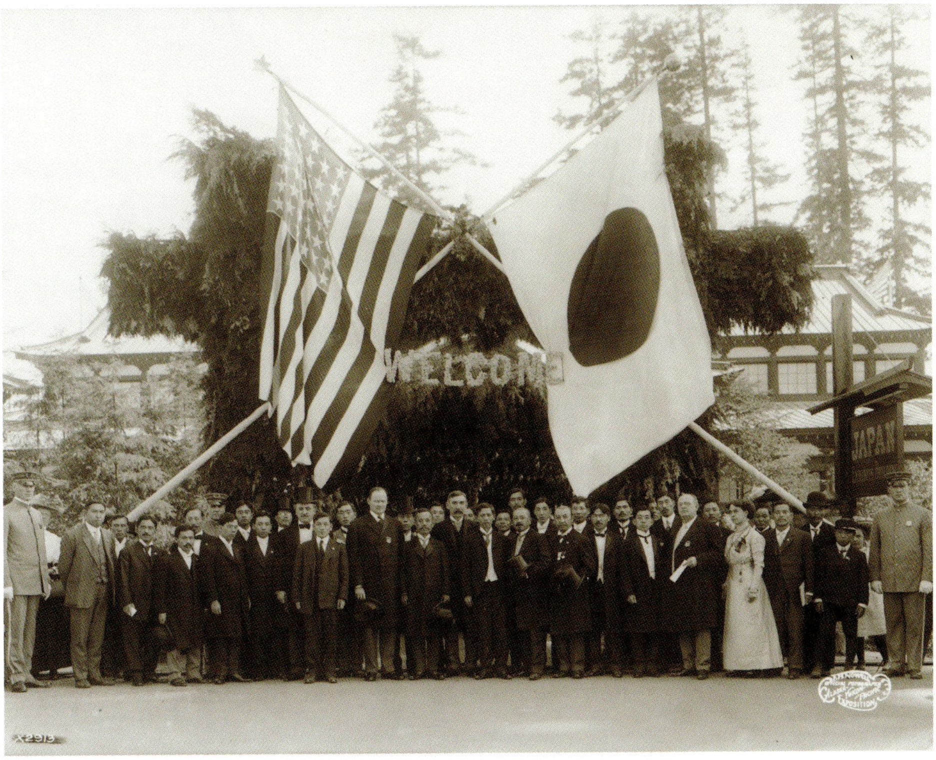

1.2 Japan Building dedication, Alaska-Yukon-Pacific Exposition, Seattle, July 21, 1909. Photo: Frank K. Nowell. Special Collections, University of Washington Libraries, PH Coll 727.416.

special relationship, city leaders credited Seattle's "cosmopolitan" mix of nationalities and looked to the leaders of the Japanese community for help in making connections to Japan.[12] Below the official veneer, however, the relationship was more problematic. In the press, they were "little brown men," even when they arrived as visiting dignitaries, whose decorum, reporters noted, was superior to that of many locals.[13] Marked differences in appearance, language, and culture, as well as the Japanese government's relationship to its people abroad, set apart the Japanese residents. White businesses, farmers, and labor did not necessarily welcome their participation and, increasingly, their economic competition. Historian Roger Daniels traces white antipathy to decades of anti-Asian racism, beginning with agitation against Chinese immigrants in the mid-nineteenth century and, after the 1882 passage of the Chinese Exclusion Act, readily transferred to the newly arriving Japanese.[14] The anti-Japanese movement began gaining momentum after 1900 as immigration to the West Coast increased. To many, the ethnic Japanese were unassimilable, forever alien to Euroamerican society. Legally and socially restricted in opportunity and connected in language and culture, most of the immigrants clustered together in Nihonmachi, or Japantown. There Fujii made his home.

Fujii's father and older brother had preceded him to Seattle, his father in 1902, and his brother the following year. Together the father and sons represented the second and third generations to leave Japan to work in the United States. An exceptionally large number of immigrants came from Hiroshima. When Japan changed its labor emigration policy in 1885, nearly thirty thousand Japanese left for Hawai'i in a decade of government-sponsored emigration, "what must rank as one of the best organized mass migrations in history."[15] Most came from the largely rural Hiroshima and Yamaguchi Prefectures in southwest Japan, and more came from Hiroshima than anywhere else, a pattern that would influence West Coast immigration.[16] When contract labor was abolished in 1900 following the American annexation of Hawai'i, thousands sailed to the mainland for greater opportunity.[17] Labor on the mainland paid up to ten times that in Japan, making prospects attractive despite the approximately one-hundred-dollar expense of the trip.[18] Fujii, his father, and brother became part of the subsequent wave of migration.

Of the three, only Fujii remained to become a first-generation settler, an Issei. His father and brother were *dekasegi*, or sojourners, among those who saved money in order to return to Japan.[19] His father worked as a laborer in the construction industry. The three of them most likely took rooms in one of the many residential hotels for single men, a business increasingly dominated by Issei. The local Hiroshima Prefecture organization was the largest of its kind in Japanese Seattle and provided immigrants an important means of socializing and support services, as well as a strong sense of group identification.[20] For eight years the young Fujii worked for the Main Fish Company in Nihonmachi and, in time, rose to salesman.

Nihonmachi lay at the southern edge of Seattle's downtown, growing alongside Chinese, and later Filipino, settlements in a tightly packed pan-Asian community. It spread north from Jackson and Main Streets up the steep south slope of Yesler Hill (now First Hill) and east and south from its center at Fifth and Sixth Avenues. Some residents scattered farther throughout the city; a few prominent families moved into established neighborhoods like Capitol Hill, while others, such as nursery owners, moved north and south, where more land was available. Within several years of Fujii's arrival, the number of ethnic Japanese, collectively called Nikkei, grew from 2,990 in 1900 to 6,217 in 1910, and to 7,874 in 1920. Fujii's family typified the changing population; although many, like his father and brother, returned to Japan, further immigration and

American-born children added to the net population gain, as would Fujii's wife and daughters.[21]

Like many immigrant groups with a shared language and culture, Seattle's Japanese community was in many respects closely knit; yet it contained distinct divisions of class, education, and gender, divisions that were further layered by individuals' familial origins in Japan, their current relationships to Japan, and their relationships to white society. Both nations made claims upon the Issei: Japan in holding them as subjects living abroad; the United States in viewing them as a racial Other. Subject to Japan but bound to the social, economic, and political realities of their American home, the Issei had a dual relationship to the two nations, responding actively, selectively, and strategically to the priorities of each nation and to changing international political relations. Early Issei leaders represented an established urban mercantile class who had a cosmopolitan vision of transpacific cooperation and fervently distinguished themselves from the laboring "masses" from rural Japan, who were focused on survival and more reflexively connected to Japan.[22] Regardless of class, however, all were defined by race in relationship to white America.[23] Japan, moreover, had its own racial definition of the Issei and their offspring, whom it claimed by "blood."[24]

Community relationships in Seattle, as elsewhere on the West Coast, changed throughout the early twentieth century in response to shifting relations between Japan and the United States, as American exclusionary politics gained headway after 1900. A signal change in community organization followed the Gentlemen's Agreement of 1907–8, in which Japan agreed to halt labor immigration to the United States by issuing passports only to designated categories of people.[25] Negotiated over many months, the agreement was intended to mollify American exclusionist demands as well as to serve Japan's aim of reversing the trend toward permanent settlement.[26] One of the outcomes was the Japanese government's greater reliance upon its diplomats in America and its delegation of the responsibility to watch over its subjects already in the country to the Japanese Association of America. A partnership between the Japanese diplomatic corps and the Issei elite established a network throughout the West in which local chapters of the Japanese Association were responsible to regional consuls and, through them, to the national association and the consulate general in San Francisco and, by extension, to the Japanese government. The Japanese consul was the symbolic leader of the community and representative of the emperor; the Japanese Association served as the organizational center of the community on a practical, daily basis and the hub of the many trade associations.[27] Both promoted acculturation and excellence in business practices and education.[28] As historian Eiichiro Azuma describes, the leadership aimed to "transform the masses of laboring men and women into imperial subjects, who could simultaneously partake fully of American life and citizenship."[29] The agreement did not stop further restrictions of Issei rights; nor, in Azuma's view, did the elites' idealized vision significantly influence the majority of working-class immigrants. Rather than aligning themselves with one side or the other, the Issei continued a dynamic process of selectively accommodating the nation to which they were subjects and the one where they made their home.

Events of the following years progressively limited Issei rights. Nativist reaction flared after World War I, when veterans returned to compete for jobs in an economic downturn. Following California's lead, Washington passed the Alien Land Law in 1921, which banned Issei from owning, leasing, or renting real property.[30] The Issei protested the legislation in lawsuits but lost them all.[31] In a further setback in 1922, the U.S. Supreme Court declared that the Japanese were not "white" and thus were ineligible for naturalized citizenship as framed by the U.S. Constitution.[32] Excluded from naturalization, the Issei had no means to represent themselves in the political process. "This state of powerlessness," asserts historian Yuji Ichioka, "is a central theme in Japanese immigrant history."[33]

The final blow, with the greatest impact on relations within Japanese America and on international relations, was the National Origins Act of 1924. Aimed at maintaining a majority American population with northern European ancestry, the act established a system of quotas that favored northern over southern and eastern Europe and barred altogether those "ineligible for citizenship," in effect ending immigration from Asia. The most visible consequence in the Nikkei community was the age gap between the first and second generations as the Issei, not joined by new arrivals, became an increasingly older population. Cut off from rights of land ownership and citizenship, the Issei had little option but to commit their efforts and aspirations to their American-born children, who were collectively named Nisei to distinguish the new generation.[34] The Issei were exhorted to instill Japanese moral values in their children with the expectation that they would serve as a bridge of understanding across the Pacific. When the Nisei began to come of age in the 1930s, both generations navigated dual relationships to the two nations even as age and generation added layers of complication to existing divisions of economic and social class.[35] The institutionalization of racial exclusion reinforced, although negatively, the high degree of social cohesion that Issei-led community building had produced. Confronting exclusion, the Issei began to view themselves as "the Japanese in America," a body apart, barred from full participation in white America and distanced from Japan by their experience living in the United States.[36]

Seattle's Nihonmachi shared the social cohesion common to Nikkei communities throughout the West but was also notable for its exceptional level of entrepreneurship. By 1930 there were reportedly more than nine hundred individual businesses. Stated in different terms, nearly half (46 percent) of the income earners were small business owners.[37] Businesses were also notable in their concentration. A majority of Seattle's Issei within the trades were engaged in hotel management, groceries, and dry cleaning, and increasingly these Issei-run businesses dominated their respective industries in the city.[38]

Fujii joined Nihonmachi's entrepreneurs when he established his own wholesale and retail fish business in 1917, the first of three small businesses he would operate in the next twenty-five years (his wife initiated the third). For three or more years he maintained a stall at the Pike Place public market, where, despite efforts to marginalize them, Japanese farmers and merchants made up three-quarters of the vendors.[39] By 1926 he had moved his business to a storefront, the Fujii Fish Market, at Twelfth and Jackson Streets, which was an active business district dominated by Issei merchants (fig. 1.3). The location was significant. Several blocks east of the center of Nihonmachi, it was in close proximity to institutions such as the Seattle Buddhist Temple and the Japanese Language School but far enough from the center to enable regular interchange with other ethnic groups. The African American newspaper *Northwest Enterprise* described Jackson Street as the "leading thoroughfare of the South business district," which, although it was often scorned by other city residents, was

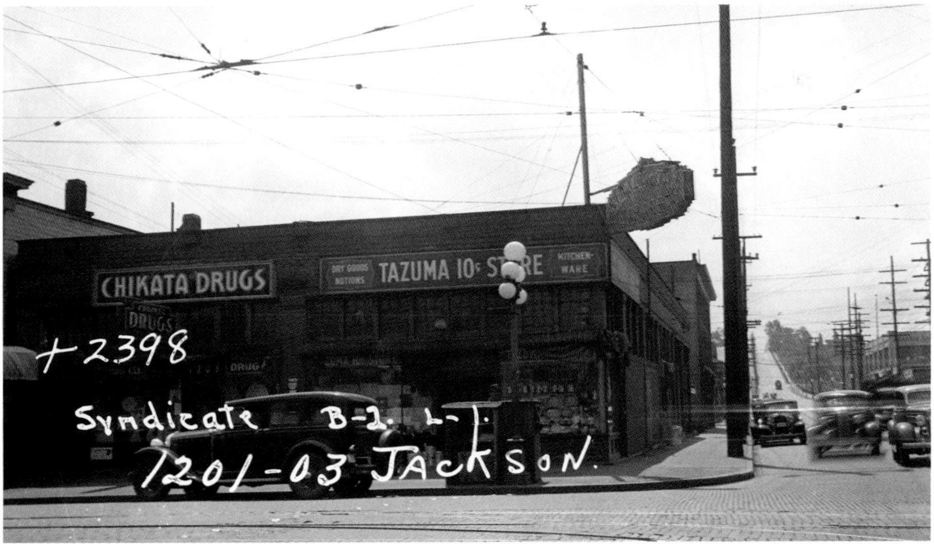

1.3 Twelfth and Jackson Streets, Seattle, 1937. Washington State Archives, Puget Sound Regional Branch.

where "Filipinos, Japanese, Negroes, and whites mingle."[40] Kamekichi Tokita, who managed a hotel at the outbreak of World War II, believed it was to his advantage to live at the periphery of Nihonmachi, where he had regular dealings with a white clientele and was removed from the insular, rumor-prone center.[41] With the exception of a two-year absence, Fujii lived and worked in the neighborhood until World War II.[42]

Fujii made one return trip to Japan after ten years in Seattle. He traveled to Hiroshima for six months in 1916, a trip during which he is thought to have addressed problems with his military registration.[43] In seeking help from a city official, he met the official's daughter and his future wife, Fusano Marumachi (1896–1995). Fusano was from an old samurai family. She had completed three years of high school and was well educated in the traditional arts of *koto* (a thirteen-string instrument), *kendo* (swordsmanship), and *naginata-jutsu* (halberd fighting).[44] Family stories recount that Fujii and her father developed a friendship through their mutual love of books; and although Fusano was engaged to a naval officer, she and Fujii, with little to his name but books, became attracted to one another. Overcoming her father's initial resistance, they were married in Hiroshima, and in 1916 they sailed separately from Kobe to make a home in Seattle.

For the first few years they lived on the south slope of First Hill, near where Fujii had lived as a single man. It was at this time, having returned from Japan, that he opened his own business as a fish merchant, and by the mid-1920s he established a home and shop at Twelfth and Jackson. Their daughter Satoko was born in 1917; and in 1919, a second daughter, Masako, was born. Although Fujii was Buddhist, he believed his daughters would benefit in the United States by being Christian, and so they were baptized in the Roman Catholic Church, a common practice among Issei parents, according to the pastor and memoirist Daisuke Kitagawa.[45] They lived a block away from Bailey Gatzert Elementary School, whose student body was predominately Nisei; and later, the girls could walk up the hill to Broadway High School, where a quarter of the students were ethnic Japanese.[46]

Culturally and spatially, Fujii was a denizen of Nihonmachi, while his roles as a businessman and an artist connected him to the larger community. The neighborhood had a vibrant cultural and intellectual life. Fujii subscribed to *Hokubei Jiji* (North American Times), one of five Japanese-language newspapers in the 1920s and one of three, including the English-language *Japanese American Courier*, that would continue until World War II. The papers, often the Issei's only source of world news, consistently represented the Japanese perspective on events and reinforced community cohesion in publicizing organizations such

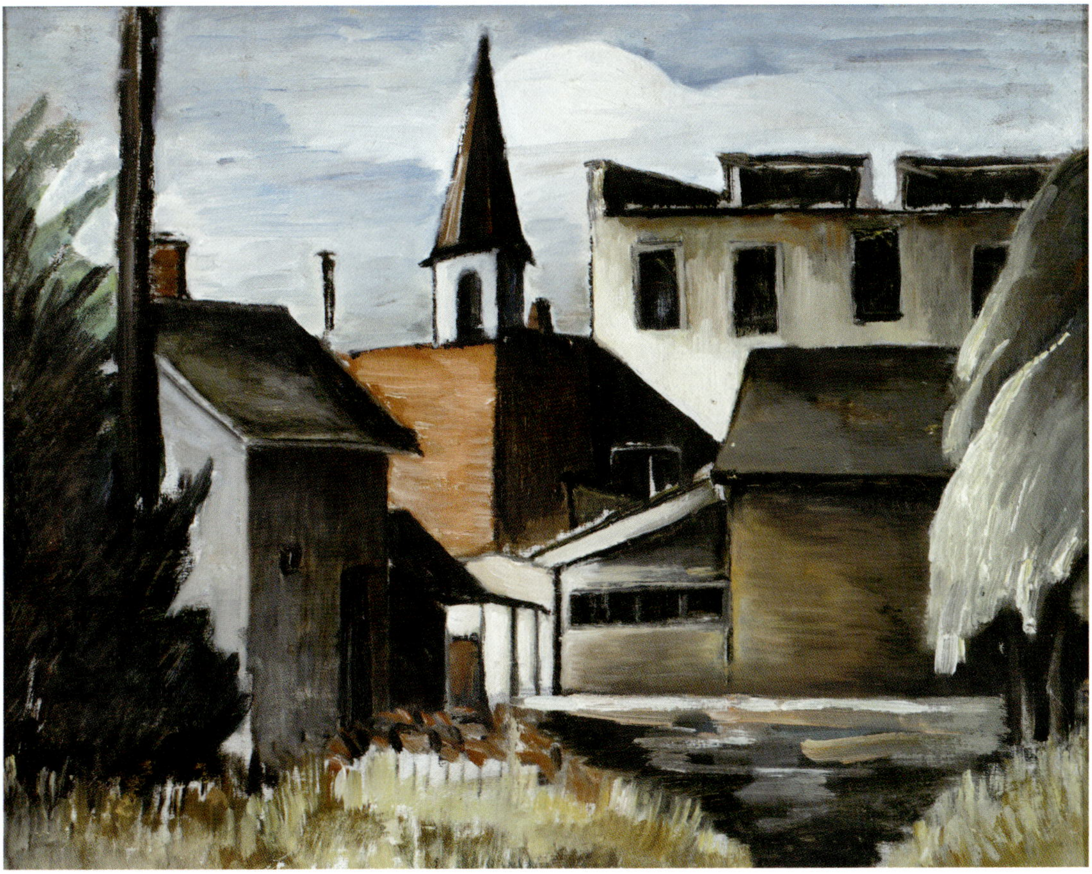

1.4 Title unknown (steeple of Church of Our Lady of Good Help viewed from Nihonmachi), early or mid-1930s. Oil on canvas, 16 × 20 in. Private collection. Photo: Richard Nicol.

as the Japanese Association and the consulate.[47] He and Fusano surely attended events at the Nippon Kan, the purpose-built theater and community center. *Noh* and *Kabuki* as well as contemporary Japanese drama appeared regularly at the Nippon Kan.[48] Fusano, who had brought her *koto* to Seattle, must have followed music and dance performances there with interest.

The visual arts were equally vital, with Western practices thriving alongside older Japanese forms. Members of the Issei-dominated Seattle Camera Club, led from 1925 to 1929 by Dr. Kyō Koike, exhibited and published their pictorialist photographs to international acclaim.[49] Concurrently a number of Fujii's peers, including Kenjiro Nomura and Kamekichi Tokita, formed a club to exhibit their paintings together.[50] Whether or not Fujii was formally a part of the group, given the demands of a young family and a business, his artistic skills developed alongside theirs. The first of his paintings exhibited to a mainstream audience in 1930, as chapter 2 describes, are fully realized modernist compositions that give clear evidence of his engagement (see, for example, fig. 1.4).

BECOMING AN ARTIST

Issei painters working in the Western tradition had been well recognized in Seattle's mainstream since the early twentieth century. A number of them gathered in the studio of Fokko Tadama, who had emigrated from the Netherlands in 1909 and established one of the city's two main teaching studios. Issei painters represented five of thirty-one artists in the Seattle Fine Arts Society's first annual juried exhibition for local artists, in 1914.[51] Among the best known were Yasushi Tanaka and Toshi Shimizu, who exhibited also in Nihonmachi venues, San Francisco's Panama-Pacific International Exposition, and in solo exhibitions at the Seattle Fine Arts Society and the Washington State Art Association. The two of them became mentors to young Kenjiro Nomura when he began studying in Tadama's studio in 1916.[52]

Writing from the perspective of the mid-1930s, an editor of the *Japanese American Courier* looked back to three periods of notable artistic success among Nikkei painters. He identified the first as that of the artists associated with the Tadama studio at the time of World War I. The second was that of the group of young painters in the 1920s, including Nomura and Tokita, who formed a club, Shunjukai, named for their spring and autumn exhibitions. Among those of the third and then-current wave of the 1930s, he cited Nomura and Tokita, who by that time had accumulated significant honors; Fujii, who had won recognition in Seattle and San Francisco; their colleague Keijiro Miyao; and the younger Shiro Miyazaki.[53] Nomura and Tokita had already emerged as leaders, and increasingly Fujii was linked with them, comprising a trio.

Fujii's formal entrance to the Seattle art scene was the acceptance of his painting at the juried *Sixteenth Annual Exhibition of Northwest Artists* (commonly called the Northwest Annual) at the Art Institute of Seattle in 1930. The following spring he exhibited in the annual juried exhibition of the San Francisco Art Association, held at the California Palace of the Legion of Honor. That fall he showed three paintings at the Northwest Annual, where one was awarded honorable mention, the equivalent of second prize. For the next several years he exhibited in all but one annual. The years 1935 and 1936 were ones of peak recognition. When a number of progressive Seattle artists organized the Group of Twelve to advance the "best painting in the Northwest," Fujii was invited to be a member.[54] In 1936, Fujii, together with Nomura and Tokita, was among ten artists selected to represent Washington State in the *First National Exhibition of American Art* in New York City.

This trajectory of professional recognition was disrupted when, about 1937, Fujii moved to Chicago.[55] Nothing indicates whether the move was prompted by the Depression's continuing impact or a more personal motivation. (The *Japanese American Courier* describes him in 1935 as a "former fish merchant.")[56] The Depression had already forced changes among his colleagues; two respected painters, Shigemitzu Hamada and Genzō (Frank) Tomita, had moved away, and in 1936 Nomura and Tokita closed their sign-painting shop, which had been a lively gathering place for Nikkei painters. Fujii and his family spent about two years in Chicago, which had a small ethnic Japanese population of about four hundred. In early 1937 he exhibited *Hillside*, its title evocative of a Seattle subject, at the Art Institute of Chicago's annual exhibition for regional artists.[57] Within a year he was engaged in a new business, the Fujii Restaurant. Family stories relate that when Fusano saw him painting pictures on a display case he had begun to give a new coat of paint, she asked if he did not want to be an artist rather than a cook or merchant.

In 1939, Fujii and his wife returned to Seattle and resettled at Twelfth and Yesler in their former neighborhood. His daughters, having graduated from high school, remained in Chicago to work, although they would return to Seattle sometime before April 1942.[58] Recognizing his desire to devote time to painting, Fusano took the lead in supporting the couple. She opened a flower shop, Mary Rose Florist (based on the American name of their older daughter), where Fujii assisted but was freed from primary responsibility.[59] It was the most successful of their businesses.

For the next two years Fujii once again exhibited in the Northwest Annuals. The title of his 1941 entry, *East of Wenatchee*, names a locale in the Columbia River country in central Washington, an area he had visited and painted before his departure for Chicago and to which he had since returned.

WARTIME

The 1941 Northwest Annual closed on November 2. A month later, on December 7, Japan attacked the American Pacific fleet in Pearl Harbor, an event that irrevocably changed Fujii's life and that of all ethnic Japanese on the West Coast. Within four days American neutrality collapsed as the United States became engrossed in war against Japan, Germany, and Italy. Immigrants from the three nations who were not naturalized citizens were declared "enemy aliens." Of these, however, only those from Japan had no choice about citizenship. And of the American-born children of these immigrant groups, only those of the ethnic Japanese also became targets of suspicion. Nikkei of all generations were seen by many as members of an enemy race, without consideration for place of birth or years invested in the United States. It provoked a profound identity crisis for the Issei, who had committed their lives to their adopted country but were legally barred from naturalized citizenship. They remained subjects of Japan and, to varying degrees, culturally Japanese.

The attack on Pearl Harbor inflamed nearly a century of entrenched anti-Asian racism, which escalated rapidly amid wartime propaganda. Increasingly, many made no distinction between the vicious depictions of the enemy nation Japan and the ethnic Japanese in America. In an environment of fear intensified by Japan's seemingly unstoppable military forces, President Franklin Roosevelt issued Executive Order 9066 on February 19, 1942, giving authority to the army to establish military zones "from which any or all persons may be excluded," targeting although not naming people of Japanese descent on the West Coast.[60]

The question of mass exclusion had been a contested one within Roosevelt's administration. Within two weeks of Pearl Harbor, the head of the Western Defense Command, Lieutenant General John L. DeWitt, who was determined to avoid blame such as that placed on the military commanders at Pearl Harbor, proposed that all enemy aliens be removed from the region and confined in the interior. Aiming more broadly, Major General Allen W. Guillon, head of the army's military police, and his chief spokesperson, Major Karl Bendetsen, pressed the case for the mass exclusion of Japanese Americans.[61] Both pressured the "insecure, inconsistent, and indecisive" DeWitt, who disliked the idea but was increasingly persuaded by Guillon and Bendetsen.[62] Opposing mass exclusion was Attorney General Francis Biddle, who argued against the abrogation of citizens' rights and, as late as February, told Roosevelt that mass exclusion was unwarranted. After weeks of interdepartmental feuding and concessions to military demands, Biddle relinquished his stand in a statement to Secretary of War Henry Stimson, saying that military necessity, under conditions only vaguely suggested, could legally justify the removal of all persons from designated areas.[63] DeWitt, by that point fully onboard, reported to Stimson: "The Japanese race is an enemy race, and while many second and third generations born on American soil, possessed of United States citizenship, have become 'Americanized,' the racial strains are undiluted."[64] In blunter terms, he would later declare, "A Jap's a Jap."[65]

When the first exclusion orders were posted on March 24 on Bainbridge Island, across Puget Sound from Seattle, they and all others covering the West Coast exclusionary zone targeted "all persons of Japanese ancestry, both alien

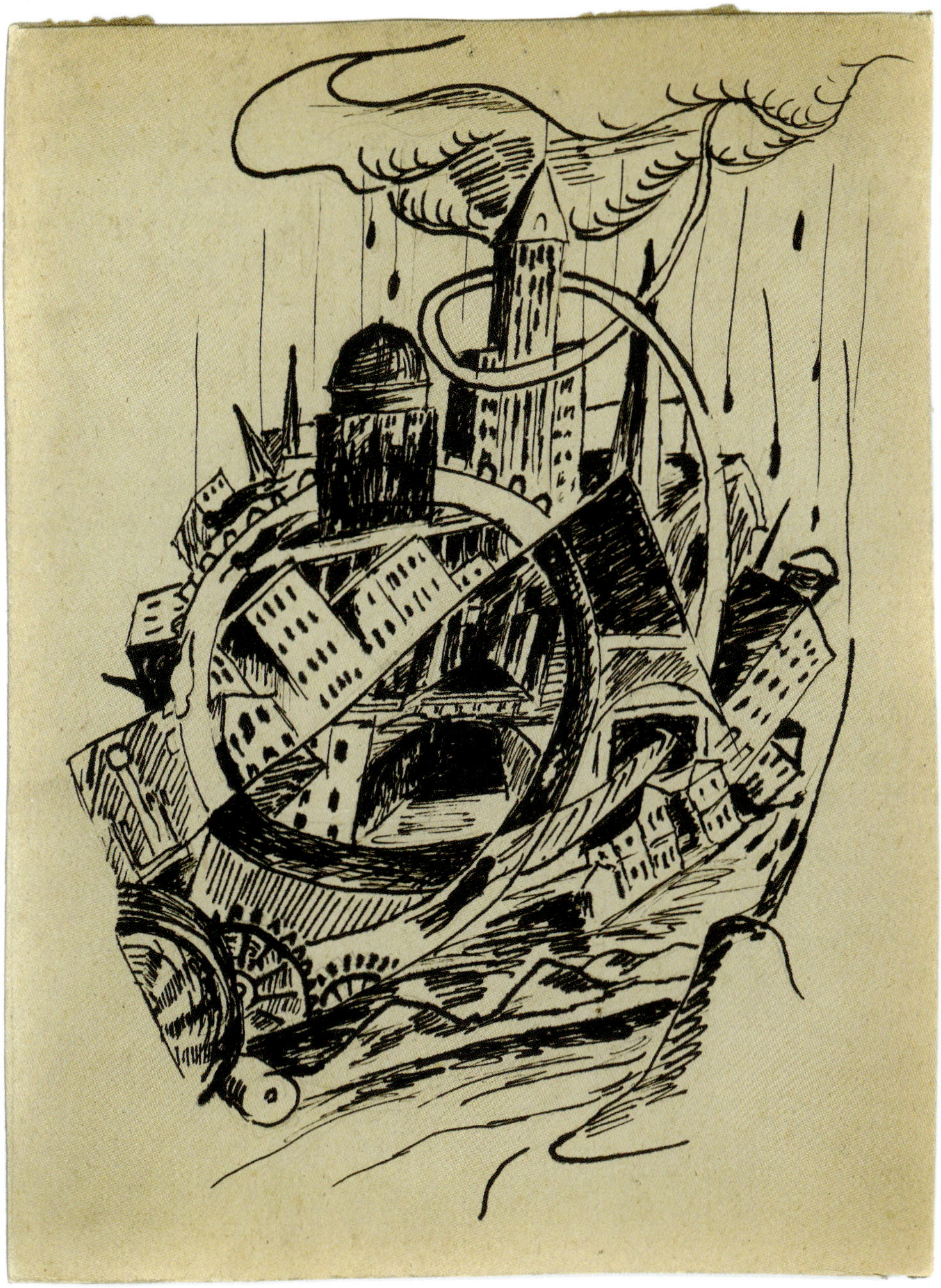

1.5 Seattle in wartime, undated. Ink on paperboard, 10¾ × 8 in.

and non-alien." The convoluted term "non-alien" masked the issue of citizenship as the order swept up first, second, and third generations. Over the next five months DeWitt issued a series of orders that determined the successive stages of exclusion and incarceration. It is DeWitt whom Fujii names as the authority confining him and his family.

As early as December 7, 1941, the FBI began arresting Issei men considered to be leaders in the Nikkei community.[66] The Japanese Association and the Japanese Chamber of Commerce, which shared offices in the center of Nihonmachi, were immediately shut down, one of many closures that took place during this time. Stepping into the leadership void, young Nisei men in Seattle gathered around James Sakamoto, a founder of the Japanese American Citizens League and the editor of the *Japanese American Courier*. Within days of the bombing they organized the Emergency Defense Council to demonstrate their loyalty as U.S. citizens and, in doing so, cooperate with government intelligence. When exclusion of the entire West Coast Nikkei population was made evident by Executive Order 9066, the league's national executive secretary, Mike Masaoka, declared that "we will have no hesitation complying" with orders for mass removal.[67] Sakamoto, aligned with the national organization, formed a coterie of Nisei who became an exceptionally disciplined group. Government authorities, who knew little about the ethnic community, turned to them for help and would continue to do so during the first months of the incarceration. Charged with the daily management of affairs at the Puyallup temporary detention center, the Nisei loyal to Sakamoto would maintain tight control.

The first exclusion orders were posted in Seattle on April 24, with departure scheduled for May 1, and in Fujii's neighborhood on May 3, with departure for May 8 and 9.[68] In the few days' interim, heads of families reported for registration, where, under the surveillance of armed soldiers, their family names were replaced by numbers and numbered tags assigned to each family member. Altogether 110,000 people of Japanese descent, two-thirds of whom were American citizens, were forcibly ordered from their homes in the western half of Washington and Oregon, all of California, and part of Arizona.[69] Most sold businesses, farms, and personal possessions at deep losses, abandoning the fruits of many years' work, while a few were able to make arrangements to protect their property. All packed the required warm clothing, basic eating utensils, and bedding and what few additional possessions they could carry. They lined up, were herded onto buses, and were taken away under armed guard (fig. 1.6).

On May 9 the Fujiis boarded a bus bound for Puyallup, thirty miles south of Seattle, where the Western Washington State Fairgrounds had been converted to a hastily built temporary detention site, the Puyallup Assembly Center. The

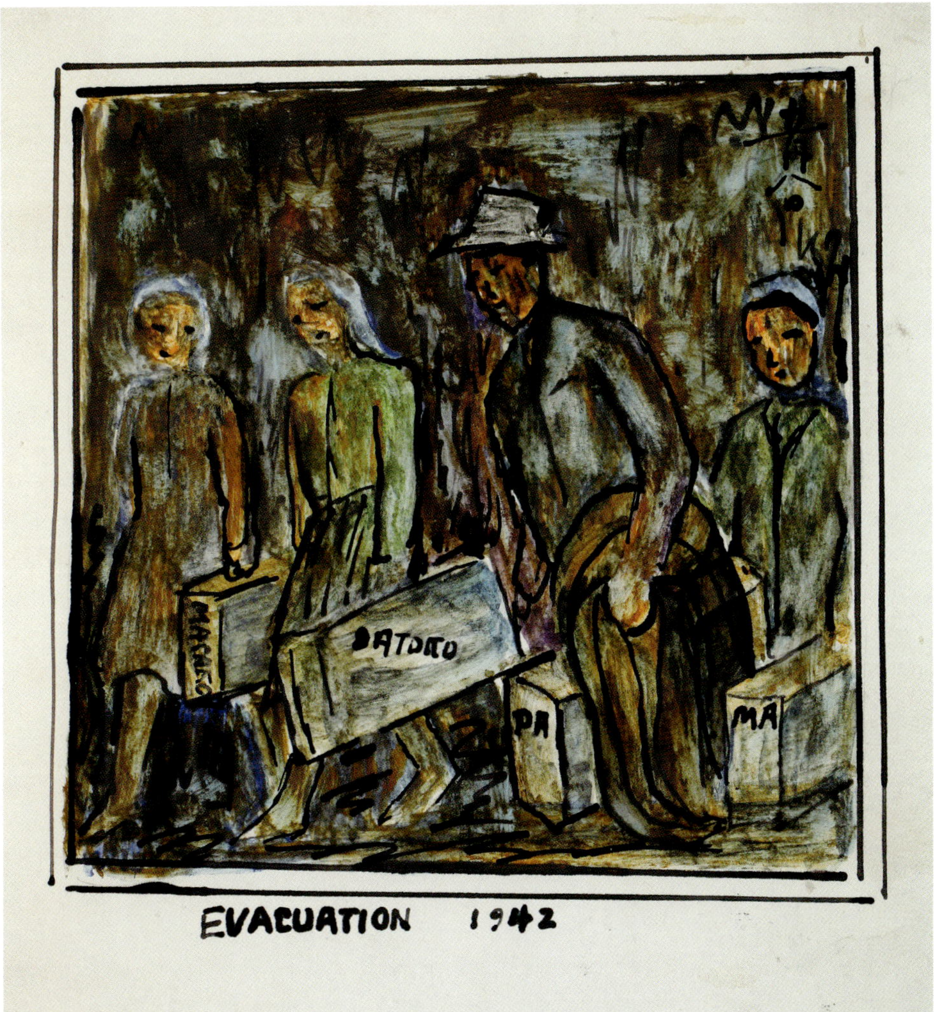

1.6 "Evacuation, 1942." Diary frontispiece. Ink and watercolor on paper, page measures 8 × 5½ in., image 4¼ × 4 in.

site filled the fairground, its parking lots, and additional leased private land, altogether over eighty acres (fig. 1.7).[70] Embellishing the official euphemism *assembly center*, army public relations staff named it "Camp Harmony." By May 16 it held 7,376 people, the majority from Seattle, others from the rural Puyallup Valley, and a small number from Alaska.[71] No one yet knew where they would go from there.

The Puyallup Assembly Center was one of seventeen temporary holding grounds built and controlled by the army's Wartime Civil Control Administration, the agency of the Western Defense Command charged by DeWitt with the

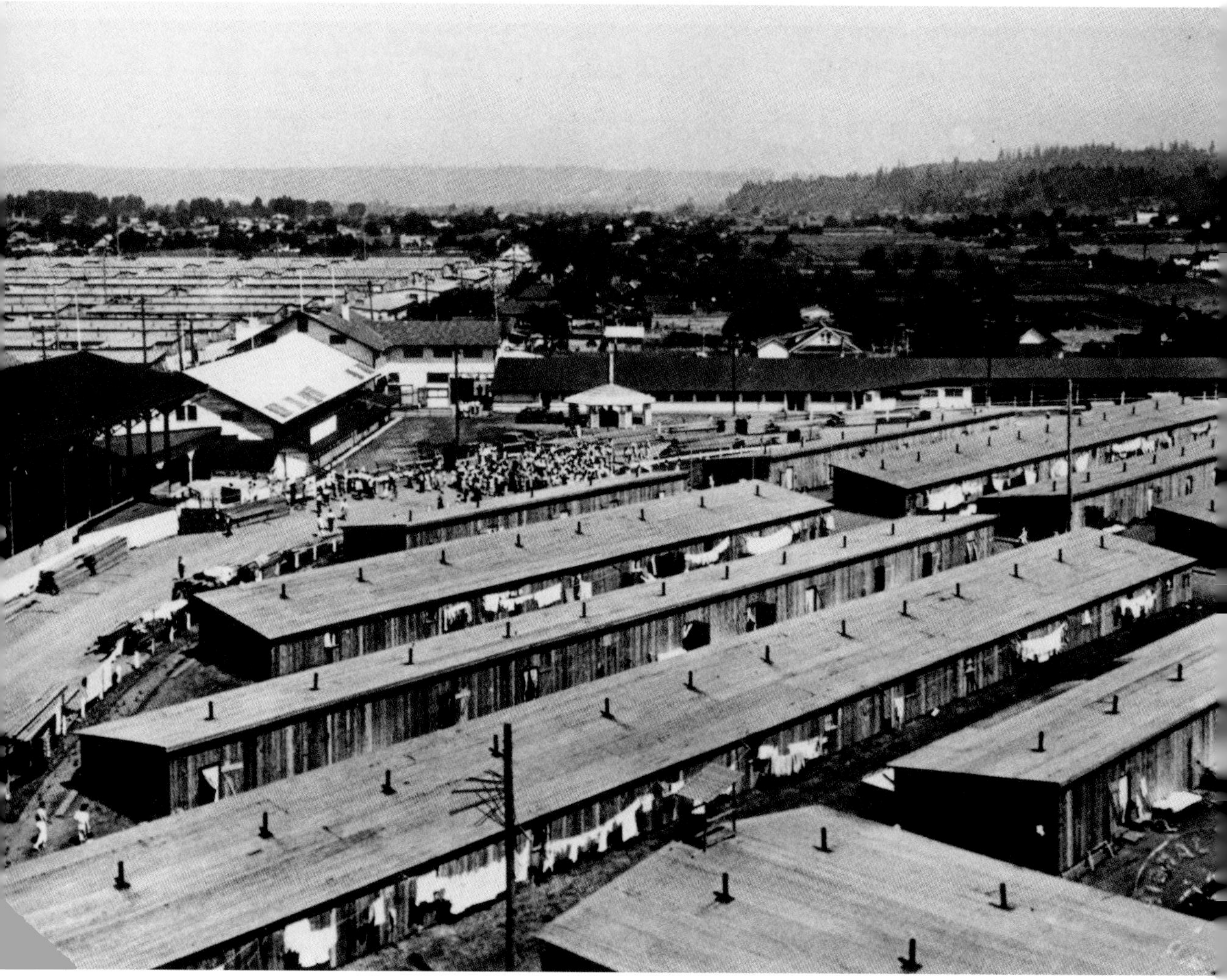

1.7 Puyallup Assembly Center, Washington, 1942. Denshō, courtesy of Library of Congress Prints and Photographs Division, LC-USZ6-1654, http://encyclopedia.densho.org/sources/en-denshopd-i217-00021-1/.

Nikkei's forced removal. The eruption of racist reaction and the momentum for their removal meant that exclusion orders had been issued before plans to house and feed everyone were finalized, and that interim measures were required. All but two of the detention sites were built on leased fairgrounds or racetracks, which had acreage, water, plumbing, and basic administrative facilities.[72] Animal stalls, grandstands, and flimsily built barracks provided housing for inmates.

Although all of the temporary camps were claustrophobically crowded, Puyallup was especially confined. Puyallup city streets divided the center into four separate areas, each surrounded by eight-foot-tall barbed-wire fences and guard towers, and each containing one or more communal mess halls, latrines, showers, and laundries. Nikkei who could show sufficient reason to move from one area to another had to pass through a guarded gate and be escorted across the street.[73] The communal facilities, shoddy construction, and crowded conditions meant a severe loss of privacy, chronic sanitation problems, and, as Fujii's diary relates, crushing humiliation. Officially the assembly centers were portrayed as "convenient gathering point[s] . . . where evacuees live temporarily while awaiting the opportunity" for their further "relocation."[74] Even before they were completed, however, they were called "concentration camps."[75]

Facing incarceration of unknown duration and an unknown final destination, Fujii began an illustrated diary, which provides the first personal insight into his life. Keeping a diary was a centuries-old practice in Japan and had become commonplace by the nineteenth century, and now Fujii turned to it at a time of personal crisis.[76] His diary is composed of ink drawings that are usually accompanied by a text or brief caption. He began with a drawing of the Mary Rose Florist shop, declaring they had been forced to sell their business and then forced to leave their home.[77] At Puyallup, he methodically recorded the spaces and events around him, a practice he continued until his release from incarceration; and at some point, he re-created many of the compositions in watercolor. Among his first drawings of Puyallup are the "dirty, dirty" shower, the communal latrine, and the long lines. He calls himself and others "beggars" as they wait in line, bowls in hand, for food.[78] In other drawings his family lines up inside their barrack for the twice-daily roll call, and a throng of diminutive figures awaits passage at the gate. Throughout, in the herding of people, their literal and figurative diminishment, the constant surveillance and control, and the unsanitary conditions and noise of communal living, his sense of degradation is palpable (figs. 1.8, 1.9).

Area B, to which the Fujiis were assigned, was one of the two smaller zones, built to accommodate eleven hundred people but lacking open space for recreation except along the fence.[79] The guards had orders to shoot anyone who breached the ten-foot zone between a double line of fences. Parallel rows of twenty-foot-wide wooden barracks were laid directly on the ground, each divided into single-room units by eight-foot walls that fell short of the roof. Each unit was equipped only with bed frames and a wood stove; inmates were given cotton sacks to fill with hay for mattresses. A single lightbulb overhead and a small window on the back side lit the interior. One group upon arriving mistook the barracks for chicken coops. Others called them rabbit hutches.[80] To Fujii they were cattle stalls. At night, the light between the wall boards reminded

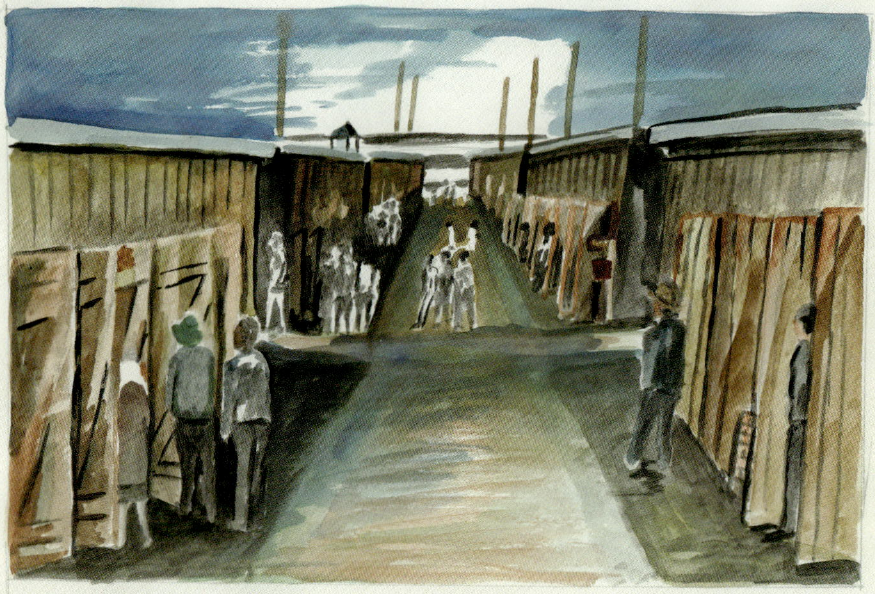

1.8 Puyallup, "Third Street." Watercolor and ink on paper, 7 × 10 in. (See diary 29.)

him of a birdcage. What most impressed him, however, were the tall barbed-wire fence, machine guns, and soldiers. "When war comes, do people become horrible like this? Thinking about that, I became wretched" (diary 9).

In August, Fujii and his family, along with other incarcerees from Seattle and Alaska, received word of their pending transfer by train from Puyallup to the Minidoka Relocation Center in south-central Idaho.[81] The train cars were old, decommissioned ones, some, as illustrated in Fujii's diary, with the ornate decoration of another era. After a hot, three-day trip they arrived on August 20 at a "desertlike place we know not where, with neither trees nor houses" (diary 53).[82] As everyone was transferred from train cars to buses for the final segment of the trip, Fujii again expressed the powerlessness of being herded from place to place.

Minidoka was situated in the Gooding Reclamation District, 33,500 acres of high-desert federal reserve land, where annual temperatures, the government reported, ranged from 30 degrees below zero to 104, and sandstorms sometimes obliterated the sky, making it so dark that work stopped.[83] For a month, from mid-August to mid-September, families arrived from Seattle, Portland, and Alaska; in time the population peaked at 9,397.[84] Minidoka was unusual among the ten long-term camps for its predominately urban population, a homogeneity

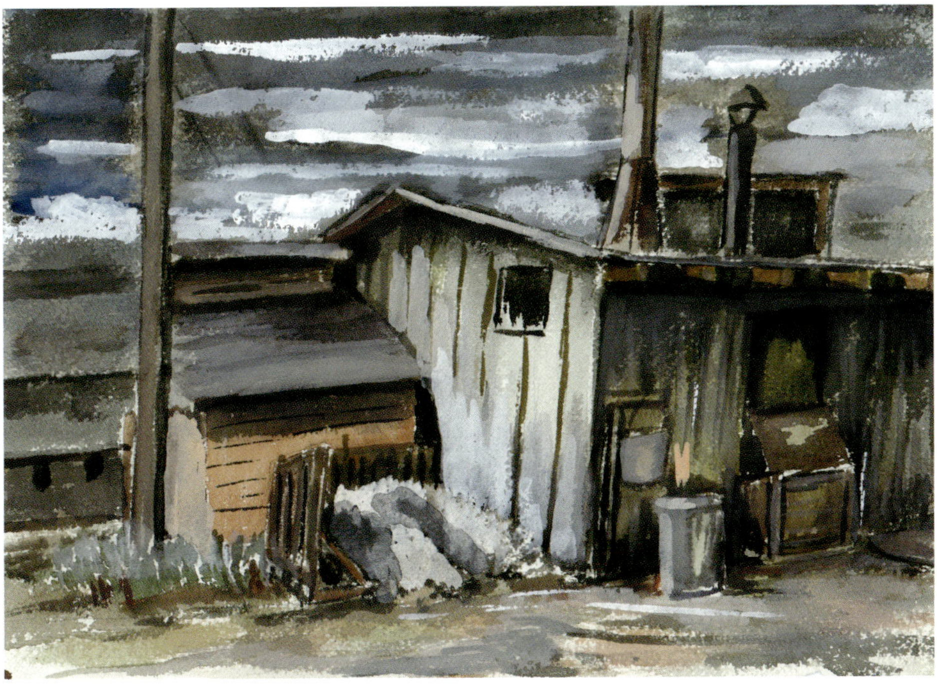

1.9 Puyallup, side of the mess hall. Watercolor and ink on paper, 10 × 13¾ in. (See diary 19.)

that would contribute to a relatively less strife-ridden environment compared to other sites. The camp itself was built on 950 acres alongside the North Canal of the Snake River. It was unfinished when the Nikkei arrived, without plumbed toilets and with housing still under construction, leaving five hundred people in temporary quarters. Two food-related epidemics swept the community before plumbing and sewage treatment were completed in January 1943. The local War Relocation Authority (WRA) director, Harry Stafford, would judge the lack of readiness to be Minidoka's greatest failure.[85]

When basic construction was finally completed, the camp consisted of thirty-six blocks of barracks that stretched three miles in an arc alongside the canal (figs. 1.10, 1.11).[86] Each block had twelve barracks and housed about 250 people, who shared a mess hall, a recreation hall, and a combined laundry, latrine, and bathhouse building (fig. 1.12). The single-room barracks were wood-frame structures covered by tar paper, so poorly constructed that Milton Eisenhower, the first director of the WRA, wondered if they would last the duration of the war.[87] They were equipped only with army cots and, finally, when winter had set in, with wood- and coal-burning stoves. Families made furnishings with salvaged materials and eventually received shipments of a few possessions

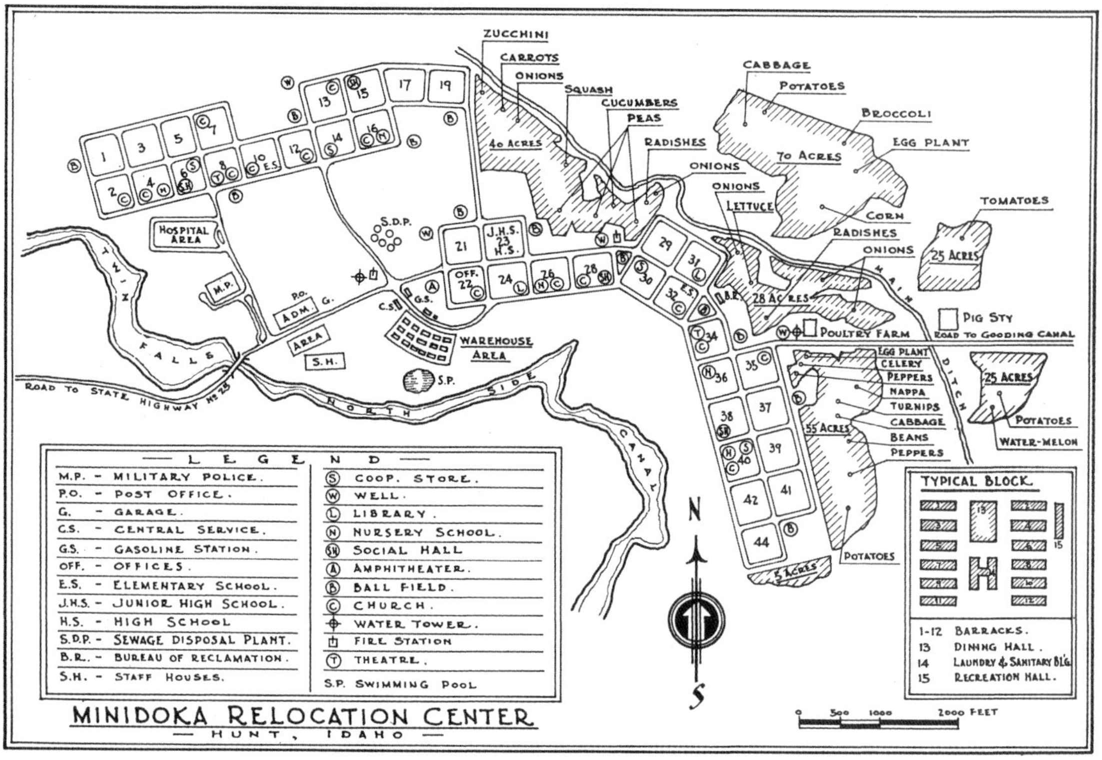

1.10 Allen Kichio "Anky" Arai, map of Minidoka Relocation Center, illustrated in *Minidoka Interlude*, 1943.

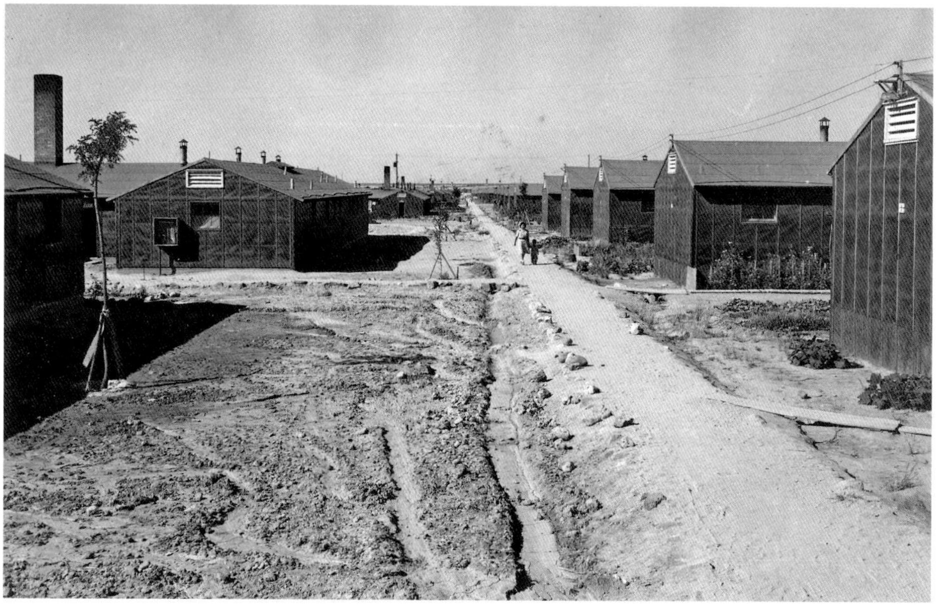

1.11 Minidoka Relocation Center, looking westward from Block 44, 1943. Denshō, denshopd-i37-00747, courtesy of the National Archives and Records Administration (Number 210-G413). http://archive.densho.org/main.aspx.

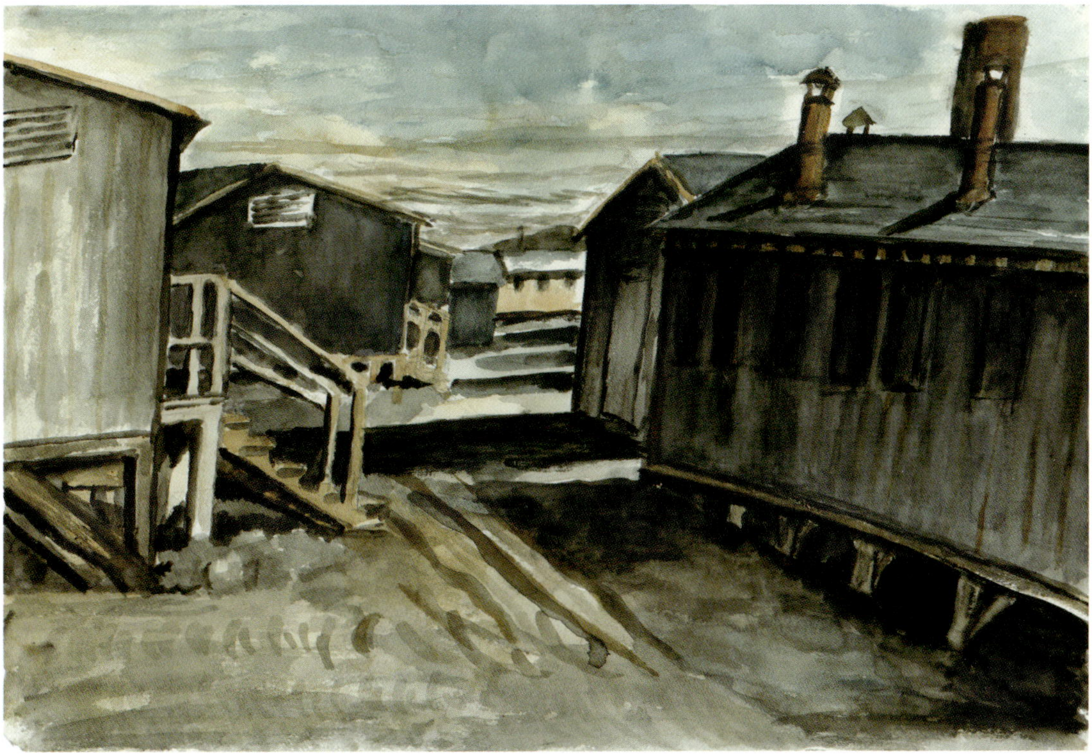

1.12 Minidoka barracks, Fujii's barrack on left(?). Watercolor on paper, 10½ × 14¾ in.

left in storage. By late fall, five miles of barbed wire bordered the camp, and eight guard towers held armed sentries, with the fence and the guns turned in toward the "residents."[88] The fence was a compound insult, built after the Nikkei's arrival and even briefly electrified, without authorization, by the contractor after Nikkei farmers working adjacent fields cut through the wire.[89] As months and years passed, many structures, utilitarian and recreational, were built by the Nikkei themselves, as were the extensive agricultural fields, animal pens, produce storehouse, and irrigation system that provided fresh food.

The Fujiis lived in Block 17 (as at Puyallup, the blocks were filled sequentially as people arrived). Almost immediately their family configuration shifted. On September 1, Satoko, their older daughter, married Denkichi Kita (1901–1959) and left the household. Theirs was the first marriage at Minidoka.[90] Kita, an Issei fourteen years older than she, had immigrated in 1915 and worked as a farm laborer in South Dakota before moving to Seattle in the 1930s.[91] Because wartime created an acute shortage of labor, the pressure from farmers at harvest time was great enough that as soon as inmates arrived at Minidoka, the War Relocation Authority offered temporary leave to harvest Idaho's sugar beets.[92]

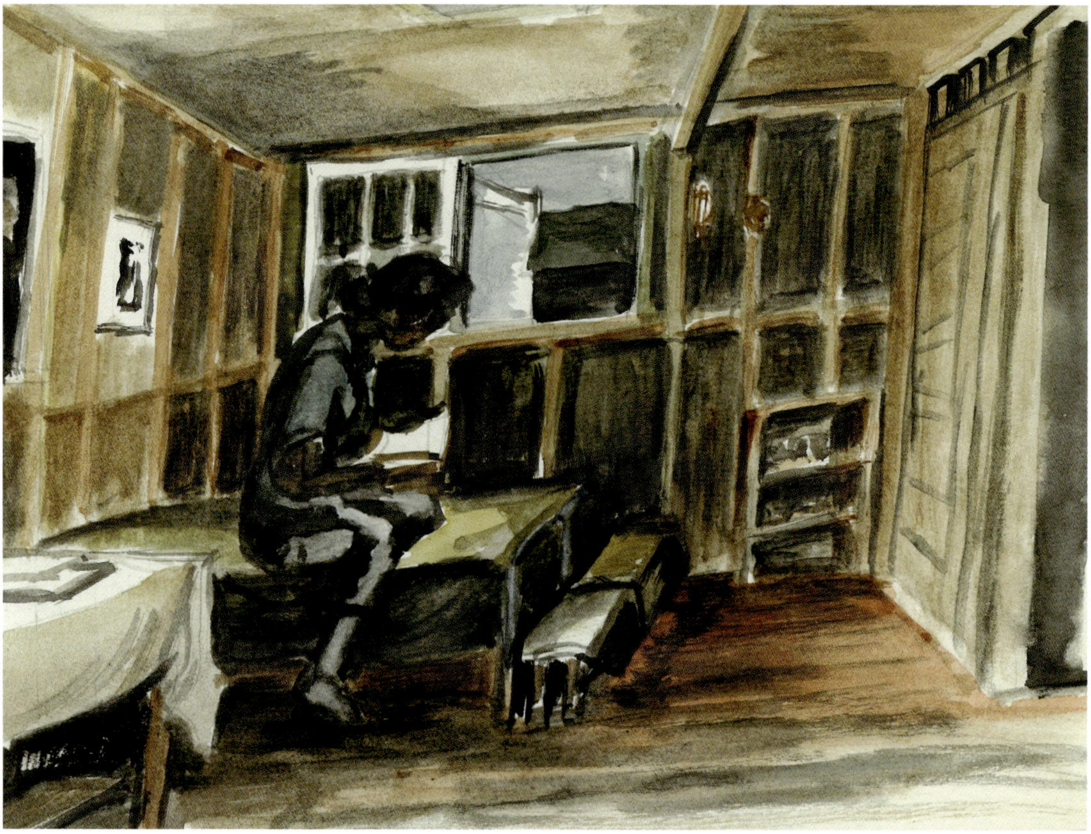

1.13 Masako in the family barrack, before her departure from Minidoka in August 1943. Watercolor on paper, 5 × 6½ in.

No record tells whether Kita accepted the work, but when in spring 1943 the WRA authorized "indefinite leave" from camp for jobs in the interior, he and Satoko left Minidoka for Ogden, Utah, which had a thriving sugar beet industry. In August that year Fujii's younger daughter, Masako, left to work in the aircraft industry in Minneapolis and, the next spring, joined the Women's Army Corps (fig. 1.13).[93] Fujii and his wife spent the remaining time at Minidoka alone.

Minidoka and the nine similar long-term detention camps were operated by the War Relocation Authority, a civilian agency charged with administering the camps and directing resettlement outside the restricted coastal zone. Army military police guarded the site. Advance publicity employed the mythos of the American West to proclaim the "relocation center" a "pioneer community," where "basic housing and protective services" were provided by the government.[94] The Nikkei were not prisoners but "colonists" or "residents," language adopted by the camp newspaper, the *Minidoka Irrigator*.[95] WRA officials served as administrators but assigned Nisei the role of managing community affairs, an arrangement similar to but more participatory than what had prevailed at Puyallup. Adults of both generations were encouraged to enlist in the Work Corps, where jobs were ranked unskilled, skilled, and professional and ranged from farm laborer to mess hall manager to doctor. The inversion of generational authority, however, produced continual tension and often conflict.[96] Fujii subtly disparaged the situation, but his artist-friend Tokita was more forthright, declaring, "Working under a Nisei was the last thing I wanted to do."[97]

Fujii, by then over fifty years old and without dependent children, was among the elders at camp and did not take a paid job.[98] He was, as he ironically called himself, "the carefree artist," dedicated to recording and interpreting his experience of more than three years at Minidoka. In the fall of 1943 he joined a volunteer team to produce a book about camp experience, the *Minidoka Interlude*.[99] His drawings of Minidoka and Puyallup, many based upon the diary, fill the endpapers and section title pages.

Fujii's pictorial record of Minidoka and Puyallup extends well beyond the diary. In some one hundred fifty extant watercolors and individual ink drawings, he reworked the diary drawings in a different medium and in sizes that range from about three by five inches to ten by fifteen inches. He expanded his exploration of Minidoka in many new compositions and in several began to experiment with abstraction. He also produced paintings in oil, some of which he finished for exhibition at Minidoka. Rather than the product of a carefree artist, and more than the literal recording of place, his work demonstrates his dedicated search for the formal means adequate to the full expression of his experience.

Some administration officials, like Biddle, had recognized from the beginning that there was no evidence of disloyalty among the vast majority of Nikkei and no justification for mass removal. By late 1942, as Japan was increasingly on the defensive, the policy of confinement became more questionable. Nevertheless, dissension within the government, along with national politics, kept the camps open for three more years. In early 1943 the WRA issued a mandatory "loyalty questionnaire"—a problematic (and protest-ridden) process that attempted to separate disloyal from loyal inmates—and the army began recruiting the Nisei, rendering continued incarceration even less tenable.[100] By spring of that year the WRA began a concerted campaign to move people out of camps and relocate them in the Midwest and East, far from the West Coast. Such a campaign required reversing a public attitude that had reviled the ethnic Japanese to one of acceptance. DeWitt, however, was unwilling to open the Western Defense Zone to resettlement. Moreover, Roosevelt faced an election the next year in which he sought an unprecedented fourth term and wanted to avoid an

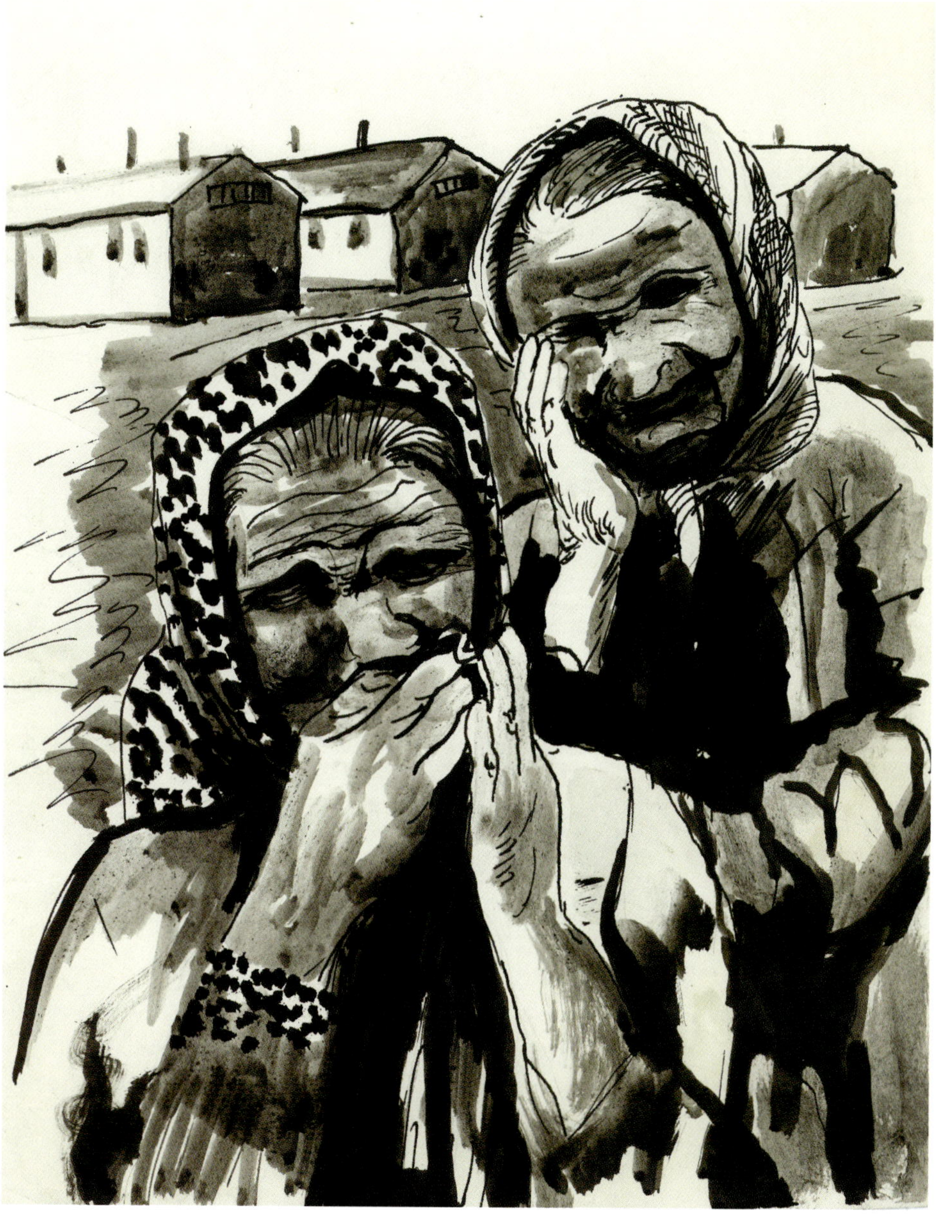

1.14 Grieving women. Ink on paper, 11 × 8½ in.

issue as contentious as opening the West Coast. Only after Roosevelt's victory in 1944 was action taken to allow Nikkei to return to the West Coast, although, even then, in the face of widespread opposition on the coast.[101] On December 17, 1944, DeWitt's replacement as head of the Western Defense Command, Delos Emmons, declared the region reopened to Japanese Americans as of the first of the year; and on January 2, WRA director Dillon Myer announced imminent preparations to close the camps by the year's end.

Many young adult Nisei, like Satoko and Masako, had already left the camps, some to serve in the armed forces, and others for work and school elsewhere in the country under the dispersal and resettlement policy of the WRA. They left behind mostly elders and families with young children.[102] The speed and finality of the announcement aroused widespread anxiety among those who remained (fig. 1.14). Dispossessed of homes and livelihoods, they had nowhere to go and were alarmed by reports of resistance to their anticipated return and of racist violence. Sympathetic groups outside the camps protested that the transition from confinement to uncertain new beginnings, particularly for the Issei, required government support in housing and services.[103] People left at an increasing rate in 1945 as the WRA began to cut services to a bare minimum, but some remained, fearful of the alternatives. By the time of Japan's surrender in August, about forty-four thousand Nikkei, one-third of the peak wartime population, remained until they were evicted.[104]

"The hearts of the people in the camp began to tremble," Fujii wrote in his diary. "Every day people went out. . . . On the other hand, there were those . . . who did not know what to do with themselves. Families were also fighting . . . anxiety, anxiety" (diary 97). Fujii and his wife lived for months in uncertainty about their unknown future, until they were abruptly issued termination papers and given three days to leave.[105] He writes of the seeming irony of freedom: "We who were moved here from the Puyallup Assembly Center in Washington State on August 18, 1942, unexpectedly on December 18, 194[4], are released from this camp by an official American government proclamation, and the road to a free life is opened to us" (diary 96).[106] He was not alone; some would describe resettlement as even more difficult than incarceration.[107] His departure from Minidoka marks the end of the diary, the last words we have in his voice.

BEGINNING ANEW

Taking the first steps to reunite the family, Fujii and Fusano moved to Ogden, where Satoko and Denkichi Kita were living after having gained work releases from Minidoka. The challenge of starting over is only hinted at by Fujii's communications with the WRA in his attempt to locate four boxes and a card table, all that he and Fusano had remaining. They received fifty-eight dollars as an assistance "grant" toward resettlement.[108] In Ogden they joined a newly expanded Nikkei community. Ogden and Salt Lake City, forty miles to the south, had a small but active ethnic Japanese population dating from the late nineteenth century, when workers were recruited for the railroads, mines, and farmlands. When in 1943 the WRA authorized early releases from relocation centers, Utah became a destination; Salt Lake was second only to Chicago in the number of Nikkei who arrived to resettle.[109] Ogden, a transcontinental railroad hub and the center of Idaho's sugar beet industry, grew overall by 30 percent during the war and immediate postwar years.[110] Fujii, however, did not stay. About 1948, he, Fusano, and the Kitas made a final move to Chicago. There they were joined by Masako, whose military duty had ended after the war. For the first time in five years the family was together again.[111]

In contrast to Seattle's picturesque but constrained geography, Chicago spreads across the flat prairie land, a sprawling metropolis of many communities and neighborhoods defined by industry and workplace, ethnicity, religion, and migration history. Nearly a fifth of the 1940 population was foreign-born. The city's initial settlement had been shaped by the Chicago River and its two branches, which divided the fledgling city into north, west, and south districts, designations that remained even as development reshaped the land. By World War II, the Near North Side, once an area of industry, warehouses, and workers' housing, had turned to a derelict neighborhood of poor, crowded tenements as industries moved from the city center.[112] The neighborhood became the home of a new Nikkei community and the Fujiis and their daughters.

During World War II, Chicago replaced the West Coast as the center of Japanese American life.[113] The city's small ethnic Japanese community dated from the 1893 World's Columbian Exposition and by 1940 numbered fewer than four hundred.[114] Wartime policy led the change. The WRA from its inception had a dual mission of administering the incarceration camps and resettling as many inmates as possible elsewhere in the country. Its stated practice encouraged dispersal and assimilation in order to prevent the reformation of concentrated communities such as those of the prewar West Coast. Although wartime Nikkei farm labor had helped save crops in the intermountain states, fierce popular resistance to permanent residence led the WRA to prohibit further resettlement there.[115] Chicago, with its industrial base, plentiful jobs, and a relatively tolerant racial environment for Japanese Americans, became the WRA's resettlement headquarters. The agency chose the Near North Side and the South Side as areas that might absorb the newcomers with the least resistance. With the

WRA's active involvement, nearly twenty thousand Nikkei, the great majority of them young adult Nisei, gained early release from camps to settle there.[116] They were joined by Issei and Nisei families, such as the Fujiis and Kitas, after the war, so that even as some returned to former homes on the West Coast, the community remained substantial.

The WRA's resettlement program was augmented by church groups sympathetic to the newly arrived Nikkei and by a Nisei group that would become the Chicago Resettlers Committee.[117] All focused on job and housing assistance. Housing discrimination proved to be a significant problem, and despite the admonition to assimilate, the Nikkei, like many new groups, relied upon one another and tended to congregate. As others arrived after the war, they found living accommodations nearby. A new Japanese American community rose under Nisei leadership. The concentrated old Nihonmachi and the social control of Issei authority, however, were gone forever.[118] Until 1950 the Nikkei population centered on the Near North Side and two South Side neighborhoods, and, in time, it moved farther north and west as the South Side became predominately African American.

Housing conditions, as well as discrimination, were an issue. The Near North Side represented some of the city's most distressed housing, which was only beginning to be addressed in the 1950s.[119] An anchor in the neighborhood was a sixty-year-old community center, the Olivet Institute, noted for its service to the ethnically diverse population (fig. 1.15). A flyer places it "Right in the Middle of Need," and its newsletter describes the context: "A ten minute walk north from Division Street carries one in rapid succession thru [*sic*] neighborhoods in which live people of many racial, religious, and national backgrounds. In the midst of this, serving all people who need it, is the Olivet Institute."[120] Olivet was the first community center in the city opened to ethnic Japanese after the war, and in 1946 it became home of the two-year-old Midwest Buddhist Temple, led by Issei minister Reverend Gyodo Kono, himself a resettler.[121] Nisei found Olivet a welcoming place for sports, dances, social events, and club meetings. The Gakka Guild, a young artists' group formed to "promote cultural activities among Nisei," met Friday nights at the Olivet Institute.[122] Olivet's programs expanded as the social isolation of the aging Issei became apparent, and again as the Nisei began families. By the 1950s it provided multigenerational services to the Near North Side community.

Fujii and his wife initially lived on West Huron Street, the Kitas a half mile away on North Clark amid the recently populated Japanese American neighborhood. Masako—who had married, borne a son, Tami, and divorced—moved into the same building as her parents, so that once again the entire family lived

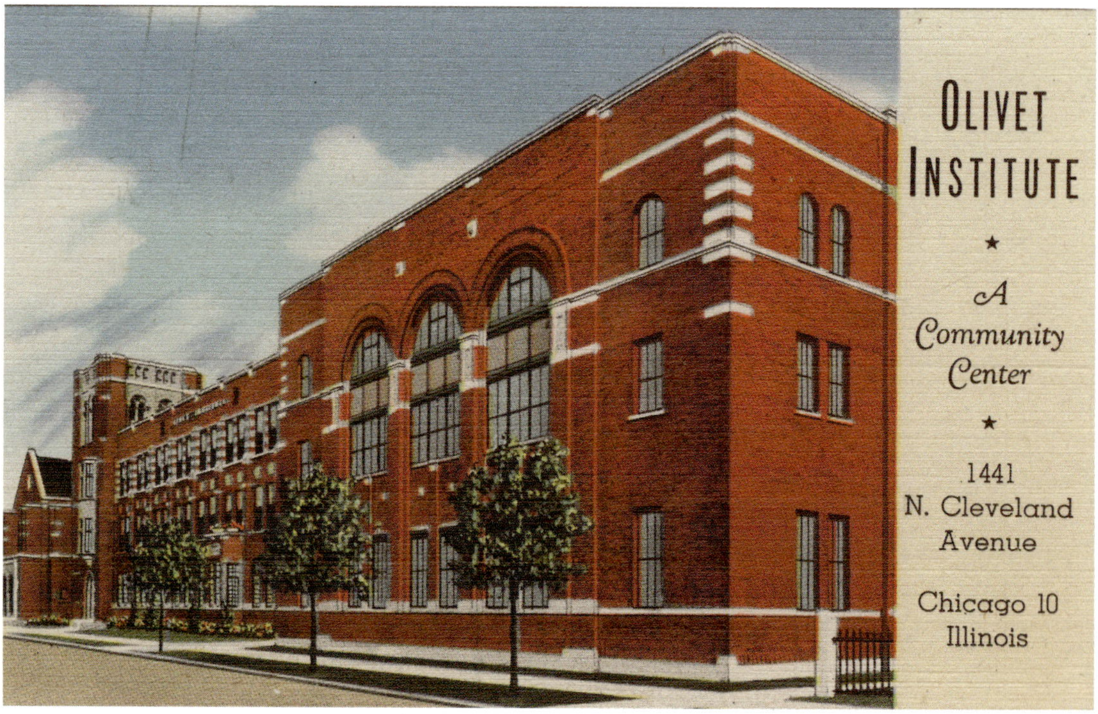

1.15 Olivet Institute, Chicago. Postcard, 1944. Curt Teich and Co., Chicago. Olivet Community Center records, Chicago History Museum.

in proximity to one another. For several years the Fujiis cared for their grandson while their daughter worked. Fujii himself found work at a lithography company but retired after a short while.

In 1951 the Fujiis and the Kitas moved together into a house of their own at 1443 North Larrabee Street, farther north but still within the Near North Side (fig. 1.16).[123] Fujii and his wife lived in the apartment upstairs; Satoko, her husband, and their young son, Sandy, born in 1950, lived on the ground floor. The front room of the upstairs apartment was closed off from the rest of the living quarters and reserved as Fujii's private space. On Saturdays the entire family gathered in the Fujiis' kitchen for breakfast, where they had extended discussions around the table. Masako continued to join them after moving to suburban Elmhurst for work. She, more than Satoko, shared their father's artistic and intellectual interests, and their conversations sometimes turned to D. T. Suzuki, whose book and lectures at Columbia University in the 1950s popularized Zen Buddhism for an American audience.

Outside the home, the Fujiis made a place for themselves in the immediate neighborhood (figs. 1.17, 1.18). The Olivet Institute, which the family visited

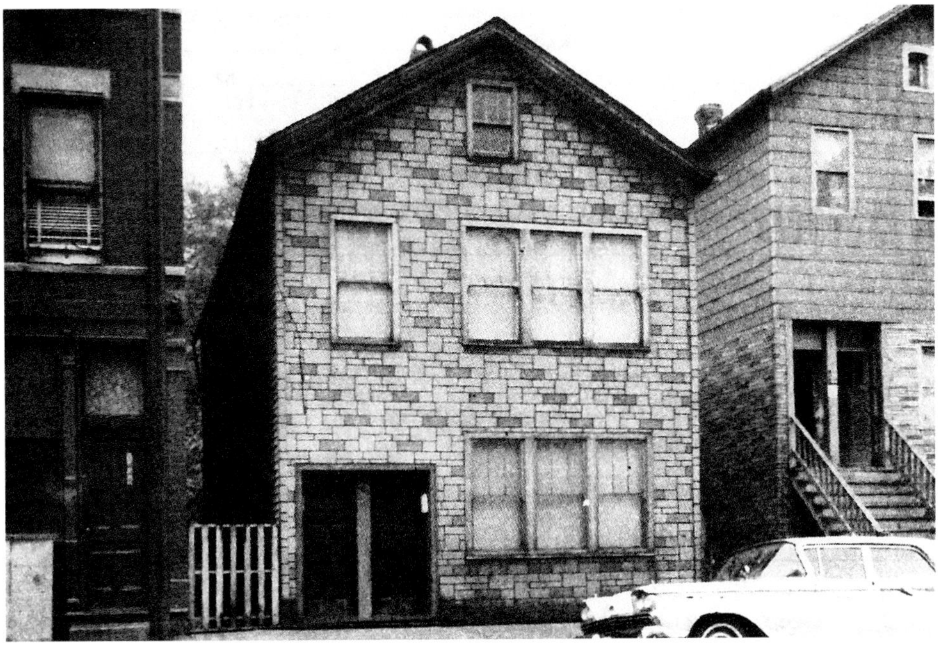

1.16 Fujii-Kita home at 1443 North Larrabee Street, Chicago, early 1960s. Courtesy of Sandy and Terry Kita.

frequently, was within walking distance. Fujii particularly enjoyed the Japanese films shown there. It also housed a small branch of the Chicago Public Library, where, apparently, sometime in the 1950s he accepted an opportunity to exhibit his work.

The Fujii and Kitas surely also joined in the social events of the larger Nikkei community. In the late 1940s the Chicago Resettlers Committee annual picnics attracted as many as three thousand people representing three generations. Two hundred performers participated in the 1949 Bon Odori celebration, a community expression of ancestral bonds that had endured through the years of incarceration.[124] In general, however, the cultural life of Chicago's Japanese American community was shaped primarily by and for Nisei. A new pictorial magazine, *Nisei Vue* (1948–1949), explicitly named the audience it addressed; another, *Scene* (1949–1955), aimed for a broader diasporic readership as it emphasized Nisei stories of success. Business groups, membership organizations and special interest groups, schools, and families celebrated at banquets and special occasions documented by Nisei photographers such as James Numata, whose photographs appeared in *Scene*.[125]

The only record of Fujii's public participation of any kind is his representation in two art exhibitions. He had first exhibited in Chicago during his

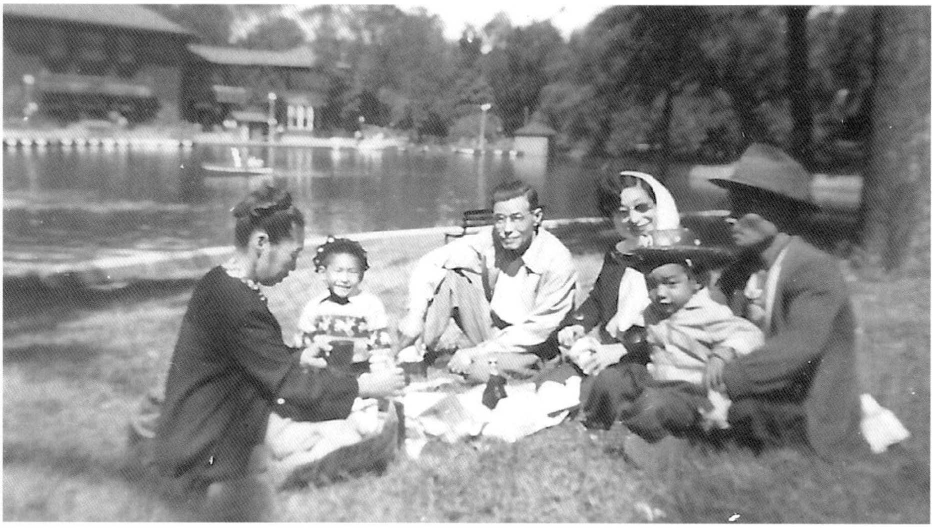

1.17 Family at Lincoln Park, Chicago, ca. 1953. *L to R*: Fusano Fujii, Tami Nelson, Takuichi Fujii, Mary Rose Satoko Kita, Sandy Kita, Denkichi Kita. Courtesy of Sandy and Terry Kita.

earlier move there, in 1937, when a painting was accepted at the Art Institute of Chicago's annual juried exhibition for artists in the Chicago area, an event the institute had sponsored since 1897. In 1957 and 1958 the institute closed a section of the building for renovation and, for two years during construction, cosponsored open, nonjuried exhibitions at Navy Pier with as many as thirty local art organizations.[126] Both were huge undertakings. The first exhibition attracted more than 1,500 artists, who displayed a total of 2,671 works; the second limited artists to one entry apiece and drew 2,126 artists. Fujii took the opportunity to enter both exhibitions, with paintings titled *Momentum, Ecstasy*, and *Work*. The titles suggest abstraction in their reference to states of being (the third title could refer to labor or an untitled "work" of art), although there is no means to identify them with his extant late paintings. Nor is there evidence to indicate whether he knew any of the thirteen or fourteen Nikkei artists among the hundreds of entrants.[127] When construction was completed the next year, the institute returned to its customary juried exhibitions, selecting fewer than two hundred artists. Five were Nisei who would establish well-recognized careers.[128]

Fujii continued to paint until the end of his life. Disciplined in his practice, he retired each day to his private space. Nonetheless he took time for his younger grandson, whom he encouraged to draw; he discussed art with his grandson when he showed promise and introduced him to the Art Institute collection.[129]

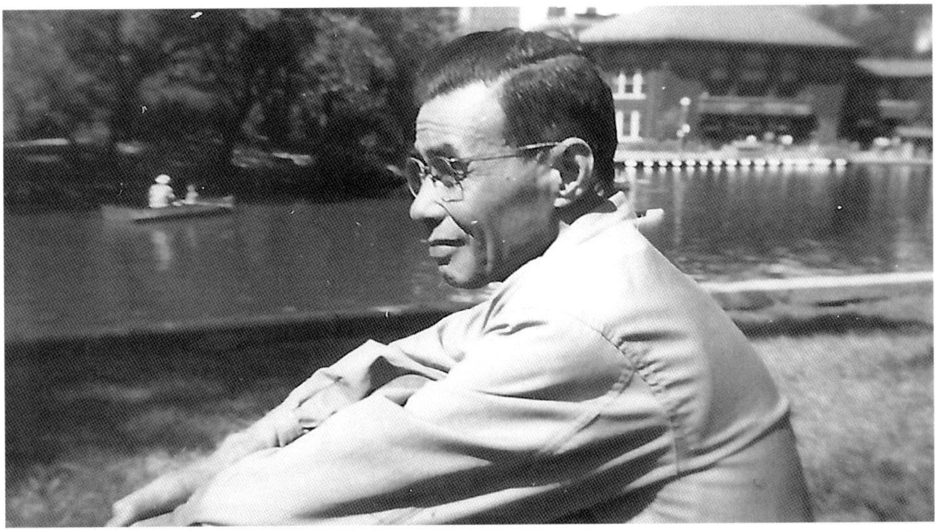

1.18 Takuichi Fujii, Chicago, ca. 1953. Courtesy of Sandy and Terry Kita.

Throughout the 1950s and early 1960s he experimented with various styles of abstraction and, in his last few years, produced a series of bold black-and-white abstract expressionist paintings.

Fujii died of metastasized lung cancer in 1964. In Seattle, where his artistic career had begun, he was all but forgotten, long thought to have returned to Japan.[130] A single historical list names him among Illinois artists.[131] His legacy lies instead in the drawings and paintings stored by his wife, his daughter Satoko, and then by her son.

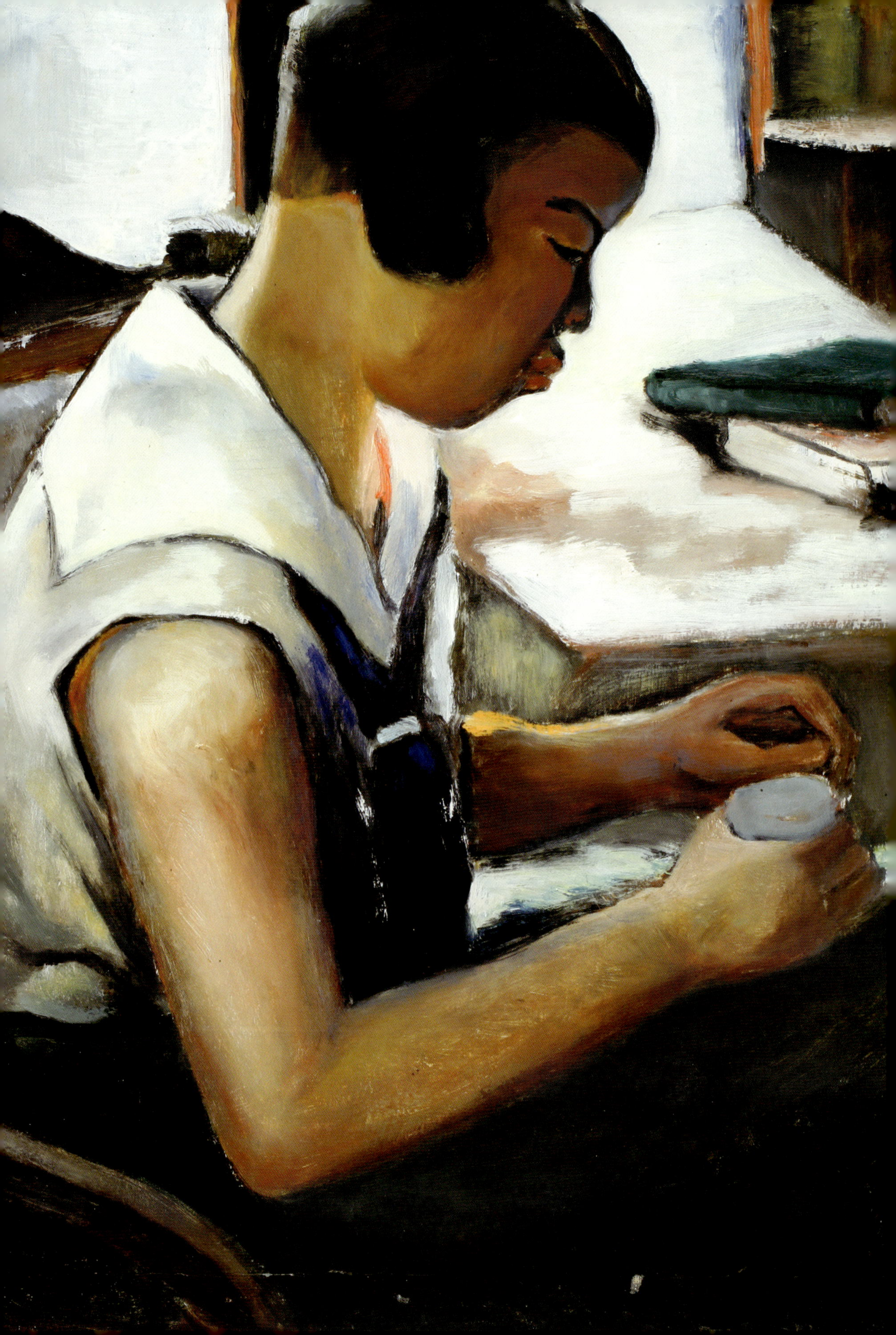

2 Painting and Recognition in the 1930s

Fujii was already a mature painter when his work first came to public attention. In the words of his colleagues Kamekichi Tokita and Kenjiro Nomura, he was "one of the most active painters who seems to be working on an individual creation."[1] Fujii's paintings in the 1930s indeed vary in subject and formal inflection, implying the search for a personal style. During these years he painted alongside Tokita, Nomura, and fellow artists on Sunday sketching trips, shared painted critiques, and visited exhibitions in their company. He found ideas in the example of his colleagues, the art on display, and the art magazines he read, but he determinedly sought his own direction. Amid his growing recognition in the mid-1930s, his statement reads as a manifesto:

> My aim in painting is to remain true to my own ideas and keep away from the influences of other painters. However, in seeing and studying the work of others, I learn from them.
>
> I am not interested in skill or technique as an end in itself, but in a combined thing, a co-ordination of my visual experiences with my knowledge of forms of art.[2]

Only twelve paintings, plus black-and-white reproductions of two more, remain from the 1930s, the years of Fujii's public introduction and recognition.[3] They picture urban and rural landscapes, fishing boats, and still lifes in the modernist-inflected American realism of the time. A self-portrait and a portrait

Opposite: *High School Girl* (detail), ca. 1934–1935. Oil on canvas, 22¾ × 29 in. Wing Luke Museum Collection, gift of Sean Callahan. Photo: Richard Nicol.

of his daughter are singularly personal images. Three paintings, including one in reproduction, are dated and provide the bare bones of a chronology. Together they show the 1930s to be a time of formal exploration and increasing confidence.

ESTABLISHING A RECORD

Fujii had had private schooling in brushwork as a youth, and he declared himself self-taught in oil painting.[4] His Western art practice was gained at least in part alongside his colleagues. The early urban and waterfront landscapes in particular demonstrate his close working relationship with Nomura and Tokita in their distinctive choice of content and viewpoint.

Nomura's and Tokita's sign-painting shop, the Noto Sign Company, was the gathering place for Nikkei painters. Most were Issei, in time joined by a few of the younger generation. All had other jobs, and most owned their own businesses. Nomura and Tokita, their profession amenably matched to their artistic practice, were the mainstays of the informal group and the most recognized during the 1930s. Tokita was heralded as "the leader of the Japanese artists" at the time of his first solo exhibition at the Art Institute of Seattle in 1931 (a second solo exhibition followed in 1935). Nomura, after winning first prize at the institute's 1932 annual regional exhibition, was given a solo exhibition and chosen as one of four painters to represent Washington at the new Museum of Modern Art in New York.[5] Their studio was the base for Sunday painting trips around the city and its environs, after which they and fellow artists met at the sign shop to critique one another's work and socialize (fig. 2.1). Although they called themselves "Sunday painters," the seriousness with which they addressed their work belies any connotation of dilettantism. George Tsutakawa, then a student, later described the shop: "I used to drop by after school or weekends, and those guys were always working, seven days a week. . . . And we'd sit there and talk about art. [Nomura and Tokita] were already . . . very knowledgeable, and they have studied European art, American painting, and they were doing some very fine work."[6] Fujii's active participation in the group is evident in both subject and style of their paintings and in snapshots from the field.

Fujii first came to public notice with the selection of his painting *Bridge* for the juried *Annual Exhibition of Northwest Artists* in 1930. More recognition quickly followed. The next year he exhibited *Fishing Boats* at the San Francisco Art Association's *53rd Annual Exhibition* and Seattle's Northwest Annual, where it won honorable mention and was illustrated with award winners in the *Town Crier*, Seattle's arts and culture magazine (fig. 2.2). In addition to *Fishing Boats*,

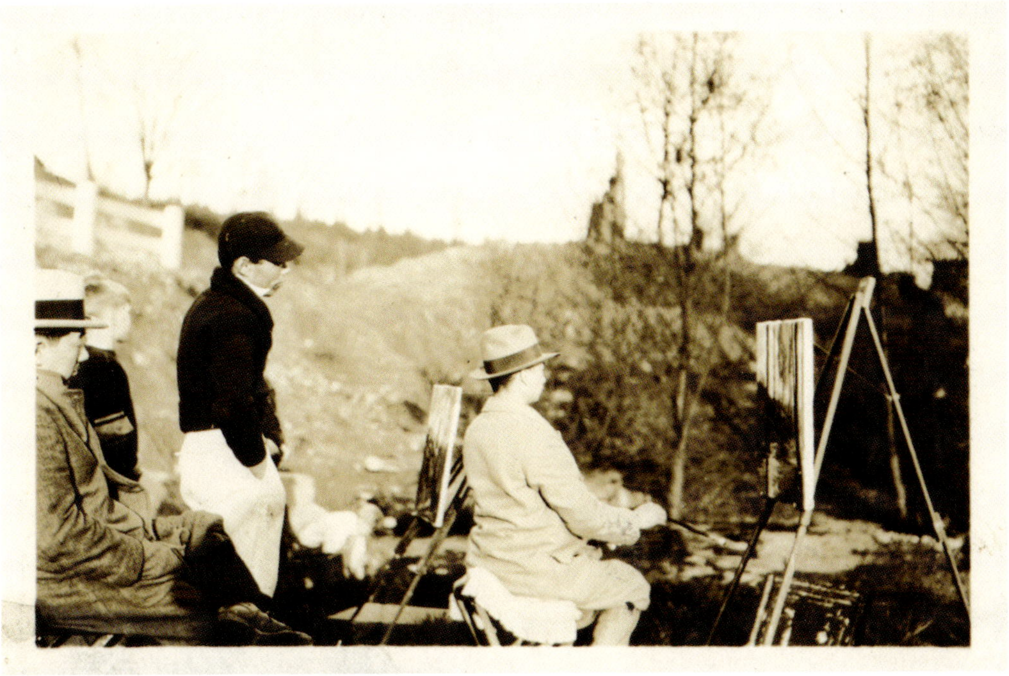

2.1 Fujii (*standing L*) and Kenjiro Nomura *(R)* on a Sunday field trip, 1930s. Kamekichi Tokita papers, Archives of American Art, Smithsonian Institution.

two more of his paintings, *Reflections* and *Moorings*, hung in the Northwest Annual, prompting exhibition reviewer Kenneth Callahan to observe that Fujii "paints chiefly marines."[7] He exhibited in San Francisco and Seattle again in 1932, this time with landscapes.

Of these early paintings, *Fishing Boats* remains only in reproduction, and we can only guess that the title *Bridge* identifies a signed but undated painting of the West Seattle Bridge (fig. 2.3). These show Fujii to be an accomplished painter, while they also reveal the close working relationships among the artists. *Bridge* is a complex study of structure, light, and shadow that resembles a nearly identical painting by Nomura.[8] One can imagine the two men painting side by side, discussing the challenge of representing fleeting direct and reflected light on the bridge understructure. The dramatically cropped viewpoint echoes a compositional device favored by Tokita. *Fishing Boats* displays the blocky planes of boats stacked laterally across the picture surface, and it shares with paintings of the same subject by Nomura and Tokita a modernist emphasis of the elements of pictorial construction rather than verisimilitude. The contrasting forms of the boats, docks, and moving, reflective surface made the fishing terminal at Salmon Bay a favorite painting site for the artists' Sunday field trips.

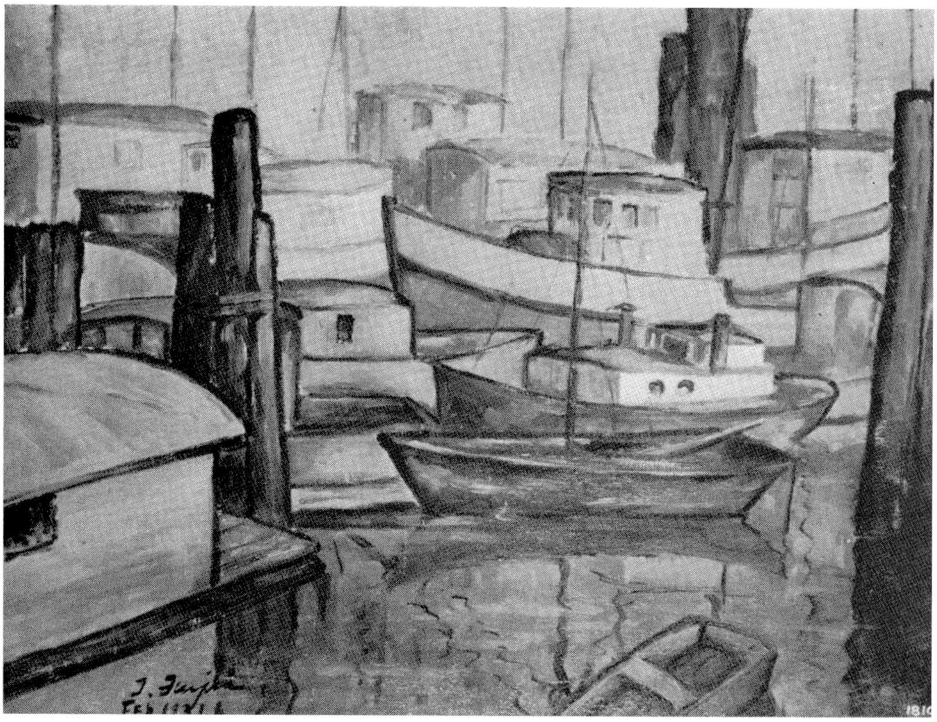

2.2 *Fishing Boats*, 1931. Photographic reproduction. Takuichi Fujii, Northwest artist files, Dorothy Stimson Bullitt Library, Seattle Art Museum. Published among Northwest Annual award winners, *Town Crier*, December 5, 1931.

Fujii's urban landscapes picture the neighborhood in and around Nihonmachi. Here the massed blocking of forms lends an intimacy to his subjects. Two feature a nearby landmark, the red steeple of the former Church of Our Lady of Good Help. One is viewed from the diagonal, steep slope of Yesler Way, the effective boundary of Nihonmachi and "the line" that separated the predominately white downtown from the multiethnic working-class district to the south. In the other, the geometry is pronounced in his pedestrian's perspective of the back side of buildings with the steeple rising in the distance (see fig. 1.4). Cast sunlight heightens the definition of forms, which are outlined in black; the colors are warm and subdued, ochre, rust, and buff against a pale-blue sky. Citing Fujii's "well balanced values," Callahan praised his attention to the relative light and dark of colors, a sensitivity Fujii would have developed during his youthful study of ink painting.[9] In this and other urban landscapes, he pictures the less public areas rather than the street facade. His viewpoint is that of one who belongs, who is familiar with the neighborhood's backyards and alleys and at home as he paints them.

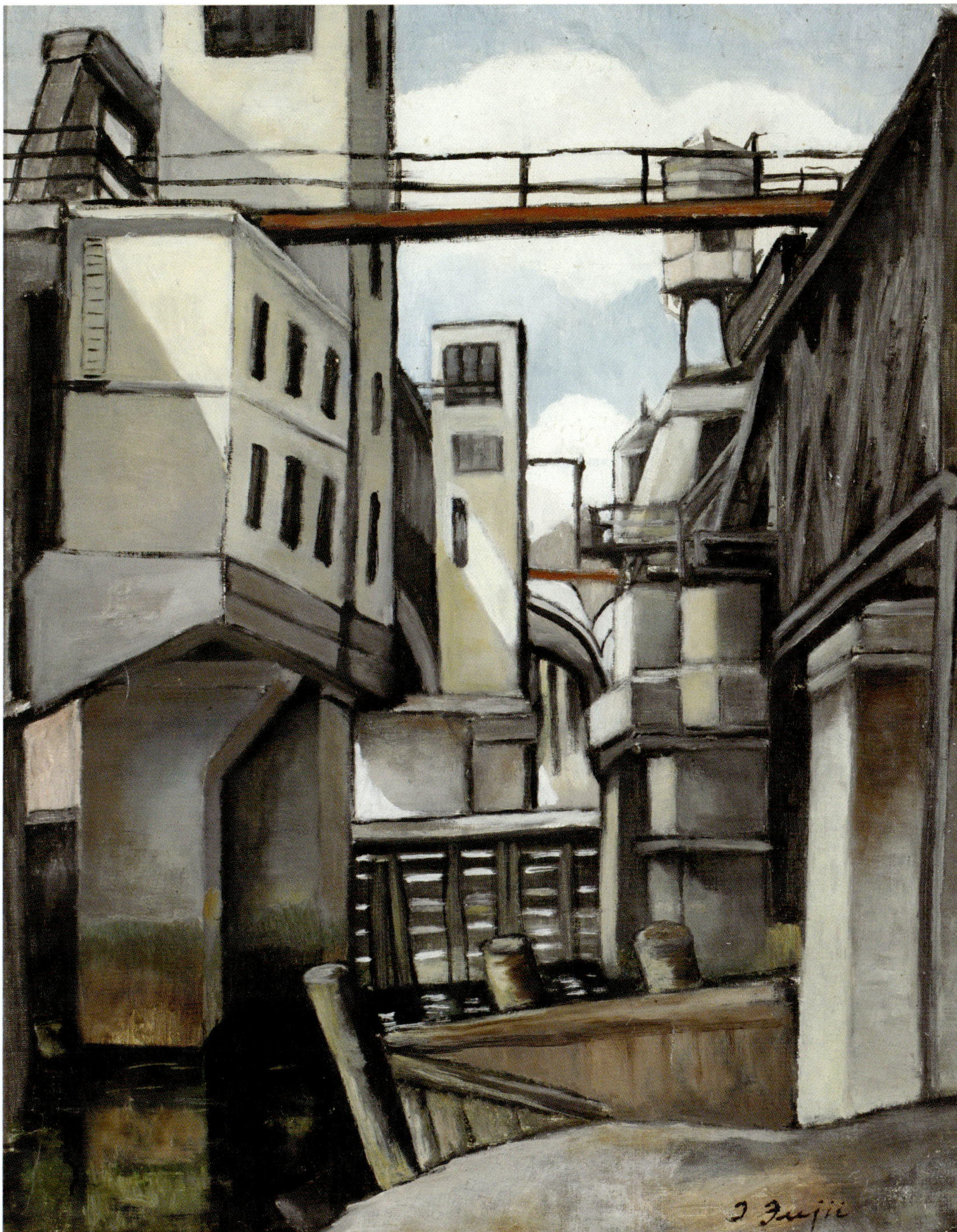

2.3 Title unknown (West Seattle Bridge), ca. 1930. Oil on canvas, 23 × 18 in. Private collection. Photo: Richard Nicol.

Fujii's landscapes fit readily into American art of the time. Throughout the 1920s there was an increasing call for a specifically "American" art and an intense debate about what it constituted. Art in the United States, some critics argued, had matured enough to be an independent force rather than a stepchild of Europe, just as the nation itself had emerged to be a global power. After World War I, artists such as Edward Hopper, Charles Burchfield, and Georgia O'Keeffe turned their attention to the small towns and rural areas of America, finding inspiration in the particularities of place. When Midwest painters Thomas Hart Benton, John Steuart Curry, and Grant Wood rose to prominence at the end of the decade, "American Scene" painting, which focused upon local place and culture, spread quickly across the country and soon dominated artistic production in the 1930s. Fujii's and his colleagues' paintings found recognition in this context but maintained their modernist premise, eschewing the literalism that burdened much regionalist production. Their work, as the artists' peers recognized, maintained a keen tension between the particularities of content and the formal elements of composition.

THE ART ESTABLISHMENT

In Seattle of the 1930s, the outstanding, and nearly the only, art writer and critic was Kenneth Callahan. Callahan, a young practicing artist, had lived in San Francisco, where he was introduced to European avant-garde art, and had visited Asia and Europe when working aboard freighters. He returned to Seattle in 1928 and quickly befriended the older, more experienced painters Ambrose and Viola Patterson, Mark Tobey, and others. His writing career began with his marriage to journalist Margaret Bundy in 1930, and from then throughout the 1940s he was the primary voice in advocating and later defining a Northwest regional style. He argued passionately to an often reluctant public for the acceptance of modern art. He was a steadfast supporter of Nomura's, Tokita's, and Fujii's work, and Fujii would count him as his most important ally.[10]

Fujii made his entry into the Seattle art community at the Art Institute of Seattle, newly located in the Capitol Hill neighborhood. The Art Institute was the outgrowth of the old Seattle Fine Arts Society, which had shed the exclusive *Society* to signal an expanded public commitment and renamed itself in emulation of the art institutes in Chicago, Cleveland, and Pittsburgh.[11] A highlight of its exhibition program was the Northwest Annual, which had been a mainstay of the Fine Arts Society's program, and which each year offered prizewinners a one-month solo exhibition. It was here that Fujii found opportunity.

John Davis Hatch Jr. was the Art Institute's first professional director. Only twenty-one at the time of his hiring, Hatch nevertheless led organizational development and an ambitious artistic program that laid the foundation for the successor organization, the Seattle Art Museum, which would open in 1933. His tastes were catholic, his artistic bias with the progressive and innovative; he continually sought to bring outstanding contemporary American art to Seattle.[12] Asian art was a particular focus of the institute, and under Hatch the institute produced three major Asian art exhibitions. The first, Japanese art from local collections, was praised by "visiting authorities" as one of the finest they had seen, and it included "what is probably one of the best private collections of Japanese art in this country," that of Shigetoshi Horiuchi, an importer and the manager of *Taihoku Nippo* (Great Northern Daily News).[13] Another major lender to the exhibition was Richard E. Fuller, who was president of the institute's board during most of Hatch's tenure and the future founding director of the Seattle Art Museum. Hatch also took special interest in Issei artists in the United States, presenting the Paris-influenced figurative paintings of Noboru Foujioka, Seattle photographs by Kyō Koike, and prints of the California landscape by Chiura Obata. He subsequently wrote to Foujioka about his interest in organizing an exhibition of "as many as 150 paintings . . . of the outstanding Japanese artists" in the United States, which unfortunately was not realized.[14]

Most critically for Fujii, Hatch actively supported artists in the Northwest and encouraged the Issei artists, writing the director of the San Francisco Art Association upon Nomura's, Tokita's, and Fujii's acceptance at the San Francisco Art Association annual that he was "pleased to see such a representation from the Northwest, especially among the Japanese."[15] His relationships extended to the personal, as when he reported the artists' enthusiastic response to an exhibition. "You will be pleased," he wrote exhibiting artist Fred Varley, "when I tell you that three Japanese painters, who are considered the most serious artists in Seattle, were in the galleries the other day and were particularly moved by your three or four latest pieces of the Indian country."[16]

Building upon the Art Institute's success, Fuller and his mother, Margaret MacTavish Fuller, pledged funds to build a museum even as the nation sank into the Depression; and in June 1933, the new Seattle Art Museum opened in nearby Volunteer Park. Fuller assumed the combined role of president and director, as well as its main funder, a position he would hold for forty years. Leading the opening ceremonies, he declared continuing support for the region's artists: "I think that the encouragement of local art is one of the most important functions of any museum. We sincerely hope that the Seattle Art Museum will be an inspiration to local talent and, at the same time, will succeed in bringing their finest achievements to the recognition of the public."[17] His steadfast support of Nomura, Tokita, and Fujii directly influenced their public exposure.

Fuller's attention to local artists was surely encouraged and guided by Callahan, whose role greatly expanded with the opening of the museum. He had multiple responsibilities, serving as deputy director, curator, registrar, exhibition preparator, and museum publicist. As publicist, he submitted press releases and exhibition reviews to local publications and national art magazines and served as a regular columnist for the *Seattle Times*, where Fujii's name appears.

Fujii exhibited annually at the Art Institute and the Seattle Art Museum from 1930 to 1935. Shortly after he began exhibiting, Callahan noted the "strongly accented line" that characterized his, as well as Nomura's and Tokita's paintings.[18] In a review of the San Francisco Annual in 1932, Callahan called attention to Fujii's two paintings on view and declared of the show overall: "Although I can be accused of provincialism, I can state without prejudice that the works of the Seattle artists in many cases stand out as personal interpretations in a maze of affectation and imitation."[19] After installing the 1934 Northwest Annual, he reported that the "natural grays obviously felt by the painter" in Fujii's *Country Lane* required extra lighting in the museum gallery, "resulting in quite startling changes in color."[20] "The Japanese group of Northwest painters," he declared the next year, "can always be depended upon for a strong showing. . . . Tokita and Fujii are well represented."[21] Fujii, Nomura, and Tokita were typically grouped together by their shared style and subject matter, but Callahan took care to note that their paintings were distinguished by individual interpretation, and that each was an artist "of considerable importance."[22]

In reviewing the work of Fujii and his colleagues, Callahan and others struggled to reconcile paintings of obviously American style and content with the artists' Japanese names and appearance. Initially reviewers denied any "Oriental" influence. Callahan wrote of Tokita: "The pictures are sympathetic, sincere interpretations of nature as he sees it through occidental eyes."[23] Shortly after that, the artists were praised as having "adapted themselves to the occidental world, yet maintained a definite racial quality" in their painting.[24] The implication was that they had innate access to Japan's artistic heritage, and that its influence appeared naturally in their work, most noticeably in the use of black line and nuanced color. Race, art historian Jacqueline Francis argues, was embedded in modernism's oppositional stance as it broke from Western academic practice, and had particular significance for American art in the 1930s. Those who supported American modern art looked for and embraced signs of racial difference

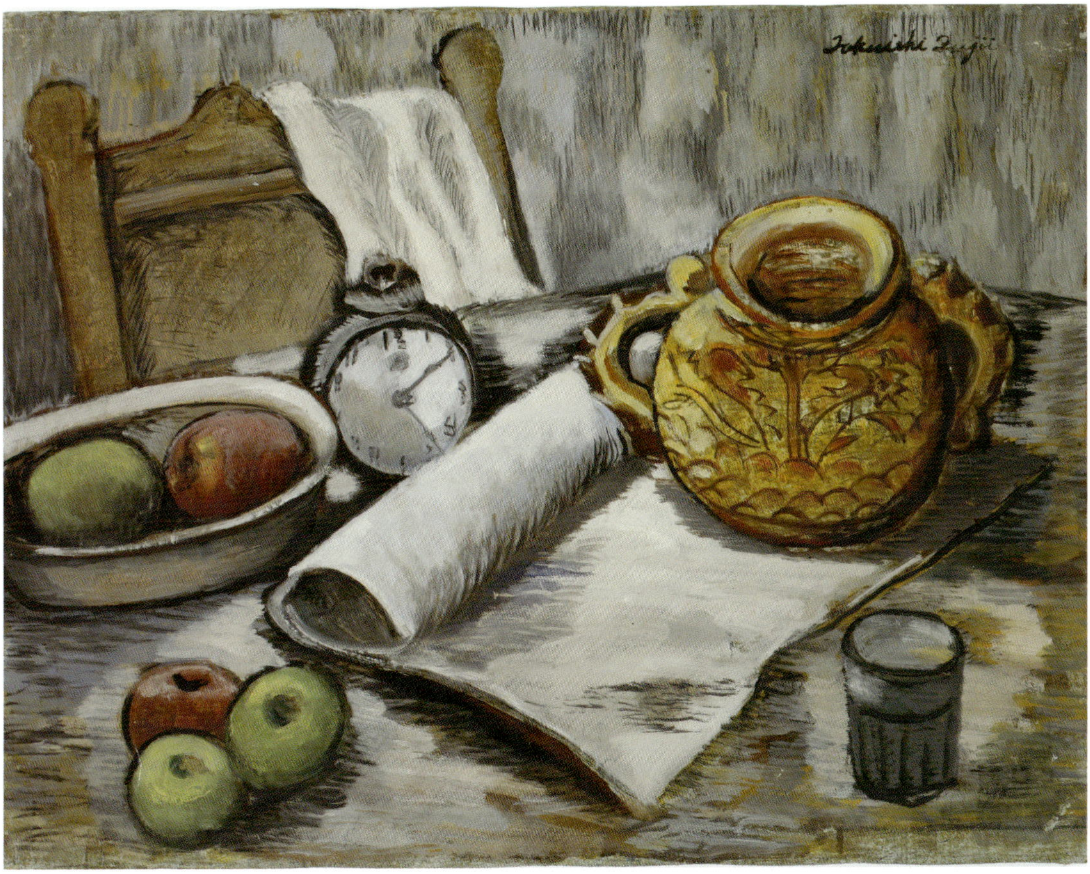

2.4 *Still Life*, ca. 1935. Oil on canvas, 22 × 26 in. Private collection.
Photo: Richard Nicol.

as evidence of the exotic and primitive that offered new modes of expression.[25] Although a number of their Euroamerican peers were foreign-born, the three Issei artists were set apart by their visible and cultural difference, continually linked in the press by ethnicity, and, in the racially charged consciousness of the 1930s, typically identified as a block.[26]

Newspapers in Nihonmachi followed the success of the Issei painters. To the Japanese-language *Taihoku Nippo* (Great Northern Daily News), they were "our artists." The English-language *Japanese American Courier* reiterated the mainstream news, including racially based characterizations of their work, as they consistently named the artists as belonging to "this community."[27] In Nihonmachi their ethnic identity and generation were a source of pride.

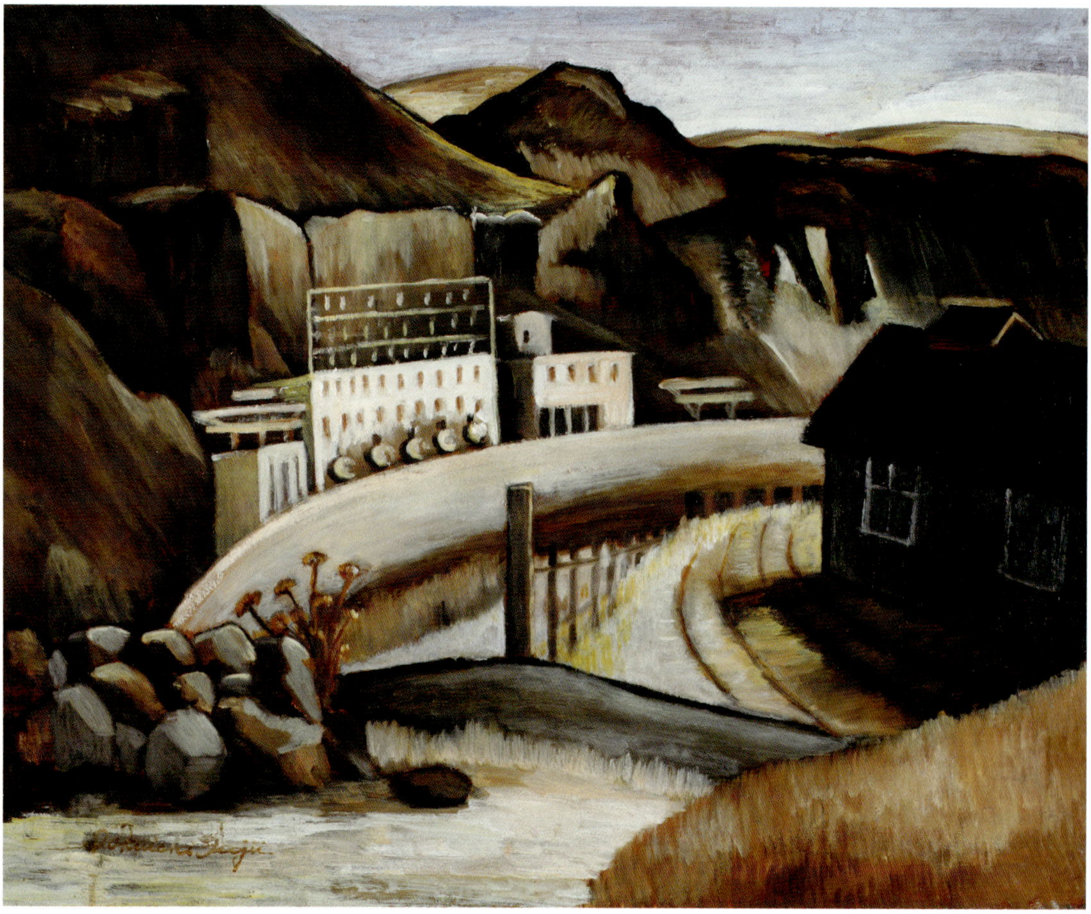

2.5 *Rock Island Dam*, ca. 1935. Oil on canvas, 27 × 33 in. Wing Luke Museum Collection, gift of Sean Callahan. Photo: Richard Nicol.

A PEER AMONG MODERNISTS

The years 1935 and 1936 represent the peak of Fujii's participation and recognition. His daughters were grown, freeing him from the level of family responsibility that young children demand, and he began to take painting trips farther afield. Above all, the paintings demonstrate an artist's dedication to his craft.

Among the twelve extant paintings of the 1930s are three still lifes that are concentrated studies of form. They are composed of common household objects arranged in a similar relationship, with the shapes outlined in black, the surfaces visibly brushed. One still life was among Fujii's three paintings accepted at the 1935 Northwest Annual. It features a ginger jar, which Fujii would paint again years later; the open mouth of the jar suggests the shift-

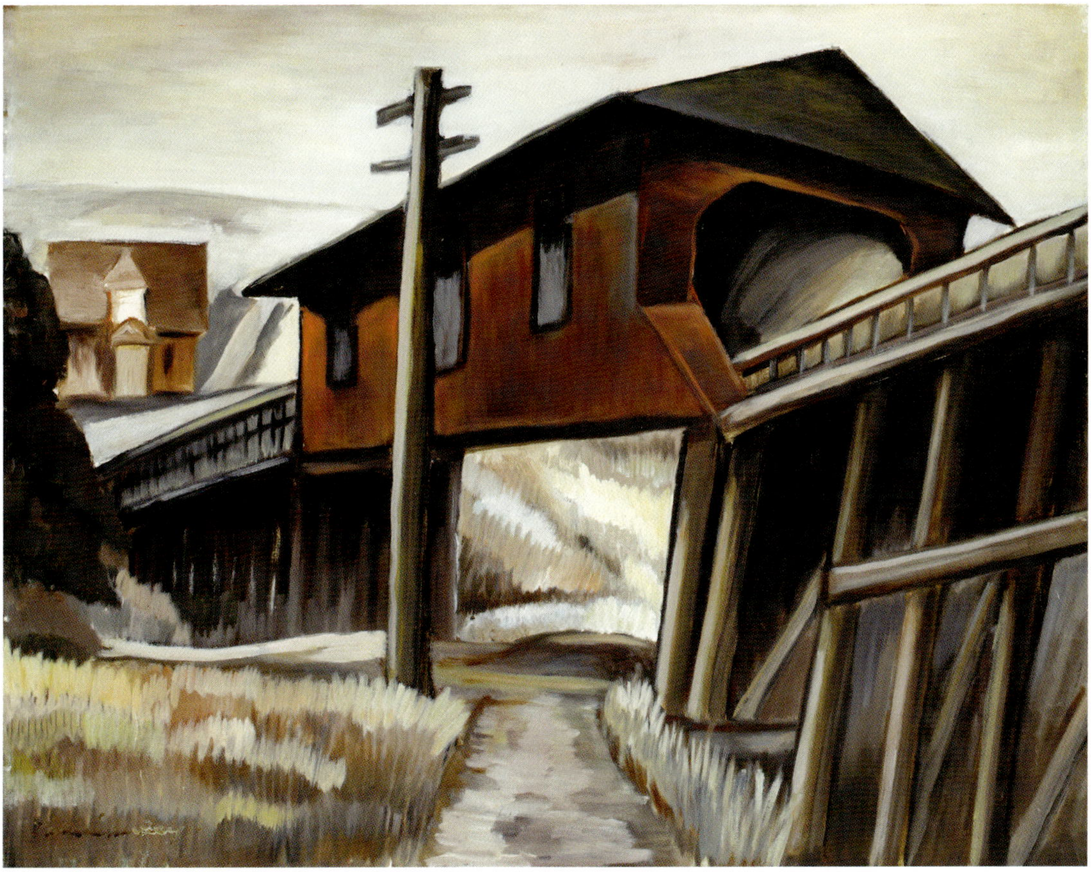

2.6 Title unknown (Allentown Covered Bridge), ca. 1940(?). Oil on canvas, 25 × 31 in. Collection of David F. Martin and Dominic Zambito. Photo: Richard Nicol.

ing perspective of vision, a modernist gesture in the classic representation of volume on a two-dimensional surface. To Callahan, it was "an extremely satisfying painting" (fig. 2.4).[28]

The study of form and composition is fully realized in two landscape paintings. *Rock Island Dam* pictures the first dam to be built on the Columbia River in central Washington (fig. 2.5). The dam was a pilot project in an ambitious undertaking to harness the river for energy and irrigation. For four years newspaper stories had recounted the heroics of the job, and in 1933 they heralded its completion. Fujii pictures the dam over the crest of a broad curve, one of a series of arcs that step diagonally into the distance. Rather than portraying the intervention in the landscape of such massive recent construction, the stark geometry of the dam nestles between golden fields and the basalt cliffs of the river. Across the face of the dam a staccato pattern of brief notations connotes its power-generating function, while a small foreground building offers refuge in the vast landscape. The colors are those of the dry country, ochre, sienna, and umber against the deep grays of rock.

The painting is a striking complement to Fujii's only other extant rural landscape, that of a covered bridge (fig. 2.6).[29] Here the curving plane of a bridge sweeps diagonally across the breadth of the painting to the foreground, a modest structure made monumental. The palette is reduced to smoky dark red and umber, lending weight to the compositional vigor. Both landscapes represent his prewar production at its most robust and dynamic.

Rock Island Dam became Fujii's single opportunity to exhibit in New York. Fuller was chair of the local committee to select work of art for the *First National Exhibition of American Art*, which opened at Rockefeller Center in May 1936.[30] Fujii's painting was one of ten to represent Washington State. Given the ongoing deep Depression, *Rock Island Dam* would have pictured for eastern viewers not only the grandeur and modern achievement of a distant corner of the country but also the product of government investment in industry during economic struggle.

One of two figurative paintings from the 1930s, *High School Girl* offers a glimpse of Fujii's personal life, the only record of it he left before World War II (fig. 2.7). His daughter (which one is uncertain) sits for a painting that is both a portrait and a formal study. She is seated in profile before a window, her eyes downcast, schoolbooks on a table, her clothes and haircut those of a young contemporary woman. The facial profile bears an unmistakable resemblance to her mother's, and the eyes identify her ethnicity, making the portrait one of family, generation, and ancestry. She is also an object of the artist's observation, in which the silhouetted curve of head and shoulders and the columnar shape of an arm rest within the angular geometry of her surroundings. Elsewhere Fujii pictures himself in a self-portrait as the artist-observer, twisting dynamically in the act of looking and painting as he fills a compressed work space; it is the active complement to the former study in stillness.

High School Girl was displayed at Mills College in Oakland, California, as part of an exhibition of paintings by the Group of Twelve, a newly organized group of Seattle university-affiliated and independent painters committed to modernism.[31] Fujii, together with Nomura and Tokita, was among those invited to join the group. Led by Callahan and Ambrose Patterson, the group held rotating exhibitions in the Penthouse Gallery atop the downtown Textile Tower. Callahan, by then well established as the city's main art writer, made sure that news of their activities appeared in the papers. In 1936, the group's first full

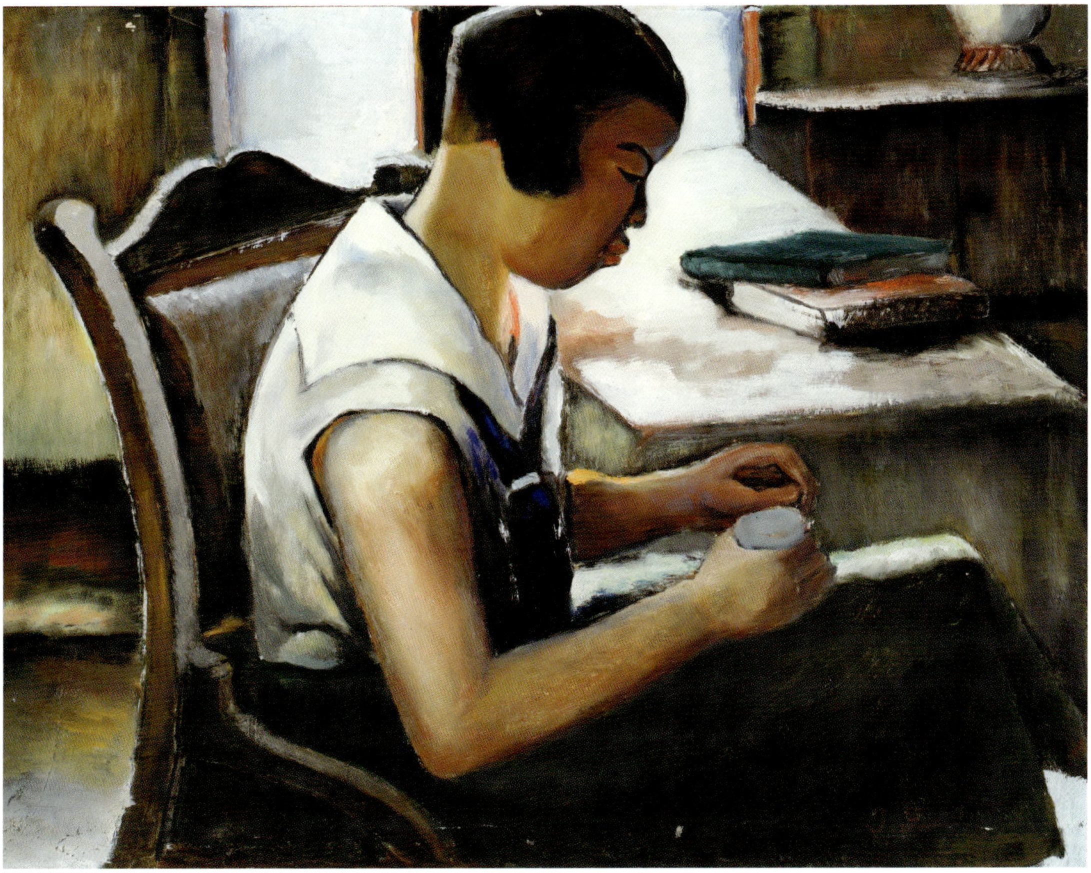

2.7 *High School Girl*, ca. 1934–1935. Oil on canvas, 22¾ × 29 in. Wing Luke Museum Collection, gift of Sean Callahan. Photo: Richard Nicol.

year together, they presented two exhibitions at the Tacoma Art Association, predecessor to the Tacoma Art Museum, and two at the Seattle Art Museum, the second of which traveled to Oakland. The 1937 catalogue, *Some Work of the Group of Twelve*, contains one reproduction and a statement by each of the artists and remains the primary record of their collective effort.[32]

The catalogue also secures Fujii's place among peers who regarded themselves as the region's advanced painters. Even during his temporary move to Chicago in the late 1930s, his paintings and name continued to appear along with the others'. His artist statement, quoted in part at the beginning of this chapter, is the sole record of intention given in the artist's voice, and it reveals his fundamentally conceptual understanding of art. Declaring that he learns from but wants not to be influenced by other painters, he continues,

> It is the truth in Nature I am after, not the superficial aspects of Nature or man, but the basic truths of the structure of life.
>
> To me, the most important element in painting is in its power to raise the observer above the everyday affairs of life into a higher plane of existence.[33]

Fujii's statement evokes the Japanese, and more broadly Asian, conception of painting as essentially abstract, an expression of the essence or mood of nature that exists on a continuum with human experience.[34] It also reflects modernism's insistence that painting is nature reimagined by the artist; it is a construction, a product of the artist's hand and conceptualization. It is to be experienced by the viewer as a dynamic space of active perception. "All art, and in particular painting," Fujii declares, "can only be expressed through visual contact."

The Group of Twelve promoted familiarity and to some extent social relationships among the Issei and white artists. Margaret Callahan described with delight Fujii's, Nomura's, and Tokita's occasional visits at the Callahans' home.[35] Years later Viola Patterson recalled her admiration of the three: "They were all painting in the western manner . . . with sensitivity for color and form, and they were very, very good."[36] Language and social practice, however, limited interactions; they remained the "three Japanese artists."

With the increasing attention to Fujii's work, director Richard Fuller offered him a one-person exhibition at the Seattle Art Museum in 1935. Fujii accepted, and later agreed when the exhibition was deferred to 1936 because of a scheduling conflict. As fate would have it, however, Fujii decided for unknown reasons to move to Chicago and so withdrew from the planned show. "Thank you for the opportunity you have given to me (one man show)," he wrote Fuller. "I am sorry to disappoint you but I had plan [*sic*] to travel to East in a few days."[37] His decision may have had an effect more lasting than simply the cancellation of an exhibition, for the museum typically purchased paintings from artists' solo exhibitions to add to the collection. Soon after his move Fujii exhibited in the regional annual at the Art Institute of Chicago, but neither there nor in Seattle did a painting of his enter the collection, an absence that would contribute to his work's disappearing from sight.

Fujii returned to Seattle in 1939 with new resolve and his wife's support to dedicate himself to painting. Twice more, in 1940 and 1941, his work was selected for the Northwest Annuals. Although no painting can be dated with certainty to these years, *Bridge*, exhibited at the 1940 Annual, perhaps identifies his large painting of a covered bridge. His entry for the 1941 Annual was a watercolor titled *East of Wenatchee*, indicating that he had resumed field trips to central Washington. His companion on occasion was George Tsutakawa, whose contemporaneous paintings picture the same country. Tsutakawa recalled the trips with Issei or "Sunday painters": "Lots of us artists—some of them were Sunday painters, you know—had to get ready for the Northwest Annual. With a bunch of painters, we used to take a trip back east of the mountain [Cascade Mountains], around Dry Falls and Wenatchee and Grand Coulee Dam. . . . And then we did watercolor and oil paintings, quite a few of them, in those days. And we'd try to finish one or two up for the Northwest Annual, hoping that they'd be accepted."[38] Fujii's friendship with Tsutakawa would be critically influential during the war.

The 1941 Northwest Annual was the last time Fujii exhibited his paintings to a broad public. Throughout the 1930s, in themes of landscape and domesticity, he had explored form and composition as he aimed for "individual creation." The war brought a profound personal crisis that prompted an extended, deeply reflective visual exploration.

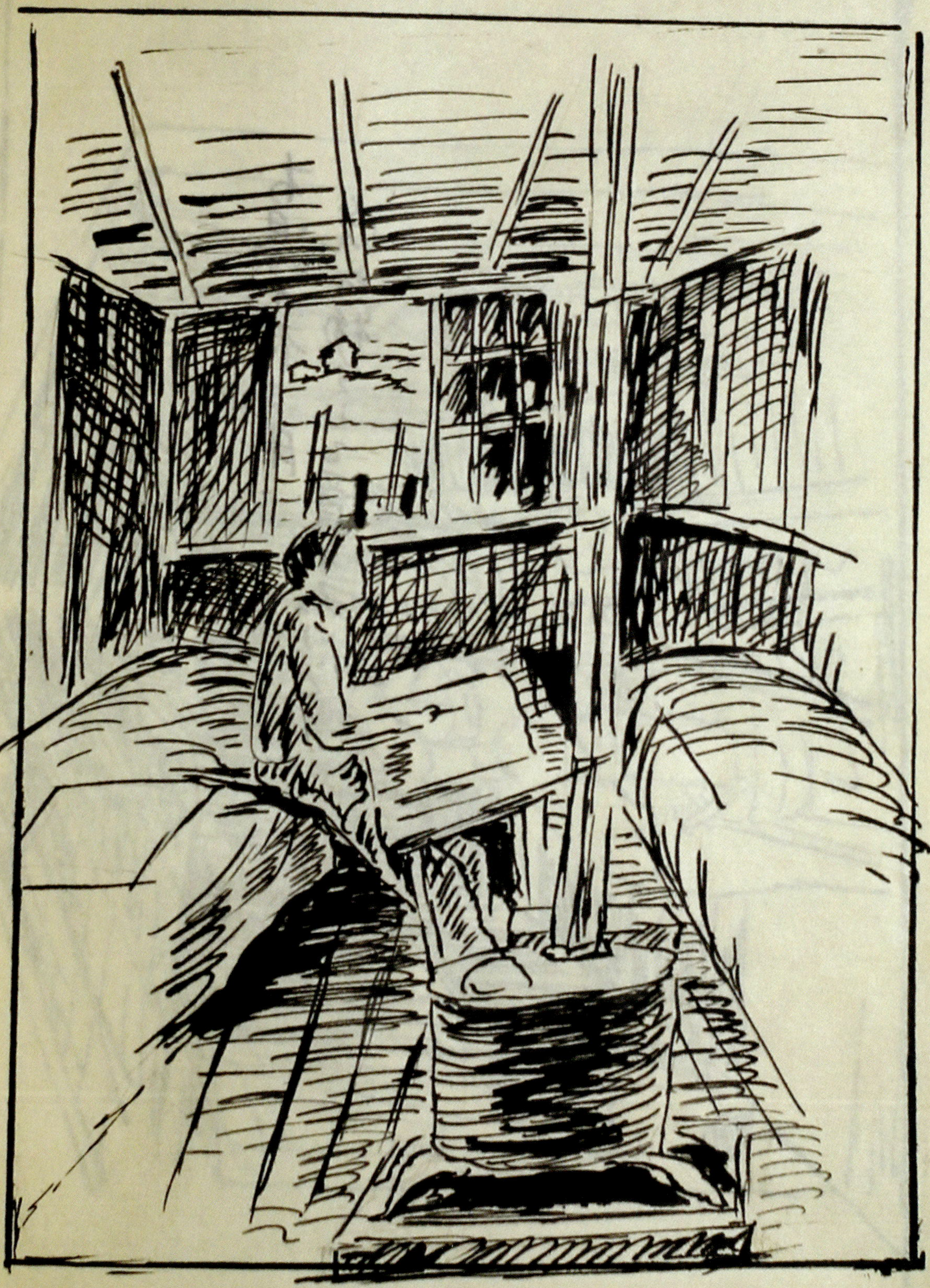

3 An Issei Diary of World War II

Fujii was fifty years old when the United States declared war in response to Japan's aggression. For thirty-five years he had lived in the United States, where he had made his way as a small businessman, reared a family, and established himself as a respected artist. The war brought the loss of his home, his business, his artistic status, and his personal freedom. Confronting such losses, he began recording his experience in drawings and paintings—all together more than four hundred images. They represent his continual effort to reconcile his lifelong aspirations with the condition of imprisonment, and they do so in their extended observation, reiteration, and elaboration as well as in number.

The central, generating project of Fujii's wartime work is an illustrated notebook that serves as a diary, nearly four hundred pages of text and ink drawings, 252 drawings in all, which begin with the family's forced move from Seattle and end with the closing of Minidoka. These drawings, or "sketches" as Fujii calls them, provide the starting point for related work in several formats: a sketchbook of ten watercolors of Puyallup; nearly fifty small, postcard-size watercolors of Puyallup and Minidoka; a portfolio of thirty-eight larger watercolors approximately ten by fourteen inches and matted as if for display; and thirty-four additional watercolors and ink drawings.[1] All those of Puyallup and many of Minidoka are based upon compositions in the diary, while others of Minidoka are fresh views. The diary subsequently served as the basis for illustrations in a book, *Minidoka Interlude*, produced in the camp

Opposite: Self-portrait in barrack. Diary entry, Puyallup. Ink on paper, 8 × 5½ in. (See diary 49.)

in 1943. Fujii's wartime work expands yet further to encompass oil paintings and sculpture, some for exhibition and others of a more personal intent.

The diary and related wartime work are together the defining achievement of Fujii's artistic production. The paintings of the 1930s, with their representation of place, family, and domesticity, provide an instructive prologue to his artwork in a time of crisis. In the wartime work, too, are the first experiments in abstraction. From then until the end of his life, he sought in abstraction a means of personal expression reflective of his time and place.

THE DIARY

Sometime after the posting of evacuation orders, Fujii began recording his experiences in a small notebook, in what became an extended mapping, narrative, and interpretive project. Although the entire project is undated, the specificity of the drawings and his methodical survey of place establish with near certainty that he began in Puyallup. He initially left the opening pages empty to account for his ultimate destination, which he and others would not know until August. Eventually the notebook was titled "MinidokaXX"; it opens with a hand-drawn map of the United States and a dotted trail leading to the Idaho barracks.[2] The illustrations are a combination of quick sketches and developed drawings. All but the final eight illustrated pages are accompanied by brief texts, which in many instances identify a place or event and elsewhere reveal feelings of sorrow, disgust, anxiety, longing, or hope. The cumulative document is an evocative personal record and a pungent critique.

Throughout the diary, Fujii's fluid and varied use of line recalls his early schooling in brushwork, although here his medium is India ink rather than sumi. Some scenes are represented with the barest notation. A flourish at the top creates a skyline. Elsewhere lines thicken, occasionally spreading in dense black. In many drawings a straight line borders the drawing and defines the field, containing the black and defining the form of white spaces within it. Indeed, the quality of line is one of the pleasures of looking at the diary in the original.

Art historian Sandy Kita characterizes Fujii's illustrated journal as an art diary in the Japanese literary tradition. Rather than a daily account of experiences, the text and illustrations together are a means of conveying personal thoughts and emotions that one would not reveal in other circumstances. Like poetry, in which the deepest feelings are expressed, the illustrations reveal dimensions of experience and emotion not evident in the writing. Elsewhere the text is essential to understanding the full meaning of the image. Text and image complement one another, each augmenting the meaning of the other. As

Kita further points out, the diary draws upon the long history of combining text and image in Japanese art and literature, which reaches from classical literature of the twelfth century to the popular imagery of eighteenth-century ukiyo-e and the modern era.[3]

Fujii's diary of World War II begins with a short litany of dates. The entries themselves are undated but unfold sequentially and are marked by the critical dates in his experience: the day of his family's move from home to incarceration, their transfer from a short-term to a long-term confinement site, and the announcement of the latter site's closure. Amid these markers, text and images gather force in their sequence, reiteration, viewpoint, and emphasis. We are drawn into the dark picture by their accumulation. Nearly half of the diary drawings are of Puyallup, although its duration was short in relation to that of Minidoka. The proportionate representation of the two was only partly a matter of the Minidoka years' becoming routine. Puyallup, like other assembly centers, was the initial shock that compelled the Nikkei's adaptation to the poorly constructed, crowded, communal conditions. The experience of the assembly center helped them brace for subsequent long-term confinement.[4] Moreover, although Fujii's diary is undated, a comparison of the events it depicts with the dated diary of his friend and fellow inmate Kamekichi Tokita indicates that the Minidoka section of Fujii's diary is heavily weighted to the first and last months in camp—through the fall and winter of 1942 and following the January 1945 announcement of the camp's closure. Only fourteen entries, each with two illustrations per page, pertain to 1943 and 1944.

The opening pages of the diary, which appear to be a retrospective selection of meaningful events, are some of the most personal images, and the texts accompanying them among the longest in the diary. A double frontispiece displays a watercolor of the Fujiis' business, Mary Rose Florist, and on the facing page his family of four carry their suitcases labeled "Masako," "Satoko," "Ma," and "Pa" (see fig. 1.6). The shop appears twice in the opening pages, a reiteration that emphasizes the impact of their loss. One of the longest texts describes the stripped, dispossessed, and anxious beginning of their journey. It is the only entry he formally titled (diary 4):

> AN EVENING OF RELUCTANCE
> Finally, tomorrow morning, we must say farewell to this house to which we have become so accustomed. Naked, having disposed of our shop, furniture, everything, in a muddle we packed only the absolute minimum of personal belongings, clothing, and bedding. Our home, which is now empty, feels sad and cold in the dim light.

> Since we had no bed, we got out our coats and, making a temporary bed, slept together like sardines in a can. But because we could not sleep, we were up before dawn. Having taken our last breakfast, we waited for the time to pass. All my family looked anxious.

Tokita writes similarly of nakedness, humiliation, and vulnerability after selling his business: "I feel as if my clothes have been stripped off or something."[5] The forced sale of business assets, means of livelihood, and personal possessions brought many to financial ruin; it was but the beginning of a long period of deprivations.

The transition from freedom to imprisonment is movingly traced in text and images. He records the gathering of neighbors, soldiers' arrival, and the fact of his daughters' leaving the city of their birth. The herding of people and attendant loss of individuality are evident in the line of figures that climb uphill out of sight as they wait to board buses for Puyallup. Riding through the countryside, he contrasts with more sorrow than irony the seeming quietude of Nikkei farmers still working in fields to their fated destination in a "concentration camp." Once the family arrived at Puyallup, Fujii seems to have embarked upon a survey of Area B, to which they were assigned, as if he were trying to absorb and come to terms with the conditions of their incarceration.

The diary unveils its story immediately. From Seattle to Puyallup to Minidoka, military guards stand duty over the Nikkei, often looming in size over diminished figures massed together. Among his first drawings of Puyallup is the view from the single window of his barrack, "this cattle stall," where he sees a barbed-wire fence, armed sentries on patrol, and, in the field beyond, a soldier sleeping next to a machine gun that is aimed at the barracks. On the following page he pictures a young man lecturing the new arrivals on camp organization, his head tilted back in a confident manner. Fujii tells us the man is a member of the Japanese American Citizens League, a Nisei, who had cooperated with the government and was now charged with management duties. He adds that the JACL's leadership had been determined in advance of others' arrival, alluding to the Issei's exclusion from decision making. In the two drawings, Fujii lays out the new order to which he is subjected: under the guns of the government and under the direction of the younger generation (diary 9, 10).

In the diary and related watercolors and larger drawings, he surveys Area B from all four sides and the activities of its inmates. He pictures each of the corridors, or "streets," between barracks, where the sentries, barbed-wire fence, and guard tower often loom in the picture (figs. 3.1, 3.2, 3.3).[6] He reports sarcastically the edginess of the white soldiers and the fear expressed by Puyallup

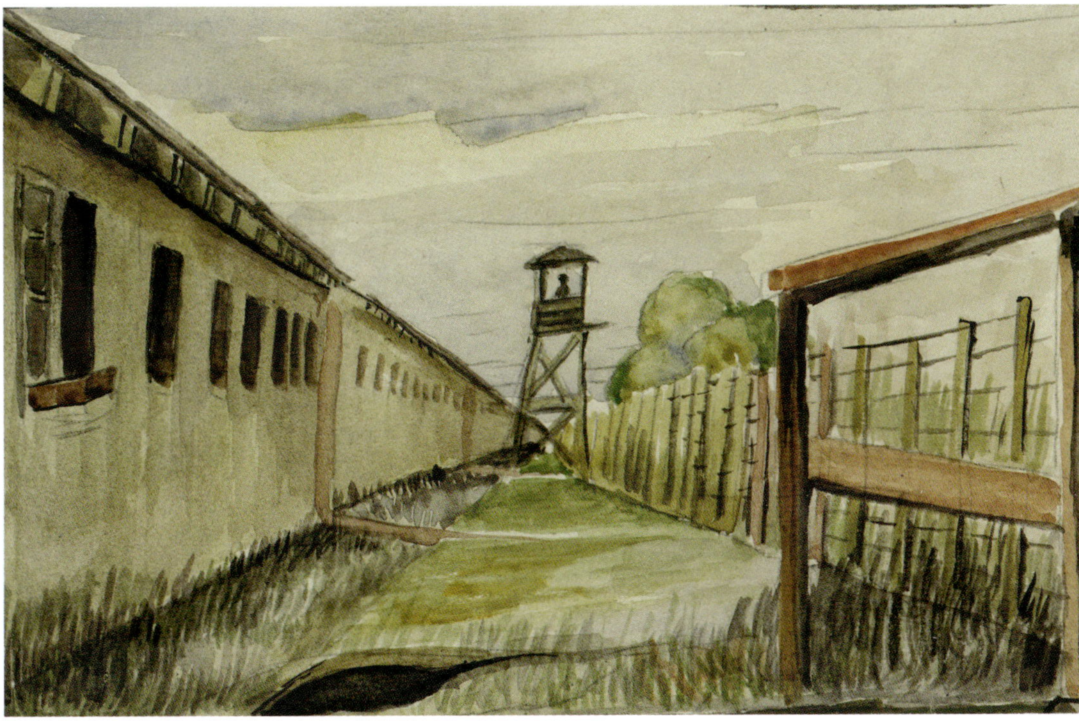

3.1 Puyallup, "The south side of the camp: the place where there was a tall watchtower." Watercolor on paper, 4 × 6 in. (See diary 15.)

townspeople. He wanders among the buildings to record the daily routine and activities as people seek to accommodate to imprisonment. Some activities like the twice-daily roll call were mandatory; others such as standing in lines for meals were daily trials. Some were practicalities designed to help people cope with living conditions, such as making *getas* (raised wooden shoes) to walk muddy paths in the unusually wet spring; some were organized activities led by the Nisei; and still more were diversions to fill the time. He comments wryly on gossip, romance, and a family fight, where even then, there was no privacy. The voices of a crowd, "Tweet, tweet, tweet," once again elicit an animal metaphor.[7] Two pages depict him in the act of drawing, on a rooftop and in his barrack, as amid surveillance and military control he declares his determination to represent his own image and his experience (diary 44 and 49).

The sequence and repetition of imagery deepen the meaning of the visual narrative. The fence and the sentries are omnipresent at Puyallup as subjects themselves or the framework of activity. The narrow space between the fence and the barracks, the only space for recreation in Area B, often converges at a watchtower. Elsewhere dark hatching, as in a drawing Fujii identifies as "Camp

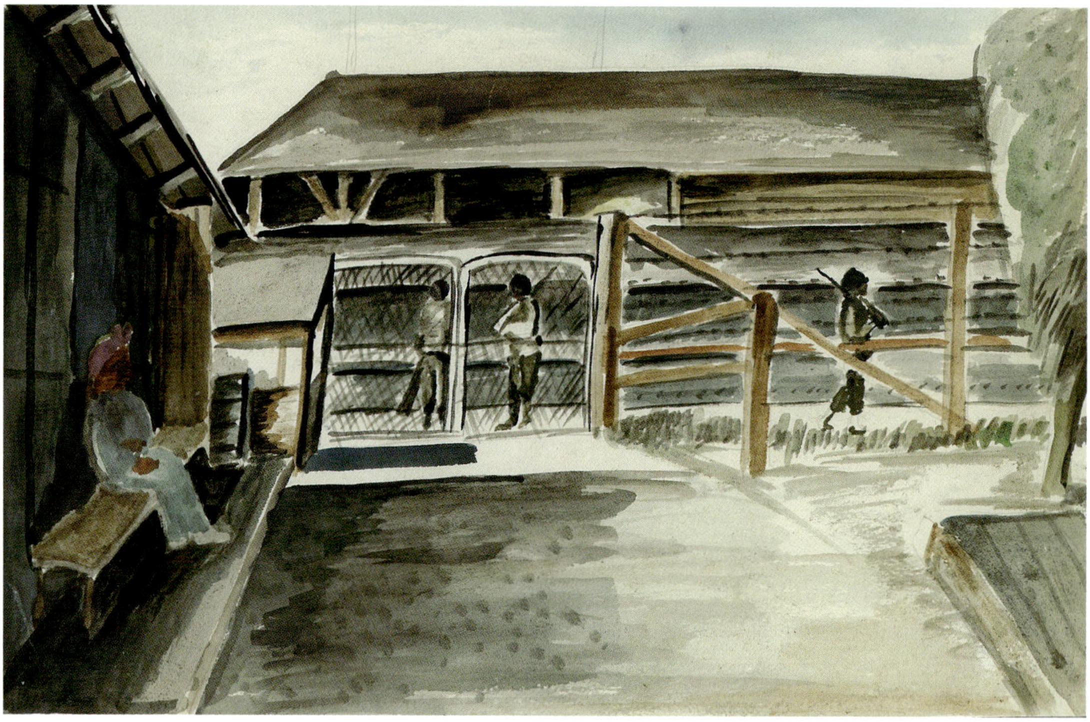

3.2 Puyallup, "This is the front gate. It was strictly guarded." Watercolor on paper, 7 × 10 in. (See diary 18.)

guard," adds to the scene's foreboding (diary 26). One after the other, scenes of seemingly interminable rows of barracks drawn in acute one-point perspective convey an oppressive sense of conformity and enclosure. The lack of hygiene and privacy are repeated themes in images of the latrine, the shower, and the mess hall with its interminable lines of people. The drawings of Puyallup are seldom as personal as those of leaving Seattle; rather than picturing his family, the majority focus on his new environment. Much of the diary's impact is in its systematic survey and retracing of the site, together with the intimacy of scenes such as those in the latrine.

Throughout the diary Fujii distinguishes between his and the younger generation. The generation gap in Nikkei communities since the barring of immigration in 1924 was exacerbated by wartime conditions, which undermined not only the Issei men's customary community leadership but also their authority within the family. No longer able to support their families, subject to the army's control and communal living on a mass scale, they watched as young adult Nisei assumed leadership positions. Issei Yamato Ichihashi, a former professor at Stanford incarcerated at Tule Lake, describes the tension over Nisei

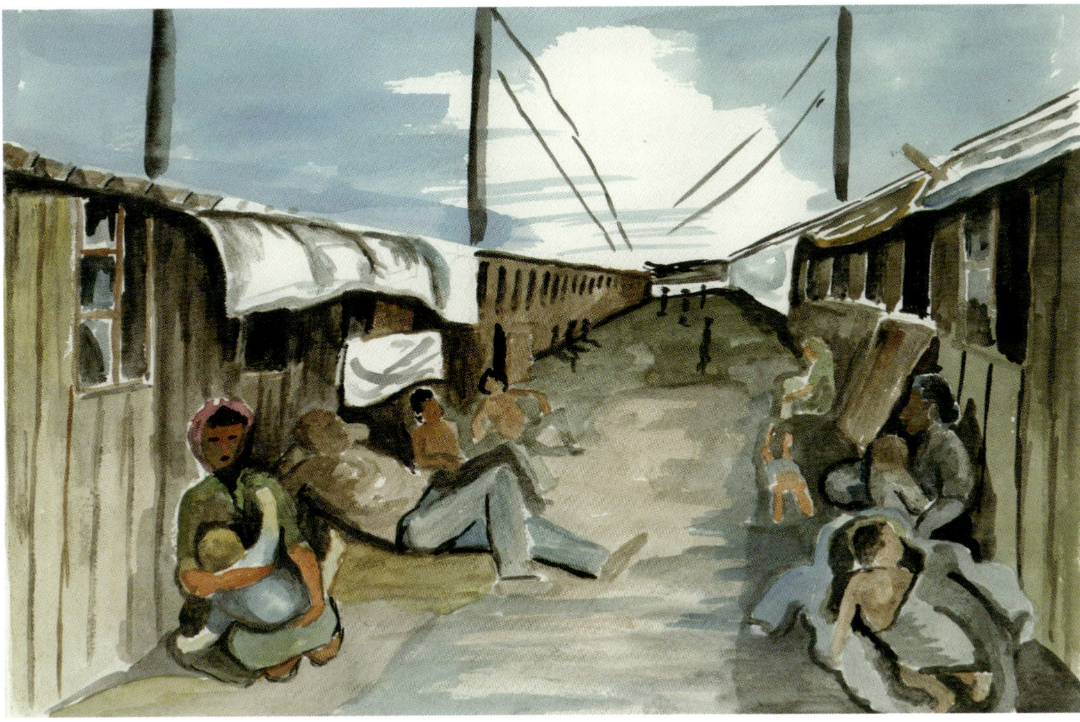

3.3 Puyallup, "An afternoon in the middle of summer." Watercolor on paper, 7 × 10 in. (See diary 30.)

management, highlighting the language difference: "Consequently there exists a feeling of dissatisfaction on the part of the colonists, many of whom are issei and aliens for whom nisei seem to have no respect. There has arisen a number of difficulties. Personally I think that the issei are not blameless; some of them are hard on nisei citizens. . . . Linguistic difficulties are one great source of misunderstanding, and the oldsters do not like to be ruled by kids, especially their own sons and daughters!"[8]

Fujii sometimes points to politically charged situations, as in his entry about the JACL spokesman, while elsewhere comparisons point to cultural practices rather than political differences. In sequential drawings, he pairs activities representing the generations, such as Issei playing checkers and Nisei playing cards, or a Bon Odori performance to honor ancestors and a "young people's dance" (diary 43). Once at Minidoka he delights in the Nisei's encouragement as he pounds *mochi* for rice cakes, "without which it is not New Year's day for us Japanese" (fig. 3.4, diary 88). For the Issei and Nisei, Japanese cultural practices and the connections they fostered to a shared heritage had been an important part of daily and ceremonial lives in prewar years.[9] Celebrations such as Bon Odori

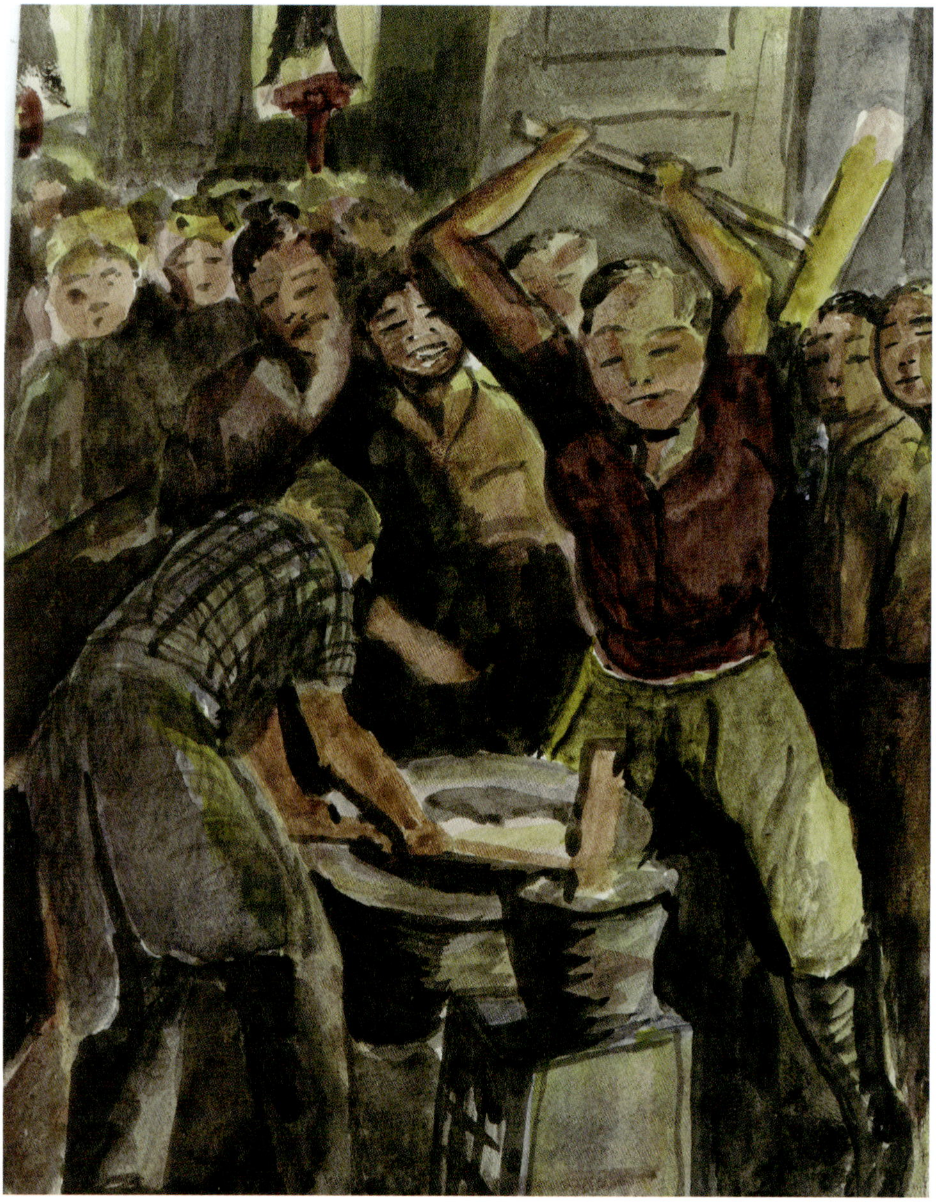

3.4 Minidoka, "Mixing with the young second-generation Japanese Americans, we pounded the [*mochi*] shouting enthusiastically." Watercolor on paper, 6¼ × 4½ in. (See diary 88.)

and the New Year were community-wide events that reinforced the continuity of cultural practice and community identification in confinement.

Two drawings at Puyallup, however, tell of deeper divides about loyalty: one is a Nisei's exhibition of a painting, the other a tale about tombstones (diary 34, 47).

Degrees of political loyalty to the United States and Japan were experienced differently by and within each generation. Class, education and intellectual interests, urban and rural origins, prewar relationships with the two nations, and presumptions about the meaning of a Japanese or American victory were formative influences in an individual's political stance. Moreover, individuals' positions shifted throughout the war in reaction to its progress, presumed outcome, and one's envisioned place in the postwar society of either nation.[10] The community of "Japanese in America," in which the two generations had complementary roles in bridging between nations, was overwhelmed in wartime.[11] While some Issei held resolutely to Japan's invincibility in war, the majority, to whatever degree predisposed to be loyal to the country of their youth, shifted throughout the war as they regarded its progress and eventual outcome.[12]

The position of Nisei varied widely with age, education, and family histories. Denied the bicultural fluidity they had exercised in the 1930s, many quickly declared their loyalty as American citizens.[13] Nisei who had been educated in Japan, and who were known as Kibei, returned with a complicated relationship to the nations of their birth and maturity and were assumed by the U.S. government to be loyal to Japan.[14] Determined to prove their loyalty as American citizens, leaders of the JACL, typically educated and urban businessmen and professionals, had adopted a policy of ultrapatriotism and accommodation of government plans before removal.[15] Once at camp, those who appeared to work too closely with the Wartime Civil Control Administration or WRA administrations or who proclaimed their loyalty too loudly could be accused of being *inu* ("dogs"), or traitors to the Nikkei, and were sometimes threatened or beaten. Some of the bitterest division was between American-loyalist Nisei leaders and pro-Japanese Kibei; when protest broke into violence at some of the camps, Kibei were readily assigned blame.[16]

Thus when Fujii relates that a dispute arose over a Nisei's painting, *Buy War Bonds*, he refers to complex relationships of generation, class, culture, and politics. The other, more ambiguous entry shows a man urinating on a tombstone built in advance of a death, the final insult, Fujii tells us, to someone declared to be a "disloyal bastard" and killed. It is rumor, he insists, and explains neither the source nor the situation, but he vividly indicates the depth of dissension.

When at last Fujii and his family boarded the train for their next unknown home, the long, hot journey fills several pages. He writes again of anxiety, so great that even the dining car raises the possibility of betrayal: "Suspiciously, today's immigrant is now being treated as a gentleman. So, it feels like something tickling my heart. After being treated like this, maybe we will be killed suddenly? Dangerous, dangerous, help us, Amida."[17] Rumors had abounded in the segregated and crowded conditions of camp, and now they did so on the train, where vulnerability and powerlessness gave quick rise to suspicion. Having been given little information, people could only speculate about their fate. The decrepit, unsanitary conditions of the trains in which they were transported added to the misery and the utter incongruity of dining car service.[18]

As Fujii reaches Minidoka, the diary's sequence of drawings, like the opening sequence at Puyallup, tells of control and imprisonment. The approach to the site is marked by armed sentries who stand front and center during the passengers' transfer from the train to buses. "We have become 'bus people,'" Fujii remarks sardonically of having been moved en masse. He represents his first glimpse of Minidoka in a dynamic yet intimate perspective, framing the camp's two water towers in the bus windshield as he peers over the driver's shoulder (diary 54). In an early drawing of Minidoka, ink washes darkly over the army police headquarters near the front gate, where the symbol of liberty, the American flag, waves overhead in the black sky (diary 73). The reality of his situation is verified for Fujii when, posting his nameplate at his barrack, he finds the lock on the outside of the door and observes, "I see that this relocation center is a prison" (diary 58). He pictures himself as an artist at work and firmly establishes himself as a witness in mapping the barracks and buildings, the sites of authority, and the Nikkei's routine. At both Puyallup and Minidoka, he specifies his point of view with such statements as: "This is the back street seen from the front gate," and "Block 19 from the place where I live," grounding his testimony in the physical reality of his experience (diary 19; unpublished diary entry; see also fig. 3.5).

As Fujii surveys his new home, the confinement of Puyallup gives way to desert space, but the communal latrine that deprives one of dignity and assaults the senses is a constant here, as at Puyallup. Among his first diary illustrations of Minidoka are the latrine (for three months only an outhouse), the lines to the mess hall, and the games to pass time. When plumbing is finally completed for the combined latrine, shower, and laundry buildings, he fills eight pages with drawings of the fixtures and infrastructure (fig. 3.6). The texts paired with these drawings are simple labels, but the accumulation alone alludes to the pressing need for the most basic services and the Nikkei's dependent status. As he did at Puyallup, Fujii methodically traces the grounds and buildings, including again the hated barbed-wire fence.

The impact on the Nikkei of being fenced in is hard to overstate. It appears often in artists' depictions of camp life, a cruelly arbitrary rupture of the landscape. Chiura Obata shows a cyclone fence towering over inmates at Tanforan, and Kenjiro Nomura paints the barbed-wire fence at Minidoka stretching into the distance until it disappears. At Topaz, Miné Okubo pictures the insult of

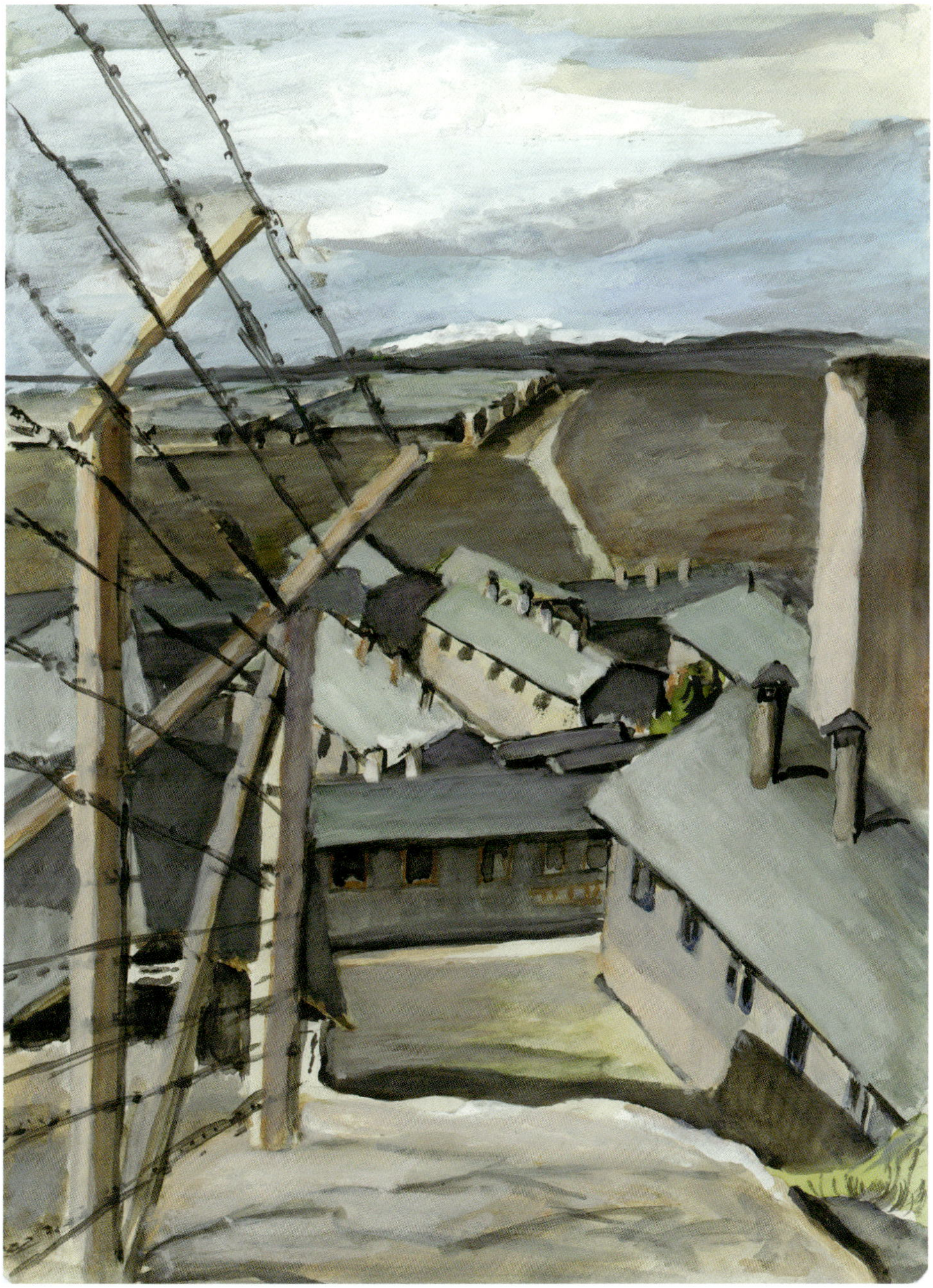

3.5 Minidoka, "This is the barbed wire and [the scene] around Block 24." Watercolor on paper, 13½ × 10 in. (See diary 74.)

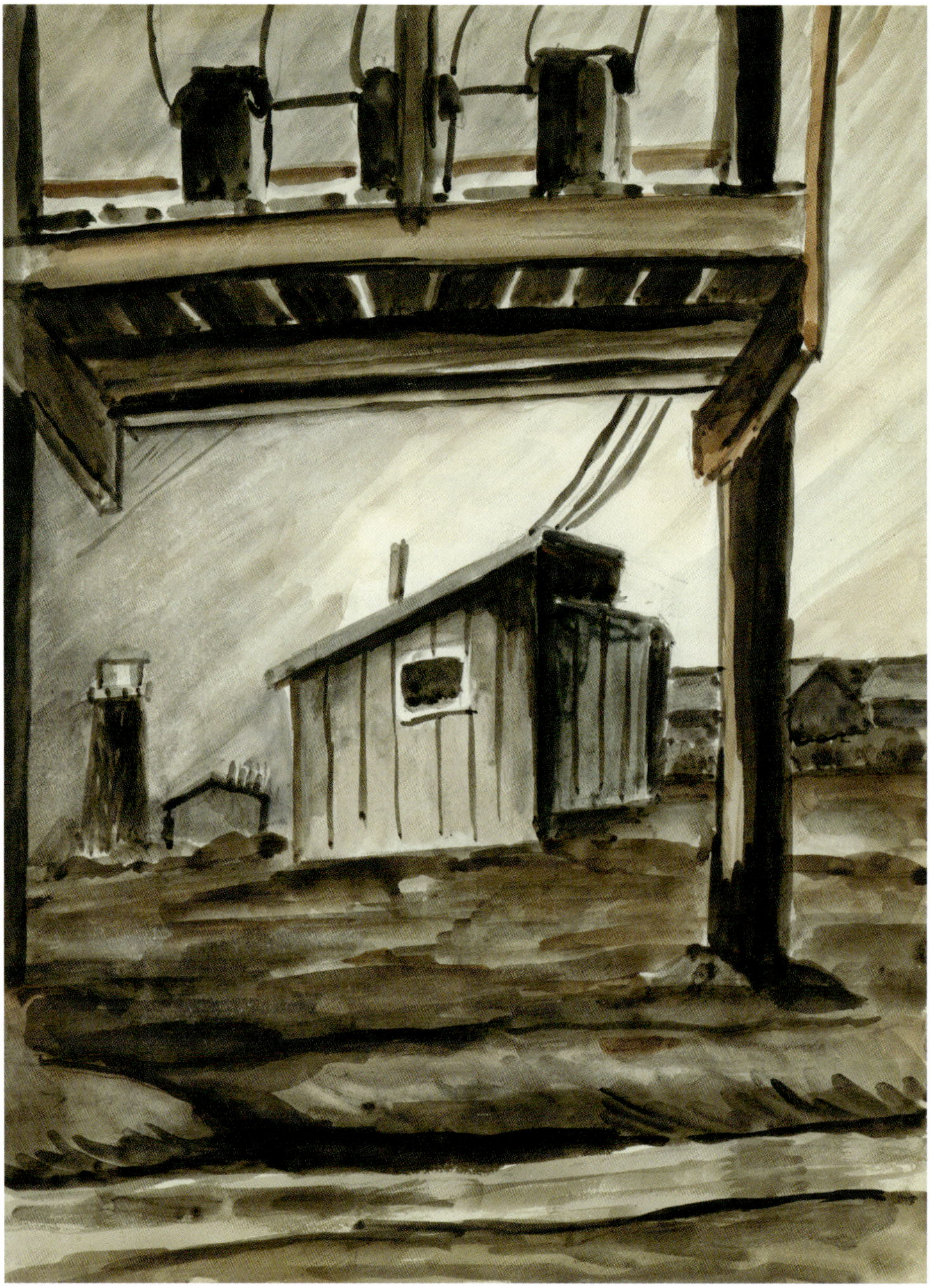

3.6 Minidoka, transformer and pump house. Watercolor on paper, 14 × 10 in.

people building the very fence that would confine them. Images of children next to the barbed wire add poignancy to an already charged site, as in Estelle Ishigo's watercolor *Boys with a Kite* at Heart Mountain and Toyo Miyatake's photograph *Boys behind Barbed Wire* at Manzanar.[19] These are occasional images, however, within larger bodies of work. Fujii features the fence repeatedly from the moment of his arrival at Puyallup, emphasizing its omnipresence, the authoritarian control that determines inside and outside, and the bitter irony of playing games next to but not in an open field. The understatement of his text—one in which two women play improvised tennis while a sentry marches outside is captioned only: "One evening moment"—heightens the disparity (diary 32).

Minidoka was not fenced when the Nikkei arrived, but camp construction continued and, by November, barbed-wire fencing surrounded both the residential blocks and the perimeter of camp, which was patrolled by sentries. Inmates, formerly confined within posted boundaries, could move outside the perimeter fence between sunrise and sunset. In May 1943, following persistent protests, the fence around the residential blocks was removed, although the perimeter fence remained.[20]

Fujii's tone shifts somewhat once he begins to explore the desert and finds solitude and pleasure in the landscape (fig. 3.7). The empty landscape is at first fearful, and even when it becomes familiar it arouses feelings of loneliness, "as if lost on the Pacific Ocean" (diary 86). He portrays himself gazing into the desert, a solitary upright figure in a landscape that recedes in textured registers to the horizon (diary 81). More often Fusano is his companion in exploring. Personal incidents such as a rattlesnake bite that caused his hospitalization become extended graphic narratives. He finds metaphors for emotions in nature: birds in winter that tell him spring is ahead; sunflowers, one clutched in Fusano's hand, that mirror the sun overhead; and on the dark side, bones in the desert, in which he sees both beautiful forms and reminders of death. In the final weeks of incarceration, with the increasing inevitability of Japan's loss and the pending closure of camp, the sunflowers become drooping stalks that echo the stooped figures of Fujii and Fusano.

Fujii makes almost no explicit reference to the course of the war, with the exception of a drawing of men gossiping in the latrine, and even there it is unclear whether his words represent his point of view or the rumors. The final eight pages of drawings are without text, leaving open to surmise the context in which people gather around a man reading a newspaper, bend deeply in walking the grounds, or lean together toward a radio. No words tell of the bombing of Hiroshima, his thoughts of family there, or Japan's surrender. One drawing, unique in the diary, is an abstract vortex of spinning Japanese and American

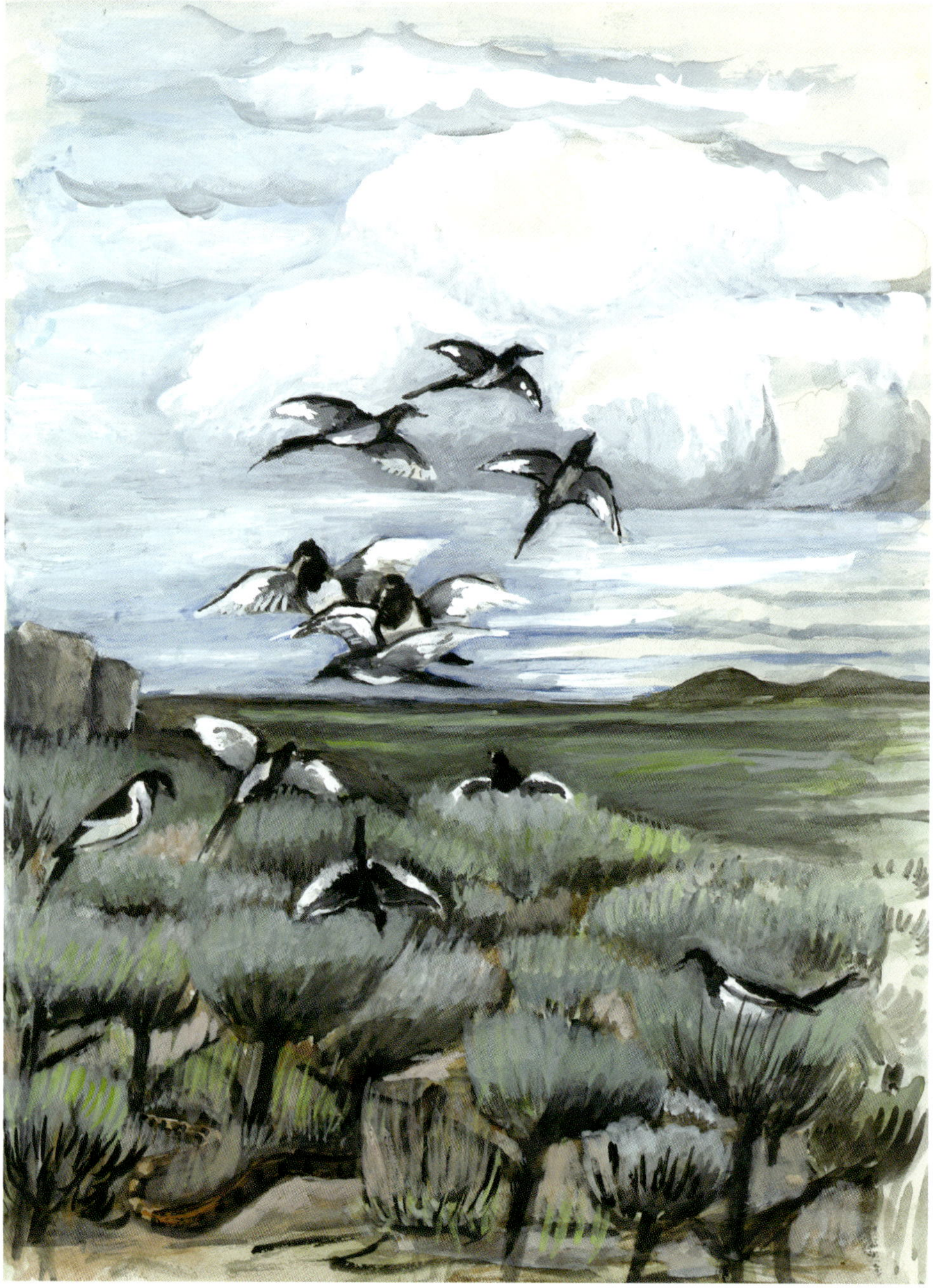

3.7 Minidoka, "A fight between birds and a snake." Watercolor on paper, 14½ × 10½ in. (See diary 82.)

flags, as if no naturalistic image could represent the magnitude of such events and the tumultuous emotions surrounding Japan's loss (diary 109). For Issei Noboru Shirai, Japan's capitulation, although anticipated, brought unstoppable tears.[21] Loss and disorientation stir a startling image in another's poem:

> By the window
> Father floats up
> over the ashes of home.[22]

Three days after Hiroshima, Nagasaki was bombed. Six days later, August 15, the emperor broadcast Japan's acceptance of Allied terms by radio, the first time the Japanese people had ever heard his voice, and on September 2 Japan signed its unconditional surrender. Fujii's diary ends a month later as he and his wife hunch dejectedly, awaiting departure from camp. A calendar on the wall marks the date October 2; their bags are packed once again. They board a truck and then a train as camp demolition is under way and the animals the community had raised for food are left to starve.

GENERATION AND FAMILY

In both image and word Fujii's diary is exceptional in its understatement. Explicitly and implicitly his awareness of age and generation pervades the diary. He tells of concern for his daughters as they leave their Seattle home, his unease with Nisei leadership in camp, the generations' differing activities, and the conflicting political loyalties. His cultural identification with Japan is evident in his references to *getas*, *yōmeishu*, and pounding *mochi*, but he says little directly about his own loyalty or his relationship to the competing factions within the camp. Looking at examples of what is and what is not expressed offers further insight into the circumstances of which he writes.

Fujii's diary says surprisingly little about his family. With the exception of illustrations of Fusano at his side, the only diary entries about his family after leaving Seattle are their moving into barracks at Puyallup and Minidoka. Fujii makes no mention of Satoko's leaving the household to marry or the couple's leaving Minidoka altogether. Although he portrays Masako twice in paintings—a small watercolor of her reading in the Minidoka barrack and a cubist-influenced composition in oil of her standing before the barrack window—she appears in the diary only when departing Minidoka at the end of a military leave. His daughters instead are present as an absence. He remarks as he pictures himself looking for mail: "This is the heart of people who have children. Just hearing someone's footfalls, one checks the mailbox." And the emptiness doubles with the realization there was no mail delivery: "Today is Sunday, isn't it?" (diary 105).

The forced removal and confinement disrupted the family unit from the beginning. Communal living deprived families of the private household, where family values and discipline were taught. Fathers no longer provided for their families, and mothers no longer served family meals. Youth banded together in age groups, eating together in the mess halls and roaming the grounds to escape the confinement of single-room barracks.[23] As months wore into years and families continued under pressure, problems became increasingly evident; Issei diarist and professor Yamoto Ichihashi, who was frequently asked to advise on community issues, expresses disgust for unruly children, gangs of teenage boys, and what he calls the loose morals of young women as he records cases of juvenile delinquency, pregnancies out of marriage, and divorce.[24] More indirectly, Fujii records the consequences of the loss of discipline in drawings of a guard tower accidentally set on fire by four-year-olds and of young people vandalizing the library (diary 101). The circumstances, however, were not entirely detrimental. In significant constructive ways, young Nisei, no longer marginalized by their Caucasian peers, found new opportunities for participation and leadership in school, sports, and activities, contributing, in one sociologist's view, to their greater ability to adapt after the war.[25]

Families, such as the Fujiis, with adult children were split in another way as sons and daughters departed for work, school, and military service, leaving elderly parents alone.[26] With the WRA actively urging resettlement, the shrinking of the young, able population was felt at the camp in labor shortages and the depletion of professional skills such as doctors, nurses, and dentists.[27] By late 1943 those remaining were mostly elders and families with young children. Fujii and Fusano could have been among those described by Okubo as she left Topaz in early 1944: "Only the very old or very young were left. . . . I thought, 'My God! How do they expect those poor people to leave the one place they can call home.'"[28] Although Fujii says little about his daughters' absence, he indicates the importance of his partnership with Fusano by making her increasingly visible in the latter part of the diary.

The diary also shows him to be keenly aware of the loss of peers. Well before the Nisei were declared eligible for military service, illness, old age, and the stress of imprisonment took Issei, and occasionally younger people, with uncomfortable frequency. Fujii depicts a row of gravestones for "the first sacrifices among the relocated," and says of the open grave in the foreground, "Always, the graves are ready." He repeats the diary image in two watercolors, which one might take simply as part of his survey of place were it not for the concluding diary text,

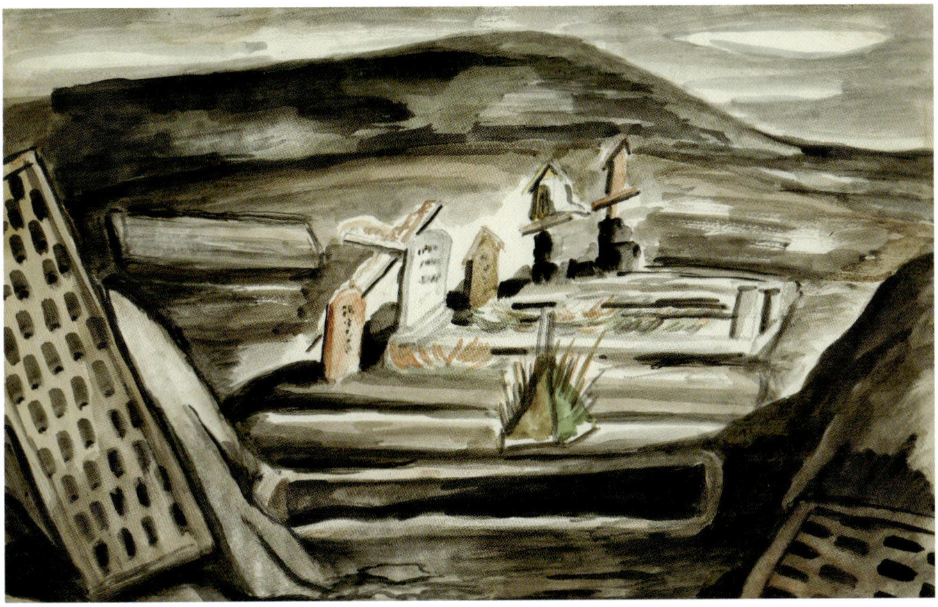

3.8 Minidoka, "Here are the gravestones of several of the dead, the first sacrifices among the relocated. Always, the graves are ready." Watercolor on paper, 10 × 14 in. (See diary 92.)

"Everyone, please quickly . . ." (fig. 3.8, diary 92).[29] Even here, in the time constraint on funerals, he points to WRA control. He again cites the time limit in picturing the first memorial service for Nisei soldiers. Ichihashi was so struck by the deaths that he tracked their numbers. "I am hardened by the phenomenon," he wrote in 1944. "I have attended more funerals in the camps than I have in [the rest of my] lifetime."[30] Fujii's is a quiet but mournful protest of the stressful living conditions and the control that circumscribed all of their lives. The void of the open grave that centers his image is paralleled by a poem by Keiho Soga, interned in a Department of Justice camp:

> The barren wasteland
> Raged by sandstorm,
> I weep for my friend
> Who sleeps there alone,
> Eternally.[31]

In the poet's spare words and the artist's equally spare image, the loss of an individual becomes emblematic of the enormity of loss that military confinement represented.

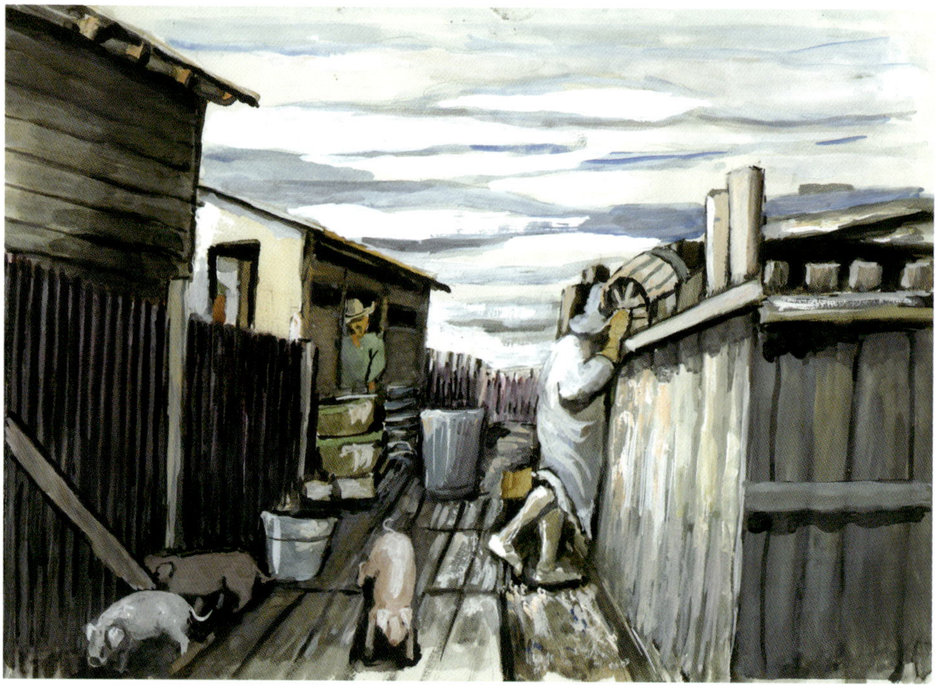

3.9 Minidoka, hog farm. Watercolor on paper, 10 × 13½ in.

Fujii does not dwell upon the endemic conflict with authorities and among inmates experienced at all of the camps, but several entries depict underlying tensions and acts of resistance.[32] He represents a strike by coal haulers with the sympathetic image of an old woman gathering bits of coal, commenting simply that people were "greatly inconvenienced" (diary 102). Coal delivery was a continual issue at Minidoka. Tokita writes after his arrival about the failure to distribute coal that occurred because "nobody wants to carry coal for $16 a month," and, amid a shortage of coal as the first winter grew bitterly cold, of the selfishness of inmates who took more than their ration (while admitting he did the same).[33] Fujii's drawing is a rare if not unique instance of his copying a photograph from the camp newspaper, where the caption reads, "While community leaders argue and harangue each other about the shortage of coal, the delivery of coal, the kind of coal, et cetera, the 'little people' take what they get and keep themselves out of controversies."[34] The newspaper's Nisei bias is revealed in the diminishing language that describes "a wizened old lady" who scrapes up coal for "her little pot-bellied stove." By isolating the large, sensitively rendered figure on the page, Fujii lends dignity to the woman and her labor. In effect aligning himself with the little people, he asserts his agency by continuing to witness and draw as he confronts the tensions of confinement.

In yet another way, Fujii registers his resistance to government control. The survey of buildings that characterizes his work calls attention to the Minidoka inmates' own construction projects, along with the labor they contributed to building infrastructure for the WRA. He pictures the completion of a baseball field (there were nine at Minidoka), a playground, a swimming pool, an irrigation canal, agricultural fields that eventually reached 740 acres, a large root cellar, and, at last in 1945, a gymnasium (fig. 3.9).[35] Although the WRA publicized such projects as evidence of successful "pioneering" communities, architectural historian Lynne Horiuchi argues that the environment the Nikkei built themselves differed fundamentally from the military-style encampment meant to imprison. The appropriation of space, materials, and building process represents an alternative kind of community planning that she calls "insurgent citizenship," a resistance to surveilled confinement. Segregated and isolated because of ancestry, with their movements controlled by fences, restricted zones, and communal facilities for the basic functions of living, they nevertheless created a dynamic space planned and occupied on their own terms, even as they had to cooperate with authorities to accomplish their goals.[36] To the extent that Fujii represents a constructive, integrated community, he accommodates an image the WRA wanted to project publically; but more critically, he contributes to the collective resistance as he draws and names these sites at both Puyallup and Minidoka.

AN ISSEI PERSPECTIVE

Fujii's point of view and accomplishment are further evident when his work is considered alongside comparable work by other artists. Among those who produced substantial bodies of work similar in scope to Fujii's, the most prominent are Chiura Obata and Miné Okubo. Representing the first and second generations, respectively, both sketched from the beginning of their incarceration with the intent to document their experiences, and both often combined image and text. The combination is essential to Okubo's *Citizen 13660*. Both, furthermore, addressed a public audience and intended their artwork for exhibition outside of camp.

Obata, an Issei like Fujii, began sketching the day he registered for removal and continued sketching and painting until his release from Topaz in 1943, all together about two hundred images.[37] His sketches and the larger paintings based upon them are typically signed with place and date; some include text in Japanese. The majority are figurative and display his academic experience in the confident representation of form and the spatial environment in which figures act, rendered in fluid strokes of modulated sumi blacks. Others are linear drawings replete with visual information.[38] Eight of his images were

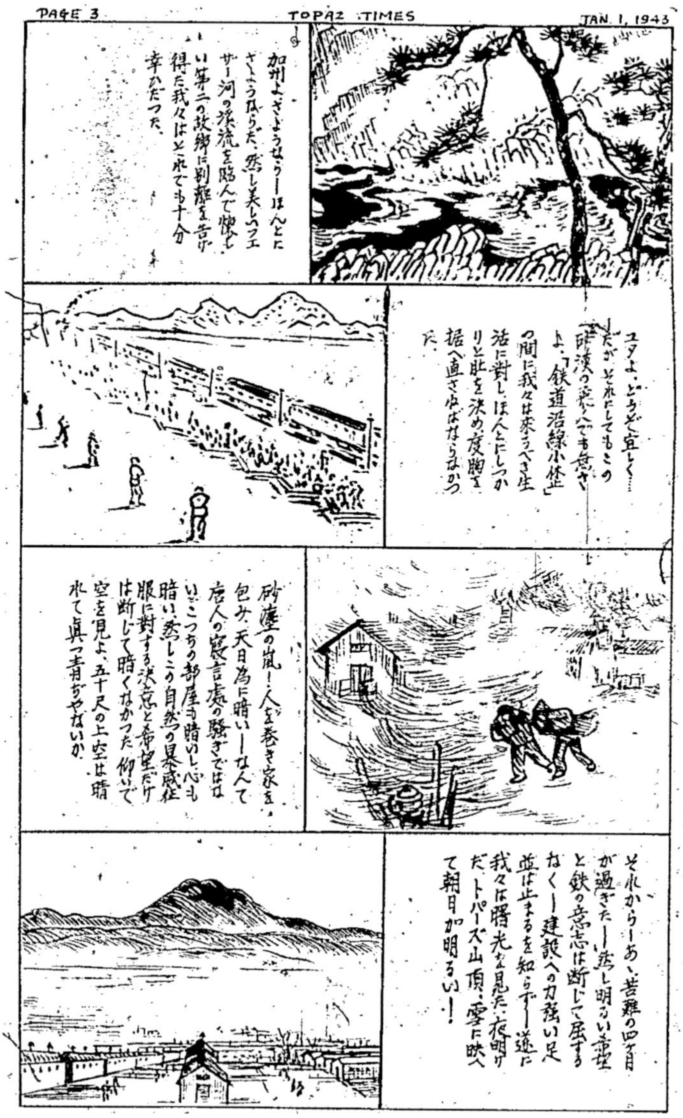

3.10 Chiura Obata, second of two illustrated pages in the *Topaz Times*, New Year's edition, January 1, 1943.

reproduced in the first New Year's edition of the *Topaz Times* with accompanying texts that tell of sorrow but reinforce spiritual uplift and natural beauty. The final one concludes, "At last, we see the beautiful dawn as reflected in the morning sun bright against snow-covered Mt. Topaz!" (fig. 3.10).[39] Although he continued the documentary work at Topaz, he increasingly turned to landscape paintings that picture the incarceration camp diminished by the vast, ethereal beauty of desert and sky.[40]

It is Okubo's primary wartime project, published in her book *Citizen 13660*, that most closely aligns in continuity and narrative trajectory with Fujii's diary. A generation younger than Obata and Fujii, Okubo relates that she began drawing for friends outside camp, but that "the humor and pathos" of the situation spurred her to address a wider audience.[41] She opens her story in Europe, where she had been studying on a University of California fellowship, immediately establishing her credentials as an accomplished and rewarded American artist. In more than two hundred pages of drawings and narrative text, she traces life at Tanforan and Topaz until her release in January 1944 to work in New York. Her study of mural painting is evident in the drawing style, with its boldly defined figures and gestures; the flattened, rhythmic pattern of figures across the page; and the placement of cropped figures in the close foreground to connect to viewers. She portrays herself on each page, usually as one of the foregrounded figures, as an emphatic, expressive witness to the events she relates. She does not mince words describing the loss of freedom and conditions at camp, but in a slyly subversive manner holds readers' attention by understatement and frequent humor. And while she has access to women's activities, whereas men do not, more broadly she is attentive to women, families, and personal interactions. Contemporary reviewers complimented her "sad and understanding humor," taking her at her word rather than seeing the disjunction between many of the drawings and accompanying texts that, as in Fujii's diary, reveals the deeper critique.[42]

Fujii's diary, by contrast, is the private endeavor of an Issei man. It is a reserved and distilled document whose force lies in evocation. He has no need to explain cultural references such as *getas* and *mochi*. Besides the obvious difference in gender-specific scenes, he, like Okubo, defines himself in relationship to family, the Nikkei community, the other generation, and the controlling white authority. Both repeatedly resist this authority in the viewpoints they represent and their autonomy as artists. While Okubo's text is characterized by understatement that is often at odds with the situation she pictures, Fujii's diary, in both image and text, is an altogether greater level of understatement. Fujii's voice is spare and allusive. As he surveys the campgrounds and names his viewpoint, he is present as a witness, but without Okubo's assertive self-portrayal and with none of her theatrical gestures such as sticking out her tongue or holding her nose.

A comparison as each looks outside the temporary detention camp is illustrative (figs. 3.11, 3.12). During the first weeks of incarceration at Tanforan, Okubo pictures herself in the racetrack grandstand looking down at the enclosing fence, the guard tower, and the streets beyond, reflecting, "We were so close to freedom and yet far from it."[43] Her eloquent opening words, expressive on their own, are followed by a description of the setting for her mainstream audience.

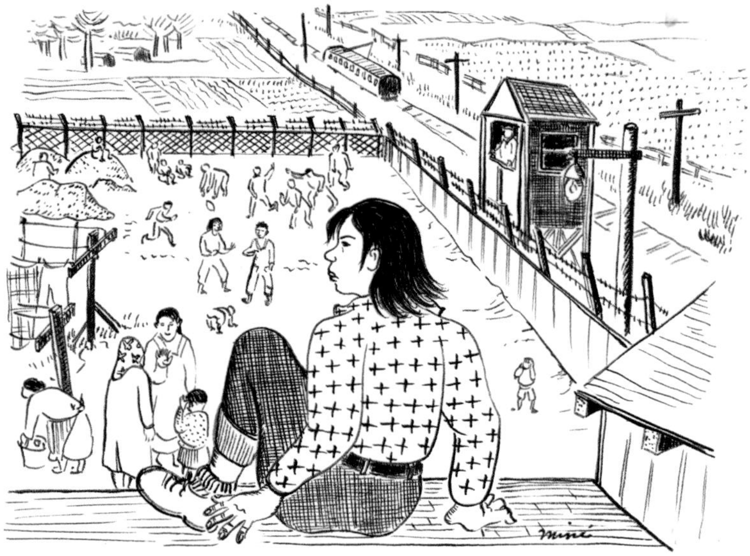

3.11 Miné Okubo, Tanforan Assembly Center, 1942. Ink on Paper, 9¼ x 13 in. Japanese American National Museum, gift of Miné Okubo Estate, 2007.62.82. Published in *Citizen 13660*, p. 81.

With similar longing, Fujii pictures the view framed by his single barrack window at the Puyallup camp, where he looks past the nearby barbed-wire fence to a farmhouse beyond, a house he would reiterate in watercolor. He writes simply, "View outside." Both artists mourn the loss of freedom. While Okubo explains for her readers, Fujii evokes, without naming, his loss of freedom, possessions, and home.

The distillation and allusion of Fujii's text in a few instances, such as the epigraph that introduces this book or his looking for mail, have the evocative and metric character of poetry. Poetry was widely practiced by Issei men and women before the war and became an important means of expression in wartime. Some, like Keiho Soga, were already well known through publication, while others, such as Tokita, turned to poetry during incarceration.[44] Prized for evocative allusion, haiku, a common form composed of seventeen syllables, is usually nature-based and often refers to seasons. A modern and widespread form of haiku, senryu, which addresses human nature, had developed a strong following in the Northwest. (A group of farmers in Yakima, Washington, are believed to have introduced the form in the United States.)[45] Originating in folk poetry, senryu was revived in the early twentieth century with greater emphasis on social relations. "A *senryu* poet," writes Teruko Kumei, who has collected and studied the form, "is an observer and a recorder of daily life" who "analyzes his/her raw emotion with critical distance."[46] Senryu poetry, Kumei

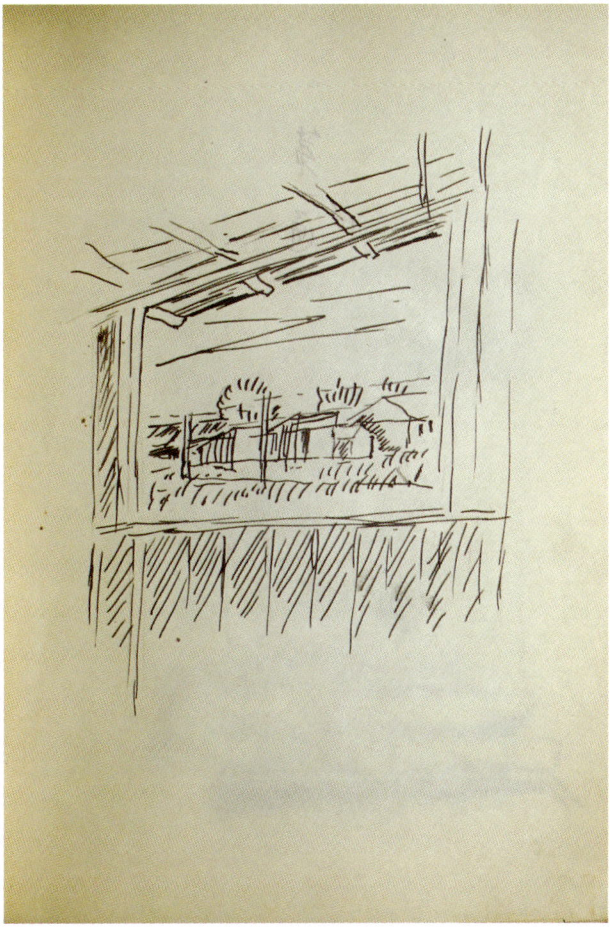

3.12 Fujii, "View outside." Diary entry, Puyallup. Ink on paper, 8 × 5½.

emphasizes, was practiced by "ordinary people, ranging from immigrant leaders to seasonal workers" and published widely in Japanese immigrant newspapers.[47] Although Fujii's text does not have the true form of poetry, a few exemplary entries demonstrate a shared sensibility with his poet-peers and link him in another way to generation.

Yet more broadly, literary scholar Stephen Sumida proposes that Fujii's diary as a whole can be seen as an epic, in the manner of the great medieval Japanese epic *The Tale of the Heike*.[48] Like an epic, the diary presents a long narrative account of a crucial time in the history of a people. It is vast in scope, engaging great nations and great themes, and transcends the local and particular in telling a story of lasting moral force. Fujii would have known the medieval tale but surely not foreseen that his effort to record his experience would be similarly compared, nor that the history of his people during World War II would retain the currency it has today.

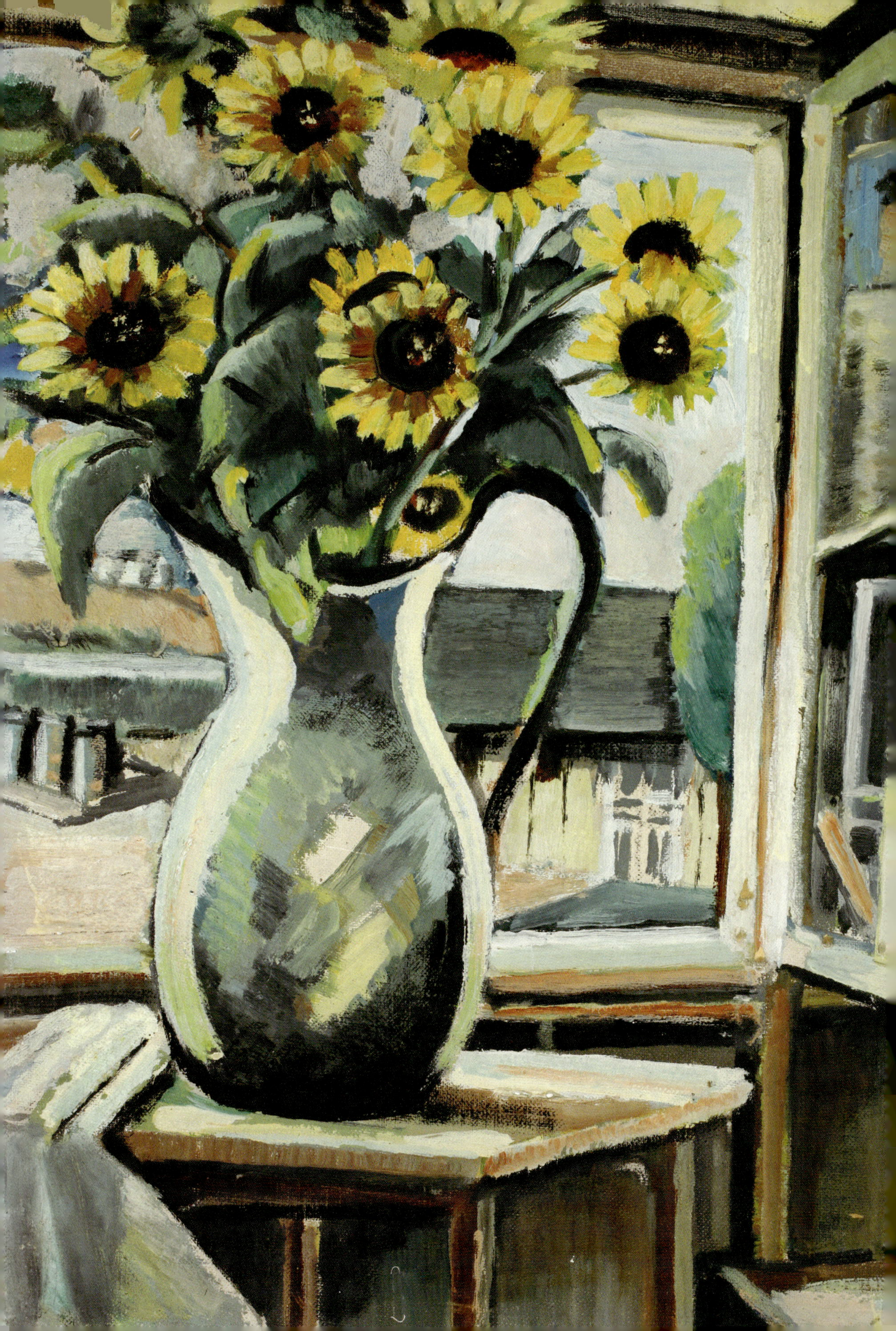

4 Public and Private

EXPANDING UPON THE DIARY

GIVING its enthusiastic endorsement, the *Minidoka Irrigator*, the camp newspaper, announced a forthcoming art exhibition in November 1943: "The exhibition promises to be an interesting and attractive one with notable and highly acclaimed artists participating. From among the ten best artists in the state of Washington, Messrs. Fujii, Tokita, and Nomura will have their masterpieces on display."[1] The three had been the most recognized Nikkei artists in Seattle before the war. The characterization of "ten best" harkens back to better times, when their paintings represented Washington State in the *First National Exhibition of American Art* at New York's Rockefeller Center.

Although Fujii's wartime production was primarily a private endeavor, his public participation left its mark in exhibition and print. He alludes in his diary to his recognition in camp when, surrounded by artwork, he works on a painting, saying only, "Communal life—if one is asked one cannot say no" (diary 105). The November exhibition was at least the third one organized by inmates since their arrival at Minidoka.[2] The largest was held in June of that year at the library in nearby Twin Falls, affording an opportunity to display camp residents' talents to an outside audience. Among the more than three hundred objects exhibited were paintings, drawings, ikebana, and "vases, tables, lamps, bird and animal figures[,] and inlaid work fashioned from the twisted branches of the bitter-bush."[3] Fujii's painting of sunflowers was prominently displayed next to landscapes by Nomura and Tokita. The *Twin Falls Times-News* emphasized that the creative projects had been produced at the end of work days, as if to forestall charges that the incarcerees passed their time with leisurely pleasures. The exhibition, the *Minidoka Interlude* later

Opposite: Sunflowers (detail), 1943. Oil on cardboard, 15½ × 11½ in. Photo: Richard Nicol.

recounted, "was received by the Twin Falls public with astounding praise."[4]

Art and craft exhibitions were popular activities, as they were at other camps. Although neither Minidoka nor Puyallup had schools of the kind Obata established, both had organized activities that included art and craft classes and exhibitions. The activities centers were staffed by Nisei as part of their management of the camps' daily affairs. Ed Tsutakawa, a former art student at the University of Washington, led art classes at both sites and years later described his pleasure in being able to order the finest art supplies for himself through the WRA administration at Minidoka.[5]

Fujii's diary pictures several exhibitions, and in one image drawn at Puyallup he depicts the ironic scene of men and women looking at paintings on the wall as they themselves are the object of a sentry's gaze (diary 33). Censorship was a fact of incarceration. The Code of Wartime Practices developed by the U.S. Office of Censorship specified "war prisoners, internees, civilian prisoners" as among those whose work was subject to censorship in "everything published and circulated inside the United States."[6] Although initially artists' activity was sometimes regarded with suspicion—Ed Tsutakawa recalled a soldier at Puyallup poking him with a bayonet as he sketched—whatever doubt the government had about allowing artists to depict camp life was dispelled by the public relations value of putting their works on display.[7] Obata's success at Tanforan set a powerful example: a month after the school opened in May 1942, student work was exhibited in Oakland and Berkeley, while inside Tanforan an exhibition of art and crafts drew nine thousand attendees and coverage in the *Oakland Tribune*, with a drawing in reproduction and the caption "Their art is American."[8] Elsewhere the government employed inmates to document camp life. Henry Sugimoto painted in secret until he found that camp administrators, who in fact knew of his activity, wanted to film him at work as evidence of the successful "relocation" of Japanese Americans. In May 1943, as the WRA increased its efforts to resettle inmates in the Midwest and East, the Society of Friends in Cambridge, Massachusetts, sponsored a two-week exhibition of art from all ten camps, which was accompanied by a brochure written by WRA historian Ruth McKee. Her essay is a rosily apologetic account of incarceration giving context, even motivation, for the creative work on display to a public far from the region where that incarceration took place: "Public opinion within the states where the centers were located dictated the enclosure of the communities with barbed wire fences and the presence of military guards at the boundaries." Depending upon the site, it continues, the landscape might offer "solace in the scene," such as at Manzanar, where one "could gaze upon the majestic grandeur of the Sierras."[9] First prize went to Obata's *New Moon*, a bird's-eye view of Topaz and snow-covered mountains that McKee might have had in mind. There is no indication whether Fujii participated, but little in his Minidoka work suggests he would have submitted a majestic landscape.[10]

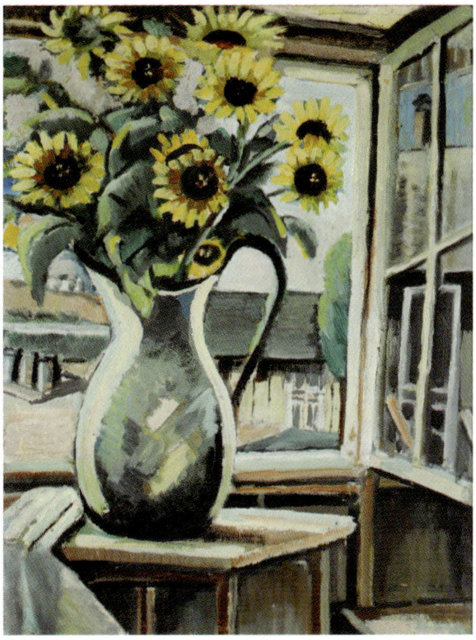

4.1 Sunflowers, 1943. Oil on cardboard, 15½ × 11½ in. Photo: Richard Nicol.

Fujii's painting in the Twin Falls exhibition is one of the few he produced in oil during the war. A pitcher of sunflowers stands by the open window of his barrack, recalling the pleasure in the flowers he expresses in the diary (fig. 4.1). The robustly painted outline and hatched surface of the pitcher display his confident handling of paint and, in the vitality of the brushwork, intimate his future interest in abstraction. What at first glance is a simple still life reveals its complexity in the representation of nearby buildings seen in the open window, where reflective surfaces and receding space vie in lively pattern. Sunflowers and barracks, organic and angular in form, are contrasting signs of natural and unnatural and, implicitly, freedom and control. While produced for public display, the painting is redolent of the intimacy of his barrack, the view he experienced daily, and the flowers Fusano picked on their walks. It is the only wartime painting that can be positively identified as one intended for exhibition and provides a bridge between his private and public life.

"MAY WE DEDICATE THIS BOOK"

Fujii portrays himself in the diary sketching in public view and indicates that his practice was a common sight to those around him. When a member of the camp's community activities division, which was charged with organizing classes and events to help maintain morale, proposed creating a souvenir yearbook, the group turned to Fujii for illustrations. High school students at all ten incarceration camps produced yearbooks filled with the typical mix of classes and activities and ranging in tone from cheerful to somber.[11] This one was different, initiated and produced primarily by and for adult Nisei.[12] The timing of the publication in fall 1943 was significant. Amid the government's extended

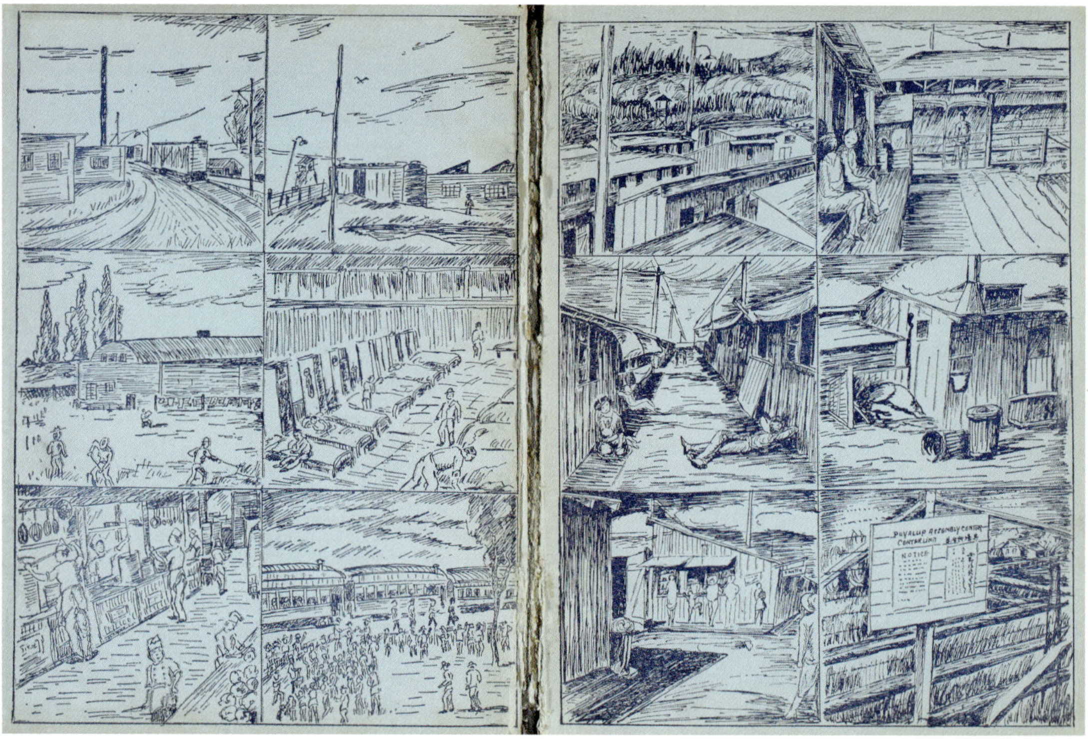

4.2 Endpapers of *Minidoka Interlude*, published at the Minidoka Relocation Center, 1943. Each 10½ × 7½ in. Fujii's well-worn copy is pictured.

discussions about resettlement, Roosevelt declared in September that the West Coast would be reopened to "loyal evacuees . . . as soon as the military situation will make such restoration feasible."[13] The Nisei who organized the yearbook knew most of them would soon leave; the book would truly be a souvenir of what they left behind them.

Proposed by Tom Takeuchi, *Minidoka Interlude* was conceived as an enduring account of the community's constructive adaptation and contributions despite the conditions in which they lived. Takeuchi wrote an impassioned foreword outlining events leading to exclusion, the conditions and costs of incarceration, and the Nisei's preparedness to contribute to American democracy.[14] A production team sold ads to finance publication, located suppliers and contractors, and organized group photographs under R. Ochi's direction. The book is composed of group portraits of residential blocks, work crews, school classes, sports teams, and activities. In their numbers alone, the people assembled by block expose the pressures of communal living. The staff thanks WRA reports officer John Bigelow and others for their support; like all camp publications, the book was subject to WRA review and censorship.

Six of Fujii's drawings of Puyallup fill one of two endpapers of *Minidoka Interlude*; on the other are six drawings of Minidoka in a similar style and which are not found in the diary. They are arranged in a grid across the page, a format recalling Obata's publication of drawings in the *Topaz Times* earlier that year. Additional drawings create a collage on the pages that divide sections (figs. 4.2, 4.3). Unlike the photographs that comprise the book's content, the drawings picture the means of military confinement, including the armed guards outside the gate and General DeWitt's orders posted on the boundary fence at Puyallup, potent symbols of the government's control. In more filmic fashion, Fujii's design for the section title page flows as if along a road from two Northwest landmarks, Seattle's Smith Tower and the Astoria Column in Oregon, to the entry gate of Minidoka. The gate is framed by a watchtower, a sentry, the stone administration building, and fences on either side and spreads graphically across the page, a visual and physical barricade to the life inside.[15] In a center inset, he pictures himself as the artist-observer drawing inside his barrack, reiterating a diary entry from Puyallup.

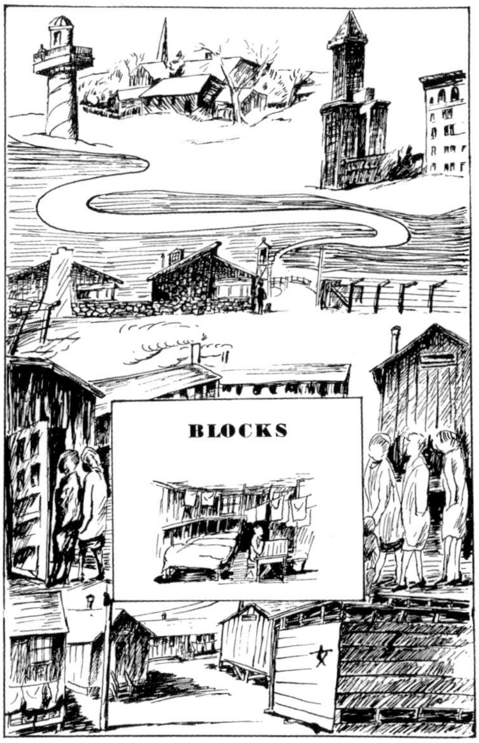

4.3 Section title page of *Minidoka Interlude*.

The yearbook was planned as a determinedly positive document that represents Minidoka as an "interlude," a challenging period of lost time in the Nisei's striving to make a place for themselves in American society. The philosophy is embodied in the dedication: "May we dedicate this book . . . to a truly free and democratic America, where men shall be judged by their actions, not by their race, color, or creed; to our homeland, and the homeland of our children." Takeuchi's foreword that follows clearly addresses the Nisei: "As we look back, we seem to have lost everything dear in our life. . . . However, we still have our Citizenship, our ideals and our future."[16]

Despite his participation in the project, nothing indicates that Fujii shared this view; nor did he share their legal status. To the contrary, his diary echoes with references to loss, and its last pages are filled with images of anxiety. Fujii's constructive focus is found instead in his commitment to recording and interpreting his experience in the body of paintings, drawings, and sculpture that expand upon the diary.

THE CAMPS IN WATERCOLORS

Among his first diary drawings at Minidoka, Fujii portrays himself sitting before an outdoor easel while Fusano stands at his side with a sketch pad (diary 68). The results of his practice are the nearly one hundred thirty watercolors, along with additional ink drawings, that are based upon and extend the diary's view. Although none are dated, most if not all appear to have been made during the war. A number of watercolors depict scenes not shown in the diary and are specific enough to indicate they were produced on-site. Moreover, while the watercolors of Puyallup are based closely upon diary compositions, the majority of those of Minidoka have no parallel in the diary, suggesting that Fujii undertook the watercolor project as a whole once he was settled in Idaho, perhaps in the 1943–1944 interval when his diary drawing slowed significantly. Some may have been painted in retrospect; several watercolors of Puyallup and Minidoka are made on the textured paper he used in picturing Ogden after the war, raising the possibility that they were made at the same time. Other hints are enticing but inconclusive. A watercolor "self-portrait" of his drawing table, chair, and wastebasket pictures the handmade portfolio that would hold matted paintings of Puyallup and Minidoka, a project that could have been undertaken in Minidoka, Ogden, or Chicago (see fig. 1.1).

Fujii seems to have returned to and ruminated upon subjects in the diary with special meaning or aesthetic interest. More than half of the watercolors are small, in the range of four by six or five by seven inches, and despite their size have a presence many times greater. Sometimes a painted image reiterates one in the diary and also appears in more than one size, as if Fujii were rethinking not only the composition but also his comprehension of the conditions in which he now lived. A watercolor may be a cropped version of the diary drawing, tightening the intimacy of the viewpoint and the sense of enclosure; occasionally a detail becomes an independent composition. In many of the watercolors the formal elements of painting take precedence as Fujii emphasizes compositional design and the fluid translucency of the medium.

The watercolors, together with several large ink drawings, focus more on buildings than people, and as in the diary, the clustering of subjects suggests

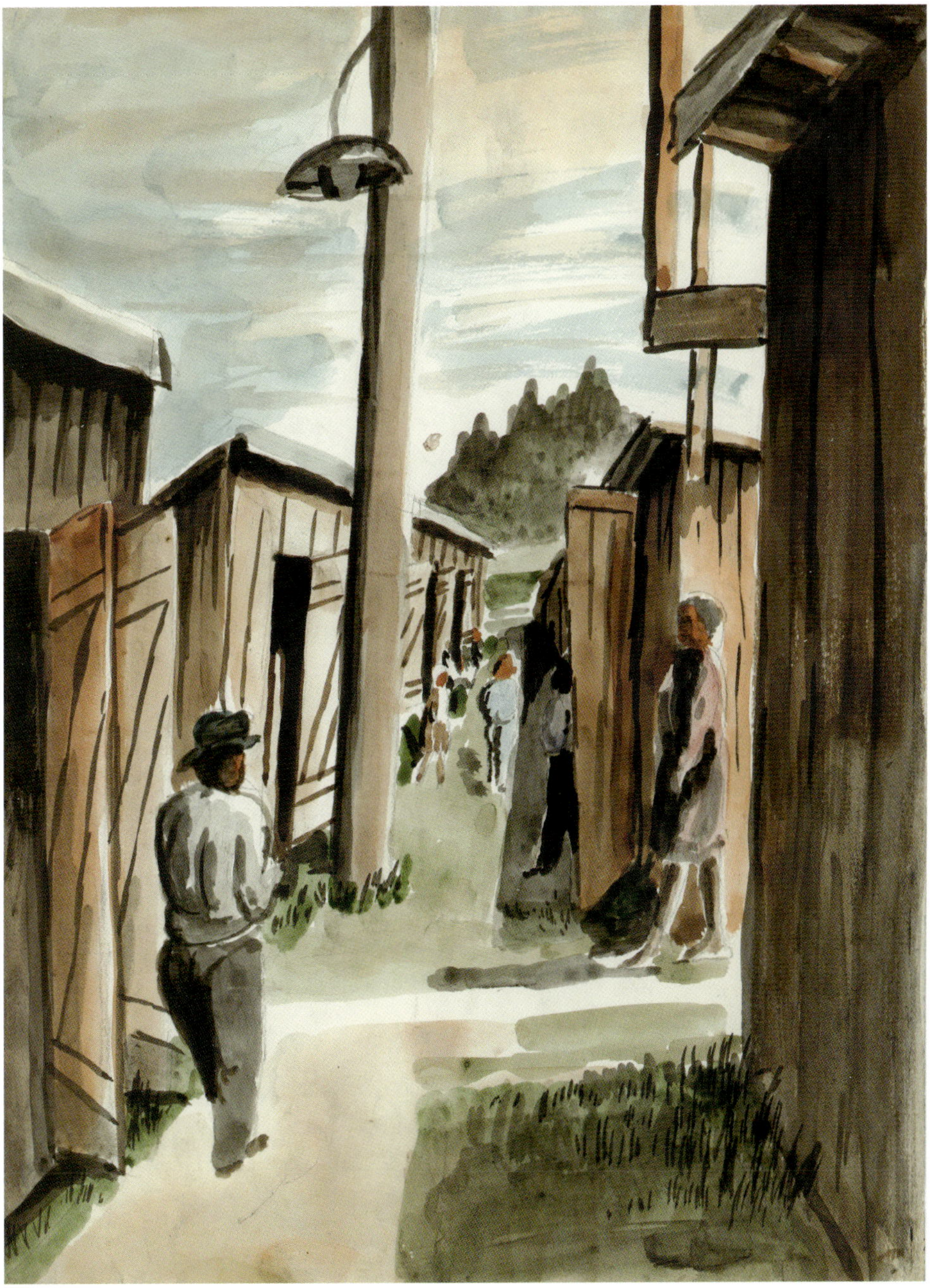

4.4 Puyallup, man standing by barracks. Watercolor on paper, 14 × 10 in.

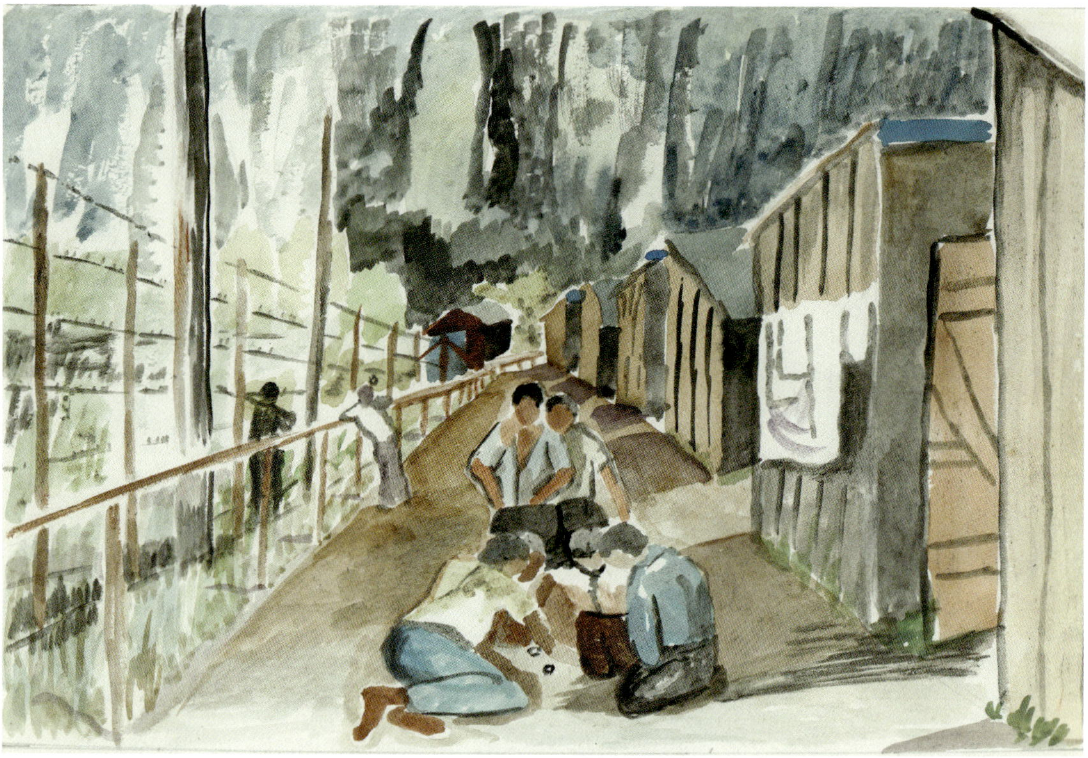

4.5 Puyallup, boys playing marbles. Watercolor on paper, 6¾ × 9¾ in.

Fujii's effort to cope with confinement. Nearly a third of the watercolors and drawings of Puyallup focus on the fence, guard towers, and sentry. When figures appear in these scenes, they are constricted by narrow passageways between barracks or between the barracks and the fence (figs. 4.4, 4.5). The rain that fell interminably in late spring seems to have not only brought misery but also held artistic appeal for him. In a pair of watercolors, he capitalizes upon the patterns of laundry hung out to dry as they reflect in the puddles underfoot (fig. 4.6).

The posting of orders from General DeWitt on the Puyallup fence must have carried particular weight for Fujii, for it is the subject of three nearly identical watercolors as well as a diary drawing (fig. 4.7, diary 17). Of two small versions, the more precisely rendered one is signed, the only watercolor to bear a signature; the large version adds a cow, a pastoral contrast to military authority.[17] His portrayal of DeWitt's orders compares tellingly to a photograph of government signage by Dorothea Lange, who was among the photographers commissioned by the WRA to document the removal and confinement of Japanese Americans. In Lange's photograph, a notice of visiting conditions hangs at the main gate of

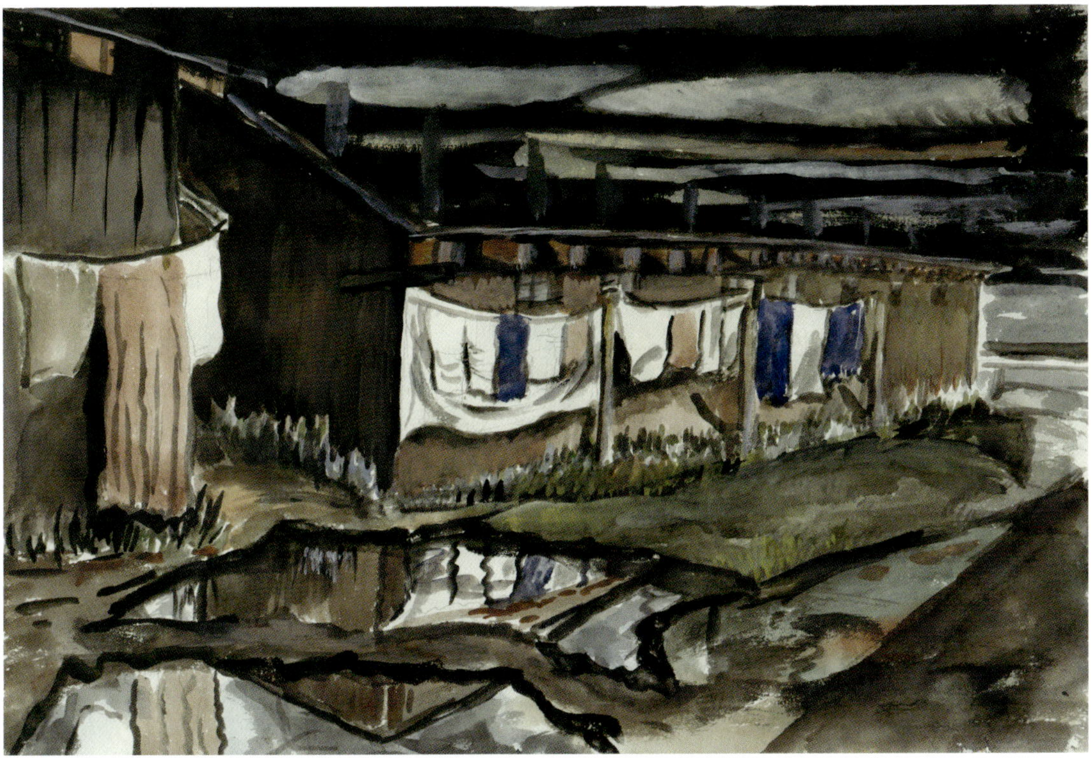

4.6 Puyallup, laundry after rain. Watercolor on paper, 10½ × 14½ in.

Tanforan, where, she writes in her caption, "the gate is guarded and controlled by U.S. soldiers." Beyond, the administration building of the former racetrack looms through the chain-link fence (fig. 4.8).[18] The sign is directed outward to those who come and go voluntarily, unlike those whom they would visit, such as the man who walks behind the sign. Lange, positioned outside, emphasizes the thin line that divides the two. Fujii's sign instead faces inside and, written in Japanese and English, addresses the Issei and Nisei generations. Mounted on a fence post, the sign fills the composition with the thrusts of its supporting structure; directly behind, the lateral lines of the rails and barbed wire of the taller outer fence reach to the top of the page. The view within the sign's authority contrasts strikingly with the freedom signaled by the fields and farmhouse seen through the fence. That the Puyallup Valley had been extensively farmed by Nikkei families implicitly heightens the loss and isolation of those inside. Even more than Lange's photograph, Fujii's images highlight the artificial but absolute line that power can draw.

After being transferred to Minidoka, Fujii traverses the camp grounds and explores the desert for his subjects. The many watercolors not paralleled in

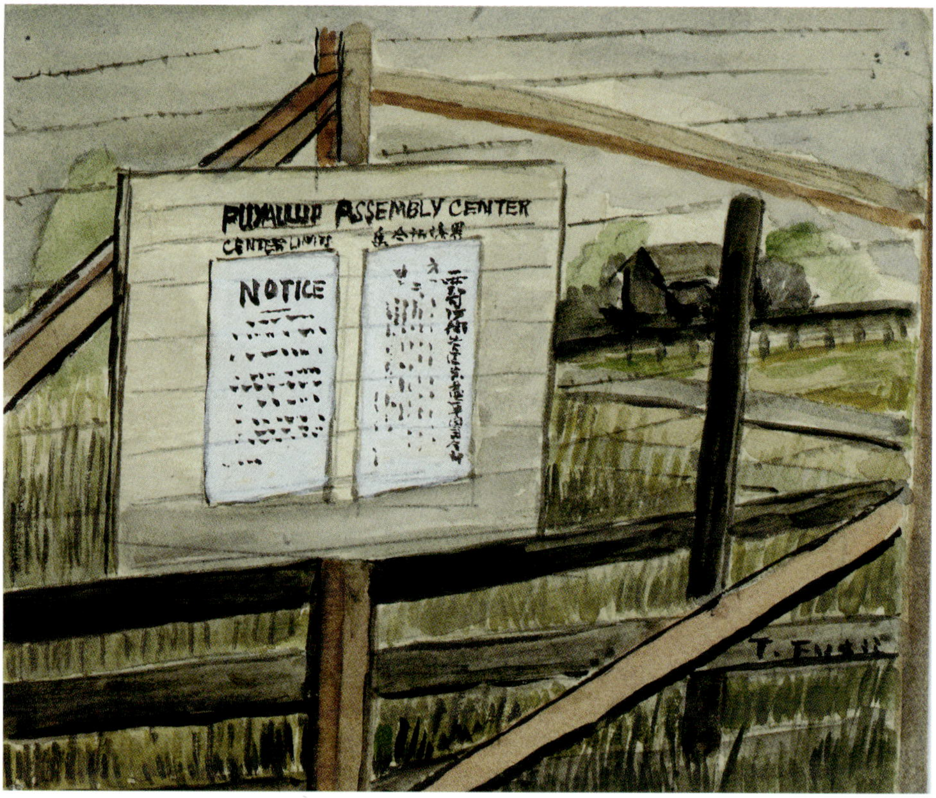

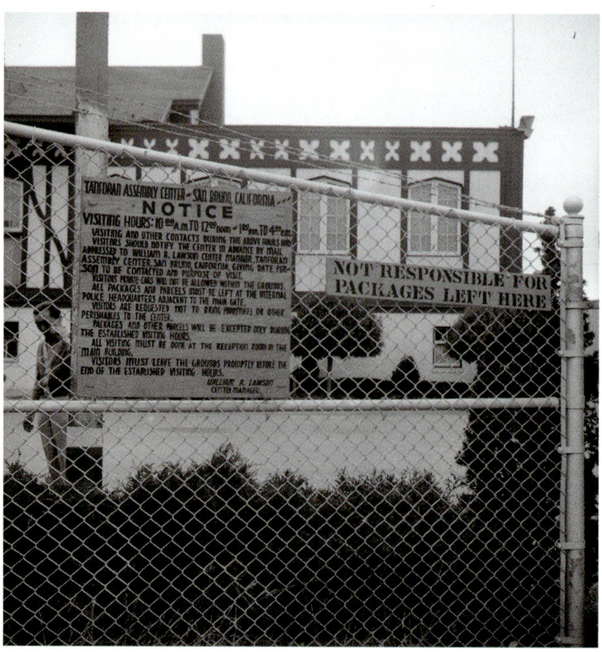

4.7 Puyallup, "This is the border of the camp. This is an announcement from Lieutenant General DeWitt. These are . . . the surroundings." Watercolor on paper, 4¾ × 5¾ in. (See diary 17.)

4.8 Dorothea Lange. "Front entrance gate, Jun. 16, 1942, Tanforan Assembly Center, California." Photograph. Denshō, courtesy of National Archives and Records Administration, Ctrl. #: NWDNS-210-G-C601, NARA ARC #: 537906, WRA; ddr-densho-151-56.

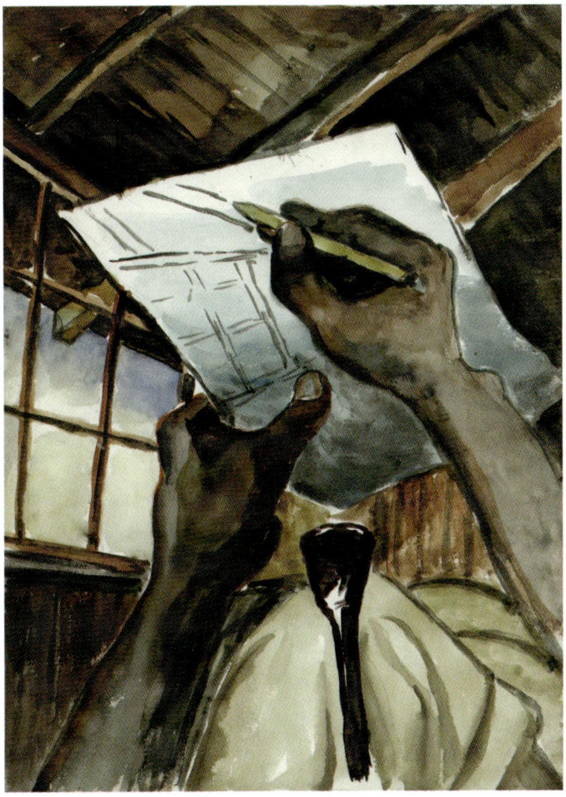

4.9 Minidoka, drawing by flashlight. Watercolor and paper, 14¾ × 10½ in.

diary drawings radiate from Fujii's barrack to the camp and landscape at large. In a startling perspective, Fujii looks down at his hands while he draws his room, as if making the viewer a participating witness to his situation. Another looks out his doorway to blocks of barracks in the distance (figs. 4.9, 4.10, 4.11). Many picture the facades, stairs, and spaces between barracks, likely in the immediate vicinity of Fujii's own barrack, as he traces his surroundings time and again. A number of paintings feature the hillside over which his barrack looked, which he calls dryly, a "rough spot in the road" (diary 70).[19] In both the diary and the watercolors, he gives evocative expression to the landscape transformed by weather and seasons: people bend in the whiteout of a sandstorm; rain puddles into reflecting pools, blocking passageways; and from his barrack window, snow makes a "silver world" of tar-paper barracks. In the watercolor version, the diary's snowy scene is framed by his barrack window, bringing an intimacy to the view and strengthening the composition with the lines of the window frame that lead from inside to outside (fig. 4.12, diary 87).

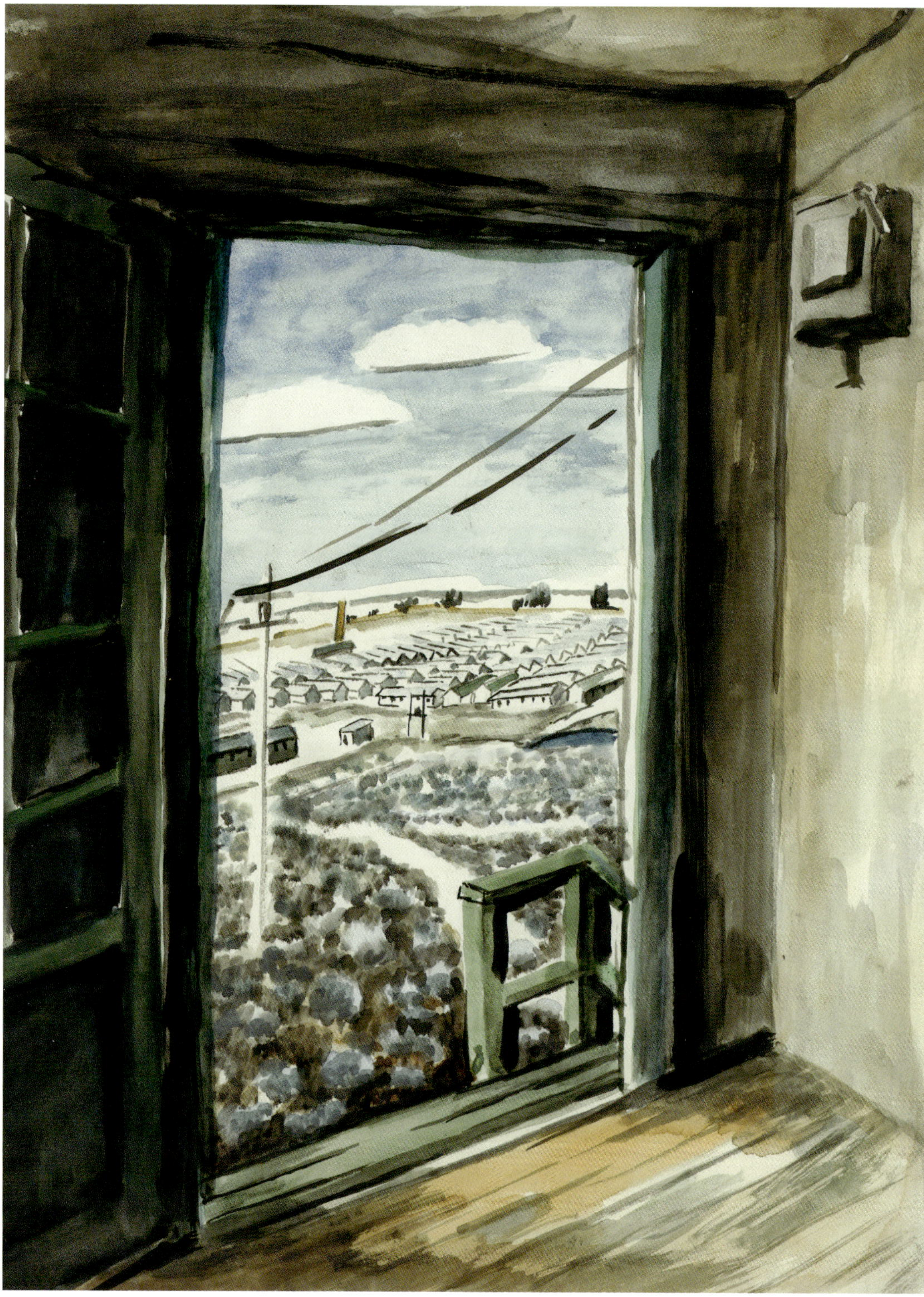

4.10 Minidoka, view from barrack doorway. Watercolor on paper, 14 × 10 in.

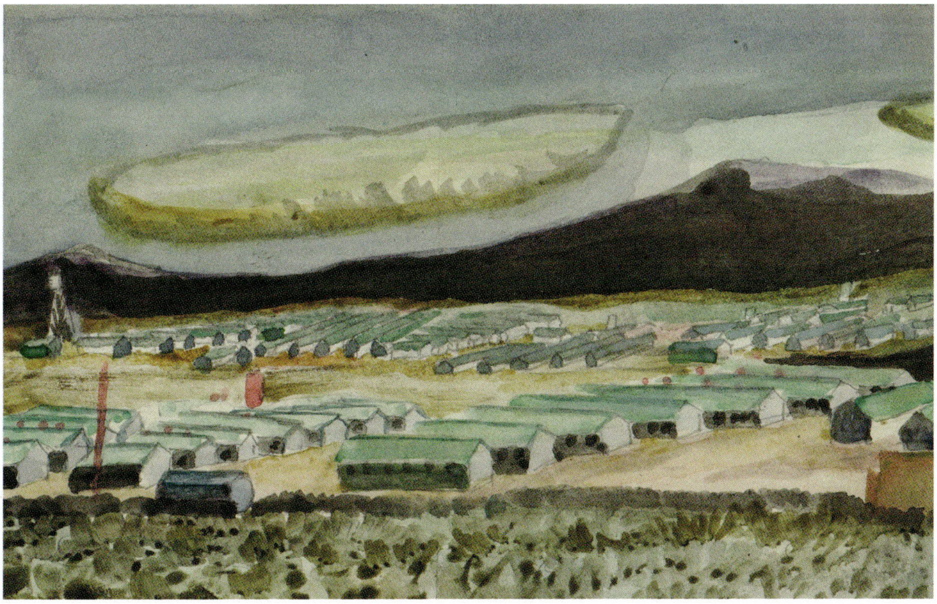

4.11 Minidoka, Blocks 19 and 21. Watercolor on paper, 4½ × 6½ in.

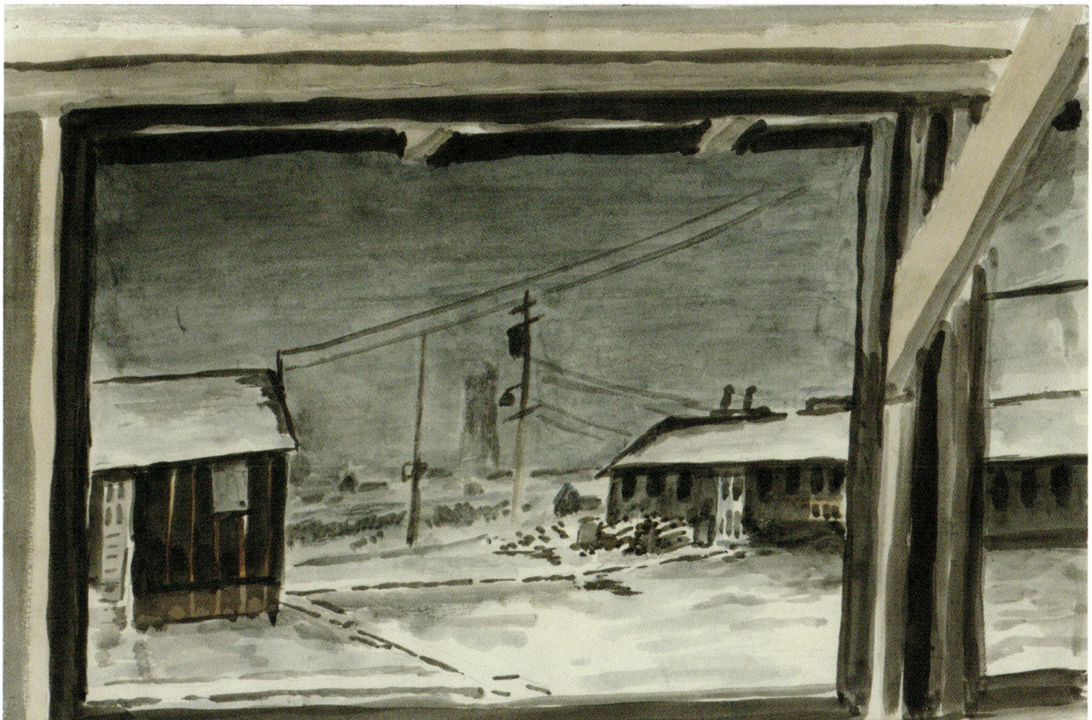

4.12 Minidoka, "This is the silver world I saw. It is still [snowing]." Watercolor on paper, 10 × 14 in. (See diary 87.)

The attention to the built environment and its inherent geometry evident in Fujii's paintings of the 1930s is amplified in his wartime watercolors. The rectilinear blocks of pictorial construction recall his city paintings of the 1930s, while the strokes of watercolor against white paper are alive with a sense of touch. The formal and expressive components of composition are sometimes pronounced, as shadows take independent life as geometric pattern. In a few paintings, buildings and shadows, foreground and distance, merge into abstract compositions of color and shape. Where he is drawn to formal experimentation, the most striking images employ geometry for expressive effect.

Here again the fence is exemplary as it appears in the diary and two related watercolors. In all three versions, a fence that Fujii locates at Block 24 fills the left half of the composition, its top section angled toward the barracks to reinforce security. Its shadow fills the lower register of the diary drawing, where the barracks, compressed within the confines, climb from low foreground to the sky (diary 74). A large watercolor repeats the scene with a naturalistic perspective that stretches to the Caribou Mountains on the horizon (see fig. 3.5). In another watercolor, however, the same fence frames a kaleidoscopic view of camp motifs—barracks and block buildings, water towers and guard towers, the stone entrance building at the main gate, agricultural tools, and children's swings (fig. 4.13). Rendered in muted red, blue, and brown, Minidoka is seen as a fractured, tumultuous montage, the embodiment of disorientation and instability. The fractured and tilted forms recall American paintings of the early twentieth century that convey the disorienting speed and scale wrought by modern technologies. Fujii employs their expressionist value but retains the legibility of individual motifs as he depicts the totalizing prison environment.

Two watercolors, which are the most brilliantly colored ones in his entire oeuvre, complicate the view he presents. These picture Victory over Japan Day celebrations in Seattle's Chinatown following Japan's surrender on August 15, 1945 (August 14 in the United States), with people lining the street as a parade passes by buildings adorned with flags and buntings. On the back is written "Seattle 1945 / King Street," leaving no doubt about the identification of the subject, which he could have known only in photographs. The scene in the second version becomes one of tumult and instability as the buildings on the left tip precariously over the crowd (fig. 4.14). Despite the disjunction, the rendering is precise; he names the Chinese benevolent association and the plumbing company that occupy the tilting buildings and places the flags of the Allies in clear view. Although his diary does not put words to events at the end of the war, the

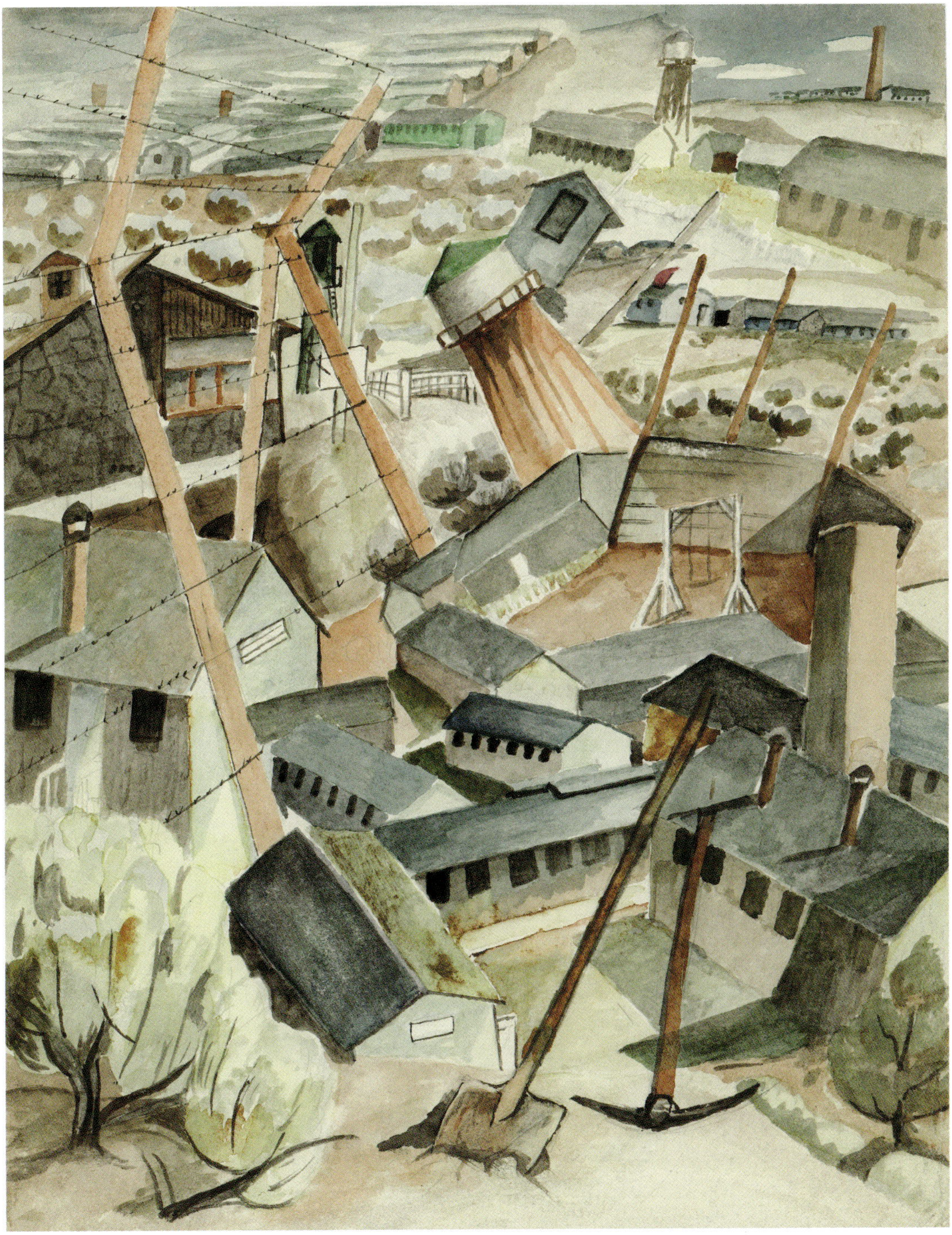

4.13 Minidoka, montage with barbed-wire fence. Watercolor on paper, 11½ × 9 in.

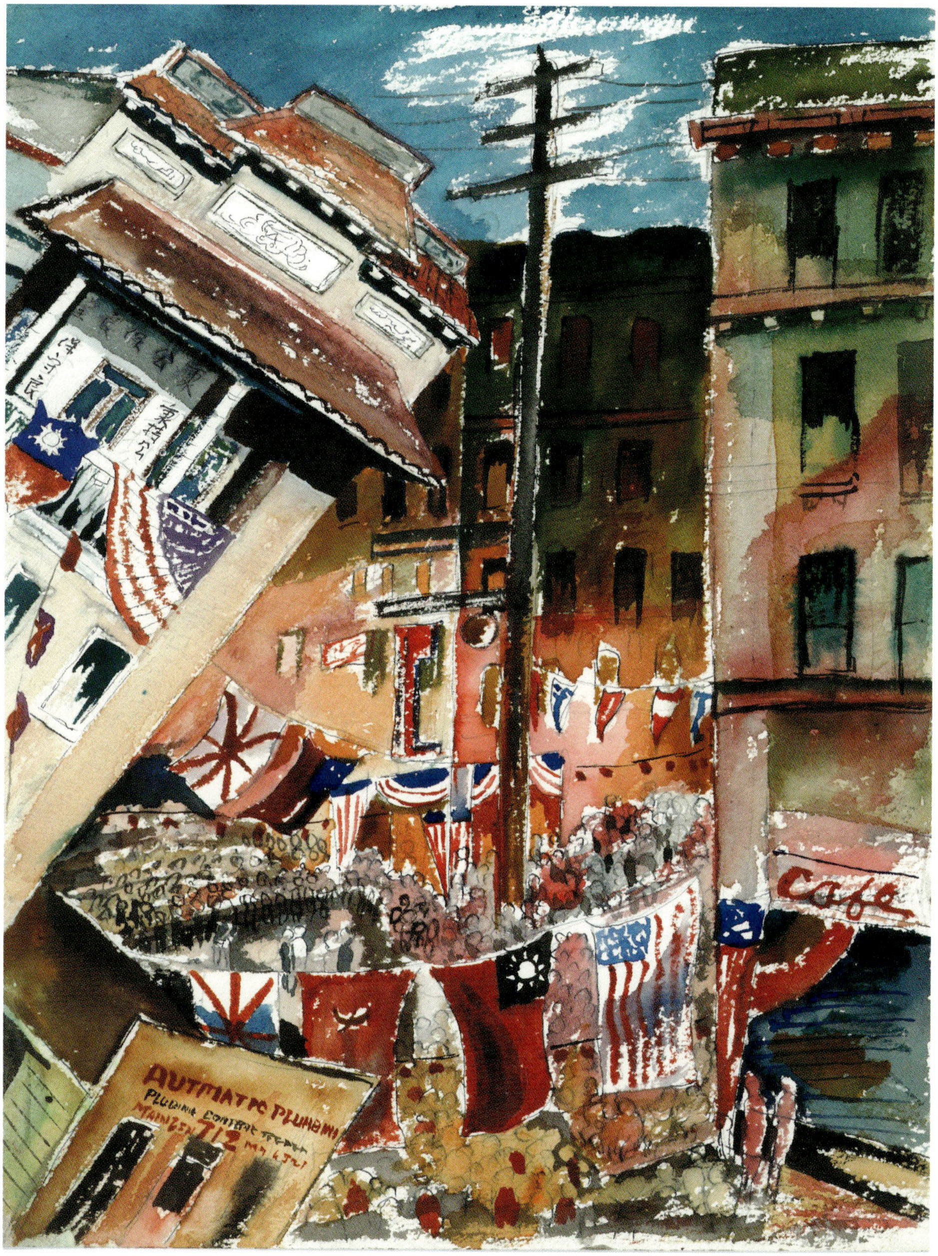

4.14 Victory over Japan Day celebration, Seattle, August 14, 1945. Watercolor and ink on paper, 12 × 9 in.; inscribed on reverse, "Seattle 1945 / King Street."

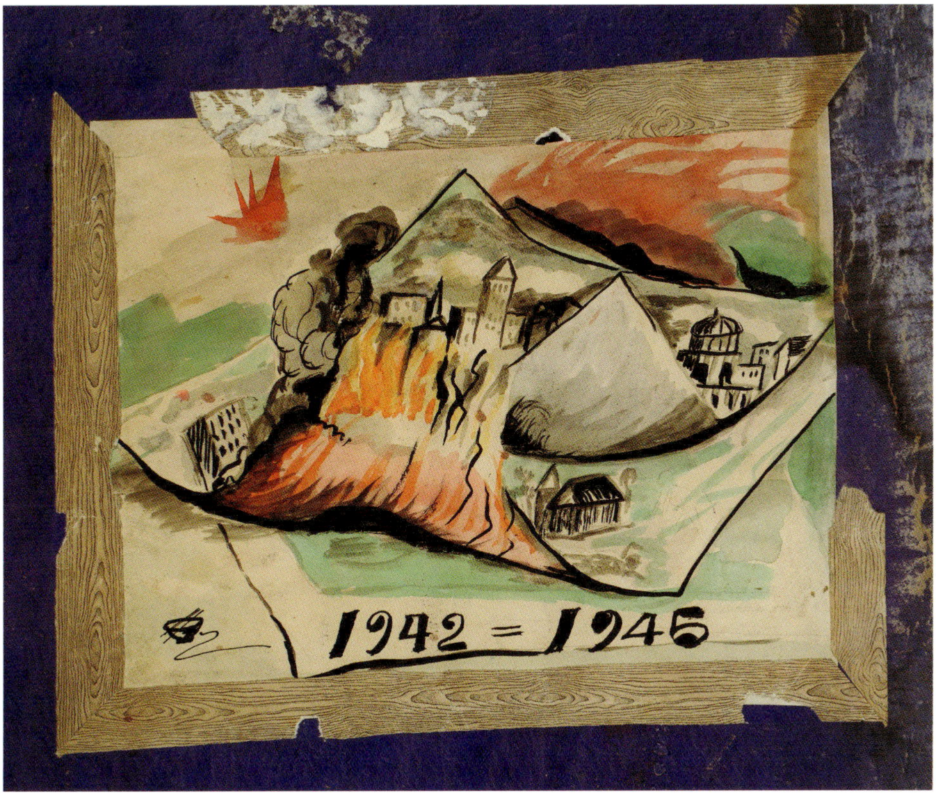

4.15 *1942–1945*, cover illustration (detail of portfolio). Ink and watercolor on paper with tape, mounted on paperboard, portfolio measures 22 × 17 in., image 7½ × 9½ in. Photo: Richard Nicol.

drawing of spinning Japanese and American flags, described in the preceding chapter, suggests a precedent to the King Street watercolors, and the final pages of the diary picture a continuing sense of despair as he and Fusano are swept up in the machinations of the camp's closure. Whatever Fujii's reasons for picturing the celebration, he shows that, for him, the end of the war did little to increase his sense of security.

Fujii eventually kept forty-two of the watercolors in a large portfolio, the same one that appears in a painting of his desk and chair. In a searing indictment of his experience, a drawing on the cover pictures buildings of downtown Seattle burning like paper in red and orange flames, just as his life there had gone up in flames (fig. 4.15). The portfolio is titled "1942–1945," and in the corner he has drawn a rice bowl and chopsticks as his signature. Guilty of nothing but his Japanese ethnicity, he names the sole identity by which he has been labeled and confined.

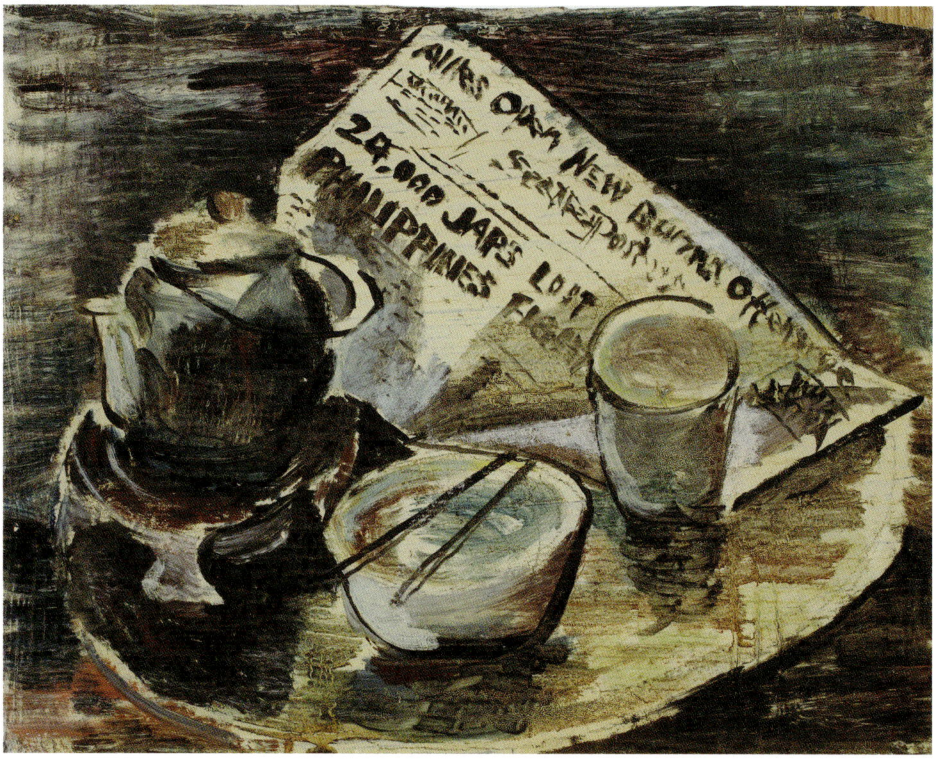

4.16 Still life with newspaper headline, "24,000 Japs Lost," ca. 1944. Oil on cardboard, 14¼ × 18 in. Photo: Richard Nicol.

TELLING HIS OWN STORY

Two paintings and a pair of sculptures, stylistically and materially distinct from the others, broaden the personal insight Fujii allows us. The paintings are oil on scrap cardboard that raise issues of loyalty. One, which is loosely brushed in earthy brown and blues, pictures a teapot and a bowl of rice with chopsticks—the same bowl that appears elsewhere as a signature—together with a *Seattle Post-Intelligencer* newspaper reporting a 1944 Japanese defeat in the Philippines (fig. 4.16). The other, more abstract and less easily identified with a specific event, is composed of a skeletal guard tower in cubist lines and a newspaper whose headline of a battle is only partly legible. The two paintings depicting war news alongside Japanese or camp motifs tell of the conflicting and shifting positions Issei experienced during the course of the war.

The dilemma for Fujii is illustrated by a comparison of the 1944 paintings to his still lifes of the 1930s, which are composed of everyday objects that might be found in any American household, such as a shopping basket, a water pitcher,

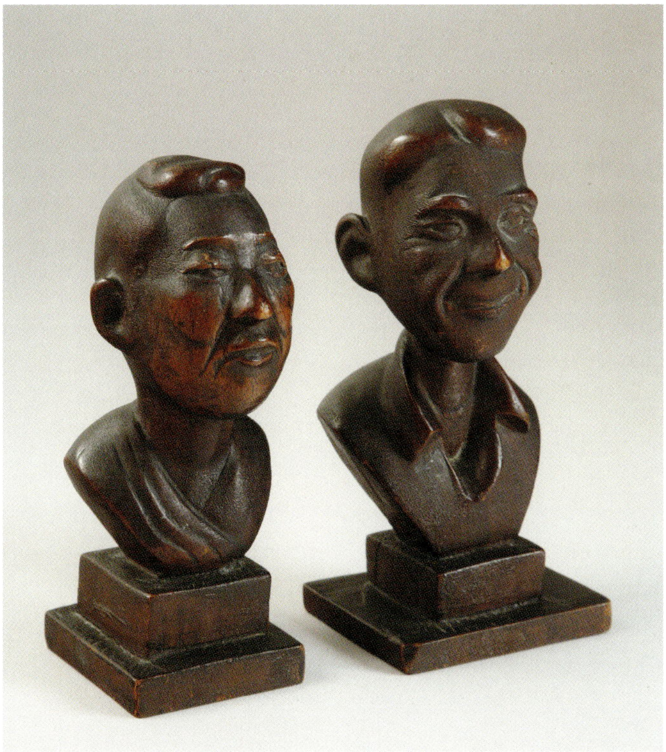

4.17 Fusano and Takuichi Fujii, ca. 1943–1945. Carved wood, the taller, 9 × 4 × 3¼ in. Photo: Richard Nicol.

and an alarm clock. Where once he could align his ambitions with the new country, he had lost nearly everything at the hands of its government and was confined to a segregated and isolated community under armed guard. That Fujii experienced yearning for the country of his youth is unquestionable. In a rare explicit expression of emotion, he writes toward the end of his diary (and the war) of library books sent from Japan: "When I hold them in my hands and look at these nostalgic books in my present situation of having been sent here, I feel like tears well up."[20] Despite such expression of loss, Fujii, like the majority of Issei, demonstrated no intention to return to Japan when facing decisions such as how to complete the loyalty questionnaire.[21] Unlike the domestic sociability associated with the 1930s paintings, these are images of mournful introspection. Incarcerated during the war because of his ethnicity, unable to gain citizenship in his adopted country, Fujii must have felt his position to be even more tenuous in the face of accumulating Japanese defeats. The paintings might be interpreted as acts of self-assertion in claiming his heritage, or as expressions of vulnerability in the political circumstances he depicts, although there is little further evidence to support a conclusion. Twice elsewhere the rice bowl appears as a signature in self-reflective images that tell of the artist's continual examination of what it meant to be a Japanese immigrant in the United States in wartime (see figs. 1.1, 4.15).

In an altogether different mode and mood, Fujii portrays himself in a unique double portrait that is among the few sculpted objects he made in camp. Busts of Fusano and Fujii stand side by side, carved of wood salvaged at Minidoka in dimensions that suggest they were once fence posts (fig. 4.17).[22] The individual features are carefully rendered. Fusano looks firmly ahead, her head tilted upward, while Fujii's face crinkles in a large smile in an image that transcends the circumstances of their incarceration. Years later, the darkly stained surface has become polished by accumulated touching. The pair calls to mind diary drawings in which Fusano accompanies him as he sketches, the two of them venturing into the desert and, finally, awaiting Minidoka's closing. The attention to expression and use of a sculptural medium suggest the commemoration of a special occasion, although there is no confirming evidence; but in their robust presentation, the sculptures radiate the sustaining strength of their subjects' relationship. They celebrate a private life in circumstances where there was little privacy. They embody resilience despite loss and deprivation. A contrast to the somber tone of the diary and paintings, they signal with comparable force Fujii's refusal to succumb to the oppressive conditions of incarceration.

Artistic production during wartime incarceration in itself is an act of resistance. It is an active rather than passive response to surveillance and control, an insistence upon self-representation at a time of enforced conformity.[23] Cultural activist and critic bell hooks writes, "As subjects, people have the right to define their own reality, establish their own identities, name their history. As objects, one's reality is defined by others, one's identity created by others. . . . Oppressed people resist by identifying themselves as subjects, by defining their reality, shaping their new identity, naming their history, telling their story."[24] Fujii locates himself, specifies his viewpoint, names his experience, and frames his visual representation as he tells his story. He insists upon the validity of his perspective however much it conflicts with the official portrayal of community and protection. Moving about the camps with the intimate viewpoint accessible to neither outsiders nor administrators and guards, he portrays the reality of being incarcerated. In addition to the overt signs of military confinement and living conditions, the space between the diary's image and text reveals the unspoken expression of emotion and critique—what is said not by either image or text alone but in relationship to one another—allowing some insight into Fujii's perspective as an Issei inmate. His perseverance alone in continuing the diary through the discouraging months of Minidoka's closing, the surrender of

Japan, and his and Fusano's departure is eloquent testimony to his determination to bear witness and tell his own story. While loss and confinement fill the pages of his diary, and his daily routine was under the government's control, in his extensive body of wartime work Fujii claims a place for himself as an autonomous and creative subject.

EXHIBITING MEMORIES

Sometime after the war ended and Fujii's family was reunited in Chicago, the Olivet Institute appears to have hosted an exhibition of his paintings.[25] The block-long community center, located in the Near North Side neighborhood that had become home to Nikkei resettlers, housed a small branch of the Chicago Public Library, where Fujii's work hung. No record of the exhibition remains, and one can only conjecture that this was the occasion of his matting and labeling forty-two watercolors of Puyallup and Minidoka that filled a large portfolio, the same portfolio he pictured in the representation of his work space. Olivet's program director, Abe Hagiwara, was a highly regarded recreation leader and was well positioned to encourage such a project. He had moved from Minidoka to the Midwest himself, undoubtedly knew Fujii's contribution to *Minidoka Interlude*, and surely took an interest in his war-related work.[26] He would have appreciated also that Fujii's work offered a rare reflection on the war for the Nikkei community.

Although a few Issei and Nisei were willing to address their experiences of incarceration, most did not speak of the painful years as they tried to put the past behind them.[27] Behind the reluctance, a sense of shame had begun to spread even as people were herded into assembly centers, an internalizing of the racist blame that had put them there. It would be some of the younger Nisei and the Sansei generation, amid the civil rights movement and self-assertions of ethnic identity, who urged their parents and grandparents to tell stories and began to construct a critical history. Fujii's decision to exhibit the paintings, and his effort to prepare the work, whether or not he repainted some images for the occasion, represents a willingness to display his experience to the public. For Chicago's Nikkei, having resettled from various government camps, the exhibition would have represented a potent act of remembrance.

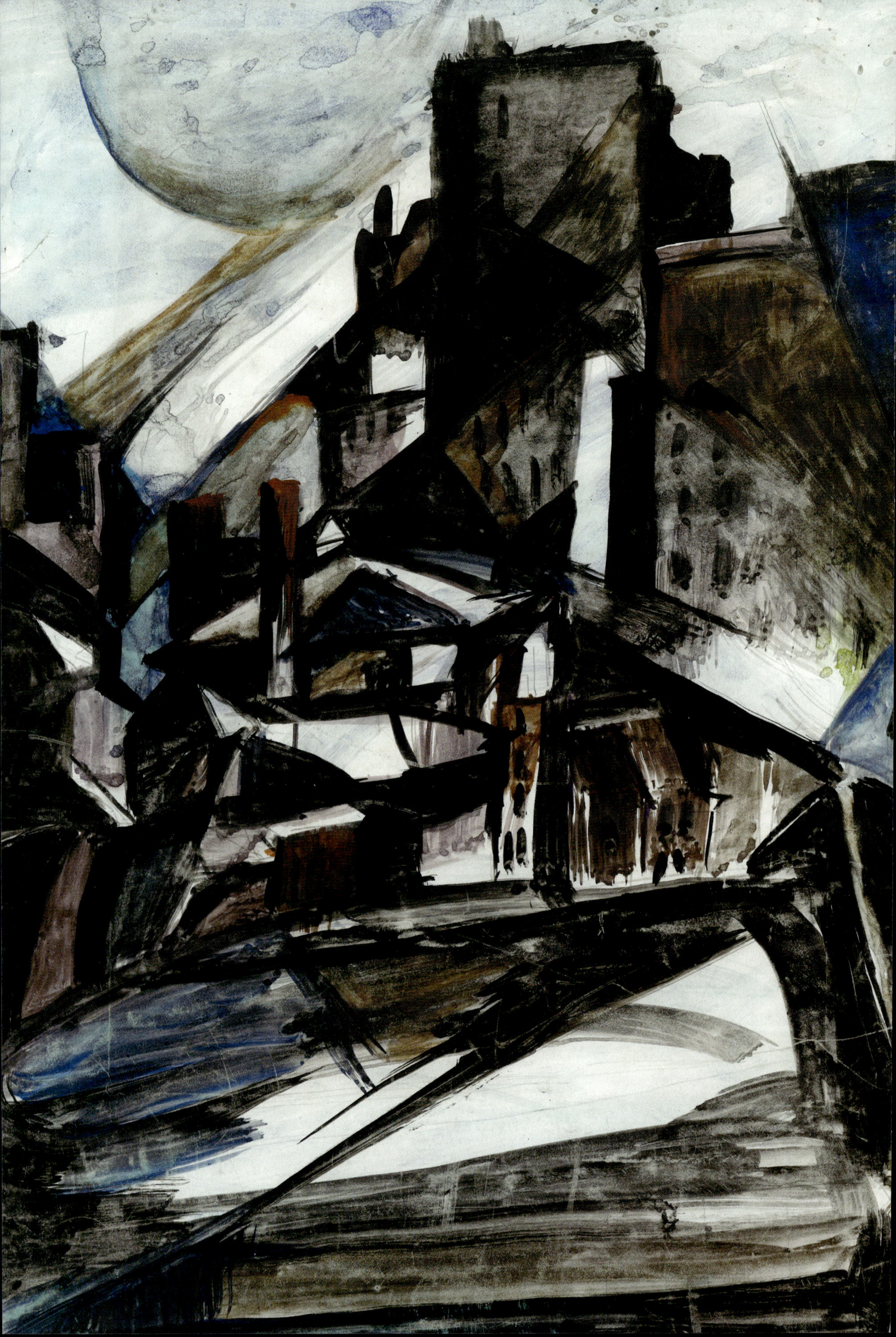

5 Abstract Expressions

FUJII found rhythms in the shapes of shadows, the repetition of rooftops, and the curve of the land at Puyallup and Minidoka. In many of the watercolors, formal considerations drive the composition as much as content, and in a few, volume and shadow become pure design. For the remainder of his life, in the much smaller body of work that he produced after leaving Minidoka, Fujii experimented with various forms of abstraction. These culminate in gestural nonobjective paintings that are at once surprisingly fresh work and a distillation of his lifetime endeavors.

Landscape continued to hold his attention as his interest in abstraction developed. His short time in Ogden is represented by six watercolors of urban landscapes. While most are naturalistic, one pictures downtown buildings as an interlocking puzzle of planes defined by slashes of black (fig. 5.1). Painted predominantly in blue, brown, and black, the Ogden scenes appear coolly distanced, as if Fujii were trying to take stock of a new home but hadn't embraced it.

Paintings and drawings from Chicago are more personal. He painted his backyard there as he watched the seasons change from the kitchen window, using the expressive possibilities of translucent and saturated watercolor to match the lushness or sparseness of seasons (fig. 5.2, 5.3). In darkly hatched ink drawings he portrays himself and Fusano in middle age: introspective self-portraits in his studio (fig. 5.4) and a nude portrait of Fusano, a rare intimate representation of an Issei woman. The watercolors and drawings convey a firm, confident hand, the result of years' practice. Other paintings in watercolor and oil venture into a wide-ranging exploration of abstraction.

5.1 Opposite: Ogden buildings, ca. 1946–1947. Watercolor on paper, 11 × 8 in. Photo: Richard Nicol.

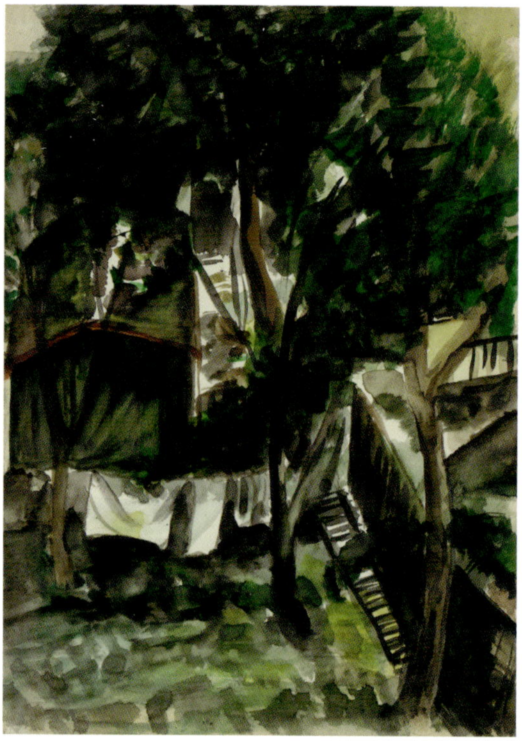

5.2 Chicago backyard in summer, ca. 1950s. Watercolor on paper, 14 × 10 in.

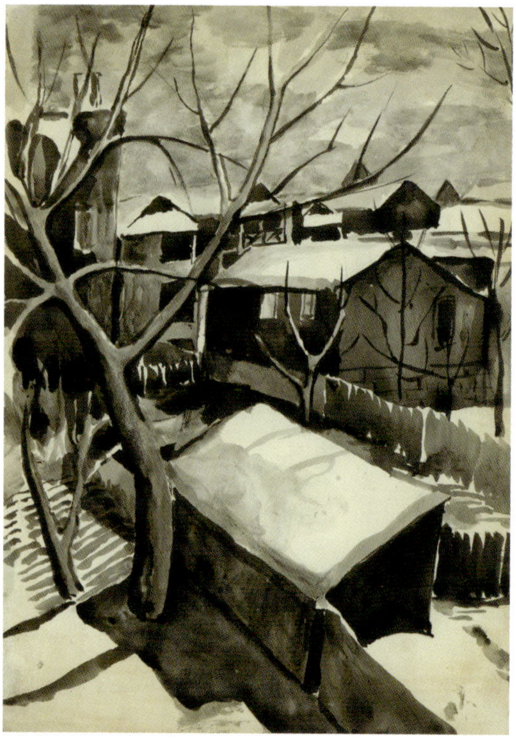

5.3 Chicago backyard in winter, ca. 1950s. Ink on paper, 14 × 10 in.

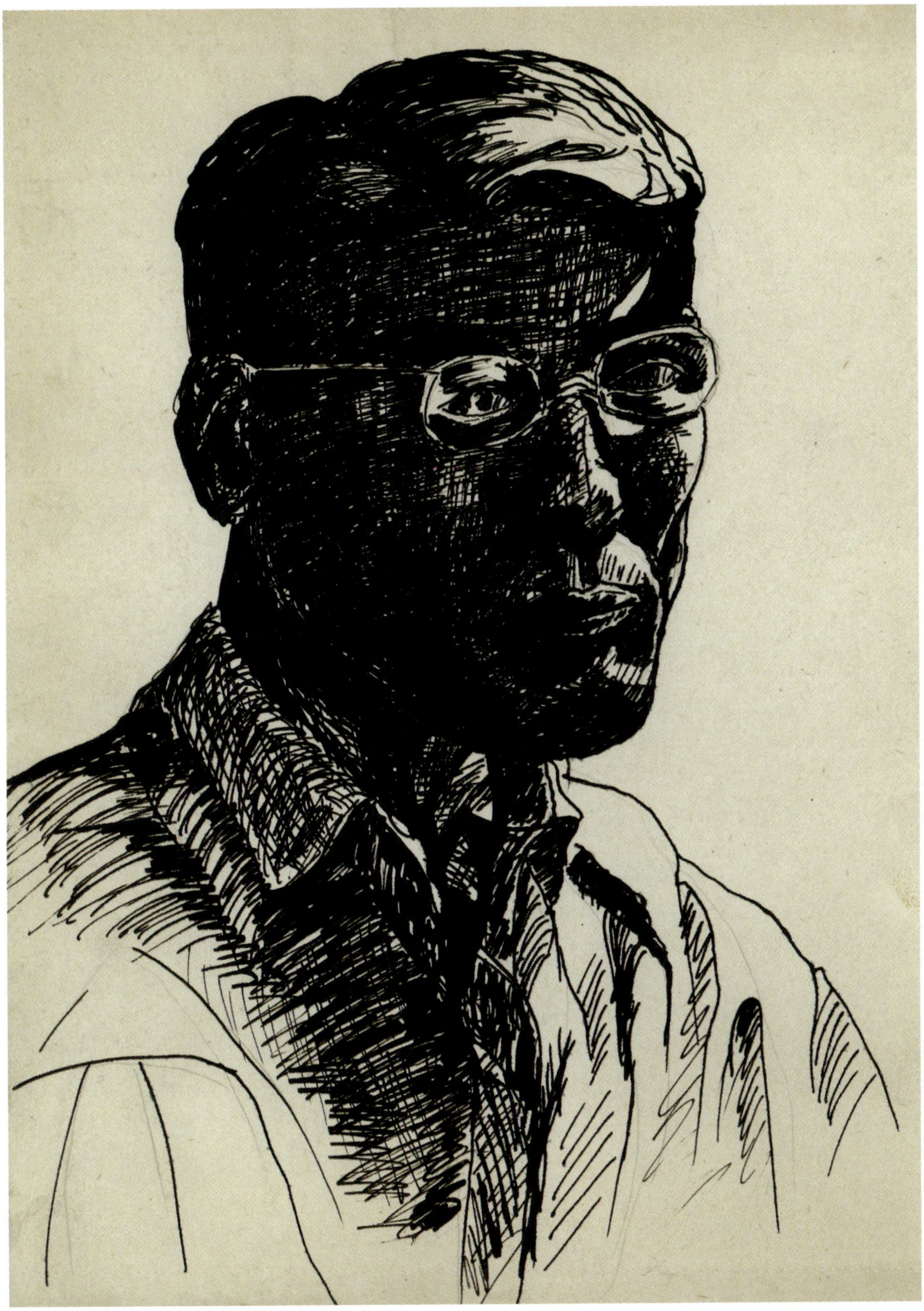

5.4 Self-portrait, ca. 1950s. Ink on paper, 12 × 8½ in.

LOOKING AT THE AVANT-GARDE

The date of the Minidoka montage cannot be determined with certainty, nor can that of a dozen colorful abstractions that show influences such as Kandinsky, Miró, Picasso, and Léger. The materials vary, as the dates surely do, likely ranging in the 1940s and 1950s. Some may have been produced during the war, complements or antidotes to the many images of incarceration. Most are watercolor on paper, one uses a tablet backing, and another is oil on corrugated cardboard like that of two war-related still lifes. In the absence of personal papers to provide clues to chronology and intent, the paintings are mute testimony to Fujii's creative search.

An important source of ideas and encouragement was Fujii's younger Seattle friend, George Tsutakawa (1910–1997). In the 1930s and early 1940s both men had enjoyed painting trips to the dry open country of central Washington. After the declaration of war, Tsutakawa, a Nisei, was inducted into the army, while Fujii began life under military surveillance and members of Tsutakawa's family were sent to Minidoka, Tule Lake in California, and Lordsburg, New Mexico. Tsutakawa, fluent in Japanese, was eventually assigned to the Military Intelligence Service at Fort Snelling, Minnesota. During the war years Tsutakawa began reading philosophy in a search for the deeper meanings of art. He wrote an artist friend:

> Lately I have been studying abstraction and nonobjective painting, and have almost reached the point where I believe [this] . . . form of art is the answer to the science and philosophy of art. The art of purely symbolic forms, nonobjective colors, lines and space (perfect harmony and balance) and abstract thought can only be equal to the best of music (absolute music), purest religion and the most profound philosophy. I have made several attempts at nonobjective in watercolor and tempera and find them very interesting. . . . I am convinced that there is nothing so satisfying as well-constructed abstraction, because it can express the ultimate truth and essence of time, space and matter.[1]

Tsutakawa took several leaves in 1943 and 1944 to see relatives at Minidoka and also visited Fujii there.[2] Once stationed in Minnesota, he traveled regularly to Chicago, where he frequented the Art Institute; and he made his first trip to New York, where he was deeply impressed by the work of Kandinsky and Miró then on view.[3] The experience rekindled his optimism about nonobjective painting. "I am convinced," he wrote, "that there lies an endless future for artists, scientists, writers and thinkers—mostly artists in this case."[4]

His friendship with Fujii is evident in a book and a painting of his own that he gave to the older artist, which are among the few items in Fujii's extant personal papers. The book, inscribed to Fujii in 1944, was Rosamund Frost's *Contemporary Art: The March of Art from Cézanne until Now* and is replete with illustrations.[5] The painting is an assemblage of organic and geometric shapes redolent of Kandinsky's work of the 1920s, dated in 1943 as Tsutakawa began his study of nonobjective art. It represents a critical turn in his thinking and his regard for Fujii in making the gift. Although no letter or diary entry tells of their conversation, Fujii's subsequent paintings pay homage to Tsutakawa's example.[6]

These paintings, mostly watercolors, include colorful assemblages of rectangles, triangles, arcs, and diagonals that suggest landscape elements. Others recall Kandinsky's early abstractions with floating fields of color and dynamic, linear notations of narrative or representational elements (fig. 5.5). In cubist-related still lifes, household objects merge with their surroundings in precisely rendered interlocking planes. Elsewhere, curving lines surround an eye, the

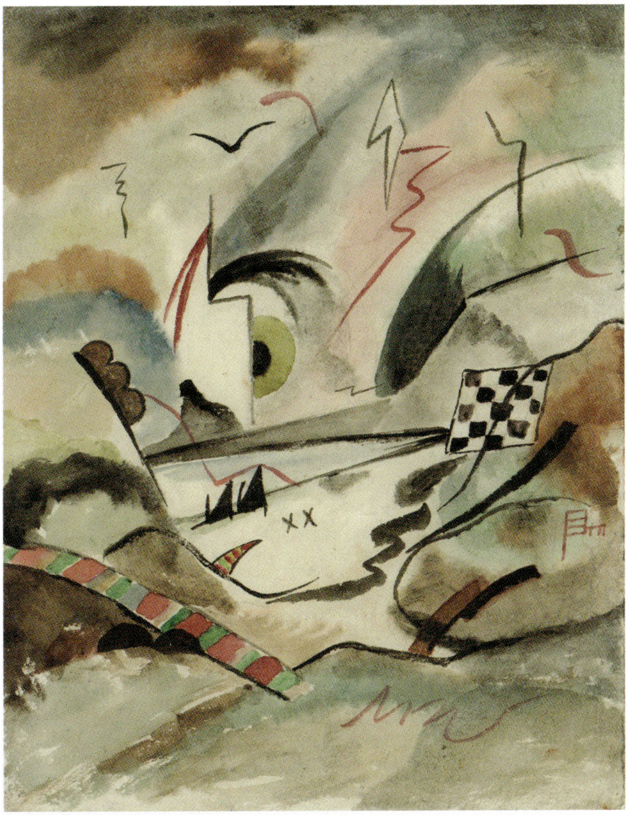

5.5 Abstraction with checkerboard, ca. 1940s–1950s. Watercolor on paper, 11 × 9 in.

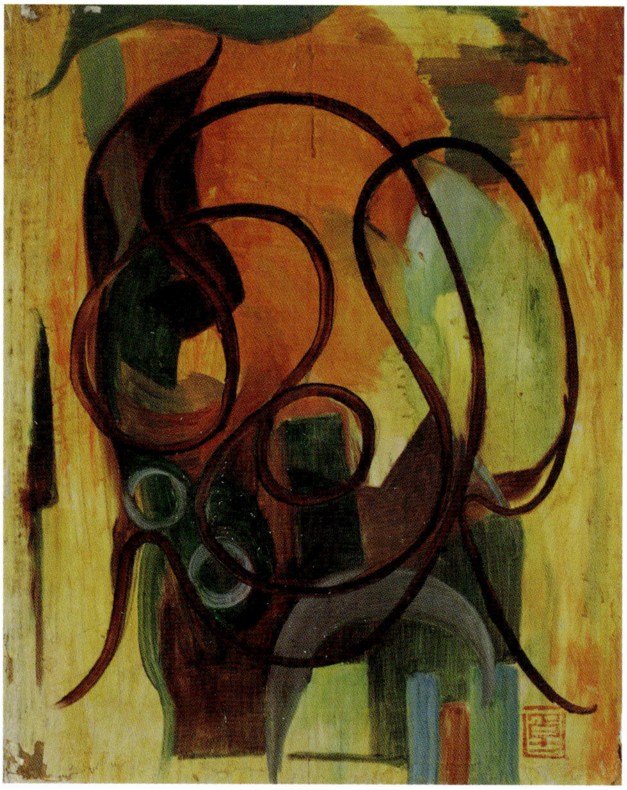

5.6 Biomorphic abstraction, ca. 1940s–1950s. Oil on corrugated cardboard, 22 × 17 in. Signed with kanji-style seal. Photo: Richard Nicol.

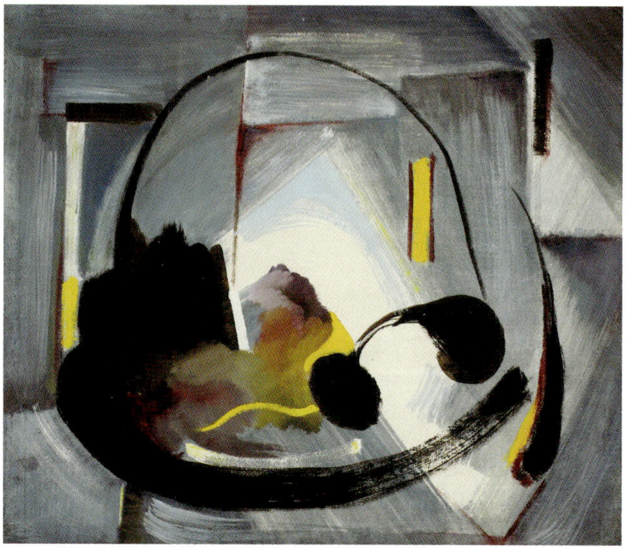

5.7 Abstraction, ca. 1950s. Oil(?) on cardboard, 21 × 24 in. Photo: Richard Nicol.

nipple of a breast, and perhaps a knee to reveal a figure; in an oil painting on cardboard, a continuing sinuous line traces a voluptuous figure that suggests the influence of Picasso's surrealist work (fig. 5.6). Several larger paintings vary from geometric to fluidly curvaceous abstract compositions and were surely produced in the more stable circumstances of Chicago. In one, on a ground of broadly brushed planes of blue gray, the fluid gestural strokes of black look forward to the abstractions of his final years (fig. 5.7).

Once Fujii was settled in Chicago, he could have found outstanding examples of modernist painting at the Art Institute of Chicago. He had exhibited there in 1937 and, by family accounts, must have visited in later years. Although the museum and its patrons had been known for decades for entrenched conservatism, new leadership and curatorial vision under Daniel Catton Rich and Katharine Kuh brought pioneering exhibitions and acquisitions to the Art Institute in the 1940s and 1950s.[7] Even in earlier years, a few adventurous collectors had bequeathed superb paintings by Cézanne, Van Gogh, and Kandinsky, the last in the artist's dynamic early style that Fujii's watercolors emulate. Besides Kandinsky, one finds tantalizing hints in Fujii's work of the precise machine shapes of Léger's *The Red Table*, the biomorphic figures of Miró's *Personages with Star*, and Van Gogh's *The Bedroom*, in which a chair and a bed assume the artist's persona—all part of the museum collection by 1952.[8] The American modernist John Marin was well represented in a large gift from the Alfred Stieglitz estate; his fractured, vividly colored watercolors portray the city with the destabilizing energy found in Fujii's rendition of V-J Day celebrations. In the early 1950s the work of a new generation of artists, the abstract expressionists, began to enter the collection. Fujii, whose study of brushwork dated to his youth, surely responded to the free but disciplined gestural mark in the Art Institute's paintings by Jackson Pollock and Willem de Kooning.

ABSTRACT EXPRESSIONIST GESTURES

Like many artists, Fujii painted alternately in realism and abstraction, but it was abstraction in which he found his final expressive means. In bold strokes of black enamel on white-painted ground, he produced a series of dynamic compositions in gestural abstraction (figs. 5.8, 5.10). Nine of these paintings remain. Measuring two by three feet horizontally or vertically in orientation, they project a monumentality that belies their physical dimensions.

By the time Fujii produced these paintings, in the 1960s, abstract expressionism was a familiar artistic language. It had emerged in postwar New York as a radical stylistic breakthrough with universalist ideals, prompting critic

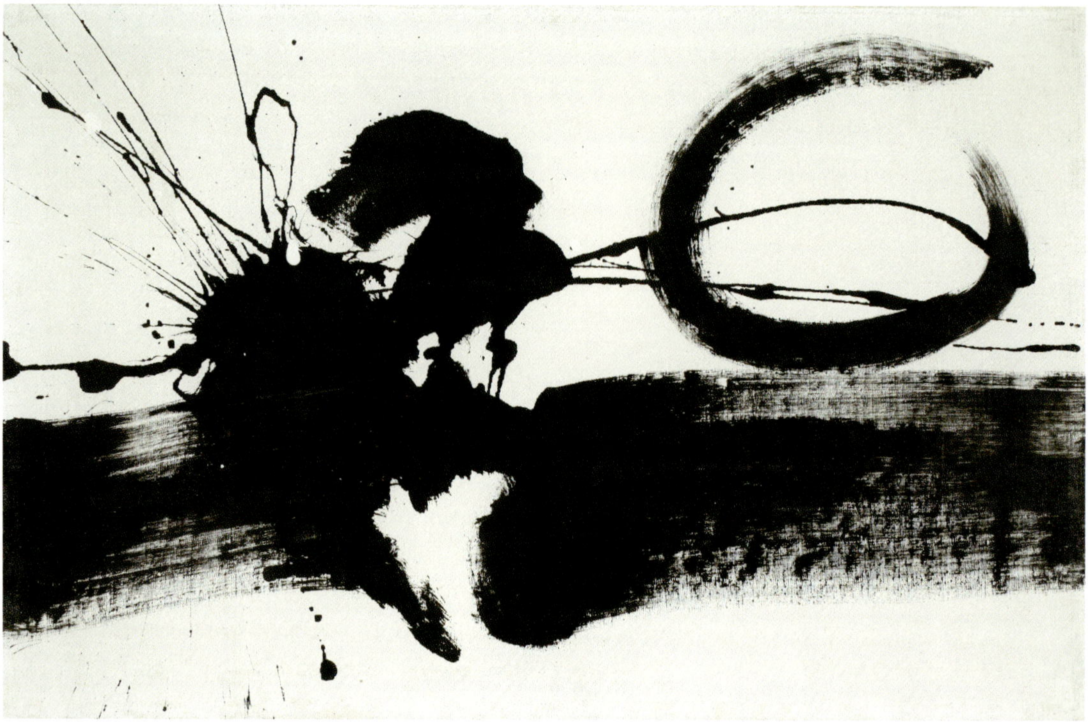

5.8 Abstraction, early 1960s. Enamel on canvas, 24 × 36 in. Photo: Richard Nicol.

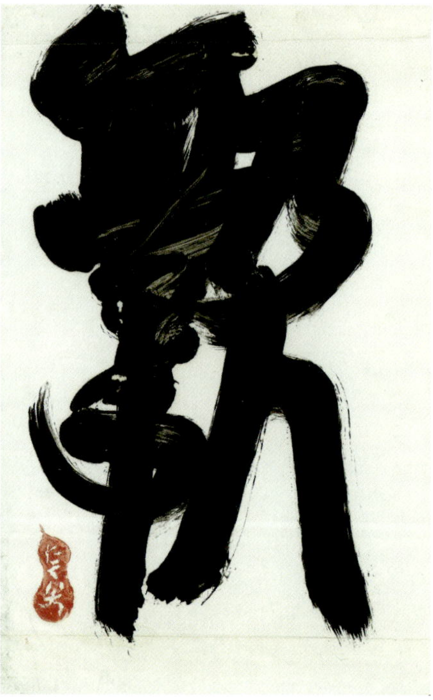

5.9 Calligraphy. Ink on paper, 14¼ × 8¾ in. Signed with hiragana-style seal.

Clement Greenberg to declare that New York had supplanted Paris as the cultural capital of the West.[9] The spontaneous gesture, emotive color, and expansive scale of abstract expressionism were said to signal the United States' artistic triumph, paralleling its economic and political dominance. As art departments multiplied with the postwar expansion of colleges and universities, what had originated as avant-garde innovation spread nationwide. At the Art Institute of Chicago's survey exhibition of American art in 1957, curator Frederick Sweet noted that abstract expressionism was the dominant style of younger and mid-career painters.[10]

In philosophical premise and the value placed in spontaneity, abstract expressionism was often understood as having affinities to Asian art. Artists during and after the war aspired to universal imagery that transcends national and cultural boundaries and sought to express the essential unity of humankind and nature, a matter of ancient concern in Asian cultures. The postwar American occupation of Japan unleashed a burgeoning interest in its aesthetics and cultural practices, especially Zen Buddhism. In the Northwest, artists Mark Tobey, Morris Graves, and Kenneth Callahan pursued insights arising from their prewar visits to Asia. In New York, D. T. Suzuki gave widely attended lectures on Zen at Columbia University. Japanese artist and theorist Saburō Hasegawa demonstrated calligraphy during an extended visit to the city, speaking frequently to audiences about the relationship of Japanese aesthetic principles and Western modernism, which he believed calligraphy epitomized. Well before his visit, Hasegawa had pointed to Franz Kline's black-and-white abstractions as exemplary of the relationship he advocated and likened Pollock's skeins of paint to free-form cursive calligraphy.[11] Although such critics as Greenberg denied Asian influence in asserting the American origins of the new painting, the calligraphic gesture became a signature mark of abstract expressionism.[12]

Western artists who delved beneath style and technique were challenged to grasp the generating premise of Asian calligraphy and its corollary, painting. From an Asian perspective, both partake in the timeless flow of nature and of life and consciousness. Art is not merely a concept or the product of philosophical theory, but rather, it embodies "the spiritual, vital forces that connect all things."[13] Tsutakawa explained, in remarking on Western categories of painting genres and in particular still life, or *nature morte* in French: "This is just the opposite from the oriental concept. There's no such word [as] 'dead nature' in the orient. Everything's alive; even a piece of rock has a life."[14] In the 1930s, Fujii had stated his aim in painting in similar terms: "It is the truth in Nature I am after, not the superficial aspects of Nature or man, but the basic truths of the structure of life."[15]

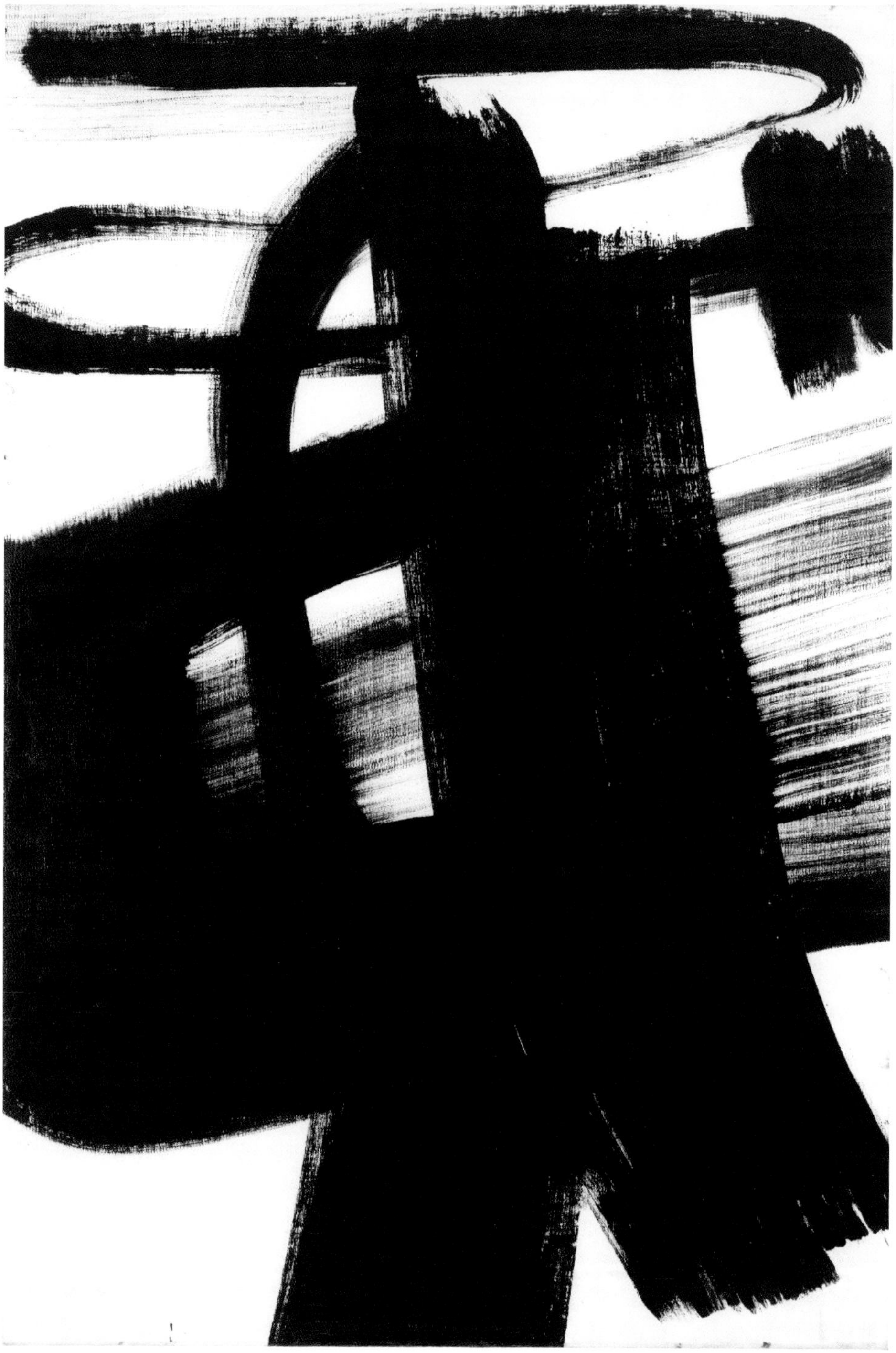

5.10 Abstraction, early 1960s. Enamel on canvas, 36 × 24 in. Photo: Richard Nicol.

At the Art Institute of Chicago in the early 1950s, Fujii could have seen major abstract expressionist paintings by de Kooning, Pollock, Kline, Tobey, and Robert Motherwell.[16] Small sumi sketches by Fujii also suggest his awareness of Hasegawa's work and harken back to his own youthful training in brushwork. A larger example of calligraphy evokes the free-form style of fifteenth-century Zen priest Sesshū (fig. 5.9). In Seattle, Mark Tobey expressed admiration for the fluid calligraphy of his friends Tsutakawa and Paul Horiuchi, which came from a lifetime of practice, and joined them at the Tsutakawa home in 1957 for sessions of sumi painting.[17] By then Fujii was thought by his former colleagues to have returned to Japan. Horiuchi would soon begin his innovative abstractions in torn-paper collage, Tsutakawa would become a renowned sculptor of fountains, and Tobey would move permanently to Europe, where his work received its greatest critical acclaim. None would know of Fujii's resolution in an exuberant series of oil paintings.

In brushstrokes as broad as six inches wide, in saturated black and the fade of a dry brush, Fujii explored the expressive spatial possibilities of a two-by-three-foot canvas. He worked on the floor, a more familiar space in Japanese than in Western domestic life, with the bodily discipline basic to the practice of calligraphy.[18] He made a brush from his wife's hair to achieve the softness he needed. The distinctions of figure and ground, line and mass, and painting and drawing are gone. From edge to edge, the entire composition is energized by the interaction of black and white, of gesture and void. His paintings represent a resolution that bridges questions of national origin, ethnicity, and cultural difference and, once again, as in the 1930s, firmly position Fujii in the art of his time.

What he had written in 1937 held true for a lifetime: art's primary aim is "its power to raise the observer above the everyday affairs of life into a higher plane of existence."

ADDRESSING INJUSTICE

After World War II, many wanted to forget the years of incarceration, and only slowly, under pressure, did the government take steps to address the injustices. The 1948 Japanese-American Evacuation Claims Act authorized limited compensation of losses of material property, with no accommodation for the loss of earnings or health, let alone the loss of freedom.[19] The 1952 Immigration and Nationality Act, also known as the McCarran-Walter Act, at last opened naturalization to the Issei, although Fujii, by then age sixty-one, did not take the step. In the context of the spreading civil rights movement of the following decades, Japanese Americans began pushing for further action, including an apology and redress, until in the changing political environment the Commission on Wartime Relocation and Internment of Civilians began an inquiry in 1980. Established by an act of Congress and signed into law by President Jimmy Carter, the nine-member commission had three charges: to review the issuance and impact of Executive Order 9066; to review military directives concerning the confinement of American citizens, including natives and permanent resident aliens of Alaska's Aleutian and Pribilof Islands; and to recommend appropriate remedies.

Two years and more than 750 testimonies later—the testimonies largely by Nisei—the commission issued its report. It was a strong and clear indictment of all three branches of the federal government at their highest level. It concludes:

> The promulgation of Executive Order 9066 was not justified by military necessity, and the decisions which followed from it—detention, ending detention and ending exclusion—were not driven by analysis of military conditions. The broad historical causes which shaped these decisions were race prejudice, war hysteria and a failure of political leadership.[20]

Spurred by its Nisei members, Congress enacted the commission's recommendations in the Civil Liberties Act of 1988, which President Ronald Reagan signed into law.[21] Its major provision awarded a $20,000 tax-free payment to each of the approximately eighty thousand survivors of wartime incarceration alive on the day of signing.

Although redress was too late for Fujii, it brought a symbolic closure to Fusano, Satoko, Masako, and their peers. What Fujii did not receive in redress money he gave in richer means: a lifetime of artwork that represents a story of perseverance and resilience. Related with an artist's sensitivity and visual acuity, it is the story of a Japanese immigrant who made a home in America, who lost his liberty and the life he had built simply because of his ancestry, and then rebuilt a home in the country that had betrayed him. Viewed from an immigrant man's perspective, it is the story of an American ethnic people who experienced events unique in American history. In a remote camp in the depth of winter, Fujii had written in his diary about sunlight in the willow trees and found hope in what it promised. He expressed that hope in making art, which, like sunlight, pervades and illuminates his story.

MinidokaXX

THE ART DIARY OF TAKUICHI FUJII

Transcription by Honda Shōjō

Translation by Sandy Kita with Honda Shōjō

Introduction to the Diary

THE NATURE OF THE WORK AND OF ITS TRANSLATION

Sandy Kita

THE art diary of Takuichi Fujii, hereafter called the Fujii diary, was part of a cache of about a hundred small and large paintings, and two wooden busts of Fujii and his wife.[1] The cache was in the apartment at 1656 Farwell Street, Chicago, where Fujii's elder daughter, who was my mother, Mary Rose Satoko Kita, had moved with her mother, Fusano, after selling the house at 1443 Larrabee Street in Chicago, where we had lived until Fujii's death. My mother gave me the cache, which I transferred to my place in October 1987.[2] My mother moved from the Farwell Street apartment to another at 1608 Sherwin Avenue upon the death of her mother in 1995. In 1999, when my mother died, some craft items that Fujii and other members of the family had made were added to the cache. Tami Nelson, the son of Fujii's younger daughter, Masako Virginia, completed the cache in 2012 when he gave me the works by Fujii in his possession, consisting of a sculpture that he recalled Fujii had told him depicted the Madonna and child and two paintings that he believed portrayed Fujii and his wife.

The Fujii diary is handwritten in India ink in Japanese, and the manuscript was transcribed by the late Reverend Honda Shōjō, who also advised me on my translation of the text. Reverend Honda's qualifications for this work are discussed here, after my own—an order of presentation chosen mainly because of my identity as one of Fujii's two grandsons, which has permitted me to add to the biography of Fujii that Barbara Johns gives earlier in this book. During my childhood, I lived downstairs at the house on Larrabee Street, where Fujii lived his last years. I did not reside upstairs with Fujii, his wife, and Tami, whom they took care of because Masako had returned to work after her divorce from my cousin's father, Dale Nelson. That said, following the death of my own father, Denkichi Kita, in 1959 and my mother's return to work as well, I did come home from the George Manierre Elementary School to them, ate with them, and in many ways was raised by them. Grandpa Fujii was my first painting teacher, and his ideas on art have influenced me throughout my life.

One of my fondest memories of Grandpa Fujii is of him at the Saturday breakfasts that he made a custom to hold with his daughters and their families. At those breakfasts we would gather in the kitchen in the rear of his apartment, eat together, and talk. Those Saturday conversations were my introduction to the art, literature, history, religion, philosophy, and so many other aspects of Western and Asian cultures. The discussions would last for hours.

It is traditional in Japan to finish a meal by pouring a bit of green tea into one's rice bowl to wash away the remaining bits of food and create a thin gruel called *ochazuke*. Connoting frugality, simplicity, gratitude for life's little gifts, and much more, *ochazuke* has as great a symbolic meaning in Japan as apple pie has here.[3] One time, absorbed in the conversation, Grandpa Fujii forgot that he was drinking coffee that morning instead of green tea, and he poured it over his rice. I think that he was seriously considering eating the mess, until Grandma, ever practical, said, "Don't eat that. Throw it out. I'll get you more." Grandpa Fujii acquiesced but not without commenting, "Okay, but, you know, it won't really be *ochazuke*."

For Grandpa Fujii, what mattered was not the rice and tea of *ochazuke* but what they represented. I learned then that things could have meanings that were more important than the things themselves. In addition it was a rule at Grandpa Fujii's table that even we children could participate in the conversation so long as we listened first, had something relevant to say, and could defend our contribution logically. In this way, Grandpa Fujii taught me not only how objects could be carriers of meaning but also that I, or anyone else for that matter, could read their deeper significance by observing carefully, considering other opinions, and then thinking for oneself. Today, I am a professor and senior scholar of Japanese art history at Chatham University, Pittsburgh, Pennsylvania. I cite my graduate training at the University of Chicago as the start of my intellectual life, but it may be closer to the truth to say that the real beginning occurred long before, at those Saturday morning conversations at Grandpa Fujii's breakfast table.

Certainly, when I studied Japanese art history under Harrie Vanderstappen, after whom the Vanderstappen Chair at the University of Chicago is named, I intuitively understood much of what I learned, not out of any superior intelligence, but because I had heard something similar discussed before at Grandpa Fujii's breakfast table. This is especially true of what would become the main focus of my research, the seventeenth- to nineteenth-century Japanese art called ukiyo-e, which is strongly identified with the city of Edo (now Tokyo) and which we in this country know best from the many woodblock prints that it produced. I have been primarily interested in applying the "early modern theory" of the Tokugawa, or Edo, period (1615–1868) to ukiyo-e. As Herman Ooms, Conrad Totman, and other historians of this period present this theory, it amounts to an acknowledgment of how our world is similar to that in certain cities of premodern Japan, such as Edo, in having a powerful monied class, high level of literacy, huge publishing industry, emphasis on image, techniques for manufacturing fame, consumer arts, systems of authority that no longer inspire confidence, and other things. My work uses the early modern theory to define ukiyo-e in a way that suggests why there may be as many as three hundred thousand such prints in this country, why some estimate that 95 percent of the Japanese art here is in the form of the print, and why even Japanese surveys of ukiyo-e show that the United States leads Japan nearly three to one in examples of this art that are publicly available.

This view of ukiyo-e of mine, which has a basis in similarities between modern American and Edo-era—or "traditional," for the purposes of this discussion[4]—Japanese culture, appeared in full form for the first time, perhaps, in my 2004 *The Moon Has No Home: Japanese Color Woodblock Prints from the Collection of the University of Virginia Art Museum.*[5] If so, it is nonetheless implicit in my 1999 *The Last Tosa: Iwasa Katsumochi Matabei, Bridge to Ukiyo-e.*[6] Indeed, thinking back forty years to my time with Grandpa Fujii, it occurs to me that a connection between modern American and traditional Japanese culture was apparent in the house at Larrabee Street, where I grew up. My mother had hung two of Grandpa Fujii's black-and-white abstract expressionist paintings in the living room, which was next to the front room of our home. In the front room, Grandpa Fujii had painted a mural in which the silhouettes of Japanese travelers marched across a bridge that stood behind a great pine tree (fig. K.1), a composition he had copied from the woodblock print of Nagakubo from the circa-1830s series *The Sixty-Nine Stages of the Kiso Highway* (Kisokaidō rokujûkyû no uchi) by Utagawa Hiroshige (1797–1858; fig. K.2).

Traditional Japanese and modern American culture were no less conjoined in Grandpa Fujii's own apartment upstairs. Grandpa Fujii kept his brushes, paints, and other art supplies in a closet-like room over the stairs leading down from his second-floor apartment to his front door on the street level. He did not paint in this space, since it was too small, but painted in the adjoining room,

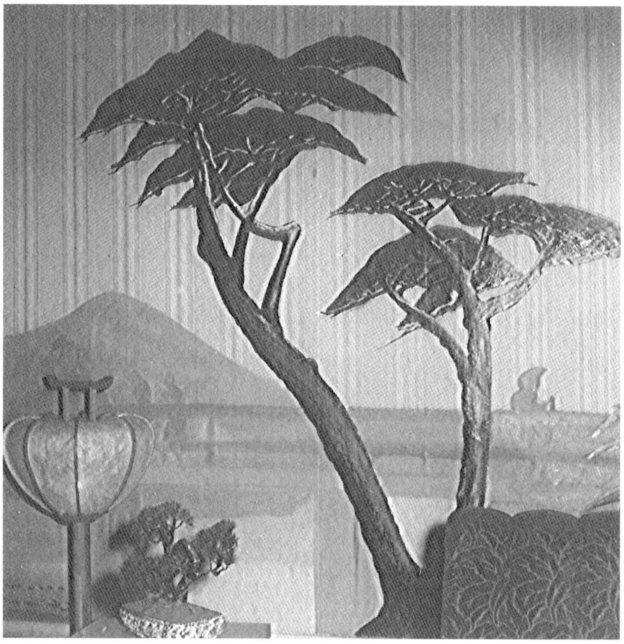

K.1 Front room of Fujii's Chicago home with his wall painting after Hiroshige, 1960. Courtesy of Sandy and Terry Kita.

in the one next to it, in the attic, and wherever else the fancy took him. The adjoining room was the front room. Separated from the rest of the apartment by French double doors, the front room had thin bamboo sheets (*goza*) laid over the floor, reproducing in this way the appearance of a traditional Japanese tatami-matted space. On one wall, Grandpa Fujii had painted a Japanese scene, covering it with sliding doors (*fusuma*) that he had decorated with traditional Japanese motifs, including a blue-and-white checkerboard pattern reminiscent of one found at the Detached Imperial Palace of Katsura. In the middle of the room stood a square, metal brazier (hibachi) filled with ashes raked into the shape of Mt. Fuji. Finally, a miniature pine tree (bonsai) that Grandpa Fujii had made, its innumerable needles carefully constructed one by one out of paper and wire, was displayed in this room, although eventually Grandpa gave it to my mother, who took it down to our place.

A bit of Japan in Chicago, the front room of Grandpa Fujii's apartment was in stark contrast to the living room next to it. Toward the back of the apartment, the living room had on the right side a sofa and the desk where Grandpa Fujii did his correspondence. On the other side, toward the front room, was the door to my grandparents' bedroom and a third French door that closed off the landing for the stairs down to the street. Around the corner, a cabinet stood between the single French door to the stairs and the double ones of the front

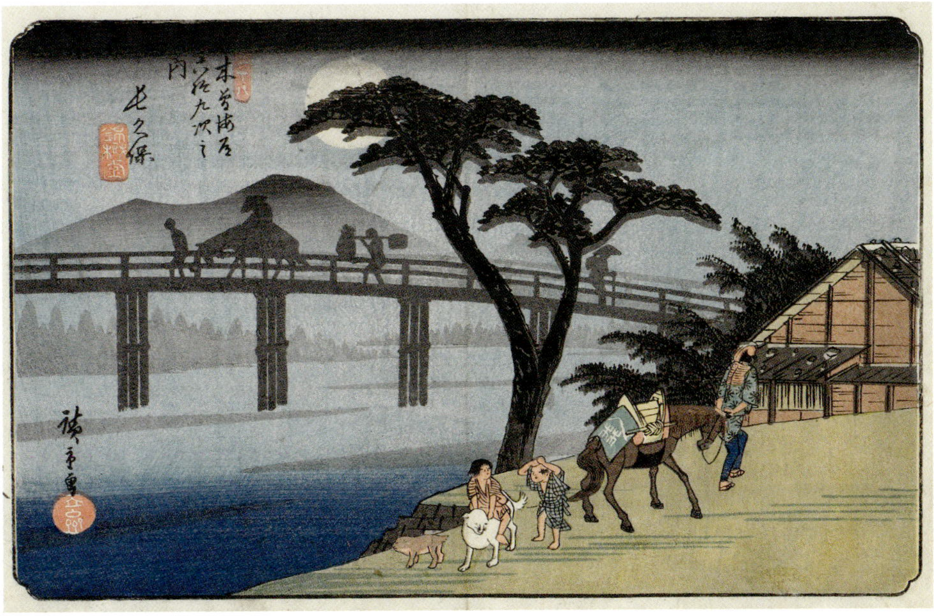

K.2 Utagawa Hiroshige, Nagakubo, no. 28 from the series *The Sixty-Nine Stages of the Kiso Highway* (Kisokaidô Rokujûkyû Tsugi no Uchi), ca. 1834–1842. Woodblock print, ink and color on paper, 8 7/8 × 13 15/16 in. Honolulu Museum of Art, gift of James A. Michener, 1970 (15618).

room. On top of this cabinet, Grandpa Fujii had installed a yard-long section of driftwood that was the perch of his pet owl. Purchased from Animal Kingdom Pet Store in Chicago under the mistaken impression that it was a small screech owl, Grandpa Fujii's bird was, in fact, a foot-and-a-half-tall great horned owl (fig. K.3). Grandpa had tamed this serious predator to the point where even we children could pet it, albeit carefully. The raptor had damaged flight feathers and could not fly, but it roamed the house at night, its huge claws clicking away. When Grandma complained about droppings on the furniture, Grandpa Fujii's solution was to weave nets out of string to create protective barriers that he hung from the ceiling. Possibly inspired by the shadows cast by the netting, he went on to paint the entire living room in a pattern of lines. From a distance, the result could be mistaken for a crude imitation of brickwork, but even as a child, I could see that it was a complex composition of interlocking rectangles. Later, I came to understand it as the work of modern abstract art that it was.

As I said, Grandpa Fujii had no specific place where he painted. He was as apt to do his traditional Japanese calligraphy in his American-modernist living room as to paint his abstract expressionist works in his traditional Japanese

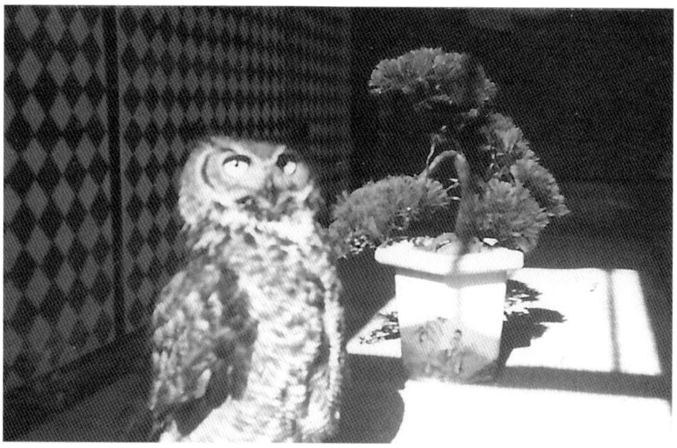

K.3 Fujii's home with great horned owl, his handmade wire and paper bonsai, and sliding doors painted by him, ca. 1960. Courtesy of Sandy and Terry Kita.

space. Grandpa Fujii did his abstract expressionist paintings using a traditional Asian brush, a huge one that he initially made out of a horsetail and then, when that proved too rough, out of Grandma's hair.[7] Grandpa Fujii also tended to discuss abstract expressionism in terms of the meaning that nonobjectivity had in Western art, on the one hand, and with regard to the importance of *fude no chikara* (the power of the brush) in Japanese ink painting, on the other.[8]

In conclusion, modern American and traditional Japanese culture were mixed in Grandpa Fujii's art, environment, and conversation, as I remember them. Not surprisingly, I see the same mixture in the Fujii diary. I begin with its traditional Japanese aspects, among which is its script. Modern Japanese is written in a combination of Chinese characters (kanji) and syllabic symbols (kana), there being two kinds of the latter: cursive (hiragana) and square (katakana). Examples of both types of syllabic script survive from the Heian period (794–1185), when cursive was the preferred form for women, who wrote much of the classic literature of that time in it. Heian-era examples of the square script are mostly Buddhist texts, and are, insofar as these are by priests, by men. Today, regardless of gender, Japanese employ the cursive script with their Chinese characters, reserving the square script primarily for foreign words. However, Grandpa Fujii used the square script exclusively, writing both Japanese and foreign words in it. In addition, he used the complicated, original, old forms of Chinese characters instead of their modern, simplified versions. He employed many old grammatical forms as well, and the proverbs, sayings, and other set expressions that he used more often belong to the Meiji period (1868–1912) of his birth than to the Taishō (1912–1926) and Shōwa (1926–1989) eras of his later years.

And yet, if the Fujii diary is traditionally Japanese in script, grammar, and expression, it is impossible to mistake it for anything other than a product of the twentieth-century Japanese community in America, since it contains so many expressions that developed only then and there. I refer to "Japlish," such as *mizutank* (*mizu* = water), *sumimasorry* (*sumimasen* = sorry), and other non-standard but common combinations of Japanese and English. The Fujii diary contains not only Japlish but also expressions that, while understood within Grandpa's family, were unlikely to be used outside it. For example, Grandpa Fujii referred to any Japanese pickle (*tsukemono*), even those that were homemade, as *fujinzuke*, an abbreviation of the brand name of a commercially canned variety.[9] Likewise, the name of the city of Poughkeepsie meant "a green olive with a red pimento in it," an expression invented by Masako. Masako was known as "Ah-chan" in the family, a pet name that derived from my babyhood inability to pronounce anything other than the *a* of *aunt*. The family word for *we* or *us* was *me-ra*. *Watashi-ra* is Japanese for *we* or *us*, being composed of the word used in Japan for *I* (*watashi*) and the pluralizing suffix *ra*. *Me-ra* is the English pronoun *me* with the pluralizing Japanese suffix *ra*.

Many of the above expressions are, as far as I can tell, unique to our family. Certainly, no one else that I have ever met calls a green olive with a pimento in it a "Poughkeepsie." Insofar as only Fujii family members would know these peculiarities of our speech, and as I am the last of us to read Japanese, this translation of the Fujii diary is likely to be the only one ever able to render these shibboleths that are in it.[10] In addition, I am a third-generation Japanese American (Sansei), and my training in and facility with the Japanese language,[11] years of residence in Japan, and decades of study of that culture have convinced me that I am, even if influenced by my Japanese heritage, essentially American in my thinking, my emotional reactions, and other fundamental aspects of personhood. As such, I believe that I complemented particularly well my collaborator on this translation of the Fujii diary: Reverend Honda. He was a first-generation Japanese American (Issei), whom I found very much my opposite in this regard, remaining essentially Japanese despite his long residence in this country, lifetime of study of Western culture, and enviable record of publication in English. Reverend Honda could explain to me the subtler implications of the wording of the Fujii diary and deepen my sense of its feel, tone, and color. As a result, it was possible for me as a native speaker of English who knew Grandpa Fujii personally to capture something of his authentic voice in this translation of the diary while remaining, nonetheless, as true as possible to the original text as we had it.

I particularly valued Reverend Honda's insights into the diary because it seemed to me that Grandpa was very much like him in being a first-generation Japanese American whose long residence here, for all it affected him, did not change his essentially Japanese character. Furthermore, Reverend Honda was close enough in age to Grandpa Fujii to recognize on sight the latter's old, unusual, nonstandard, and even miswritten Chinese characters and to be familiar with his proverbs, sayings, and other set expressions that were no longer common by my time. Like many Pure-Land Buddhist priests in this country, Reverend Honda had a day job, which in his case was as the chief research librarian in the Japanese Division of the Library of Congress. In part, it was his responsibility to answer questions on Japan from high-ranking government officials, professors in universities across the country, curators of our national and regional museums, and many others. As a result, Reverend Honda had very special skills when it came to accessing information in the collections of the Library of Congress, where we did the bulk of the research for this translation of the diary. A second benefit of Reverend Honda's career at the Library of Congress was that it gave him a wide circle of contacts in this country and Japan with whom to consult; their help in our work on the diary proved invaluable.[12] Lastly, Reverend Honda was particularly astute and experienced at explaining difficult Japanese ideas to Americans, because the Pure-Land Buddhist Temple of the Ekoji in Burke, Virginia, where he was minister, had a predominantly Caucasian congregation in his day.

By the time that Reverend Honda and I began translating the diary, we had worked together for more than twenty-five years. We translated Japanese into English and English into Japanese; but as Japan specialists, we naturally focused on the Japanese rather than American aspects of the diary in making this translation of it. We took this approach not only to make the most of our abilities but also to balance Barbara Johns's emphasis on the American reception of Fujii's artwork. That said, Reverend Honda and I did not translate the diary just as a Japanese text. We saw it as a traditional Japanese text. We did so because of our assessment of what it was and why Grandpa had made it.

Reverend Honda and I understood that we could not establish beyond doubt Grandpa Fujii's intent in creating his diary, but the Klip and Note notebook that he used, its small size, and his limited palette—the illustrations being done in pen and India ink with occasional watercolor—did suggest that the work might be "artist's notes." Supporting such a hypothesis was Grandpa Fujii's subsequent development of some of the compositions in his diary into fuller paintings. He painted wherever the fancy took him when I lived with him at Larrabee Street; and assuming that this was always the case with him, it made sense that he would carry sketching materials around with him, and that the diary might have resulted in that way naturally from his standard artistic practice.

Against such a view was the presence of a title page, the absence of any incidental writings or drawings, and the overall look of the diary, all of which indicated something more formal than simply notes. To Reverend Honda and me, the diary seemed to be a discrete project of some sort, although what the purpose of that project might be, we found difficult to decide. Barbara Johns, Lawson Inada, John Ruff, and others have commented on the fact that the diary is outstanding in the completeness with which it shows all aspects of his incarceration. The diary is a useful historical source for this reason, but whether or not a sense of history—that is, a desire to keep a complete and accurate record of events for posterity—motivated Grandpa to make his diary is another question altogether. For one thing, the diary is not a day-to-day, or even a consistent, account of his life in those years. The work does begin with Grandpa's incarceration and end with his release, but within that general time frame, he made entries as things interested him. Consequently, the diary lacks the regularity that produces that sense of objectivity, and so truth, that one would expect in a historical record. Also, Grandpa Fujii did not have, at least as far as I could tell, the sense of history of which I spoke earlier. Indeed, my recollection of him is that he was the last person to think that his experiences might be important enough to interest history. Grandpa Fujii was a most modest man, so much so that when *Who's Who in American Art* requested his information, he could not bring himself to send it in until my mother nagged him into it.

If the Fujii diary is not a historical record, neither is it a confessional writing as diaries sometimes are. Nor does the purpose of the diary appear to be to provide a safe, uncritical space where Grandpa could express himself with complete freedom because its contents would be secret. Barbara Johns has commented that Fujii was free of the need to consider an audience in his diary, and while that is true, especially compared to his larger paintings, it is also the case that in portraying the women in their shower, Grandpa was careful to note in his diary that the scene is as "gossip" had it (diary 40) and not as he saw it. Clearly, Grandpa was worried here that his drawing might cause some viewer of it to think him a voyeur, and this concern with how his diary would be received indicates that he cannot have seen it as entirely private. Still, the diary, if not private, is most definitely personal. The toilets, the sleeping arrangements, the laundry, and all the other little things that compose the fabric of everyday life are there in the diary, where we see, as well Grandpa's fear on the train to Minidoka, his triumph at catching fish, his joy in the visit of his daughter Masako, his anxious waiting for mail to arrive, and his disgust and shame with the quarters that he called "cattle stalls."

American readers of the diary may find its personal but not private nature, ahistorical content, and inconsistent chronology puzzling, but these qualities are common enough in Japanese diaries. In fact, Earl Miner contends that they are characteristic features of Japanese diary literature (*nikki bungaku*). Miner states that Japanese diary literature is rarely a day-to-day account of the lives of its writers.[13] He points out that where Western diaries that have won quasi-literary status, such as James Boswell's *The Life of Samuel Johnson*, are valued principally for what they tell us of their authors' or compilers' time[14]—that is, for their historical worth—this is not so of their Japanese counterparts. The truth of what Miner says is obvious in the very term *Japanese diary literature*, for it identifies diaries in Japan as literature, not history. Finally, one reason that Miner offers for why Japanese diaries are literature is that they are "concerned with *personal* matters—love rather than marriage, death rather than mortal battles, the family rather than public life" [italics mine].[15]

Otherwise puzzling aspects of the Fujii diary explain themselves when it is considered as an example of Japanese diary literature. For this reason, Reverend Honda and I classified it as such, something that we did all the more because the work fit not only into this general category of Japanese writing but also into a specific tradition within it. There are 252 pen-and-ink drawings in the 388 pages of the diary, and 232 of these are juxtaposed against passages of text. The diary is as much a work of drawing as of writing, so it exemplifies the tradition in Japanese diary literature of the "art diary" (*e-nikki*).

Classifying the Fujii diary as an art diary proved crucial to Reverend Honda's and my reading of it, in allowing us to understand Grandpa's feelings about his incarceration despite the fact that he said nothing direct on this matter. Seeing the diary as an art diary accomplished the above because this related it to *The Record of Travels through the Provinces* (Kaikoku michi no ki) by painter Iwasa Katsumochi Matabei (1578–1650).[16] Reverend Honda and I had previously translated this work, hereafter called Matabei's Record, and it came to mind now because it was similar to the Fujii diary in being by a painter and the only document of any substance by its writer to survive.[17] In addition, Matabei's Record tells how he went from Fukui to the old imperial capital of Kyoto and then down the Eastern Sea Road (Tōkaidō) to the new shogunal capital of Edo.[18] As the account of this trip, Matabei's Record is a travel diary (*tabi nikki*), another tradition of Japanese diary literature into which we can place the Fujii diary if we focus on how Grandpa's incarceration was, if an unwilling journey, still a move from Seattle to Minidoka.

Even more important was how Matabei expressed his feelings in his record, for that related closely to how Grandpa did the same in the Fujii diary. Like Grandpa Fujii, Matabei made no direct statements about how he felt, but a tone of sorrow, nonetheless, permeated his record, just as a consciousness of imprisonment, according to Barbara Johns, imbues the Fujii diary. That this should be so in the case of the Matabei Record was logical given the circumstances under which Matabei created it. Matabei wrote the record under circumstances that were as difficult for him as the incarceration that produced the Fujii diary was for Grandpa. Matabei was part of a group called the *machishu* or *chōshu* (literally, "city group"), who dominated politics and art in places such as Kyoto in the period from the start of the Age of Wars (1467?–1615?) to its final end with the rise of the Tokugawa clan in the Edo period. As the Tokugawa established their shogunate in the city of Edo and consolidated their power, they suppressed the *machishu*. Hiroshi Mizuo tells how the *machishu* leader Hon'ami Kōetsu (1558–1637) accepted the shogunate's gift of the property at Takagamine, knowing how that would remove him from politics, but then swore, "No command from on high shall ever make us move to Edo."[19] Around this same time, Matabei, too, withdrew from Kyoto. He went to Fukui, but after "more than twenty years there,"[20] watching the *machishu* cause fail, he had given up. The year that Kōetsu died, Matabei moved to Edo, his journey there to paint for the Tokugawa, the subject of his record.

As a former *machishu*, Matabei could not have wanted to make that journey east to Edo that he wrote about in his record, but he could hardly express such feelings in it, lest the Tokugawa take offense. What Matabei could not say openly, he could still make clear by referring cleverly to the classics of Japanese poetry and literature. Warriors such as the Tokugawa honored and respected these old court writings no less than artists such as Matabei. Consequently, references of this sort were above reproach. Thus, when Matabei reached the place called the Eight Bridges (Yatsuhashi) in Mikawa Province, he commented that he had "a well-worn cloak" and "a wife to whom I have become accustomed," and then, looking for the iris for which the place is famous, went on to say that "even the roots . . . had sadly dried up."[21] These statements by Matabei are allusions to the ninth chapter of that classic of Heian-era literature and poetry (*uta monogatari*) *The Tales of Ise* (Ise monogatari), which contains the incident of the "journey east" (*azuma kudari*) of poet Ariwara no Narihira (825–880). Narihira's journey east was no fun-filled pleasure trip, the East representing in Japan much of what the West used to here. The Western Plain (Kansai) of Japan is where the centers of culture, including Kyoto, initially developed and subsequently concentrated, whereas the Eastern Plain (Kantō), where Edo is located, was nearly the frontier in Narihira's day. To journey east was to move away from civilization; and that this is how Narihira felt about it is apparent in the poem he composed when he came to the Eight Bridges and saw the iris there:

I have a beloved wife,
Familiar as the skirt
Of a well-worn robe,
And so this distant journeying
Fills my heart with grief.[22]

Accordingly, one result of Reverend Honda's and my consideration of Matabei's Record as we translated the Fujii diary was that we did not assume that the absence of direct expressions of emotion in it meant that Grandpa's feelings about his incarceration were not to be found in his diary. In other words, placing the diary in the context of Matabei's Record heightened our awareness of the importance of considering what the diary implied as well as said.

However, the implications of the diary could not be elicited from Grandpa Fujii's allusions to classic poetry and literature, because he made so few of these. Another method was needed, and it suggested itself in something else that Matabei's Record made me, as an art historian, particularly aware of—the close relationship between literature and art in Japan.[23] The connection is apparent from Narihira's poem at the Eight Bridges, which reads in Japanese:

Karagoromo
kitsutsu narenishi
tsuma shi areba
harubaru kinuru
tabi o shi zo omou

The poem is acrostic, its first syllables spelling out the word *kakitsubata*, or "iris."[24] In this way, the poem inscribes its connotations of longing and sorrow on the object of the iris, so that to portray this flower is to evoke those emotions. A tradition of depicting the iris at the Eight Bridges developed, and the many images of this subject that it produced were crucial to my reading of the implications of the Fujii diary.

For instance, there is a hanging scroll of iris by *machishu* Ogata Kenzan (1663–1743) titled *Eight Bridges* (Yatsuhashi) that is now in the Fujii Family (no relation) Collection, Kyoto, and which has been designated an important cultural property.[25] Kenzan's brother Ogata Kōrin (1658–1716) made a set of two six-fold screens of iris that is now in the Nezu Museum in Tokyo, these works being national treasures and among Japan's most famous paintings.[26] Kōrin used the same motif, of the iris at the Eight Bridges, to decorate a writing box that is another national treasure, held by the Tokyo National Museum, which also owns his hanging scroll of the same subject.[27] The Hatakeyama Memorial Museum in Tokyo has Kōrin's fan showing the iris at the Eight Bridges, and the Metropolitan Museum of Art in New York owns a pair of six-fold screens of the same subject by the same artist.[28] In addition, various members of Kōrin's Rimpa school depicted the theme, these including two works by Sakai Hōitsu (1761–1828), three by Suzuki Kiitsu (1796–1858), two by Nakamura Hōchû (fl. 1790–1818), and two by Sakai Dōitsu (1845–1913).[29]

The ninth, or "Journey East Chapter," of the *Tales of Ise* also told how Narihira went past Mt. Fuji. This incident gained a separate identity of its own, as can be seen in the book *Passes Mt. Fuji, Chapter Nine Azuma Kudari* (Journey east) that Yoshida Soan (d. 1632) published around 1608 and which is now in the New York Public Library.[30] More significantly, Narihira at Mt. Fuji became another theme in art, Sumiyoshi Jōkei (1598–1670) making the painting *Journey East: Passing Mt. Fuji* (Azuma kudari: Fuji no yama) that is part of the collection of the British Museum.[31] Bernard Leach believed that a friend of Matabei and the creator of so much of the tradition of art that Kōrin and his followers codified, Tawaraya Sōtatsu (d. 1643?), painted the theme as well.[32] So did Kōrin, two works by him showing Narihira at Mt. Fuji being known.[33] There is also a painting by Hōitsu titled *Ariwara Narihira: Journey East* (Ariwara Narihira azuma kudari zu), and this same artist is thought to have portrayed the same subject in a second work now in the Hatakeyama Memorial Museum.[34] In fact, Murashige Yasushi, in his study of Rimpa, identifies four more depictions of it by Hōitsu, not to mention paintings of the theme by Hōitsu's son Suzuki Shuitsu (1823–1889). Kiitsu and Dōitsu painted the subject as well.[35] Makers of ukiyo-e also took up the subject, an early example being the pillar print (*hashira-e*) dated 1770 by Kitao Shigemasa (1739–1820) that is titled *Journey East* (Azuma kudari), and later ones including the triptychs *A Modern Journey East* (Tōsei azuma kudari) by Kikugawa Eizan (1787–1867), *Journey East* (Azuma kudari) by Rekisentei Eiri (fl. c. 1790–1800), and *Journey East: Passing Mt. Fuji* (Azuma kudari yatsushi no Fuji) by Kitagawa Tsukimaro (d. 1830).[36]

The examples of ukiyo-e discussed here are woodblock prints and so exist in multiple copies. Added to all the paintings that there are of Narihira's journey east (*azuma kudari*), there can be little doubt of how widespread this tradition of imagery is in Japan. Unquestionably, Grandpa Fujii had in his cultural heritage as a Japanese a way to think about his unwilling journey east from the city of Seattle to the desert of Minidoka. And yet, whether or not Grandpa actually had that model in mind when he composed his diary, I could not say. Indeed, there is no absolute proof that Grandpa Fujii had ever encountered images of

Narihira's journey east, even though such images are so widespread that it is hard to believe he did not.

Still, this tradition of imagery remained important to my reading of the Fujii diary because of its broader meaning. The tale of Narihira's journey east can be understood as that of a great poet whose greatness was undiminished by his removal from the centers of poetry. When so removed, Narihira composed some of his best verse, as would poets ranging from Priest Saigyō (1118–1190) to Matsuo Bashō (1644–1694). Based on the importance of the "outsider" (*marebito*) in Japanese myth, religion, and culture, and acknowledging that artistic worth is not the same as an artist's financial or social success, there was in Japan the idea that appreciative audiences, understanding critics, and supportive institutions are not crucial for art to flourish. Quite the opposite, removing these things was seen, not as destroying an artist's creativity, but as strengthening his art, in that it purified it by making his love for it his only reason for doing it.

This idea is not confined to poetry but exists across all the arts of Japan. Kōetsu, for one, may have had it when he withdrew to Takagamine, and it seems that Sōtatsu might have had it as well, judging from how he followed Kōetsu there. It was fundamental to the aesthetic of the literati (*bunjin*), whose tradition originated in China when the Mongol hordes took over and men of the arts left the centers of culture to enter what amounted to self-imposed rural exile. While the tradition of portraying the journey east was how I happened to learn of this larger idea, and likely how Grandpa did as well, it was not the only way to do so. Many other routes of access to it existed; so many that it is all but certain that Grandpa knew this greater trope of which the tradition of portraying the journey east was but part.

That point was key to my reading of the Fujii diary, for it gave reason to believe that Grandpa saw his work, not just as a way to pass the time during his incarceration, but as a worthy project that had the backing of Japanese history and tradition. Such a possibility was important to me because of my own experience of life. When racism in academics hurt me badly, I found that I needed, more than anything else, to do the work that I saw as defining me as the person I most wanted to be. In my case, that work was scholarship; but not just any scholarly work would do. It had to be worthy. So, was it the same with Grandpa? When the internment took so much away from him, did he react as I did and need to do something worthy?

If the worthwhile work that Grandpa chose to do is the Fujii diary, Reverend Honda and I were right to approach it as a traditional Japanese text, for in such a case its links to tradition would be very much its point. Moreover, Grandpa was an artist. The work that he would need to do would be artwork. No less important, therefore, was the fact that Reverend Honda and I classified the Fujii diary as an art diary, for this meant it was as much a work of art as of literature. In turn, seeing the Fujii diary as art including Grandpa's paintings produced the feature that was perhaps most characteristic of my approach to translating its text. I always consulted the illustrations in so doing. This method was adopted because of the long history of equating images and words in Japanese art.

Modern Western artists have made much of equations of images and words, no doubt because we write in letters that have no representational capacity. By contrast, Chinese characters (kanji) often derive from pictograms; and because the art of calligraphy developed in China and then Japan, the original link between images and words was never completely forgotten. Combinations of text and pictures can be found in Japan almost as far back as the beginning of writing there. Buddhism is usually credited with bringing writing to Japan, and among its early works is the *Sutra of Causes and Effects* (E-ingakyō) in the Jōbonrendai temple in Kyoto, which dates to the eighth century.[37] In this work, passages of text appear below their illustrations, so that the combination of image and word is rather simple.

Halle O'Neal provides an example of a closer connection between image and word in Japanese art. She focuses on a twelfth-century Buddhist painting in gold of a pagoda, a work in the Chûson temple in Hiraizumi, Iwate Prefecture.[38] The pagoda is composed entirely of Chinese characters from the Sutra of Golden Light. The characters are so small that it is impossible to read them unless one is so close to the painting that one cannot see the pagoda. Since the pagoda becomes visible only when one moves so far from the painting as to make the characters impossible to read, a viewer interested in both goes back and forth, enacting in this way a performance that makes obvious the interdependence of image and word. As O'Neal notes, this interpretation of this painting fits well with sutra covers from the same time that bear decorations in the "reed style" (*ashide*), in which characters take on the forms of birds, rocks, and other objects.

Contemporaneous secular, as well as religious, combinations of images and words are known as well, an example being *The Illustrated Hand-Scroll of the Tale of Genji* (Genji monogatari emakimono), dated to the early twelfth century and now in the Tokugawa Art Museum in Nagoya.[39] Such works are identified with the tradition of yamato-e (Japanese-style painting), which also produced portraits of poets composed of the characters or syllabic letters for their names. A seventeenth-century example by Daishin Gitō (1657–1730) in the Kurt and Millie Gitter Collection turned the body of poet Kakinomoto Hitomaro (662–710) into the character for "person" (*hito*) and the glyph for "round" or "perfect" (*maru*).[40] In the diptych *Bulls* (Ushizu) by Sōtatsu, with calligraphy by Karasumaru Mitsuhiro (1579–1638), in the Chōmyō temple in Kyoto, the work has political implications when image and word are read together, but not otherwise.[41] Similarly, Okudaira Shunroku has shown how closely Sōtatu's painting and Kōetsu's calligraphy interact in the *Deer Scroll* in the Seattle Art Museum, the images overlapping the words in some places, and the words the images in others, in a way possible only if the two were done simultaneously.[42] Ukiyo-e combinations of images and words were introduced earlier, all the prints discussed then having both pictures and text. Writing is so common on ukiyo-e woodblock prints that it is hard to think of one without it. There are any number of examples by Hiroshige, whose work Grandpa copied.

More than ample justification exists in art in Japan to read the images and words of the Fujii diary together, and doing so allowed me, as it will any reader, to comprehend what Grandpa was feeling about sensitive matters upon which he may have felt he could not speak freely. Consider the entry "What it looked like when I visited a friend living in Area A" (diary 36). The statement seems innocuously objective until one considers the illustration that accompanies it—a sentry, guard house, and barbed-wire fence that are disproportionately large when compared to a crowd of inmates, their size diminishing all the more as they recede into the distance. The unusual black wash that covers most of the drawing that accompanies the entry "Headquarters of the Army Military Police" (diary 73) likewise suggests the dread that these people must have evoked in inmates such as Grandpa Fujii. Finally, the sudden change from a horizontal to a bird's-eye perspective in the illustration of the entry "This is the barbed wire and [the scene] around Block 24" (diary 74) conveys the dislocation, unreality, and unease that Grandpa Fujii must have felt on being incarcerated.

And if consulting the images when reading the words of the Fujii diary illuminates Grandpa's meaning, no less do his words give insight into the deeper significance of his images. For example, there is Grandpa Fujii's drawing of himself looking at his door. Not until one reads that the lock is on the outside, leading him to conclude that the so-called relocation center into which he has been placed is in reality a prison (diary 58), does the poignancy of the scene become apparent. Grandpa Fujii's depiction of a large muddy depression can be mistaken for mere *reportage*, until we read his laconic comment that this is a "rough spot in the road" (diary 70) and realize that it may well be caricature. Nothing could make more obvious how Grandpa felt about his incarceration than putting the scene he drew of sentries before buses against his entry: "Gasping, 'It's hot, it's hot,' [we reach a] desertlike place we do not know where, with neither trees nor houses" (diary 53).

Of course, Grandpa Fujii never told me to read the images and the words of his diary together, nor did he leave any instructions to do so. Still, I think that he would have approved of such a course of action, given how it changes the way in which his diary communicates. If it is up to us to put together his images and words, we become active participants in a conversation that we have with him, rather than passive recipients of a message that he just gives us. The Grandpa that I knew would have much preferred the former to the latter. He was never one to impose his opinions on others, and if he argued hard for his beliefs in those discussions that he loved, he was always open to dissenting opinions, for his goal was not to win but to have a true intellectual exchange. In any case, such was how things worked at his breakfast table during those Saturday morning conversations so long ago, for if all had to listen carefully and respect the opinions of others, even we children were ultimately free to make up our own minds and, in the end, to come to our own conclusions.

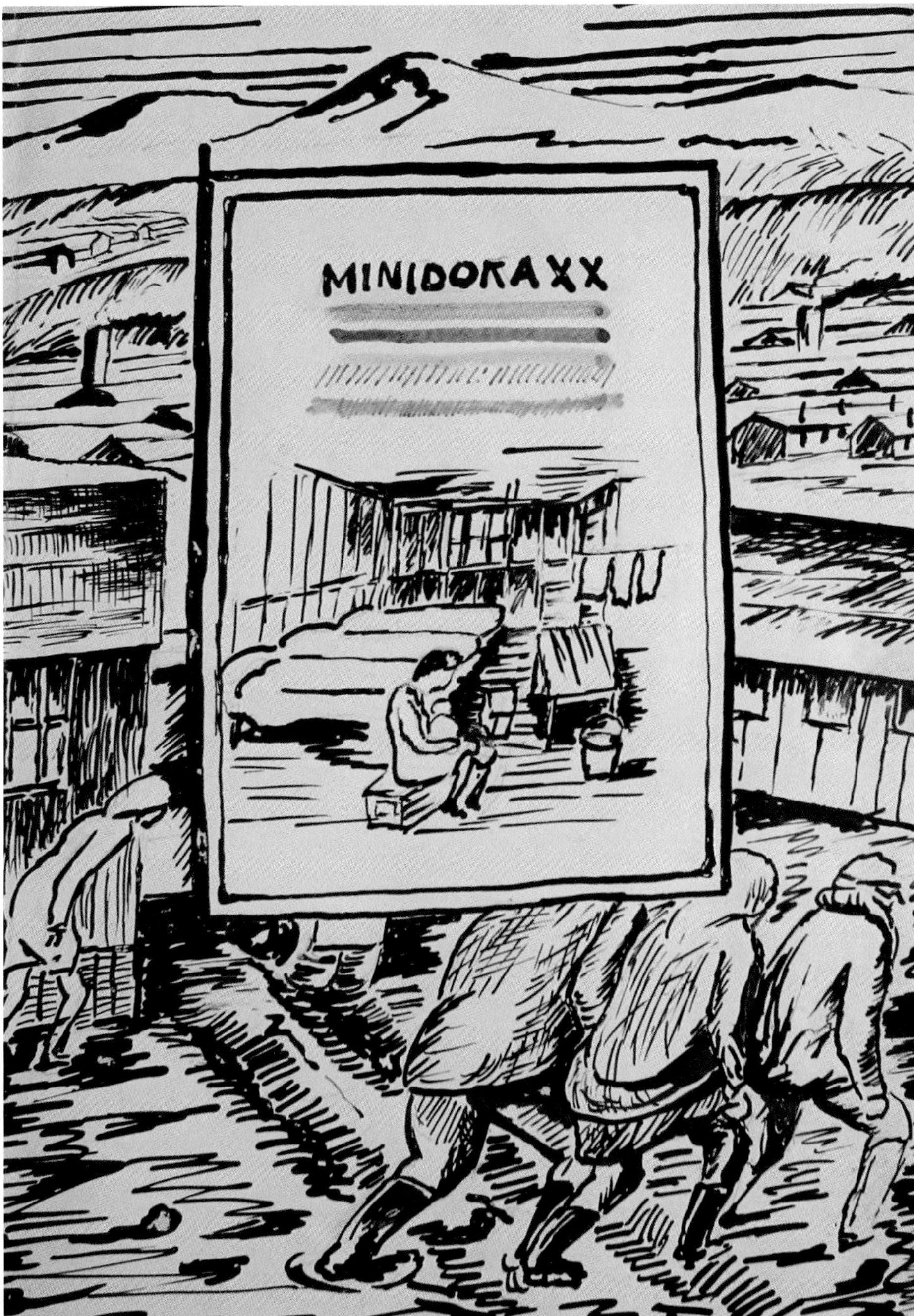

1

2

December 7, 1941: Attack on Pearl Harbor
December 8: Declaration of war against Japan
December 23: Issuing of Lieutenant General DeWitt's orders of compulsory removal of enemy aliens. Orders to leave, starting with Bainbridge and across the whole state of Washington. We are to leave behind this homeland to which we have long been accustomed and gather in shanties in Puyallup. One hundred twenty thousand Japanese Americans living in West Coast states were thus directly affected by the war.

We had the [Mary] Rose Florist [from] the time that we returned to Seattle from the East Coast two years ago until we were forced out. Shown is the appearance of the exterior around the time that we were forced out.

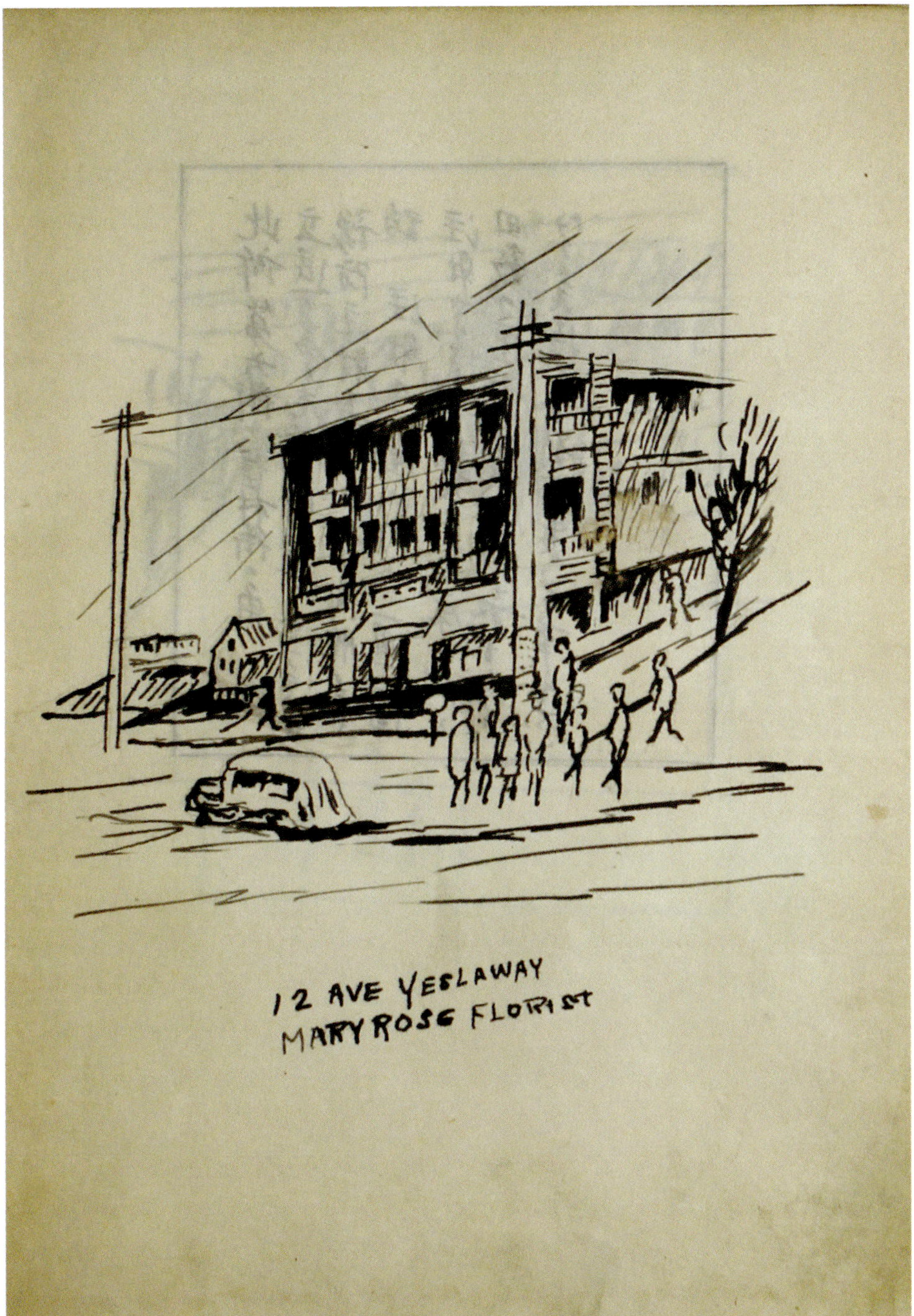
12 AVE YESLAWAY
MARYROSE FLORIST

3

This is a WCC [Wartime Civil Control Administration] program. During the evacuation, the former Japanese Commerce [Association] meeting room was where the officers were who worked mainly on investigating the Japanese. They apparently asked about the management and disposition of property and [other matters] following the evacuation.

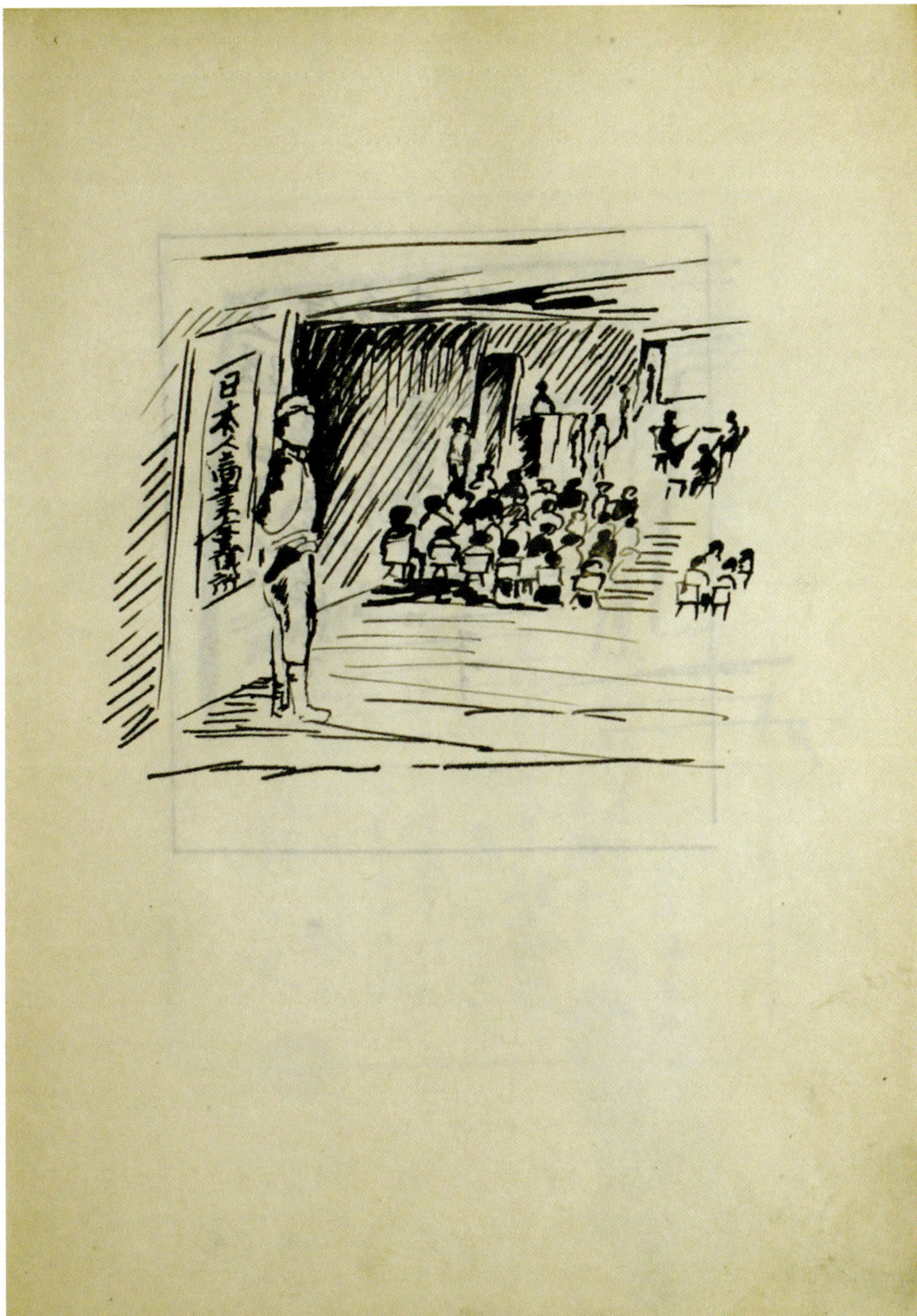

4

An Evening of Reluctance

Finally, tomorrow morning, we must say farewell to this house to which we have become so accustomed. Naked, having disposed of our shop, furniture, everything, in a muddle we packed only the absolute minimum of personal belongings, clothing, and bedding. Our home, which is now empty, feels sad and cold in the dim light. Since we had no bed, we got out our coats and, making a temporary bed, slept together like sardines in a can. But because we could not sleep, we were up before dawn. Having taken our last breakfast, we waited for the time to pass. All my family looked anxious.

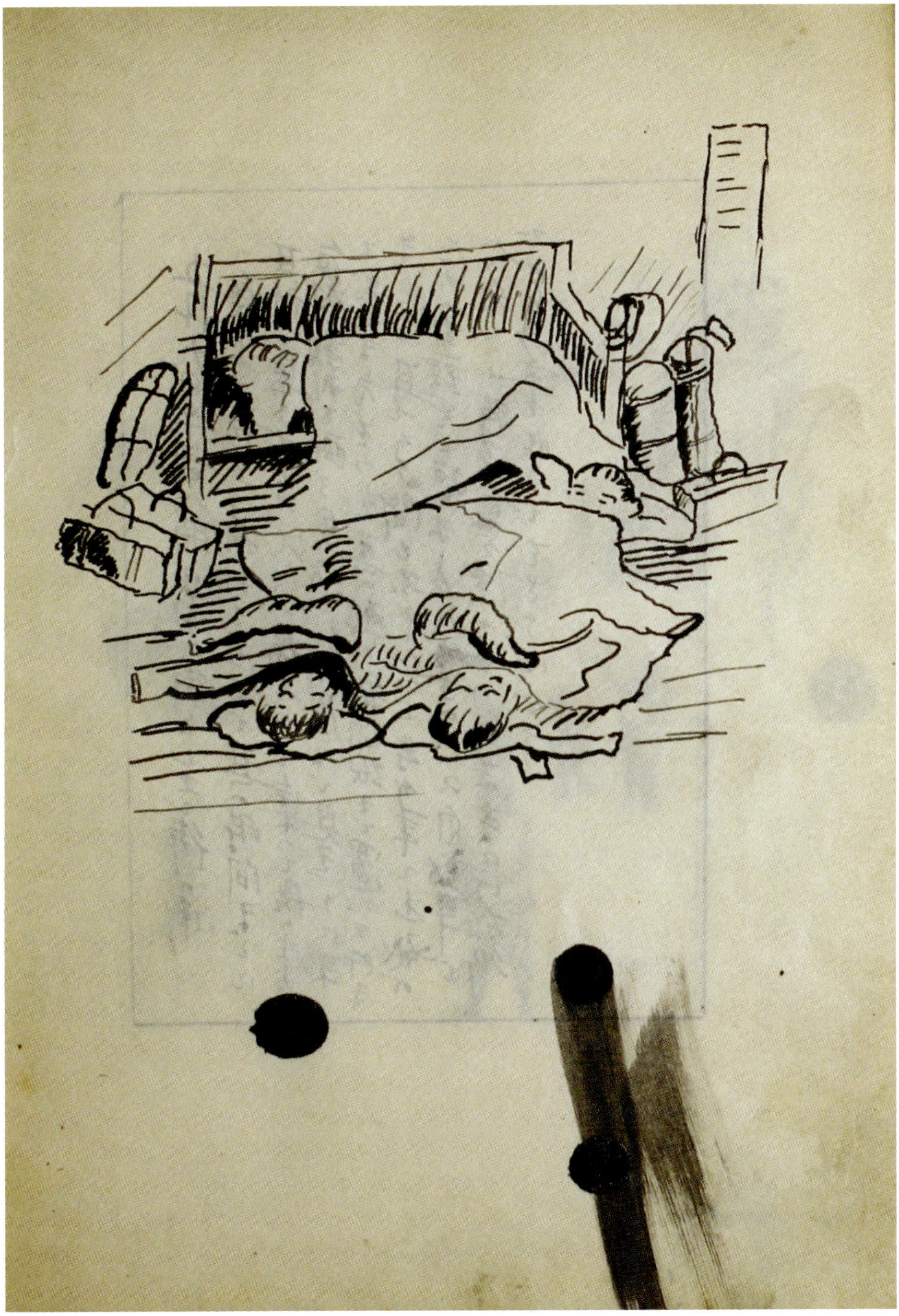

5

Since we were scheduled to meet at the corner of South Eighth and Lane Streets on May 9 at 8:00 A.M., carrying our luggage, we gathered there by that time. A great many of our neighbors were gathered there. Even the black newspaper delivery boy who had brought us the paper every morning came to see us off. He even brought us the paper that morning. Soon after that, the soldiers came and began to prepare for our departure. Splitting us up into eight autobuses, finally around ten, we said farewell to Seattle, which we would miss and which was hometown to our children.

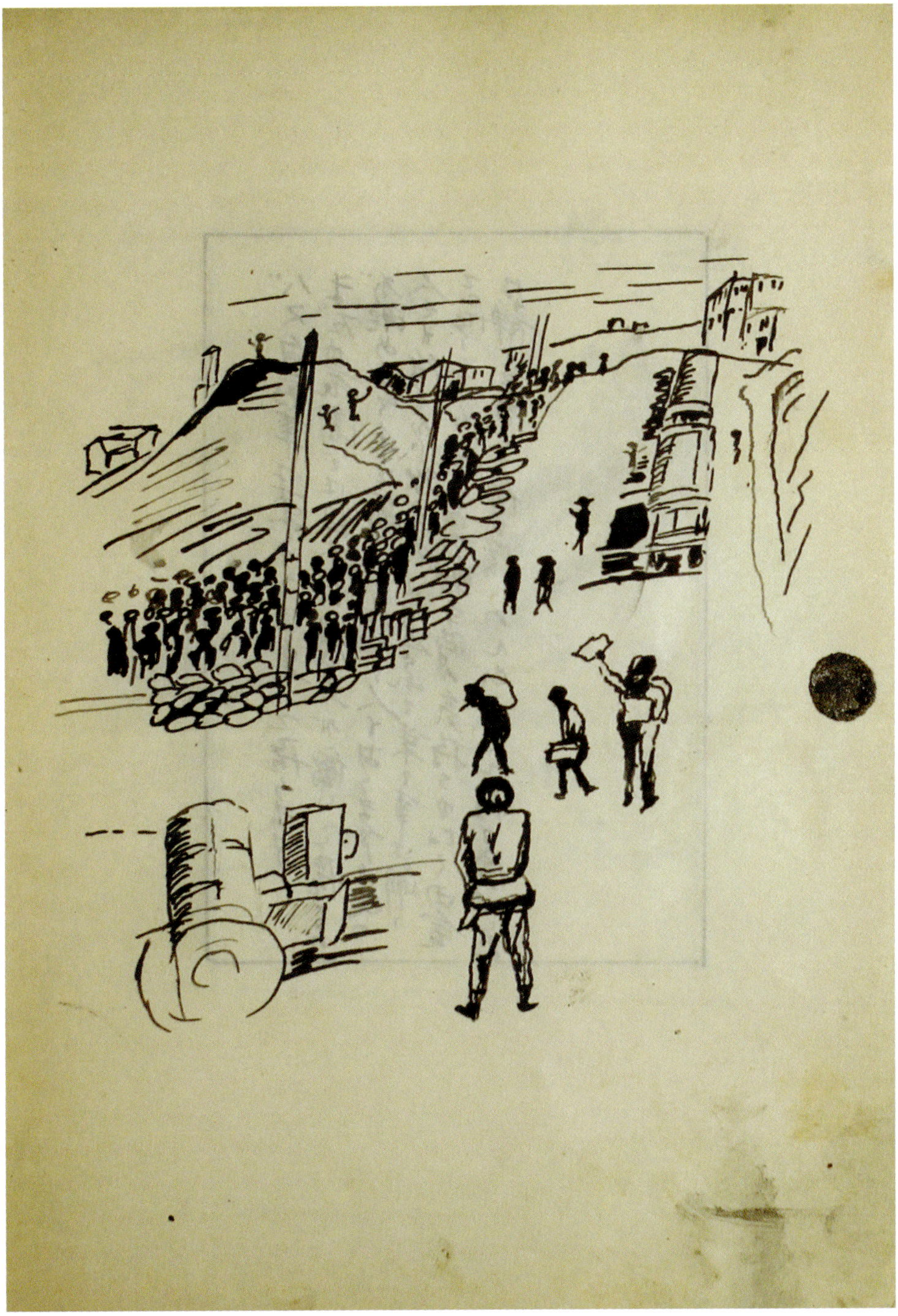

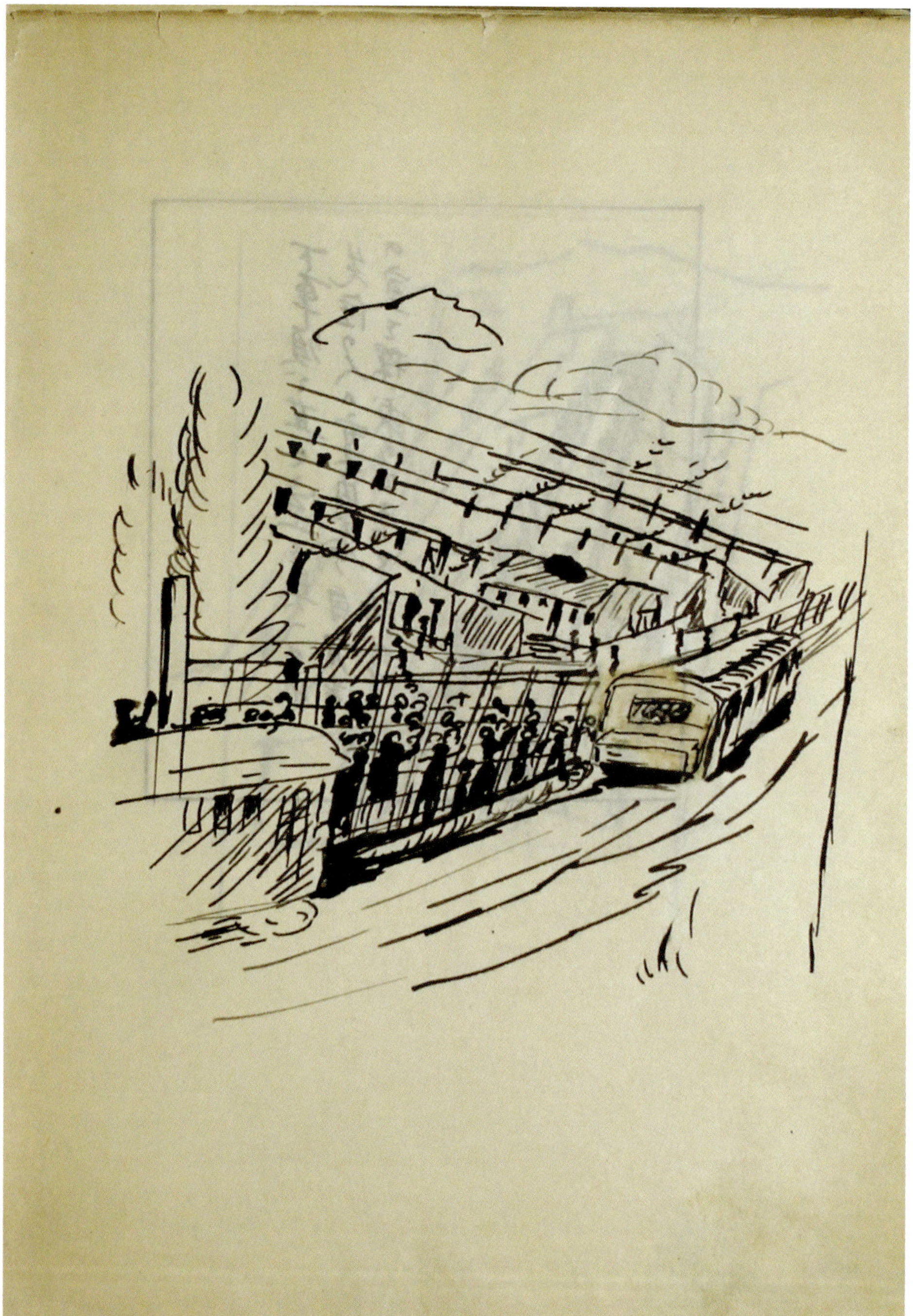

6 We arrived at the Puyallup Assembly Center. Those who had been sent here earlier greeted us from inside the barbed wire.

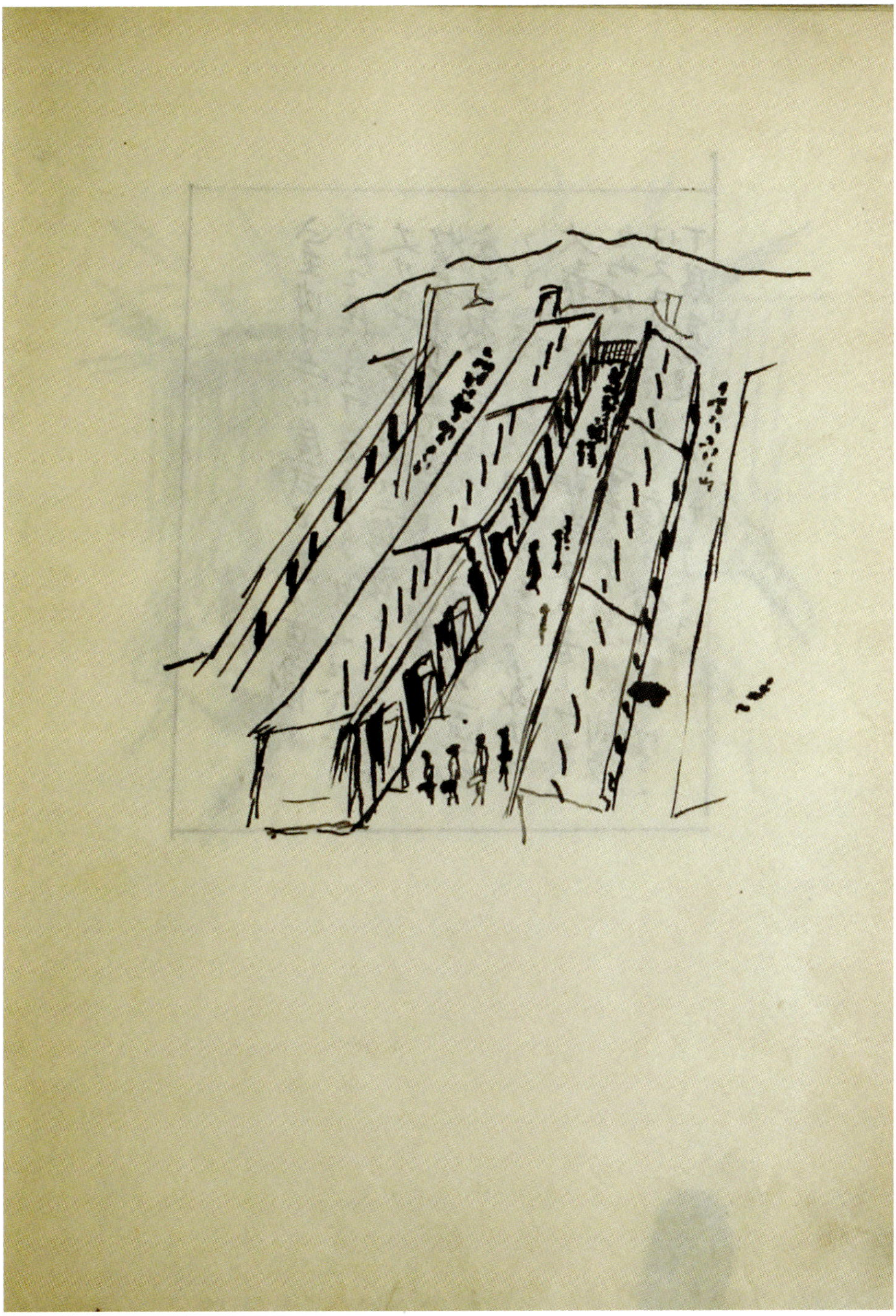

7 We were given rooms in the order in which we got off the bus and here [in the sketch] are looking for our rooms with the guidance of those already in the camp.

8

The rooms were like cattle stalls with a window in back. There was just a stove and a bed. As soon as we arrived, we looked for hay and made mattresses with it. We were to put our bedding [on these mattresses] and sleep there. Every room was divided inside the same way. Those who had big families had to endure the difficulty of these small [rooms]. There were lots of spaces between the wallboards, so when the lights were turned on at night, it looked just like a birdcage.

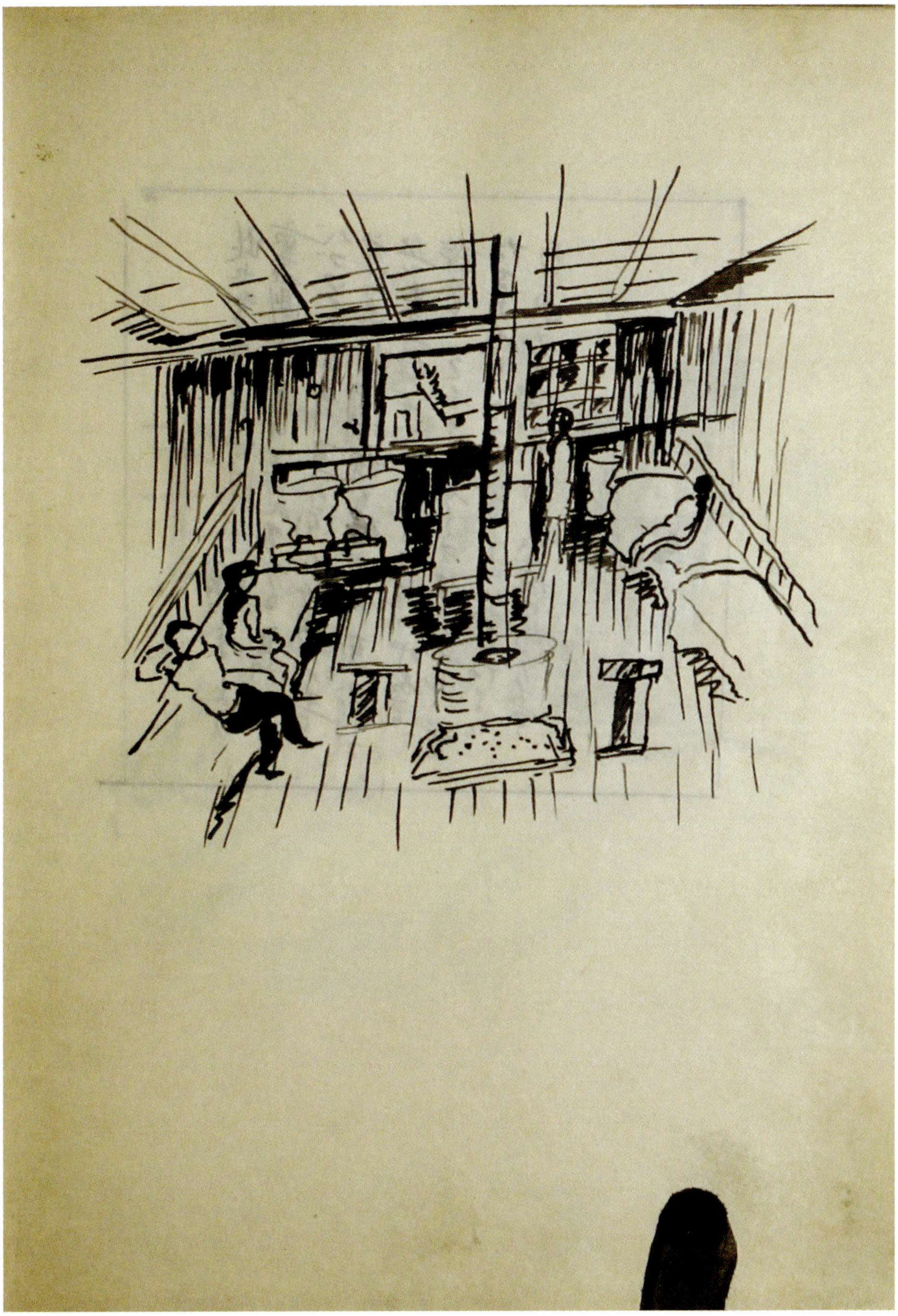

9

This cattle stall . . . let us check around. Peeking behind in back, there was a tall barbed-wire fence. Above the green grass of the pasture beyond, a machine gun was placed, and next to it, some soldiers were sleeping and others were training. When war comes, do people become horrible like this? Thinking about that, I felt wretched.

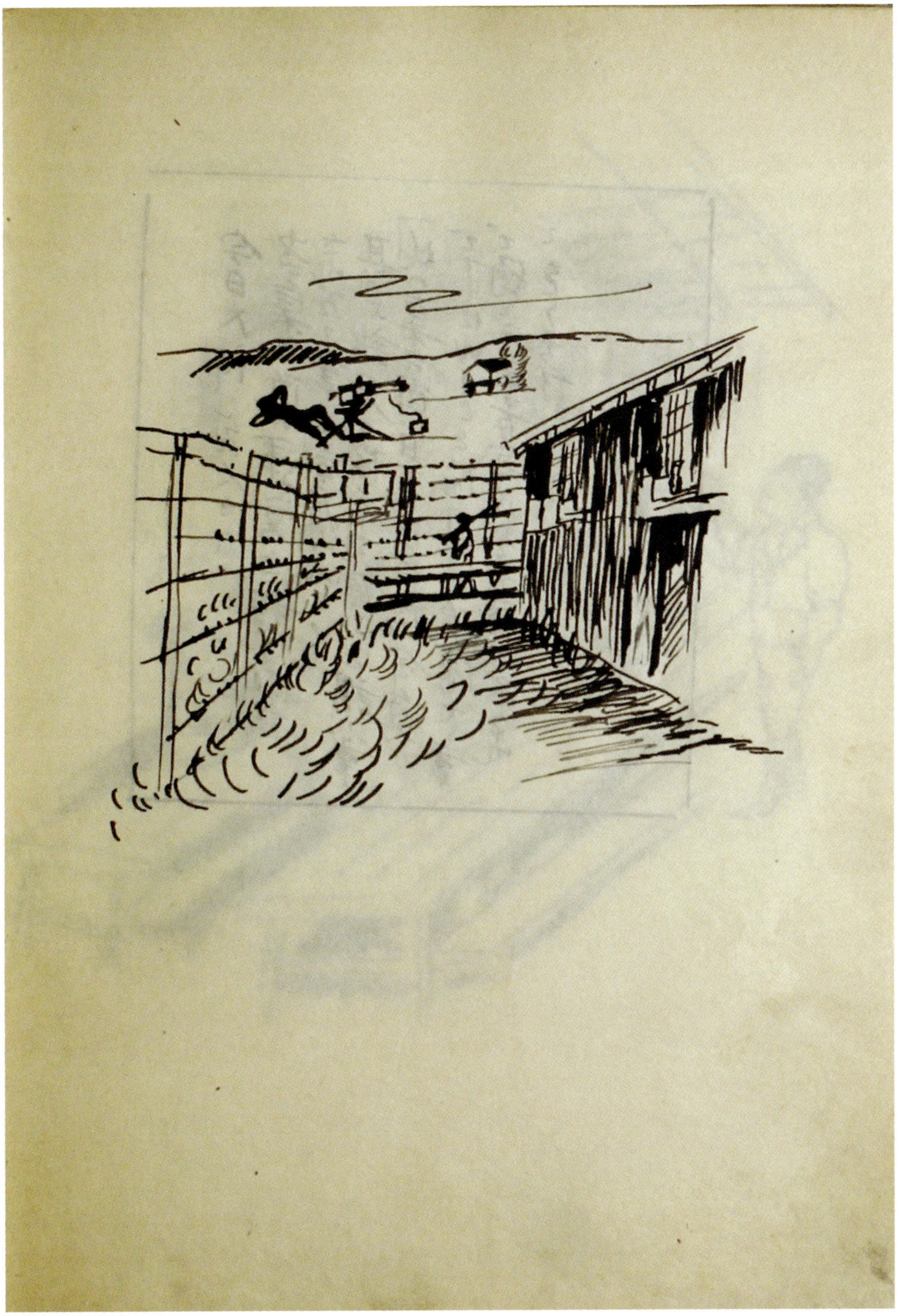

10

Those of us who had newly arrived were told various aspects of the management and organization of this assembly center, and in addition, all of us were asked to cooperate. The Japanese American Citizens League had cooperated earlier with the WCC [Wartime Civil Control Administration], so young Japanese Americans, who had prepared earlier, did everything in this camp.

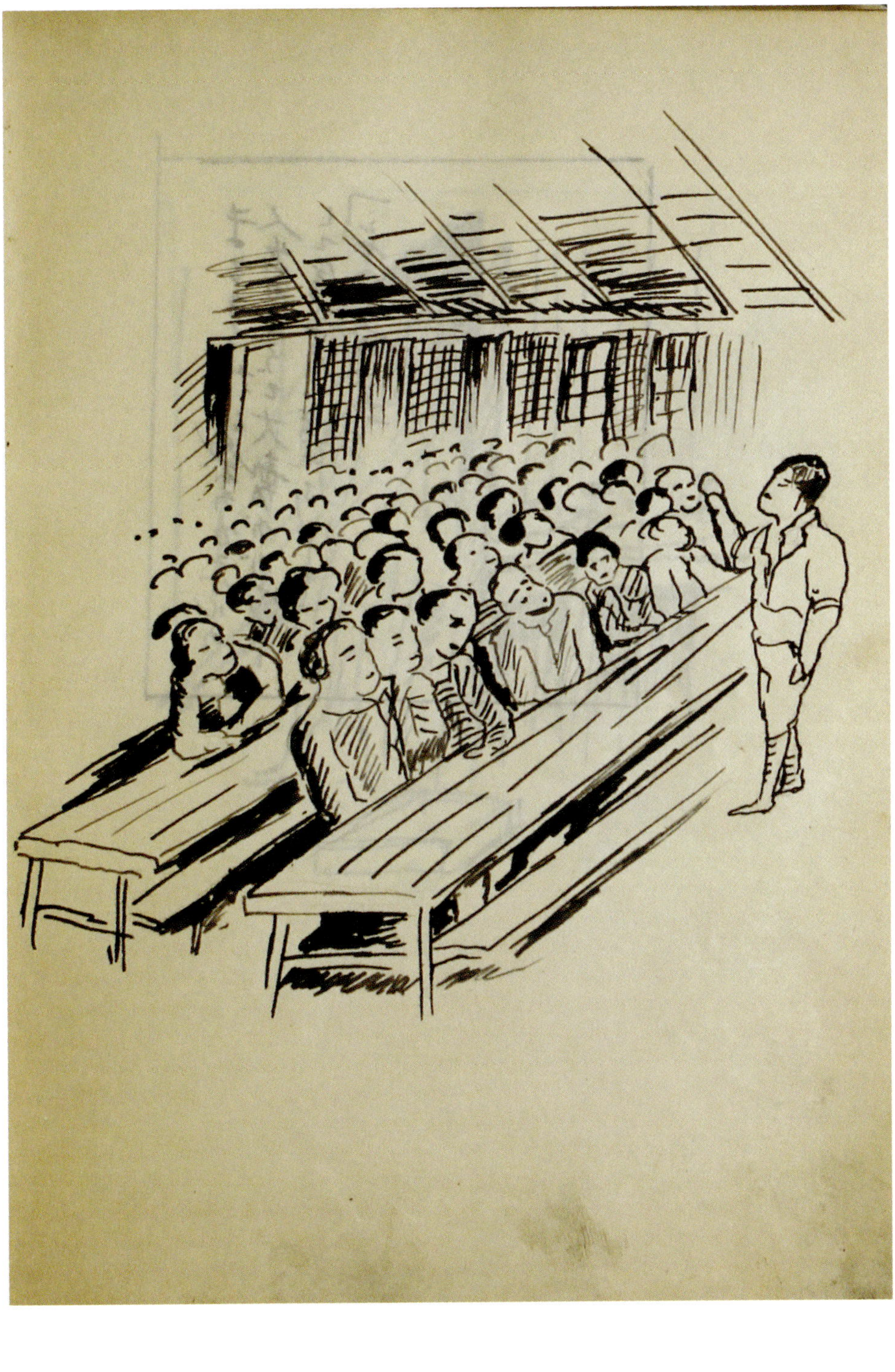

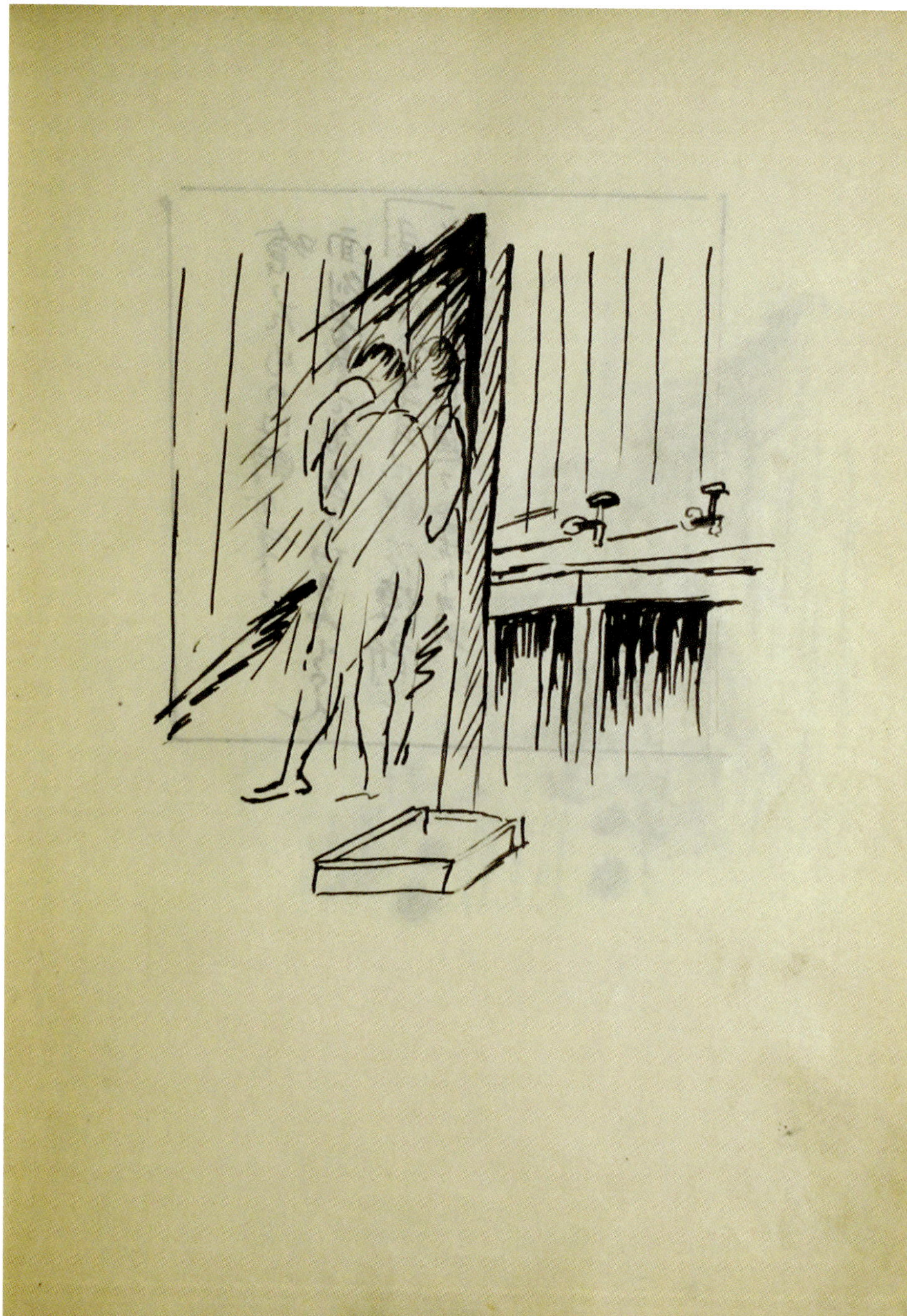

11 A great many people were noisy, just like at the carnival for the Bon Festival. This [sketch] shows a dirty, dirty shower room.

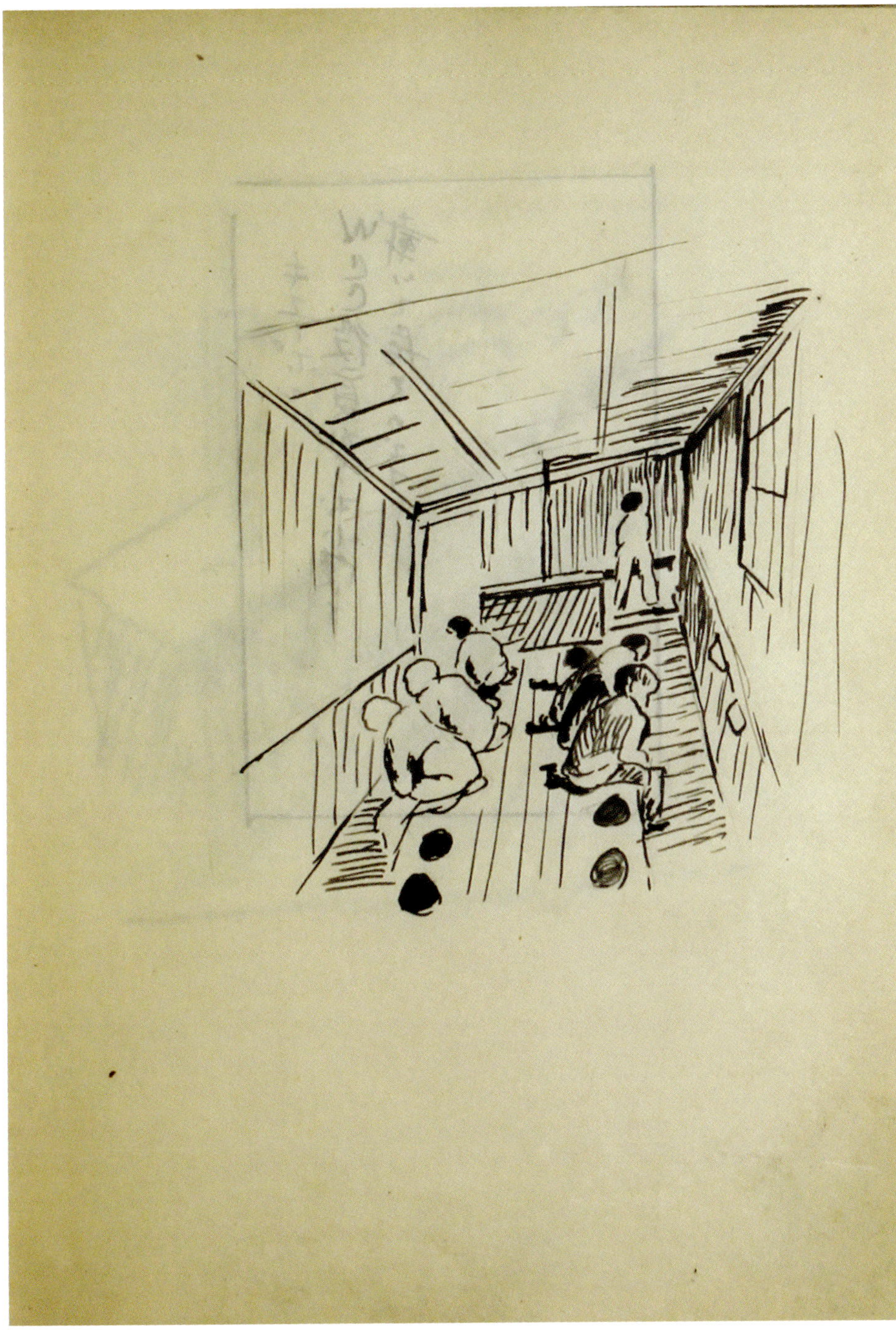

12 That which one has eaten, troublesome though it may be, we must in time put out. This is a waterwheel-style toilet. The waterwheel is always turning.

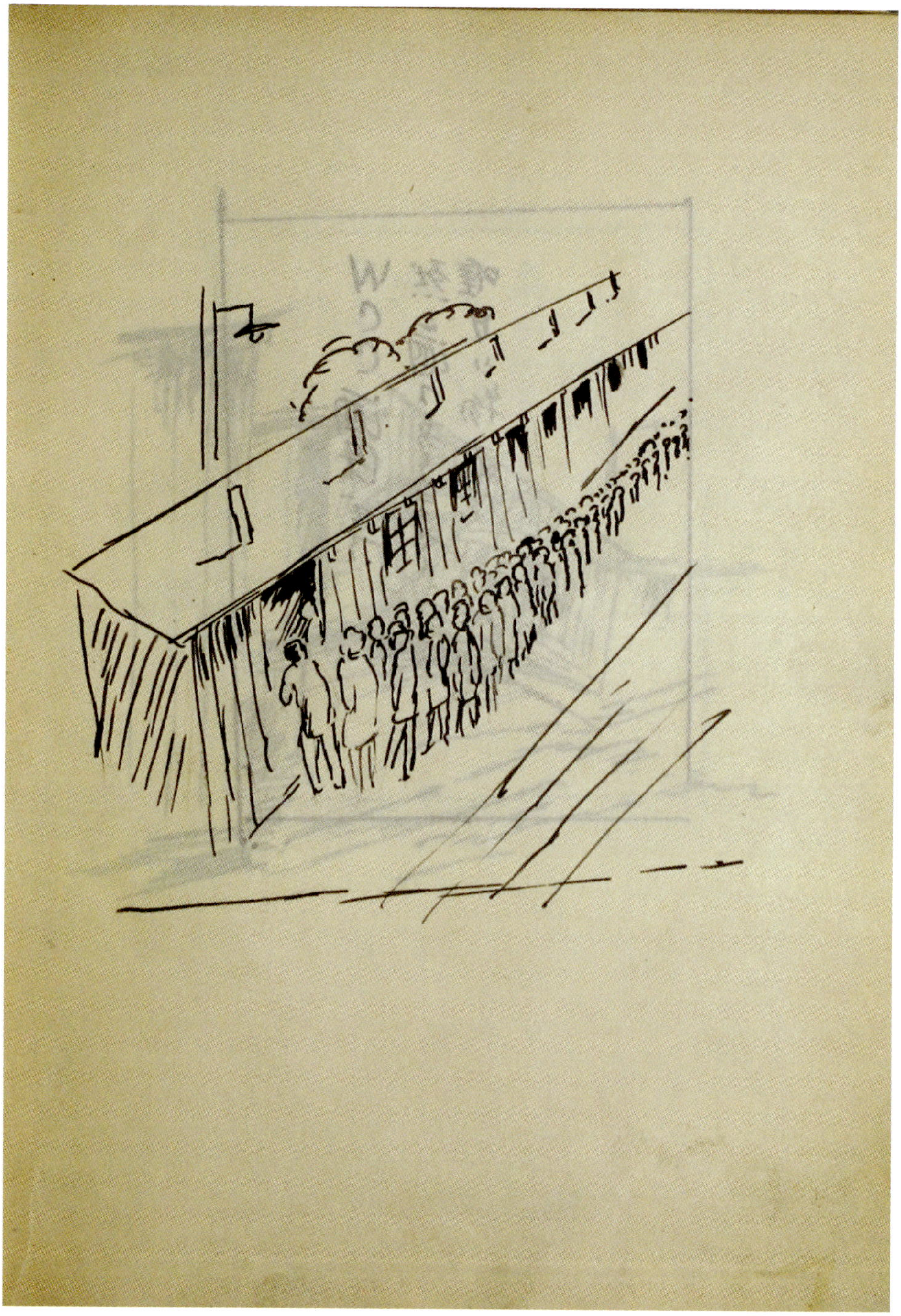

13 Coupons—we are receiving our allowance from a WCC [Wartime Civil Control Administration] person.

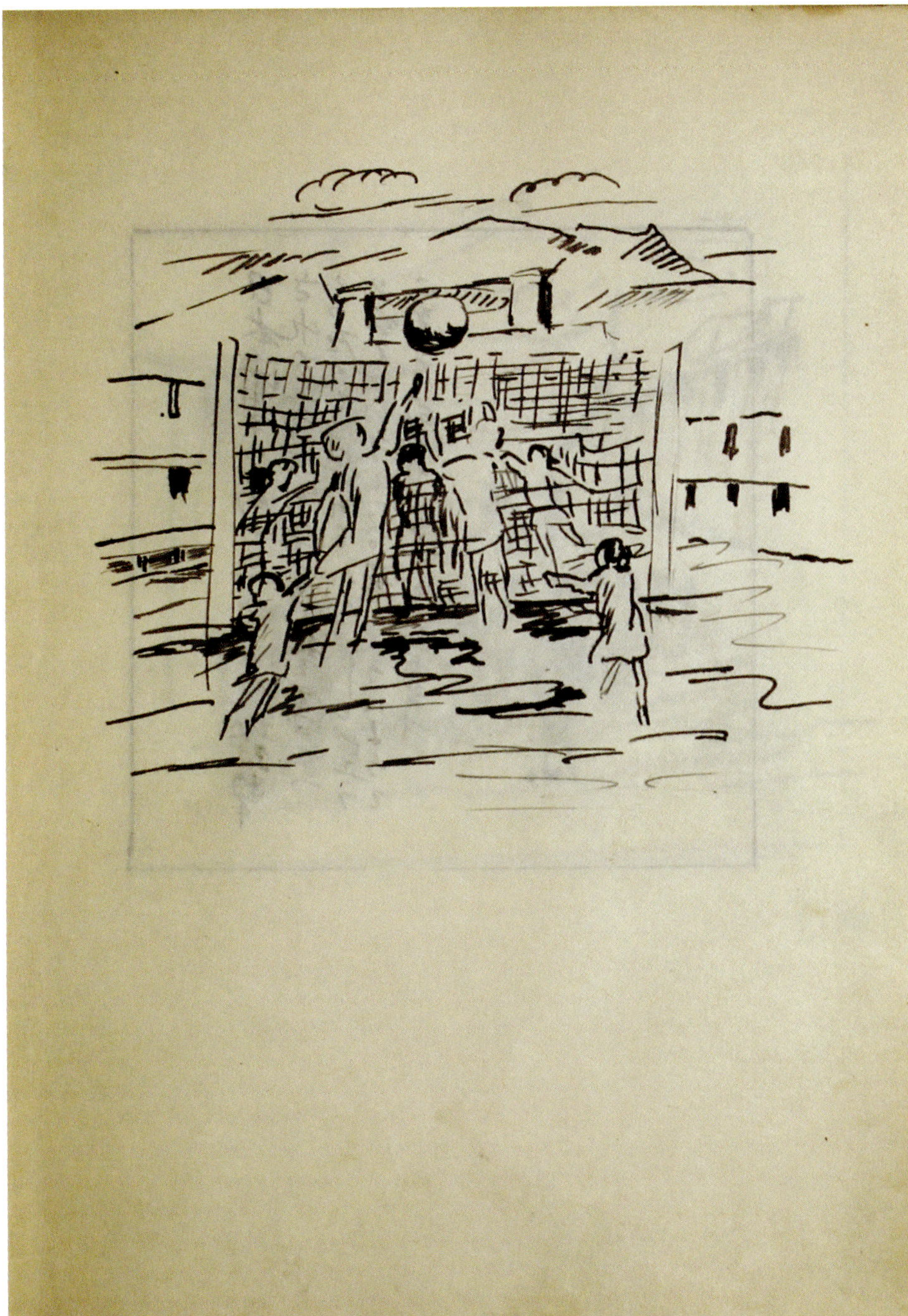

14 The children play heartily every day.

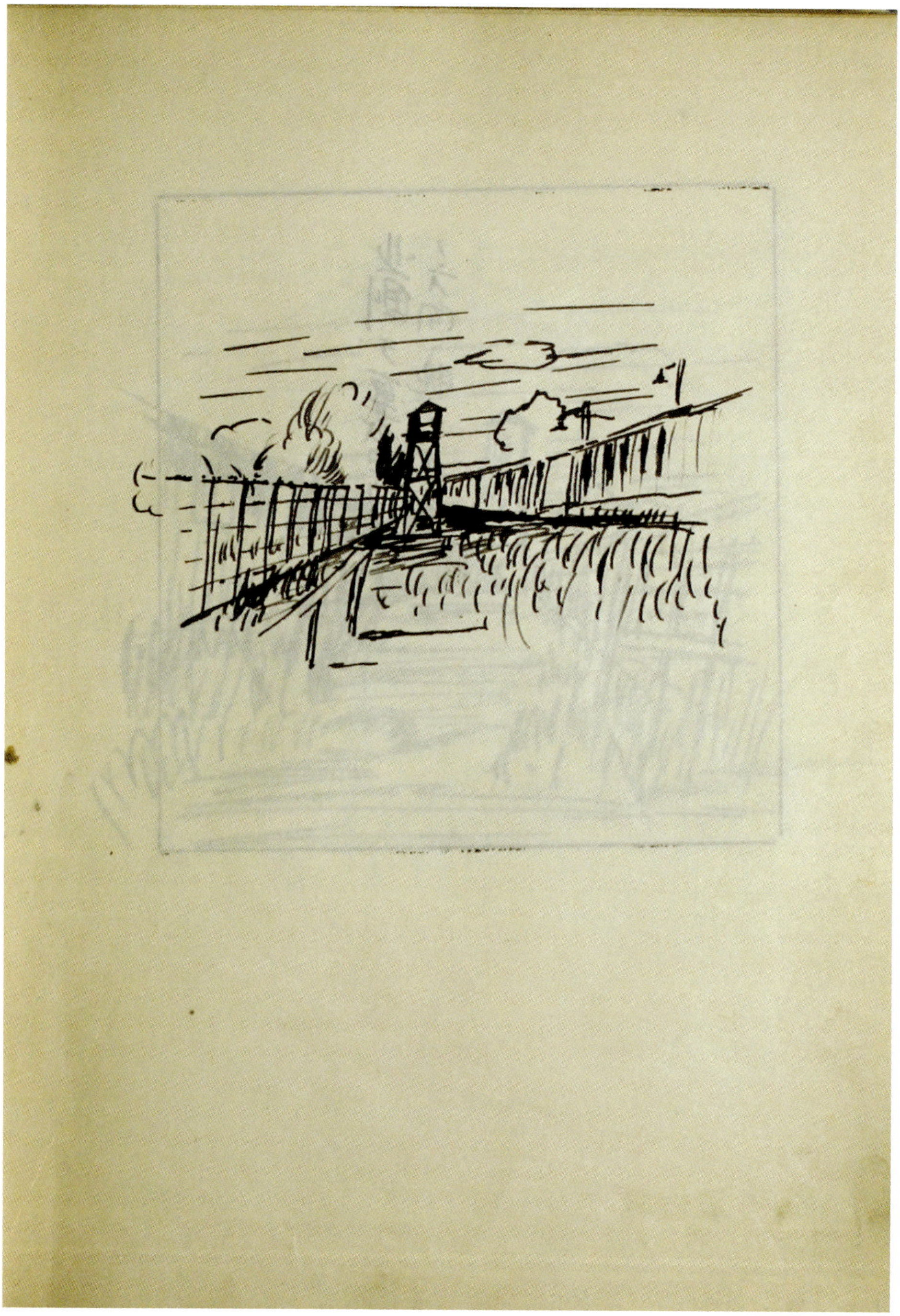

15 The south side of the camp: the place where there was a tall watchtower.

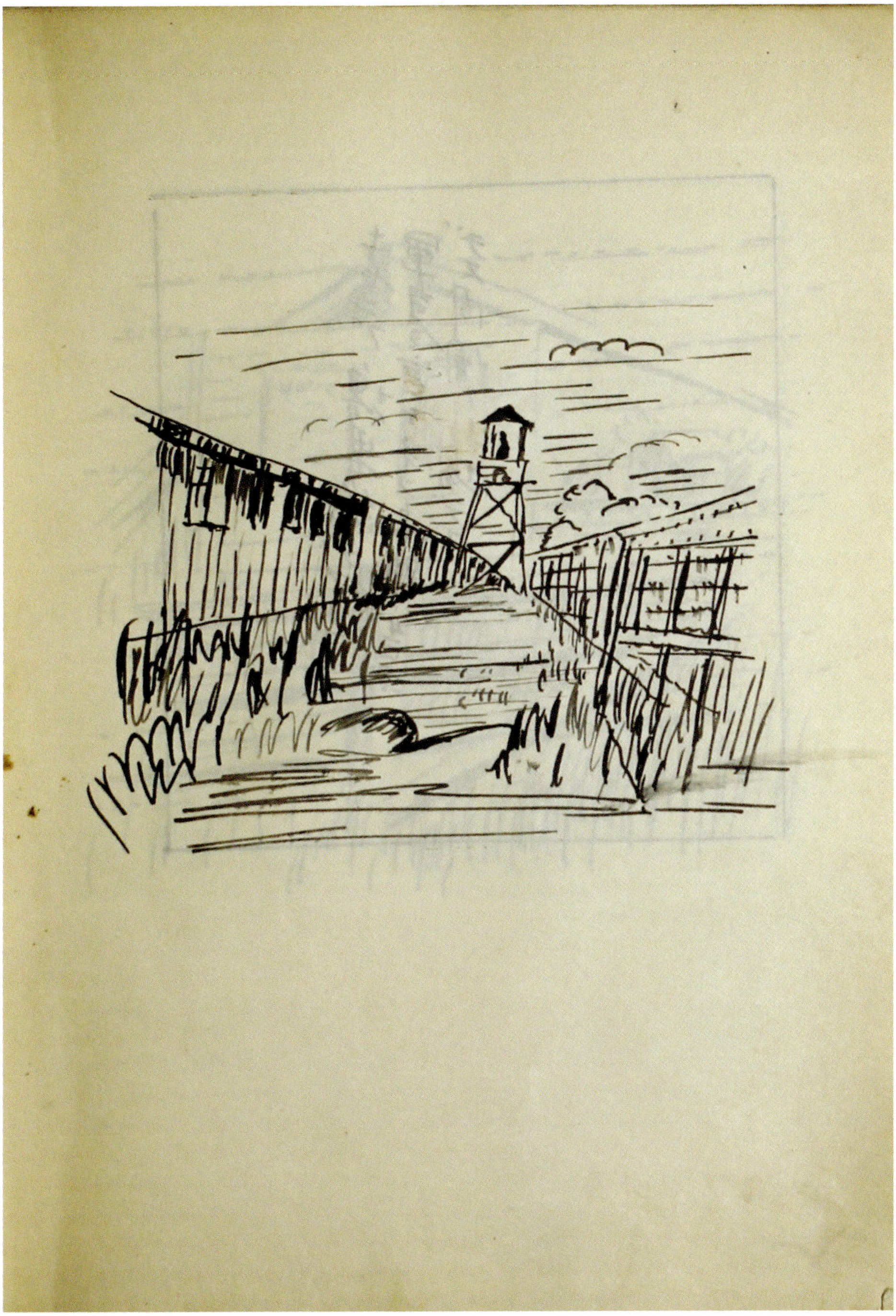

16 In the north: looking in the direction of the front gate from the back.

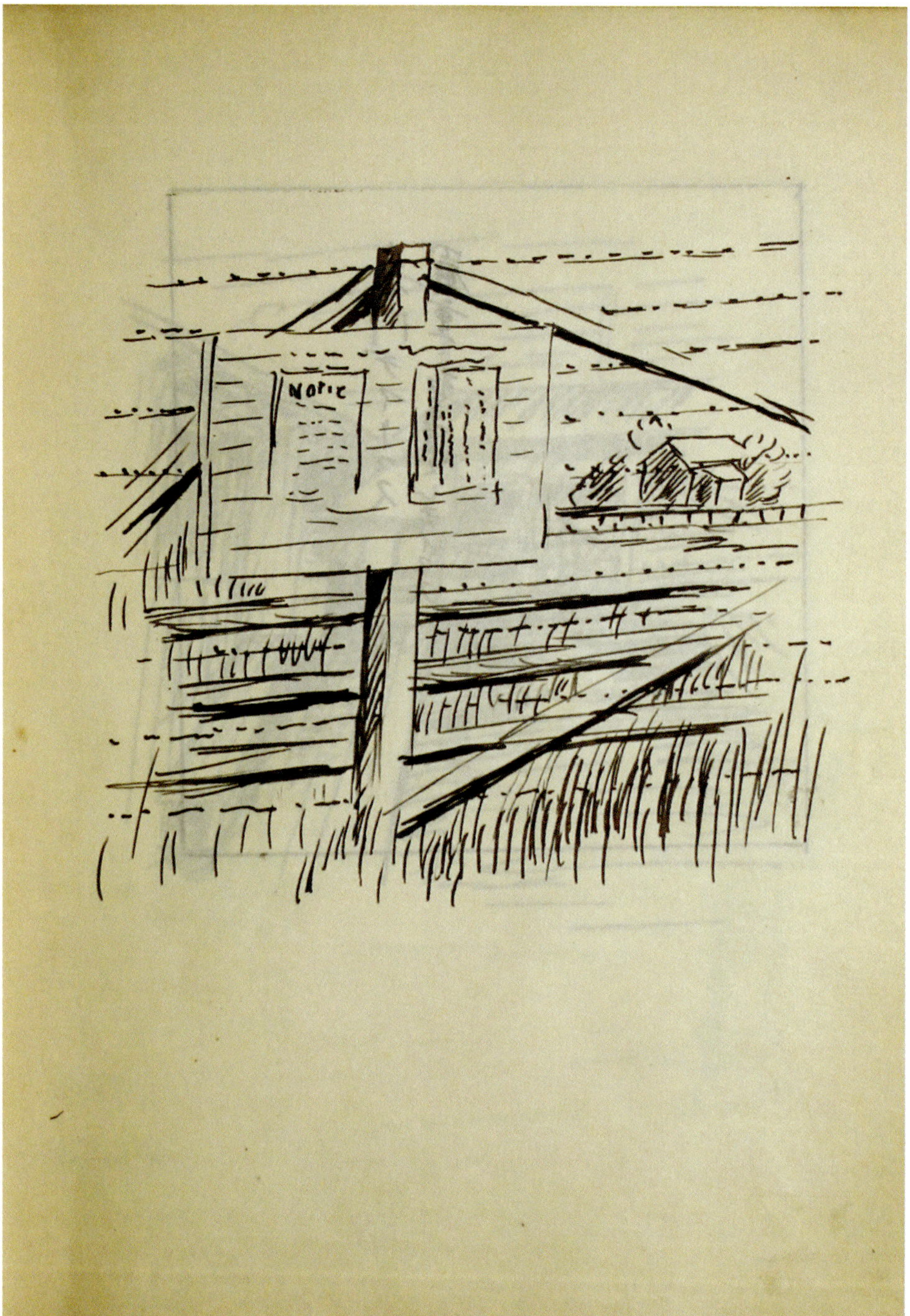

17 This is the border of the camp. This is an announcement from Lieutenant General DeWitt. These are . . . the surroundings.

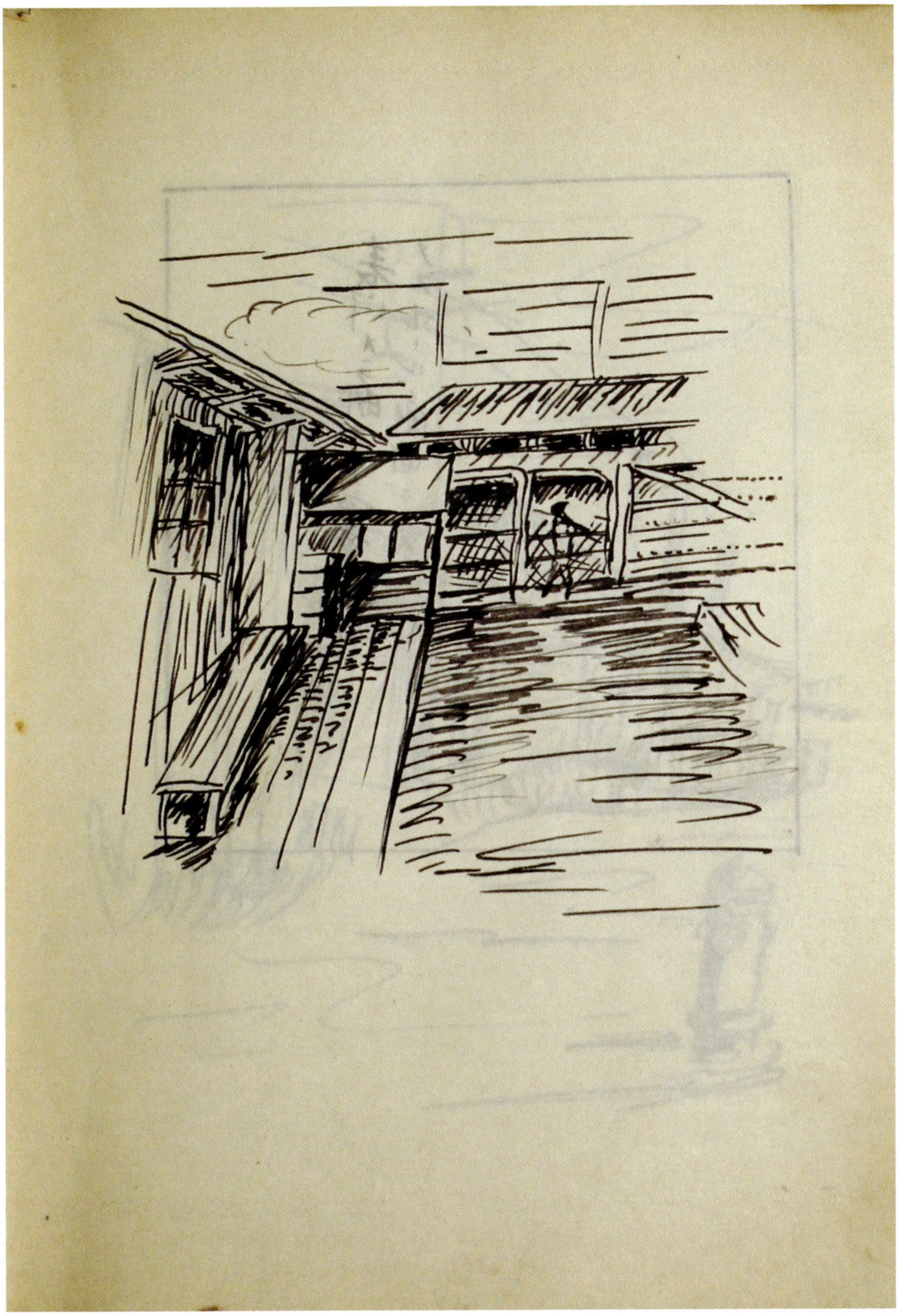

18 This is the front gate. It was strictly guarded.

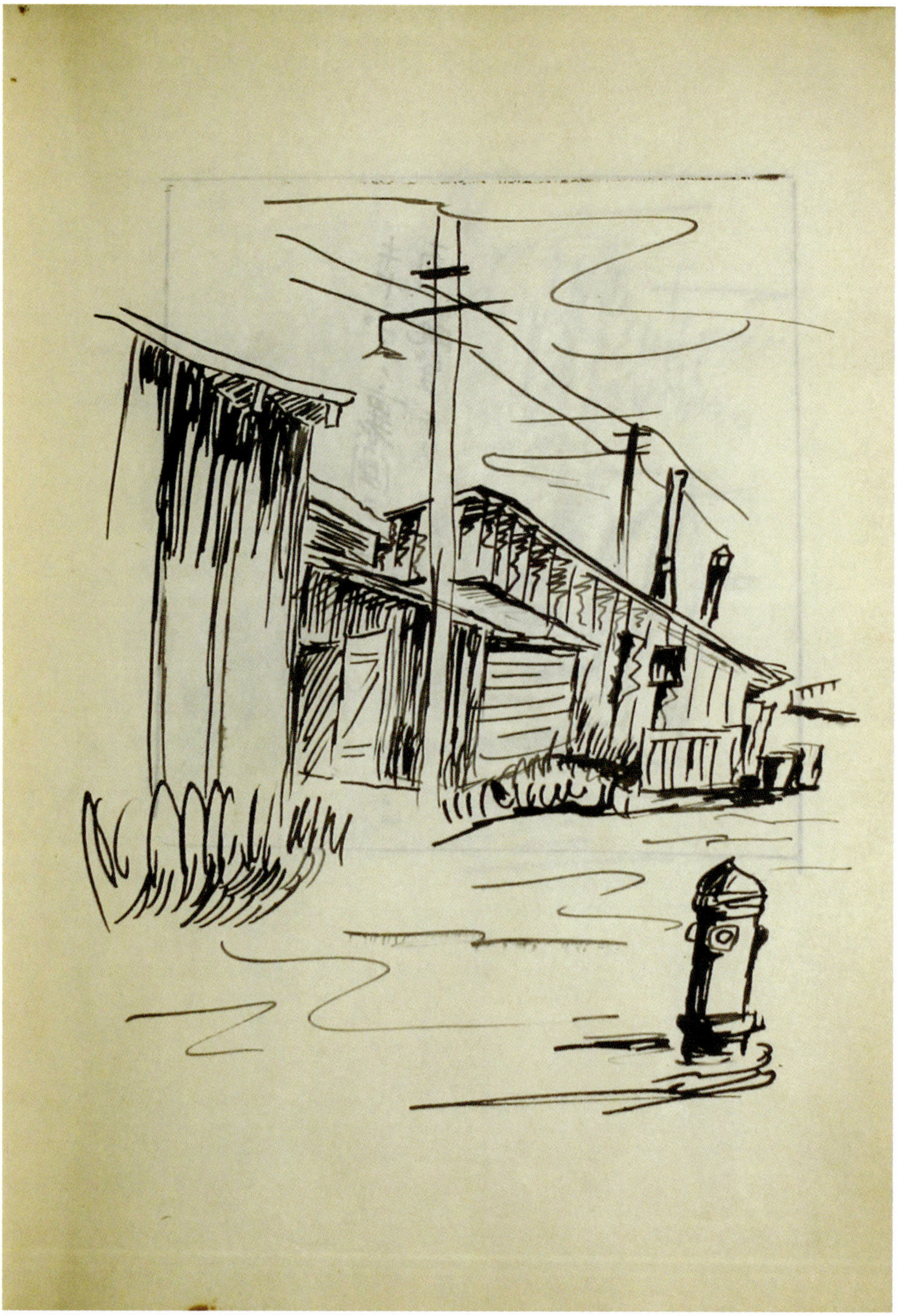

19 The back street seen from the front gate. The side of the mess hall.

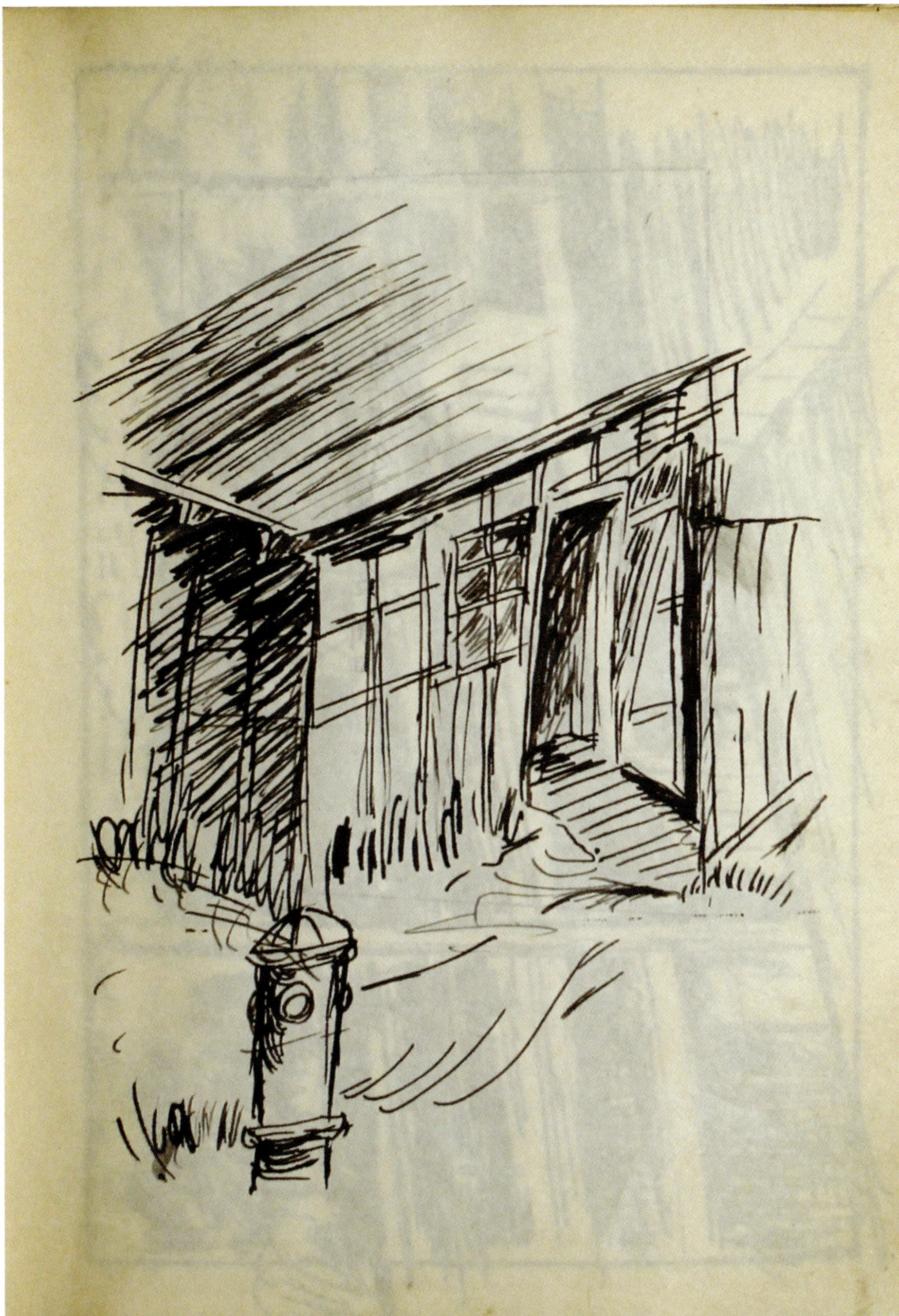

20 This is the shower hut. In the B Area, there were three such structures. Because this region had only a small population and suddenly a great number of people had been gathered here, there were problems with the sewage system every day.

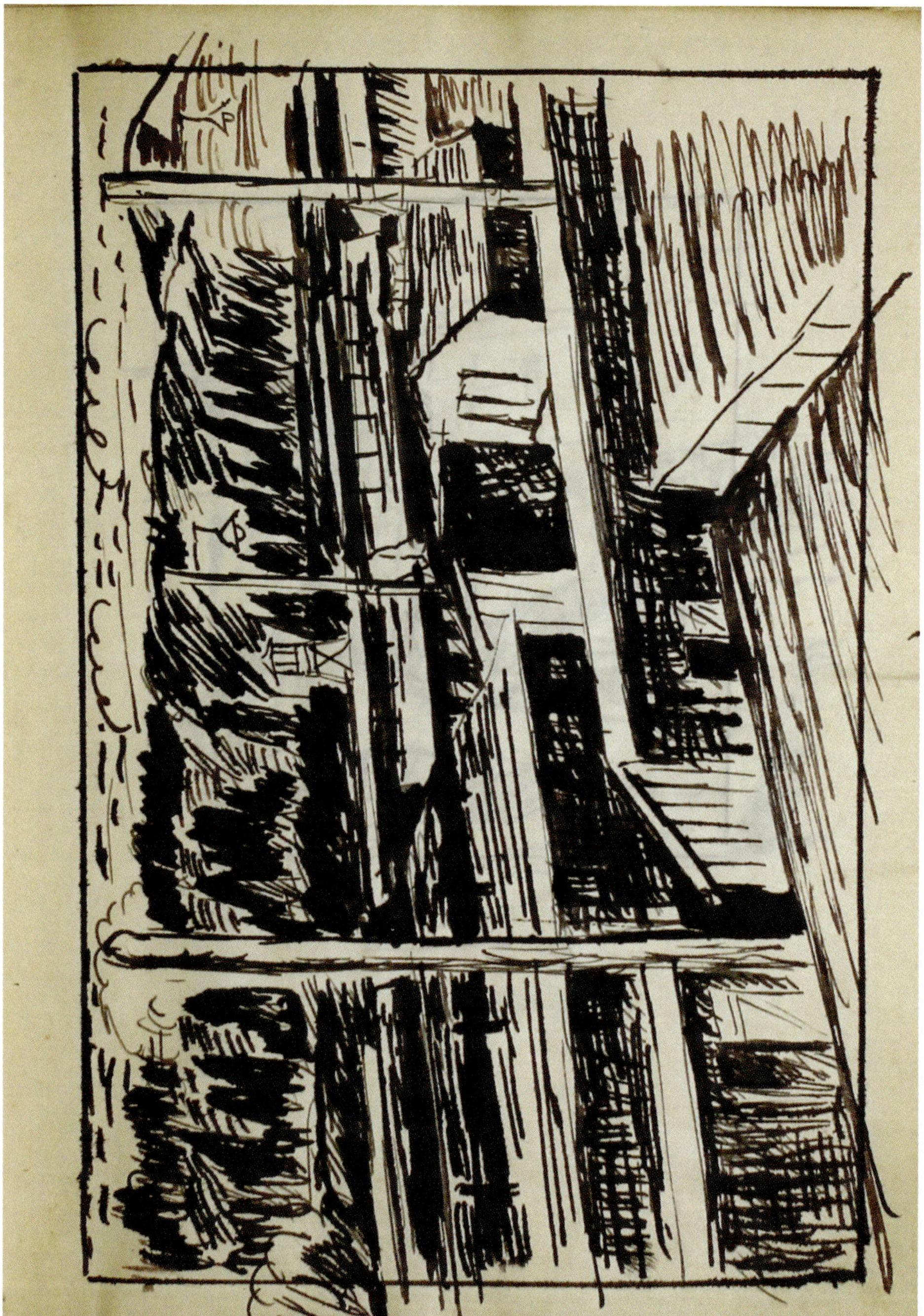

21 This is a view of the camp from a rooftop.

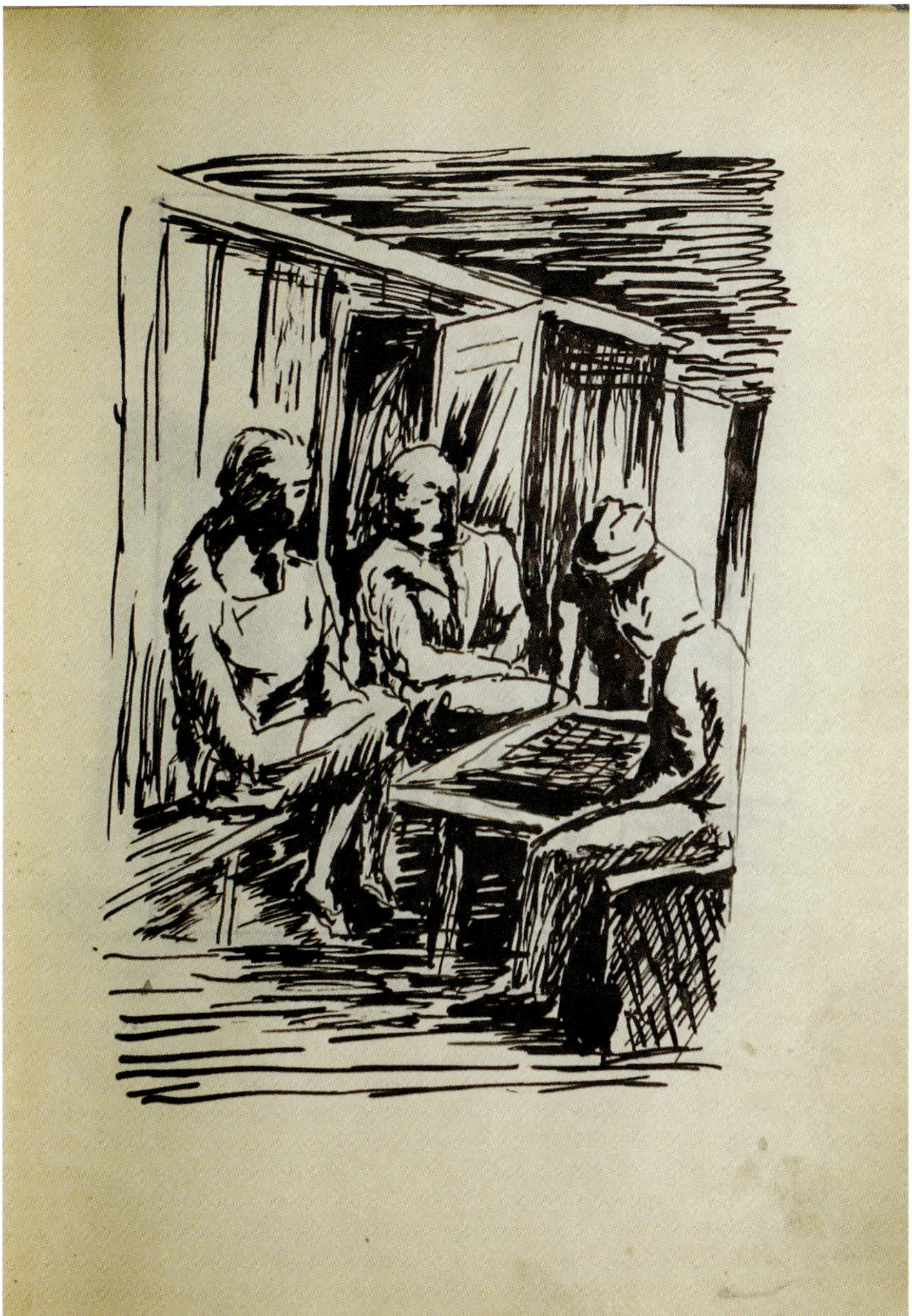

22 Game of checkers.

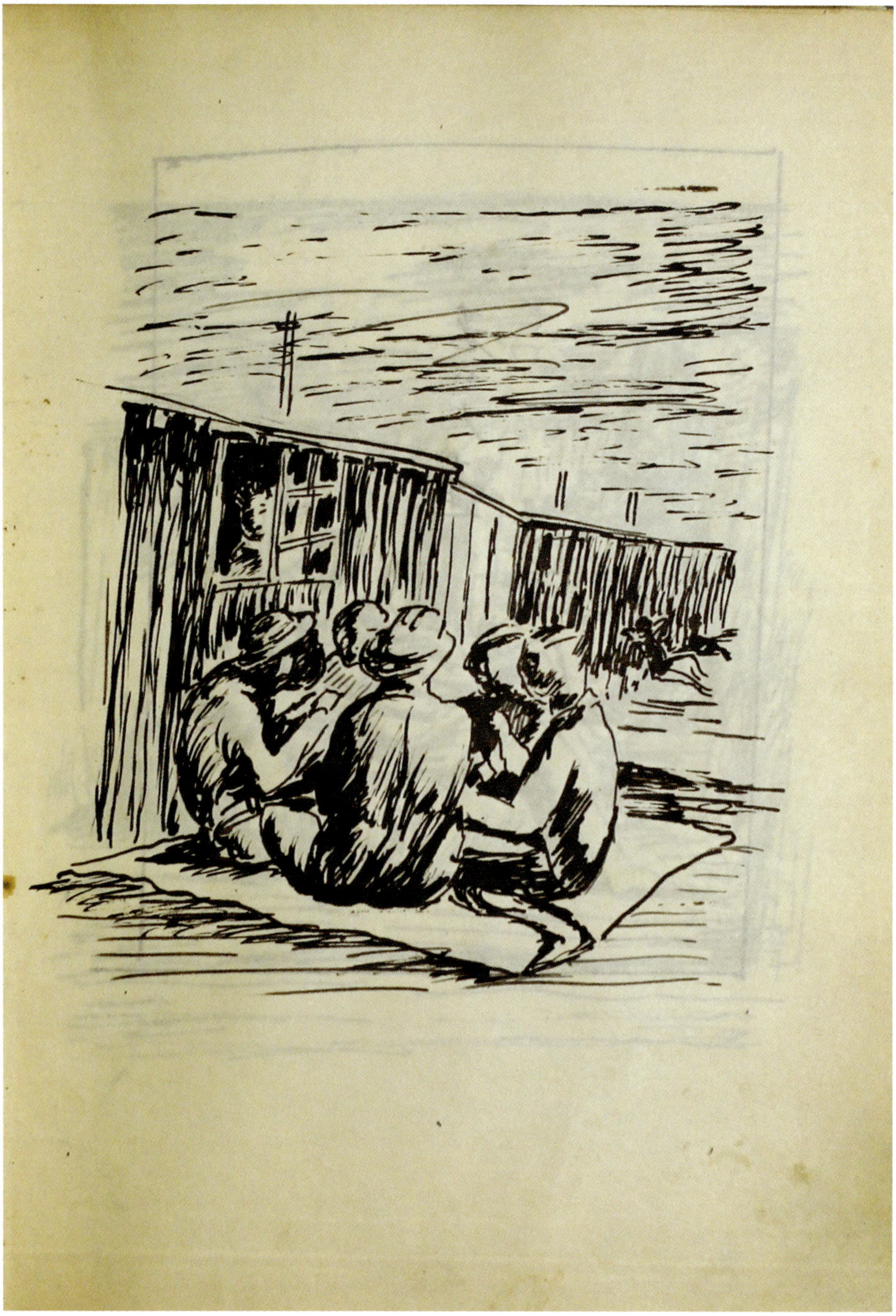

23 Young adults.

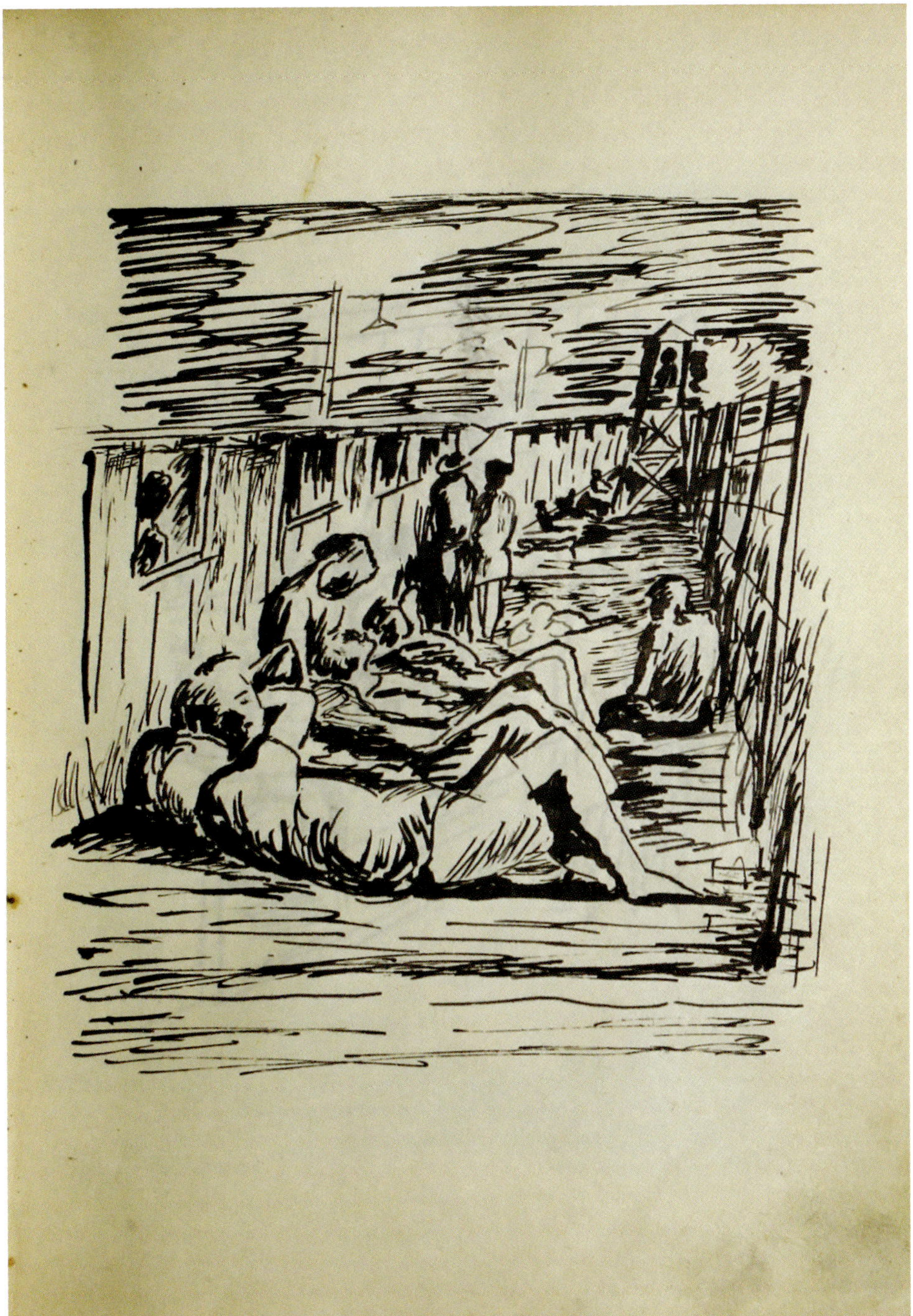

24 Young people.

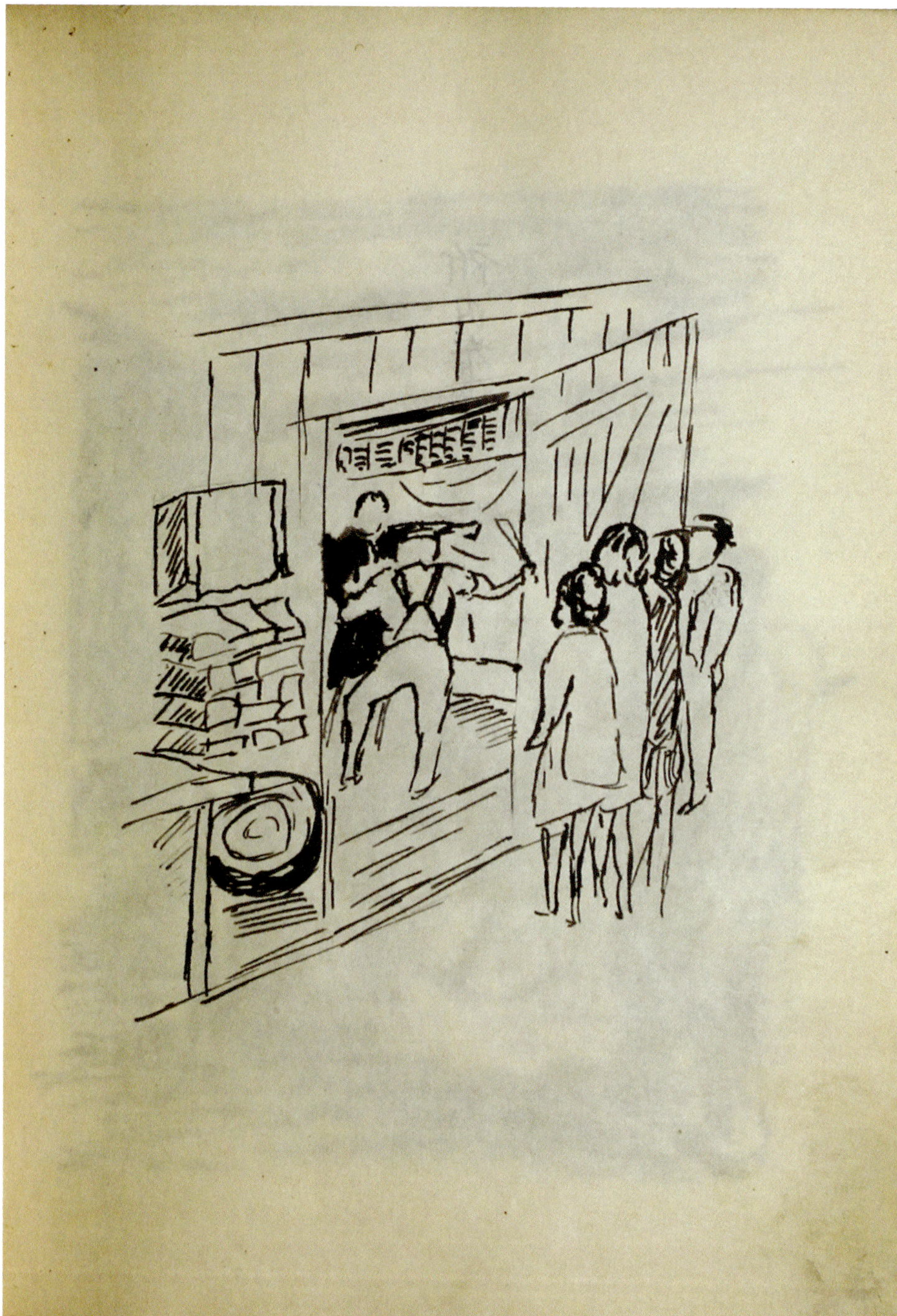

25 A fight at home.

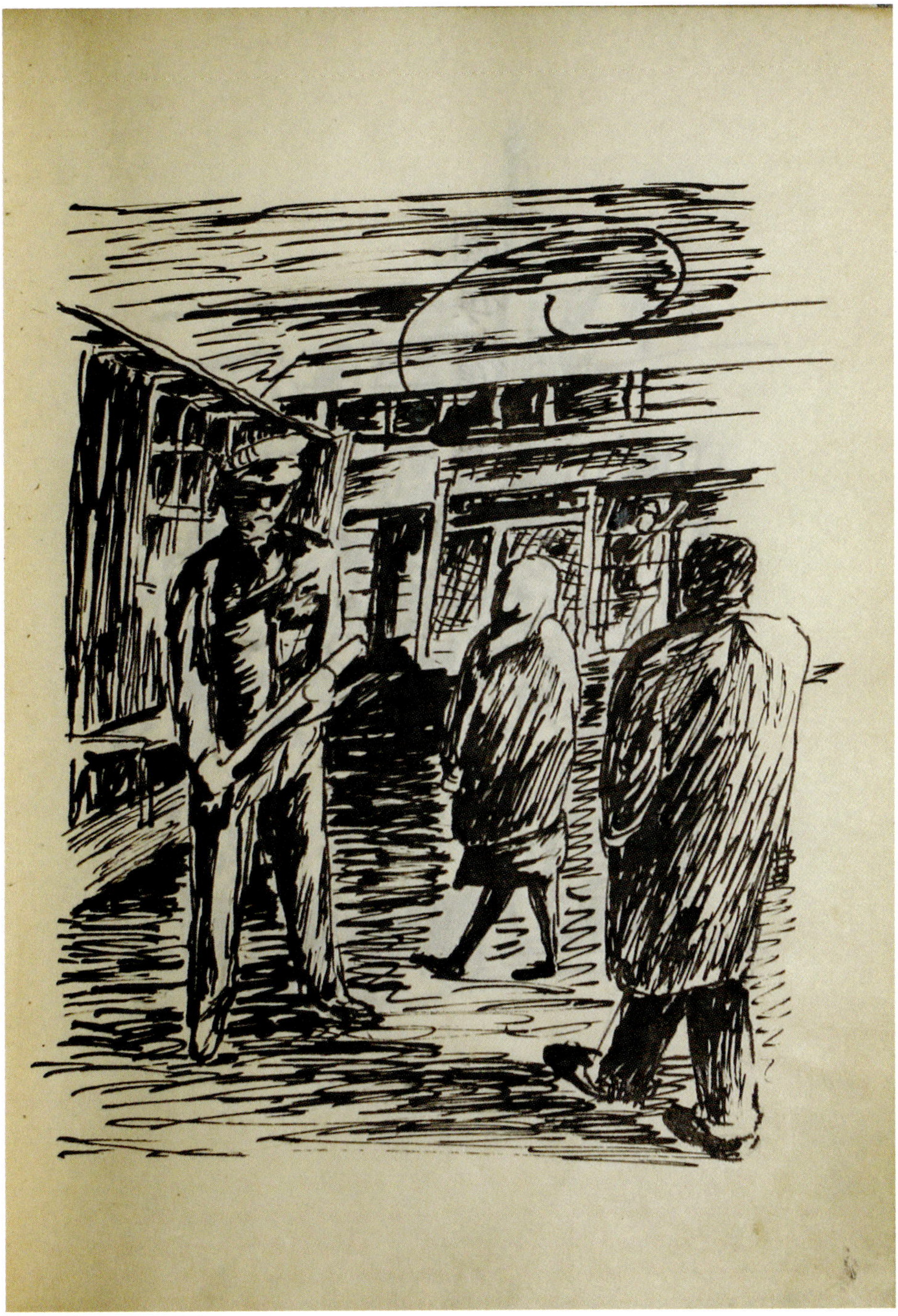

26 Camp guard.

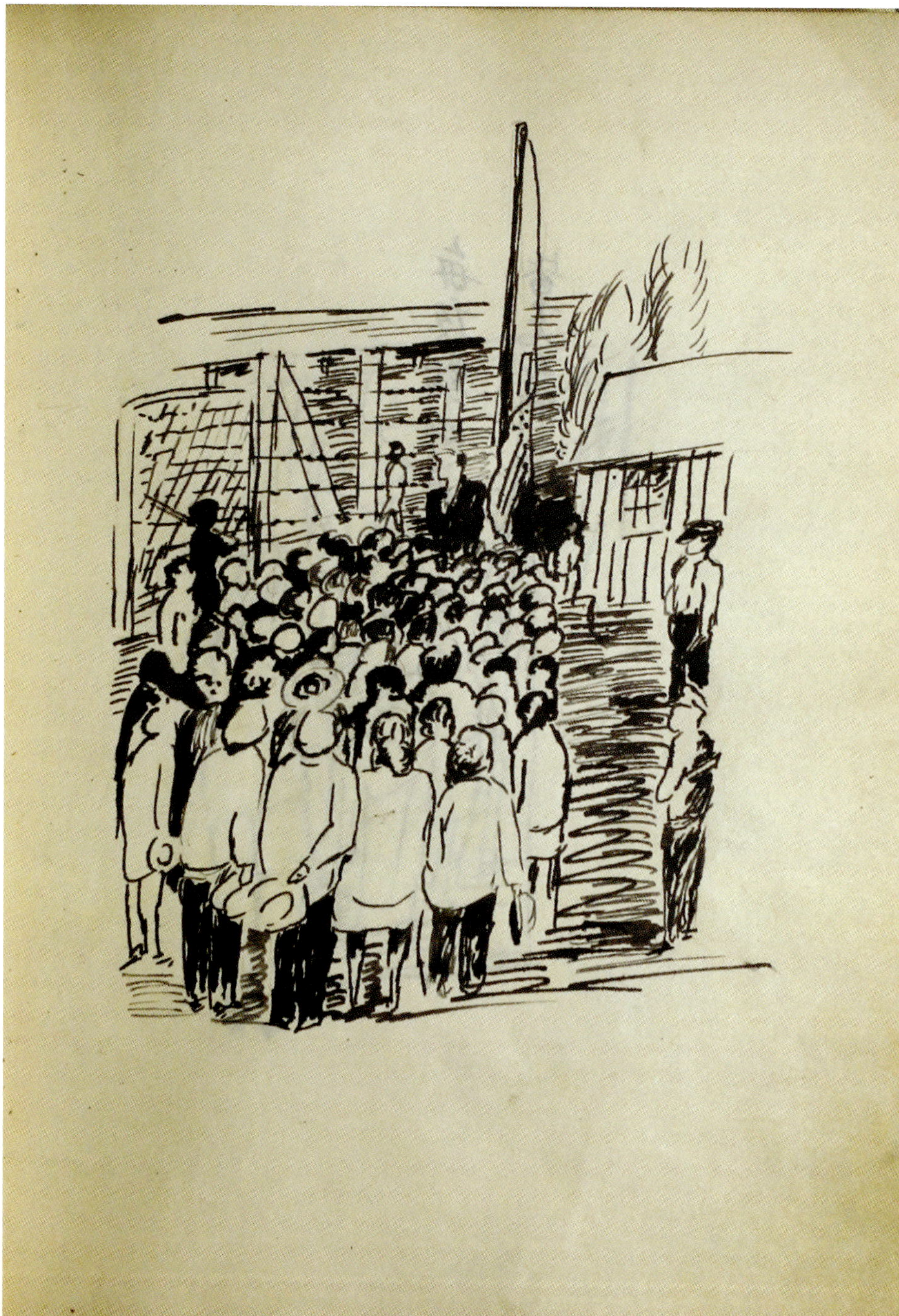

27 Raising the national flag.

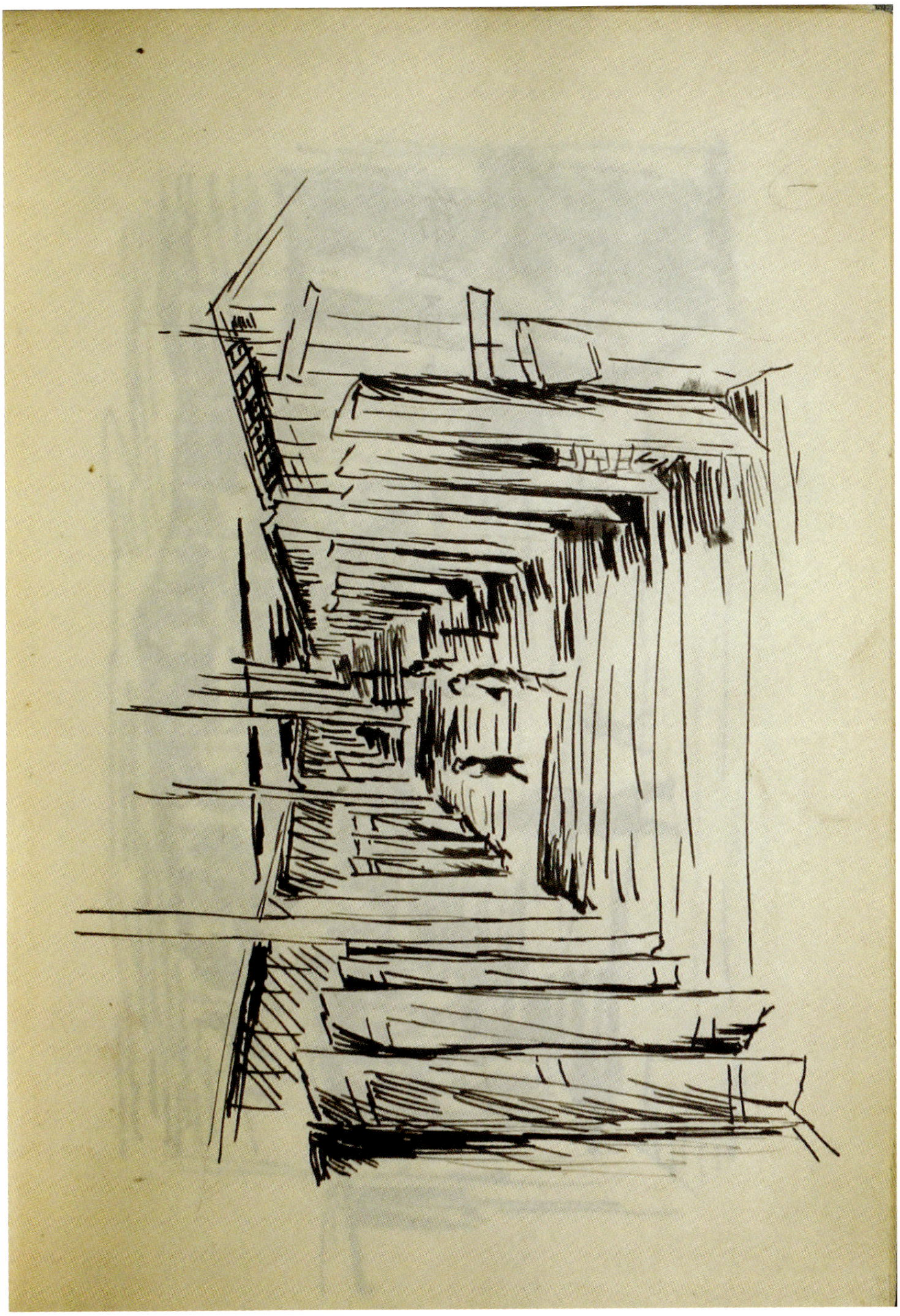

28 First Street.

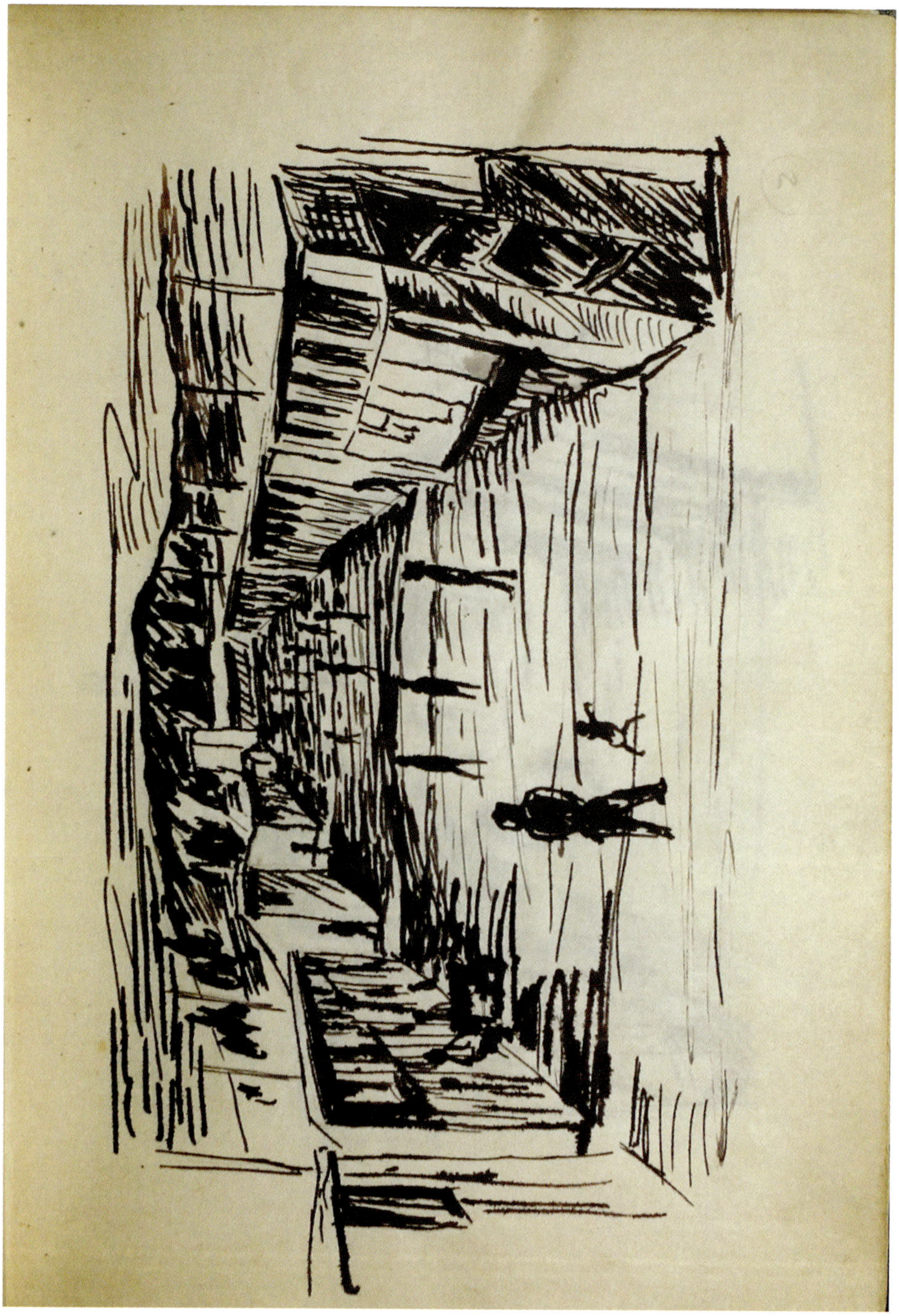

29 Third Street.

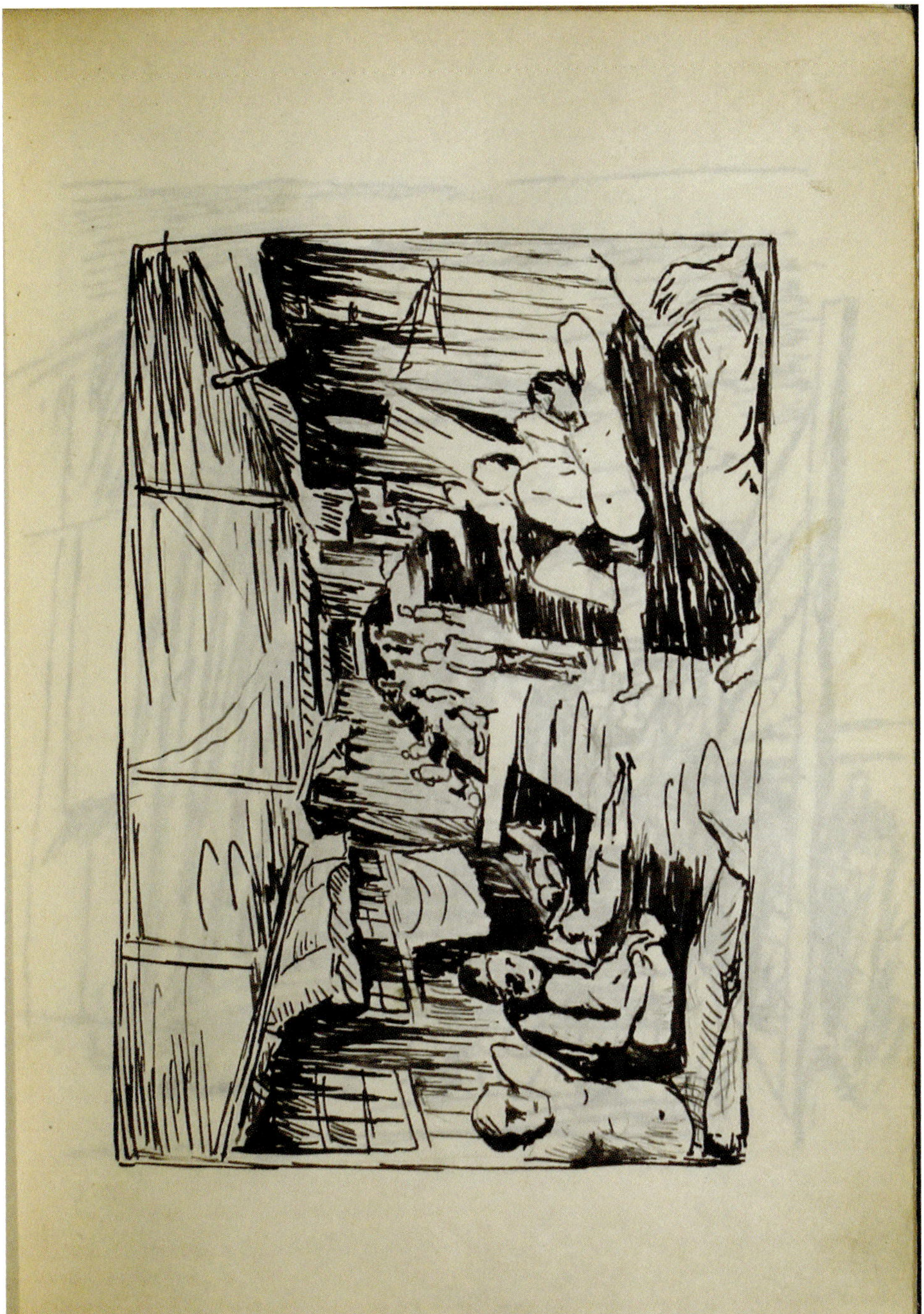

30 An afternoon in the middle of summer.

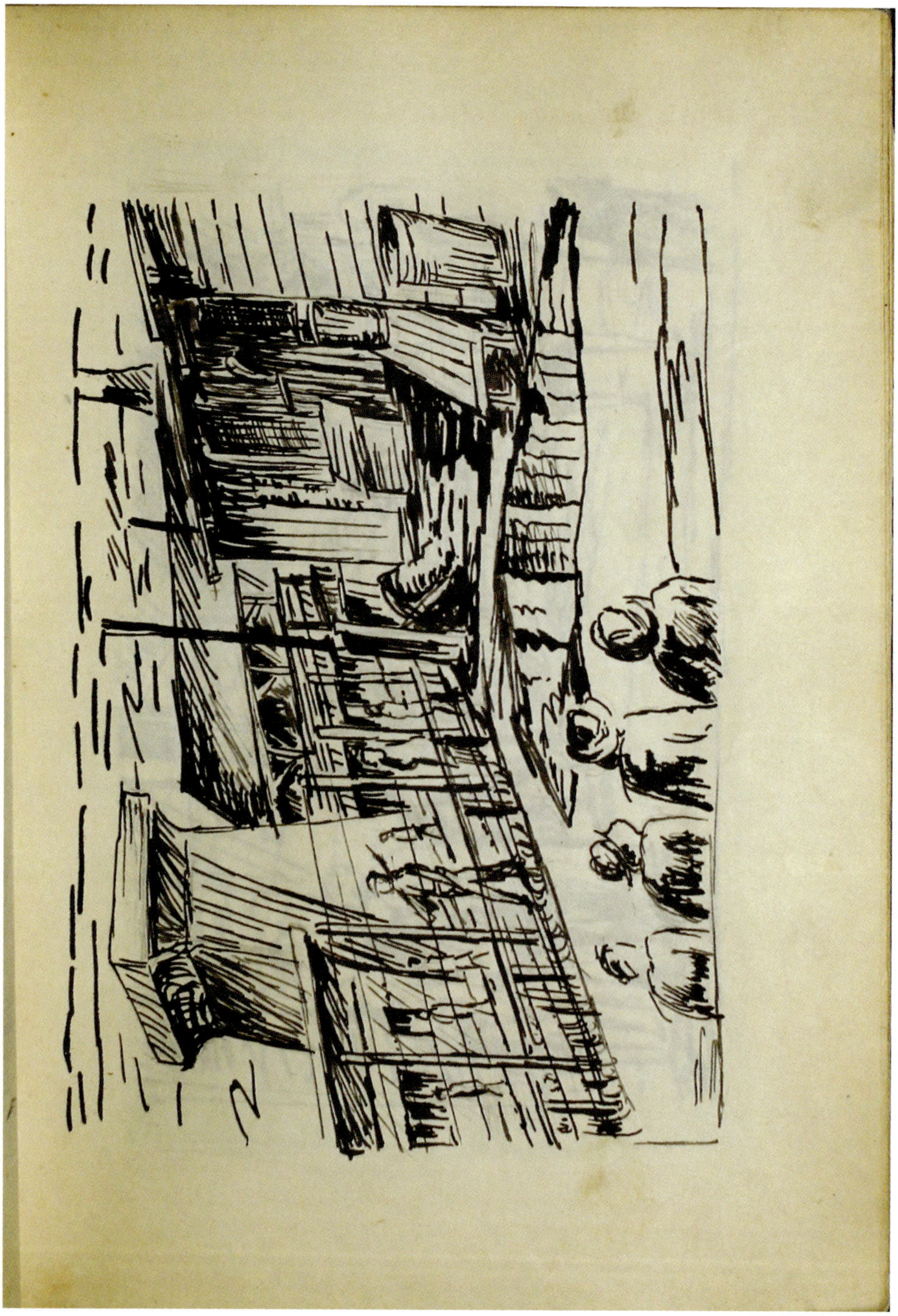

31 The mess hall after rain.

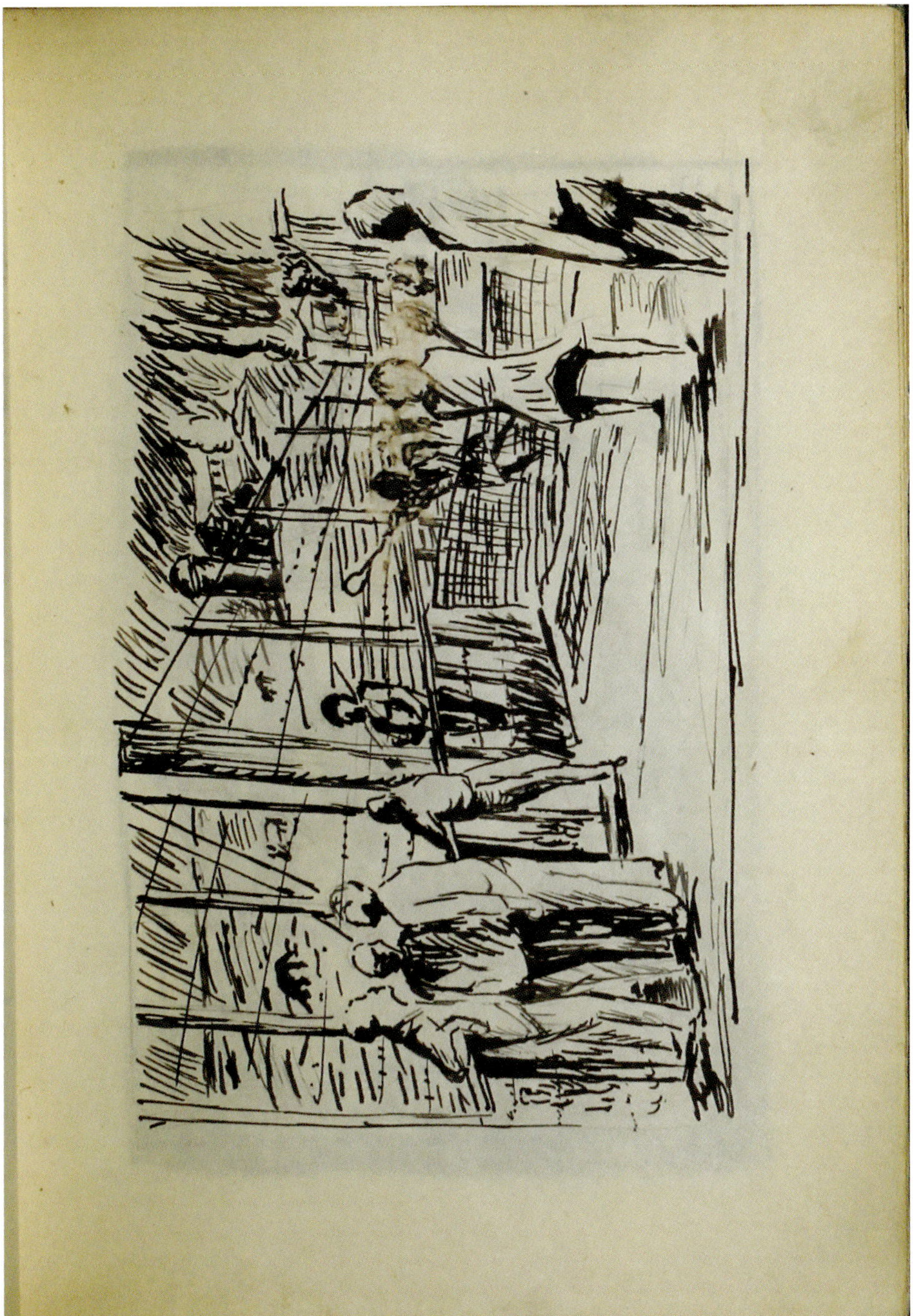

32 One evening moment.

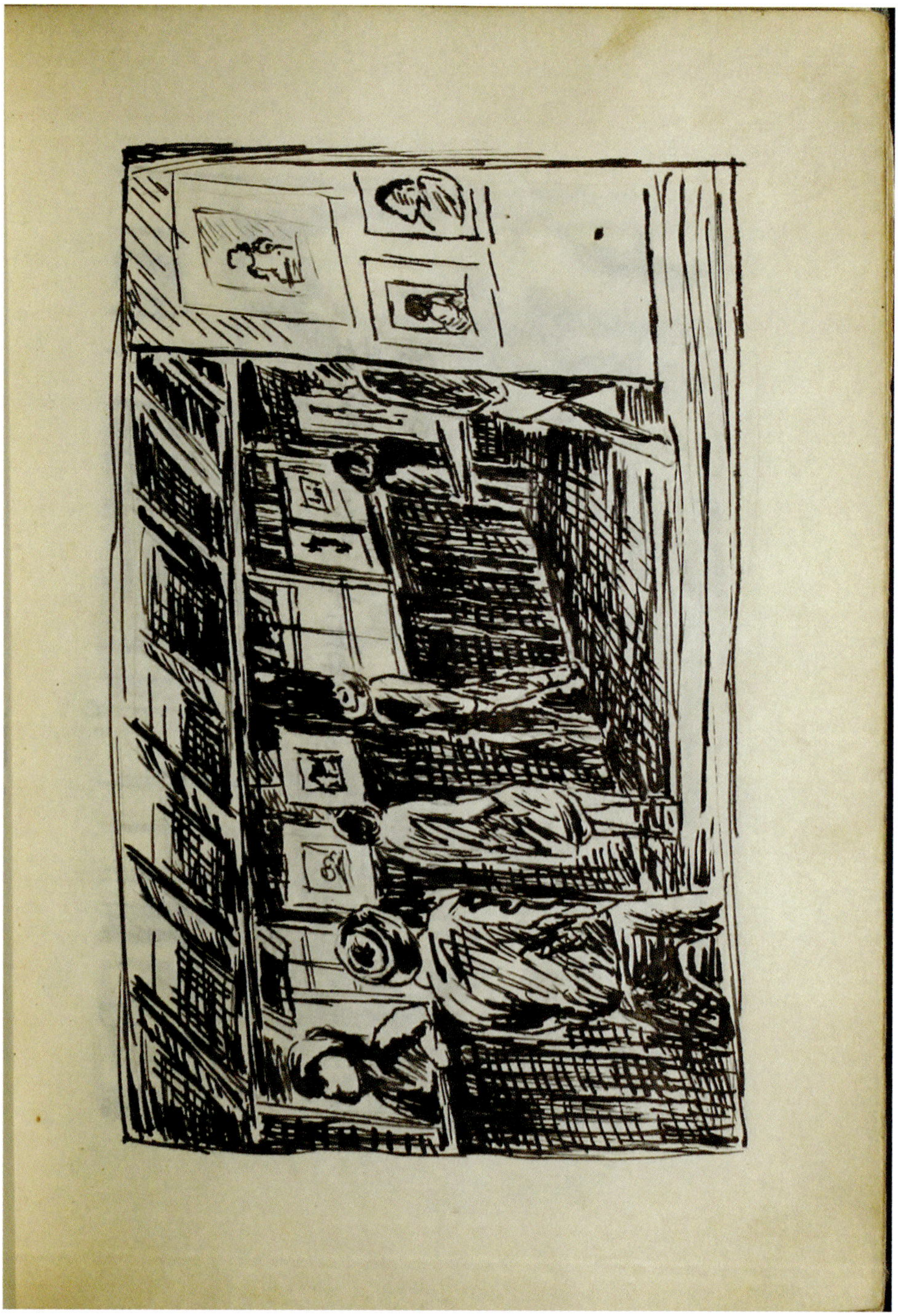

33 The painting exhibition hall.

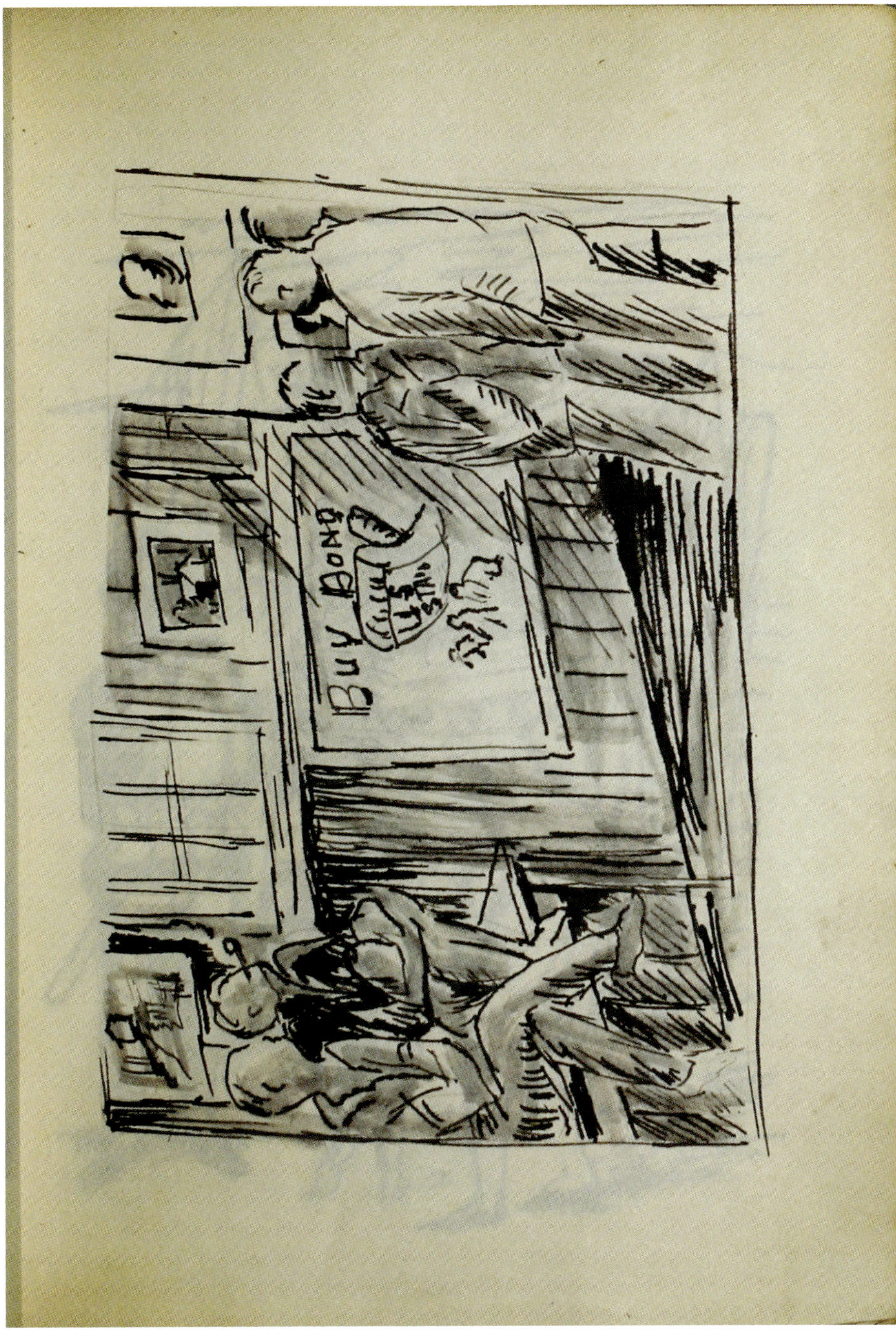

34 A work of art by a young Nisei that caused trouble.

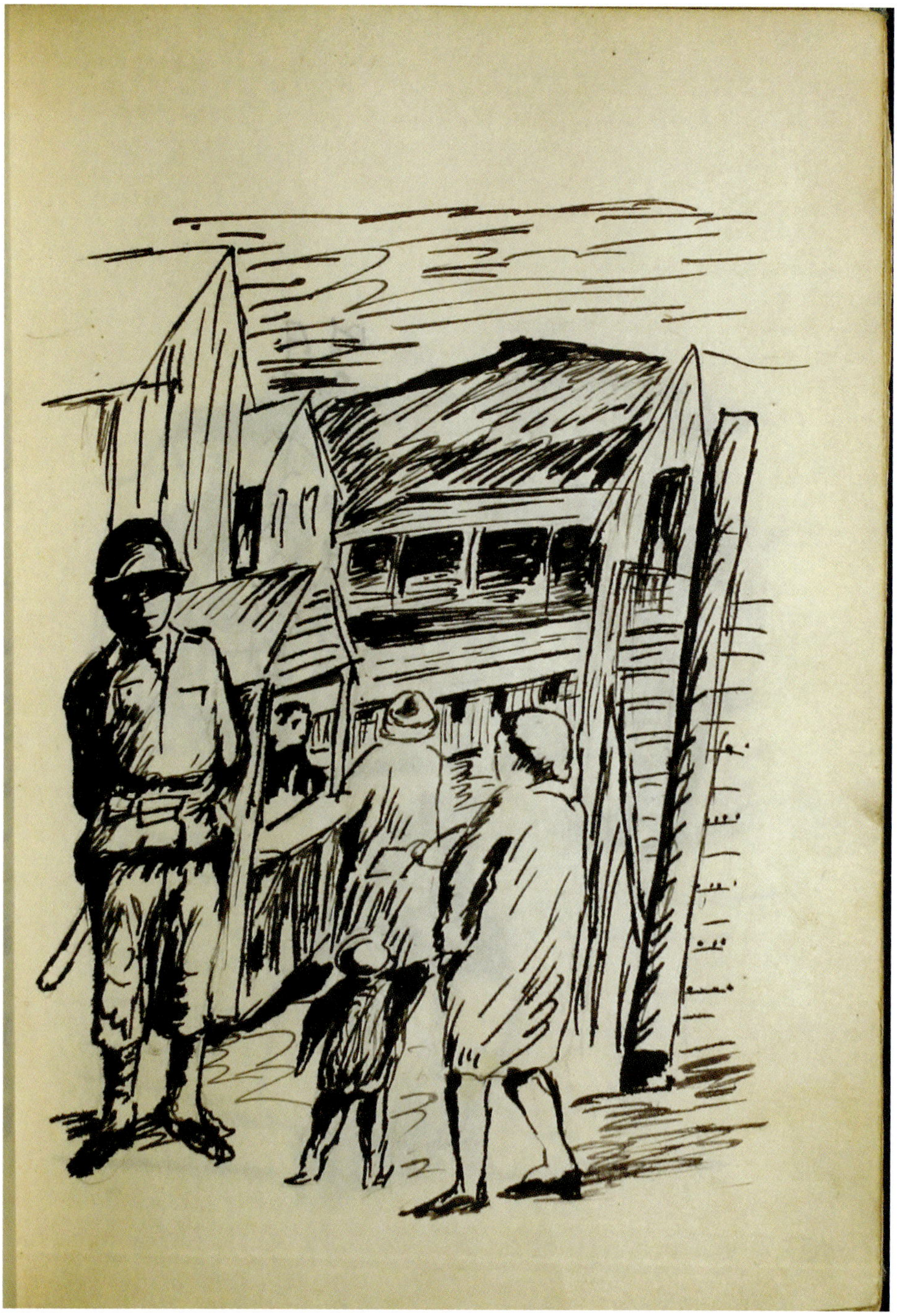

35 I went to visit a friend in Area D. Before, this area was the large yard of a local agricultural production promotion group.

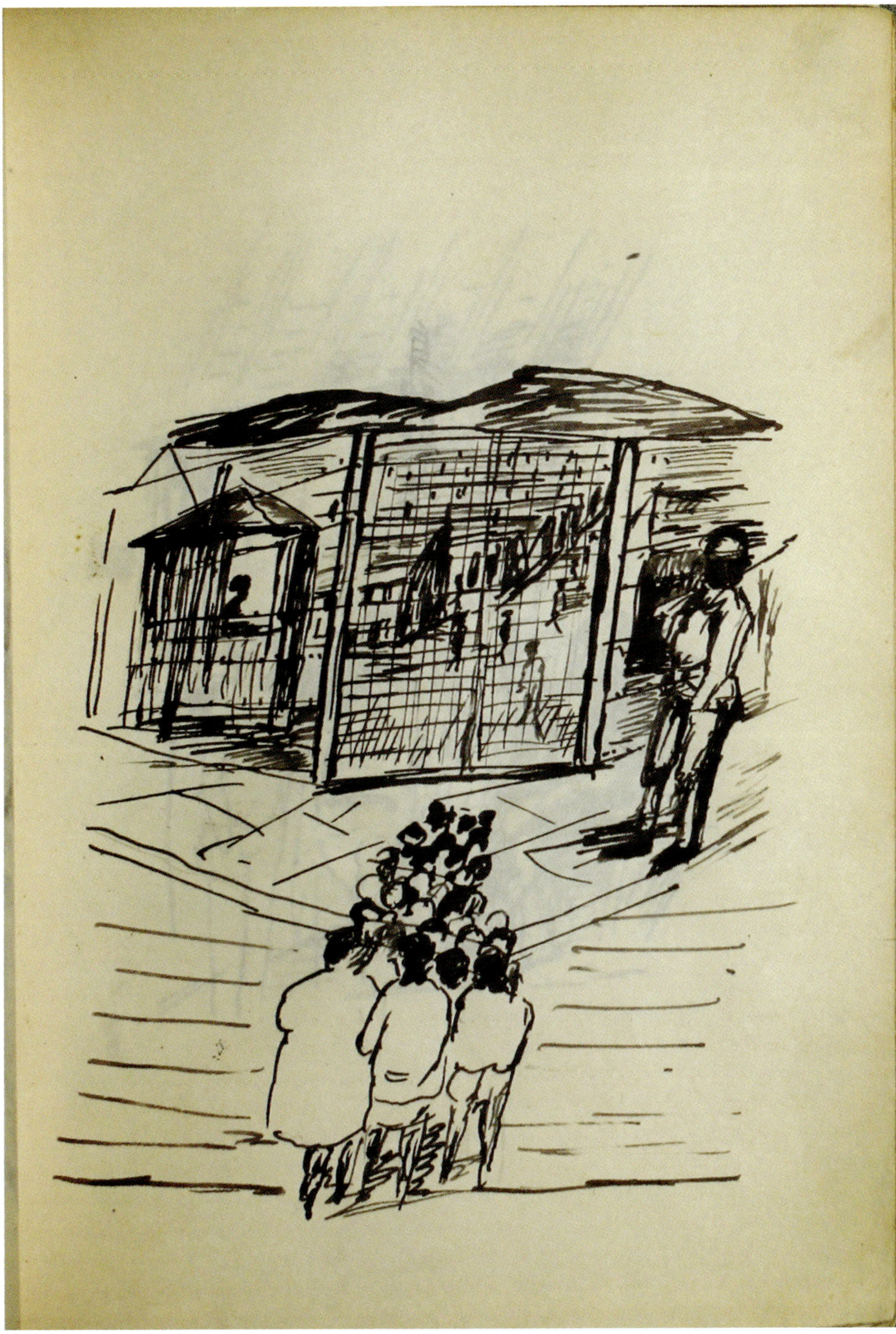

36 What it looked like when I visited a friend living in Area A.

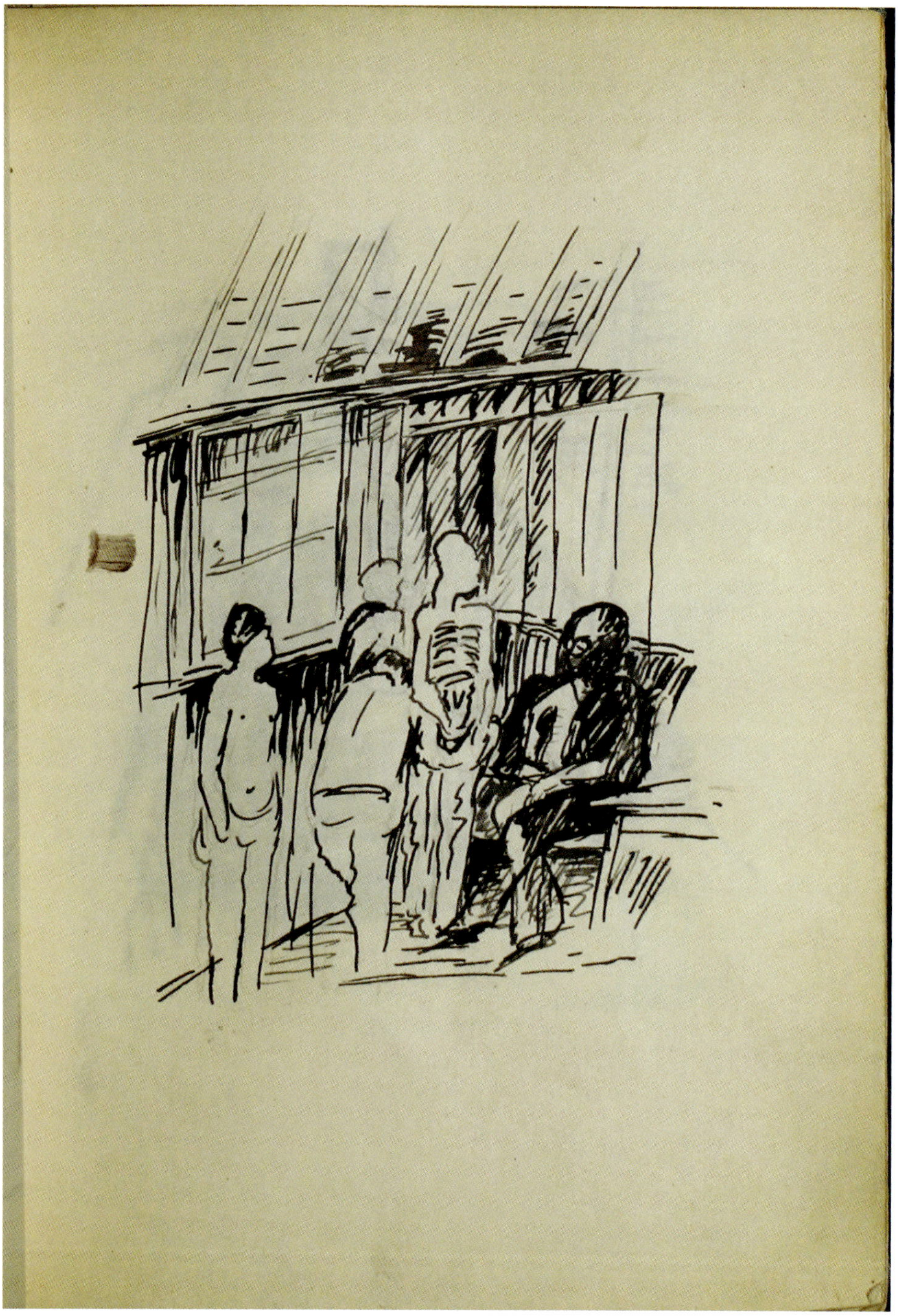

37 Health inspection.

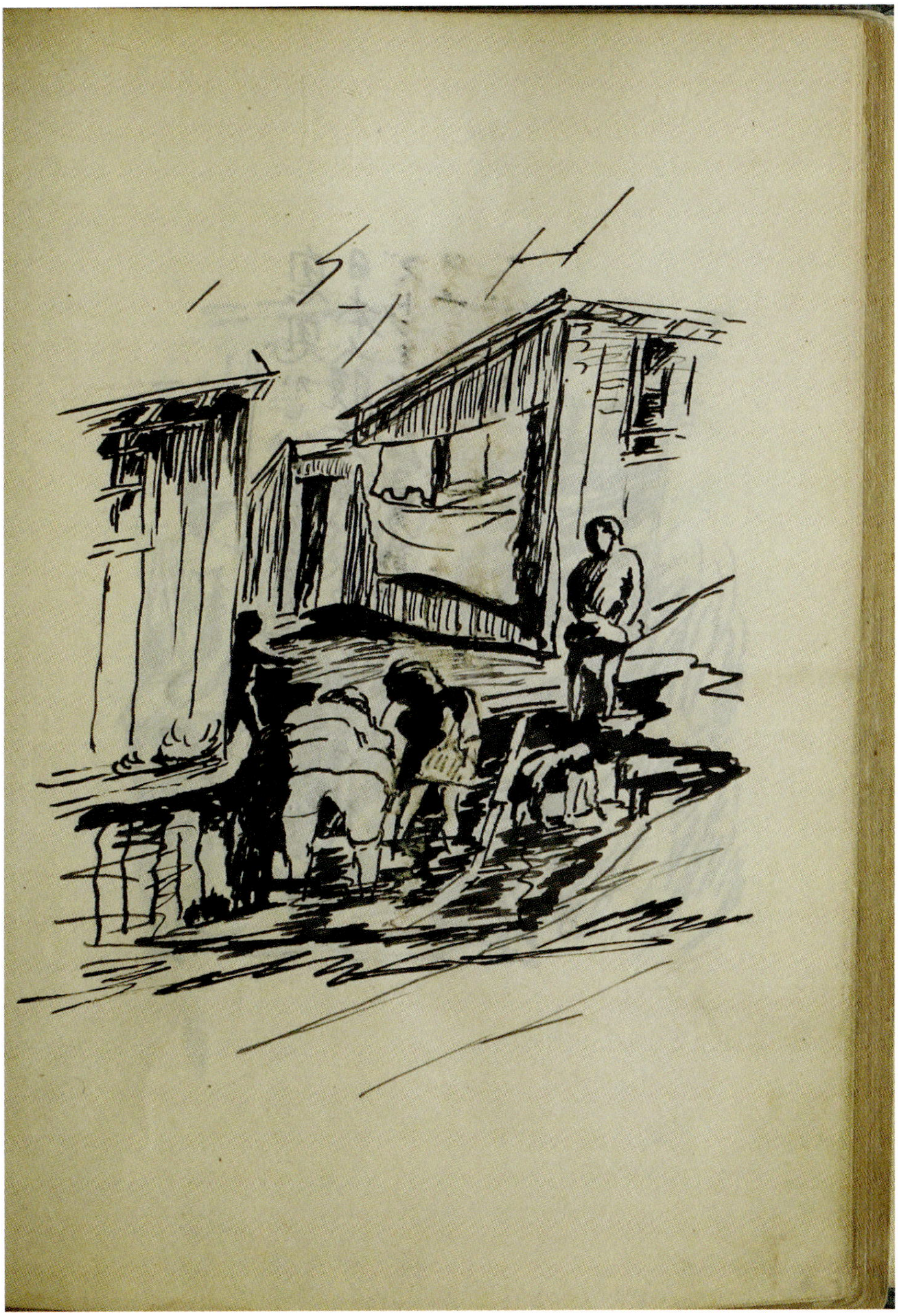

38 Children play in the water that accumulated after an afternoon rain.

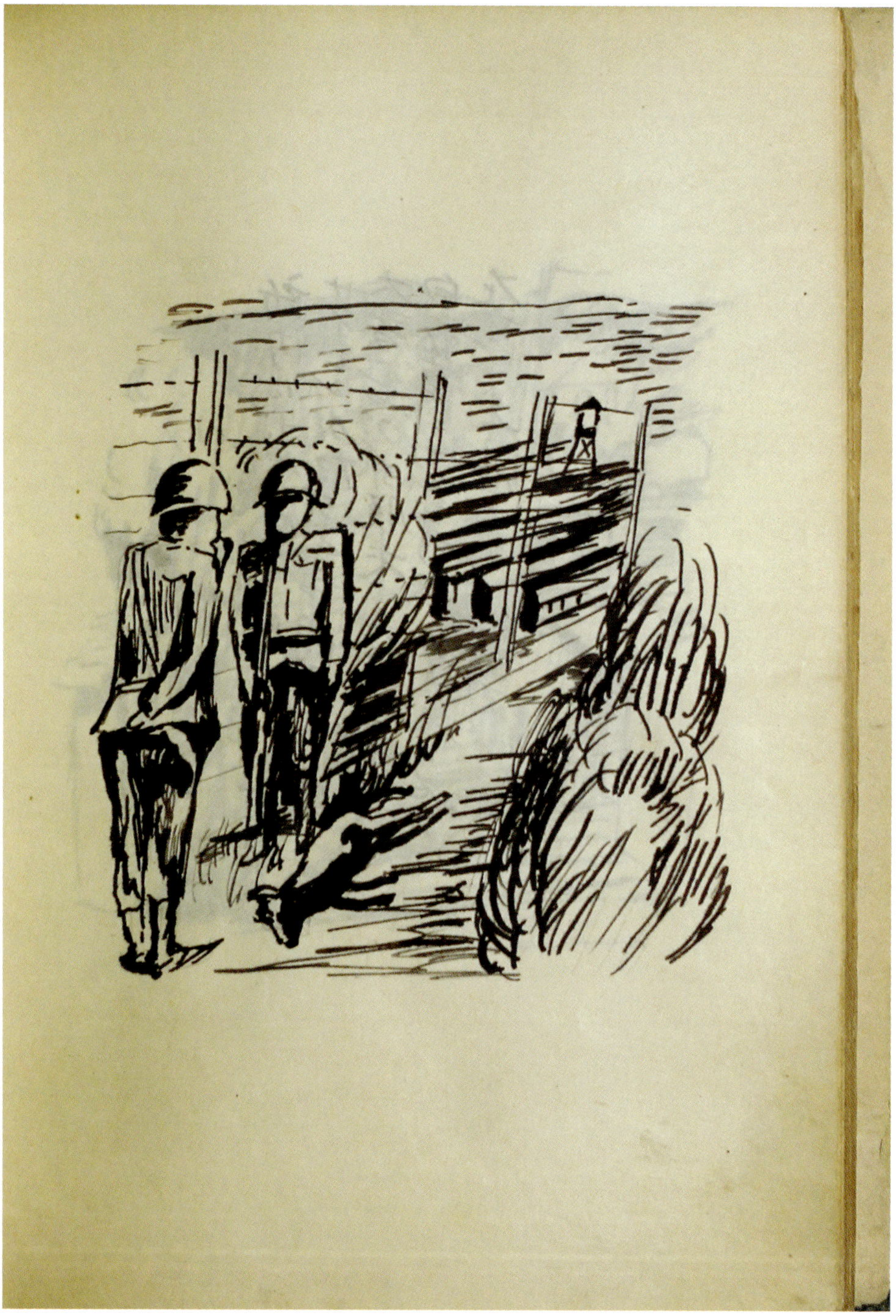

39 One night a heedless new soldier, thinking a Japanese was escaping, shot off a precious bullet with a bang. Pitiful.

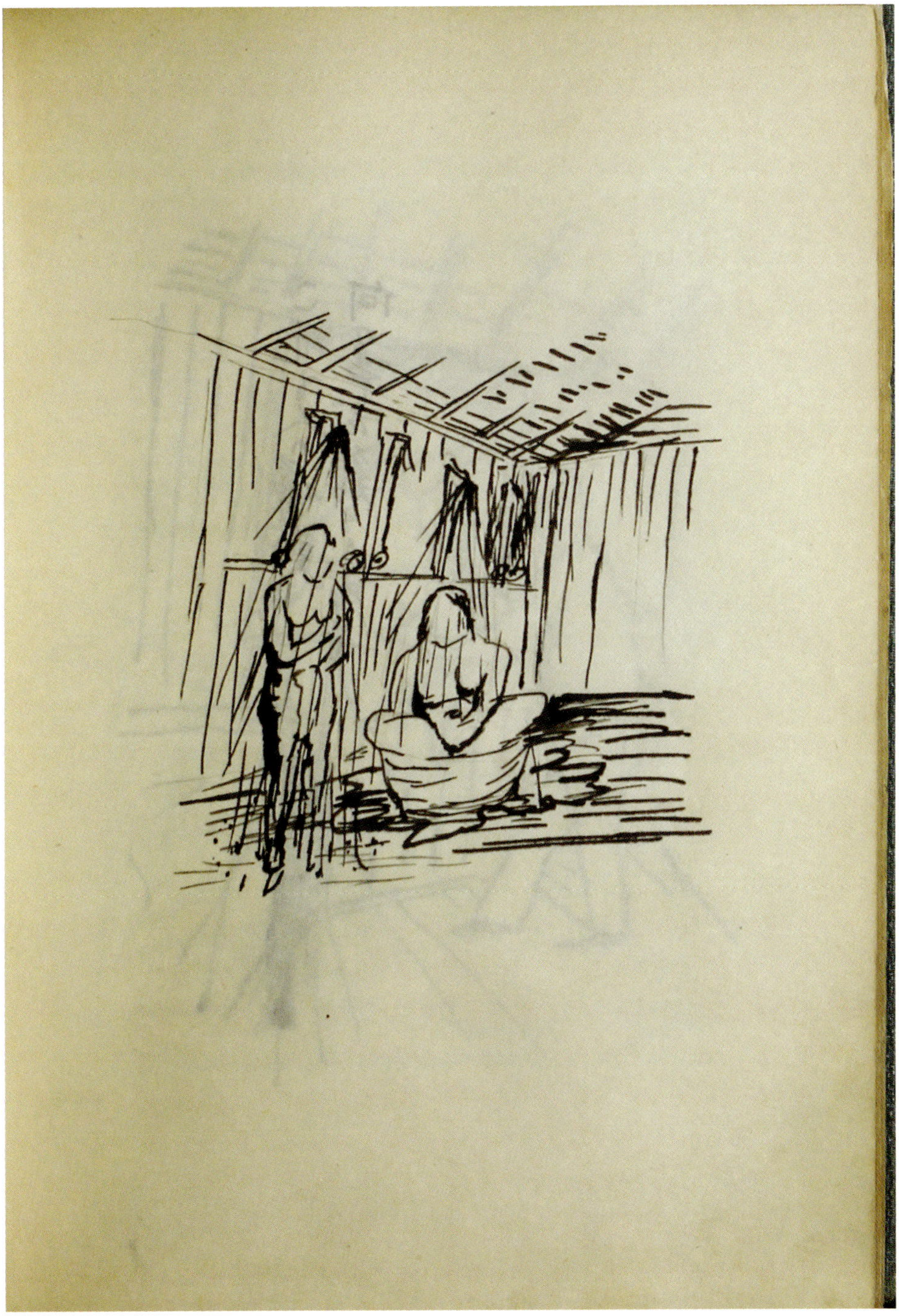

40 Shown here is the shower room of the first-generation women as the gossip of women and children has it.

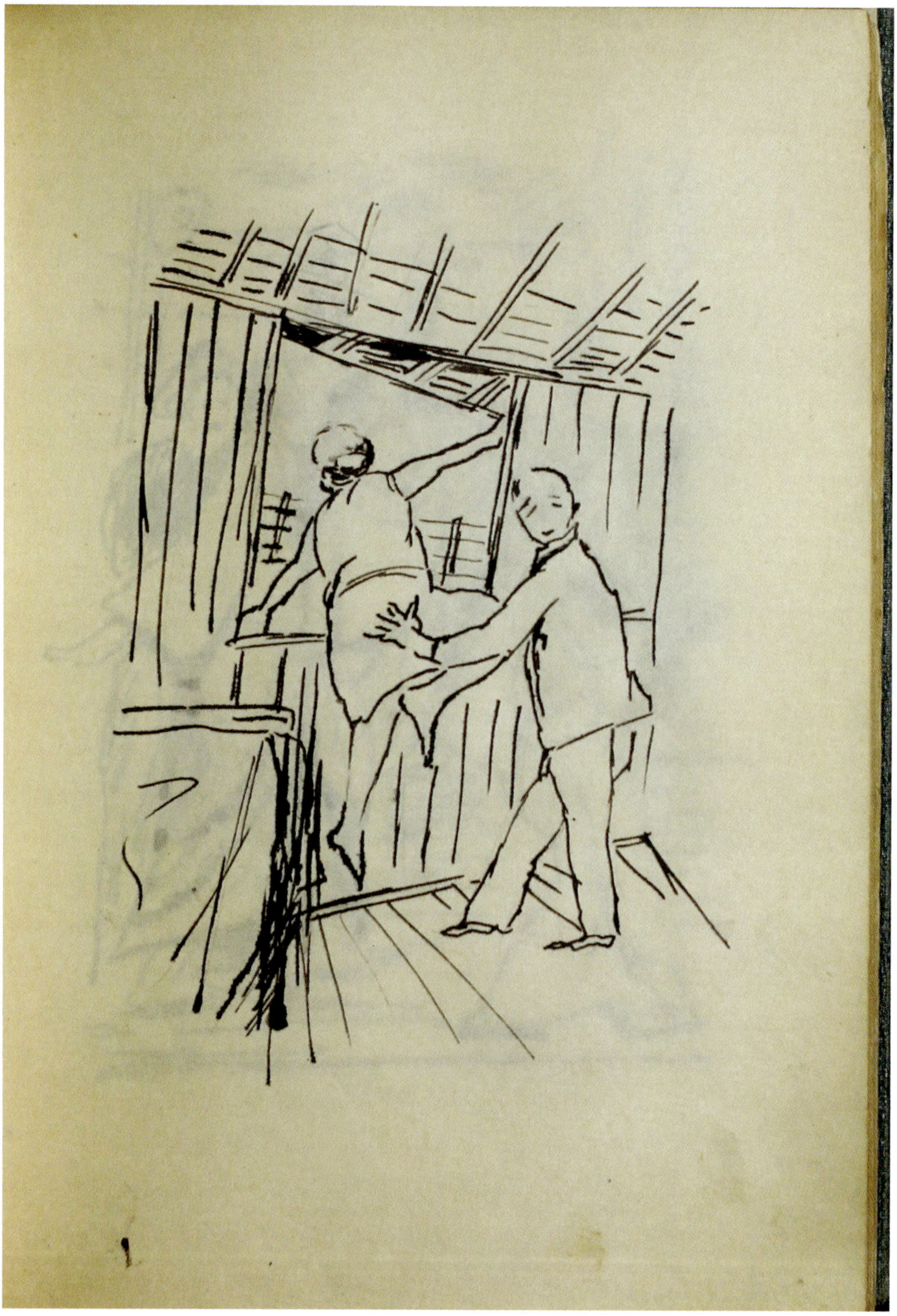

41 This is also as is rumored among people. I don't know what it is about, but . . .

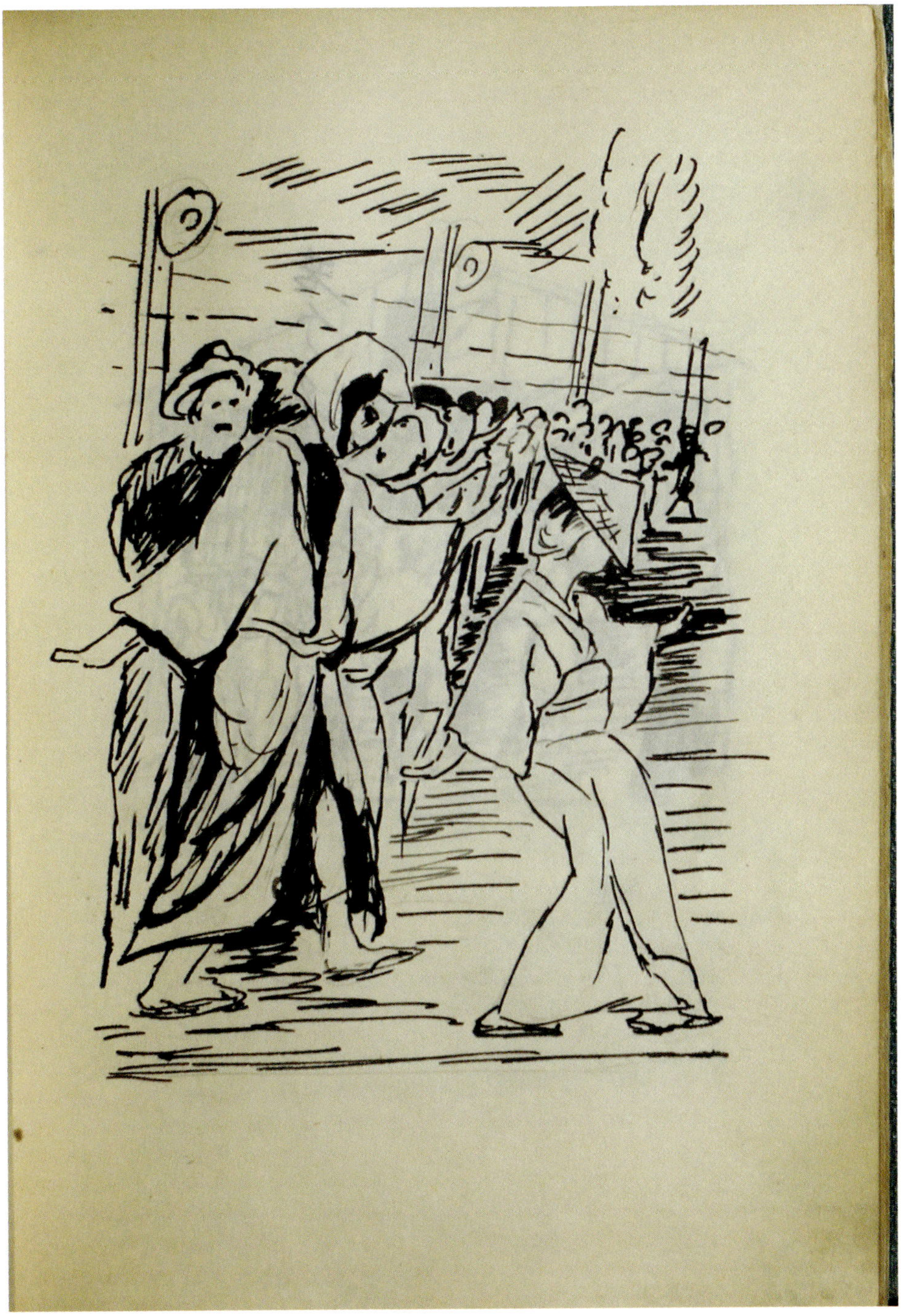

42 Bon Festival.

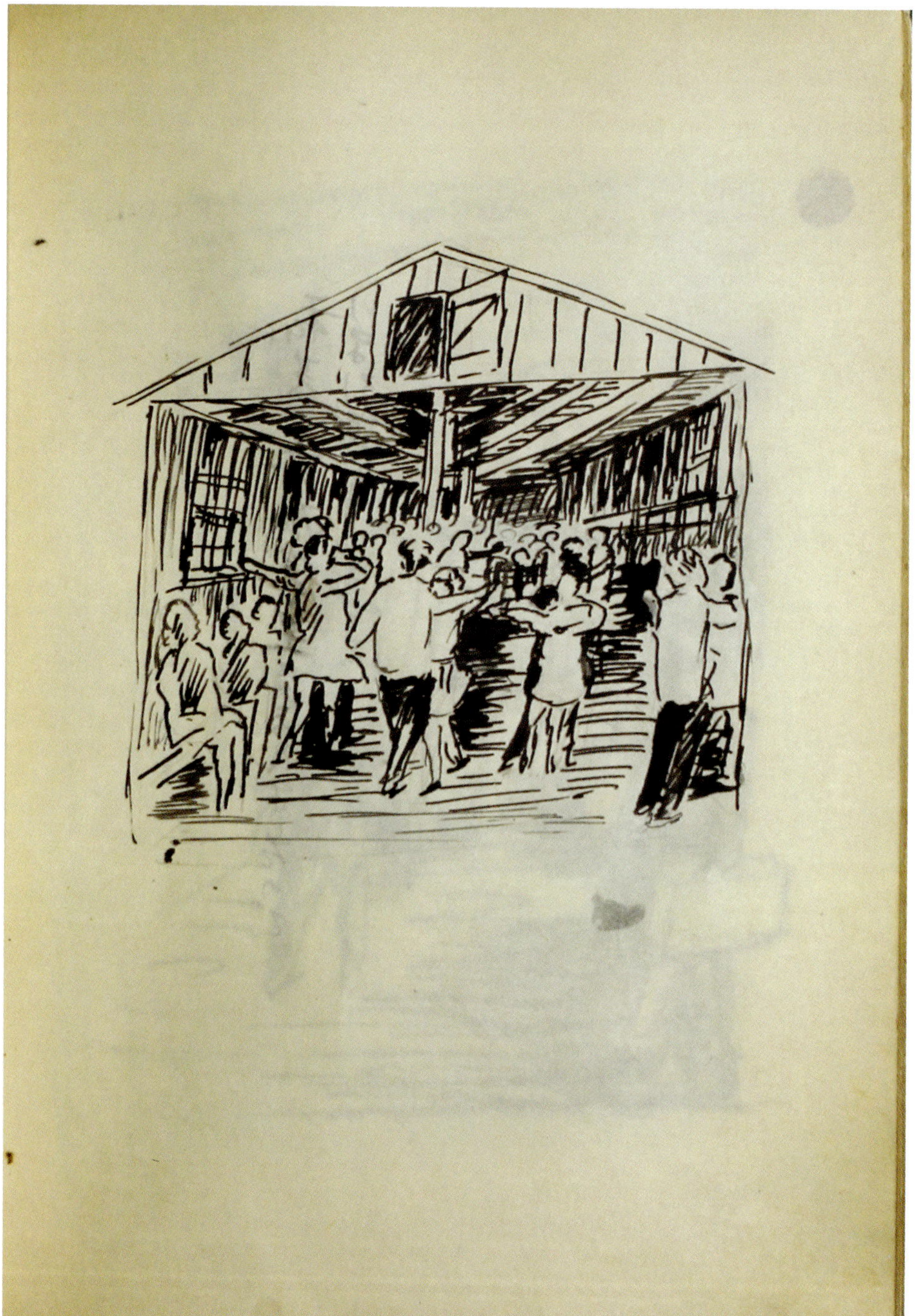

43 Young people's dance.

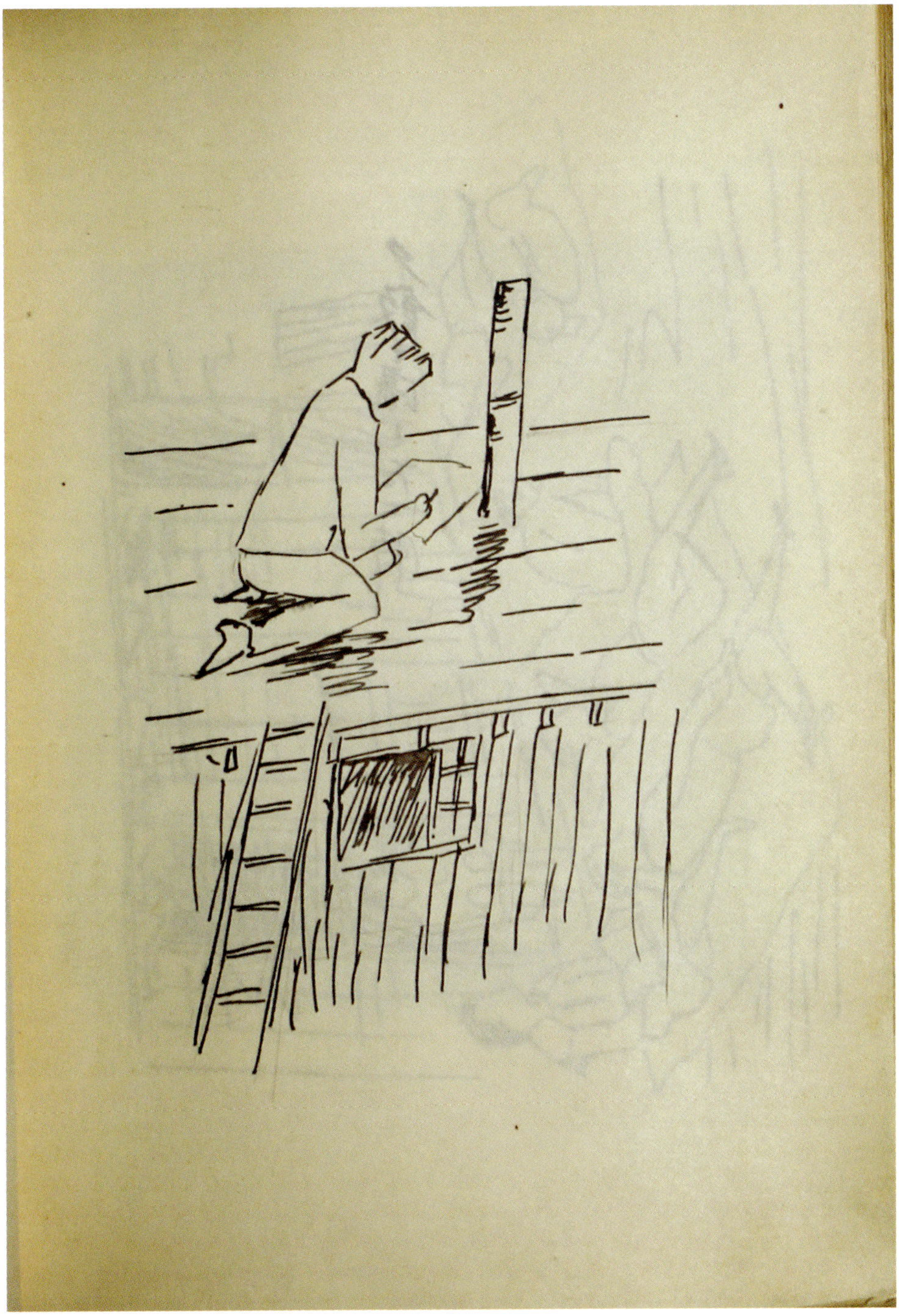

44 Me.

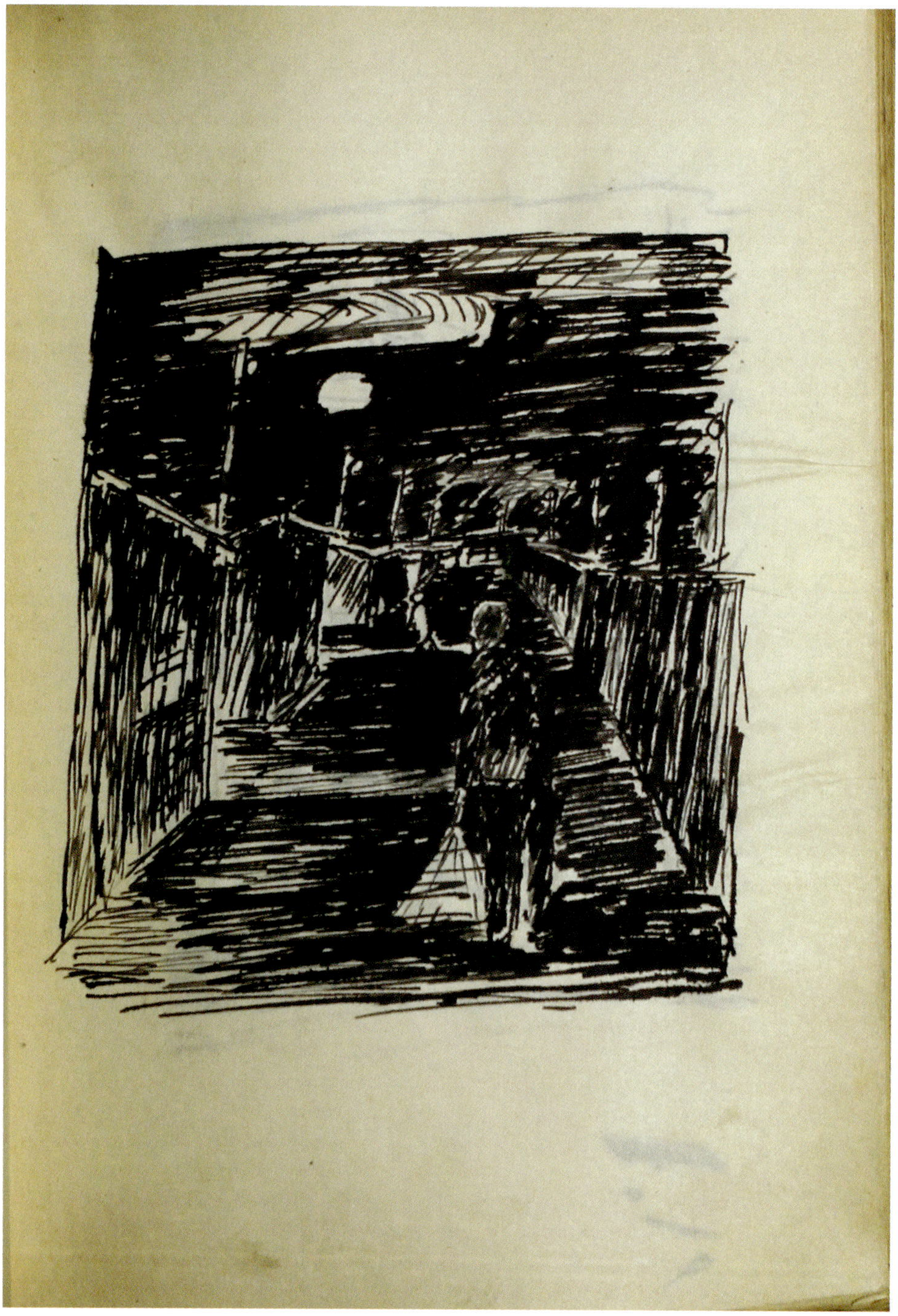

45 Going to the bathroom in a pitch-black night.

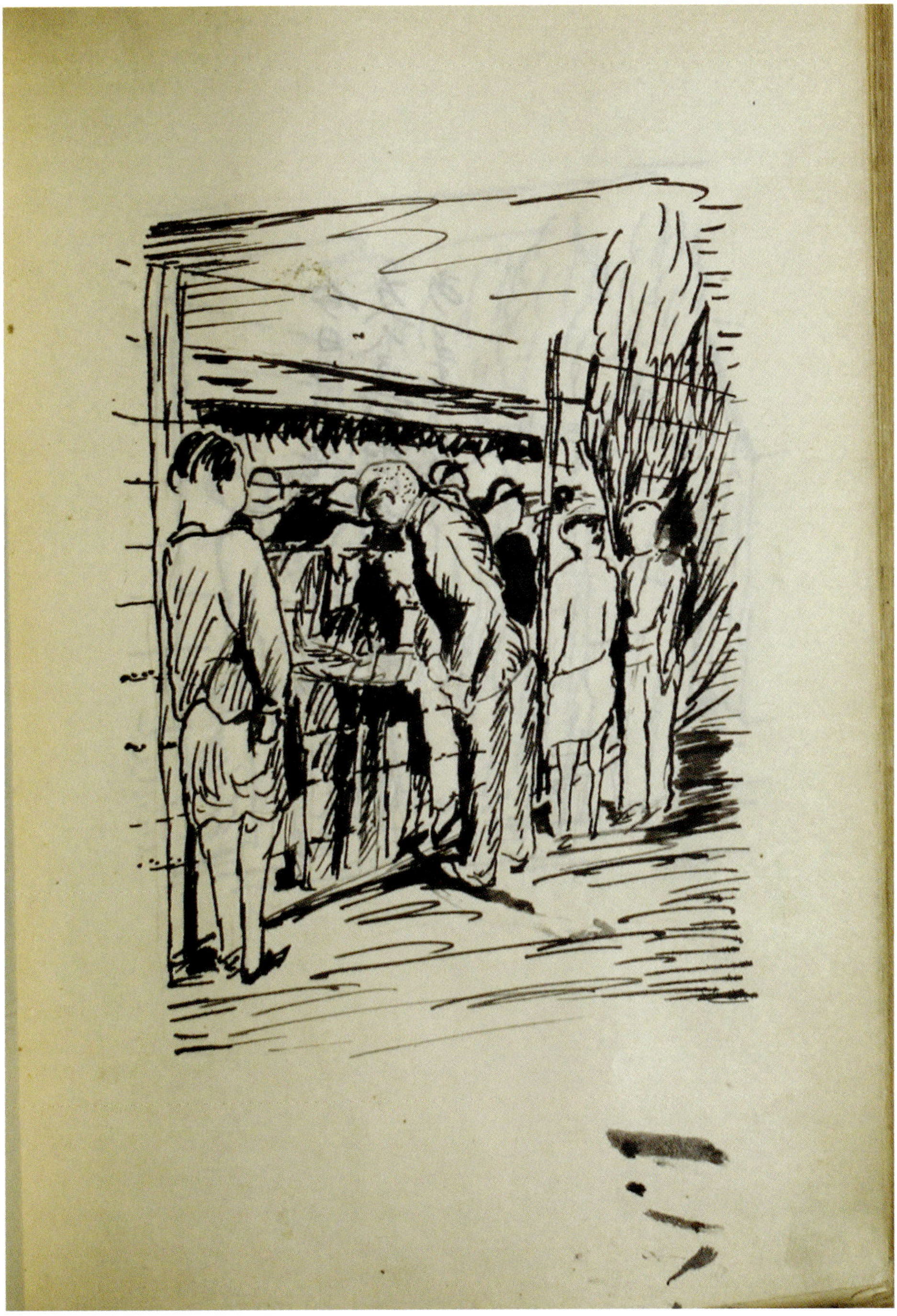

46 Black market.

47

It seems that disloyal bastards will be killed one by one. Someone whom I do not know has already erected tombstones and [otherwise] prepared. Should a memorial service be performed at the temporary tombstones of those people, there is a rumor that . . . [unknown someone] will make sure to urinate down on them every night. Whether this is the truth is not known.

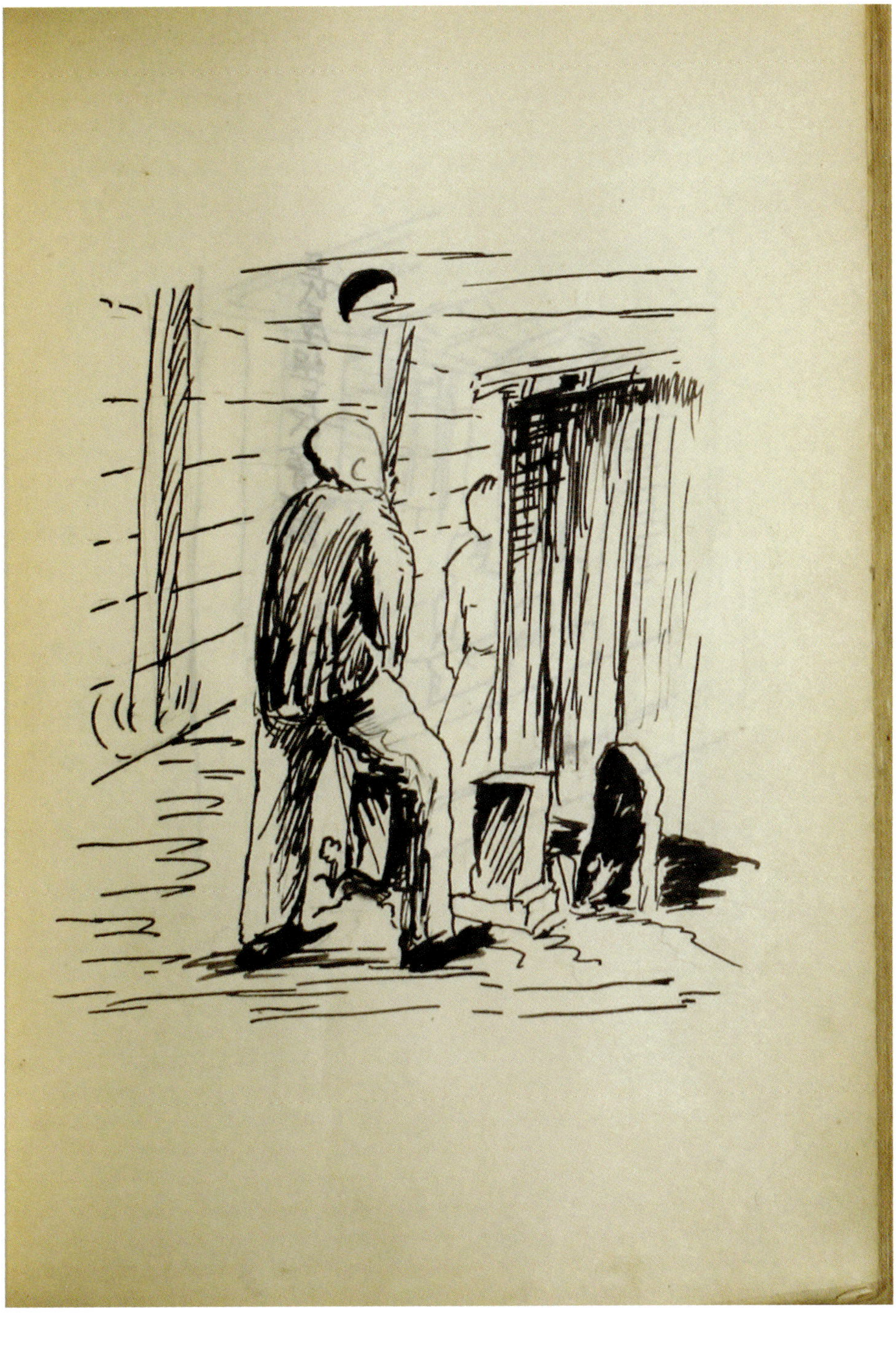

48

The star house of the star land of fairy tales. This carelessly made hut is really cheap. Made quickly from "shiplap" wood, the boards are full of knots. It has become popular to fashion various things from those wooden knots. Children have pulled all the knots out of the wallboards of house after house. Seen from the inside, the walls are full of holes, enough to make one wonder if stars had come out.

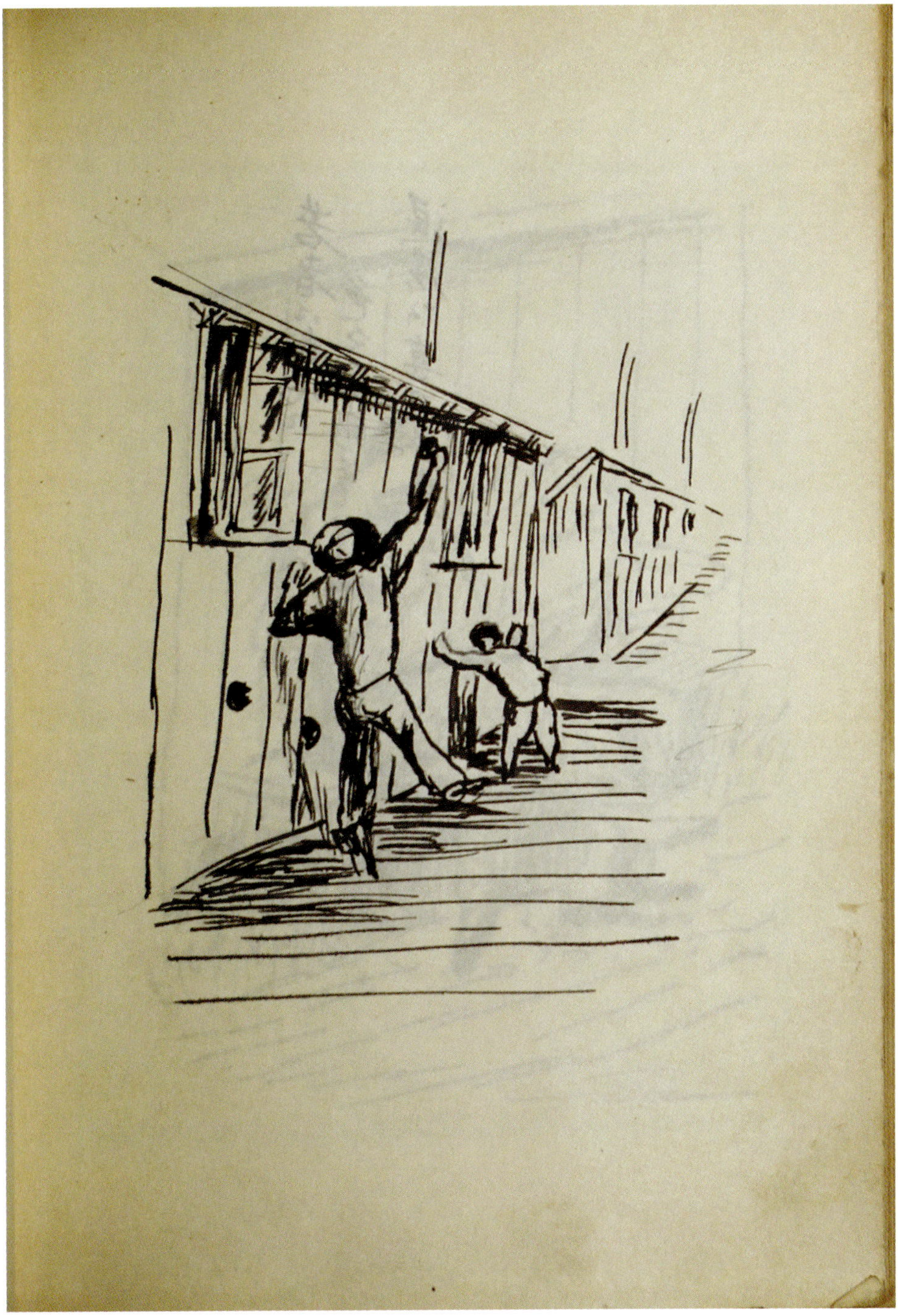

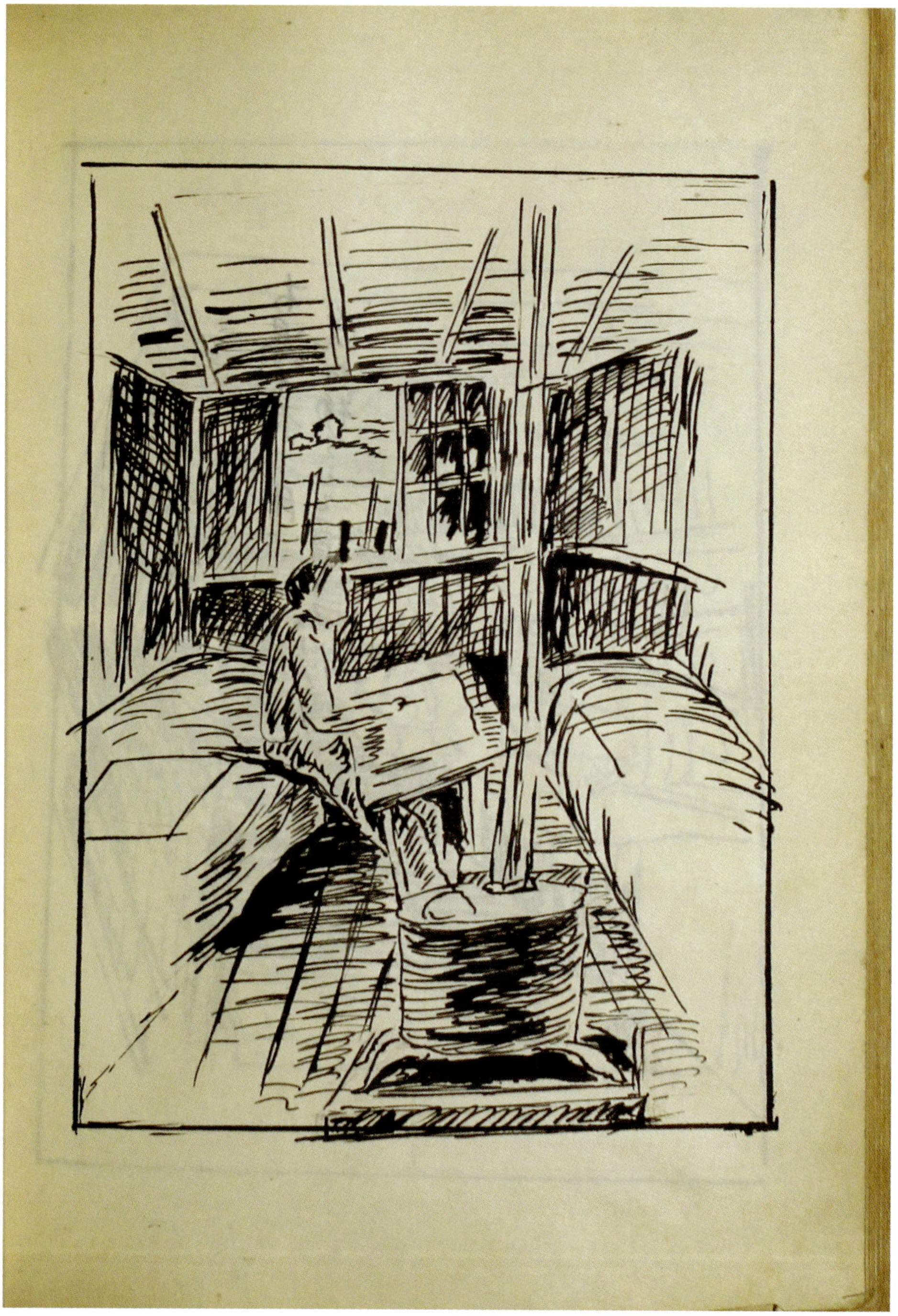

49 Hard at it, then?

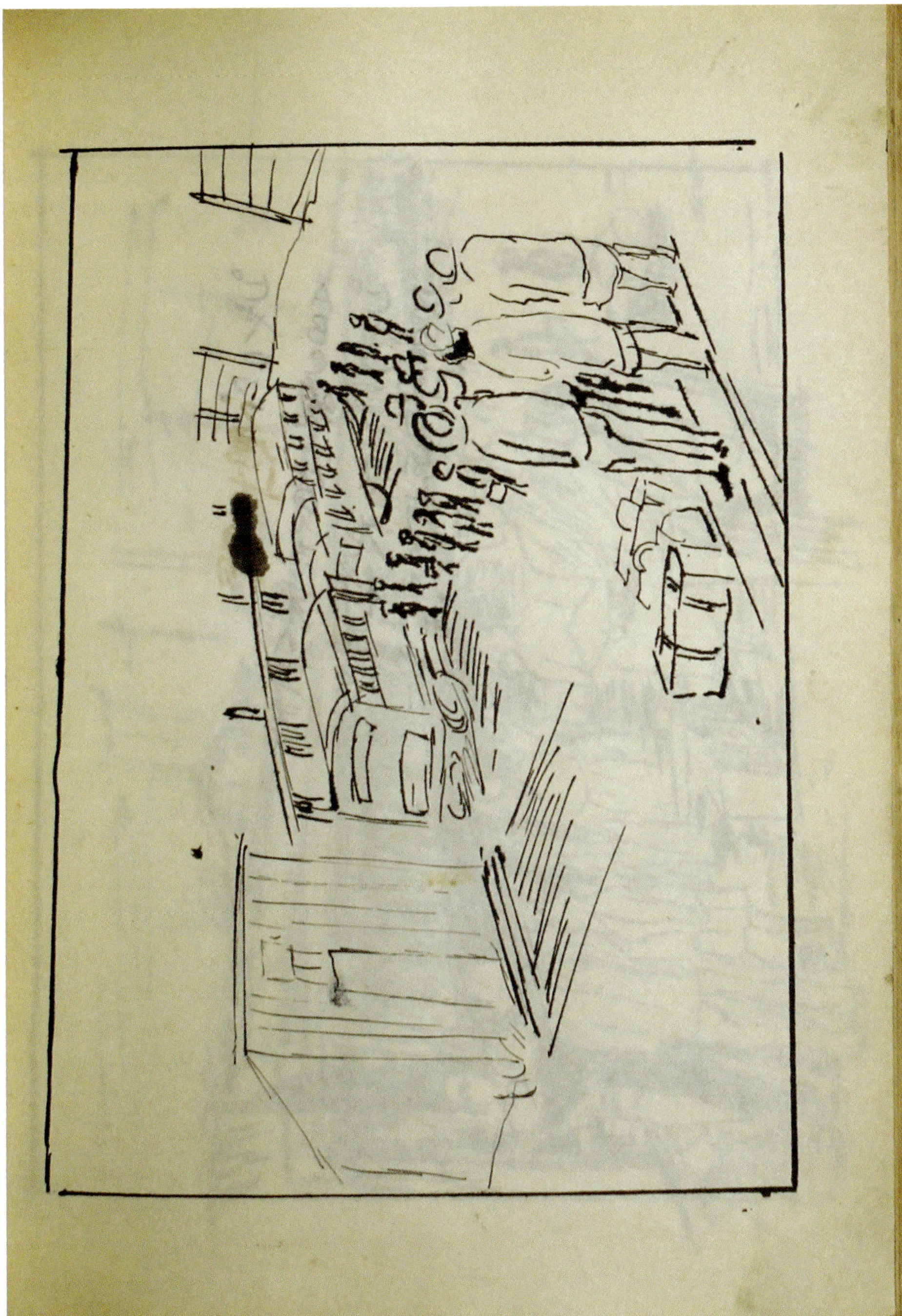

50 Finally this assembly center is going to be closed. Everyone is being moved again, to a mountainous area of the continent. Within one or two weeks all will be transported. Every day, every day, [they] take people to the railroad station by bus.

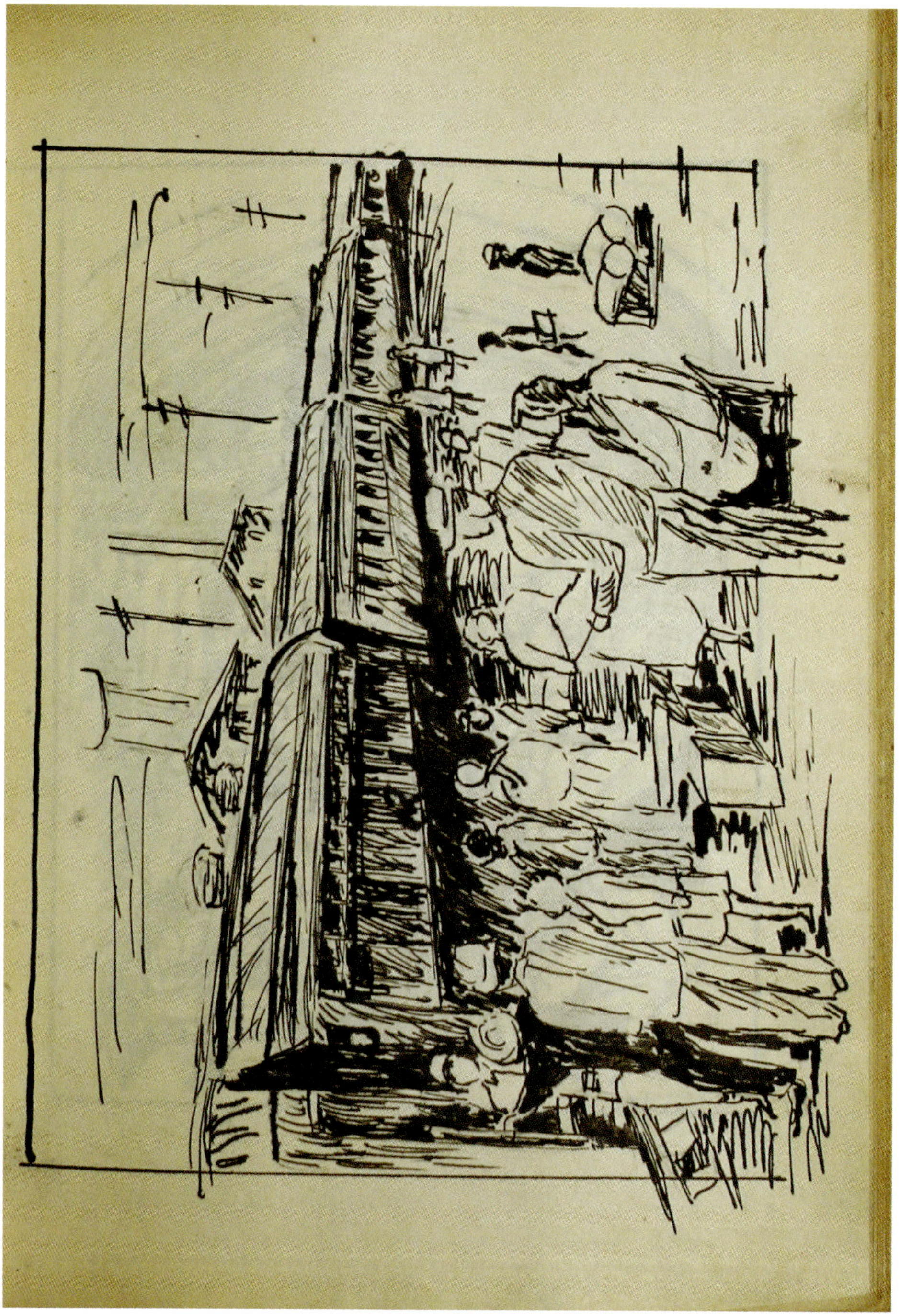

51 Puyallup. Everyone got on in A, B, C order. Good bye, Puyallup. Will the day ever come when we see this place again?

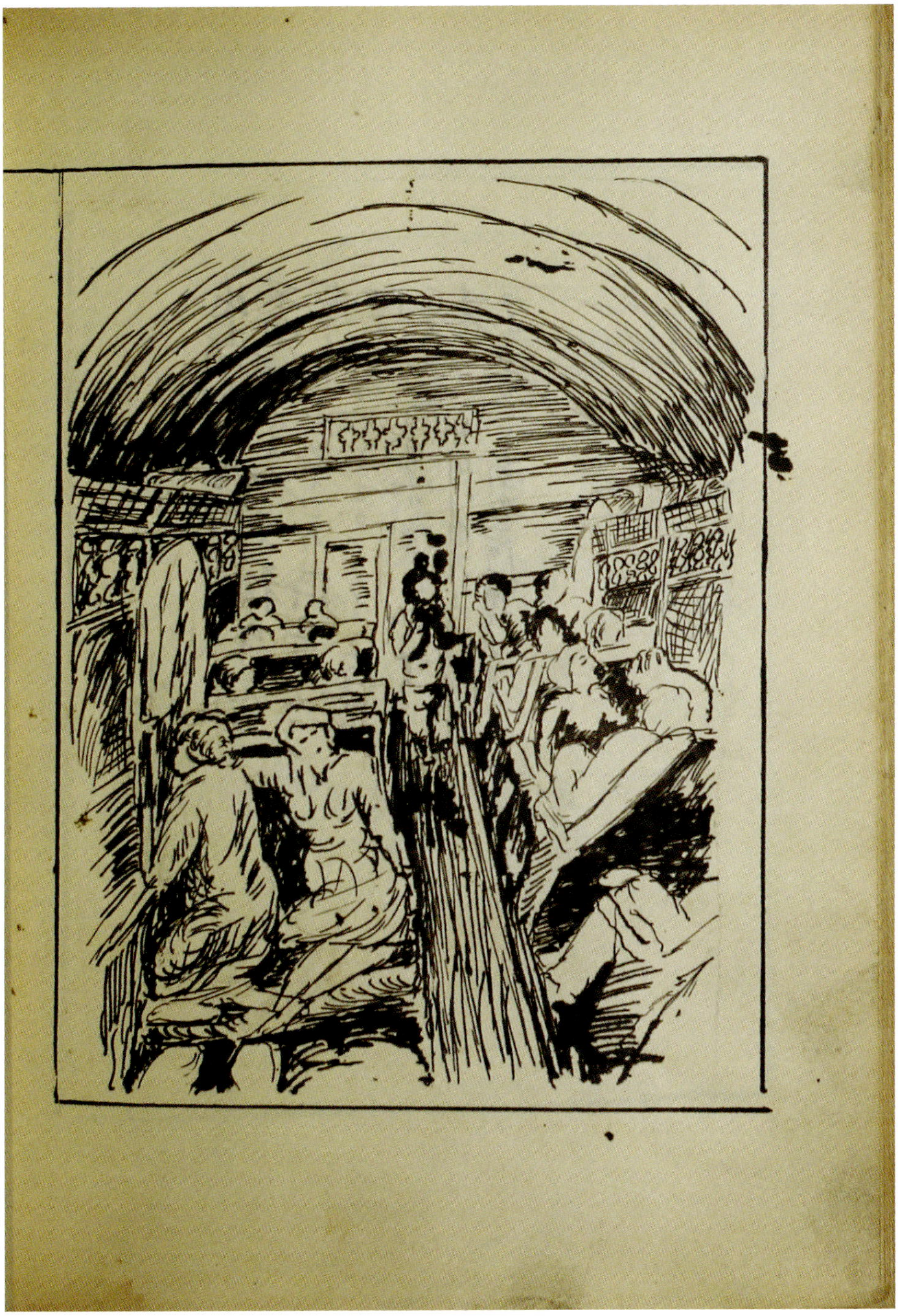

52 A hot, hot August day. The inside of the coach was so hot that we were all running around naked. Feeling anxious, [we rode] the train, going east, ever east.

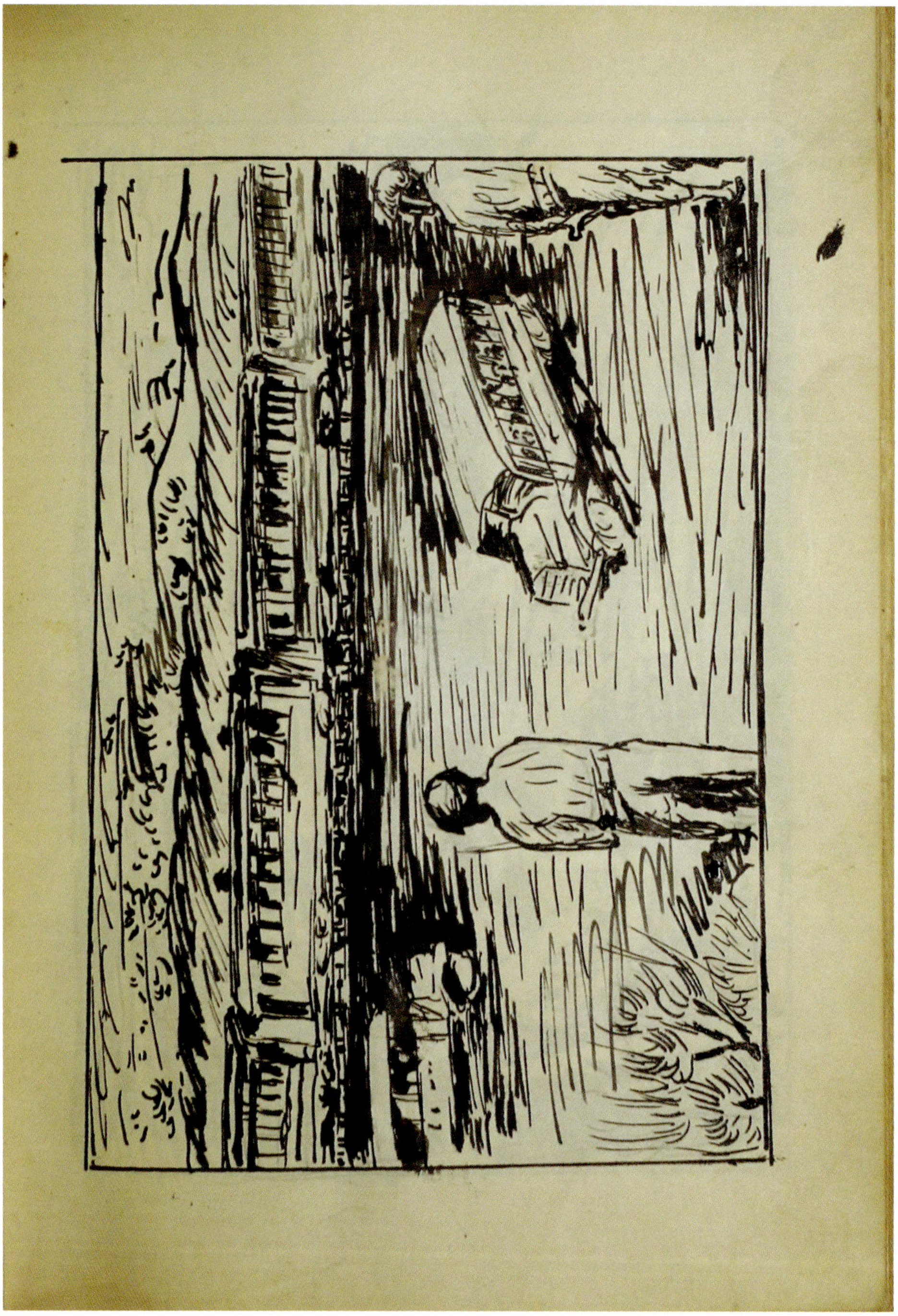

53 Gasping, "It's hot, it's hot," [we reach a] desertlike place we know not where, with neither trees nor houses. Because it is so dry, a hot wind is blowing.

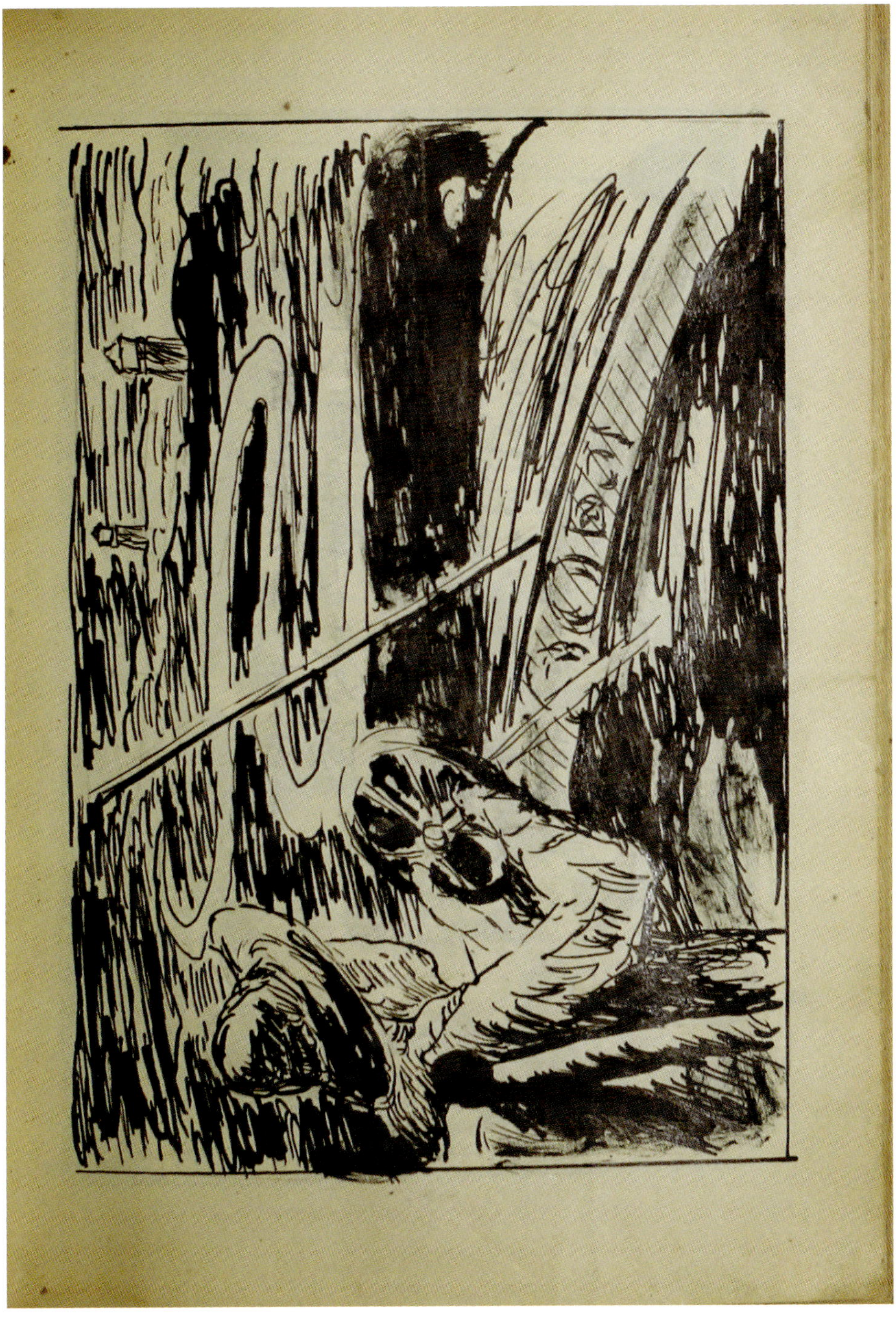

54 We have become "bus people." In front far off, we can see a water tank. There are the dwellings to which we are being transported.

55

So we have arrived. We are in the seventeenth block. There, young second-generation Japanese Americans (Nisei) who had come earlier barged into our room. Then they said the following to us: "There is not a sufficient number of houses for you all to enter. So, could you please arrange to live together with friends, relatives, and so on? If that is not possible, there is nothing that can be done. [We] may have to ask those left over to sleep outside. Thanks."

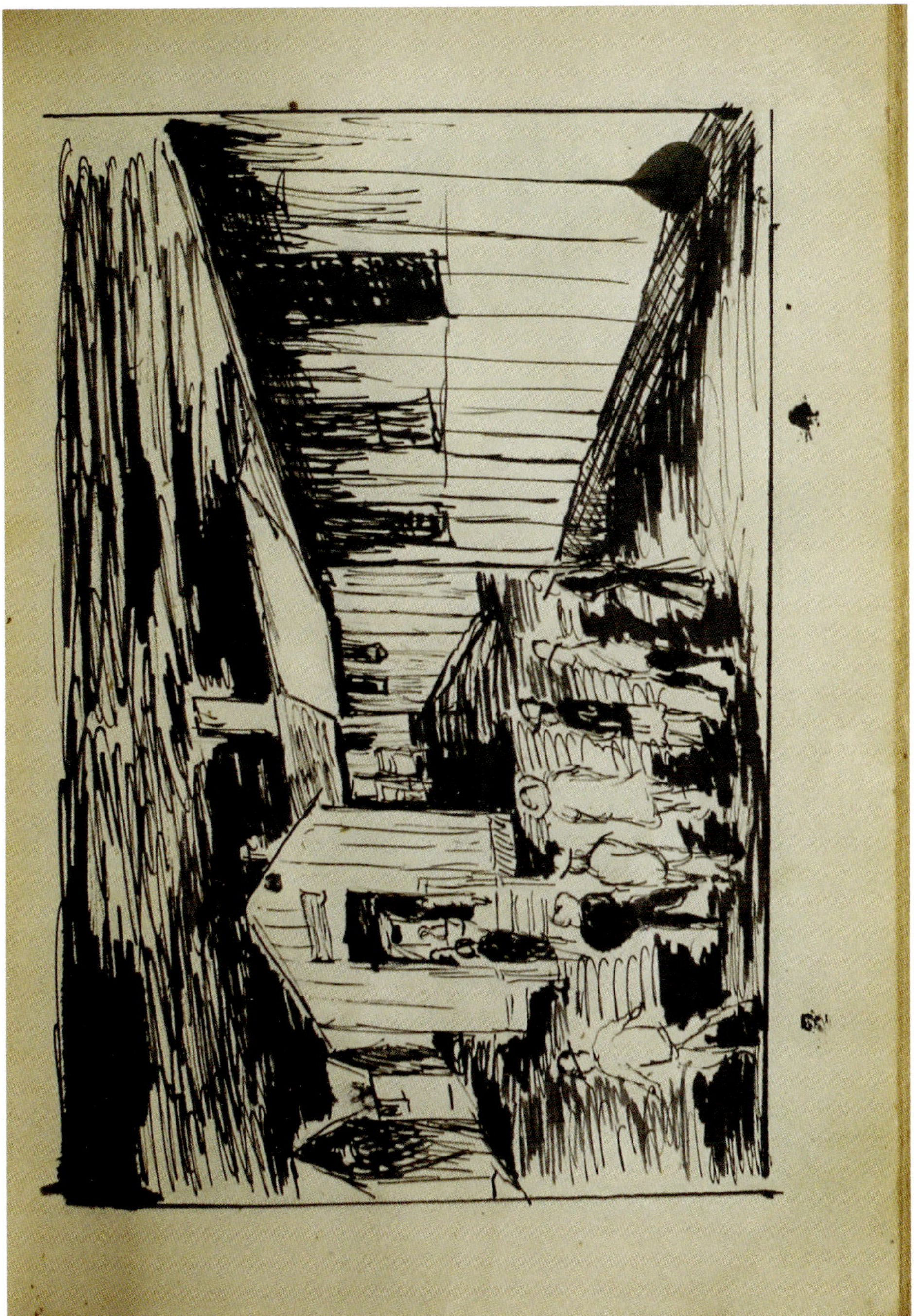

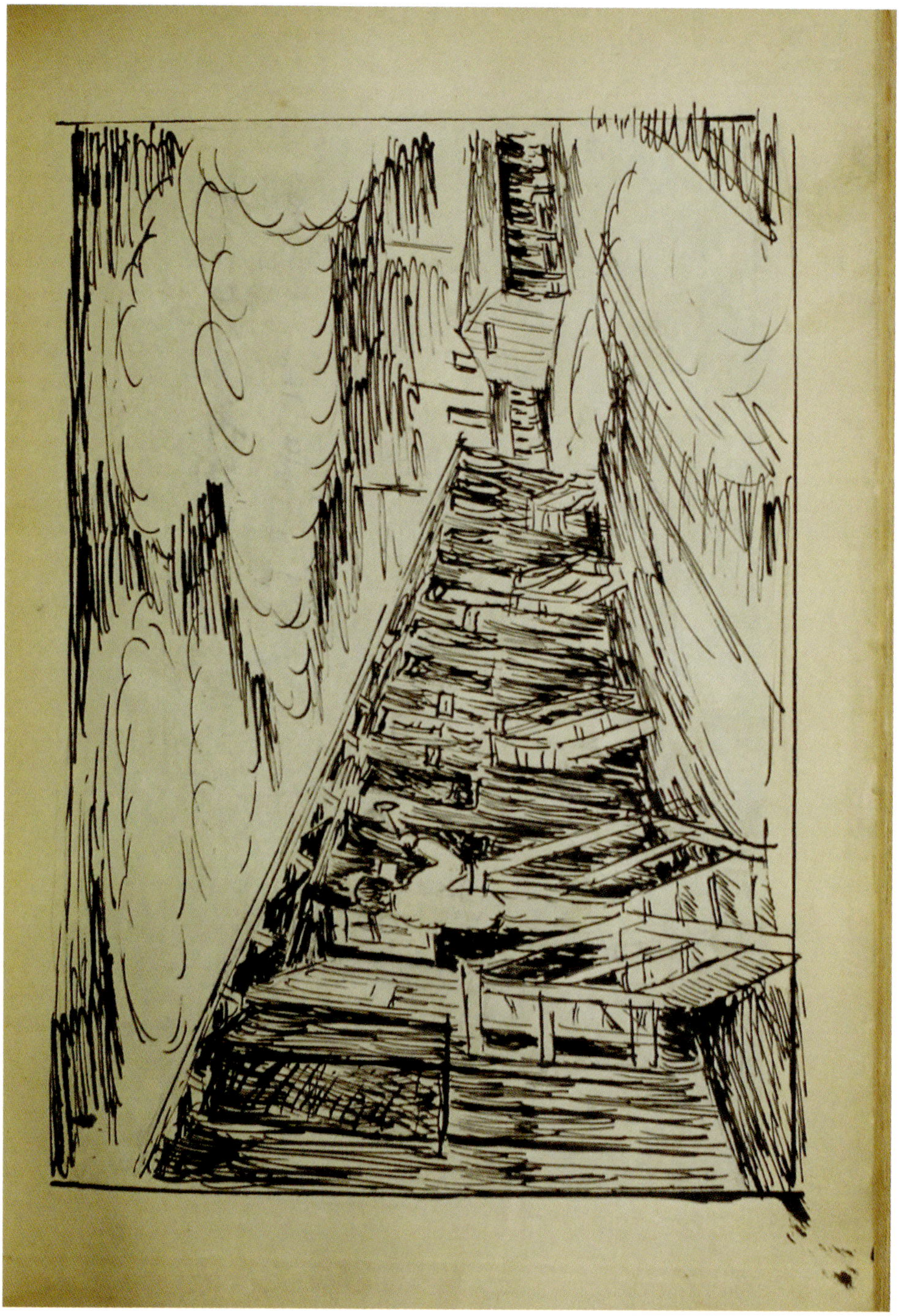

56 Finally, we were given our one room. Whew, whew. Let us at least put up our nameplate.

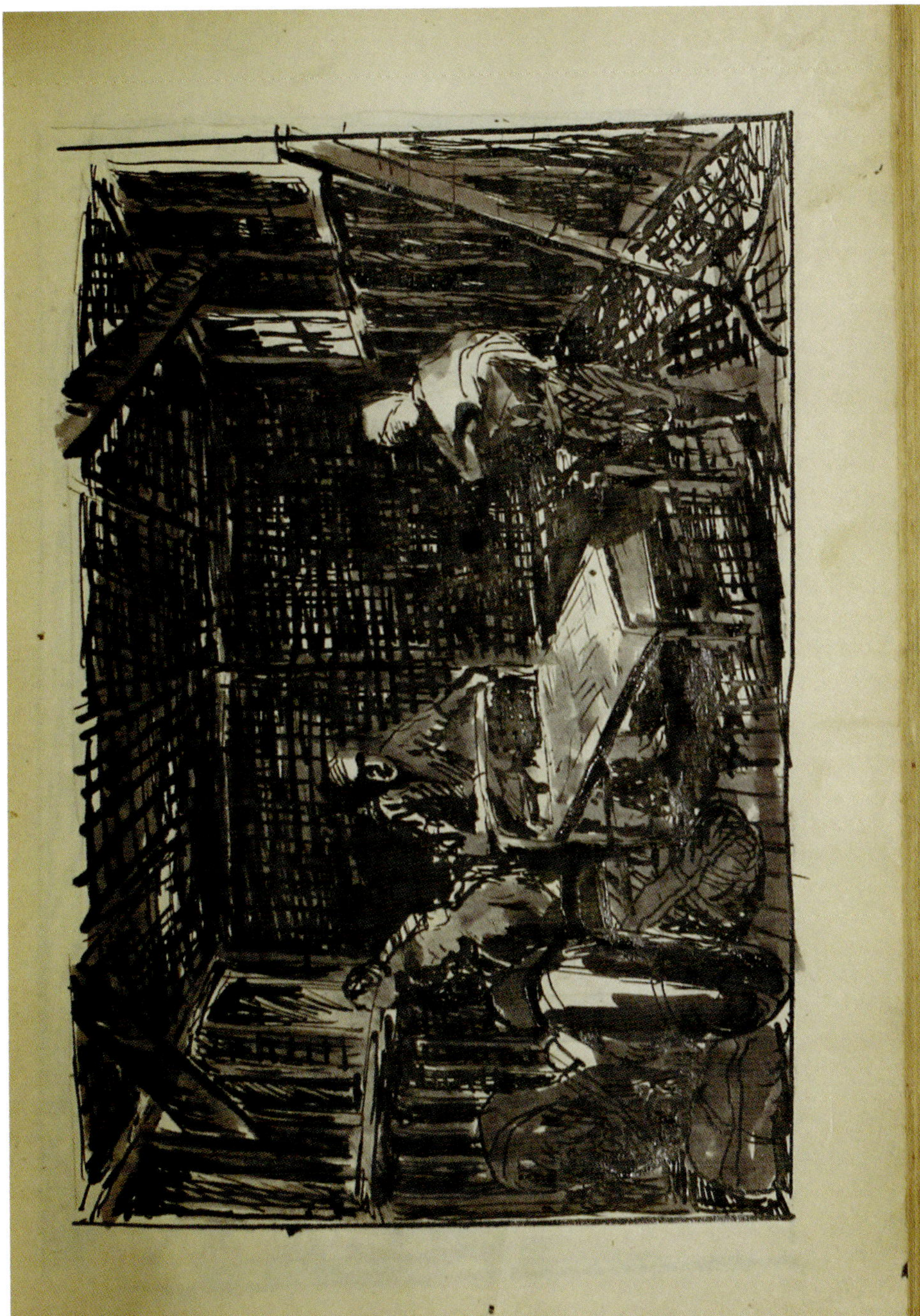

57 So everyone unpack and straighten it all up.

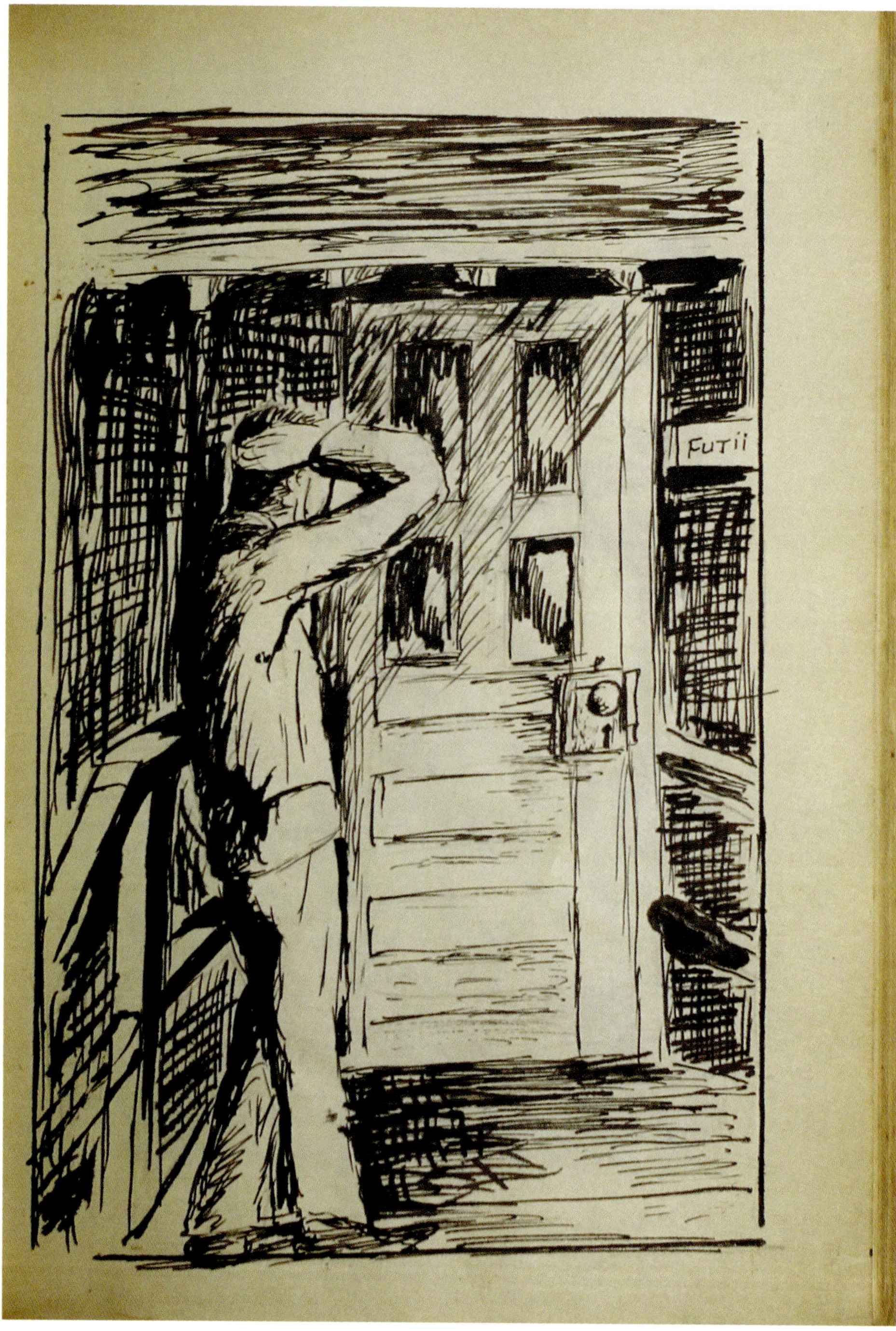

58 Indeed, this is an odd door. The lock is on the outside. I see that this relocation center is a prison.

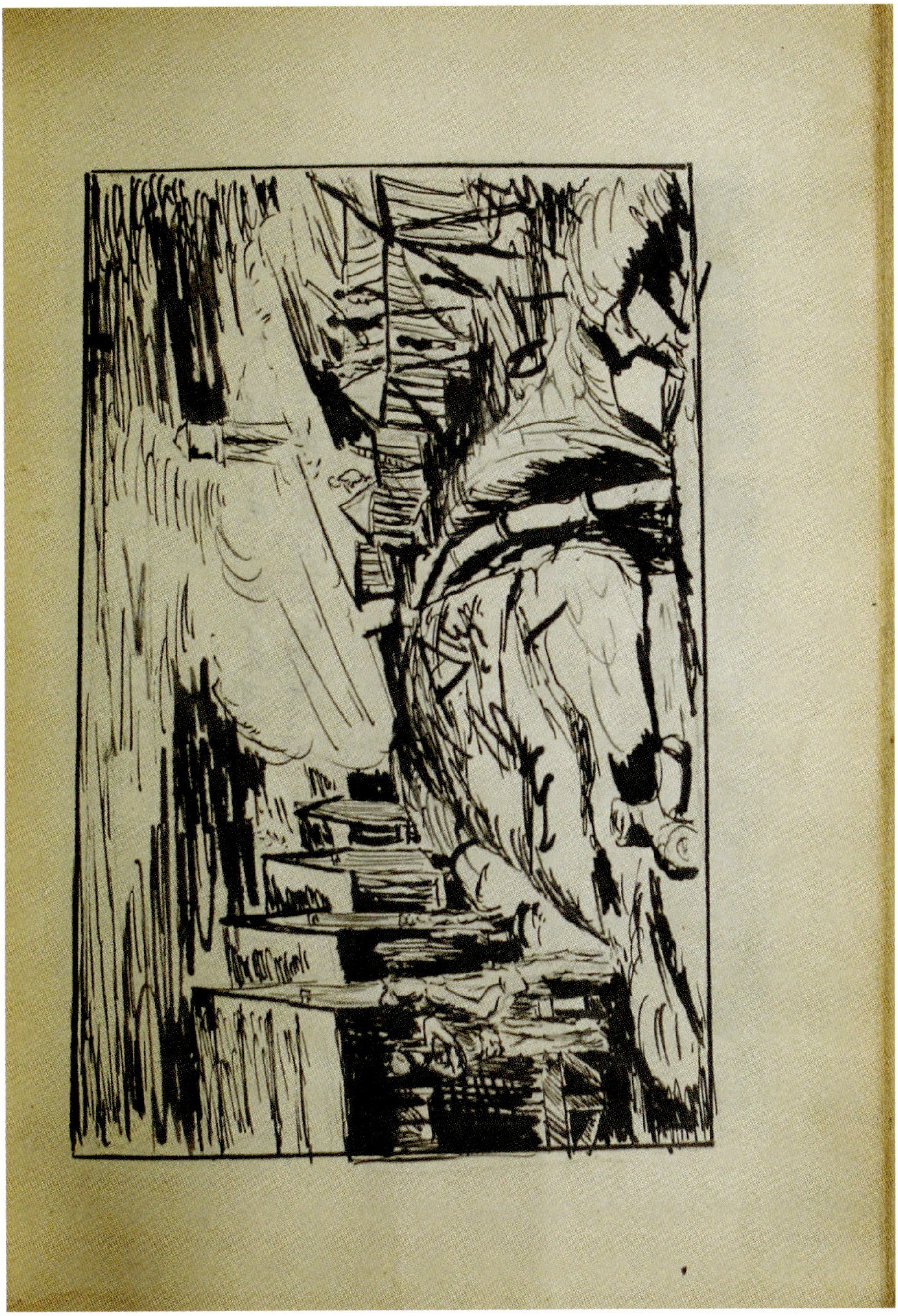

59 Even now there is construction everywhere in camp. The sound of dynamite makes it feel like war. Suddenly we are busy.

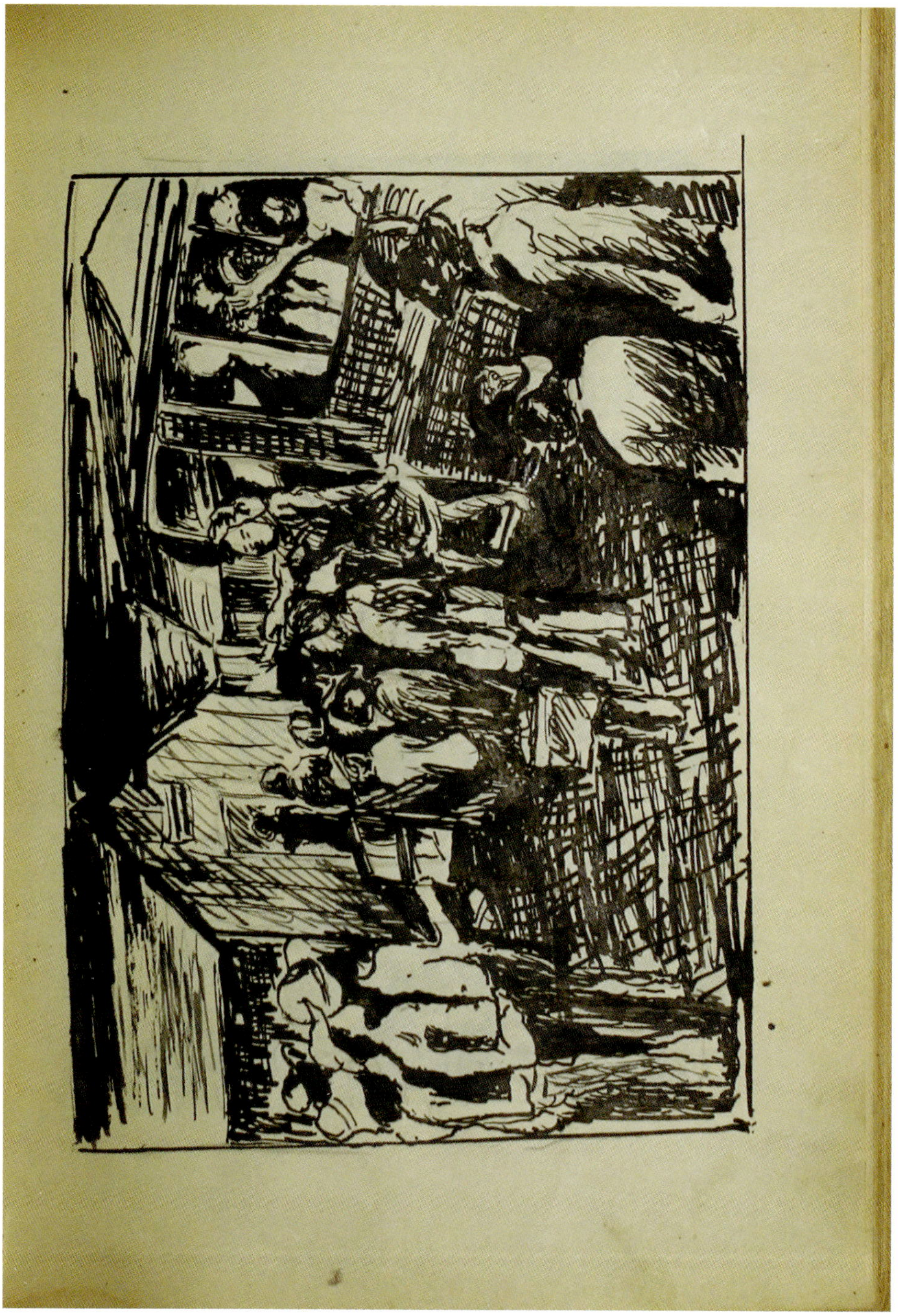

60 Every day we go to meet our brothers who were sent here later. Hiya, kid.

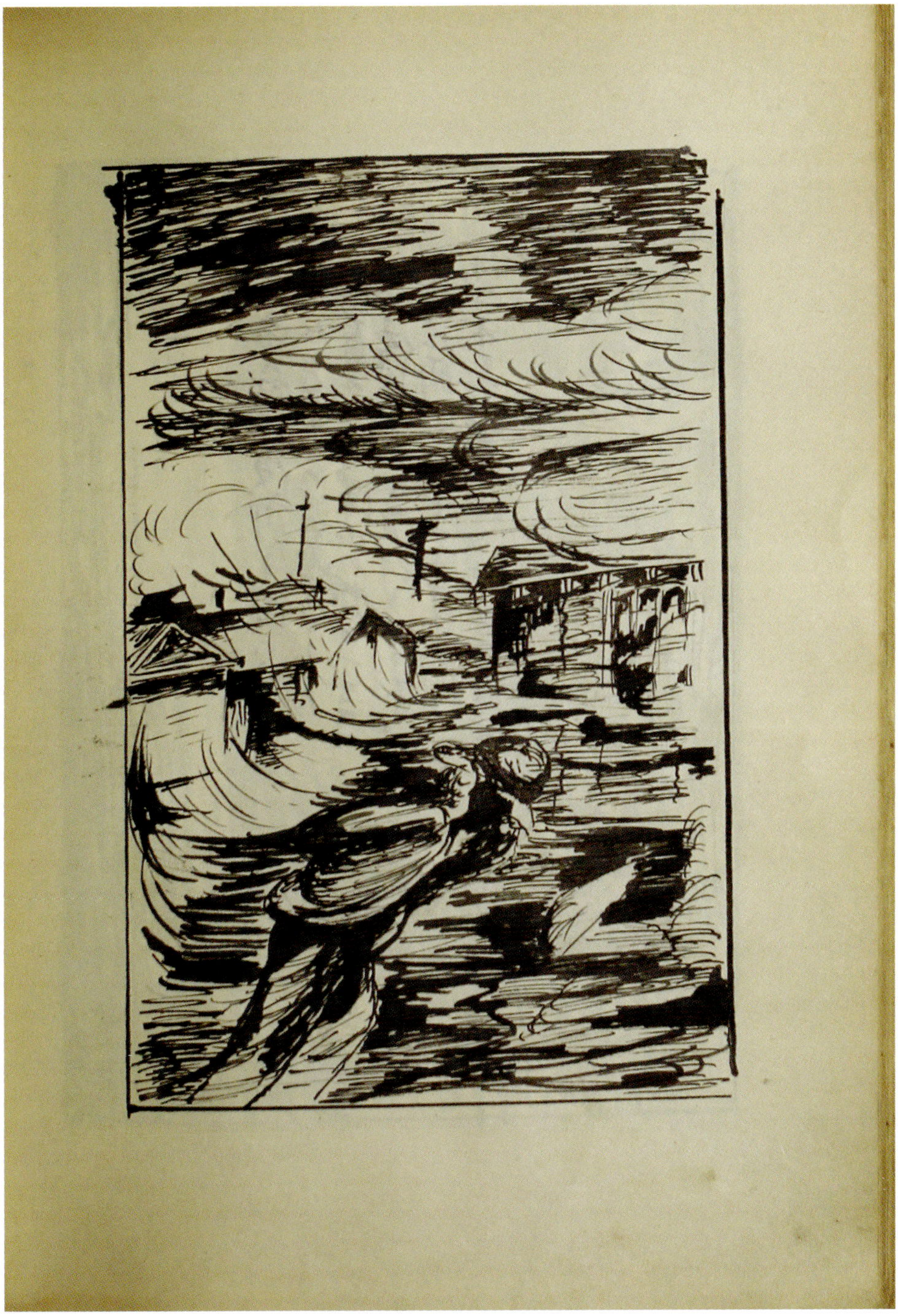

61 This area's famous phenomenon of the sandstorm can make even the day dark. It is really something.

62

This is the temporary, quickly made men's bathroom. Since we evacuated our bowels into a deep hole, it was very unsanitary. Since it was midsummer, lots of flies accumulated there. One time there was an epidemic. In addition, the road got so bad on rainy days that you could not even walk on it.

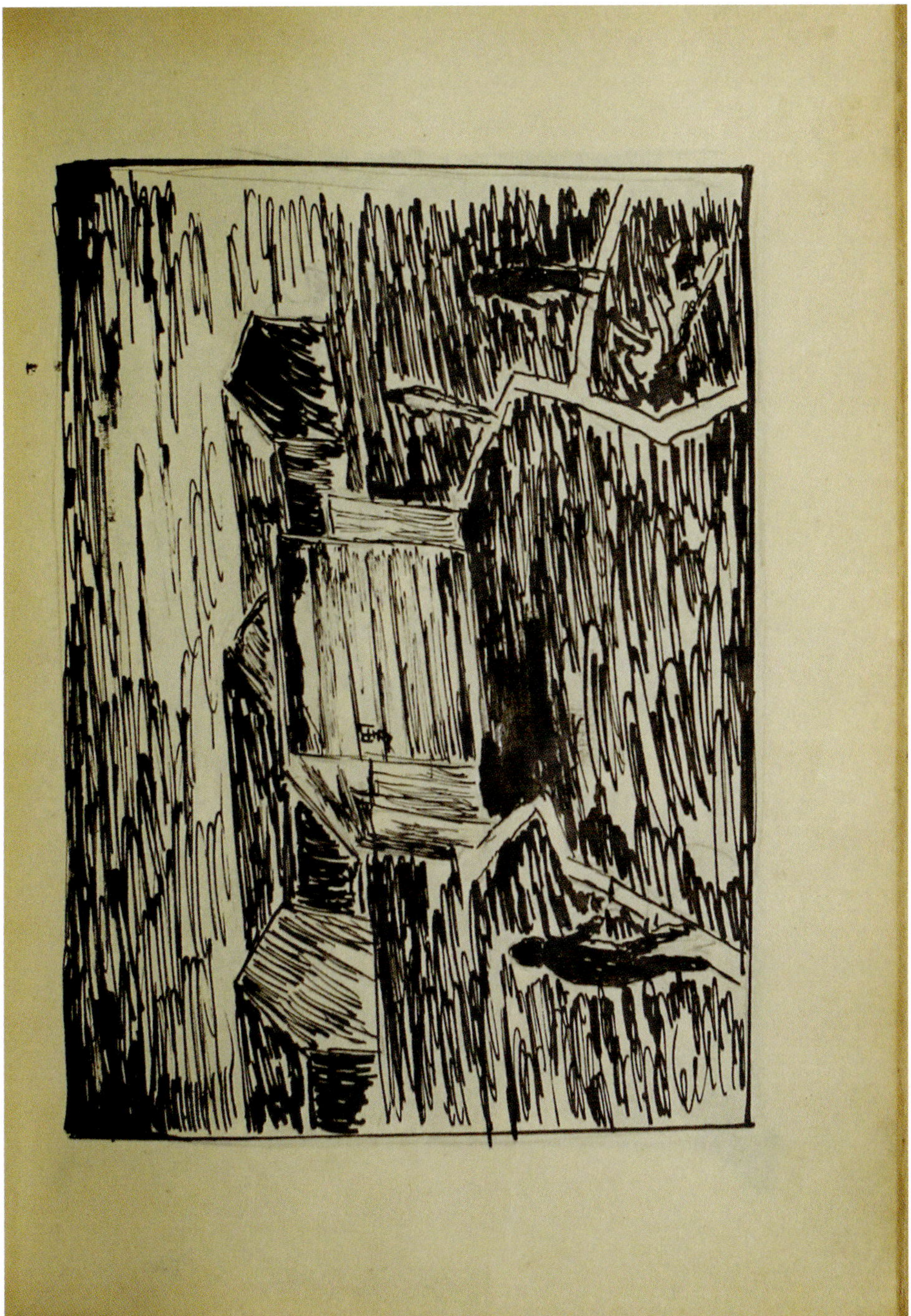

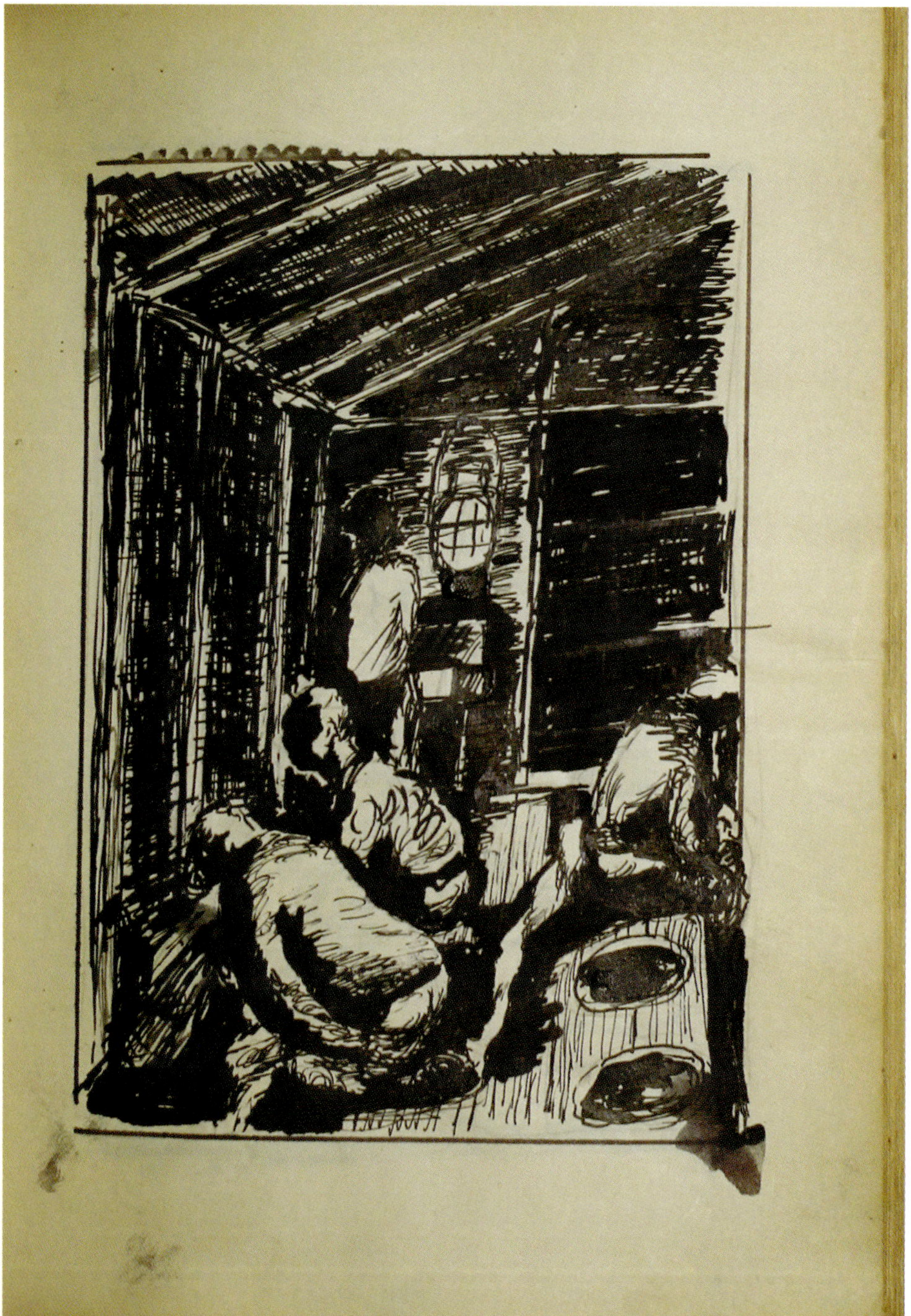

63 The toilet on a windy night: from the anus a long piece of toilet paper waves in the wind.

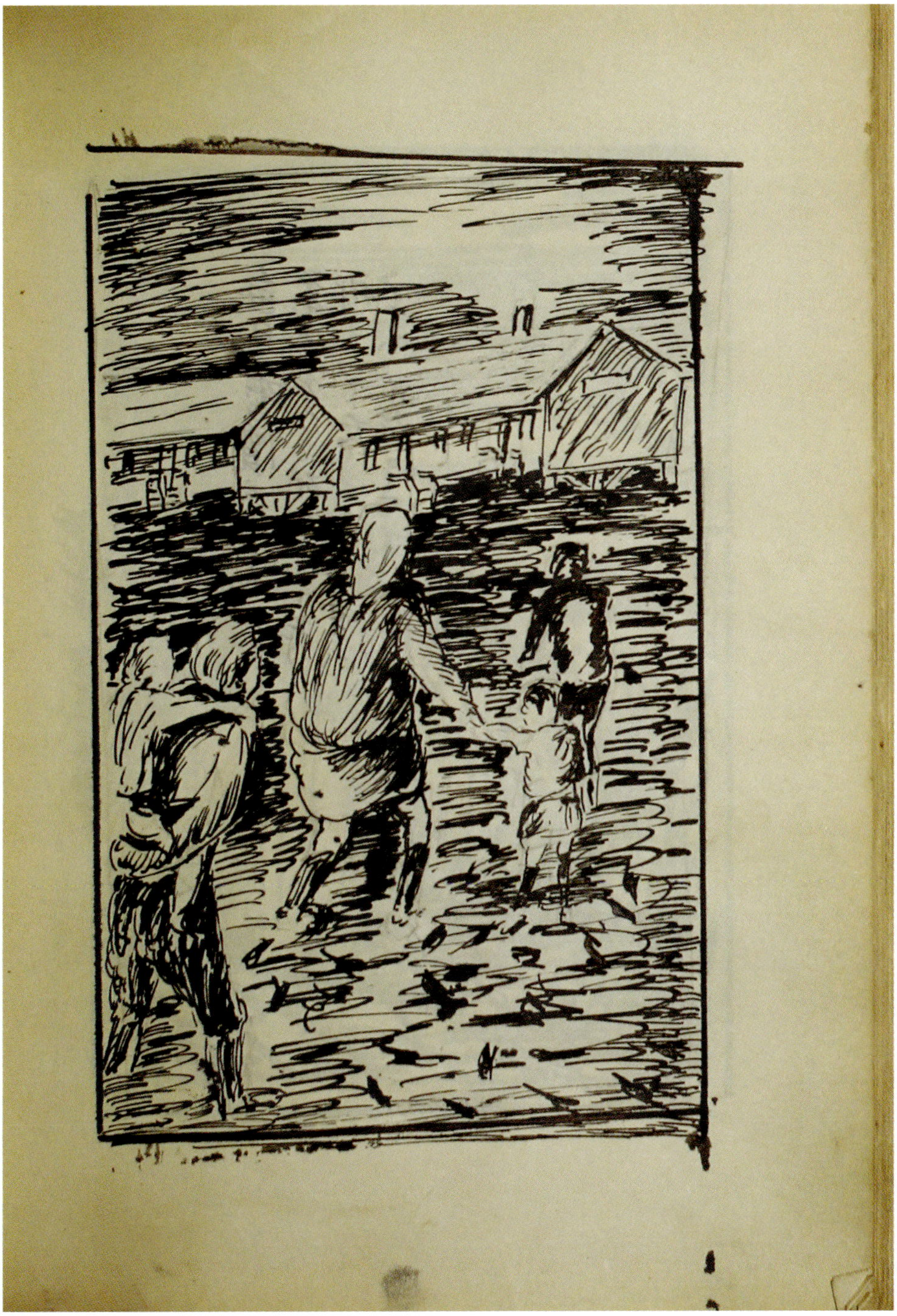

64 When rainy days continue, . . . [the ground] becomes mud.

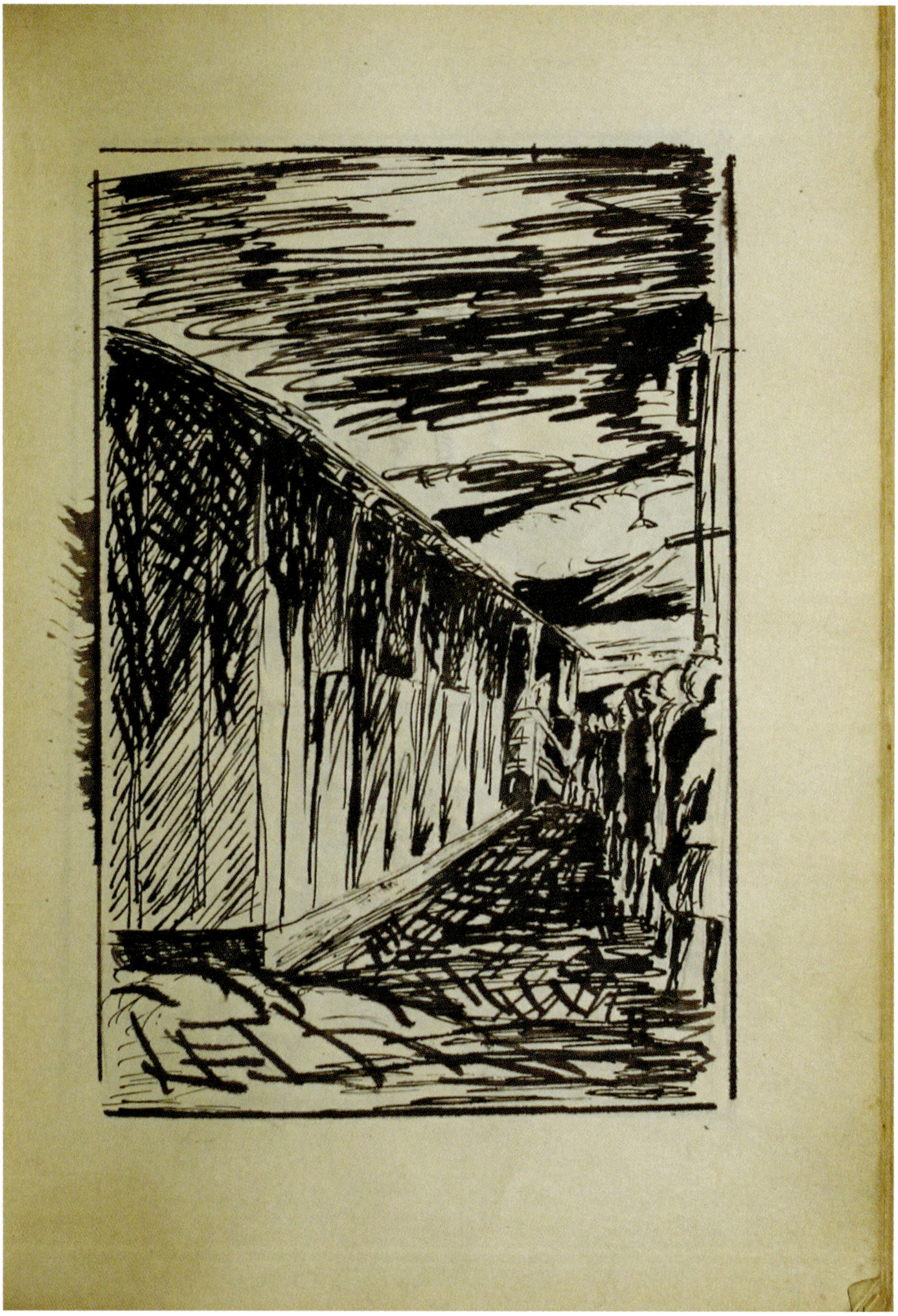

65 It seems this is to be our daily custom. Like sheep, we form a line . . . [and] enter the mess hall.

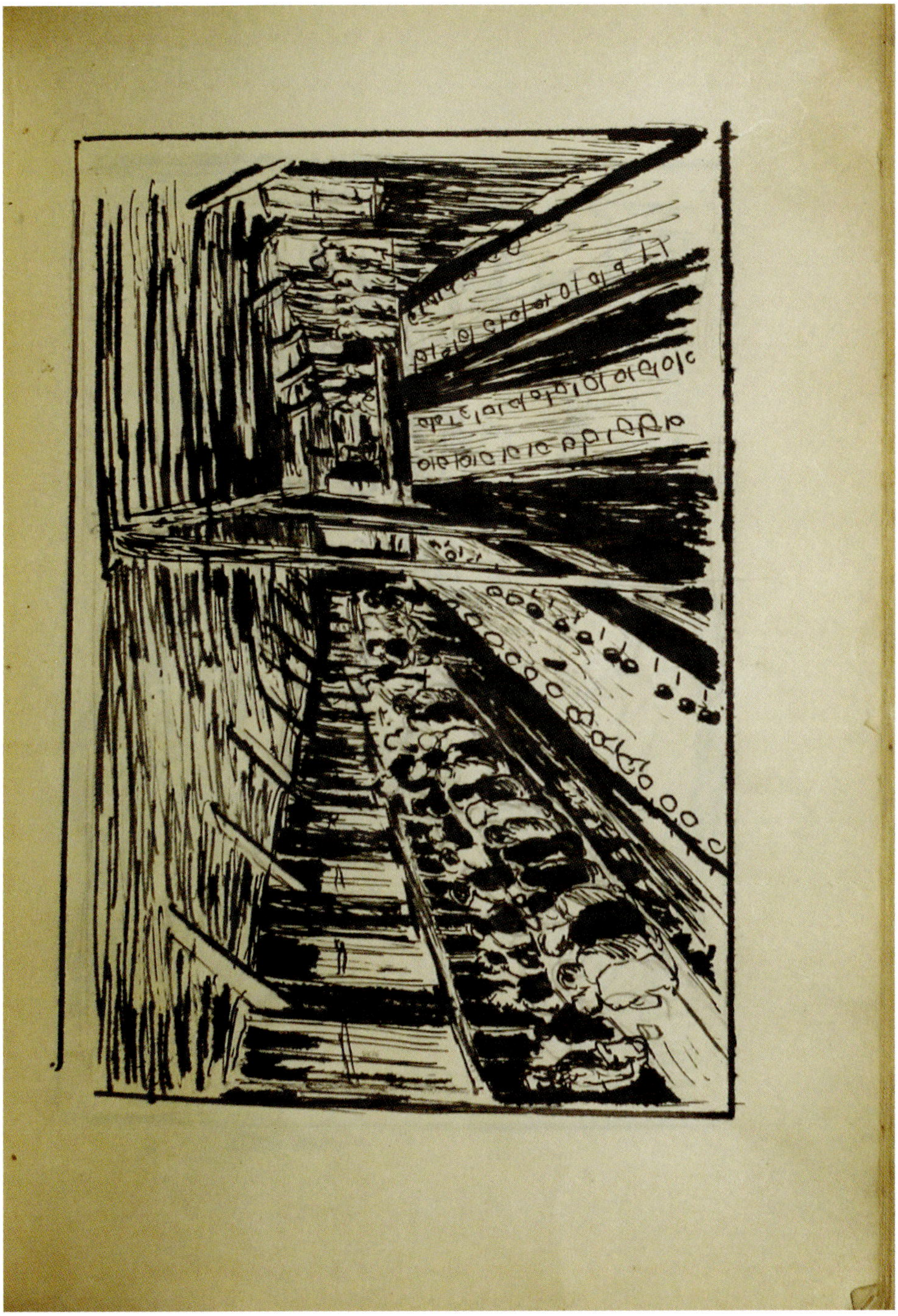

66 This is the mess hall. All form a line and bring their food [to the table] themselves. Again, after eating, they take their plates themselves to the place where they can be washed.

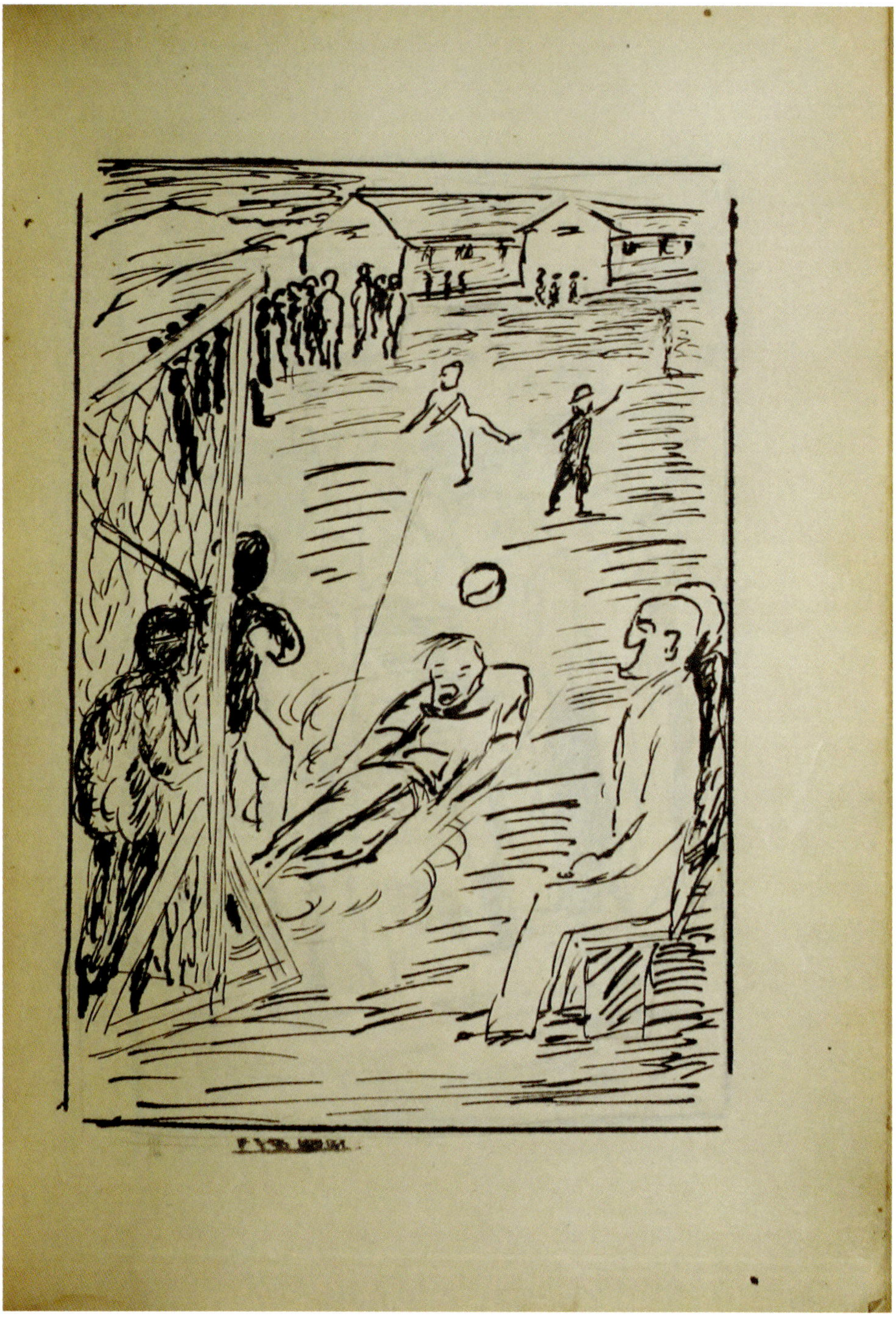

67 Five o'clock. Because the sun stays up in summer, some played baseball or looked around after finishing dinner. This is the senior baseball team. They are all laughing enthusiastically.

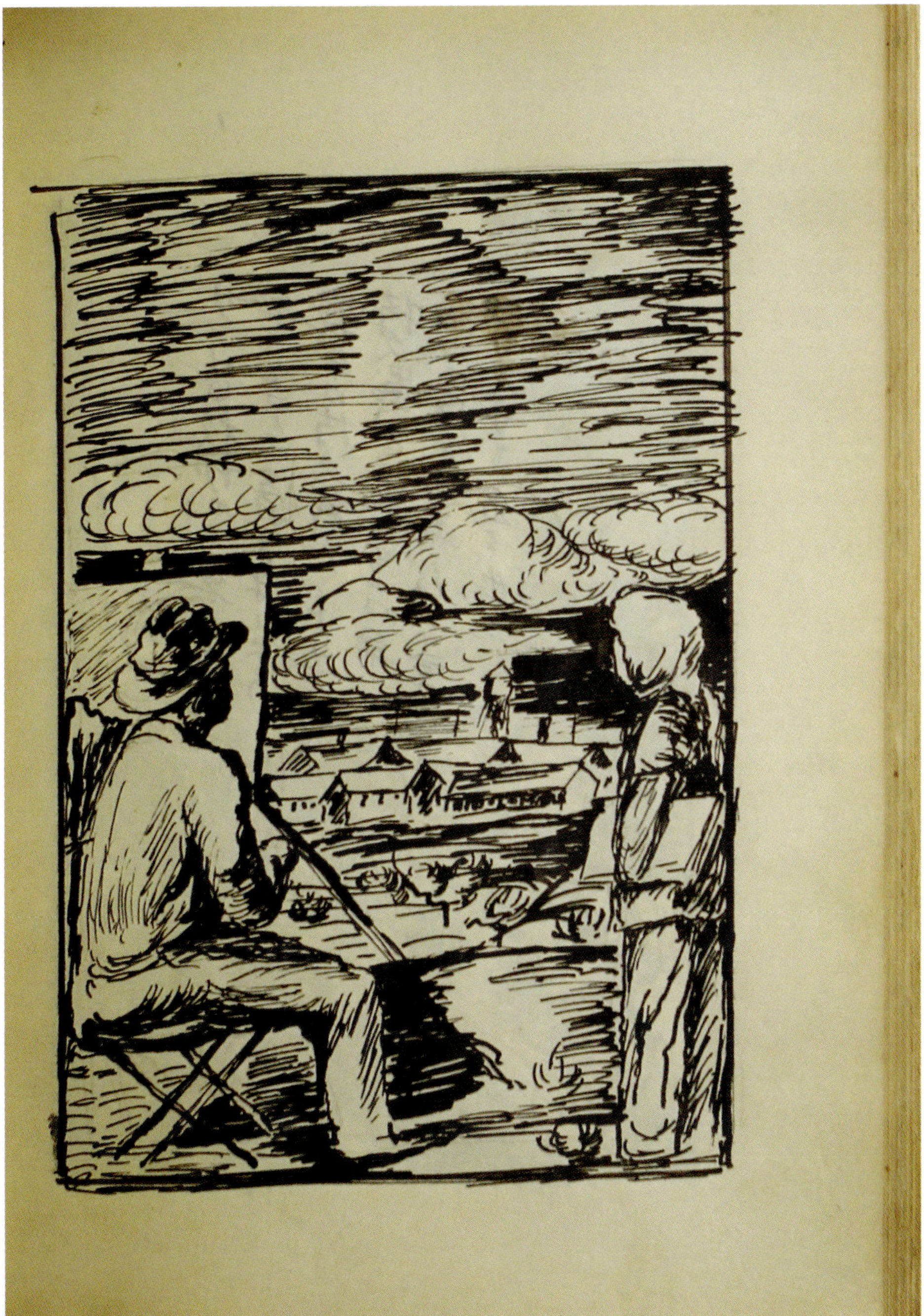

68 The carefree artist. On a bright sunny day, I am sketching a camp scene.

69

Hey, everyone, they say that they will give us some cut wood. Let us hurry up and get it. Just as this war is becoming a long one, so it is for us too. We must take quickly what can be taken. Move it, move it. Old men and old women come out.

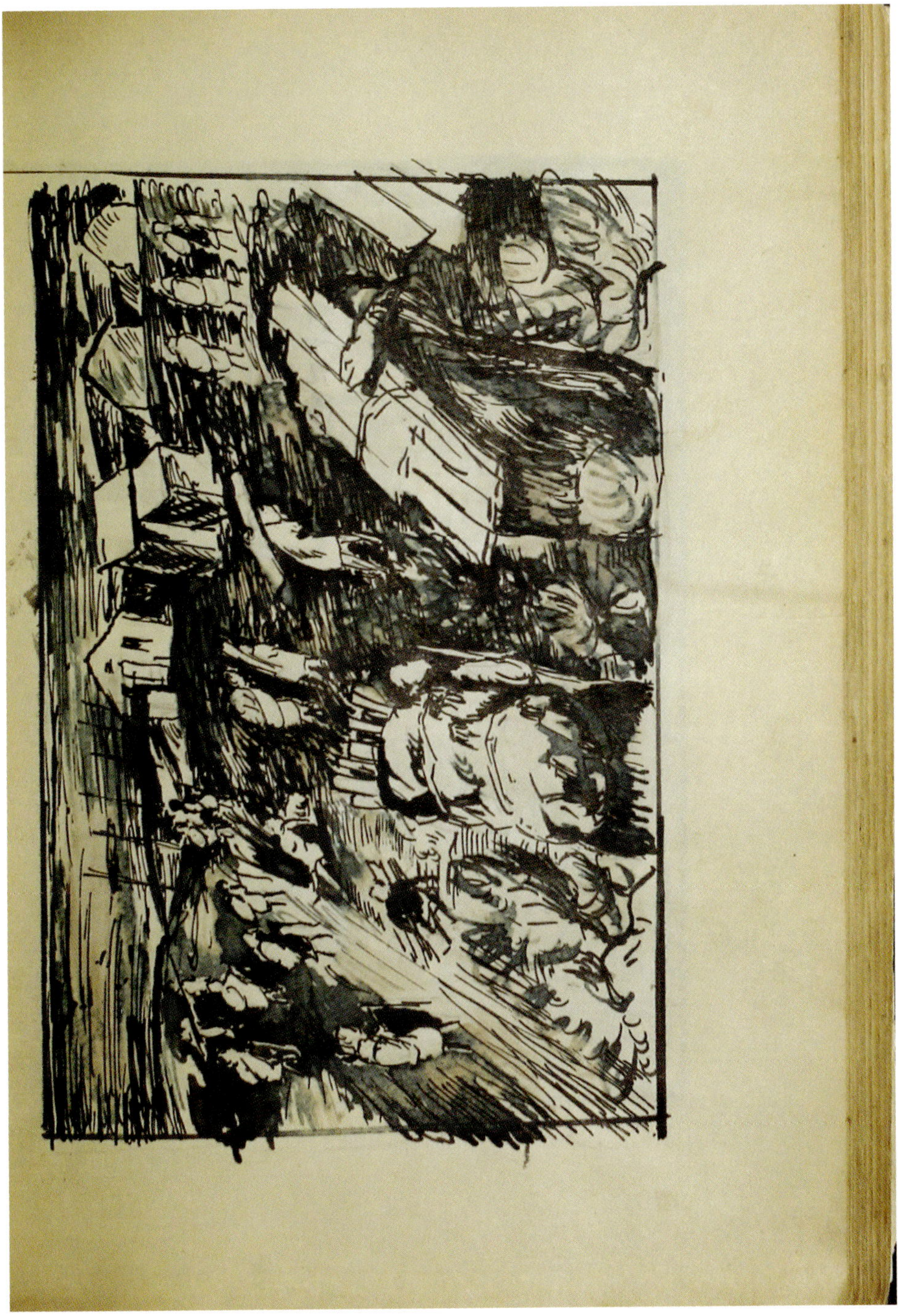

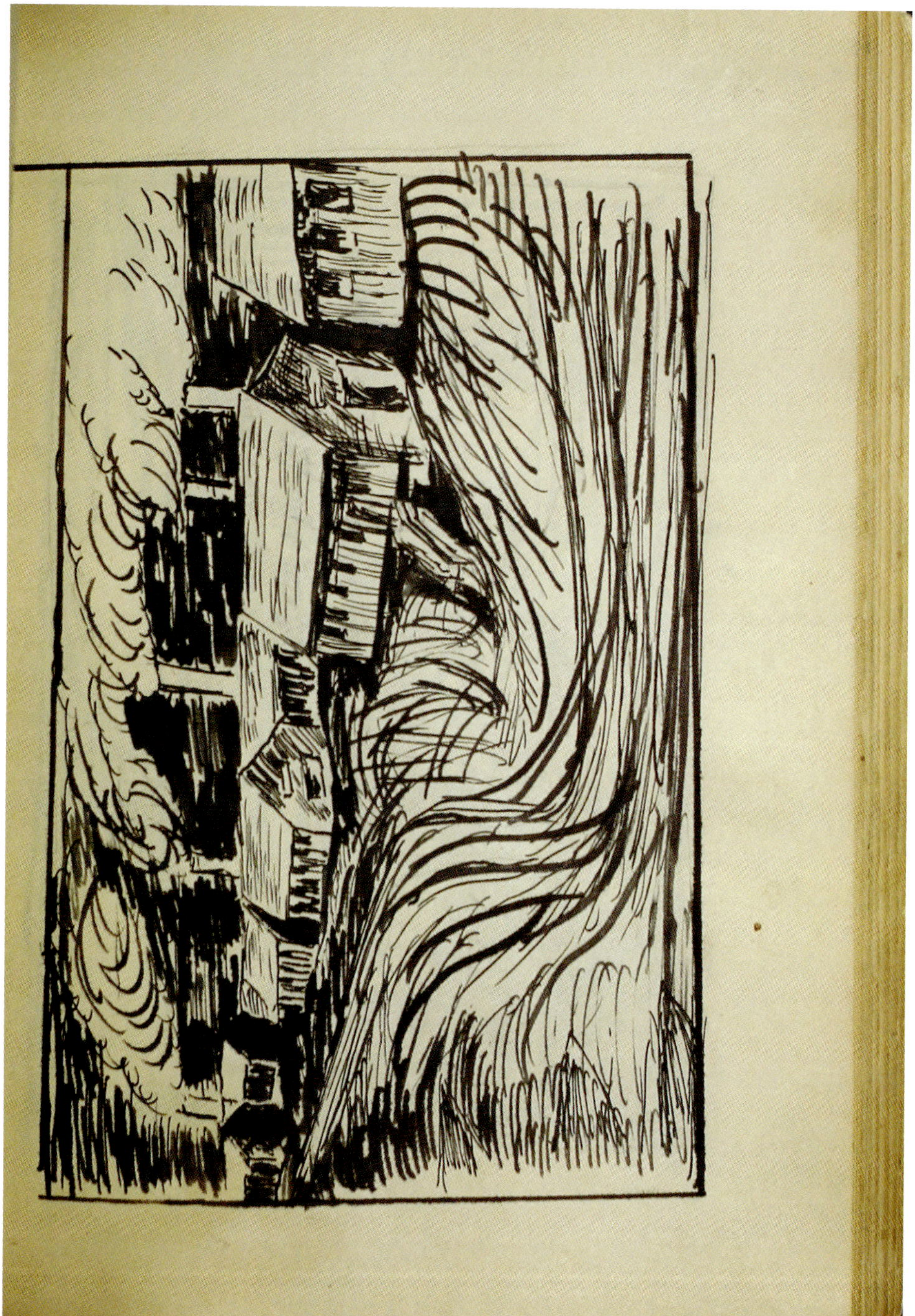

70 Rough spot in the road.

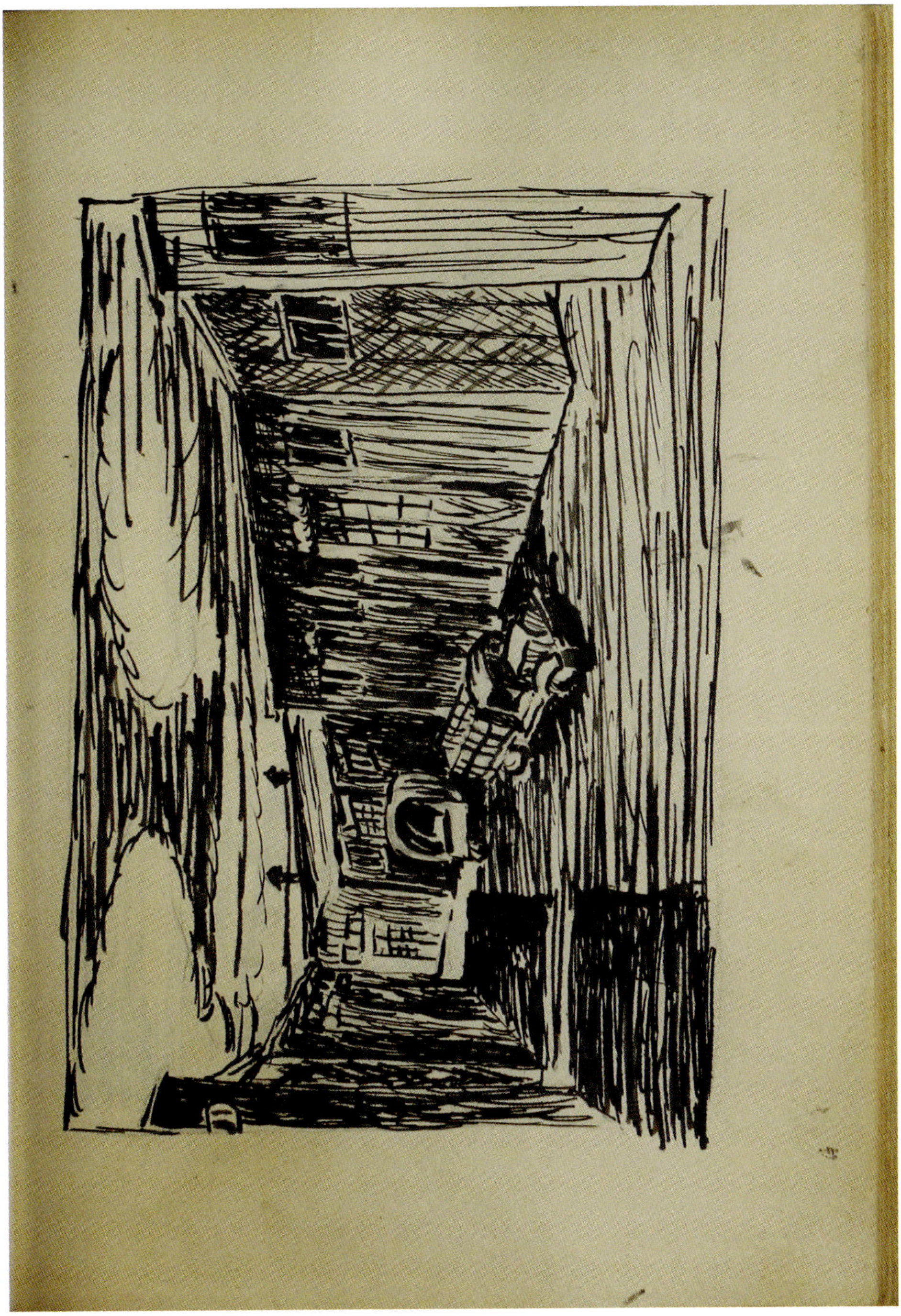

71 This is the storehouse where they keep the food and other things upon which our survival depends.

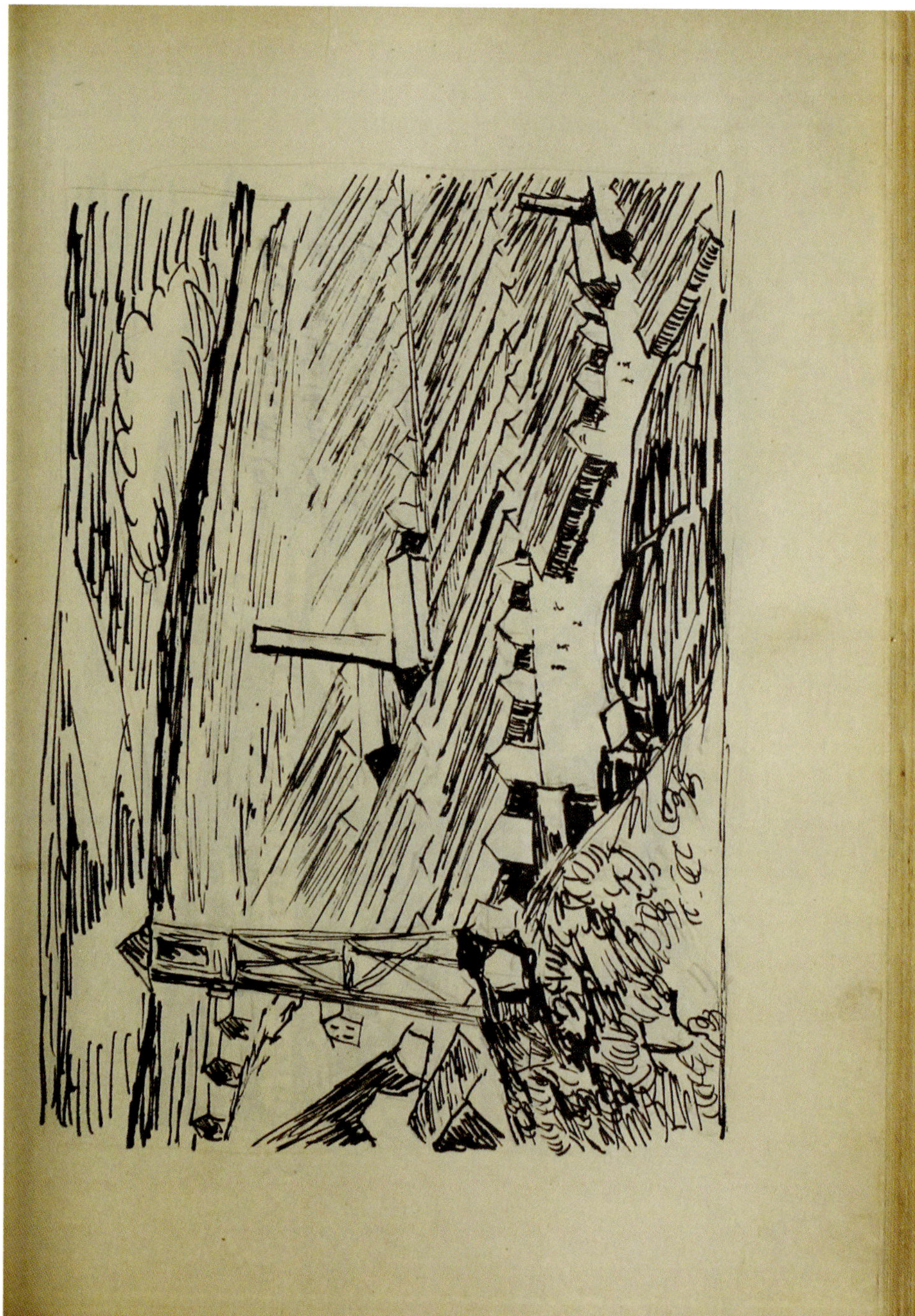

72 This is drawn to frame a view of the interior of the camp, Blocks 15 and 16.

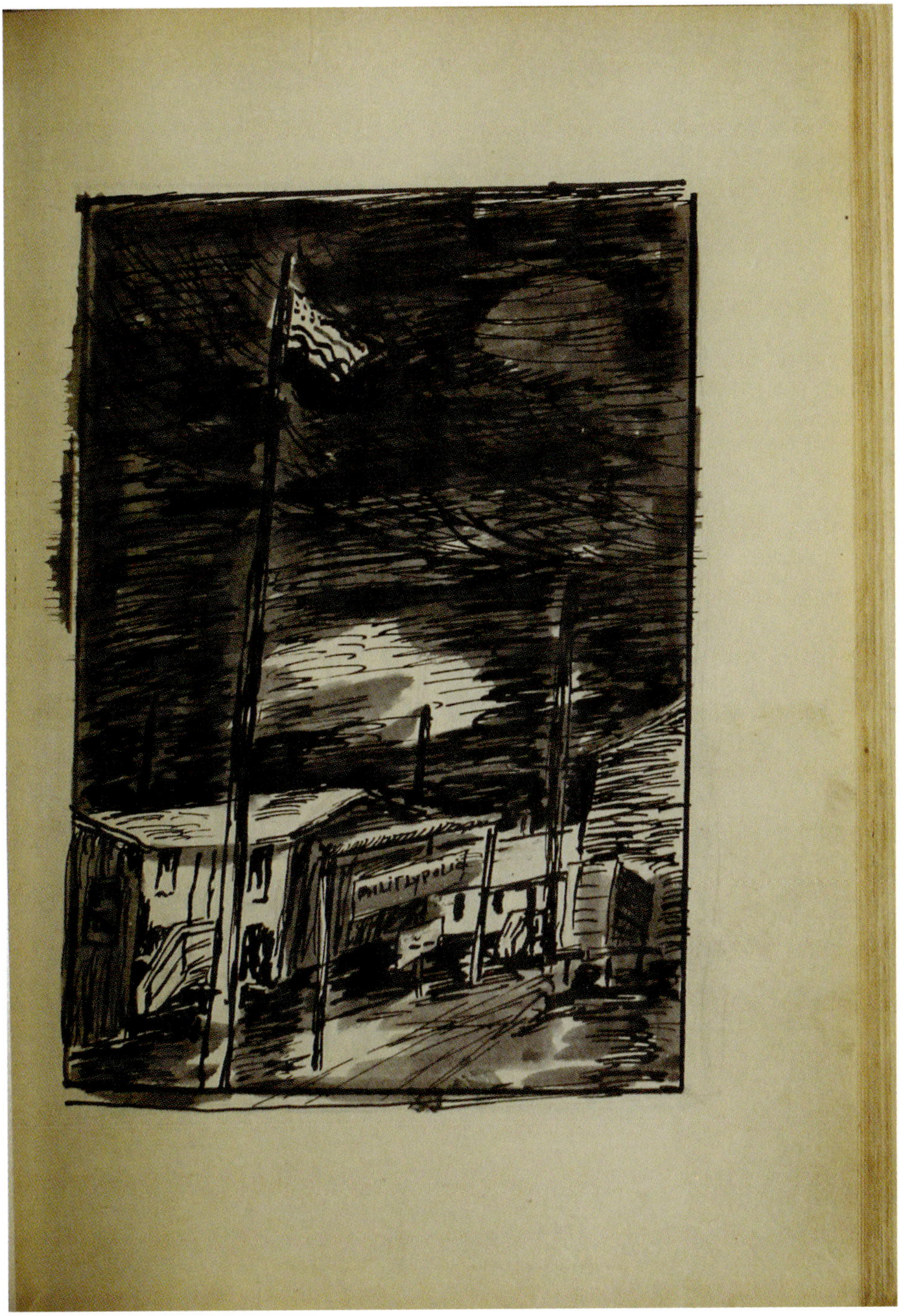

73 Headquarters of the Army Military Police.

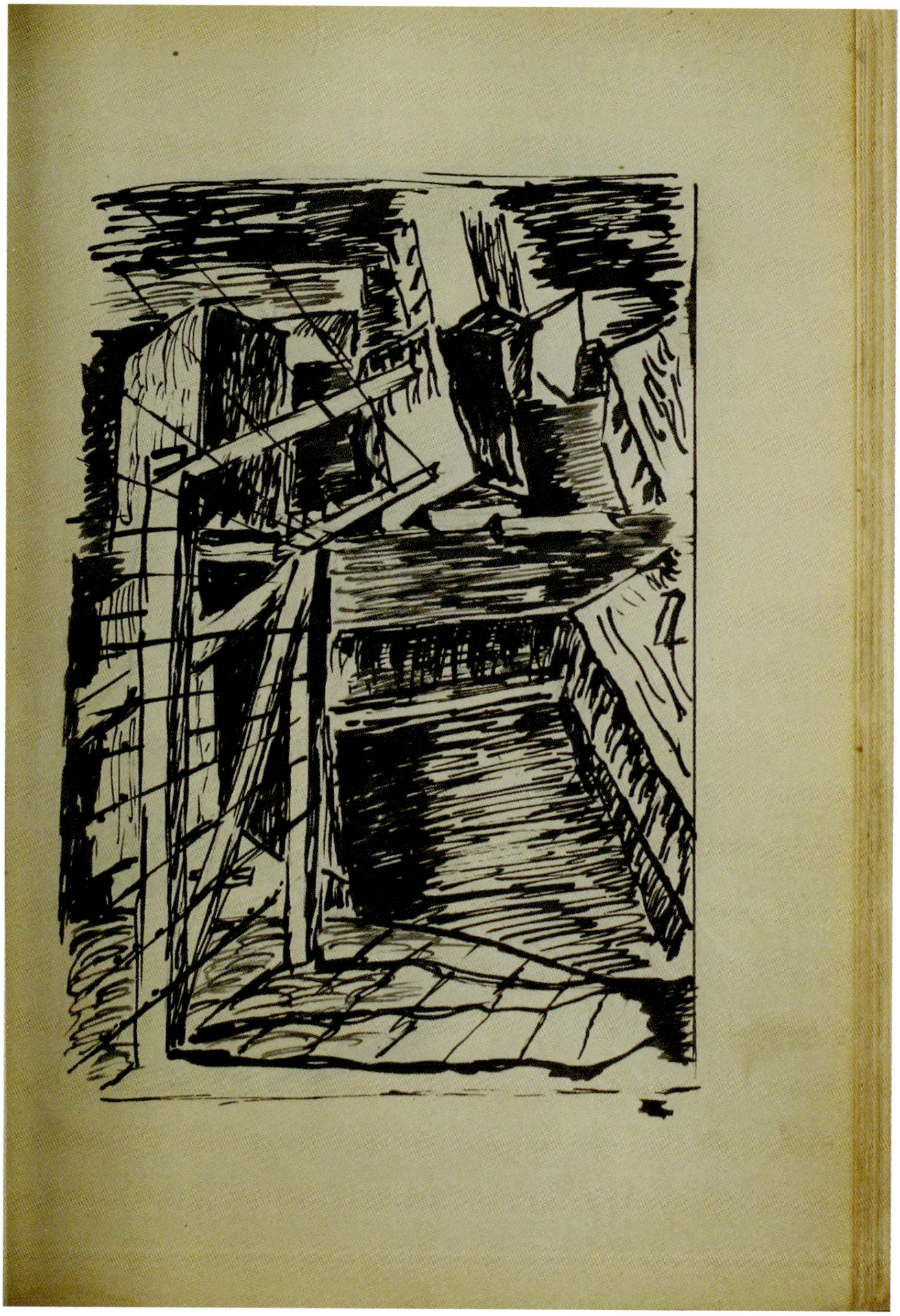

74 This is the barbed wire and [the scene] around Block 24.

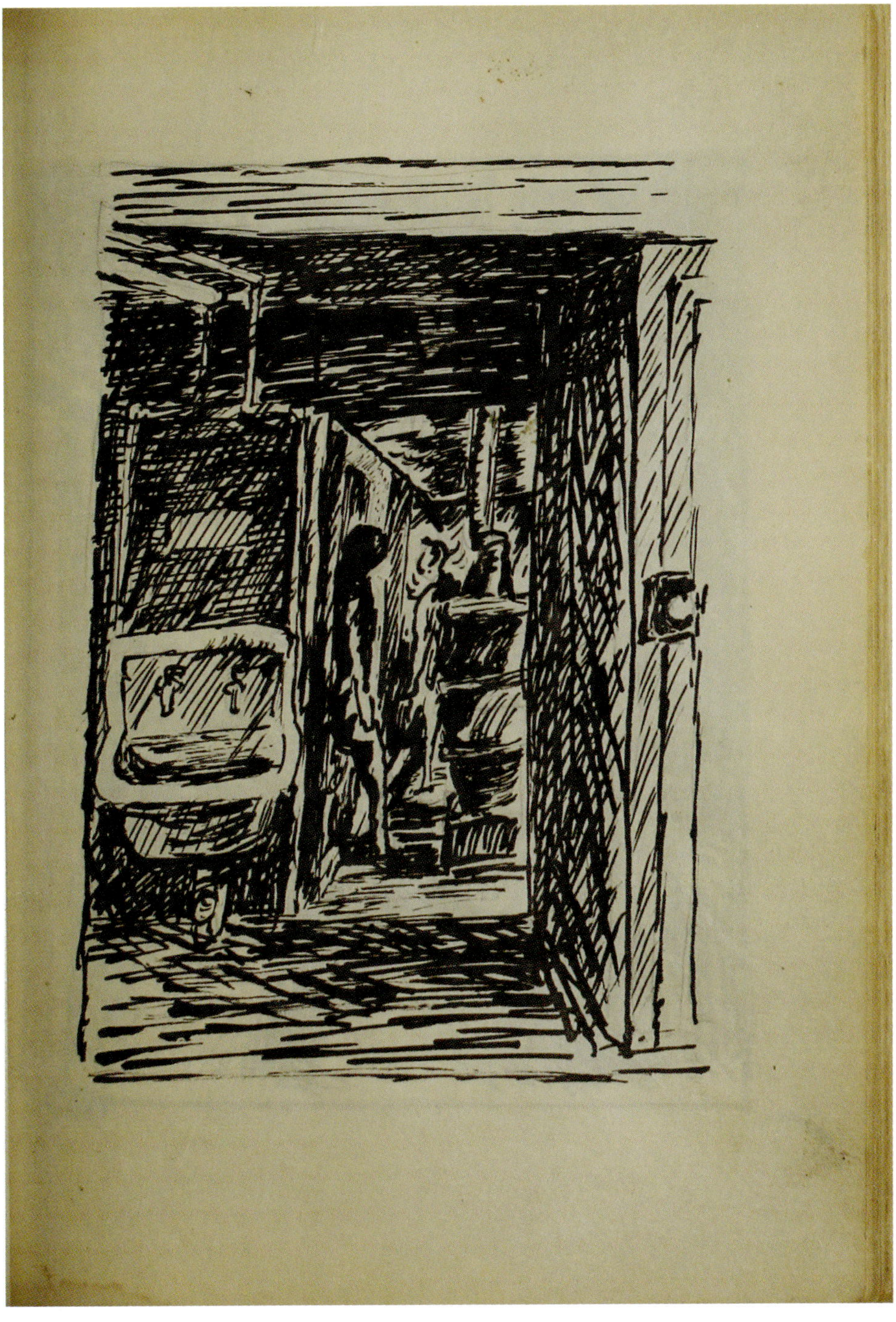

75 The men's shower room.

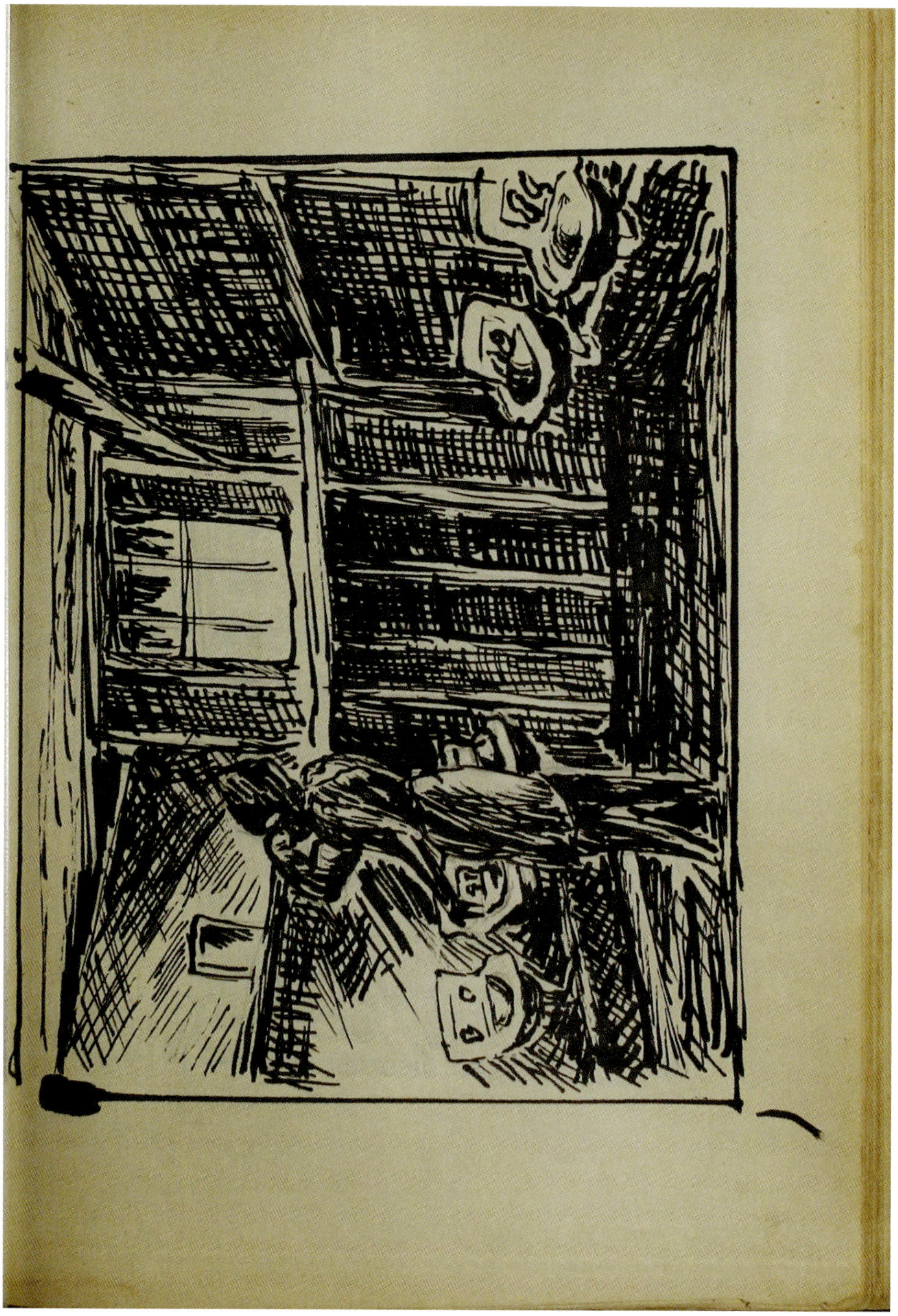

76 The first new lavatory to have been built.

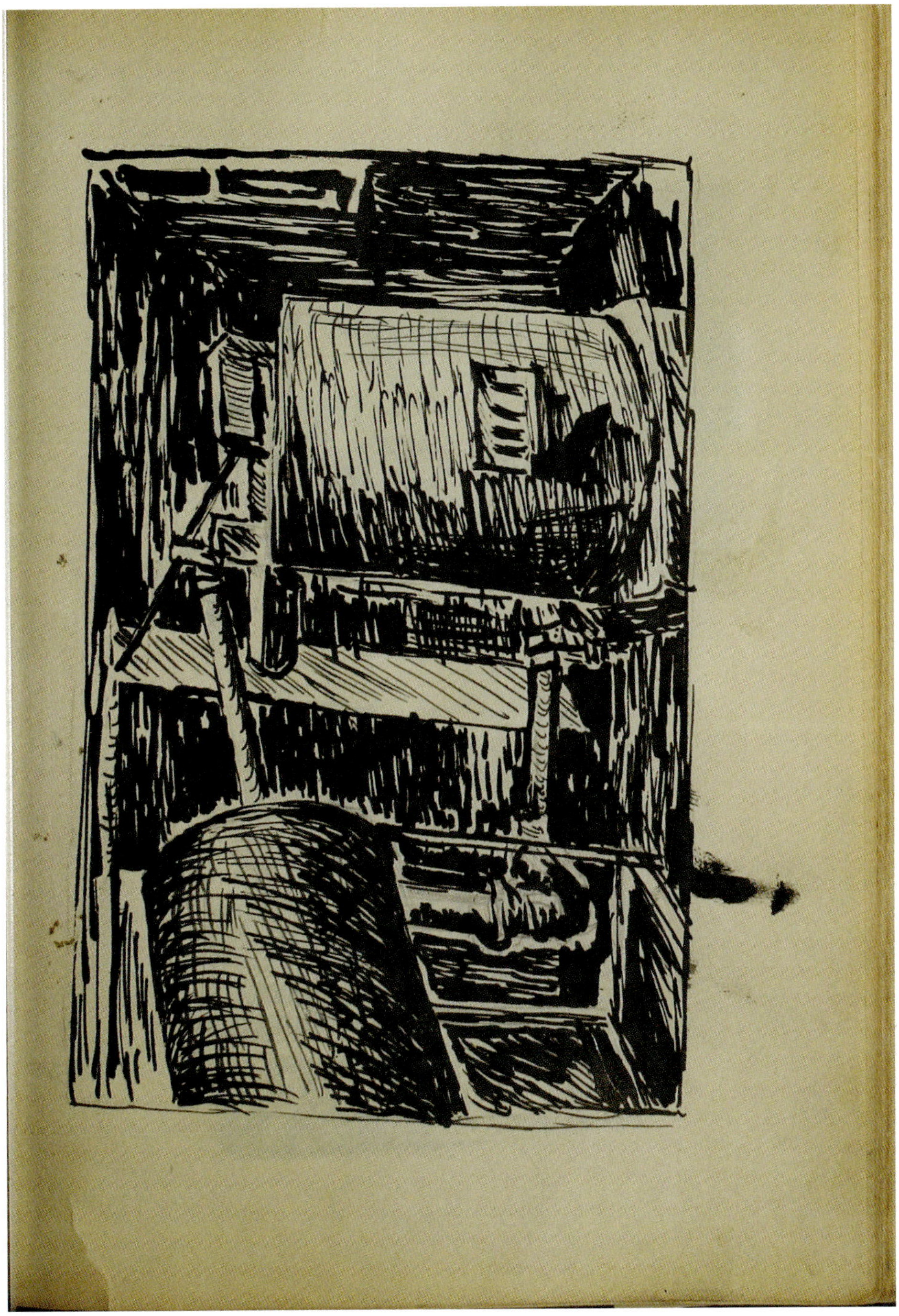

77 Boiler room.

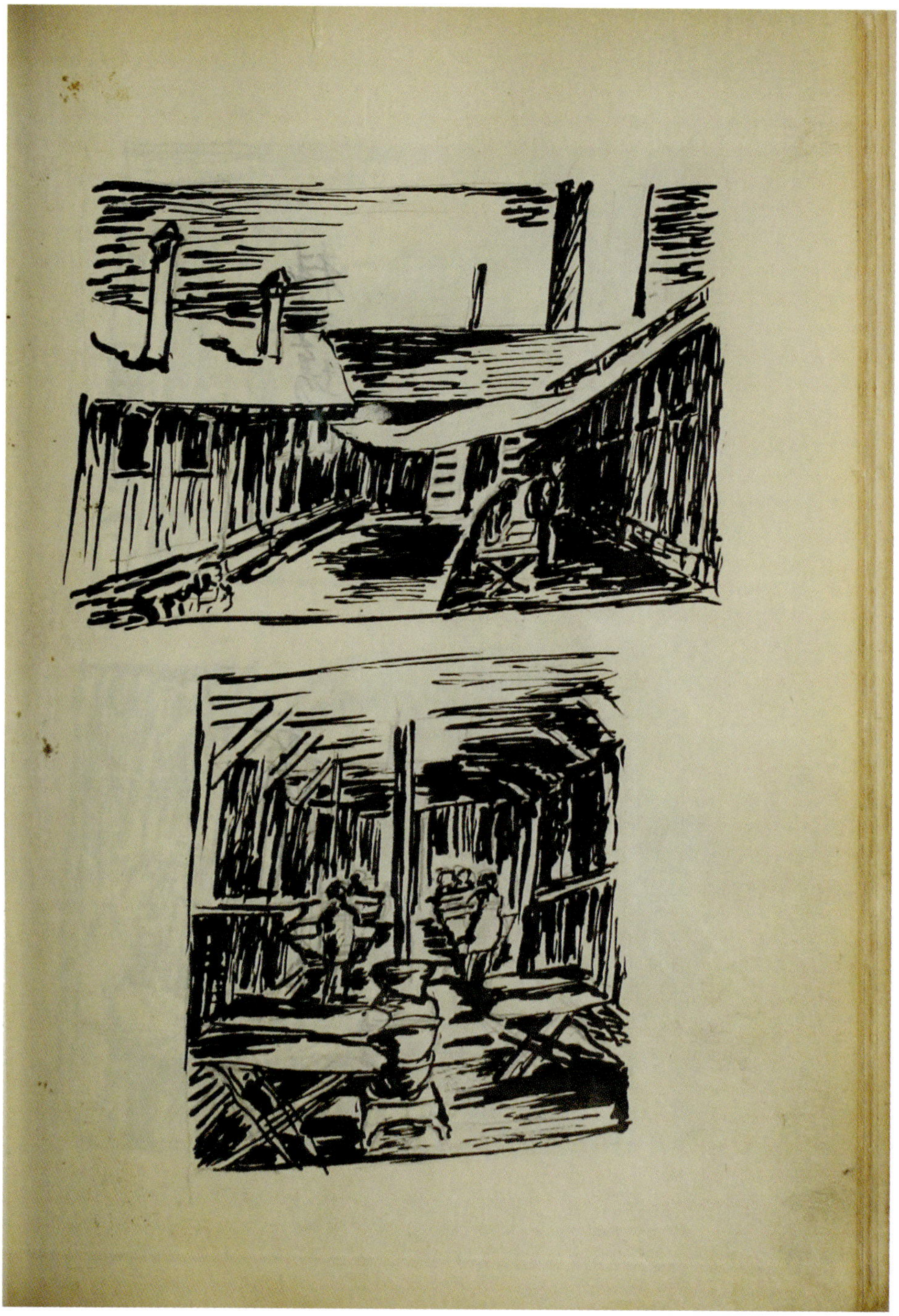

78 The shower room and lavatory built in the shape of an *H*.

The inside of the laundry.

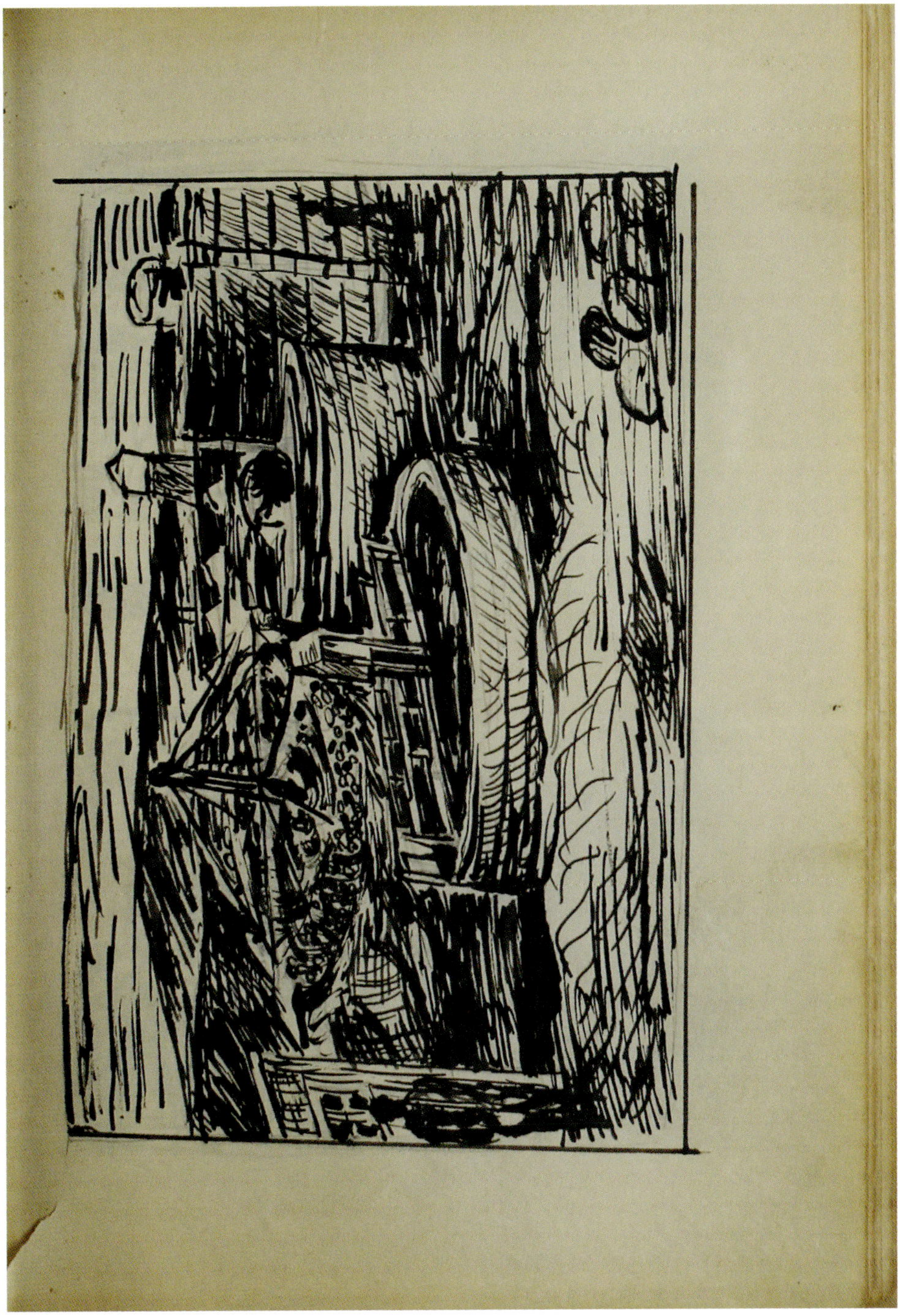

79 The sewage area. On days when the wind was bad, it was so smelly that it was hard to bear.

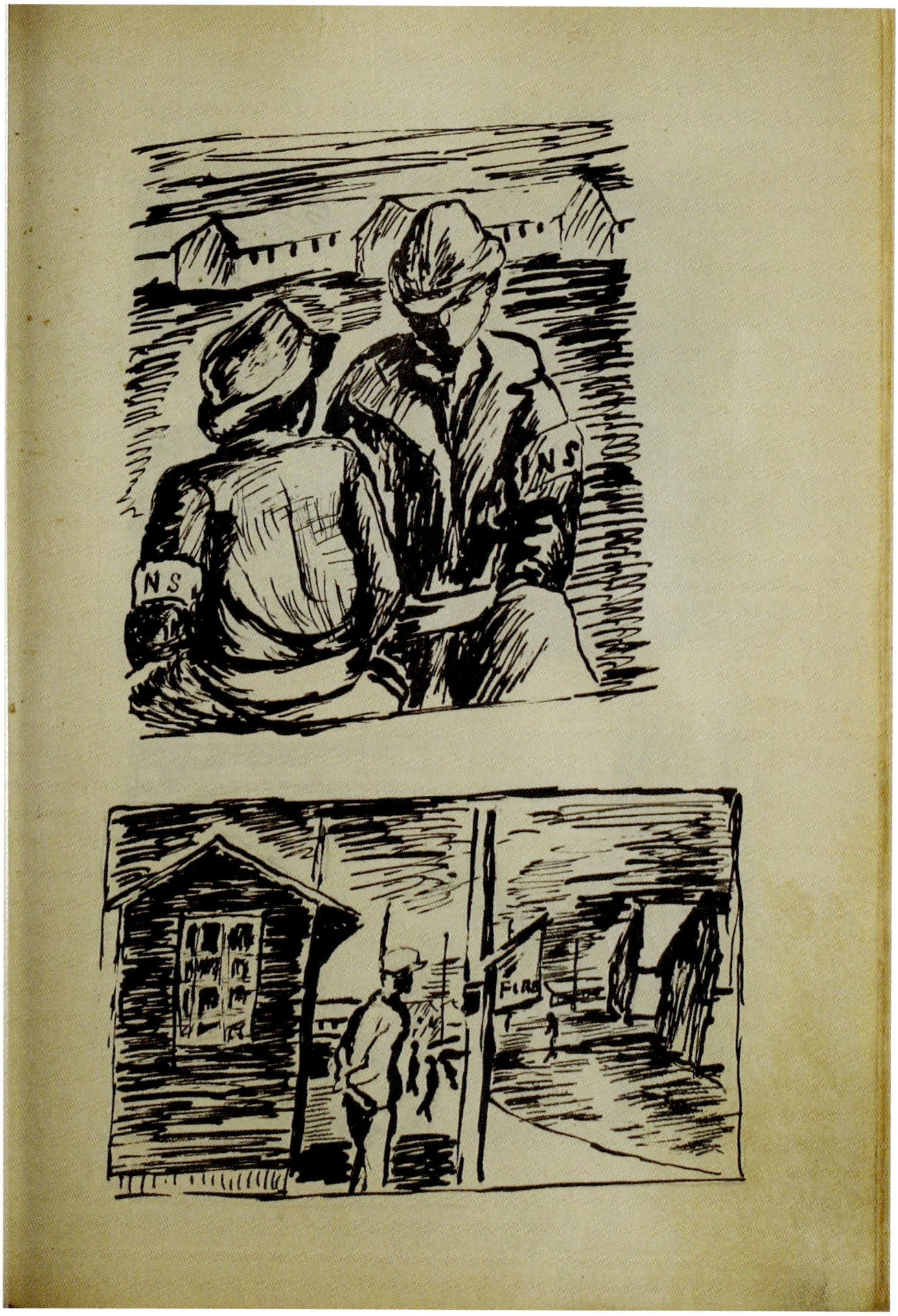

80 Dress of the Immigration and Naturalization Service Officers in the camp.

The police box number three in the camp. These are the policemen.

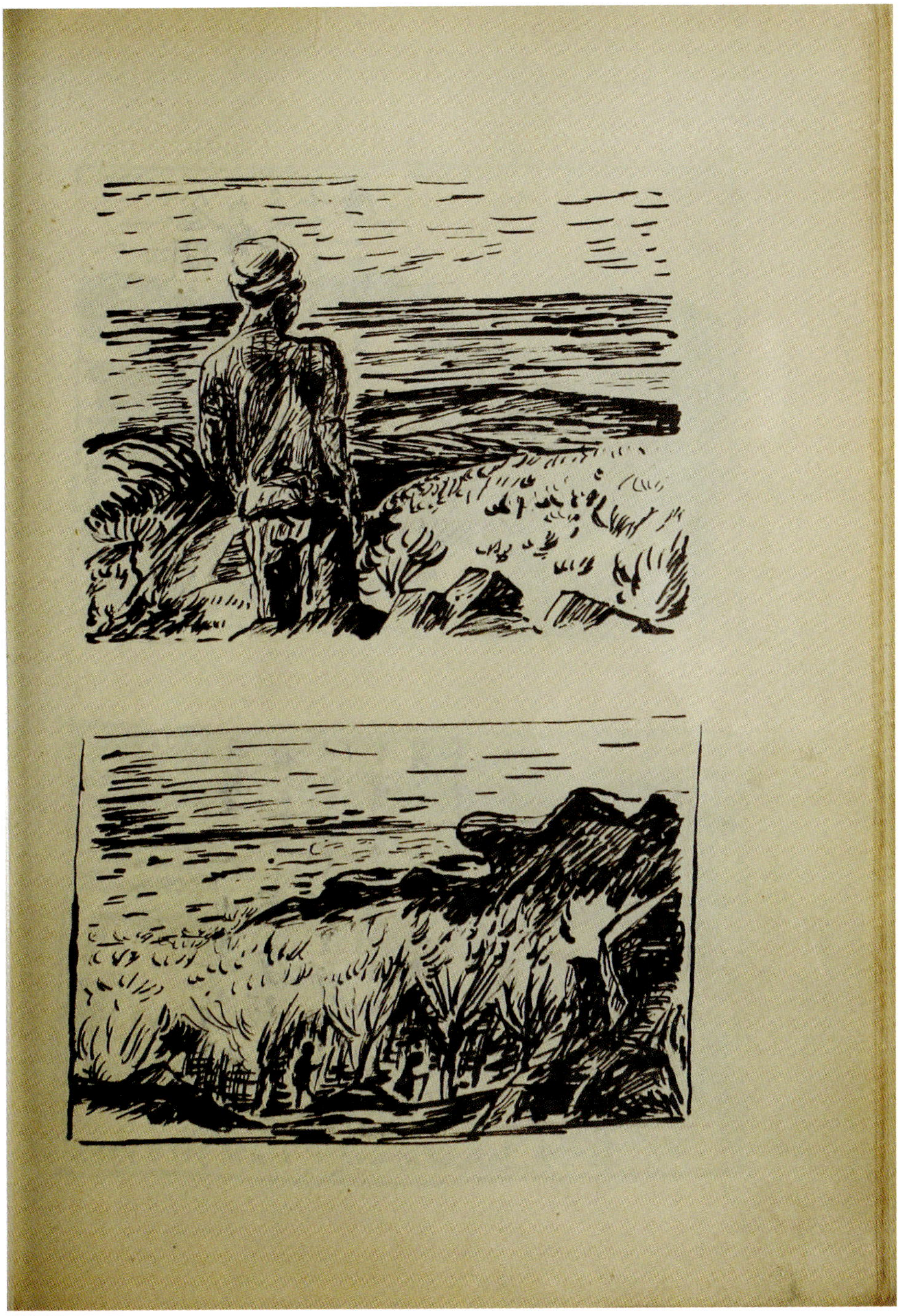

81 Here is a distant view of a wide space. Looking at the scene unchanged from its original form and without even a trace of people, a fearful feeling wells up in me.

This is the sage in a valley between two cliffs.

82

Bones of an animal. There are many coyote around here. When it becomes night, we can hear them crying out vigorously. They are the number one . . . in this area.

A fight between birds and a snake.

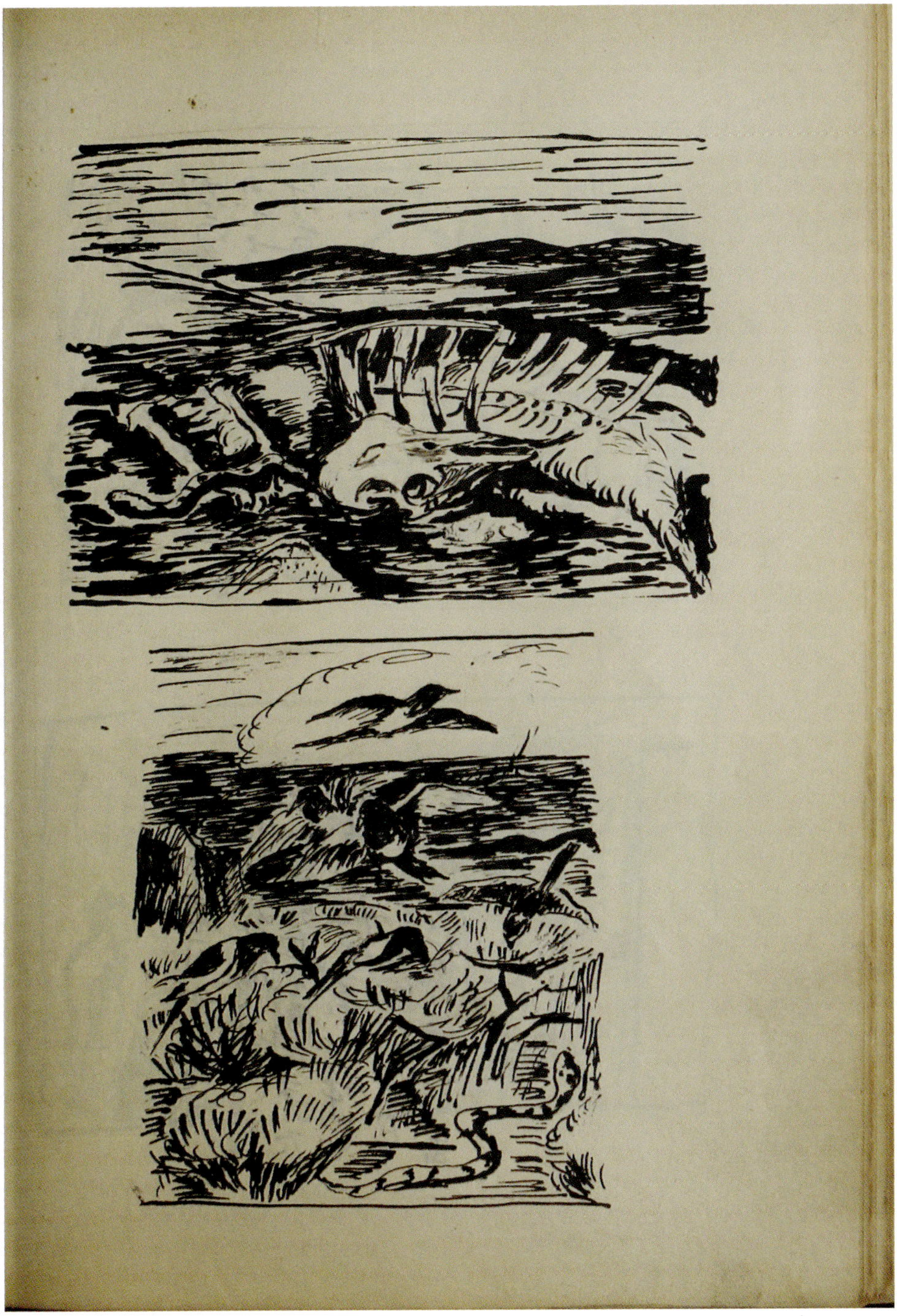

83

We ran across a rattlesnake. We were very surprised.

I am not sure if that was the reason or not, but immediately after returning home, I collapsed from blood poisoning. An ambulance was quickly called, and it was decided I would be hospitalized. Now, two strong men are taking me out.

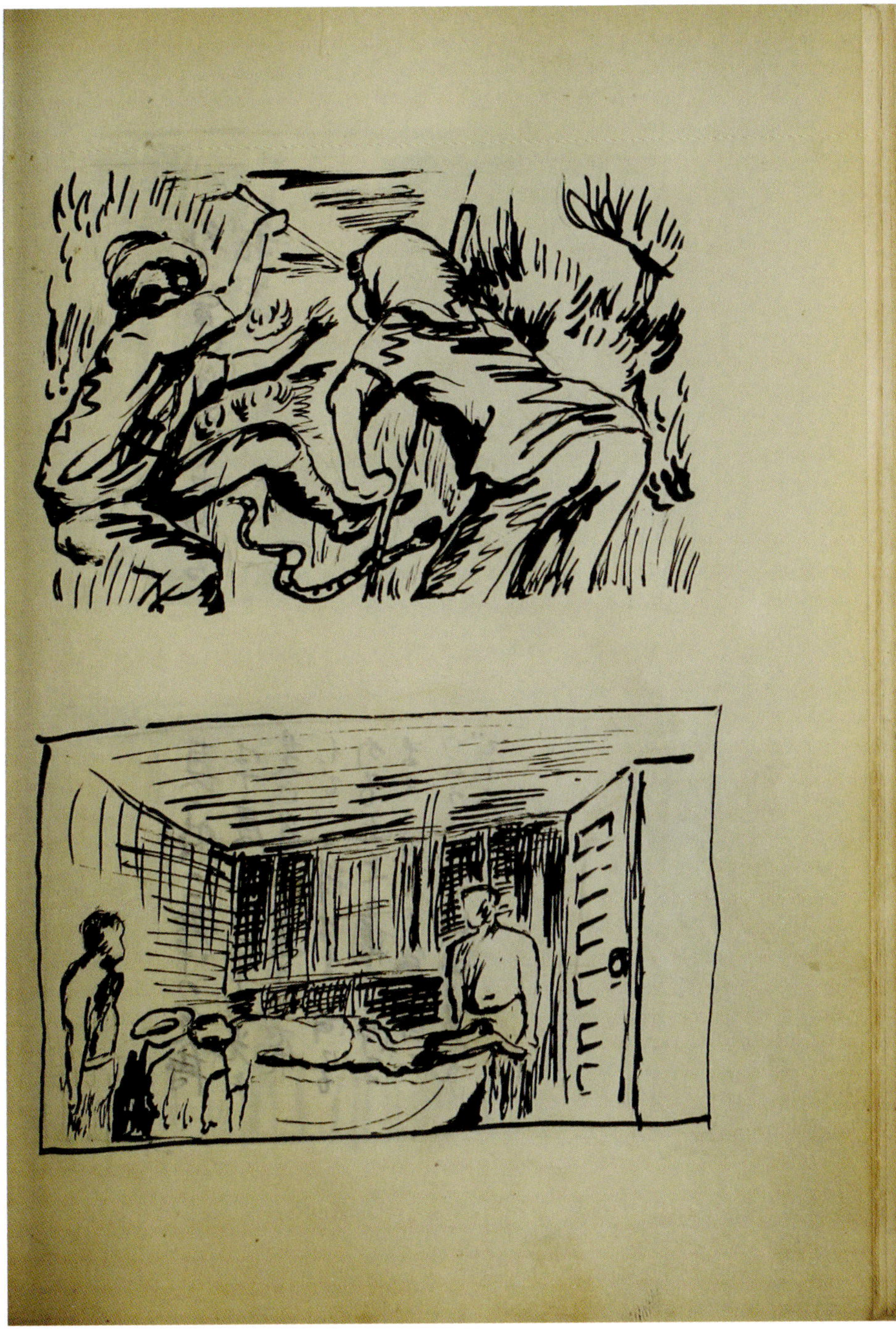

84

This is me being taken outside.

My feeling during that time of my sickness was just like a shining white cloth or flying along at high speed. This, that, and everything was rising, and because of that, I had no choice but to keep my eyes shut.

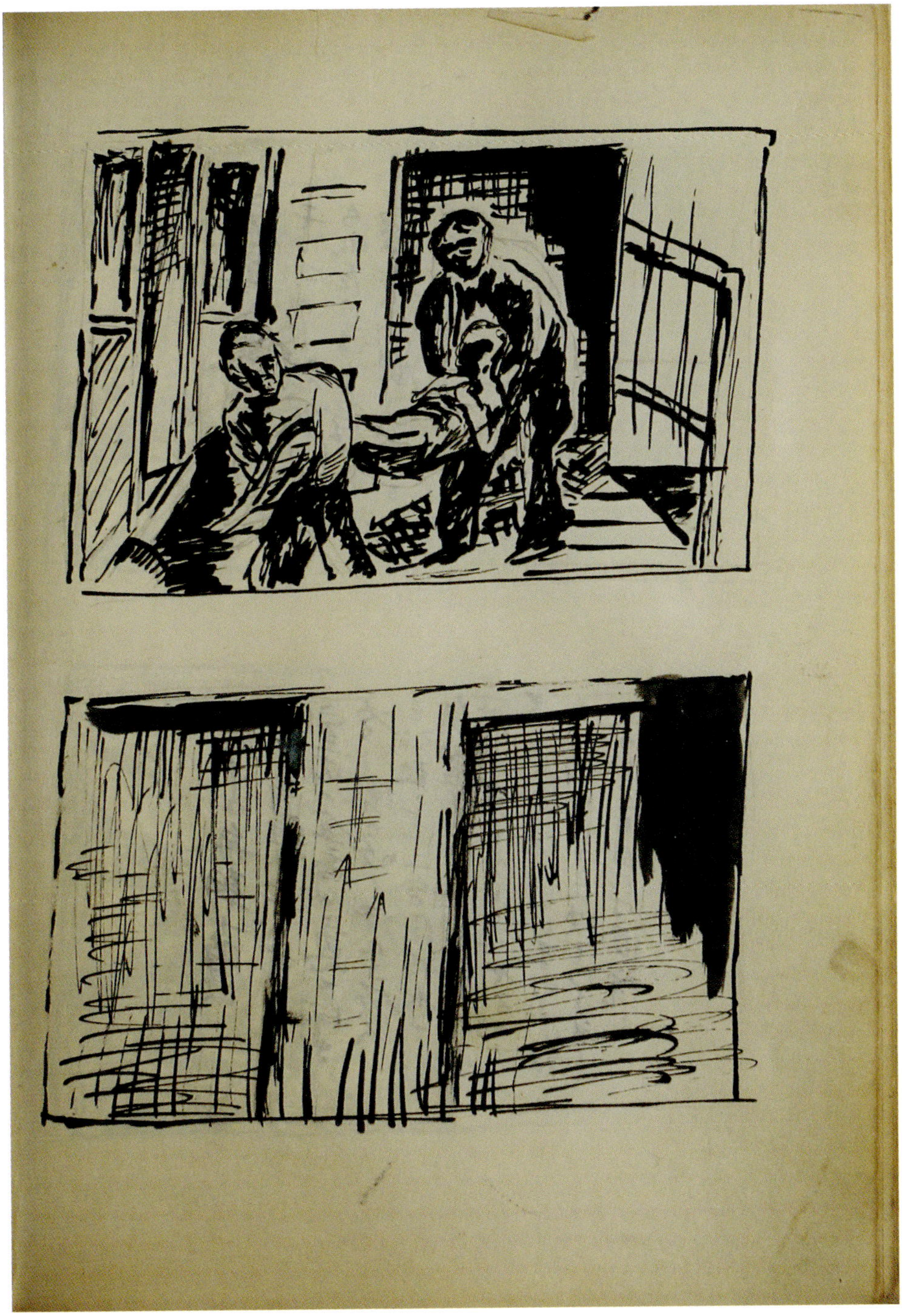

85

After they carried me to the hospital room, they threw me off the [stretcher,] so I almost fell off the other side of the bed.

In the hospital every morning around 7:00 A.M., two male nurses came in and opened all the windows in the room. Waking up the patients in the blowing cold wind, they would wipe down our bodies with [about] two glasses of cold water. This would take about an hour, and so in the end, I caught cold. My feelings immediately improved, and so [I] was released on the third day.

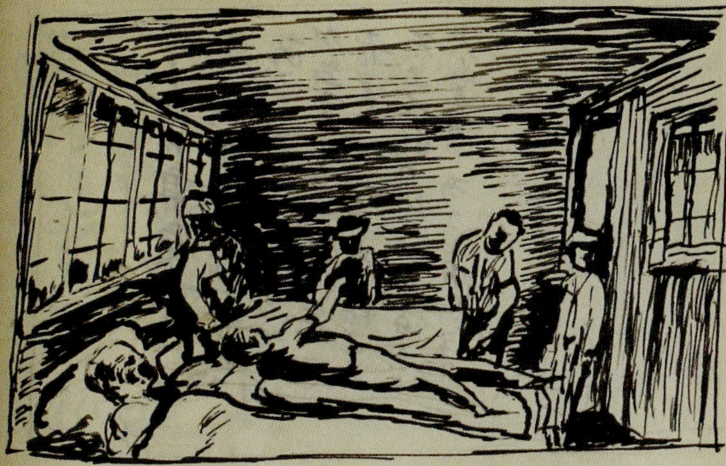

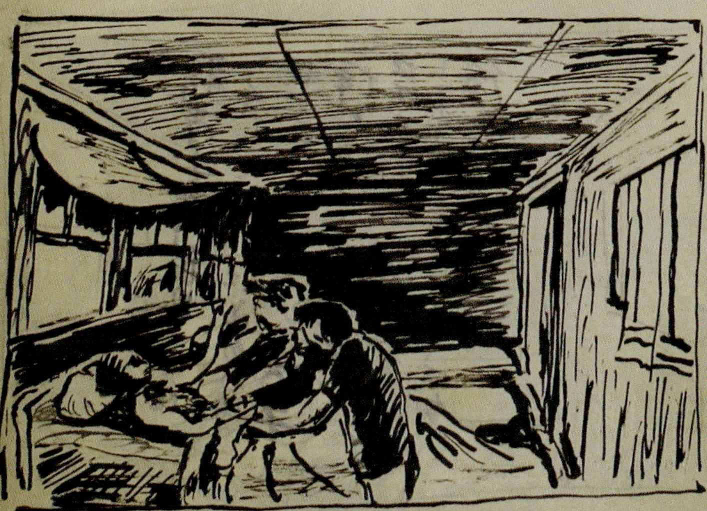

86

A four-thousand-foot plateau. As far as the eye can see, the land is flat with deep valleys formed into it everywhere. The color of the rock is red black. I think that this area was probably a volcanic field in the past.

My wife and I go walking around from mountain to mountain almost every day trying to catch an owl. I feel lonely as if lost on the Pacific Ocean. Of course, if one lost one's sense of direction, it would be dangerous.

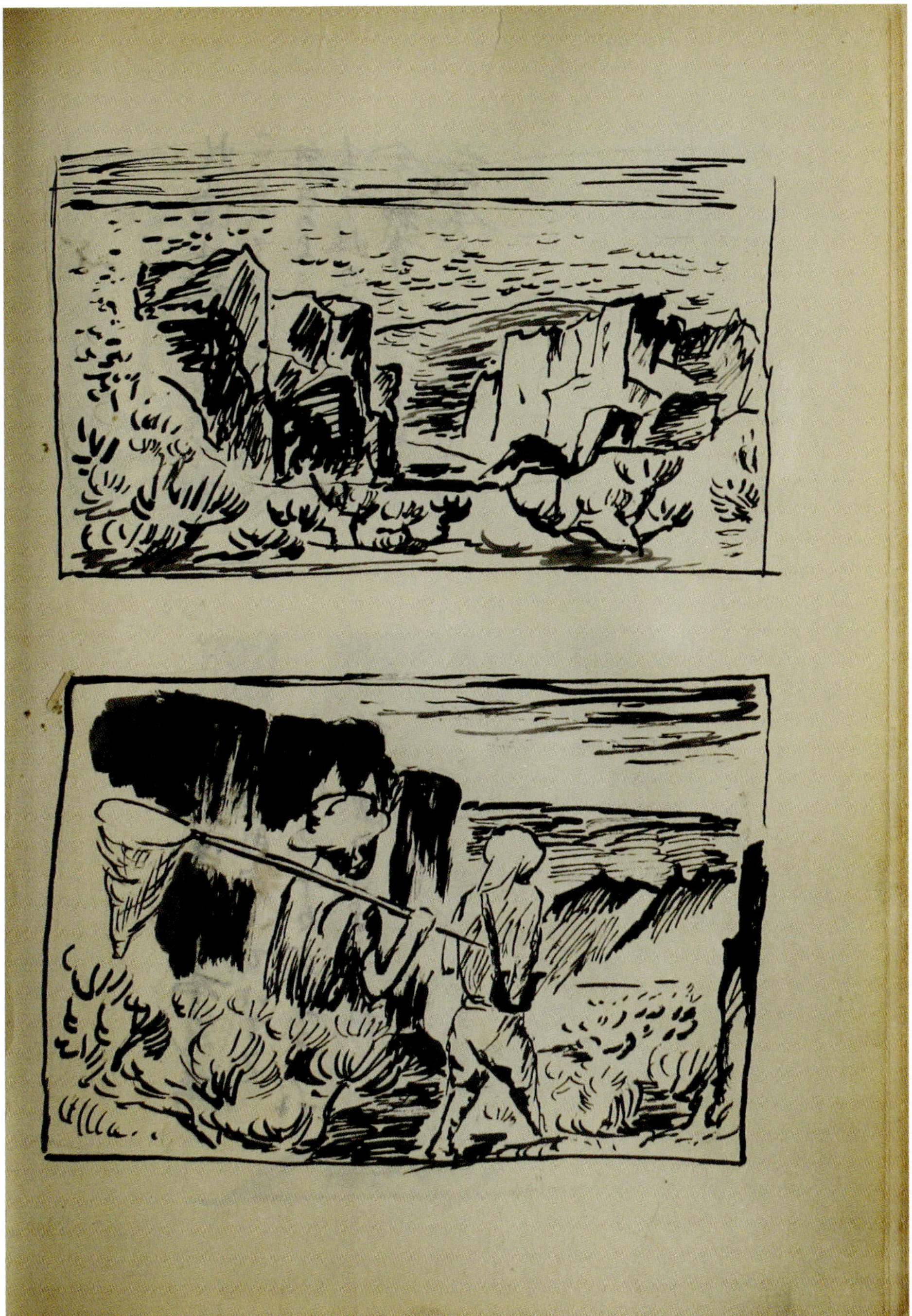

87

This is the silver world I saw. It is still [snowing.]

It is the end of the year. We will pound the rice cakes without which it is not New Year's Day for us Japanese. The rice for the rice cake is being steamed in the outside garden.

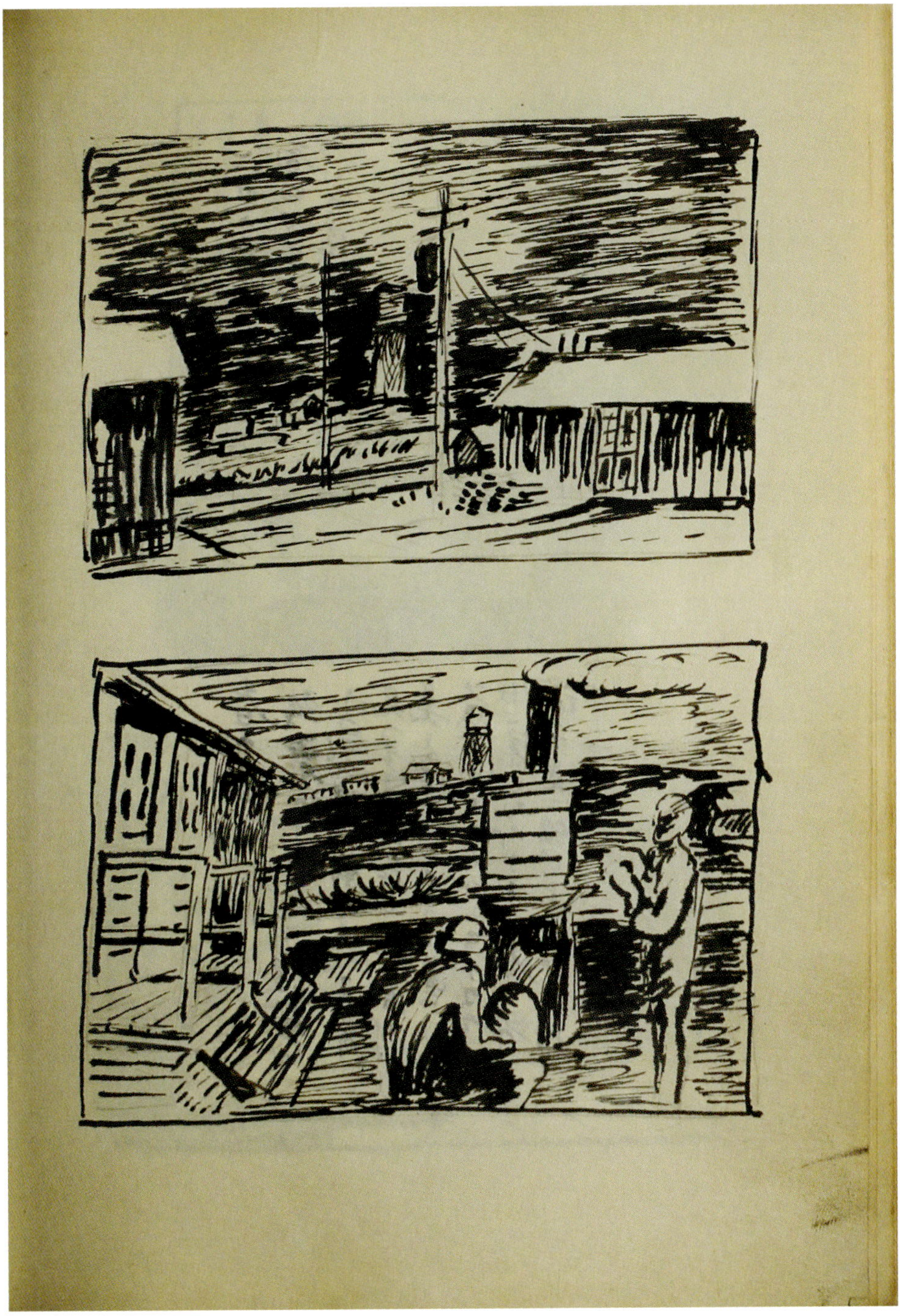

88

Mixing with the young second-generation Japanese Americans, we pounded the [*mochi*] shouting enthusiastically.

In the snow remaining in the advent of spring, I can see various kinds of birds singing and playing. The beautiful stripes of yellow sunlight peek through from among the dry willow trees. Although it is still very cold, the hope of seeing another spring gives me a warm feeling.

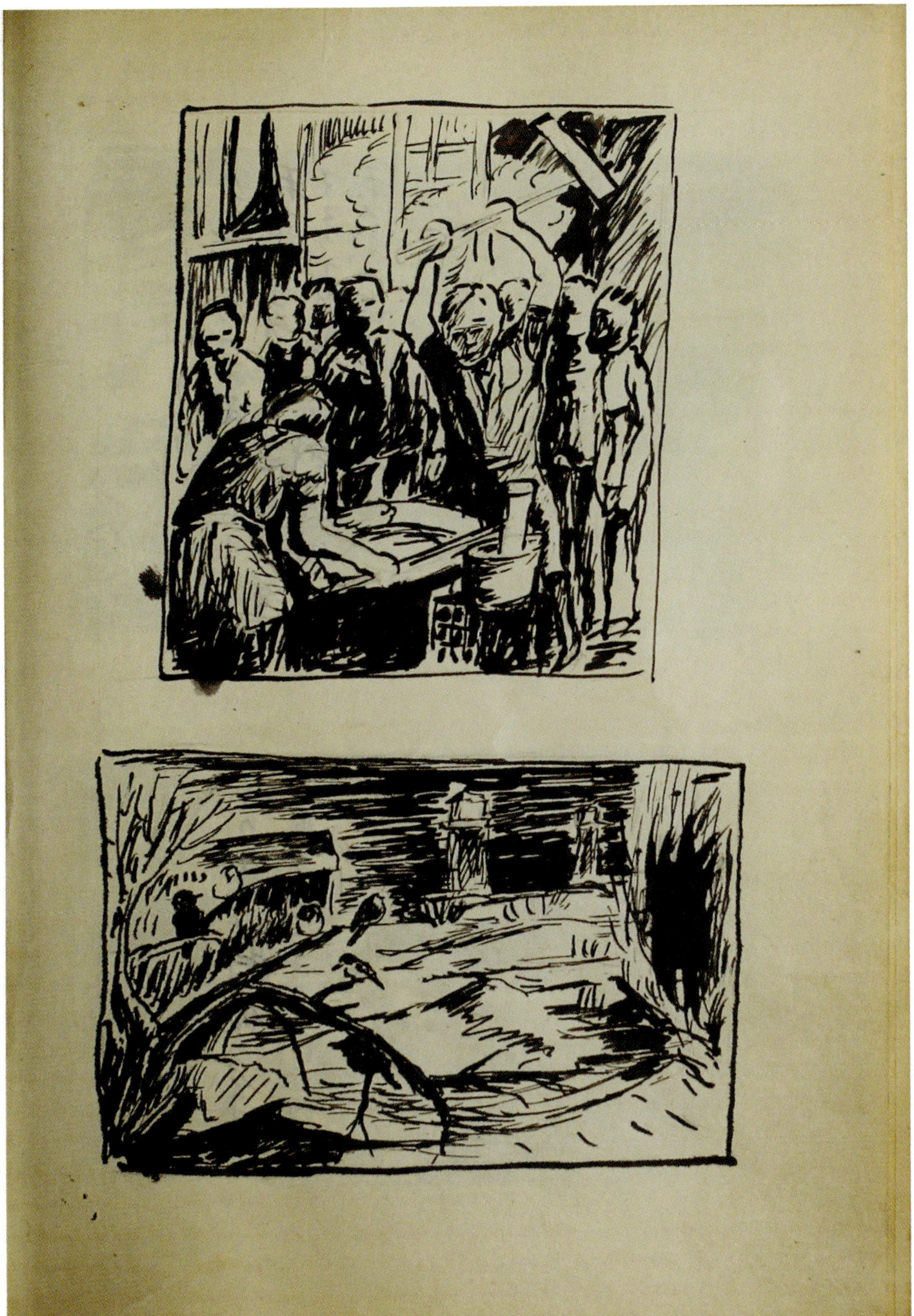

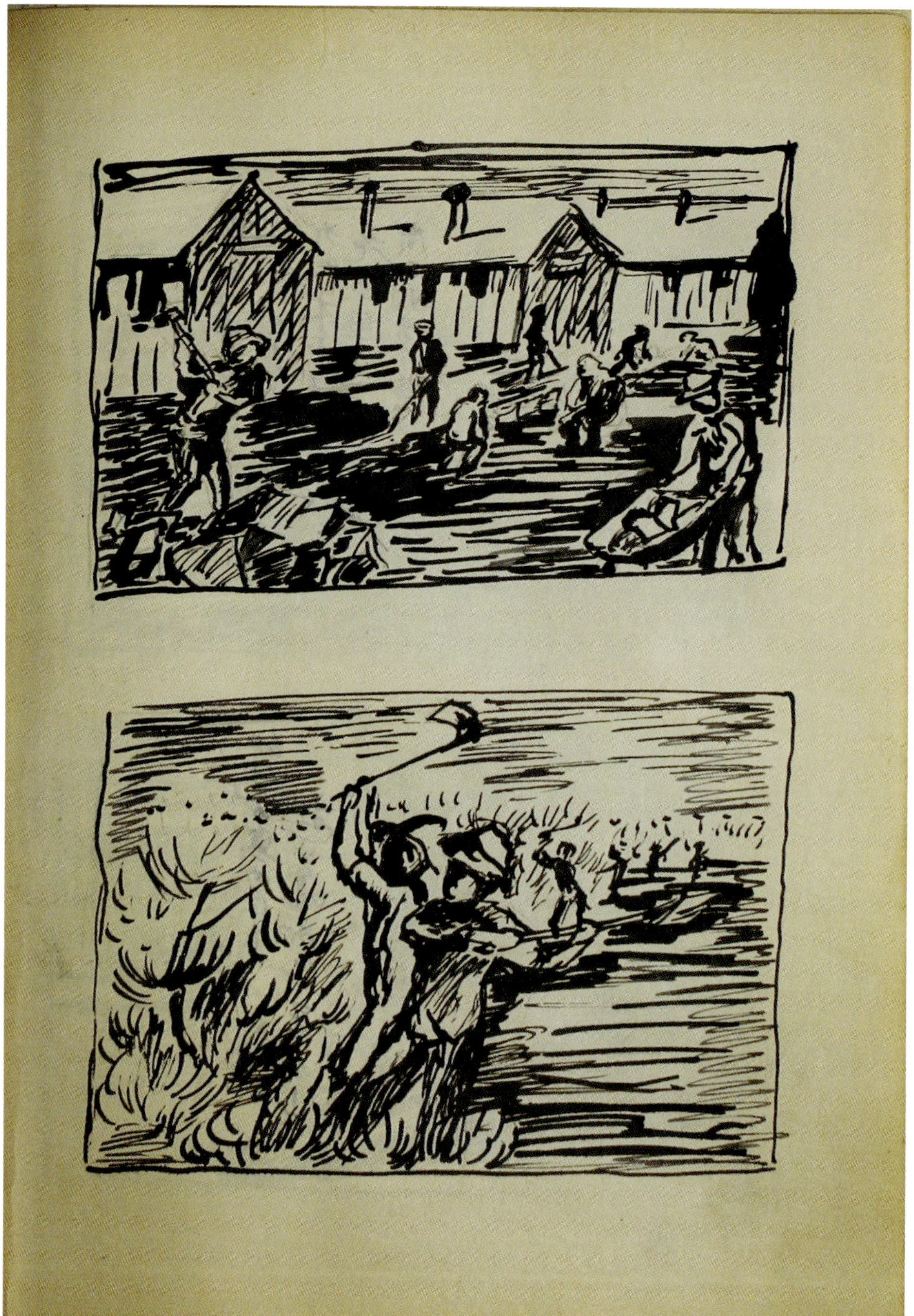

89 This is local road repair. All are volunteers.

We are making a baseball field. They are cutting and removing the sagebrush.

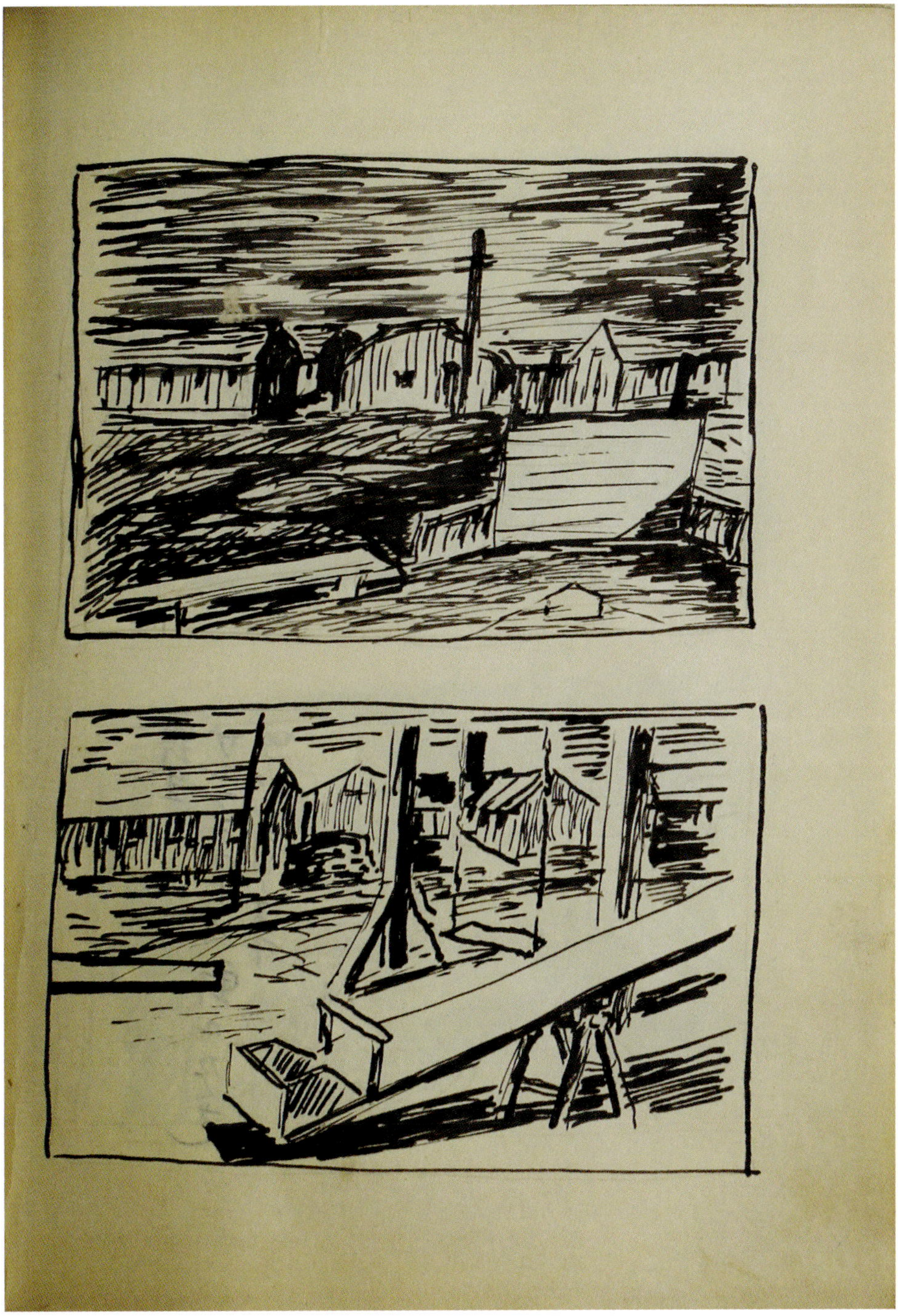

90 Humble though it is, the baseball field is done. A softball game among the old people has begun.

There is also a place for children to play.

91

The swimming pool, too, is done.

There are many wild sunflowers blooming in the fields.

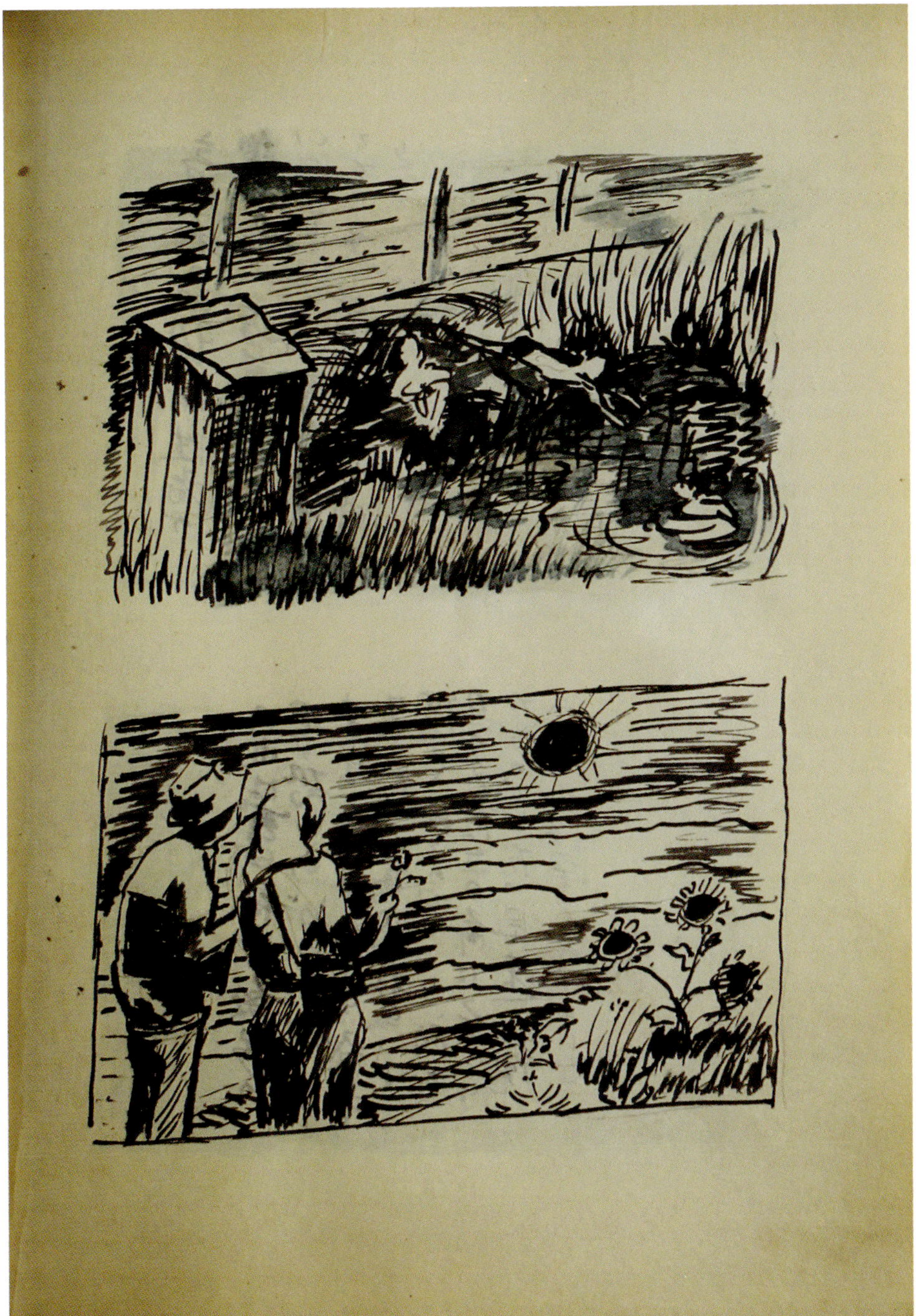

92

Here are the gravestones of several of the dead, the first sacrifices among the relocated. Always, the graves are ready. Everyone, please quickly . . .

This is a horrible tick that I picked up coming home from a walk. Having discovered it, my wife was surprised and upset. That tick got on me three days ago. Immediately, I went to the hospital to receive treatment.

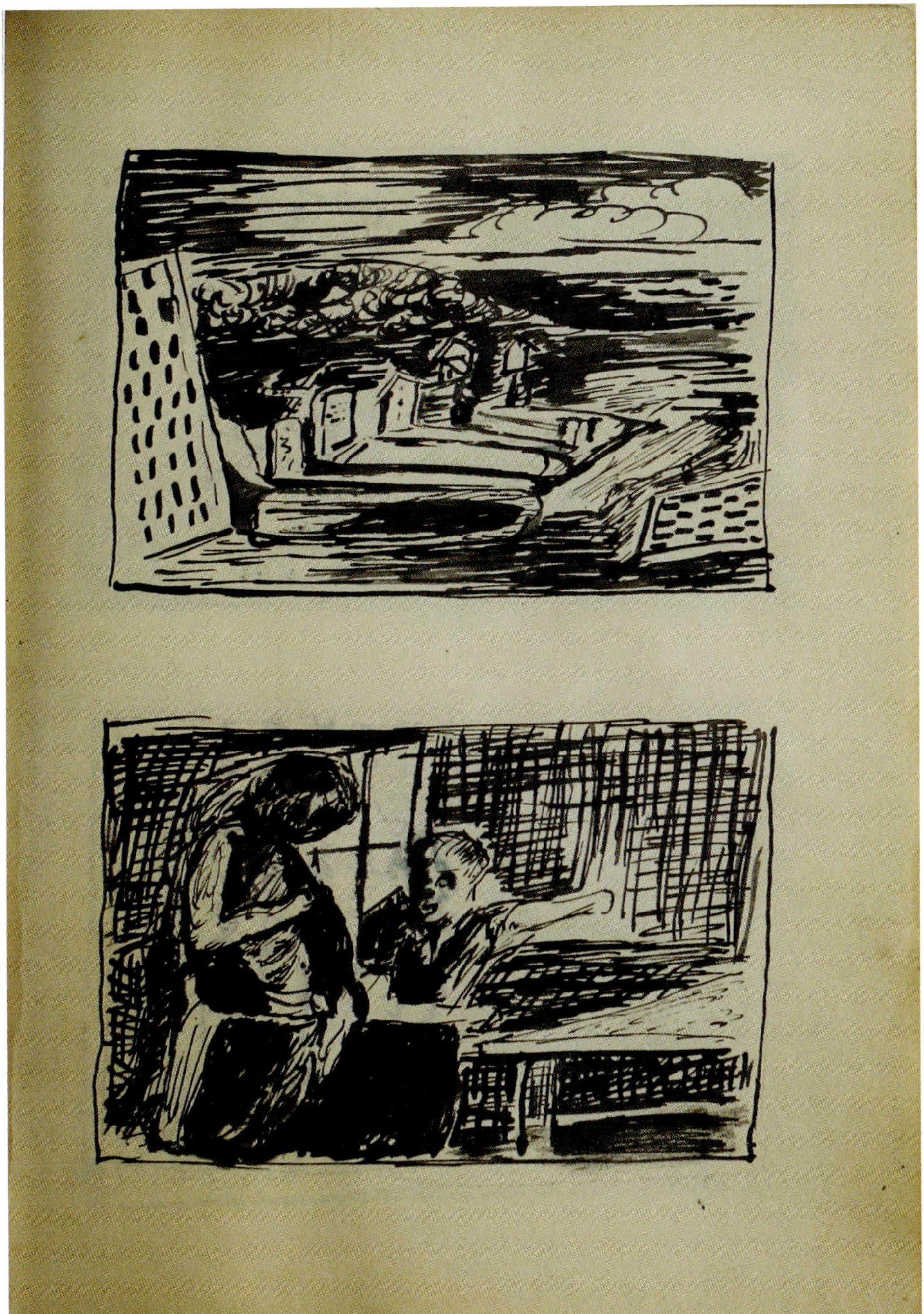

93

When we went to the river to see, many sport fishermen had gathered and were enjoying their fishing. In this river, you fish mostly for trout and sockeye. It is the only place of comfort given us who have been relocated here.

Caught . . . [some fish]. Do you see, do you see?

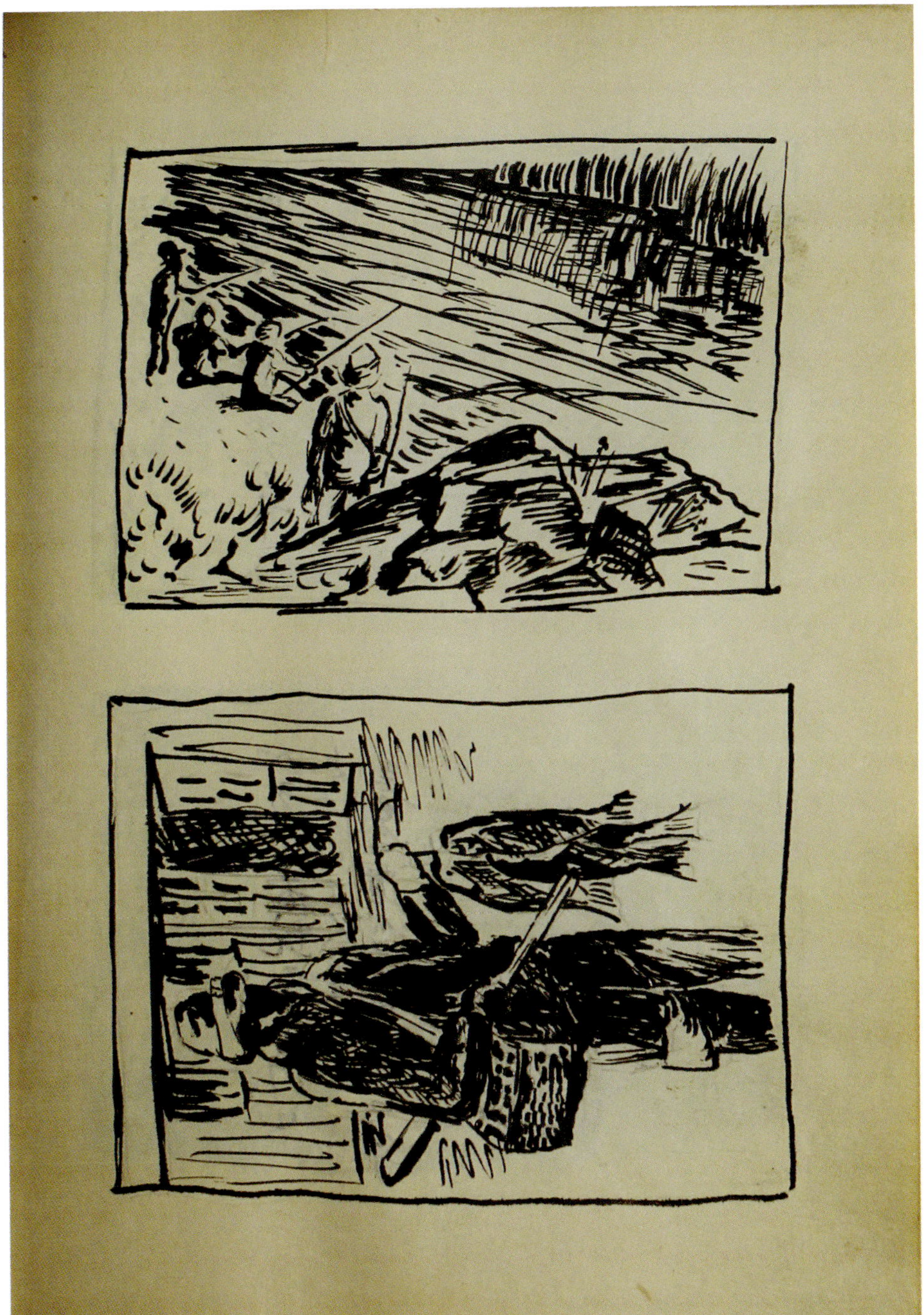

94

The inhabitants who are farmers are all participating in the work on the plan to reclaim several hundred acres at the Minidoka camp. This is the season when they are busy . . . [caring for] what they have planted. They have even brought out the grammar and middle school students and are having them work during the farmers' busy season.

The reclamation.

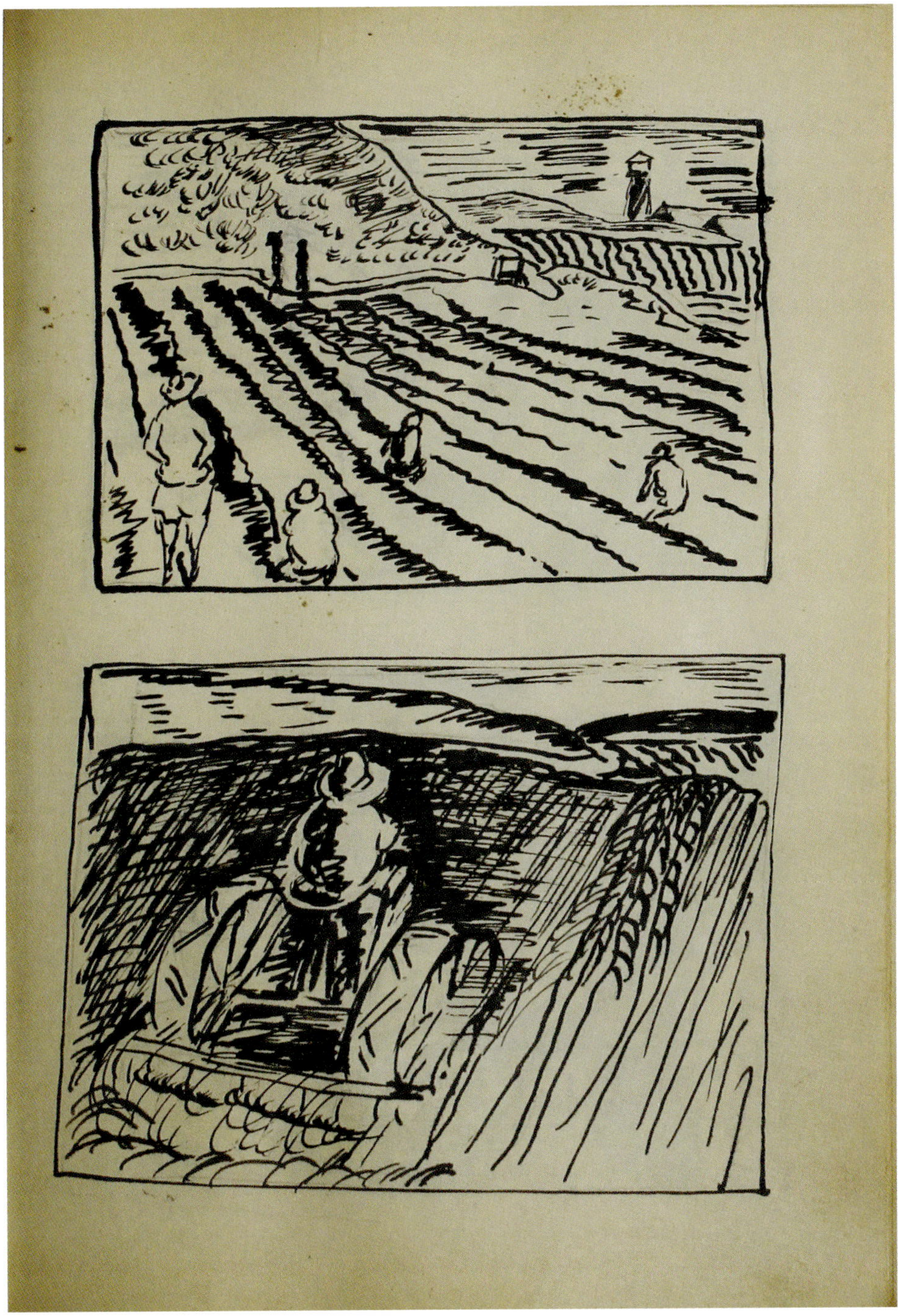

95

Carpenter's shed. Ding. They are making busy-sounding noises.

This is the place where vegetables are stored. The floor has been lowered [into the ground] so that it can be used as an icebox.

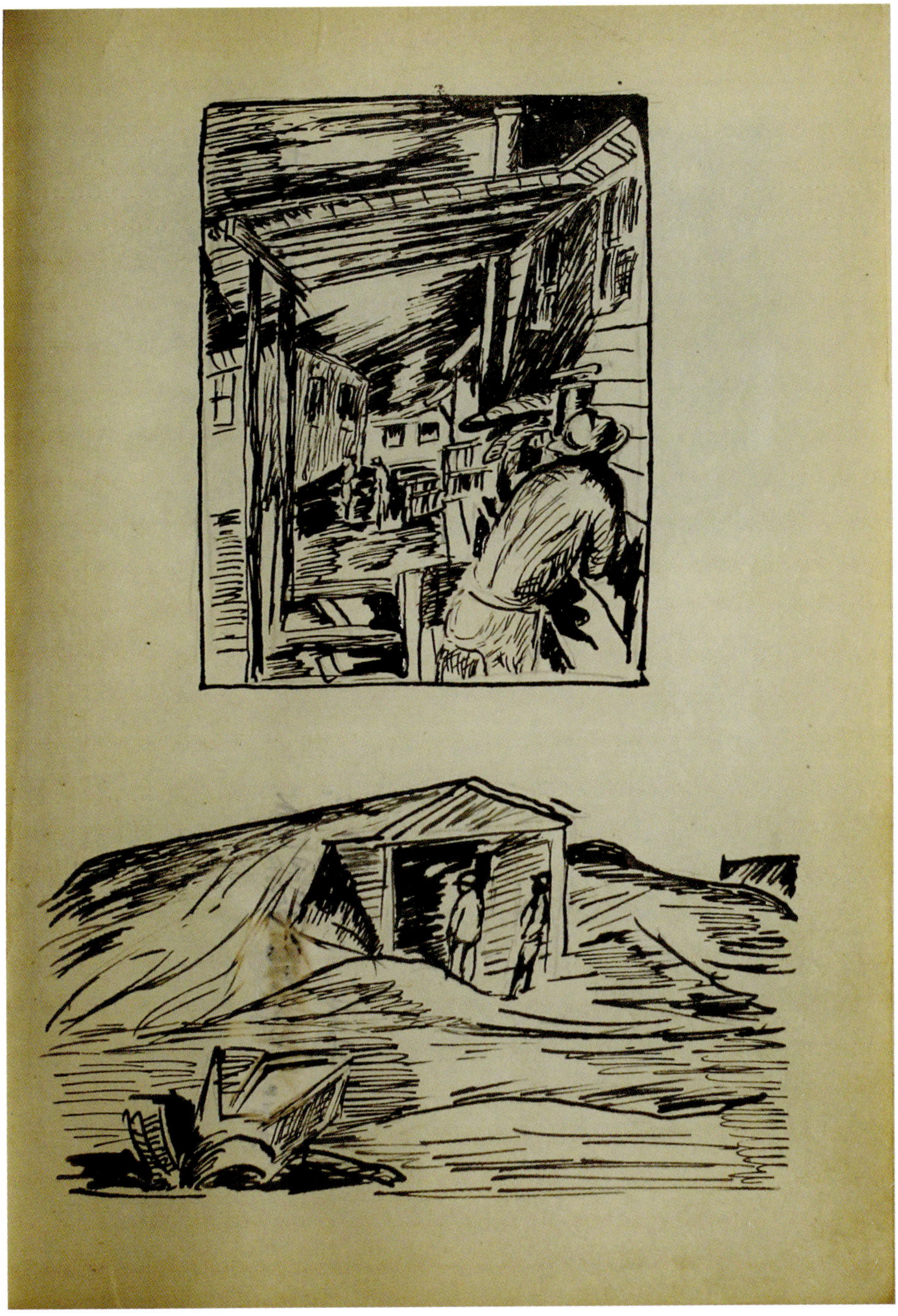

96

This is part of the entertainment for a gathering of the North American PTA . . . performed by the Hatsune group.

We who were moved here from the Puyallup Assembly Center in Washington State on August 18, 1942, unexpectedly on December 18, 1945, are released from this camp by an official American government proclamation, and the road to a free life is opened to us. This camp will be closed by December 31.

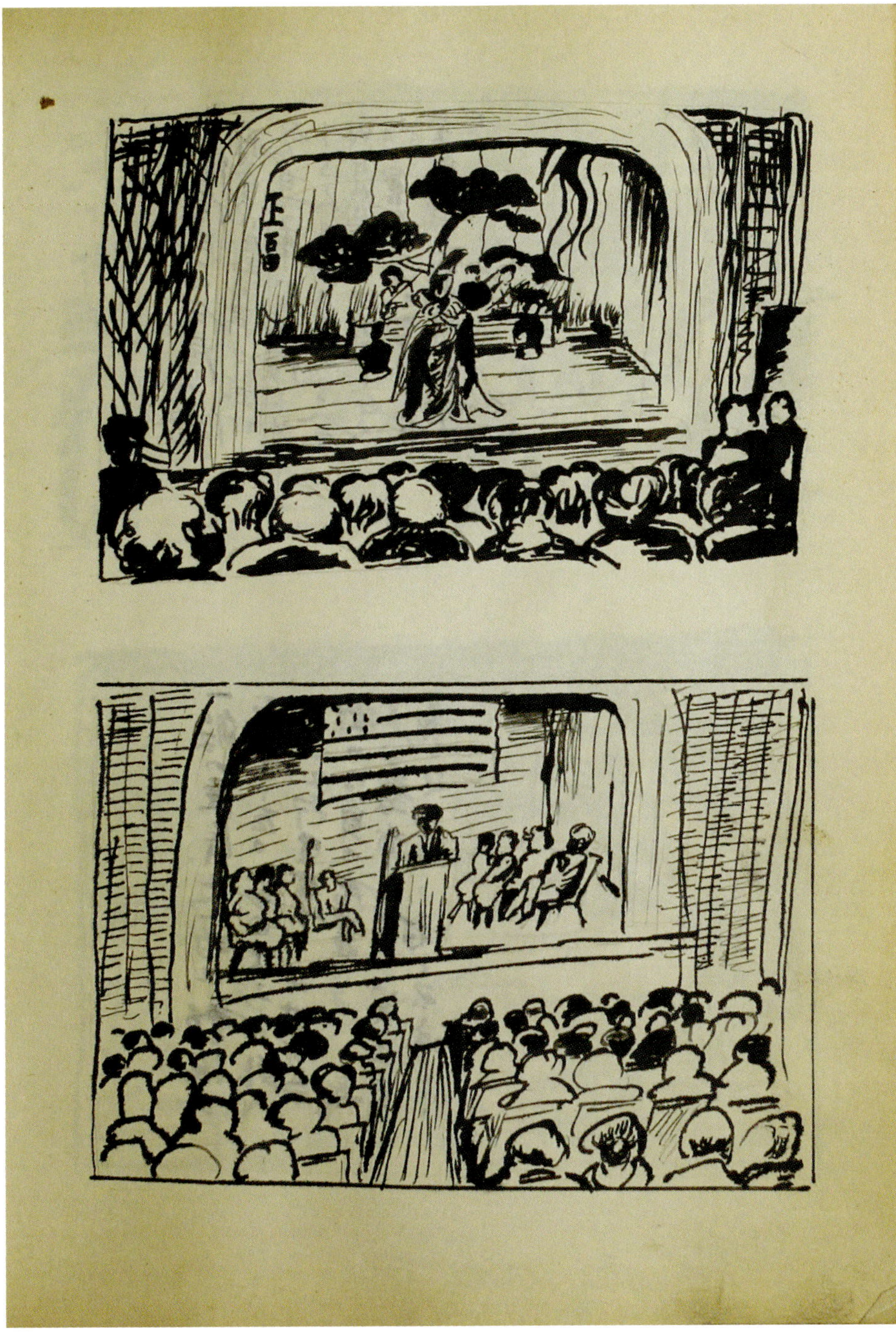

97

The general public had many doubts about this government proclamation. There were also people . . . who went to investigate this matter. On the road home after hearing a speech by WRA director Myer, suddenly there was a drubbing incident.

The hearts of the people in the camp began to tremble. Every day people went out. Again, on the other hand, there were those . . . who did not know what to do with themselves. Families were also fighting . . . anxiety, anxiety.

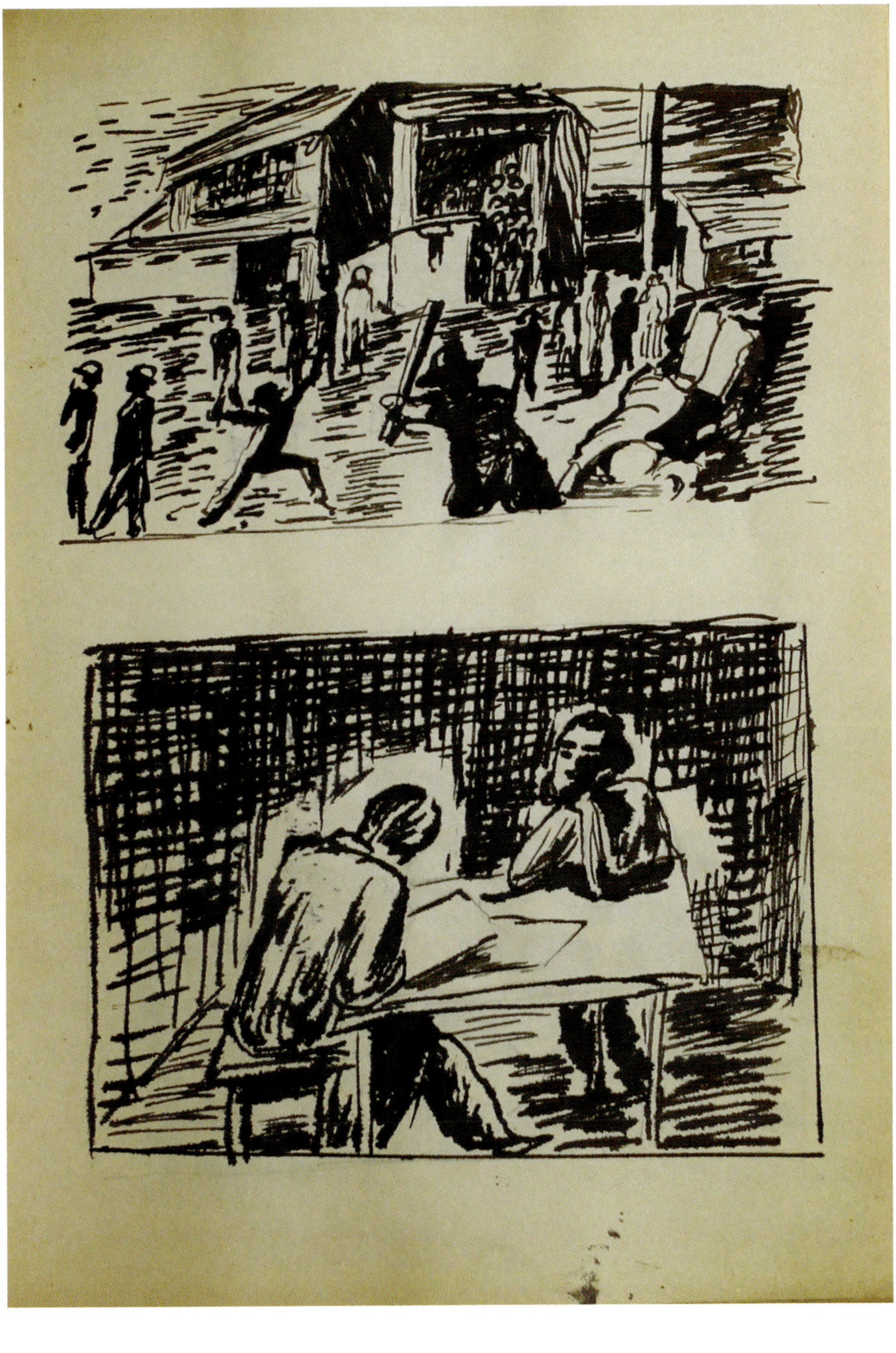

98

Incident concerning bodily injury to an old man of sixty. [Illegible], chop, [illegible].

A brawl due to drunkenness. Sitting in the cold snow, he says carelessly, "You did it, eh. I will do it too." Clang. Cherry blossoms [of blood] unseasonably fall on the snow. Children pass by laughing, "Adults—foolish."

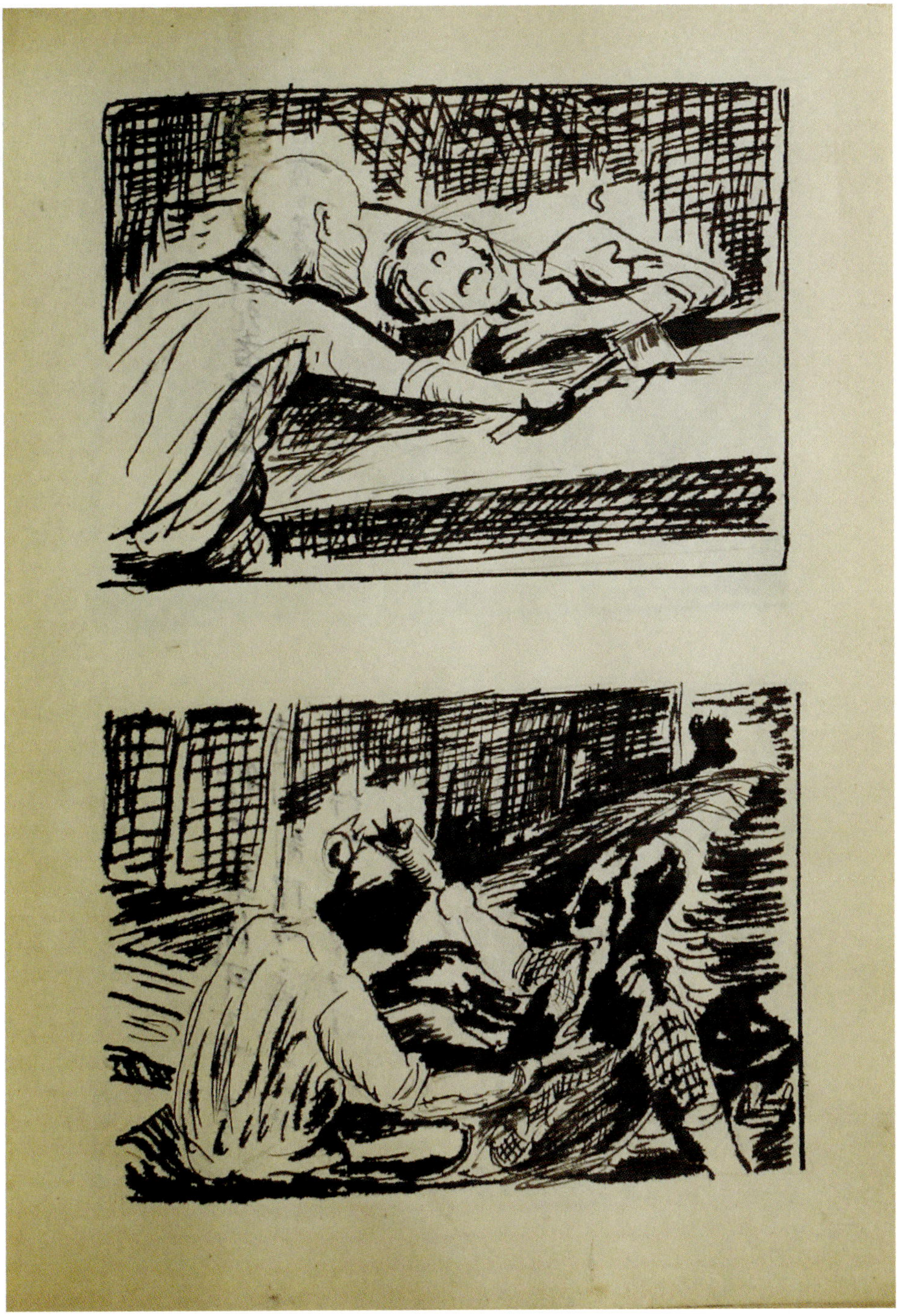

99

This is the first memorial service for those who died in the war.

It was just an ordinary funeral. The ceremony was held solemnly within the time limit.

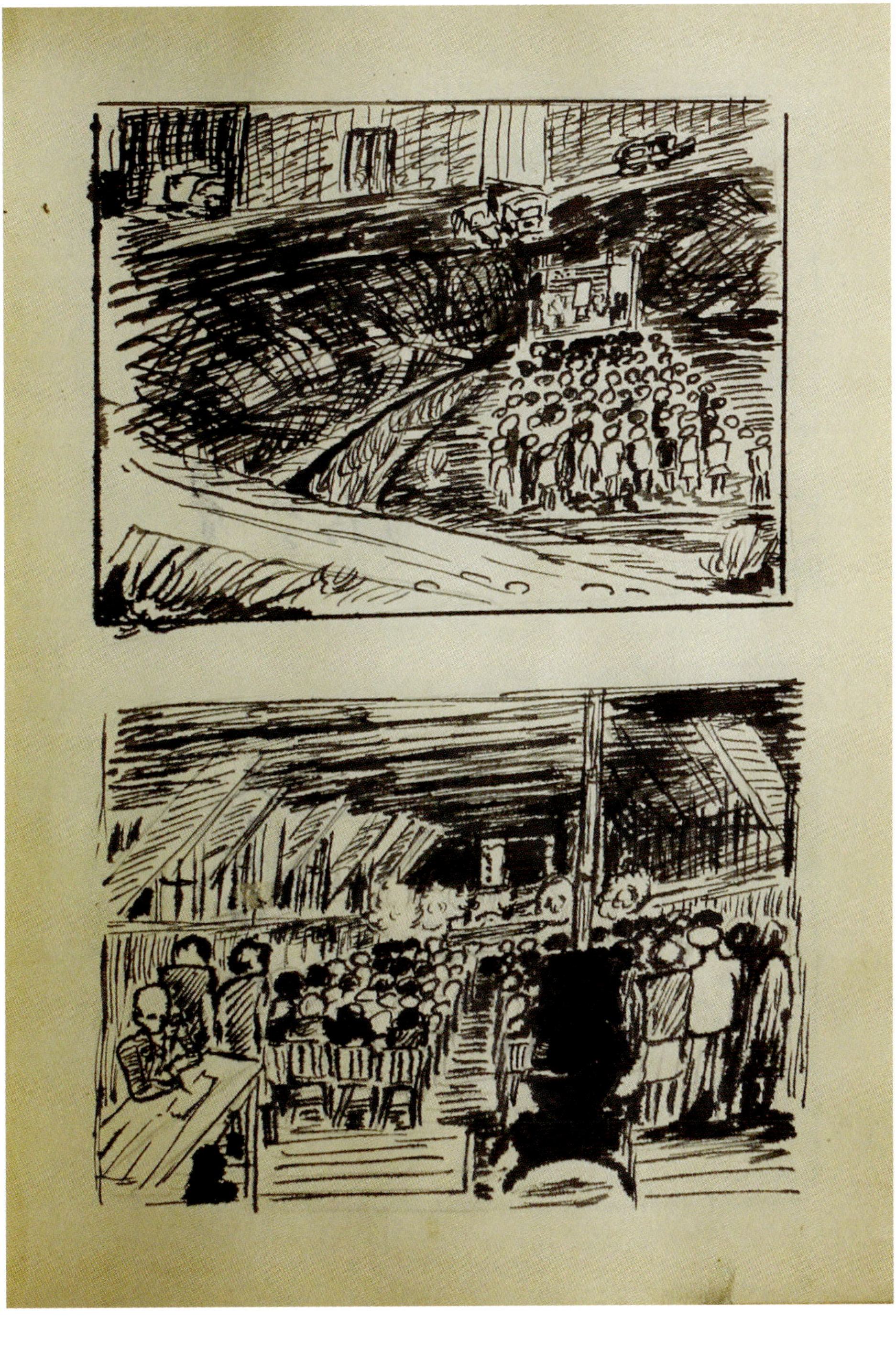

100

A place in the camp that manufactures demagogues. She is a dog. That guy is a cat. They are loyal. They are not. They are rich. They are poor. She has divorced him. She has married three times.

War news has been announced. One hundred battleships sunk. How can such things be true?

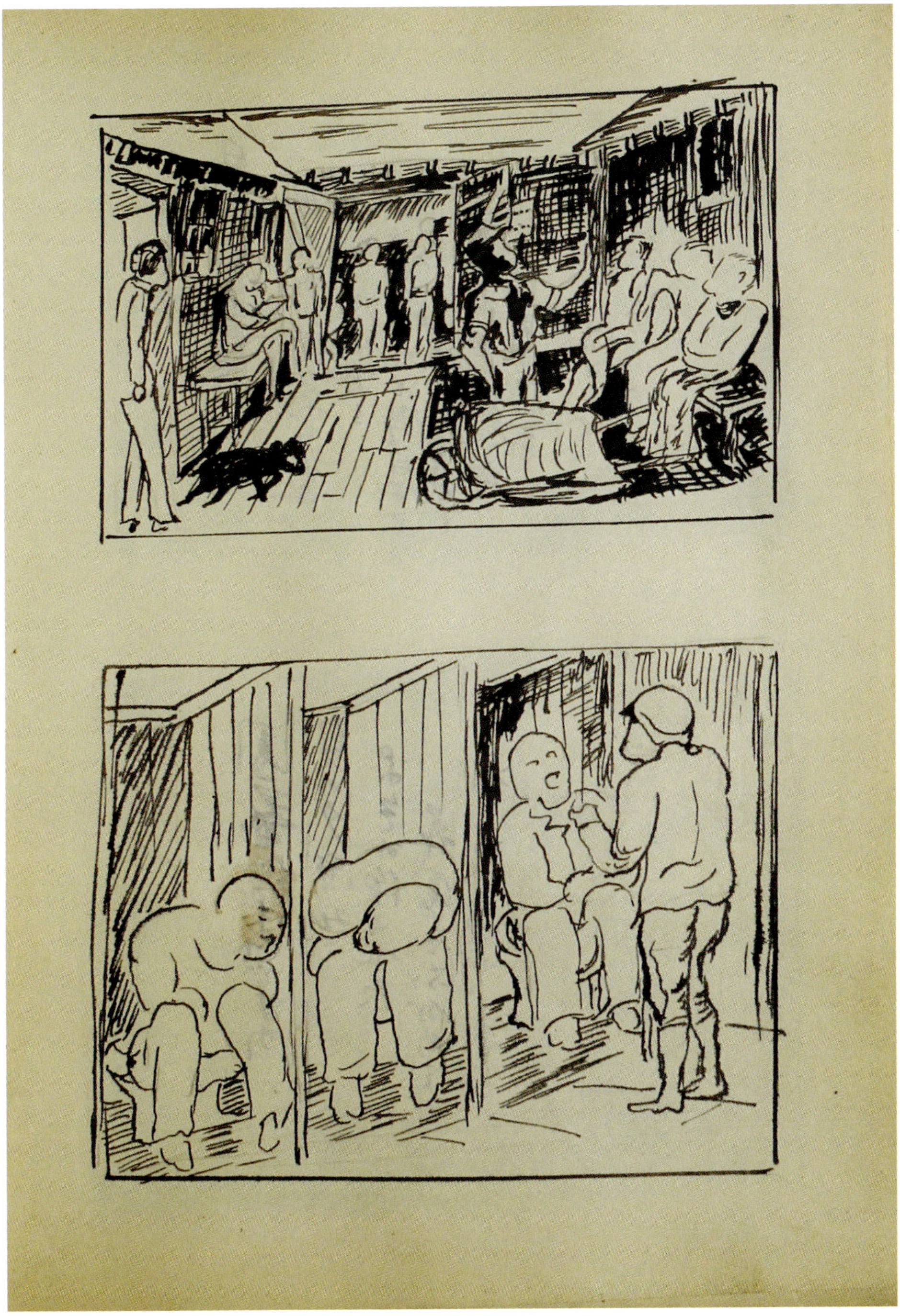

101

Resentful because one night they did not offer a convoy bus for the return home from a dance . . . there was a disturbance in which the library was vandalized.

One day around 2:00 P.M. . . . this occurred. Four-year-old children playing with fire in the end burned down the watchtower.

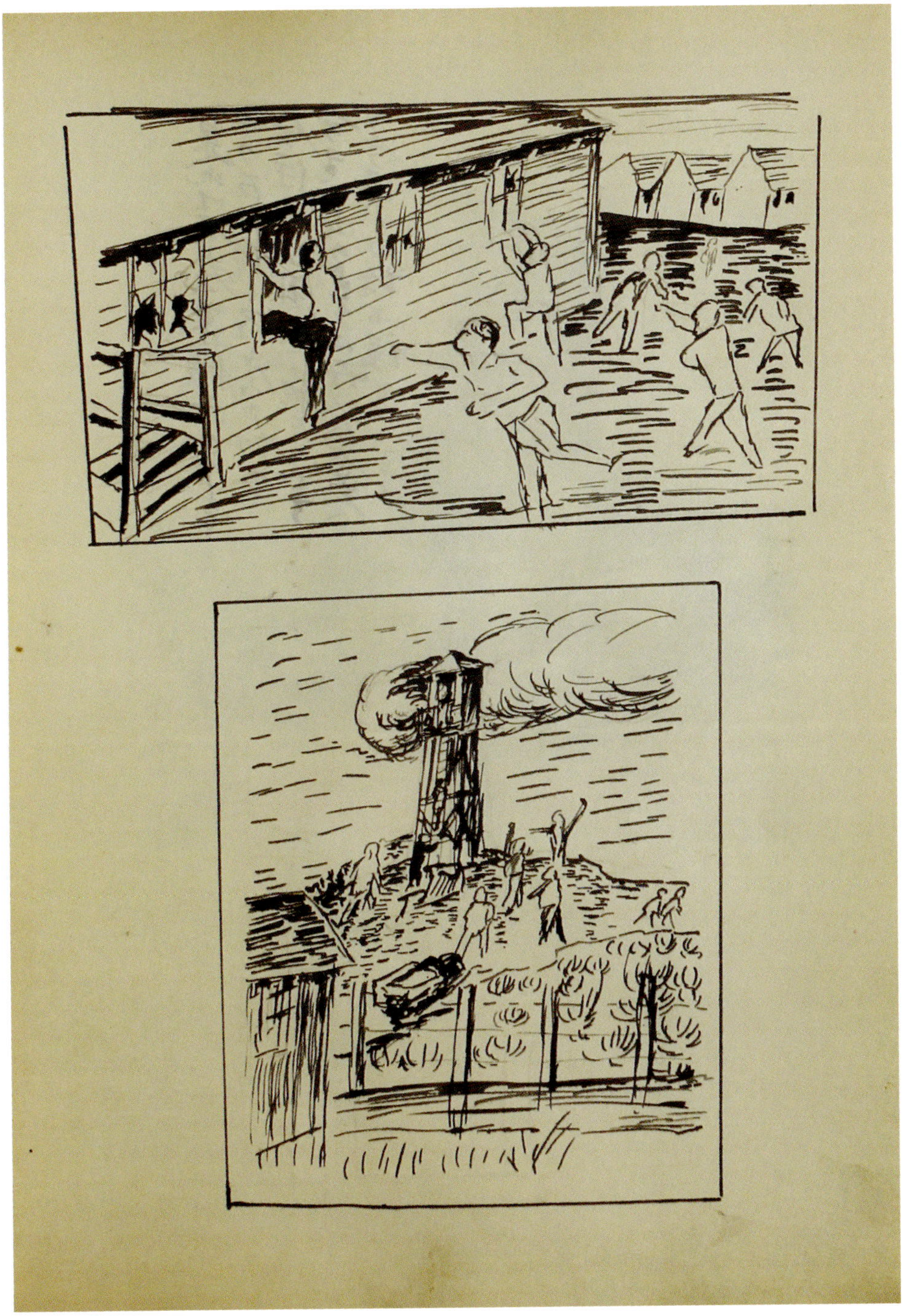

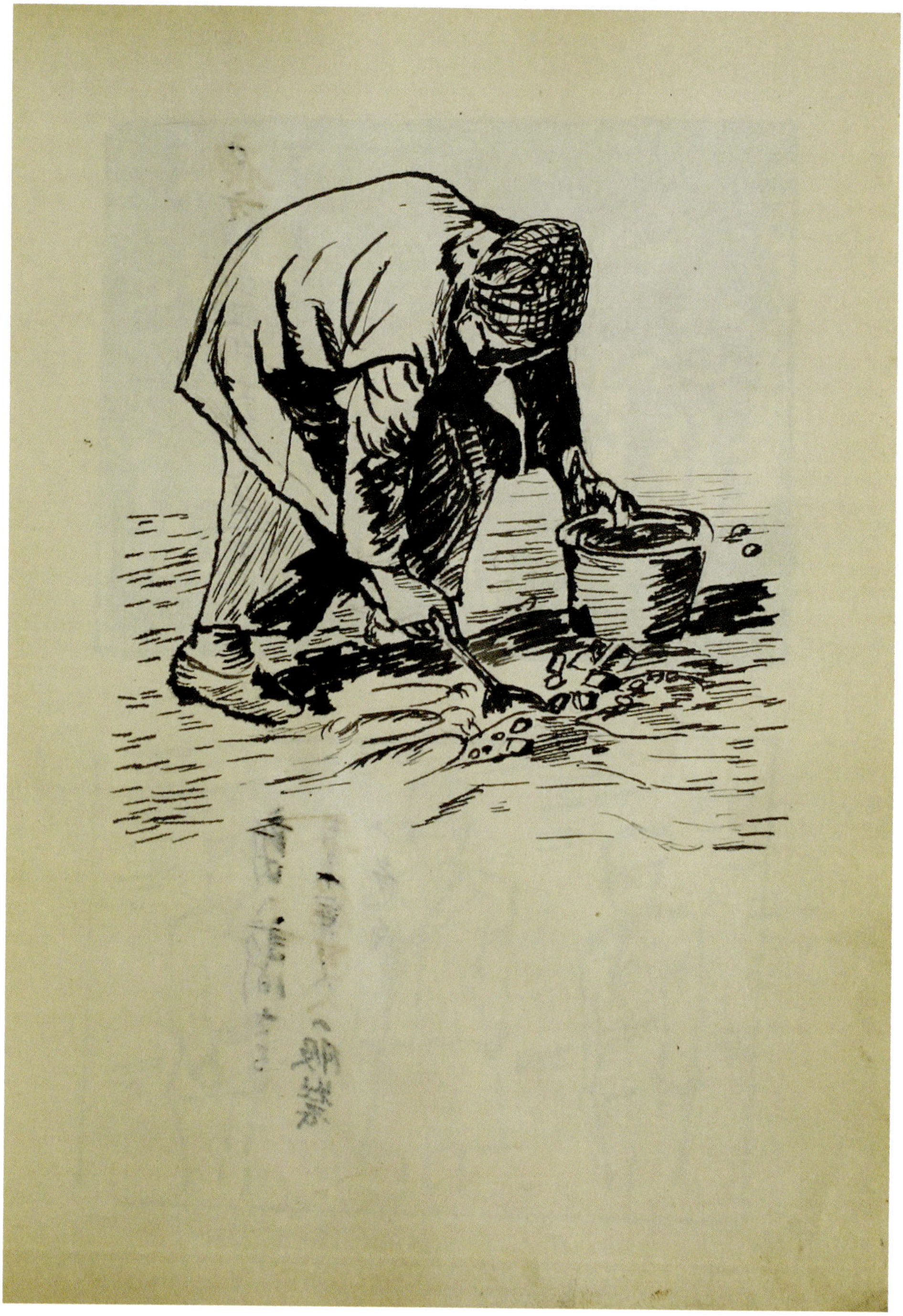

102 Because of a strike by the haulers of coal, the supply of coal was cut for a while and the people in the camp were greatly inconvenienced. Of what had been a mountain of coal, there is now not even enough to pick up.

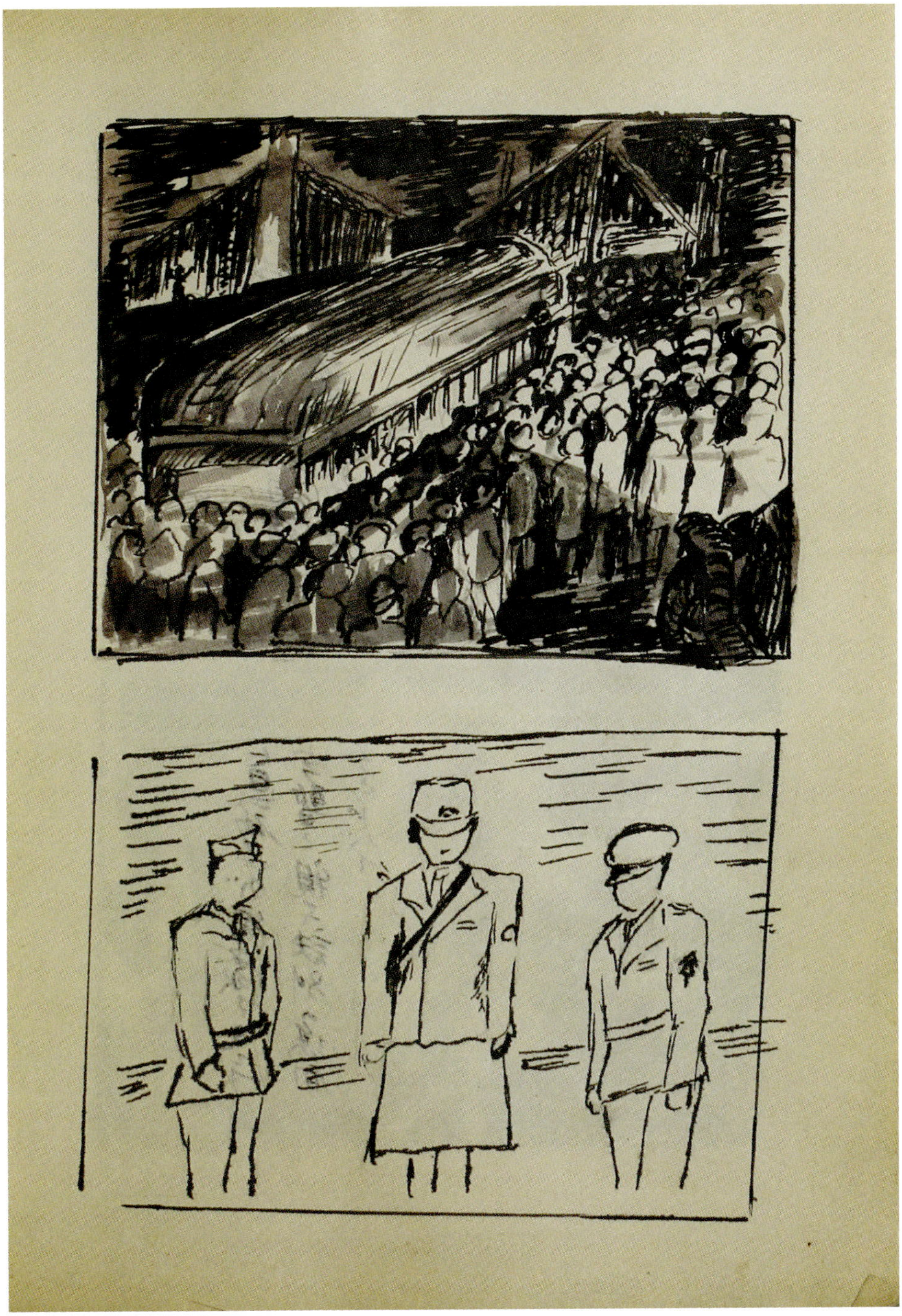

103 This is [a sketch of] people in the late afternoon seeing off soldiers going to war.

These are various uniforms of the Japanese American soldiers who visited the camp.

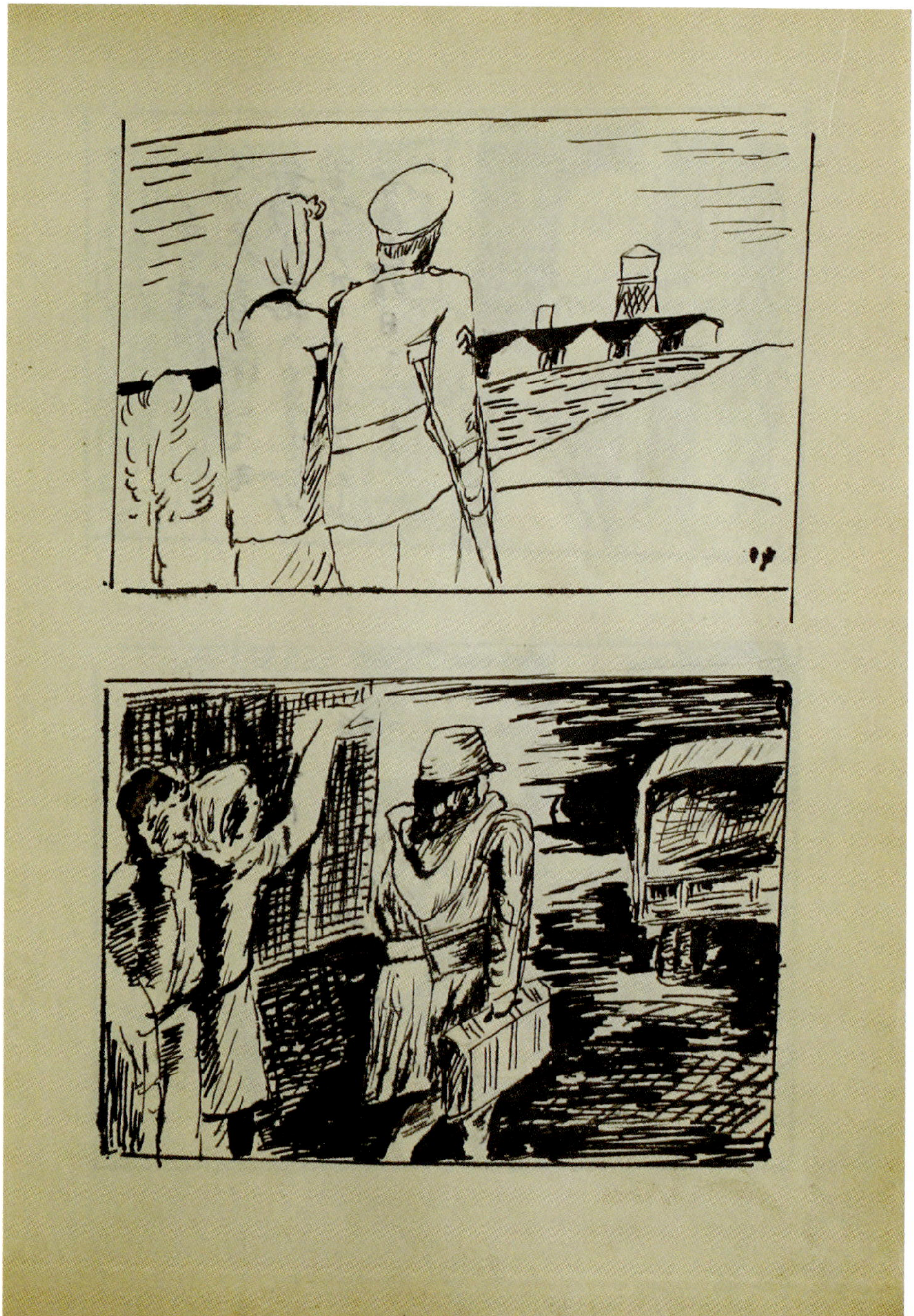

104 I occasionally see the backs of injured soldiers who have returned to the camp.

Masako is going back to the army. This will be soon. A scene of parents and children parting. Good-bye.

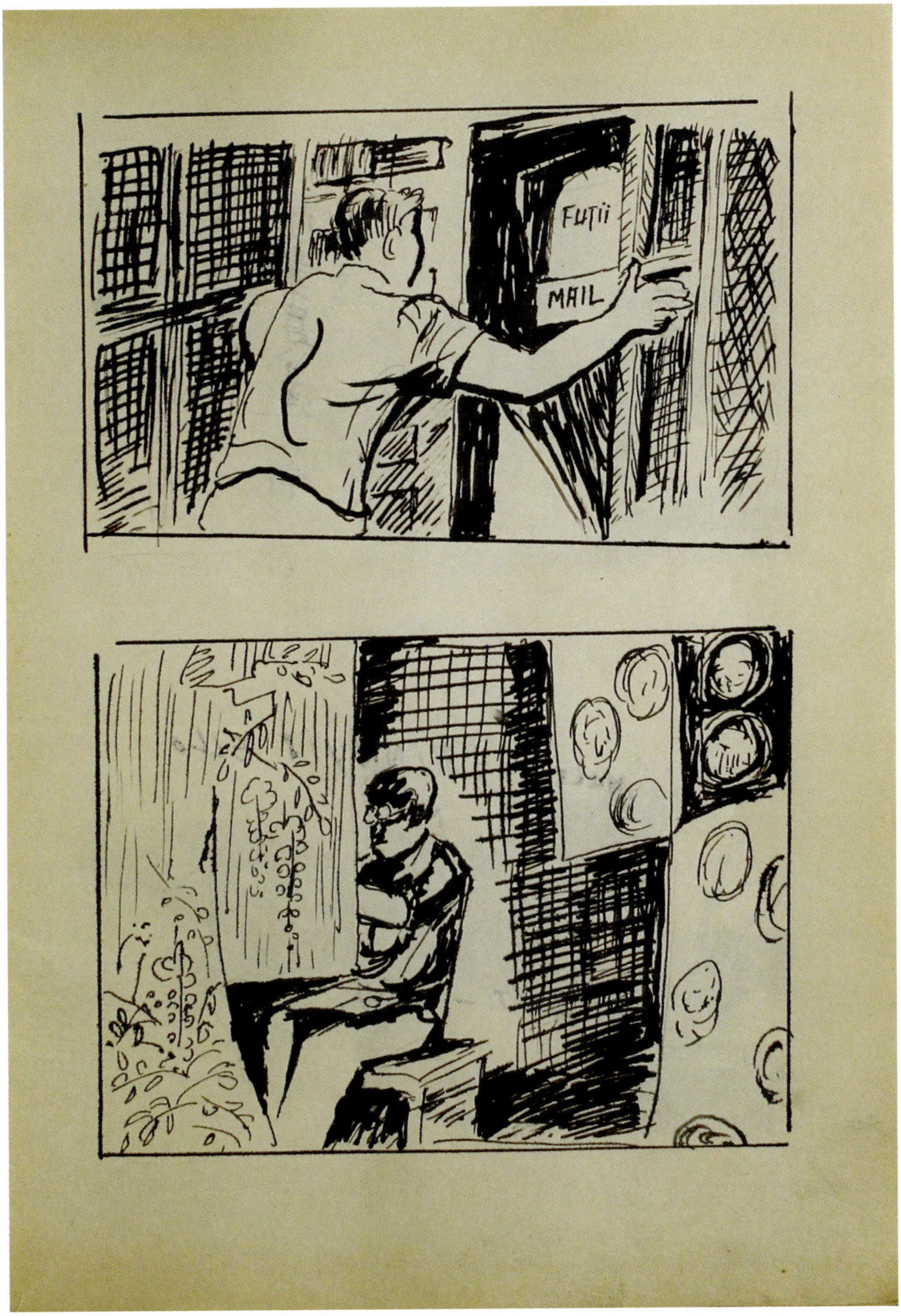

105 This is the heart of people who have children. Just hearing someone's footfalls, one checks the mailbox. "No mail today. Today is Sunday, isn't it?"

Communal life—if one is asked one cannot say no.

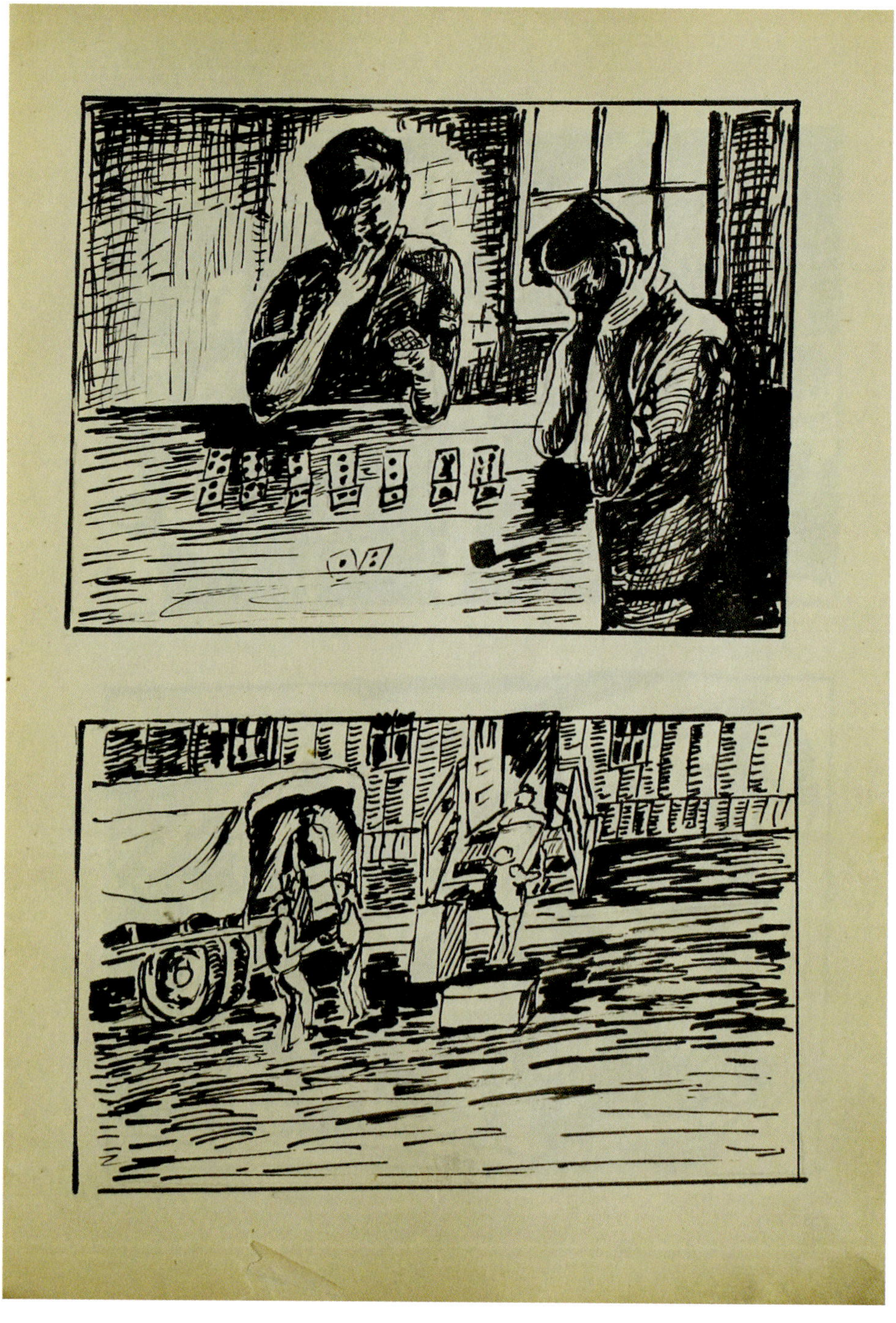

106 [no text—couple playing cards; people moving out of barrack]

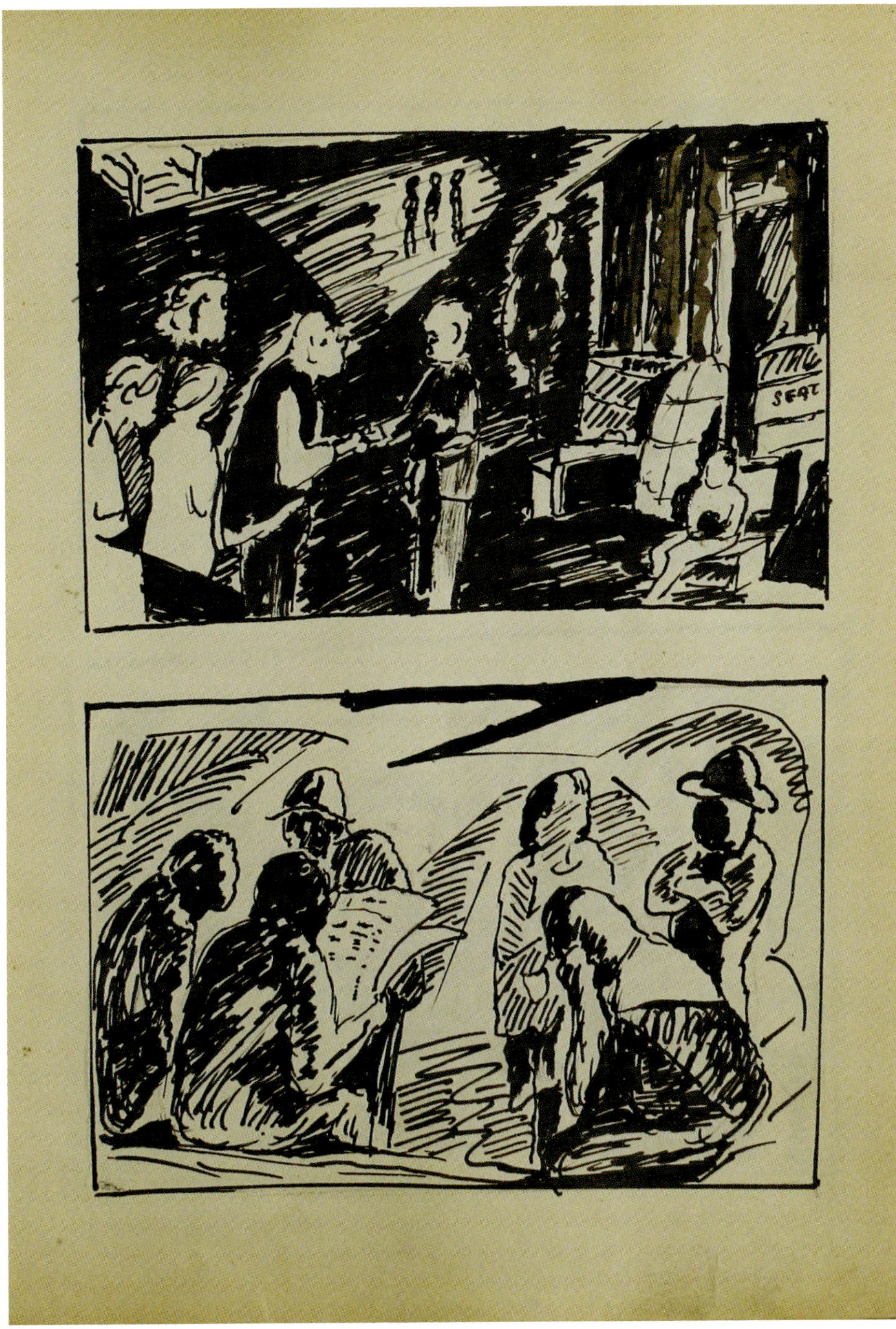

107 [no text—leaving with packs labeled "Seattle"; group reading newspaper]

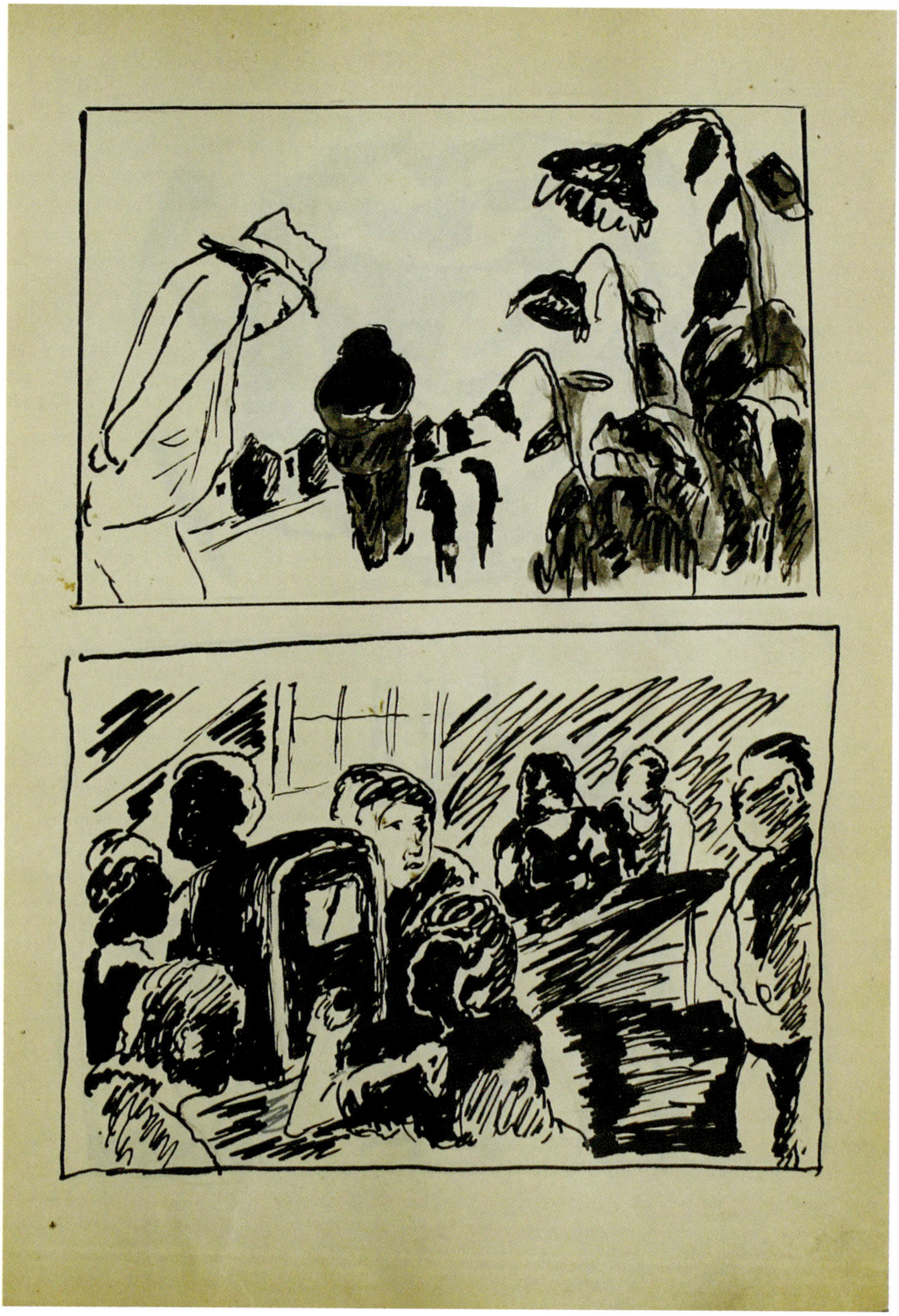

108 [no text—hunched figures walking past sunflowers; listening to the radio]

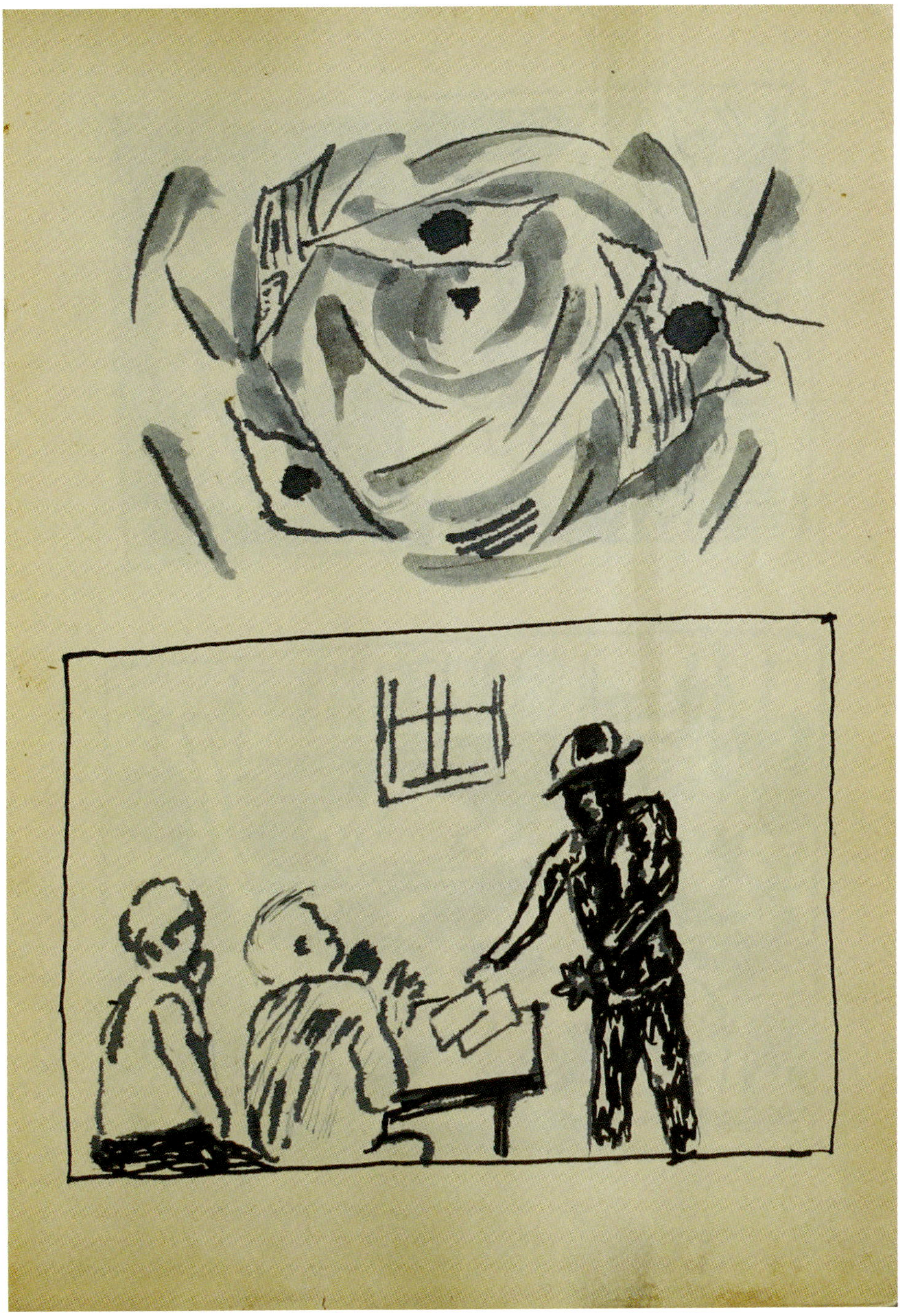

109 [no text—abstraction with American and Japanese flags; couple startled by man delivering papers]

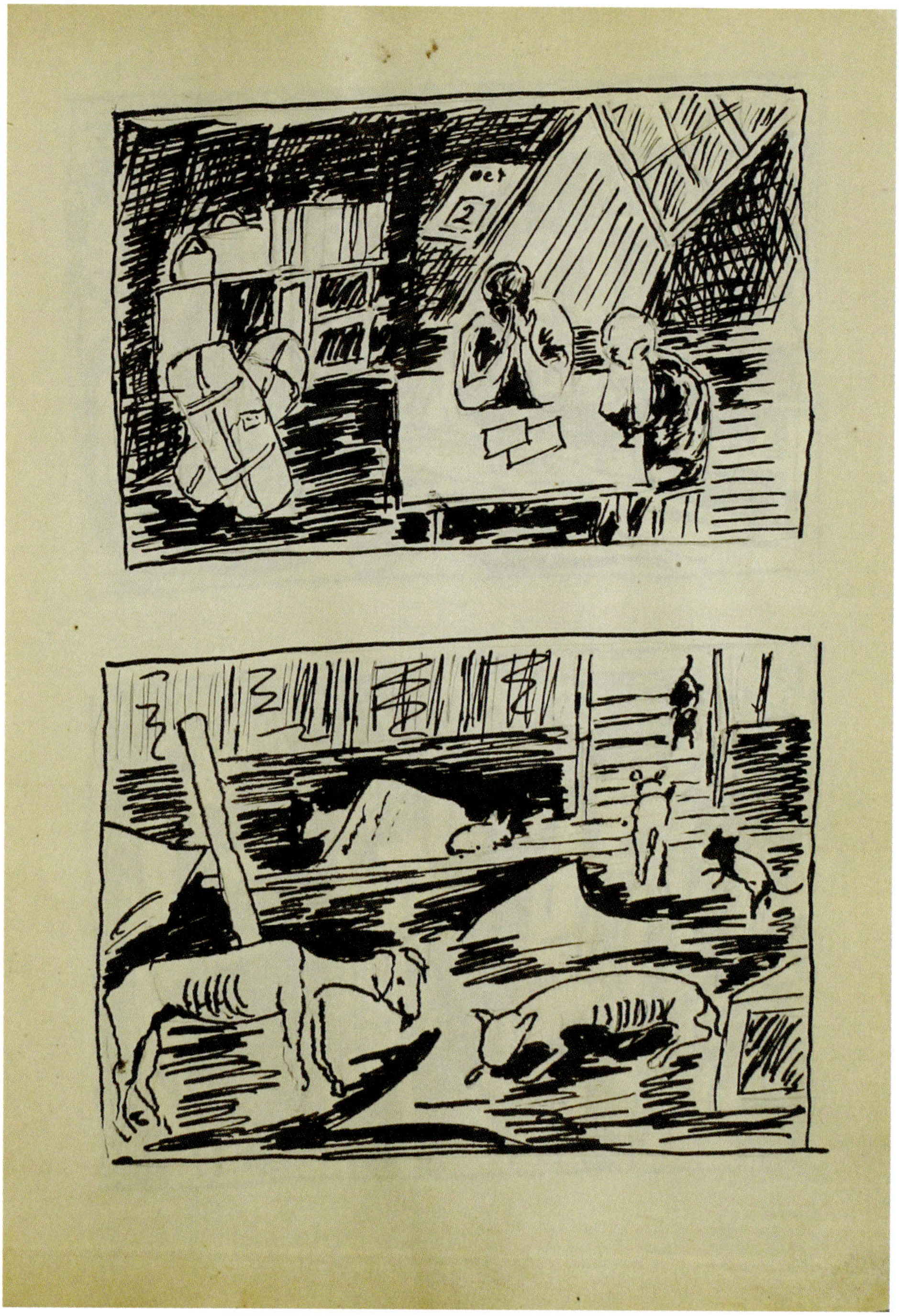

110 [no text—Fujii and wife at table, belongings packed; animals scavenge abandoned barracks]

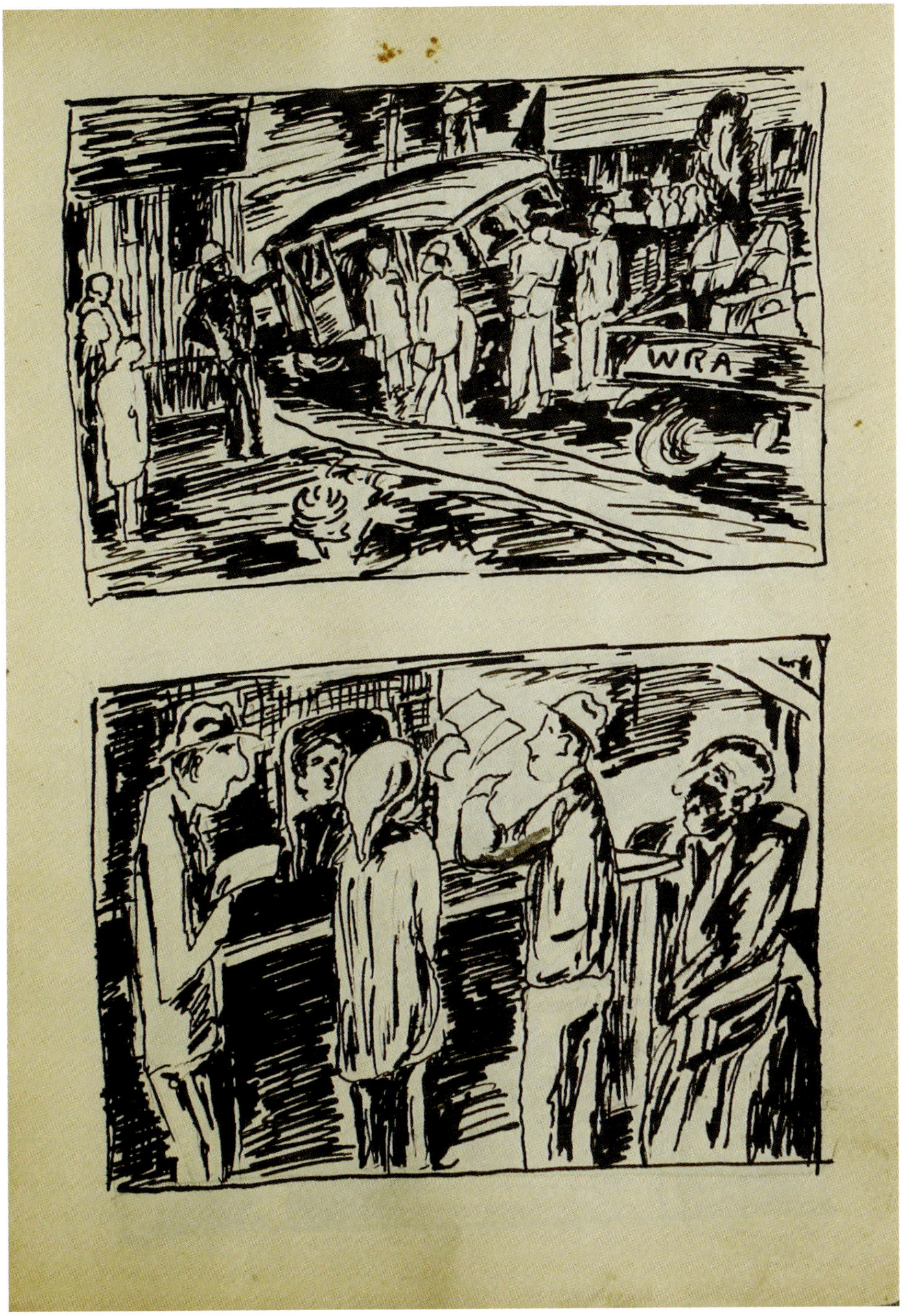

111 [no text—boarding WRA buses and trucks; men and woman with paperwork]

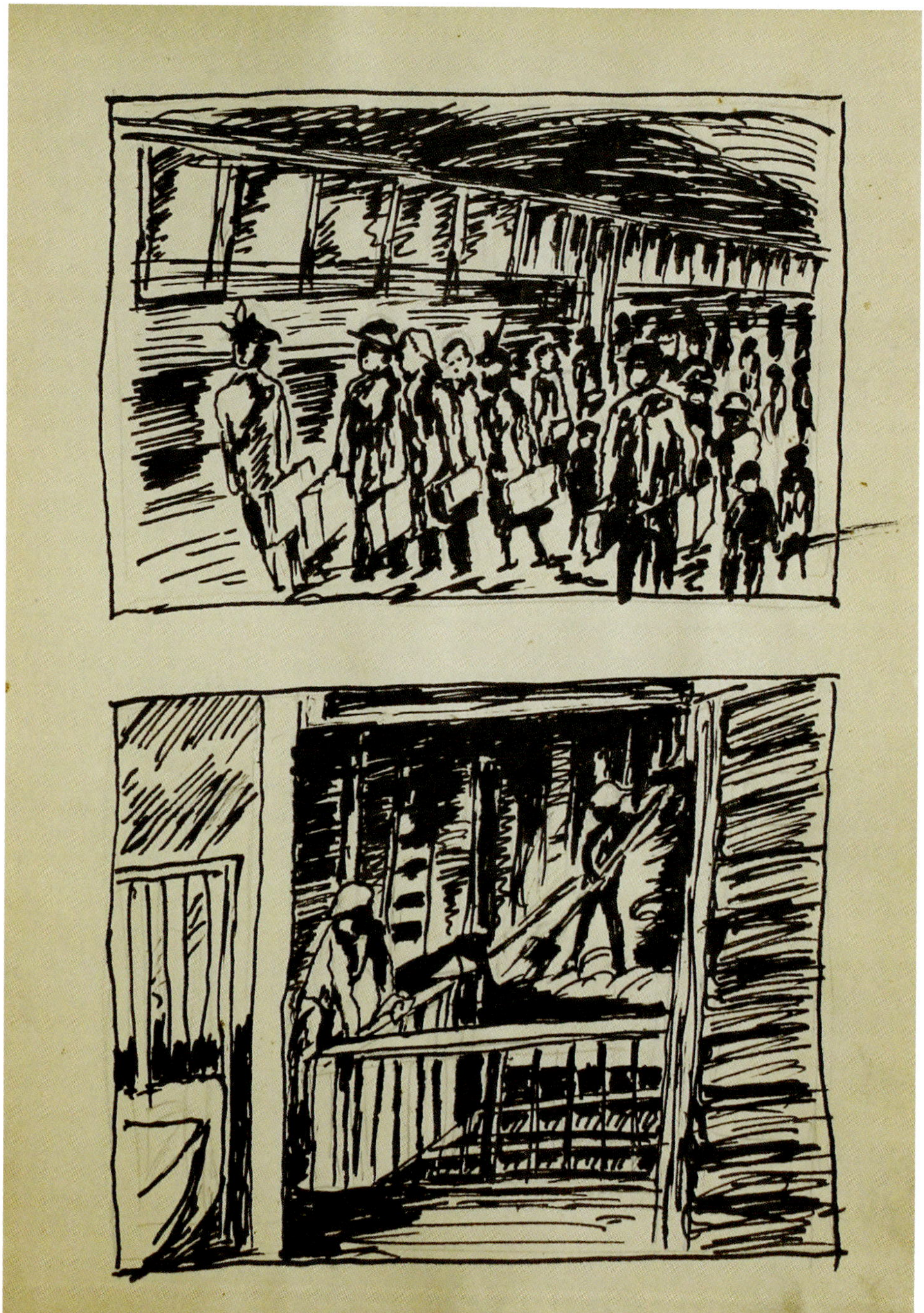

112 [no text—boarding a train; workers inside empty building]

APPENDIX 1

ARTIST STATEMENT

All art, and in particular painting, can only be expressed through visual contact; it cannot be written. My aim in painting is to remain true to my own ideas and keep away from the influences of other painters. However, in seeing and studying the work of others, I learn from them.

I am not interested in skill or technique as an end in itself, but in a combined thing, a co-ordination of my visual experiences with my knowledge of forms of art. It is truth in Nature I am after, not the superficial aspects of Nature or man, but the basic truths of the structure of life.

To me, the most important element in painting is in its power to raise the observer above the everyday affairs of life into a higher plane of existence.[1]

APPENDIX 2

EXHIBITION HISTORY

1930

Sixteenth Annual Exhibition of Northwest Artists, Art Institute of Seattle (*Bridge*)

1931

Fifty-Third Annual Exhibition of the San Francisco Art Association, California Palace of the Legion of Honor, San Francisco (*Fishing Boats*)

Seventeenth Annual Exhibition of Northwest Artists, Art Institute of Seattle (*Reflection*, *Mooring*, *Fishing Boats*—Honorable Mention)

1932

Fifty-Fourth Annual Exhibition of the San Francisco Art Association, California Palace of the Legion of Honor (*Hillside*, *Houses*)

Eighteenth Annual Exhibition of Northwest Artists, Art Institute of Seattle (*Landscape*)

1933[1]

Award winners of recent Northwest Annuals (group exhibition at museum opening), Seattle Art Museum

1934

Twentieth Annual Exhibition of Northwest Artists, Seattle Art Museum (*Boats, Country Lane*)

1935

Twenty-First Annual Exhibition of Northwest Artists, Seattle Art Museum (*Alley, Porch, Still Life*)

Group of Twelve, rotating exhibitions, Penthouse Gallery, Seattle

1936

First National Exhibition of American Art, Rockefeller Center Gallery, Municipal Art Committee, City of New York (*Rock Island Dam*)

Group of Twelve, rotating exhibitions, Penthouse Gallery

Group of Twelve, oil paintings, Tacoma Art Association, Tacoma, Washington

Group of Twelve, watercolors, Tacoma Art Association

Group of Twelve, Seattle Art Museum

Paintings by the Group of Twelve, Seattle Art Museum; traveled in 1937 to Mills College, Oakland, California, as *The Pacific Northwest Painters* (*High School Girl, Still Life*, and *Alley*)

1937

Forty-First Annual Exhibition by Artists of Chicago and Vicinity, Art Institute of Chicago (*Hillside*)

1938

Drawings by the Group of Twelve, Seattle Art Museum

1940

Twenty-Sixth Annual Exhibition of Northwest Artists, Seattle Art Museum (*The Bridge*)

1941

Twenty-Seventh Annual Exhibition of Northwest Artists, Seattle Art Museum (*East of Wenatchee*)

1943

Art Exhibit, Minidoka Relocation Center, Jerome County, Idaho

Minidoka Art Exhibit, Twin Falls Public Library, Twin Falls, Idaho (*Sunflowers*)

1957

1957 Chicago Artists No-Jury Exhibition, Navy Pier, Chicago, sponsored by the Art Institute of Chicago and Chicago Art Organizations in cooperation with City of Chicago (*Momentum*, *Ecstasy*)

1958

1958 Chicago Artists No-Jury Exhibition, Navy Pier, Chicago, sponsored by the Art Institute of Chicago and Chicago Art Organizations in cooperation with City of Chicago (*Work*)

1950s (undocumented)

Chicago Public Library branch, Olivet Institute, Chicago

1992

Lines of Inheritance: Northwest Oils and Works on Paper, 1920s–1990s, Carolyn Staley Fine Prints, Seattle (paintings of the 1930s)

1994

They Painted from Their Hearts: Pioneer Asian American Artists, Wing Luke Asian Museum, Seattle (paintings of the 1930s)

2016

Minidoka: Artist as Witness, Boise Art Museum, Boise, Idaho

2018–2021

Witness to Wartime: Takuichi Fujii, tour

NOTES

FOREWORD

1 Barbara Johns, *Paul Horiuchi: East and West* (Seattle: University of Washington Press in association with Museum of Northwest Art, La Conner, WA, 2008); Barbara Johns, *Signs of Home: The Paintings and Wartime Diary of Kamekichi Tokita* (Seattle: University of Washington Press, 2011); Barbara Johns, "Knowing Your Place: Issei Artists in Seattle; Kenjiro Nomura, Kamekichi Tokita, and Takuichi Fujii" (PhD diss., University of Washington, 2014).

2 See, for example, Kazuko Nakane, "Facing the Pacific: Asian American Artists in Seattle, 1900–1970," in *Asian American Art: A History, 1850–1970*, ed. Gordon H. Chang, Mark Dean Johnson, and Paul J. Karlstrom, 55–81 (Stanford, CA: Stanford University Press, 2008).

3 For the Puyallup camp, see Louis Fiset, *Camp Harmony: Seattle's Japanese Americans and the Puyallup Assembly Center* (Champaign: University of Illinois Press, 2009). We have no good history of Minidoka.

4 Some of the diary art was reproduced in the *Minidoka Interlude*, published by inmates in the Minidoka Relocation Center in 1943 and available in reprint from Friends of Minidoka, www.minidoka.org.

5 The work of Tetsuden Kashima, especially *Judgment without Trial: Japanese American Imprisonment during World War II* (Seattle: University of Washington Press, 2003), establishes an Issei-centered narrative.

INTRODUCTION

1 Dictionary.com, s.v. "witness," www.dictionary.com.

2 *Issei* names the generation who immigrated from Japan; *Nisei*, the first American-born generation; and *Sansei*, their children. *Nikkei* is the collective name.

3 About 110,000 people were subject to the army's orders to leave the region in spring 1942. The total number incarcerated reached 120,000, accounting for births, a small number of volunteers, transfers from other forms of detention, and inmates from Hawai'i. Michi Weglyn, *Years of Infamy: The Untold Story of America's Concentration Camps*, updated ed. (Seattle: University of Washington Press, 1996), 21n.

4 Kenneth Callahan, "Names Change but Quality of N.W. Annual Remains High," *Seattle Times*, November 18, 1956.

5 For a recent reference, see Gordon H. Chang, Mark Dean Johnson, and Paul J. Karlstrom, eds., *Asian American Art: A History, 1850–1970* (Stanford, CA: Stanford University Press, 2008).

6 The project was my PhD dissertation, "Knowing Your Place: Issei Artists in

Seattle; Kenjiro Nomura, Kamekichi Tokita, and Takuichi Fujii" (University of Washington, 2014), which addresses place and identity in the artists' 1930s production.

7 Karin M. Higa, *The View from Within: Japanese American Art from the Internment Camps, 1942–1945* (Los Angeles: Japanese American National Museum, UCLA Wight Art Gallery, and UCLA Asian American Studies Center, 1992).

8 Ibid., 15.

9 Kristine Kuramitsu, "Internment and Identity in Japanese American Art," *American Quarterly* 47, no. 4 (December 1995): 638, paraphrasing an interview with Karin Higa, February 22, 1993.

10 Monographs about the artists include Kimi Kodani Hill, ed., *Topaz Moon: Chiura Obata's Art of the Internment* (Berkeley, CA: Heyday Books, 2000) and Hisako Hibi and Ibuki H. Lee, *Peaceful Painter: Memoirs of an Issei Woman* (Berkeley, CA: Heyday Books, 2004). For more on the artists and the wartime schools, see Higa, *View from Within*, 21–29.

11 "Issei, Nisei, Kibei," *Fortune* 24, no. 4 (April 1944): 32; Miné Okubo, *Citizen 13660* (Seattle: University of Washington Press, 2014), first published by Columbia University Press in 1946 and reissued by Arno Press in 1978 and Washington in 1983 and 2014. See also Greg Robinson, "Birth of a Citizen: Miné Okubo and the Politics of Symbolism," in *Miné Okubo: Following Her Own Road*, ed. Robinson and Ellen Tajima Creef (Seattle: University of Washington Press, 2008), 166. Robinson quotes a letter from M. Margaret Anderson, Okubo's New York patron, that cites as many as two thousand drawings by Okubo.

12 In 1934, Bay Area artists Sugimoto and Masuta Narahara exhibited with Kenjiro Nomura and Kamekichi Tokita from Seattle in *Oil Paintings by Four Japanese Artists of the West Coast*, which was organized by the Seattle Art Museum and the California Palace of the Legion of Honor in 1934 and toured the West Coast.

13 Nisei who were sent to Japan for schooling, a common practice among Issei parents, are known as Kibei. For further discussion, see chapter 3.

14 Deborah Gesensway and Mindy Roseman, *Beyond Words: Images from America's Concentration Camps* (Ithaca, NY: Cornell University Press, 1987), 150–154, 166. The officer was Lieutenant Alexander H. Leighton, who subsequently published *The Governing of Men: General Principles and Recommendations Based on Experience at a Japanese Relocation Camp* (Princeton, NJ: Princeton University Press, 1945).

15 Estelle Ishigo, *Lone Heart Mountain* (Los Angeles: privately published, 1972).

16 Nomura's wartime work is the subject of *Kenjiro Nomura: An Artist's View of the Japanese American Internment* (Seattle: Wing Luke Asian Museum, 1991). The Tacoma Art Museum acquired the major part of the collection in 2013.

17 Atsushi Kikuchi, quoted in Gesensway and Roseman, *Beyond Words*, 15.

18 *1957* and *1958 Chicago Artists No-Jury Exhibition* (Chicago: Art Institute of Chicago and Chicago Art Organizations in cooperation with City of Chicago, 1957, 1958), exhibition brochures, www.artic.edu/sites/default/files/libraries/pubs/1957/AIC1957ChiArtNoJury_comb.pdf; www.artic.edu/sites/default/files/libraries/pubs/1958/AIC1958ChiArtNoJury_comb.pdf.

19 Allen H. Eaton, *Beauty behind Barbed Wire: The Arts of Japanese in Our War Relocation Camps* (New York: Harper and Brothers, 1952). See also Estelle Ishigo Papers, UCLA Special Collections, Young Research Library, Japanese American Research Project Collection: 2010, series 1, subseries 11, www.oac.cdlib.org. Eaton

enlisted artists such as Ishigo in his effort. Eaton's collection was recently in the news when its pending auction prompted an angry response among Japanese Americans whose families had been incarcerated and others who shared their concern. Some called for the collection to be returned to families or donated rather than sold. The Heart Mountain Wyoming Foundation, after trying unsuccessfully to purchase the collection at nearly twice its stated value, notified the auction house of intent to file a formal complaint. The collection was withdrawn from public auction and purchased by the Japanese American National Museum. The foundation has negotiated with the museum to allow the long-term loan of the Ishigo material. Verified Complaint, April 15, 2015, www.heartmountain.org/pressreleases_17_4287335041.pdf.

20 See n14.

21 National Museum of American History, Smithsonian Institution, 1987–2004; for an online version, http://amhistory.si.edu/perfectunion/experience/index.html.

22 Delphine Hirasuna, *The Art of Gaman: Arts and Crafts from the Japanese American Internment Camps 1942–1945* (Berkeley, CA: Ten Speed Press, 2005).

23 Gordon H. Chang, "Foreword: Emerging from the Shadows; The Visual Arts and Asian American History," in Chang et al., *Asian American Art*, ix–xv. Chang cites the additional challenge of identifying Asian American artistic production in terms of American or Asian characteristics, while noting also that recent accounts of the transnational and hybrid character of Asian America have enabled more nuanced interpretations than a blunt binary of East and West. *Asian American Art* limits its study to pre-1965 production, after which Asian American demographics changed significantly with new immigration.

24 Higa credits earlier, little-documented exhibitions in university ethnic studies departments and a few nonethnic institutions in the Bay Area, all of which emphasized history rather than art. *View from Within*, 17–18.

25 Mayumi Tsutakawa and Alan Chong Lau, eds., *Turning Shadows into Light: Art and Culture of the Northwest's Early Asian/Pacific Community* (Seattle: Young Pine Press, 1982), and Mayumi Tsutakawa, ed., *They Painted from Their Hearts: Pioneer Asian American Artists* (Seattle: Wing Luke Asian Museum, 1994). The latter includes "A Directory of Asian American Artists in Washington and Oregon (1900–1975)," compiled by Alan Chong Lau and Kazuko Nakane for the Archives of American Art, Smithsonian Institution, 1990.

26 See Elena Tajima Creef, *Imaging Japanese America: The Visual Construction of Citizenship, Nation, and the Body* (New York: New York University Press, 2004); Robinson and Creef, *Miné Okubo*.

27 Citations of the diary refer to the entries as they are numbered and reproduced in this book.

28 The date 1942 is based upon the contents of preceding pages and confirmed by events recorded in Tokita's diary, which is published in Johns, *Signs of Home: The Paintings and Wartime Diary of Kamekichi Tokita* (Seattle: University of Washington Press, 2011). A low of –20 degrees Fahrenheit was recorded that winter.

29 H. L. Stafford to Dillon S. Myer, director, War Relocation Authority, September 26, 1945, "Project Director's Narrative: H. L. Stafford Report," University of California Libraries, www.oac.cdlib.org/view?docId=ft9p300845;NAAN=13030&doc.view=frames&chunk.id=d0e76&toc.id=d0e76&brand=oac4. Some outdoor latrines remained in use through midwinter.

30 Valparaiso University in Indiana, with which Kita has a special relationship, has promised to publish a facsimile of the full diary together with the translation notes. Following the release of both books, the diary will be accessible online at Denshō.

31 The historic Issei-produced Seattle newspaper *Hokubei Jiji* (North American Times) is being scanned and its major headlines translated for posting online, a future boon to historians; but even so, references to artists typically fall to back pages and so will not appear in translation. Founded in 1902, the newspaper continues publication under the name the *North American Post*, or *Hokubei Hochi*.

32 Roger Daniels, "Words Do Matter: A Note on Inappropriate Terminology and the Incarceration of the Japanese Americans," in *Nikkei in the Pacific Northwest: Japanese Americans and Japanese Canadians in the Twentieth Century*, ed. Louis Fiset and Gail Nomura, 183–207 (Seattle: University of Washington Press, 2005), republished at www.discovernikkei.org/en/journal/2008/2/1/words-do-matter. The term *internment* is more accurately limited to the legal confinement of nationals of enemy states in camps administered by the Department of Justice. Kashima, *Judgment without Trial*, examines the several systems of imprisonment. For others' choices of terminology, see, for example, Alice Yang Murray, *Historical Memories of the Japanese American Internment and the Struggle for Redress* (Stanford, CA: Stanford University Press, 2008), 6–7; Greg Robinson, *A Tragedy of Democracy: Japanese Confinement in North America* (New York: Columbia University Press, 2009), vii–viii.

33 Stephen H. Sumida, "Hawaii, the Northwest, and Asia: Localism and Local Literary Developments in the Creation of an Asian Immigrants' Sensibility," *Seattle Review* 11, no. 1 (spring–summer 1988), 10–14, 17. Sumida's text reads, "people thought to be invisible, silent, or, worst, 'assimilated,'" a reference to prewar Hawai'i, not the West Coast of wartime.

34 Stephen H. Sumida, "Centers without Margins: Responses to Centrism in Asian American Literature," *American Literature* 66, no. 4 (December 1994): 803–815.

35 The definitive statement is Kenneth Callahan, "Pacific Northwest," *ArtNews* 45 (July 1946): 22–27, 53–55.

1. ANOTHER SPRING

1 Once the United States went to war, nearly a million legal residents who were nationals of countries at war with the United States—about 600,000 Italians, 200,000 Germans, and 60,000 Japanese—automatically became "enemy aliens" and subject to internment. Using haphazard criteria, the government confined only a fraction of them in internment camps administered by the Department of Justice—in total about 8,000 Japanese, 2,300 Germans, and 200 Italians.

2 U.S. War Relocation Authority, "War Relocation Evacuee Case File: Takuichi Fujii," U.S. National Archives and Records Administration, College Park, MD, hereafter "Evacuee Case File"); U.S. Selective Service System, "World War I Selective Service System Draft Registration Cards, 1917–1918," M1509, National Archives and Records Administration, Washington, DC, Ancestry database, "U.S., World War I Draft Registration Cards, 1917–1918," www.ancestry.com/. Fujii's birth is recorded elsewhere as ranging from 1888 to 1892.

3 On causal factors of emigration, Yuji Ichioka, *The Issei: The World of the First Generation Japanese Immigrants, 1885–1924* (New York: Free Press, 1988),

42–43; Eiichiro Azuma, *Between Two Empires: Race, History, and Transnationalism in Japanese America* (New York: Oxford University Press, 2005), 27–28; John E. Van Sant, *Pacific Pioneers: Japanese Journeys to America and Hawaii, 1850–1880* (Urbana: University of Illinois Press, 2000), 133–134.

4 Contract labor immigration to Hawai'i had begun as early as 1868, with a small group from Yokohama, but the abusive terms of contract, adding to already strained relations between the United States and Japan, prompted Japan to bar further labor emigration for nearly two decades. Daniels, *The Politics of Prejudice: The Anti-Japanese Movement in California and the Struggle for Japanese Exclusion* (Berkeley: University of California Press, 1962), 4; for a detailed account, Van Sant, *Pacific Pioneers*, 97–116.

5 S. Frank Miyamoto, *Social Solidarity among the Japanese in Seattle* (Seattle: University of Washington Press, in cooperation with the Asian American Studies Program, University of Washington, 1984), 20. First published in *University of Washington Publications in the Social Sciences* 11, no. 2 (1939): 57–130.

6 For conditions in Hiroshima, see Ichioka, *Issei*, 43–45.

7 "List or Manifest of Alien Immigrants for the Commissioner of Immigration," 1902, 1903, U.S. Immigration and Naturalization Service, Records, 1891–1957, National Archives and Records Administration, Washington, DC, Record Group 85, M1383, Ancestry database, "Seattle, Washington, Passenger and Crew Lists, 1882–1957," www.ancestry.com/ (hereafter "Passenger and Crew Lists"). His father is named on a ship manifest as a laborer, his brother, a farmer. The labels do not necessarily match their occupations in Japan. See, for example, Neil Nakadate, *Looking after Minidoka: An American Memoir* (Bloomington: University of Indiana Press, 2013), 12.

8 "Evacuee Case File"; "Passenger and Crew Lists," 1906. Fujii's War Relocation Authority (WRA) records are among the few sources of information. Some dates are inconsistent. Fujii states in information provided to the WRA that he attended Numata grammar school from 1898 to 1906 and Shudo high school from 1906 to 1908. Immigration records show that he left Japan on September 29, 1906, and landed in Seattle in October. If one accepts the 1898 date, Fujii would have been seven when he entered school. It seems plausible that he might have misspoken and could have begun grammar school in 1896 and completed two years at the higher level in 1906. On Shudo, www.shudo-u.ac.jp/english/history.html.

9 *Some Work of the Group of Twelve* (Seattle: Dogwood Press, 1937), unpaginated.

10 Sharon Boswell and Lorraine McConaghy, "Partners across the Pacific," *Seattle Times*, January 28, 1996. The reception was bigger than that given five years earlier for President Benjamin Harrison.

11 "Japs Who Come to Seek Fortune in America," *Seattle Times*, June 21, 1903.

12 Shelley Sang-Hee Lee, *Claiming the Oriental Gateway: Prewar Seattle and Japanese America* (Philadelphia: Temple University Press, 2011), 11–12. Lee views the use of *cosmopolitan* in this way as an "unconventional, even radical twist" of the term by the Seattle elite to incorporate Asian, and particularly Japanese, immigrants and the city in the discourse of cosmopolitanism.

13 R. S. Jones, "What the Visitor Sees at the Seattle Fair," *American Review of Reviews* 40 (July 1909): 66, cited in Lee, *Claiming the Oriental Gateway*, 62. For a local report, "Thousands Cheer Soldiers and Sailors," *Seattle Times*, June 1, 1909.

14 Daniels, *Politics of Prejudice*.

15 Yukiko Irwin and Hilary Conroy, "Robert Walker Irwin and Systematic Immigration to Hawai'i," in *East across the Pacific: Historical and Sociological Studies of Japanese Immigration and Assimilation*, ed. Hilary Conroy and T. Scott Miyakawa (Santa Barbara, CA: Clio Press, 1972), 41.

16 Daniels, *Politics of Prejudice*, 6; Irwin and Conroy, "Robert Walker Irwin and Systematic Immigration," 46–47; Ichioka, *Issei*, 41–51. Irwin, an American businessman with extensive experience in Japan, served as Hawai'i's consul general in Japan and oversaw the period of organized labor immigration to Hawai'i.

17 Azuma, *Between Two Empires*, 29. See also Ichioka, *Issei*, 51–52. Under U.S. law, the labor contracts violated the Constitution's prohibition of slavery and involuntary servitude. Azuma estimates that more than 130,000 immigrated to Hawai'i and the West Coast between 1895, when Irwin's role ended, and 1908. Between 1902 and 1907, an estimated additional 38,000 Japanese moved to the mainland from Hawai'i when their contracts ended.

18 On comparable rates of pay, see Azuma, *Between Two Empires*, 29; on fare, Ichioka, *Issei*, 65. Azuma estimates expenses on the basis of agents' fees and steerage fare.

19 "Passenger and Crew Lists," 1906; "Evacuee Case File." Fujii stated for the ship manifest that he would join his father, but it is unclear whether his brother, Nobuichi, was still in Seattle when Fujii arrived in 1906. By 1943, when Fujii completed a required wartime questionnaire, his father had died and Nobuichi was living in Osaka. The brothers seem not to have been close as adults; Fujii did not know his brother's address or occupation.

20 Kazuo Ito, *Issei: A History of Japanese Immigrants in North America*, trans. Shinichiro Nakamura and Jean S. Gerard (Seattle: Japanese Community Service, 1973), 145; Daisuke Kitagawa, *Issei and Nisei: The Internment Years* (New York: Seabury Press, 1967), 15. Having arrived in Seattle in 1939, Japanese pastor Daisuke Kitagawa saw membership in prefectural organizations as a kind of "tribalism" that contributed significantly to community divisiveness.

21 Census figures from Miyamoto, *Social Solidarity*, 14. American-born represented 6 percent of the total in 1910, nearly a quarter in 1920, and nearly a half by 1930. The growth rates were influenced by political relations between Japan and the United States, as this chapter relates in part.

22 Azuma, *Between Two Empires*, 5–7, 38, 41.

23 Ichioka, *Issei*, 1–2; Azuma, *Between Two Empires*, 7.

24 Azuma, *Between Two Empires*, 4.

25 Ichioka, *Issei*, 71–72, lists those eligible for passports as merchants, students, diplomats, tourists, immediate family members, Issei returning for visits, and a special category of farmers.

26 Ichioka, *Issei*, 159. For discussions of the Gentlemen's Agreement, see ibid., 71–72, 159–161; Roger Daniels, *Asian America: Chinese and Japanese in the United States since 1850* (Seattle: University of Washington Press, 1988), 125–128, 131. The year-and-a-half-long negotiations resulted in an executive agreement, in the form of correspondence in late 1907 and early 1908, that did not require congressional ratification.

27 Miyamoto, *Social Solidarity*, 58, 60; Daniels, *Asian America*, 128.

28 On acculturation redefined as a Japanese value, see Ichioka, *Issei*, 184–187.

29 Azuma, *Between Two Empires*, 11. See also Ichioka, *Issei*, 5, 163–164.

30 The 1921 law strengthened the prohibition of property ownership already imbedded in the state constitution. Additional legislation in 1923 prohibited the practice of assigning ownership to Nisei children.

Issei with real property were then forced to put their children's land in trust to a Caucasian.

31 Ichioka, *Issei*, 232.

32 Takao Ozawa v. U.S., 260 U.S. 178 (1922). See Ichioka, *Issei*, 219–226, on the case and its impact. The U.S. Constitution, which limited rights of naturalization to whites, had been amended in the nineteenth century to include Native Americans and African Americans, but the amendment did not include ethnic Asians.

33 Ichioka, *Issei*, 7.

34 On generational change, see, for example, ibid., 252–254; on identifying the Nisei generation, Azuma, *Between Two Empires*, 96.

35 Azuma, *Between Two Empires*, 12; Ichioka, *Issei*, 197. On divisions within the community from the viewpoint of a contemporary witness, Kitagawa, *Issei and Nisei*, 15–17, 35–39.

36 Azuma, *Between Two Empires*, 60–61.

37 S. Frank Miyamoto, "An Immigrant Community in America," in Conroy and Miyakawa, *East across the Pacific*, 223; Miyamoto, *Social Solidarity*, 16. Miyamoto counts professionals such asdoctors and lawyers among business owners.

38 Miyamoto, *Social Solidarity*, 18.

39 Daniels, *Asian America*, 134; "Pike Place Market Centennial," www.seattle.gov/cityarchives/exhibits-and-education/online-exhibits/pike-place-market-centennial. Efforts to exclude the Nikkei from the market continued through the 1930s; see Ito, *Issei*, 150–152.

40 "Poor Man's Playground," *Northwest Enterprise*, October 12, 1933, Denshō, denshopd-i350-00151, http://archive.densho.org/main.aspx.

41 Tokita, diary, December 26, 1941, in Johns, *Signs of Home*, 124–125. Tokita and his wife managed a hotel at Second and Jackson Streets on the western edge of Nihonmachi. His diary, dated Decem ber 7, 1941, to July 20, 1944, is published in Johns, *Signs of Home*, 109–214.

42 There is no record of whether he joined a trade association, as Issei were encouraged to do, but at the time of the war's outbreak, he had left the fish business and belonged to none. "Evacuee Case File."

43 Japanese law allowed an annual deferment from mandatory military service to anyone living abroad. Revisions at the time of the Gentlemen's Agreement required that Issei obtain a local certificate of residence in order to qualify. Ichioka, *Issei*, 13–14, 162; Azuma, *Between Two Empires*, 30, 43.

44 For Fusano Fujii's education and immigration, see "Japanese-Immigration Internee Data File: Fusano Fujii," U.S. National Archives and Records Administration, Record Group 10, http://aad.archives.gov/aad/record-detail.jsp?dt=2003&mtch=2&tf=F&q=fusano+fujii&bc=&rpp=10&pg=1&rid=6021&rlst=6021.6022.

45 Kitagawa, *Issei and Nisei*, 20.

46 *Sealth* (Seattle: Broadway High School, 1934), 16; U.S. War Relocation Authority, "Final Accountability Roster of the Minidoka Relocation Center, October 1945," Record Group 210, Records of the War Relocation Authority, National Archives and Records Service, Washington, DC, 1956. I have assumed both daughters followed the same educational track, although I have found evidence only of Satoko's attending Broadway High School. Both spoke Japanese, although according to the 1956 roster, they did not attend the Japanese Language School.

47 "Evacuee Case File"; Daniels, *Asian America*, 167–168; Miyamoto, *Social Solidarity*, 65.

48 Reviews appeared regularly in *Notan*, the newsletter of the Seattle Camera Club, 1925–1929.

49 The Seattle Camera Club met from 1924 to 1929, although its most prominent members were active in the early 1920s and well after its termination. See David F. Martin and Nicolette Bromberg, *Shadows of a Fleeting World: Pictorial Photography and the Seattle Camera Club* (Seattle: University of Washington, 2011).

50 See Johns, *Signs of Home*, 20, for a photograph of young Issei men that may depict the club. Only Tokita and Nomura have been positively identified; based upon photographs in the Nomura papers, the center figure is likely Show Toda, Nomura's first business partner. Kamekichi Tokita papers, possession of Shokichi Tokita.

51 Seattle Art Museum records, Accession 2636-1, Box 24, File: "Exhibition Catalogues, Northwest Artists," Special Collections, University of Washington Libraries (hereafter "Seattle Art Museum records").

52 Nomura's scrapbook contains photographs of himself with the two older artists. Nomura papers, possession of George and Betty Nomura.

53 Tooru Kanazawa, "Seattle's Artists of Palette and Brush . . ." [*sic*], *Japanese American Courier*, October 7, 1934. See also George Tsutakawa, interview, 1983, Archives of American Art, Smithsonian Institution, www.aaa.si.edu/collections/interviews/oral-history-interview-george-tsutakawa-11913.

Miyazaki, a Nisei, was a friend of George Tsutakawa, who describes the two of them, both students in the late 1920s and early 1930s, visiting Nomura's and Tokita's studio. Miyao, a florist, moved from Seattle to Tukwila, Washington, in the mid-1930s and no longer exhibited in the Northwest Annuals.

54 Kenneth Callahan, "Penthouse Art Gallery Plans to Show Work," *Seattle Times*, October 10, 1935.

55 Records of Fujii's 1930s residence in Chicago are inconsistent. A postcard from Fujii in June 1936 states his imminent departure, and he participated in a Chicago regional exhibition in February 1937; his WRA case file, however, dates his stay to 1938–1939. No mention of him at this time appears in Chicago city directories. Fujii to Richard E. Fuller, June 22, 1936, Seattle Art Museum records; *Forty-First Annual Exhibition by Artists of Chicago and Vicinity* (Chicago: Art Institute of Chicago, 1937), exhibition brochure, www.artic.edu/sites/default/files/libraries/pubs/1937/AIC1937ArtofChi41stAn_comb.pdf; "Evacuee Case File."

56 "Three Japanese Show Works at N.W. Art Exhibit," *Japanese American Courier*, November 2, 1935.

57 *Forty-First Annual Exhibition by Artists of Chicago and Vicinity.*

58 U.S. Bureau of the Census, "Sixteenth Census of the United States," National Archives and Records Administration, Washington, DC, Ancestry database, "1940 United States Federal Census," www.ancestry.com/.

59 Their daughters were given Christian names, Mary Rose and Virginia, upon their baptism. Outside the family, Satoko went by *Mary* throughout her life, while Masako in adulthood returned to the name she was given at birth.

60 Executive Order 9066, February 19, 1942, General Records of the United States Government, Record Group 11, U.S. National Archives and Records Admin istration, www.archives.gov/historical-docs/todays-doc/?dod-date=219.

61 Murray, *Historical Memories*, 29, on the issuance of Executive Order 9066, 30–38. See also U.S. House of Representatives, Committee on Interior and Insular Affairs, *Personal Justice Denied: Report on the Commission of Wartime Relocation and Internment of Civilians* (Washington, DC: Government Printing Office,

1982), 72–86. For a thorough account of the years before the commission's findings, Roger Daniels, *Concentration Camps: North America: Japanese in the United States and Canada during World War II* (Malabar, FL: Robert E. Krieger Publishing, 1989), 44, rev. ed., updated in 1989, of *Concentration Camps USA* (New York: Holt, Rinehart and Winston, 1971), 40, 44–73; and on DeWitt see especially 52–55. Enemy aliens were within the authority of the Department of Justice and remained so in internment camps.

62 Characterization of DeWitt, Murray, *Historical Memories*, 29; see also Daniels, *Concentration Camps*, 44. On Bendetsen's role, Daniels, *Concentration Camps*, 51–67; Murray, *Historical Memories*, 30–34; Robinson, *Tragedy of Democracy*, 69–71.

63 Francis Biddle to Henry Stimson, letter February 12, 1942, Secretary of War, Record Group 107, National Archives and Records Administration, quoted in Daniels, *Concentration Camps*, 69.

64 John L. DeWitt to Henry Stimson, "Final Recommendation," February 14, 1942, in *Final Report: Japanese Evacuation from the West Coast, 1942*, quoted in U.S. House of Representatives Committee on Interior and Insular Affairs, *Personal Justice Denied*, 6, 222.

65 Testimony before a subcommittee of the House Naval Affairs Committee, April 14, 1943. For transcript online, see "A Slap's a Slap: General John L. DeWitt and Four Little Words," blog post by Alan Walker, November 22, 2013, http://blogs.archives.gov/TextMessage/2013/11/22/a-slaps-a-slap-general-john-l-dewitt-and-four-little-words/.

66 The FBI acted on lists of names already in place. Those arrested were detained in Immigration and Naturalization Service jails, and many were eventually confined in internment camps for enemy aliens administered by the Department of Justice. Of those released without internment, those on the West Coast ended up in WRA incarceration camps. See Kashima, *Judgment without Trial.*

67 Mike Masaoka, "Statement before the Tolan Committee," February 21, 1942, cited in Murray, *Historical Memories*, 106. For an account of the league's position, see, 103–139.

68 Fiset, *Camp Harmony*, 58. Fiset provides a detailed account of preparations in Seattle and Puyallup.

69 See introduction, note 2.

70 Fiset, *Camp Harmony*, 63.

71 Ibid., 58, 84–90, 97.

72 Fiset describes the necessary conditions and the search for usable sites in Washington, ibid., 61–63. Manzanar and Tule Lake in California and Poston and Gila River in Arizona took inmates directly without intermediate temporary confinement.

73 Ibid., 101.

74 U.S. War Relocation Authority, *Questions and Answers for Evacuees: Information Regarding the Relocation Program* (San Francisco: War Relocation Authority Regional Office, 1942), Denshō, denshop-p156-00165.

75 For example, "Coast Japs Are Interned in Mountain Camp, Manzanar, California," *Life*, April 6, 1942, cited in Audrie Girdner and Anne Loftis, *The Great Betrayal: The Evacuation of Japanese-Americans during World War II* (London: Macmillan, 1969), 146. President Roosevelt used the term until news of German death camps became public. Daniels, *Asian America*, 228; for example, Roosevelt press conference, November 21, 1944, quoted in U.S. House of Representatives, Committee on Interior and Insular Affairs, *Personal Justice Denied*, 233.

76 Donald Keene, *Modern Japanese Diaries: The Japanese at Home and Abroad as*

Revealed through Their Diaries (New York: Henry Holt, 1995), 2.

77 Within two weeks new owners reopened former Nikkei businesses in the neighborhood. "Elliot Café 1209 Jackson Street," *Northwest Enterprise*, May 22, 1942, Denshō, denshopd-i35-00180.

78 Unpublished diary entry. A visitor to the United States in 1921, Kinoshita Mokutarō, only slightly older than Fujii, writes about the shame of having to carry one's own tray in a cafeteria. Keene, *Modern Japanese Diaries*, 482.

79 Fiset, *Camp Harmony*, 65.

80 Girdner and Loftis, *Great Betrayal*, 154.

81 Nikkei from Portland were also sent to Minidoka. Those from Bellevue, Renton, and other communities near Seattle were sent to Tule Lake, California, while those from Bainbridge Island were sent to Manzanar. The latter were transferred to Minidoka in January 1943.

82 Arrival date in "Evacuee Case File."

83 Temperatures the first summer reached 112 Fahrenheit and dropped to −14 in mid-November 1942. Karl Lillquist, *Imprisoned in the Desert: The Geography of World War II–Era, Japanese American Relocation Centers in the Western United States* (Ellensburg: Central Washington University, 2007), 166; online, www.cwu.edu/geography/sites/cts.cwu.edu.geography/files/chapter5minidoka.pdf; Stafford, "Stafford Report."

84 Total cited in Roger Daniels, Sandra C. Taylor, and Harry H. L. Kitano, eds., *Japanese Americans: From Relocation to Redress* (Seattle: University of Washington Press, 1991), xxi.

85 Stafford, "Stafford Report."

86 The blocks at Minidoka were numbered to forty-four but skipped some numbers. Jeffery F. Burton, Mary M. Farrell, Florence B. Lord, and Richard W. Lord, *Confinement and Ethnicity: An Overview of Japanese American Relocation Sites*, rev. ed. Publications in Anthropology 74 (Tucson, AZ: Western Archeological and Conservation Center, National Park Service, U.S. Department of the Interior, July 2000), www.cr.nps.gov/history/online_books/anthropology74/index.htm.

87 Gesensway and Roseman, *Beyond Words*, 76, no source given. On Eisenhower's tenure, see Daniels, *Concentration Camps*, 91–94. Eisenhower opposed long-term incarceration of Japanese Americans and resigned after three months.

88 For a summary of structures, Burton et al., *Confinement and Ethnicity.*

89 National Parks Service, Minidoka National Historic Site signage, Carol Ash, personal communication, November 24, 2015; Amy Lowe Merger, *Minidoka Internment National Monument: Historic Resource Study* (Seattle: National Park Service, 2005).

90 "First Wed," *Minidoka Irrigator*, September 10, 1942, 2, Denshō, denshopd-i119-00001.

91 Biographical information for Denkichi Kita, "Passenger and Crew Lists"; Department of Employment and Immigration Service, "Passenger Lists, 1865–1935," Library and Archives Canada, Ottawa, Canada, ancestry database, "Canadian Passenger Lists, 1865–1935," www.ancestry.com/; and "Records about Japanese Americans Relocated during World War II, created 1988–1989, documenting the period 1942–1946," Record Group 210, Records of the War Relocation Authority, National Archives and Records Administration, Washington, DC, ancestry database, "Japanese Americans Relocated during World War II," www.ancestry.com/.

92 The work was advertised in the first issue of the *Minidoka Irrigator*, September 10, 1942, and the first workers left in October after new leave clearance procedures were instituted. Temporary leave to work in the

fields had been first tested at Puyallup in late May. The demand for sugar beets was driven by the U.S. military, where it was needed to supply sugar for soldiers and to produce ethanol. The pressing need reversed farmers' initial opposition to Nikkei workers, who by the end of 1942 harvested 20 percent of Idaho's sugar beet crop. Daniels, *Concentration Camps*, 112; Fiset, *Camp Harmony*, 52, 112–116. See also Louis Fiset, "Thinning, Topping, and Loading: Japanese Americans and Beet Sugar in World War II," *Pacific Northwest Quarterly* 90, no. 3 (1999): 123–139.

93 U.S. Army, World War II Army Enlistment Records, Record Group 64, National Archives and Records Administration, College Park, MD, ancestry database, "U.S. World War II Army Enlistment Records, 1938–1946," www.ancestry.com/. Robinson states that only a few Nisei secured work in war industries (*Tragedy of Democracy*, 186).

94 U.S. War Relocation Authority, *Questions and Answers for Evacuees*.

95 This language appears in the first issues, September 10 and 18, 1942.

96 Stafford, "Stafford Report."

97 Tokita, diary, October 15, 1942, in Johns, *Signs of Home*, 190. Tokita had earlier praised the Nisei's assumption of leadership, but accepting their authority in personal circumstances was too much. At first working as his block's maintenance person, he eventually became a sign painter at camp, where he worked alongside Nomura, his former business partner.

98 Fixed wages were twelve, sixteen, and nineteen dollars per month for unskilled labor, skilled labor, and professional.

99 *Minidoka Interlude: September 1942–October 1943* (Hunt, ID: Minidoka Relocation Center, 1943), unpaginated. Fujii is pictured among the production team. The book, with a new introduction, was privately reissued by Tom Takeuchi (Gresham, OR, [ca. 1990]) and is available from the Friends of Minidoka, www.minidoka.org/.

100 On the questionnaire, Daniels, *Concentration Camps*, 112–116; Fujii's response, "Evacuee Case File." Both work release and military enlistment required the verification of loyalty. Framed in the guise of an "Application for Leave Clearance" and required of all inmates over the age of seventeen, the questionnaire contained two key questions that were problematic, one about willingness to serve in the armed forces, the other about swearing allegiance exclusively to the United States. Although the latter, which would have rendered the Issei stateless, was changed to "abide by the laws of the United States," the ambiguities of the wording and the process aroused widespread confusion, resistance, and protest. Fujii answered both questions positively, as did the majority at Minidoka, but made no mention of the process in his diary.

101 U.S. House of Representatives, Committee on Interior and Insular Affairs, *Personal Justice Denied*, 214–215.

102 For an account of the numbers of inmates, see "Movement into and Out of WRA Centers, 1942–1946," in *The Evacuated People: A Quantitative Description*, by War Relocation Authority (Washington, DC, 1946), 8, 128, reprinted in Daniels, *Asian America*, 242.

103 Robinson, *A Tragedy of Democracy*, 254–255.

104 Daniels, *Concentration Camps*, 167.

105 On eviction, W. A. Dougherty, memorandum, January 10, 1946, in "Evacuee Case File."

106 U.S. War Relocation Authority, "Final Accountability Roster." Mandatory exclusion orders were rescinded in December 1944 and the closure of camps was announced in January. The diary reads "December, 18, 1945"; Fujii's error

has been retained in the translation as it appears in the second section of this book to be true to his text as written. The Fujiis left Puyallup on August 18, 1942, arrived at Minidoka on August 20, and were released from Minidoka on October 2, 1945, a date pictured in diary 109. The last persons left Minidoka on October 28, 1945.

107 For example, Tom Takeuchi, introduction to *Minidoka Interlude*, in the reissued edition.

108 Correspondence between M. K. on behalf of Fujii and W. A. Dougherty, January 4, 10, 11, 1945; Dougherty regarding assistance grant, November 7 and 25, 1945, in "Evacuee Case File."

109 Charlotte Brooks, "In the Twilight Zone between Black and White: Japanese American Resettlement and Community in Chicago, 1942–1945," *Journal of American History* 86 (2000): 1655. Brooks notes, however, that Salt Lake's wartime ethnic Japanese population gain was three thousand, a fraction of Chicago's.

110 U.S. Census by decade, cited in "Ogden, Utah," Wikipedia, last modified June 12, 2016, http://en.wikipedia.org/wiki/Ogden,_Utah.

111 The first record of their residence in Chicago is 1948; Masako's, 1949. *Chicago Japanese American Year Book, 1948* and *1949* (Chicago: Joe T. Komaki, 1948, 1949), Japanese American Service Committee Legacy Center.

112 The description of the city is from Henry C. Binford, "Multicentered Chicago," in *Encyclopedia of Chicago*, Chicago Historical Society, 2005, www.encyclopedia.chicagohistory.org/pages/854.html.

113 Brooks, "In the Twilight Zone," 1655.

114 About half represented Japanese business interests, so that established residents numbered only about two hundred. Michael Daniel Albert, "Japanese American Communities in Chicago and the Twin Cities" (PhD diss., University of Minnesota, 1980), 110. I thank Roger Daniels for referring me to Albert's dissertation.

115 Ibid., 114; U.S. House of Representatives, Committee on Interior and Insular Affairs, *Personal Justice Denied*, 10. Milton Eisenhower, the first WRA director, met overwhelming opposition to Nikkei settlement when meeting with western governors in April 1942.

116 Brooks, "In the Twilight Zone," 1655. The number includes a small number of Issei. Besides Chicago, the first WRA offices were established in Cleveland, Des Moines, Minneapolis, Milwaukee, and New York; and by mid-1943, forty-two were under way. Albert, "Japanese American Communities," 89.

117 The main church groups were the American Friends Service Committee and the Lutheran Brethren Service Committee. The Nisei-led Chicago Resettlers Committee was founded in 1945 and, in 1954, changed its name to the Japanese American Service Committee in recognition of the community's changing needs.

118 Albert, "Japanese American Communities," 118, 178–182, on housing discrimination; on WRA policy, 174–177. The Nisei differed in their response to the WRA's policy of assimilation, some embracing it while most resisted it in relying upon each other. The WRA and cooperating agencies, Brooks states, viewed the prewar concentration in Japantowns as a matter of choice, while the Nisei understood it to be largely the result of social restrictions. Brooks, "In the Twilight Zone," 1657, 1679–1680, 1685. For an extended description of Chicago's Nikkei community, see Albert, "Japanese American Communities," 114–134.

119 Neighborhood groups met to address housing in the late 1940s. The neighborhood became home to the Cabrini-Green

public housing project when large high-rise complexes were added to the wartime Cabrini housing project in 1958 and 1962. The expanded project came to epitomize the pitfalls of urban redevelopment. Amanda Seligman, "Cabrini-Green," in *Encyclopedia of Chicago*, Chicago Historical Society, 2005, www.encyclopedia.chicagohistory.org/pages/199.html.

120 "Right in the Middle of Need," n.d.; *Tower Topics* 1, no. 1 (ca. 1960s): 1. Olivet Community Center records, Box 5/5, 5/7, Chicago History Museum.

121 Olivet director Wallace O. Heistad cited in Georgie Anne Geyer, "Japanese Help Out Olivet," *Chicago Daily News*, February 24, 1962, 13; Olivet Community Center records, Box 5/5, Chicago History Museum; Midwest Buddhist Temple, www.mbtchicago.org/about-the-temple/history-of-our-temple/. The congregation was founded in 1944 by Kono and several Issei and Nisei.

122 "Chicago Nisei Artists Form Gakka Guild," *Pacific Citizen*, January 10, 1948. Artists included painter-sculptor Ken Nishi, a Gakka founder; sculptor Shinkichi Tajiri; and photographer Yashuhiro Ishimoto. By the early 1950s all had left Chicago to settle elsewhere and would establish prominent careers.

123 The house may have been bought in their daughter's name. Mary (Satoko) Kita is listed in directories. (The exception is 1953, when Masako, not Mary, is listed at the Larrabee address under her married name, Nelson.) *Chicago Telephone Directory*, 1951; *Polk Cross Directory*, 1952, 1953.

124 Alice Murata, *Japanese Americans in Chicago* (Chicago: Arcadia, 2002); "Buddhist Rites of Bon Odori on Saturday to Present 200 Members in 2,500 Year Old Dance," *Chicago Tribune*, July 7, 1949.

125 The James and Mary Numata collection of nearly eight thousand photographs is in the Japanese American Service Committee Legacy Center.

126 *1957 Chicago Artists No-Jury Exhibition* and *1958 Chicago Artists No-Jury Exhibition*.

127 Numbers are based upon ethnic Japanese names.

128 They were Joseph Goto, Miyoko Ito, Atsushi Kikuchi, Arthur Okamura, and Ray Yoshida.

129 Kita, age fourteen at his grandfather's death, later found the Art Institute familiar and surmises that he went with his grandfather as a child.

130 Callahan, "Names Change."

131 Illinois Art Historical Project, www.illinoisart.org/#!e-g/cr4y.

2. PAINTING AND RECOGNITION IN THE 1930S

1 [Kamekichi] Tokita and [Kenjiro] Nomura, "Seattle's Japanese Artists," *Town Crier*, May 28, 1932, 9. Margaret Bundy Callahan, editor of the *Town Crier*, initiated a series written by "outstanding Seattle artists" and invited Tokita and Nomura to contribute.

2 Fujii, artist statement in *Some Work of the Group of Twelve*. The statement, as well as those of Nomura and Tokita, appears to be heavily edited, likely by artist and art writer Kenneth Callahan, the group's primary organizer. Fujii's command of English is noted in War Relocation Authority records as "poor"; official correspondence in English was written on his behalf, and Kita's translation of the diary in this book remains close to the author's syntax. The statement in full is reproduced in appendix 1.

3 Of the paintings located to date, two are in the collection of the Wing Luke Museum, a gift of the Callahans' grandson in 1991; the others are in two private

Seattle collections. The Callahans traded paintings with other artists in the 1930s to build their collection. See Brian Tobey Callahan, ed., comp., *Margaret Callahan: Mother of Northwest Art* (Victoria, BC: Trafford Publishing, 2009), 110; Johns, *Signs of Home*, 80.

4 Fujii, in *Some Work of the Group of Twelve*.

5 Kenneth Callahan, "Tokita's Paintings Exhibited," *Town Crier*, December 31, 1930, 15. Nomura's *Puget Sound* was exhibited in *Painting and Sculpture from 16 American Cities*, Museum of Modern Art, 1933.

6 Tsutakawa, oral history interview, 1983.

7 Kenneth Callahan, "The Northwest Annual," *Town Crier*, December 5, 1931, 35, 38.

8 Nomura's painting is in the collection of the Wing Luke Museum.

9 Kenneth Callahan, "San Francisco Annual," *Town Crier*, March 19, 1932, 8.

10 Sandy Kita, personal communication, November 11, 2011. See also ch. 2, n3.

11 [Carl F. Gould], "President's Report," 1927, Box 33/23, Art Institute of Seattle, Seattle Art Museum records.

12 For more on Hatch's tenure, see Johns, "Knowing Your Place."

13 On praise, Margaret Bundy, "Art in the Northwest," *Town Crier*, March 26, 1930, 12; on Horiuchi collection, [John Davis Hatch Jr.], "Director's Report," December 10, [1930], Art Institute of Seattle, Box 33/22, Seattle Art Museum records. The exhibitions, originally planned as a series of four, were Japanese art (1930), Chinese art (1931), and Southeast Asian art (1932); a fourth, Near Eastern art, was canceled by Hatch's resignation. They were organized by the Art Institute in collaboration with the Japan Society, the China Club, the Far East Society, and the University of Washington Oriental Department.

14 Hatch to Foujioka, November 12, 1929, Box 32/53, Seattle Art Museum records.

15 Hatch to Spencer Mackey, May 8, 1931, Box 32/65, Seattle Art Museum records.

16 Hatch to F. H. Varley, January 20, 1930, Box 32/31, Seattle Art Museum records. Hatch corresponded with Tokita after his resignation; Hatch to Tokita, December 1934, Kamekichi Tokita Papers, Archives of American Art, Smithsonian Institution (hereafter Tokita Papers).

17 Fuller, typescript for the museum opening, June 28, 1933, Box 23/Writings re: Museum Opening 1933, Seattle Art Museum records. For Fuller's account of his tenure, written in 1964, see Richard E. Fuller, *A Gift to the City: A History of the Seattle Art Museum and the Fuller Family* (Seattle: Seattle Art Museum, 1993).

18 Kenneth Callahan, "Northwest Annual Opens," *Town Crier*, September 26, 1931, 7.

19 Kenneth Callahan, "San Francisco Annual," *Town Crier*, May 14, 1932, 8.

20 Kenneth Callahan, "Seattle Art Museum," *Seattle Times*, October 14, 1934.

21 Kenneth Callahan, "The Art Museum," *Seattle Times*, October 5, 1935.

22 Kenneth Callahan, "The Galleries: Northwest Annual Opens," *Town Crier*, October 8, 1932, 9.

23 Callahan, "Tokita's Paintings Exhibited."

24 [Kenneth Callahan], "Artists Scored by Critic Here for Exhibition," *Seattle Times*, October 4, 1933. Callahan quotes the lead jurist for the 1933 Northwest Annual, Lloyd Rollins, former director of the California Palace of the Legion of Honor and the De Young Museum.

25 This is the thesis of Jacqueline Francis, *Making Race: Modernism and "Racial Art" in America* (Seattle: University of Washington Press, 2012); see 7 and 27–48. Francis's study specifically addresses New York in the interwar period.

26 Seven of the twelve founding members of the Group of Twelve were foreign-born. See *Some Work of the Group of Twelve.*

27 "Opening Ceremony of the Seattle Art Museum Tomorrow Night" (translated), *Taihoku Nippo* [Great Northern Daily News], [June 1933], Kenjiro Nomura papers, possession of George and Betty Nomura; "Critic Praises Paintings Done by 2 Japanese," "Tokita's Canvas Wins 3rd Prize," and "Artistic Recognition," *Japanese American Courier*, all October 7, 1933.

28 Kenneth Callahan, "Seattle Art Museum," *Seattle Times*, June 30, 1935.

29 The subject is likely the former Allentown Covered Bridge in Tukwila, south of Seattle. Nomura's son, George, identified the subject in his father's paintings. Personal communication, November 11, 2012.

30 The exhibition was organized by the volunteer Municipal Art Committee of New York as the first of an annual series. It was mounted three years and was ended by the 1939 New York World's Fair, followed by World War II.

31 Mills College Art Museum records, Mills College, Oakland, CA.

32 Both Nomura and Tokita state their intent to combine influences from Japanese and Western practice; Tokita specifies his interest in commonalities between French modernist Paul Cézanne and the fifteenth-century Zen master Sesshū Tōyō.

33 Fujii, in *Some Work of the Group of Twelve.*

34 On the conception of painting, Jeffrey Wechsler, "From Asian Traditions to Modern Expressions: Abstract Art by Asian Americans, 1945–1970," in *Asian Traditions, Modern Expressions: Asian American Artists and Abstraction, 1945–1970*, ed. Wechsler (New York: Harry N. Abrams, in association with the Jane Voorhees Zimmerli Art Museum, Rutgers, the State University of New Jersey, 1997), 105–115.

35 Brian T. Callahan, ed., *Margaret Callahan: Mother of Northwest Art* (Victoria, BC: Trafford Publishing, 2009), 56. The visits ended as political tensions between Japan and the United States increased.

36 Viola Patterson, oral history interview, July 10, 1972, Special Collections, University of Washington Libraries, Accession 2563-2, v.f. 1396B.

37 Postcard to Fuller, June 22, 1936, Box 1/40, Seattle Art Museum records.

38 Tsutakawa, oral history interview.

3. AN ISSEI DIARY OF WORLD WAR II

1 The totals represent what remains. The watercolors in the portfolio, for example, are numbered up to forty-two.

2 The title page reads "MinidokaXX," which Kita, the diary's translator, has retained. The *X*'s appear to be graphic placeholders to center the title on the page. Below are rows of shading as if placeholders for additional text.

3 Sandy Kita, "Introduction to the Diary," 134–138 in this volume; Kita writes more on the history of image and text in an unpublished version of the introduction and diary, 2011, copy in author's possession.

4 Fiset, *Camp Harmony*, 167; Robinson, *Tragedy of Democracy*, 132; and for example, Okubo, *Citizen 13660*, 50.

5 Tokita, April 18, 1942, in Johns, *Signs of Home*, 178.

6 To maximize the reproduction of Fujii's work, references to diary entries are illustrated by watercolors of matching content and composition.

7 Unpublished diary entry.

8 Yamato Ichihashi to Payson Treat, November 20, 1942, in Gordon H. Chang, ed., *Morning Glory, Evening Shadow: Yamato Ichihashi and His Internment Writings, 1942–1945* (Stanford, CA: Stanford University Press, 1997), 160.

9 Lon Kurashige describes the intergenerational spirit of an *ondo* dance, part of Bon celebrations, during Nisei Week in prewar Los Angeles. *Japanese American Celebration and Conflict: A History of Ethnic Identity and Festival in Los Angeles, 1934–1990* (Berkeley: University of California Press, 2002), 50.

10 Brian Masaru Hayashi, *Democratizing the Enemy: The Japanese American Internment* (Princeton, NJ: Princeton University Press, 2004), 8; Hayashi cites examples at Manzanar and Poston, 122, 167.

11 Azuma, *Between Two Empires*, 209.

12 Ibid., 273–274n5.

13 Ibid., 213; Kurashige, *Celebration and Conflict*, 67–68; Robinson, *Tragedy of Democracy*, 37–39. See also Kitagawa, *Issei and Nisei*, 14, 35–36. A number of Nisei as well as Issei had supported Japan's territorial expansion in the 1930s. From Japanese pastor Kitagawa's perspective, the Issei, who knew nothing of contemporary Japan, were loyal to the nation they had known in youth rather than its current reality.

14 Daniels, *Asian America*, 176–177, 258–259; Hayashi, *Democratizing the Enemy*, 34.

15 On characterization of JACL leaders, Kurashige, *Celebration and Conflict*, 31.

16 Daniels, *Asian America*, 258; Robinson, *Tragedy of Democracy*, 161–163; on camp violence, see for example, the confrontation at Manzanar in Robinson, *Tragedy of Democracy*, 133–135.

17 Unpublished diary entry; see also diary 52. Fujii, a Buddhist, appeals to a principal form of the celestial Buddha.

18 On composition and conditions of the trains, see Fiset, *Camp Harmony*, 158–160.

19 For illustrations, Obata, *Talking through the Wire Fence*, in Hill, *Topaz Moon*, 48; Nomura, *Guard Tower*, in *Kenjiro Nomura*, 26; Okubo, *Citizen 13660*, 155; Ishigo, in Higa, *View from Within*, plate 18; Miyatake, in Jasmine Alinder, *Moving Images: Photography and the Japanese American Incarceration* (Urbana: University of Illinois Press, 2009), 87–89. *Boys behind Barbed Wire*, in Alinder's assessment, "may be the most frequently reproduced photograph of the incarceration."

20 Minidoka National Historic Site signage. See also Tokita, November 6, 1942, in Johns, *Signs of Home*, 193.

21 Noboru Shirai, *Tule Lake: An Issei Memoir*, ed. Eucaly Shiry and Valerie Samson, trans. Ray Hosoda (Sacramento, CA: Muteki Press, 2001), 166.

22 Hakushu, *Yuta Nippo*, October 15, 1945, quoted in Teruko Kumei, "'A Record of Life and a Poem of Sentiments': Japanese Immigrant 'Senryu,' 1929–1945," *Amerikastudien / American Studies* 51 no. 1 (2006), 47.

23 Kitagawa, *Issei and Nisei*, 86–88; Jeanne Wakatsuki Houston, *Farewell to Manzanar* (Boston: Houghton Mifflin, 1973), 34. Kitagawa's and Houston's memoirs are two of several first-person accounts that describe the disruption to families.

24 For example, Ichihashi diary entries January 3, 8, February 8, and April 5, 1943, January 14, 1944, in Chang, *Morning Glory, Evening Shadow*, 167, 169, 178–179, 303–304. Ichihashi held firmly to a patriarchal code of honor and authority; his anger over his own son's marrying without his approval led to their estrangement for twenty years. Diary and footnote, August 25, 1943, in ibid., 252. At Heart Mountain, Estelle Ishigo relates a tragic instance of an unwed mother taking her newborn to the incinerator: "The breaking of home was complete[,] the alienation of child from parent." Ishigo, *Lone Heart Mountain*, 57.

25 Harry H. L. Kitano, *Japanese Americans: The Evolution of a Subculture* (Englewood Cliffs, NJ: Prentice-Hall, 1969), 48–49.

26 Fiset, *Camp Harmony*, 115–116; Robinson, *Tragedy of Democracy*, 182–184. Temporary work releases began as early as May 1942 in response to acute labor shortages in agriculture. Robinson outlines the stages by which leave was liberalized between July 1942 and February 1943. Some Nisei were released for Military Intelligence Service beginning July 1942. Nisei were declared eligible for military service in January 1943 and began to be drafted in January 1944.

27 For example, Ichihashi to Payson Treat, September 22, 1944, in Chang, *Morning Glory, Evening Shadow*, 364–365.

28 Okubo, *Citizen 13660*, 209; Kitano, *Japanese Americans*, 36, quotes WRA director Dillon Myer in 1945: "Over the past three years, we have watched some of these formerly enterprising, energetic people become steadily obsessed with feelings of hopelessness, personal insecurity, and inertia." See also Ichihashi to Treat, in ibid., November 26, 1944, 383.

29 The translators' use of ellipsis denotes illegible text. Regulation of funerals differed at camps and eased with time. Okubo writes of guards at Tanforan barring all but family members; *Citizen 13660*, 58. See also WRA photograph of a Minidoka funeral in *Executive Order 9066*, 95.

30 Ichihashi, draft letter to Jessie Treat, in Chang, *Morning Glory, Evening Shadow*, 310. Brackets in the cited text.

31 Keiho Soga, "Death at the Camp," in Nakano and Nakano, *Poets behind Barbed Wire*, 61.

32 Daniels, *Concentration Camps*, 105. Daniels writes, "From the very beginning of their confinement, the evacuated people were in conflict, both with their keepers and with each other. These conflicts started even before the evacuation began, grew in the Assembly Centers, and were intensified in the concentration camps."

33 Tokita, October 8 and November 13, 1942, in Johns, *Signs of Home*, 188, 195. Tokita also elaborates on a feud about management of the mess hall in his block and expresses disgust with the conduct of some Issei and Nisei. Tokita, in ibid., 208–209, 211.

34 *Minidoka Irrigator*, December 23, 1944. Given Fujii's attention to the figure, one might speculate that Fusano is the subject of the photograph.

35 For an inventory of the site, see Burton et al., *Confinement and Ethnicity*.

36 Lynne Horiuchi, "Dislocations: The Built Environments of Japanese American Internment," in *Guilt by Association: Essays on Japanese Settlement, Internment, and Relocation in the Rocky Mountain West*, ed. Mike Mackey (Powell, WY: Western History Publications, 2001), 255, 258, 259. She credits the term to James Holton, "Spaces of Insurgent Citizenship," in *Making the Invisible Visible: A Multicultural Planning History*, ed. Leonie Sandercock, 37–56 (Berkeley: University of California, 1998). The WRA held up these efforts as evidence of the camps' purported humane conditions and the inmates' cooperative self-reliance.

37 Hill, *Topaz Moon*, 19.

38 Obata's extensive writings in English and Japanese provide additional information about individual images and serve as captions in *Topaz Moon*. My characterization is based on published material; I have not reviewed his personal papers, which remain in the family.

39 *Topaz Times*, New Year's edition, January 1, 1943.

40 Obata's *Moonlight over Topaz* won first prize at the Cambridge Friends' May 1943 exhibition of art from the ten camps. In May also, JACL representatives presented paintings by Obata to Eleanor Roosevelt and WRA director Dillon

Myer. "A Japanese Art Exhibit," *Friends Bulletin*, May 1943, Friends Meeting at Cambridge, [MA]; Hill, *Topaz Moon*, 87.

41 Okubo, *Citizen 13660*, 53.

42 Alfred McClung Lee, "Concentration Camp, U.S. Model," *Saturday Review*, September 28, 1946, 12. For a discussion of the reviews, Greg Robinson, "Miné Okubo and the Politics of Symbolism," in Robinson and Creef, *Miné Okubo*, 168–170.

43 Okubo, *Citizen 13660*, 81.

44 For examples, Tokita in Johns, *Signs of Home*, 200, 203–205.

45 Sumida, "Hawaii, the Northwest, and Asia," 12–13; Teruko Kumei, "Transformation of Japanese Immigrants in Senryu Poems," *Japanese Journal of American Studies*, no. 16 (2005): 31. Sumida notes that references to seasonal nature in haiku are part of its local character (11).

46 Kumei, "Transformations," 30.

47 Ibid., 30–31.

48 Sumida, personal communication, November 20, 2015.

4. PUBLIC AND PRIVATE

1 "Project Artistic Talent on Display Next Week," *Minidoka Irrigator*, November 20, 1943, Denshō, denshopd i119-00065.

2 Additional references to exhibitions in *Minidoka Irrigator*: "Art Exhibit Scheduled in January," December 19, 1942; "Skills Hobbies of Hunt Residents to Be Shown in Twin Falls Exhibit," June 19, 1943; "Project Artistic Talent on Display Next Week," November 20, 1943; "Art Exhibit Schedule Given," November 27, 1943, Denshō, denshopdi119-00020, -00044, -00064, and -00065.

3 "Hunt Residents Display Work at Library Exhibit," *Twin Falls (ID) Times-News*, June 25, 1943.

4 "Art and Handicraft Exhibits," *Minidoka Interlude*, unpaginated.

5 Ed Tsutakawa interview, June 8, 2006, Denshō Visual History Collection, denshovh-ted-01-0018. Ed Tsutakawa was a cousin of artist George Tsutakawa, (see chapters 2 and 5). Others often made do with inexpensive or salvaged materials. Artist Henry Sugimoto, lacking supplies at the Fresno Assembly Center, used bedsheets in lieu of paper or canvas. Higa, *The View from Within*, 33.

6 U.S. Office of Censorship, "Code of Wartime Practices for the American Press," 2nd revision (Washington, DC: U.S. Government Printing Office, 1943), 7, cover page, Denshō, Bigelow Family Collection, ddr.densho.org/ddr.densho/156/169.

7 Ed Tsutakawa, interview, 2003-2004, Denshō Visual History Collection, denshovh-ted_g-01-0004.

A photographic representation of the camps was a more complicated matter, less obviously the maker's interpretation and more readily accepted as a factual document, even though viewpoint, focus, framing, cropping, and labeling subject the image to manipulation. Historian Jasmine Alinder calls photography of the incarceration "a representational battleground," which varied from criminalizing to ennobling Japanese Americans. The government initiated its own extensive photo documentation as soon as mass removal began, altogether as many as twenty-five thousand images by government staff, military, and commissioned photographers. Issei photographer Toyo Miyatake, an exception inside the camps, gained special dispensation to photograph at Manzanar. The ban on inmates' possession of cameras at most camps was lifted by 1944. Alinder, *Moving Images*, 1; on Miyatake, ibid., 75–102. Miyatake is featured in a film, *Toyo's Camera*, directed by Junichi Suzuki (2008); for a synopsis and trailer, www.siff.net/cinema/junichi-suzuki%E2%80%99s-nisei-trilogy/toyos-camera.

8 Hill, *Topaz Moon*, 43–45; Hill reproduces the news article by H. L. Dungan, "500 Students in Tanforan Art School," *Oakland Tribune*, July 12, 1942.

9 "A Japanese Art Exhibit," *Friends Bulletin*; Ruth E. McKee for the War Relocation Authority, "By-Product of War," [May 1943], Denshō, Bigelow Family Collection, ddr.densho.org/ddr.densho/156/174.

10 I have been unable to locate records of participants in the exhibition other than prizewinners.

11 Yearbooks are found on various websites; see, for example, University of California, California Digital Library, http://calisphere.cdlib.org/search/?q=relocation+center+yearbooks. For a list of yearbooks, National Archives, Record Group 210, Records of the War Relocation Authority, Relocation Center Yearbooks, 1048635.

12 In deference to the Issei, the back of the book includes seventeen pages of Japanese text as well as several pages of advertisements in Japanese.

13 Franklin D. Roosevelt, U.S. Senate, 78th Congress, first session, Doc. 96, "Message from the President of the United States," September 14, 1943, cited in Robinson, *Tragedy of Democracy*, 249. For an account of the government debates about ending exclusion, see ibid., 247–254.

14 Tom Takeuchi, "By Looking Back, We Look Forward," *Minidoka Interlude*, unpaginated. The foreword, little cited in historical accounts, provides a first-person Nisei perspective after one year at Minidoka. See also Tomiko Takeuchi, interview, May 13, 2014, Denshō Visual History Collection, denshovh-ttomiko-01-0009. In 1989, Tom Takeuchi committed the funds he received from the federal government's redress payment to reissuing the book and distributing free copies to colleges and libraries in Multnomah County, Oregon. His daughters realized the project after his death in early 1990.

15 Thanks to Jennifer Hills at the Twin Falls Public Library for identifying the Astoria Column. An earlier sketch for the section page shows Mount Rainier flanked by the Smith Tower and the Astoria Column. Collection of Sandy and Terry Kita.

16 *Minidoka Interlude*, unpaginated.

17 The version with the cow is framed in a mat, raising the possibility that it was painted later. A fourth watercolor on textured paper depicts only a farmhouse like that in the background of the other three.

18 Dorothea Lange, "Front entrance gate, Jun. 16, 1942, Tanforan Assembly Center, California," photograph, Denshō, courtesy of National Archives and Records Administration, Ctrl. #: NWDNS-210-G-C601, NARA ARC #: 537906, WRA; ddr-densho-151-56.

19 Minidoka was located on the Snake River Plain, the remains of an ancient lava flow that left an irregular terrain of small hills and depressions. Karl Lillquist, *Imprisoned in the Desert: The Geography of World War II–Era, Japanese American Relocation Centers in the Western United States* (Ellensburg: Central Washington University, 2007), www.cwu.edu/geography/geography-japanese-american-relocation-centers. See chapter 5, "Minidoka."

20 Unpublished diary entry.

21 "Evacuee Case File," "Application for Leave Clearance." Fujii was among the majority at Minidoka who responded positively to the 1943 loyalty questionnaire (the "Application"). Although the key questions about loyalty were so problematic that they do not necessarily reflect an individual's position, nothing in Fujii's diary or associated production connects him to the hard line right or suggests

he considered leaving America and his American family.

22 The sculptures are among several three-dimensional objects in Fujii's wartime work. These include the figures of a nude woman and child carved into a twisted branch and stone-fruit pits in the form of small animals. All are in the collection of Sandy and Terry Kita.

Salvaged fence material inspired a poem by Tokita: "Pulling up posts and tearing out the barbed wire / We use them to make our clothes lines." Kamekichi Tokita, "Conflict of Loyalties," unpublished manuscript (2006), possession of the Tokita family.

23 See, for example, the following essays: Vivian Fumiko Chin, "Gestures of Noncompliance: Resisting, Inventing, and Enduring in *Citizen 13660*," and Heather Fryer, "Miné Okubo's War: *Citizen 13660*'s Attack on Government Propaganda," in Robinson and Creef, *Miné Okubo*, 67–81 and 82–98. In the same volume Robinson points out how resistance has become imbedded in the critique of Okubo's work and calls attention to the accommodation, and to a degree, collusion, her work represents. Greg Robinson, "Miné Okubo and the Politics of Symbolism," 159–176.

24 bell hooks, *Talking Back: Thinking Feminist, Thinking Black* (Boston: South End Press, 1989), 43. My quoting hooks follows Elena Tajima Creef's example in *Imaging Japanese America*, 76.

25 The exhibition at Olivet is not confirmed by written records. My account is based upon Sandy Kita's memory of his grandfather's having had a show in a library, which he associates with the name "Olivet." I have constructed a hypothetical narrative by drawing upon the history of the Olivet Institute.

Based upon the variety of paper employed, some watercolors could be new iterations of earlier work. Until their recent conservation, all remained matted to uniform sizes, and clear plastic film still covered a few images.

26 Albert, "Japanese American Communities," 121–122; "Democracy at Work," Bancroft Library, University of California, Berkeley, http://content.cdlib.org/ark:/13030/ftod5n9916/. Hagiwara, originally from Alaska, left Minidoka for Cleveland, where he ran the boys' programs at the YMCA. Hired by the Chicago Resettlement Committee, he began a successful citywide recreation project and, in 1950, became Olivet's program director.

27 Amy Iwasaki Mass, "Psychological Effects of the Camps on Japanese Americans," in Daniels et al., *Japanese Americans: From Relocation to Redress*, 159–162; Edison Tomimaro Uno, introduction to *Executive Order 9066*, 9–13; Weglyn, *Years of Infamy*, 268–273.

5. ABSTRACT EXPRESSIONS

1 Tsutakawa to William and Margaret Gamble, November 20, 1943, Tsutakawa papers, estate of George Tsutakawa (hereafter Tsutakawa papers).

2 Tsutakawa papers. The visits are described in letters to the Gambles, 1943–1945. Fujii's barrack number at Minidoka appears in Tsutakawa's address book, and his name in miscellaneous papers.

3 Martha Kingsbury, *George Tsutakawa* (Seattle: University of Washington Press and Bellevue Art Museum, Bellevue, WA, 1990), 47.

4 Tsutakawa to William Gamble, June 7, 1945, Tsutakawa papers.

5 Rosamund Frost, *Contemporary Art: The March of Art from Cézanne until Now* (New York: Crown, 1942). Inscribed copy, possession of Sandy and Terry Kita.

6 Tsutakawa papers; Tsutakawa, oral history interview, 1983. Tsutakawa also visited

relatives held in Lordsburg and Tule Lake. In later interviews he made no mention of having visited Minidoka, although his trips there are well documented in his personal papers. He and Fujii apparently lost contact; when interviewed in 1983, he talked at some length about Nomura and Tokita but could not remember Fujii's name.

7 Katharine Kuh, *My Love Affair with Modern Art: Behind the Scenes with a Legendary Curator*, ed. Avis Berman (New York: Arcade Publishing, 2006); Sue Ann Prince, "'Of the Which and the Why of Daub and Smear': Chicago Critics Take on Modernism," in *The Old Guard and the Avant-Garde: Modernism in Chicago, 1910–1940*, ed. Prince (Chicago: University of Chicago Press, 1990), 95–117.

8 Art Institute of Chicago, www.artic.edu/aic/collections/.

9 Clement Greenberg, "The Decline of Cubism" (1948), in *The Collected Essays and Criticism*, ed. John O'Brian, vol. 2 (Chicago: University of Chicago Press, 1986), 215.

10 Frederick A. Sweet, foreword to *62nd American Exhibition* (Chicago: Art Institute of Chicago, 1957), www.artic.edu/sites/default/files/libraries/pubs/1957/AIC1957PandS62ndAn_comb.pdf.

11 Bert Winthur-Tamaki, *Art in the Encounter of Nations: Japanese and American Artists in the Early Postwar Years* (Honolulu: University of Hawai'i Press, 2001), 35–39, 56–61. Kline himself denied any Japanese influence.

12 William Seitz thus characterized the painting style in 1955. "Abstract-Expressionist Painting in America: An Interpretation Based on the Work and Thought of Six Key Figures" (PhD diss., Princeton University, 1955), 34–35, cited in Bert Winthur-Tamaki, "The Asian Dimensions of Postwar Abstract Art," in *The Third Mind: American Artists Contemplate Asia, 1860–1989*, ed. Alexandra Munroe (New York: Solomon R. Guggenheim Foundation, 2009), 147. On Greenberg, Winthur-Tamaki, *Art in the Encounter of Nations*, 46, 56–57.

13 Wechsler, "From Asian Traditions to Modern Expressions," 105. Wechsler's essay informs my discussion. Tseng Yuho notes that true calligraphy artists, beyond having a practical knowledge of calligraphy, must know thousands of characters and have a highly developed sense of spatial design. "'Abstraction' in the Traditional Art of East Asia," in Wechsler, *Asian Traditions, Modern Expressions*, 25.

14 George Tsutakawa, interviewed in *Northwest Visionaries*, directed by Kenneth R. Levine (Seattle: Iris Film and Video, 1979), DVD.

15 Fujii, in *Some Work of the Group of Twelve*.

16 These include de Kooning's *Excavation* and *Woman*, the former a purchase prize at the institute; Pollock's *Number 3* and *Ocean Grayness*, and Kline's *Painting* of 1952, along with *Solstice* by Japanese-born Kenzo Okada.

17 Mark Tobey to Paul Horiuchi, 1961, C. Paul Horiuchi papers, possession of Paul M. Horiuchi. For examples of Tobey's work in sumi, Seattle Art Museum collection, www.seattleartmuseum.org/eMuseum/code/emuseum.asp?style=browse&currentrecord=1&page=search&profile=objects&searchdesc=mark%20tobey&quicksearch=mark%20tobey&newprofile=objects&newvalues=1&newcurrentrecord=101; on Tobey's positioning of his work, Winthur-Tamaki, *Art in the Encounter of Nations*, 49–50.

18 His working on the floor is based on Kita's slim memory of his practice.

19 U.S. House of Representatives, *Personal Justice Denied*, 118–119. Payment of claims amounted to $37 million, only 25 percent

of the total amount submitted in more than twenty-six thousand claims. So many records were lost that by 1954 a calculation of the economic loss seemed futile.

20 Ibid., 18.

21 Cosponsors of the Senate bill included Daniel K. Inouye, Spark Matsunaga, and S. I. Hayakawa; those of the House bill included Norman Mineta and Robert Matsui. See Tetsuden Kashima, foreword to *Personal Justice Denied*, xv–xxv, for a summary of the process and impact. The many groups involved, and varying viewpoints leading to the legislation, are the subject of Alice Yang Murray's *Historical Memories*.

INTRODUCTION TO THE DIARY

1 Japanese names are given as in Japan, surname first, except where the opposite is more common in the United States. Long vowels are marked with a macron, except for Japanese words in common use in the United States. In the following translation of the diary, illegible parts of the diary are marked as such, whereas missing sections are indicated by an ellipsis. Proper English is substituted for "Japlish." Where a sentence requires an additional word to be understood, that term is given in brackets. This is also done where a descriptive title is added to illustrations without caption.

2 The cache was in a Bekins Company cardboard shipping box that bears a United Parcel Service label dated October 11, 1987.

3 The meaning of *ochazuke* in Japan can be judged from the featured role it has in Ozu Yasujirō's 1952 movie *The Taste of Green Tea over Rice* (Ochazuke no aji).

4 Purists may object to my description of ukiyo-e or other Edo-era cultural forms as "traditional," since they are comparatively late developments in the long history of Japan. However, the Edo period produced so many of the things that Americans now think of as traditionally Japanese that the usage is perhaps justified. For instance, *nigiri sushi* and tempura are Edo-era developments, and sleeping on futons and eating white rice became common among the general populace only at that time. Many young Japanese, as well as Americans, see these things as traditionally Japanese. The examples are, in any case, types of "invented" or "constructed" traditions. Ukiyo-e, too, is a special case in this regard, because certain images from the genre are so well known, not just here, but internationally, that they have become fundamental parts of far more than just the Japanese visual vocabulary. See Christine Guth, *Hokusai's Great Wave* (Honolulu: University of Hawai'i Press, 2015).

5 *The Moon Has No Home: Japanese Color Woodblock Prints from the Collection of the University of Virginia Art Museum* (Charlottesville: Fralin Museum of Art of the University of Virginia, 2003).

6 Sandy Kita, *The Last Tosa: Iwasa Katsumochi Matabei, Bridge to Ukiyo-e* (Honolulu: Univeristy of Hawai'i Press, 1999).

7 For so many of the details of Grandpa Fujii's Larrabee Street apartment and his life there, I have Tami Nelson to thank. So often his memory was so much better than mine that his generosity in sharing his knowledge was appreciated more than I can say.

8 As far as I can remember, Grandpa Fujii indicated no rejection of Asia in discussing his development of abstract expressionism. So much was the opposite case that I was quite surprised when I learned about Clement Greenberg and others' ideas about how abstract expressionism was supposed to be a "purely American

art," best represented by its East Coast practitioners who denied any Asian influence. Needless to say, my recollection of Grandpa Fujii's views on this matter accord better with the scenario of the development of abstract expressionism in the work of Jeffery Wechsler in the past and Alexandra Munroe more recently. See Wechsler, *Asian Traditions, Modern Expressions,* and Alexandra Munroe, *The Third Mind.*

9 Grandpa Fujii tended to drop vowels, pickled plums (*umeboshi*) being, for example, *meboshi. Fujinzuke* is presumably Fukujinzuke, or Kikuya fukujinzuke produced by the Niko Company, Ltd., Nishi-ochiai, Shinjuku-ku, Tokyo. I owe this information to the Japanese American artist of the internment Hiro, who says it is her favorite food and still had old cans of it available.

10 Tami has children, but neither he nor they read Japanese.

11 My mother was born here, but my father came from Wakayama in Japan; so counting from him, I am a second-generation Japanese American (Nisei), leading to my joking reference to myself as a *sansei no niseimono*—that is a "fake" (*niseimono*) Sansei.

12 Among the many whose aid Reverend Honda and I must acknowledge, we especially thank the late Konishi Jin'ichi. Reverend Honda had an especially close relationship with him because Konishi annotated his *Pre-Meiji Works in the Library of Congress: Japanese Literature, Performing Arts, and Reference Books: A Bibliography* (Washington, DC: Library of Congress, 1997) and collaborated on his subsequent bibliography of works in that same institution on the visual arts. The latter is available in Japan, and the Library of Congress has promised to bring out the complete text online. To date, only my introductory English-language captions have appeared in Sandy Kita, *The Floating World: Shadows, Dreams, and Substance* (New York: Harry N. Abrams in association with Library of Congress, 2001).

13 Earl Miner, "The Traditions and Forms of the Japanese Poetic Diary," *Pacific Coast Philology* 3 (April 1968): 38–48.

14 Ibid.

15 Ibid.

16 Kita, "Kaikoku michi no ki." The illustrations in Matabei's Record no longer survive, but that does not change the work's status as an art diary, since the text is marked with the places where the pictures had been.

17 When Reverend Honda and I were translating Matabei's Record, the question arose of whether, given its importance in the study of this artist, its survival could be entirely accidental. That is, did Matabei's Record alone, of all his writings, survive because it was so important, or did it become important because it was the only writing to survive? The same question arose with regard to the Fujii diary, particularly since it was the only work that was wrapped in the cardboard Bekins moving box in which the cache of Grandpa's paintings, of which it was part, was found.

18 It is not likely that Grandpa knew Matabei's Record, which is a rather specialized text of interest mainly to ukiyo-e scholars. They know it as one of the earliest Edo-period Tōkaidō diaries—that is, a diary of a journey down that road which Hiroshige so famously portrayed in his 1833–1834 series of woodblock prints *The Fifty-Three Stages of the Eastern Sea Road* (Tōkaidō gojûsan tsugi). As noted, Grandpa copied a composition from Hiroshige's *Kisokaidō* series and he had access to the Tōkaidō prints as well. Another account of travel down that road

is Jippensha Ikku's (1765–1831) farcical *Shanks Mare* (Tōkaidō hizakurige) about the misadventures of Kita and Yaji. Since I have the same name as one of the protagonists of that story, I have an especially strong memory of a copy of this book being in the house at Larrabee Street and of it being illustrated with the prints from Hiroshige's Tōkaidō series.

19 Hiroshi Mizuo, *Edo Painting: Sotatsu and Korin*, trans. John M. Shields, vol. 18, *Heibonsha Survey of Japanese Art* (New York: Weatherhill, 1972), 69.

20 Matabei's Record, 329.

21 Ibid., 336–337.

22 Helen Craig McCullough, *Tales of Ise* (Stanford, CA: Stanford University Press, 1968), 73.

23 Matabei's Record made me think of the connection between literature and art because I used that text against this artist's paintings in my book on him to establish him as the first artist of ukiyo-e, on the one hand, and the last Tosa—that is, the final *machishu* master—on the other.

24 The phonetic syllable for *ha* is also read *ba*.

25 Yamane Yūzō, *Sōtatsu to Kōrin*, vol. 14, *Genshoku nihon no bijutsu* (Tokyo: Shogakkan, 1969), plate 113.

26 Ibid., plates 68–70.

27 Murashige Yasushi, ed., *Rimpa Painting*, vol. 4, *Scenes from Literature, People* [Rimpa 4: jinbutsu] (Kyoto: Shikosha Art Books, 1991), plates 5 and 7.

28 Ibid., plates 3 and 6.

29 Kobayashi Tadashi, ed., *Rimpa Painting*, vol. 2, *Seasonal Flowering Plants and Birds* [Rimpa 2: Kachō] (Kyoto: Shikosha Art Books, 1990). For the two works by Hōitsu see plates 126, 130; for the two by Hōchū, see plates 128–129; for the three by Kiitsu, see plates 131–133; and for the two by Dōitsu, see plates 127 and 134.

30 See their online digital collection at http://digitalcollections.nypl.org/items/510d47e3-e797-a3d9-e040-e00a18064a99.

31 See their collection online at www.britishmuseum.org/research/collection_online/collection_object_details.aspx?objectId=790212&partId=1.

32 Bernard Leach published "an early painting by Sōtatsu" with an inscription by Karasumaru Mitsuhiro that he says was "inspired by the old poet Narihira, beloved of Kenzan." The subject of this work is clearly that of Ariwara Narihira at Mt. Fuji. See Bernard Leach, *Kenzan and His Tradition* (New York: Transatlantic Arts, 1967), color plate D.

33 Murashige, *Rimpa Painting*. Kōrin's paintings are plates 17–18.

34 Hōitsu's first painting appears as *The Courtier Ariwara Narihira on His Trip to the Eastern Region* (Ariwara Narihira azuma kudari zu) in *Sakai Hōitsu ten* (Tokyo: Nihon keizai shinbun, 1977), plate 29. The second appears as *Mt. Fuji Episode from the Tale of Ise*, in Howard A. Link, with catalogue by Tōru Shimbo, *Exquisite Visions: Rimpa Paintings from Japan* (Honolulu: Honolulu Academy of Arts et al., 1980), plate 40.

35 Murashige, *Rimpa Painting*. For Hōitsu, see plates 19–22; for Kiitsu, plates 23 and 25; for Shuitsu, plate 24; and for Dōitsu, plate 26.

36 These works survive in a number of private and public collections, but I chose the examples given because copies of all of them were available for sale online at the time of this writing.

37 Akiyama Terukazu, *Japanese Painting* (Geneva: Albert Skira, 1961), 28.

38 Halle O'Neal, "Performing the Jeweled Pagoda Mandala: Relics, Reliquaries, and a Realm of Text," *Art Bulletin* 97, no. 3 (September 2014): 279–300.

39 Akiyama, *Japanese Painting*, 72.

40 Stephen Addiss, *Zenga and Nanga: Paintings by Japanese Monks and Scholars* (New Orleans: New Orleans Museum of Art, 1978), plate 10.

41 Sandy Kita, "Bulls of the Chōmyō-ji: A Joint Work of Art by Sōtatsu and Mitsuhiro," *Monumenta Nipponica* 47, no. 4 (Winter 1992): 495–519.

42 Okudaira Shunroku, "Sōtatsu's Gold and Silver Paintings: The Interaction between Painting and Calligraphy," in *Sōtatsu*, ed. Yukio Lippit and James Ulak (Washington, DC: Arthur M. Sackler Gallery, Smithsonian Institution, 2015), 43–63.

APPENDIX 1

1 *Some Work of the Group of Twelve* (Seattle: Dogwood Press, 1937), unpaginated.

APPENDIX 2

1 Only a partial list of the 1933 Northwest Annual remains.

BIBLIOGRAPHY

*Denotes reference to Fujii or his family.

*"10 Seattle Art Works at Show." *Seattle Times*, May 15, 1936.

**1957* and *1958 Chicago Artists No-Jury Exhibition*. Chicago: Art Institute of Chicago and Chicago Art Organizations in cooperation with City of Chicago, 1957, 1958. Exhibition brochures. www.artic.edu/research/1957-exhibition-history; www.artic.edu/research/1958-exhibition-history.

Abstract and Surrealist Art: Fifty-Eighth Annual Exhibition of American Paintings and Sculpture. Chicago: Art Institute of Chicago, 1947. Exhibition catalogue.

Albert, Michael Daniel. "Japanese American Communities in Chicago and the Twin Cities." PhD diss., University of Minnesota, 1980.

Alinder, Jasmine. "Camera in Camp." In Muller, *Colors of Confinement*, 83–101.

———. *Moving Images: Photography and the Japanese American Incarceration*. Urbana: University of Illinois Press, 2009.

Anderson, M. Margaret. "Concentration Camp Boarders, Strictly American Plan." *New York Times*, September 22, 1946.

Art in Chicago, 1945–1995. Organized by Lynne Warren. London: Thames and Hudson; Chicago: Museum of Contemporary Art, 1996.

Art Institute of Chicago. www.artic.edu/aic/collections/; www.artic.edu/research/exhibition-history.

"Artistic Recognition." *Japanese American Courier*, October 7, 1933.

**Artists of Chicago and Vicinity: Forty-First* and *Sixty-Second Annual Exhibition*. Chicago: Art Institute of Chicago, 1937, 1959. Exhibition brochures. www.artic.edu/research/1937-exhibition-history; www.artic.edu/research/1959-exhibition-history.

Azuma, Eiichiro. *Between Two Empires: Race, History, and Transnationalism in Japanese America*. New York: Oxford University Press, 2005.

Binford, Henry C. "Multicentered Chicago." In *Encyclopedia of Chicago*. Chicago Historical Society, 2005. www.encyclopedia.chicagohistory.org/pages/854.html.

Boswell, Sharon, and Lorraine McConaghy. "Partners across the Pacific." *Seattle Times*, January 28, 1996.

Brooks, Charlotte. "In the Twilight Zone between Black and White: Japanese American Resettlement and Community in Chicago, 1942–1945." *Journal of American History* 86 (2000): 1655–1687.

*Bryant, Elizabeth. "Endangered Heritage: NW Art of the '30s." *Reflex* 6 (May–June 1992): 23–24.

"Buddhist Rites of Bon Odori on Saturday to Present 200 Members in 2,500 Year Old Dance." *Chicago Tribune*, July 7, 1949.

Bundy, Margaret. "Art in the Northwest." *Town Crier*, March 26, 1930, 12.

Burton, Jeffery F., Mary M. Farrell, Florence B. Lord, and Richard W. Lord. *Confinement and Ethnicity: An Overview of Japanese American Relocation Sites.* Rev. ed. Publications in Anthropology 74. Tucson, AZ: Western Archeological and Conservation Center, National Park Service, U.S. Department of the Interior, July 2000. www.cr.nps.gov/history/online_books/anthropology74/index.htm.

Callahan, Brian T., ed. *Margaret Callahan: Mother of Northwest Art.* Victoria, BC: Trafford Publishing, 2009.

"The Art Museum." *Seattle Times*, September 13, 1936.

[Callahan, Kenneth]. "Artists Scored by Critic Here for Exhibition." *Seattle Times*, October 4, 1933.

*Callahan, Kenneth. "The Art Museum." *Seattle Times*, October 5, 1935.

*———. "The Art Museum." *Seattle Times*, October 30, 1938.

*———. "The Galleries: Northwest Annual Opens." *Town Crier*, October 8, 1932, 9.

*———. Letter to the editors. *Life* 4, no. 25 (June 20, 1938): 6.

*———. "Names Change but Quality of N.W. Annual Remains High." *Seattle Times*, November 18, 1956.

*———. "The Northwest Annual." *Town Crier*, December 5, 1931, 35, 38.

*———. "Northwest Annual Opens." *Town Crier*, September 26, 1931, 7.

———. "Pacific Northwest." *ArtNews* 45 (July 1946): 22–27, 53–55.

*———. "Pacific Northwest Painters." *Art and Artists of Today* 1 (September–October 1937): 6–7, 17.

*———. "Penthouse Art Gallery Plans to Show Work." *Seattle Times*, October 20, 1935.

*———. "San Francisco Annual." *Town Crier*, March 19, 1932, 8.

*———. "San Francisco Annual." *Town Crier*, May 14, 1932, 8.

*———. "Seattle Art Museum." *Seattle Times*, October 14, 1934.

*———. "Seattle Art Museum." *Seattle Times*, June 30, 1935.

———. "Tokita's Paintings Exhibited." *Town Crier*, December 31, 1930, 15.

Card, Laura. "Miné Okubo's Illustrations for *Trek* Magazine: Sites of Resistance." In Robinson and Creef, *Miné Okubo*, 131–144.

*Chang, Gordon H. "Deployments, Engagements, Obliterations: Asian American Artists and World War II." In Chang et al., *Asian American Art*, 110–139.

———. "Foreword: Emerging from the Shadows; The Visual Arts and Asian American History." In Chang et al., *Asian American Art*, ix–xv.

———, ed. *Morning Glory, Evening Shadow: Yamato Ichihashi and His Internment Writings, 1942–1945*. Stanford, CA: Stanford University Press, 1997.

*Chang, Gordon H., Mark Dean Johnson, and Paul J. Karlstrom, eds. *Asian American Art: A History, 1850–1970*. Stanford, CA: Stanford University Press, 2008.

**Chicago Japanese American Directory*. Chicago: Chicago Shimpo, 1954, 1967.

**Chicago Japanese American Year Book*. Chicago: Joe T. Komaki, 1948, 1949, 1950.

"Chicago Nisei Artists Form Gakka Guild." *Pacific Citizen*, January 10, 1948.

"Chicago's Annual Bars Japanese." *Art News*, November 23, 1922, 7.

Chin, Vivian Fumiko. "Gestures of Noncompliance: Resisting, Inventing, and Enduring in *Citizen 13660*." In Robinson and Creef, *Miné Okubo*, 67–81.

Conroy, Hilary, and T. Scott Miyakawa, eds. *East across the Pacific: Historical and Sociological Studies of Japanese Immigration and Assimilation*. Santa Barbara, CA: Clio Press, 1972.

*Cook County Clerk. Cook County Clerk Genealogy Records. Chicago, IL: Cook County Clerk, 2008. Ancestry database:

"Cook County, Illinois Death Index, 1908–1988." www.ancestry.com/.

Cornell, Daniel, and Mark Dean Johnson, eds. *Asian/American/Modern Art: Shifting Currents, 1900–1970*. Essays by Gordon H. Chang, Karin Higa, Sharon Spain, and ShiPu Wang. San Francisco: Fine Arts Museums of San Francisco and University of California Press, Berkeley, 2008.

Creef, Elena Tajima. *Imaging Japanese America: The Visual Construction of Citizenship, Nation, and the Body*. New York: New York University Press, 2004.

Critical Past. "People Gather and Celebrate the VJ Day in Seattle, Washington," August 14, 1945. www.criticalpast.com/video/65675076161.

"Critic Praises Paintings Done by 2 Japanese." *Japanese American Courier*, October 7, 1933.

Daniels, Roger. *Asian America: Chinese and Japanese in the United States since 1850*. Seattle: University of Washington Press, 1988.

———. *Concentration Camps: North American Japanese in the United States and Canada during World War II*. Malabar, FL: Robert E. Krieger Publishing, 1981. Rev. ed., updated in 1989, of *Concentration Camps USA*. New York: Holt, Rinehart and Winston, 1971.

———. "Dorothea Lange and the War Relocation Authority." In Partridge, *Dorothea Lange*, 45–55.

———. "Japanese Immigrants on a Western Frontier: The Issei in California, 1890–1940." In Conroy and Miyakawa, *East across the Pacific*, 77–91.

———. *The Politics of Prejudice: The Anti-Japanese Movement in California and the Struggle for Japanese Exclusion*. Reprint of 2nd ed. Berkeley: University of California Press, 1962.

———. *Prisoners without Trial: Japanese Americans in World War II*. Rev. ed. New York: Hill and Wang, 2004.

———. "Words Do Matter: A Note on Inappropriate Terminology and the Incarceration of the Japanese Americans." In Fiset and Nomura, *Nikkei in the Pacific Northwest*, 183–207. Republished at Discover Nikkei, www.discovernikkei.org/en/journal/2008/2/1/words-do-matter.

Daniels, Roger, Sandra C. Taylor, and Harry H. L. Kitano, eds. *Japanese Americans: From Relocation to Redress*. Seattle: University of Washington Press, 1991.

Danovitch, Sylvia E. "The Past Recaptured? The Photographic Record of the Internment of Japanese-Americans." *Prologue* 12, no. 2 (Summer 1980): 91–103.

Dempster, Brian Komei, ed. *Making Home from War: Stories of Japanese American Exile and Resettlement*. Berkeley, CA: Heyday Books, 2011.

Denshō: The Japanese America Legacy Project. http://densho.org/.

*Department of Employment and Immigration Service. "Passenger Lists, 1865–1935." Library and Archives Canada, Ottawa, Canada. Ancestry database, "Canadian Passenger Lists, 1865–1935." www.ancestry.com/.

Discover Nikkei. www.discovernikkei.org/.

*Dorpat, Paul. "Fujii's Bridges: Now and Then." *Seattle Times*, December 4, 1994. Republished online as: "Seattle Now and Then: Coming Home to Riverside," January 21, 2012. http://pauldorpat.com/2012/01/21/seattle-now-then-coming-home-to-riverside/.

Eaton, Allen H. *Beauty behind Barbed Wire: The Arts of Japanese in Our War Relocation Camps*. New York: Harper and Brothers, 1952.

"Elliot Café 1209 Jackson Street." *Northwest Enterprise*, May 22, 1942. Denshō, denshopd-i35-00180.

Executive Order 9066. February 19, 1942, General Records of the United States Government, Record Group 11, U.S.

National Archives and Records Administration. www.archives.gov/historical-docs/todays-doc/?dod-date=219.

Executive Order 9066: The Internment of 110,000 Japanese Americans. Compiled by Masie and Richard Conrat. [San Francisco]: California Historical Society, 1972.

*Falk, Peter Hastings, ed. *Who Was Who in American Art*. Madison, CT: Sound View Press, 1985.

*"First Wed." *Minidoka Irrigator*, September 10, 1942. Denshō, denshopd-i119-00001.

Fiset, Louis. *Camp Harmony: Seattle's Japanese Americans and the Puyallup Assembly Center*. Champaign: University of Illinois Press, 2009.

*———. *Imprisoned Apart: The World War II Correspondence of an Issei Couple*. Seattle: University of Washington Press, 1997.

———. "Thinning, Topping, and Loading: Japanese Americans and Beet Sugar in World War II." *Pacific Northwest Quarterly* 90, no. 3 (1999): 123–139.

Fiset, Louis, and Gail Nomura. *Nikkei in the Pacific Northwest: Japanese Americans and Japanese Canadians in the Twentieth Century*. Seattle: University of Washington Press, 2005.

"Four Hunt Residents in Art Contest Win Honors." *Minidoka Irrigator*, May 29, 1943. Denshō, denshopd-i119-00001-00148.

Francis, Jacqueline. *Making Race: Modernism and "Racial Art" in America*. Seattle: University of Washington Press, 2012.

Frost, Rosamund. *Contemporary Art: The March of Art from Cézanne until Now*. New York: Crown, 1942.

Fryer, Heather. "Miné Okubo's War: *Citizen 13660*'s Attack on Government Propaganda." In Robinson and Creef, *Miné Okubo*, 82–98.

*Fujii, Takuichi. Northwest Artist Files. Dorothy Stimson Bullitt Library, Seattle Art Museum.

*———. Papers. Possession of Sandy and Terry Kita.

Fuller, Richard E. *A Gift to the City: A History of the Seattle Art Museum and the Fuller Family*. Seattle: Seattle Art Museum, 1993.

Gesensway, Deborah, and Mindy Roseman. *Beyond Words: Images from America's Concentration Camps*. Ithaca, NY: Cornell University Press, 1987.

Geyer, Georgie Anne. "Japanese Help Out Olivet." *Chicago Daily News*, February 24, 1962.

Girdner, Audrie, and Anne Loftis. *The Great Betrayal: The Evacuation of Japanese-Americans during World War II*. London: Macmillan, 1969.

Gordon, Linda. "Dorothea Lange Photographs the Internment." In Gordon and Okihiro, *Impounded*, 5–44.

Gordon, Linda, and Gary Y. Okihiro, eds. *Impounded: Dorothea Lange and the Censored Images of Japanese American Internment*. New York: W. W. Norton, 2006.

Grant, Nicole. "White Supremacy and Alien Land Laws of Washington State." Seattle Civil Rights and Labor History Project, http://depts.washington.edu/civilr/ alien_land_laws.htm.

Greenberg, Clement. *The Collected Essays and Criticism*. Edited by John O'Brian. Vol. 2. Chicago: University of Chicago Press, 1986.

———. "The Decline of Cubism." In Greenberg, *Collected Essays and Criticism*, vol. 2, 211–215.

**Guidebook, Chicago, The*. Chicago: Chicago Publishing Company, 1949, 1950, 1951.

Harris, Neil. "The Chicago Setting." In Prince, *The Old Guard and the Avant-Garde*, 3–22.

Hayashi, Brian Masaru. *Democratizing the Enemy: The Japanese American Internment*. Princeton, NJ: Princeton University Press, 2004.

Heart Mountain Wyoming Foundation. Verified complaint, April 15, 2015.

www.heartmountain.org/pressreleases_17_4287335041.pdf.

Hibi, Hisako, and Ibuki H. Lee. *Peaceful Painter: Memoirs of an Issei Woman*. Berkeley, CA: Heyday Books, 2004.

Higa, Karin M. Introduction to Kim, *Henry Sugimoto*, ix–xiv.

———. *The View from Within: Japanese American Art from the Internment Camps, 1942–1945*. Rev. ed. Los Angeles: Japanese American National Museum, UCLA Wight Art Gallery, and UCLA Asian American Studies Center, 1992.

Hill, Kimi Kodani, ed. *Topaz Moon: Chiura Obata's Art of the Internment*. Berkeley, CA: Heyday Books, 2000.

Hirasuna, Delphine. *The Art of Gaman: Arts and Crafts from the Japanese American Internment Camps, 1942–1945*. Berkeley, CA: Ten Speed Press, 2005.

Honda Shōjō. *Pre-Meiji Works in the Library of Congress: Japanese Literature, Performing Arts, and Reference Books*. Washington, DC: Library of Congress, 1997.

hooks, bell. *Talking Back: Thinking Feminist, Thinking Black*. Boston: South End Press, 1989.

Horiuchi, C. Paul. Papers. Possession of Paul M. Horiuchi.

Horiuchi, Lynne. "Dislocations: The Built Environments of Japanese American Internment." In Mackey, *Guilt by Association*, 255–275.

———. "Miné Okubo's *Citizen 13660* and her *Trek* Artwork: Space, Movement, Image, Text, and Their Sites of Production." In Robinson and Creef, *Miné Okubo*, 111–130.

Houston, Jeanne Wakatsuki. *Farewell to Manzanar*. Boston: Houghton Mifflin, 1973.

Howe, Graham, Patrick Nagatani, and Scott Rankin, eds. *Two Views of Manzanar: An Exhibition of Photographs by Ansel Adams and Toyo Miyatake*. Los Angeles: Wight Art Gallery, UCLA, 1978.

"Hunt Residents Display Work at Library Exhibit." *Twin Falls (ID) Times-News*, June 25, 1943.

Ichioka, Yuji. *The Issei: The World of the First Generation Japanese Immigrants, 1885–1924*. New York: Free Press, 1988.

———. "A Study in Dualism: James Yoshinori Sakamoto and the *Japanese American Courier*, 1928–1942." *Amerasia* 13, no. 2 (1986–1987): 49–81.

*Illinois Historical Art Project. www.illinoisart.org/#!e-g/cr4y.

Irwin, Yukiko, and Hilary Conroy. "Robert Walker Irwin and Systematic Immigration to Hawai'i." In Conroy and Miyakawa, *East across the Pacific*, 40–55.

Ishigo, Estelle. *Lone Heart Mountain*. Los Angeles: privately published, 1972.

———. Papers, 1941–1957. UCLA Special Collections, Young Research Library, Japanese American Research Project Collection, 2010, series 1, subseries 11. www.oac.cdlib.org.

"Issei, Nisei, Kibei." *Fortune* 24, no. 4 (April 1944): 32.

Ito, Kazuo. *Issei: A History of Japanese Immigrants in North America*. Translated by Shinichiro Nakamura and Jean S. Gerard. Seattle: Japanese Community Service, 1973.

Jacobsen, J. Z., ed. *Art of Today: Chicago 1933*. Chicago: L. M. Stein, 1932.

Japanese American National Museum. www.janm.org/.

Japanese American National Museum, Chicago Japanese American Historical Society, Japanese American Historical Society of San Diego, and Japanese American Resource Center/Museum, eds. *REgenerations Oral History Project: Rebuilding Japanese American Families, Communities, and Civil Rights in the Resettlement Era. Chicago Region*, vol. 1. http://texts.cdlib.org/view?docId=ft7n39p0cn&query=0&brand=calisphere.

"A Japanese Art Exhibit." *Friends Bulletin*, May 1943. Friends Meeting at Cambridge [MA].

*"Japanese-Immigration Internee Data File: Fusano Fujii." U.S. National Archives and Records Administration, Record Group 10. http://aad.archives.gov/aad/record-detail.jsp?dt=2003&mtch=2&tf=F&q=fusano+fujii&bc=&rpp=10&pg=1&rid=6021&rlst=6021.6022.

"Japs Who Come to Seek Fortune in America." *Seattle Times*, June 21, 1903.

Jenkins, Rupert, ed. *Nagasaki Journey: The Photographs of Yosuke Yamahata, August 10, 1945*. San Francisco: Independent Documentary Group; Pomegranate Artbooks, 1995.

*Johns, Barbara. "Knowing Your Place: Issei Artists in Seattle; Kenjiro Nomura, Kamekichi Tokita, Takuichi Fujii." PhD diss., University of Washington, 2014.

*———. *Paul Horiuchi: East and West*. Seattle: University of Washington Press in association with Museum of Northwest Art, La Conner, WA, 2008.

*———. *Signs of Home: The Paintings and Wartime Diary of Kamekichi Tokita*. Seattle: University of Washington Press, 2011.

*Kanazawa, Tooru. "Seattle's Artists of Palette and Brush . . ." [*sic*]. *Japanese American Courier*, October 7, 1934.

Kashima, Tetsuden. Foreword to U.S. House of Representatives, *Personal Justice Denied*, xv–xxv.

———. Introduction to Soga, *Life behind Barbed Wire*, 1–16.

———. *Judgment without Trial: Japanese American Imprisonment during World War II*. Seattle: University of Washington Press, 2003.

Keene, Donald. *Modern Japanese Diaries: The Japanese at Home and Abroad as Revealed through Their Diaries*. New York: Henry Holt, 1995.

Kenjiro Nomura: An Artist's View of the Japanese American Internment. Essay by June Mukai McKivor. Seattle: Wing Luke Asian Museum, 1991.

Kim, Kristine. *Henry Sugimoto: Painting an American Experience*. Los Angeles: Japanese American National Museum, 2000.

Kimura, Lillian. Oral history transcript 2004.010. Box 2/13, Japanese American Service Committee Legacy Center, Chicago.

Kingsbury, Martha. *George Tsutakawa*. Seattle: University of Washington Press; Bellevue, WA: Bellevue Art Museum, 1990.

Kita, Sandy. "Bringing Home the Changes: The Implications of New Views of Ukiyo-e for Their American Study." In *The Moon Has No Home*, 6–19.

———. "Bulls of the Chōmyō-ji: A Joint Work of Art by Sōtatsu and Mitsuhiro." *Monumenta Nipponica* 47 (Winter 1992): 495–519.

———. *The Floating World: Shadows, Dreams, and Substance*. New York: Harry N. Abrams, in association with the Library of Congress, 2001.

———. "Kaikoku michi no ki: A Seventeenth Century Travelogue by Iwasa Matabei." *Monumenta Serica* 45 (1997): 309–352.

———. *The Last Tosa: Iwasa Katsumochi Matabei, Bridge to Ukiyo-e*. Honolulu: University of Hawaiʻi Press, 1999.

Kitagawa, Daisuke. *Issei and Nisei: The Internment Years*. New York: Seabury Press, 1967.

Kitano, Harry H. L. *Japanese Americans: The Evolution of a Subculture*. Englewood Cliffs, NJ: Prentice-Hall, 1969.

Kuh, Katherine. *My Love Affair with Modern Art: Behind the Scenes with a Legendary Curator*. Edited by Avis Berman. New York: Arcade Publishing, 2006.

Kumei, Teruko. "'A Record of Life and a Poem of Sentiments': Japanese Immigrant 'Senryu,' 1929–1945." *Amerikastudien / American Studies* 51, no. 1 (2006): 29–49.

———. "Transformation of Japanese Immigrants in Senryu Poems." *Japanese Journal of American Studies*, no. 16 (2005): 81–110.

Kuramitsu, Kristine C. "Internment and Identity in Japanese American Art." *American Quarterly* 47, no. 4 (December 1995): 619–658.

Kurashige, Lon. *Japanese American Celebration and Conflict: A History of Ethnic Identity and Festival in Los Angeles, 1934–1990*. Berkeley: University of California Press, 2002.

———. "Unexpected Views of the Internment." In Muller, *Colors of Confinement*, 103–116.

Lee, Alfred McClung. "Concentration Camp, U.S. Model." *Saturday Review*, September 28, 1946, 12.

Lee, Shelley Sang-Hee. *Claiming the Oriental Gateway: Prewar Seattle and Japanese America*. Philadelphia: Temple University Press, 2011.

Lillquist, Karl. *Imprisoned in the Desert: The Geography of World War II–Era, Japanese American Relocation Centers in the Western United States*. Ellensburg: Central Washington University, 2007. www.cwu.edu/geography/geography-japanese-american-relocation-centers.

Lippit, Akira Mizuta. "Photographing Nagasaki: From Fact to *Artefact*." In Jenkins, *Nagasaki Journey*, 25–29.

Lyon, Cherstin M. *Prisons and Patriots: Japanese American Wartime Citizenship, Civil Disobedience, and Historical Memory*. Philadelphia, PA: Temple University Press, 2012.

Mackey, Mike, ed. *Guilt by Association: Essays on Japanese Settlement, Internment, and Relocation in the Rocky Mountain West*. Powell, WY: Western History Publications, 2001.

Martin, David F., and Nicolette Bromberg. *Shadows of a Fleeting World: Pictorial Photography and the Seattle Camera Club*. Seattle: University of Washington, 2011.

Mass, Amy Iwasaki. "Psychological Effects of the Camps on Japanese Americans." In Daniels et al., *Japanese Americans*, 159–162.

Matsunaga, Erik. "30 Years of Lakeview: Chicago's Japanese American Community, 1960s–1990s." Parts 1 and 2. Discover Nikkei, December 24, 2014. www.discovernikkei.org/en/journal/2014/12/24/lakeview-1 and /lakeview-2.

McKee, Ruth E. *By-Product of War*. Cambridge, MA: War Relocation Authority for the Exhibition of Relocation Center Art, [1943]. Exhibition brochure. Denshō, Bigelow Family Collection, ddr-densho-156-174.

Merger, Amy Lowe. *Minidoka Internment National Monument: Historic Resource Study*. Seattle: National Park Service, 2005.

Midwest Buddhist Temple. www.mbtchicago.org/about-the-temple/history-of-our-temple/.

*Mills College Art Museum records. Mills College, Oakland, CA.

Miner, Earl. "The Traditions and Forms of the Japanese Poetic Diary." *Pacific Coast Philology* 3 (April 1968): 38–48.

**Minidoka Interlude: September 1942–October 1943*. Hunt, ID: Minidoka Relocation Center, 1943. Reissued with an introduction by Tom Takeuchi. Gresham, OR: privately published, [ca. 1990].

**Minidoka Irrigator* (Hunt, ID). 1942–1945. Denshō, denshopd-i119-00001-00148.

Miyamoto, S. Frank. "An Immigrant Community in America." In Conroy and Miyakawa, *East across the Pacific*, 217–243.

———. *Social Solidarity among the Japanese in Seattle*. Seattle: University of Washington Press, in cooperation with the Asian American Studies Program, University of Washington, 1984. First published in *University of Washington Publications in the Social Sciences*, 1939.

Miyatake, Archie. Interviews August 31, September 1, 2012. Denshō Visual History Collection, denshovh-marchie-02-0018, 0019, 0020, 0021.

The Moon Has No Home: Japanese Color Woodblock Prints from the Collection of the University of Virginia Art Museum. Charlottesville: Fralin Museum of Art of the University of Virginia, 2003.

Muller, Eric L., ed. *Colors of Confinement: Rare Kodachrome Photographs of Japanese American Incarceration in World War II.* Photographs by Bill Manbo. Chapel Hill: University of North Carolina Press in association with the Center for Documentary Studies at Duke University, 2012.

———. "Introduction: Outside the Frame." In Muller, *Colors of Confinement*, 1–21.

Munroe, Alexandra, ed. *The Third Mind: American Artists Contemplate Asia, 1860–1989*. New York: Solomon R. Guggenheim Museum, 2009.

Murata, Alice. *Japanese Americans in Chicago.* Chicago: Arcadia, 2002.

Murray, Alice Yang. *Historical Memories of the Japanese American Internment and the Struggle for Redress.* Stanford, CA: Stanford University Press, 2008.

Nakadate, Neil. *Looking after Minidoka: An American Memoir.* Bloomington: University of Indiana Press, 2013.

*Nakane, Kazuko. "Facing the Pacific: Asian American Artists in Seattle, 1900–1970." In Chang et al., *Asian American Art*, 55–81.

Nakano, Jiro, and Kay Nakano, eds. and trans. *Poets behind Barbed Wire: Keiho Soga, Taisanboku Mori, Sojin Takei, Muin Ozaki.* Honolulu: Bamboo Ridge Press, 1983.

Nakashima, Ted. "Concentration Camp: U.S. Style." *New Republic* 106, no. 24 (June 15, 1942): 822–823.

National Museum of American History, Smithsonian Institution. *A More Perfect Union: Japanese Americans and the U.S. Constitution.* Exhibition 1987–2004. http://amhistory.si.edu/perfectunion/experience/index.html.

Nomura, Kenjiro. Papers. Possession of George and Betty Nomura.

Northwest Visionaries. Directed by Kenneth R. Levine. Seattle: Iris Film and Video, 1979. DVD.

Oh, Stella. "Paradoxes of Citizenship: Reviewing the Japanese American Internment in Miné Okubo's *Citizen 13660*." In Robinson and Creef, *Miné Okubo*, 145–158.

Okihiro, Gary Y. "An American Story." In Gordon and Okihiro, *Impounded*, 47–84.

———. "Tule Lake under Martial Law: A Study in Japanese Resistance." *Journal of Ethnic Studies* 5, no. 3 (Fall 1977): 71–85.

Okubo, Miné. *Citizen 13660*. Seattle: University of Washington Press, 2014. First published by Columbia University Press in 1946.

———. "An Evacuee's Hopes—and Memories." In Robinson and Creef, *Miné Okubo*, 40–45. Previously published in the *San Francisco Chronicle*, August 29, 1943.

Olivet Community Center records. Chicago History Museum.

"Opening Ceremony of the Seattle Art Museum Tomorrow Night" (translated). *Taihoku Nippo* [Great Northern Daily News], [June 1933]. Kenjiro Nomura papers, possession of George and Betty Nomura.

Partridge, Elizabeth, ed. *Dorothea Lange: A Visual Life*. Washington, DC: Smithsonian Institution Press, 1994.

Patterson, Viola Patterson. Oral history interview, July 10, 1972. Special Collections, University of Washington Libraries, Accession 2563-2, v.f. 1396B.

Payne, James Robert, ed. *Multicultural Autobiography: American Lives*. Knoxville: University of Tennessee Press, 1992.

Phillips, Kimberly L. "To Keep a Record of Life: Miné Okubo's Autographic *Manga* and Wartime History." In Robinson and Creef, *Miné Okubo*, 99–110.

**Polk's Chicago Directory*. Chicago: R. L. Polk, 1950, 1952, 1953.

"Poor Man's Playground." *Northwest Enterprise*, October 12, 1933. Denshō, denshopd-i350-00151
Prince, Sue Ann. "'Of the Which and the Why of Daub and Smear': Chicago Critics Take on Modernism." In Prince, *The Old Guard and the Avant-Garde*, 95–117.
———, ed. *The Old Guard and the Avant-Garde: Modernism in Chicago, 1910–1940*. Chicago: University of Chicago Press, 1990.
"Relocation Center Art Featured in Asia Magazine." *Pacific Citizen* (Salt Lake City, UT), October 16, 1943.
"Resettlers Committee Answers Many Needs." No source, n.d. [Chicago, ca. 1950]. Japanese American Service Committee Legacy Center, Scrapbook Collection, Box 4.
Robinson, Greg. *After Camp: Portraits in Midcentury Japanese American Life and Politics*. Berkeley: University of California Press, 2012.
———. "Birth of a Citizen: Miné Okubo and the Politics of Symbolism." In Robinson and Creef, *Miné Okubo*, 159–176.
———. Foreword to *Making Home from War: Stories of Japanese American Exile and Resettlement*, edited by Brian Komei Dempster, viii–xiii. Berkeley, CA: Heyday Books, 2011.
———. *A Tragedy of Democracy: Japanese Confinement in North America*. New York: Columbia University Press, 2009.
Robinson, Greg, and Elena Tajima Creef, eds. *Miné Okubo: Following Her Own Road*. Seattle: University of Washington Press, 2008.
Sakamoto, James Y. Papers. Special Collections, University of Washington Libraries, Accession 1609-001.
Sakatani, Bacon. "A Youngster's Life behind Barbed Wire." In Muller, *Colors of Confinement*, 22–34.
*San Francisco Art Association records. San Francisco Art Institute Library.
Sato, Eddie. Camp Harmony Sketchbook and Drawings. Special Collections, University of Washington Libraries, Ph Coll 664.
Scene: The Pictorial Magazine, 1949–1955.
Schulze, Franz. "Art in Chicago: The Two Traditions." In *Art in Chicago*, 14–34.
**Sealth*. Seattle: Broadway High School, 1934.
*Seattle Art Museum records. Special Collections, University of Washington Libraries, Accession 2636-1.
Seattle Art Museum reports. Dorothy Stimson Bullitt Library, Seattle Art Museum.
**Seattle City Directory*. Seattle: R. L. Polk, 1906–1941.
Seligman, Amanda. "Cabrini-Green." In *Encyclopedia of Chicago*. Chicago: Chicago Historical Society, 2005. www.encyclopedia.chicagohistory.org/pages/199.html.
Shirai, Noboru. *Tule Lake: An Issei Memoir*. Edited by Eucaly Shiry and Valerie Samson. Translated by Ray Hosoda. Sacramento, CA: Muteki Press, 2001. Originally published in 1981 in Japan.
Sims, Robert C. "Japanese Americans in Idaho." In Daniels et al., *Japanese Americans*, 103–111.
"A Slap's a Slap: General John L. DeWitt and Four Little Words." Blogpost by Alan Walker, November 22, 2013. http://blogs.archives.gov/TextMessage/2013/11/22/a-slaps-a-slap-general-john-l-dewitt-and-four-little-words/.
Soga, Yasutaro (Keiho). *Life behind Barbed Wire: The World War II Internment Memoirs of a Hawai'i Issei*. Translated by Kihei Hirai. Honolulu: University of Hawai'i Press, 2008.
Some Work of the Group of Twelve. Seattle: Dogwood Press, 1937.
Sone, Monica. *Nisei Daughter*. Seattle: University of Washington Press, 2014. First published by Little, Brown and Company in 1953.

Stafford, H. L. "Project Director's Narrative: H. L. Stafford Report." September 26, 1945. University of California Libraries. http://content.cdlib.org/view?docId=ft9p300845;NAAN=13030&doc.view=frames&chunk.id=d0e76&toc.depth=1&toc.id=d0e76&brand=calisphere&query=Project%20director%20narrative.

Sumida, Stephen H. "Centers without Margins: Responses to Centrism in Asian American Literature." *American Literature* 66, no. 4 (December 1994): 803–815.

———. "Hawaii, the Northwest, and Asia: Localism and Local Literary Developments in the Creation of an Asian Immigrants' Sensibility." *Seattle Review* 11, no. 1 (Spring–Summer 1988): 9–18.

———. "Protest and Accommodation, Self-Satire and Self-Effacement, and Monica Sone's *Nisei Daughter*." In Payne, *Multicultural Autobiography*, 207–243.

Sweet, Frederick A. Foreword to *62nd American Exhibition*, 3–4. Chicago: Art Institute of Chicago, 1957. www.artic.edu/sites/default/files/libraries/pubs/1957/AIC1957PandS62ndAn_comb.pdf.

*Tacoma Art Museum records. Washington State Historical Society.

Takeuchi, Tomiko. Interview, May 13, 2014. Denshō Visual History Collection, denshovh-ttomiko-01-0009, -0010.

Tanaka, Togo. "Chicago's Newest Citizens." In *The Guidebook, Chicago*, 90–121. Chicago: Chicago Publishing Company, 1949.

Taniguchi, Nancy J. "Japanese Americans in Utah." Discover Nikkei, February 27, 2008. www.discovernikkei.org/en/journal/2008/2/27/enduring-communities/.

Thomas, Dorothy Swaine, with Charles Kikuchi and James Sakoda. *The Salvage: Japanese American Evacuation and Resettlement.* Berkeley: University of California Press, 1952.

"Thousands Cheer Soldiers and Sailors." *Seattle Times*, June 1, 1909.

*"Three Japanese Show Works at N.W. Art Exhibit." *Japanese American Courier*, November 2, 1935.

Tokita, Kamekichi. "Conflict of Loyalties." Unpublished manuscript, 2006. Possession of Tokita family.

*———. Papers. Archives of American Art, Smithsonian Institution.

*Tokita, [Kamekichi], and [Kenjiro] Nomura. "Seattle's Japanese Artists." *Town Crier*, May 28, 1932, 9.

*"Tokita's Canvas Wins 3rd Prize." *Japanese American Courier*, October 7, 1933.

Tsutakawa, Ed. Interviews, 2003–2004, 2006. Denshō Visual History Collection, denshovh-ted_g-01-0004 and denshovh-ted-01-0016, -0017.

*Tsutakawa, George. "A Conversation on Life and Fountains." *Journal of Ethnic Studies* 4 (Spring 1976): 4–36.

———. Oral history interview, 1983. Archives of American Art, Smithsonian Institution. www.aaa.si.edu/collections/interviews/oral-history-interview-george-tsutakawa-11913.

*———. Papers. The estate of George Tsutakawa.

*Tsutakawa, Mayumi, ed. *They Painted from Their Hearts: Pioneer Asian American Artists.* Seattle: Wing Luke Asian Museum, 1994. Includes "A Directory of Asian American Artists in Washington and Oregon (1900–1975)," compiled by Alan Chong Lau and Kazuko Nakane for the Archives of American Art, Smithsonian Institution, 1990.

*Tsutakawa, Mayumi, and Alan Chong Lau, eds. *Turning Shadows into Light: Art and Culture of the Northwest's Early Asian/Pacific Community.* Seattle: Young Pine Press, 1982.

Uno, Edison Tomimaro. Introduction to *Executive Order 9066*, 9–13.

*U.S. Army. World War II Army Enlistment Records. Record Group 64, U.S. National Archives and Records Administration,

College Park, MD. Ancestry database, "U.S. World War II Army Enlistment Records, 1938–1946." www.ancestry.com/.

*U.S. Bureau of the Census. "Fourteenth . . . ," "Fifteenth . . . ," and "Sixteenth Census of the United States." U.S. National Archives and Records Administration, Washington, DC. Ancestry database, "1920 . . . ," "1930 . . . ," "1940 United States Federal Census." www.ancestry.com/.

U.S. House of Representatives. Committee on Interior and Insular Affairs. *Personal Justice Denied: Report on the Commission of Wartime Relocation and Internment of Civilians*. Washington, DC: Government Printing Office, 1982.

*U.S. Immigration and Naturalization Service. Records, 1891–1957. U.S. National Archives and Records Administration, Washington, DC. Record Group 85, M1383. Ancestry database, "Seattle, Washington, Passenger and Crew Lists, 1882–1957." www.ancestry.com/.

U.S. Office of Censorship. "Code of Wartime Practices for the American Press." Washington, DC: Government Printing Office, 1943. Denshō, Bigelow Family Collection, ddr-densho- p156-00169.

*U.S. Selective Service System. "Selective Service Registration Cards, World War II, Fourth Registration." Records of the Selective Service System, Record Group 147. U.S. National Archives and Records Administration, Washington, DC. Ancestry database, "U.S. World War II Draft Registration Cards, 1942." www.ancestry.com/.

*———. "World War I Selective Service System Draft Registration Cards, 1917–1918." M1509. U.S. National Archives and Records Administration, Washington, DC. Ancestry database, "U.S., World War I Draft Registration Cards, 1917–1918." www.ancestry.com/.

*U.S. Social Security Administration. "Social Security Death Index, Master File." Social Service Administration, Washington, DC. Ancestry database, "U.S., Social Security Death Index, 1935–Current." www.ancestry.com/.

*U.S. War Relocation Authority. "Final Accountability Roster of the Minidoka Relocation Center, October 1945." Record Group 210, Records of the War Relocation Authority. U.S. National Archives and Records Service, Washington, DC, 1956. https://research.archives.gov/id/596001.

———. *Questions and Answers for Evacuees: Information Regarding the Relocation Program*. San Francisco: War Relocation Authority Regional Office, 1942. Denshō, densho-156-00165.

*———. "Records about Japanese Americans Relocated during World War II, Created 1988–1989, Documenting the Period 1942–1946." Record Group 210, Records of the War Relocation Authority. U.S. National Archives and Records Administration, Washington, DC. Ancestry database, "Japanese Americans Relocated during World War II." www.ancestry.com/.

*———. "War Relocation Evacuee Case File: Takuichi Fujii." U.S. National Archives and Records Administration, College Park, MD.

Uyeki, Eugene S. "Process and Patterns of Nisei Adjustment to Chicago." PhD diss., University of Chicago, 1953.

Van Sant, John E. *Pacific Pioneers: Japanese Journeys to America and Hawaii, 1850–1880*. Urbana: University of Illinois Press, 2000.

Wang, ShiPu. *Becoming American? The Art and Identity Crisis of Yasuo Kuniyoshi*. Honolulu: University of Hawai'i Press, 2011.

———. "Performing Diaspora: The Body and Identity in the Work of Asian American Artists." In Cornell and Johnson, *Asian/American/Modern Art*, 23–28.

*"Washington Births, 1891–1929." Washington State Archives, Olympia, WA. Ancestry database, "Washington Births." www.ancestry.com/.

Wechsler, Jeffrey, ed. *Asian Traditions, Modern Expressions: Asian American Artists and Abstraction, 1945–1970*. New York: Harry N. Abrams, in association with the Jane Voorhees Zimmerli Art Museum, Rutgers, the State University of New Jersey, 1997.

———"From Asian Traditions to Modern Expressions: Abstract Art by Asian Americans, 1945–1970." In Wechsler, *Asian Traditions, Modern Expressions*, 58–145.

Weglyn, Michi Nishiura. *Years of Infamy: The Untold Story of America's Concentration Camps*. Updated ed. Seattle: University of Washington Press, 1996.

Winthur-Tamaki, Bert. *Art in the Encounter of Nations: Japanese and American Artists in the Early Postwar Years*. Honolulu: University of Hawai'i Press, 2001.

———. "The Asian Dimensions of Postwar Abstract Art." In Munroe, *The Third Mind*, 145–157.

Yoo, David K. *Growing Up Nisei: Race, Generation, and Culture among Japanese Americans of California, 1924–49*. Urbana: University of Illinois Press, 2000.

Yuho, Tseng. "'Abstraction' in the Traditional Art of East Asia." In Wechsler, *Asian Traditions, Modern Expressions*, 21–29.

INDEX

THE SCOTT AND LAURIE OKI SERIES IN ASIAN AMERICAN STUDIES

From a Three-Cornered World: New and Selected Poems, by James Masao Mitsui

Imprisoned Apart: The World War II Correspondence of an Issei Couple, by Louis Fiset

Storied Lives: Japanese American Students and World War II, by Gary Okihiro

Phoenix Eyes and Other Stories, by Russell Charles Leong

Paper Bullets: A Fictional Autobiography, by Kip Fulbeck

Born in Seattle: The Campaign for Japanese American Redress, by Robert Sadamu Shimabukuro

Confinement and Ethnicity: An Overview of World War II Japanese American Relocation Sites, by Jeffery F. Burton, Mary M. Farrell, Florence B. Lord, and Richard W. Lord

Judgment without Trial: Japanese American Imprisonment during World War II, by Tetsuden Kashima

Shopping at Giant Foods: Chinese American Supermarkets in Northern California, by Alfred Yee

Altered Lives, Enduring Community: Japanese Americans Remember Their World War II Incarceration, by Stephen S. Fugita and Marilyn Fernandez

Eat Everything Before You Die: A Chinaman in the Counterculture, by Jeffery Paul Chan

Form and Transformation in Asian American Literature, edited by Zhou Xiaojing and Samina Najmi

Language of the Geckos and Other Stories, by Gary Pak

Nisei Memories: My Parents Talk about the War Years, by Paul Howard Takemoto

Growing Up Brown: Memoirs of a Bridge Generation Filipino American, by Peter Jamero

Letters from the 442nd: The World War II Correspondence of a Japanese American Medic, by Minoru Masuda; edited by Hana Masuda and Dianne Bridgman

Shadows of a Fleeting World: Pictorial Photography and the Seattle Camera Club, by David F. Martin and Nicolette Bromberg

Signs of Home: The Paintings and Wartime Diary of Kamekichi Tokita, by Barbara Johns and Kamekichi Tokita

Nisei Soldiers Break Their Silence: Coming Home to Hood River, by Linda Tamura

A Principled Stand: The Story of Hirabayashi v. United States, by Gordon K. Hirabayashi, with James A. Hirabayashi and Lane Ryo Hirabayashi

Cities of Others: Reimagining Urban Spaces in Asian American Literature, by Xiaojing Zhou

Enduring Conviction: Fred Korematsu and His Quest for Justice, by Lorraine K. Bannai

Asians in Colorado: A History of Persecution and Perseverance in the Centennial State, by William Wei

The Hope of Another Spring: Takuichi Fujii, Artist and Wartime Witness, by Barbara Johns